Citizenship Education and Global Migration: Implications for Theory, Research, and Teaching

Citizenship Education and Global Migration: Implications for Theory, Research, and Teaching

James A. Banks
Editor

AMERICAN EDUCATIONAL RESEARCH ASSOCIATION

© 2017 American Educational Research Association

Published by the American Educational Research Association
1430 K St., NW, Suite 1200
Washington, DC 20005
Printed in the United States of America

Library of Congress Cataloging-in-Publication Data
Names: Banks, James A., editor.
Title: Citizenship education and global migration : implications for theory, research, and teaching / James A. Banks, editor.
Description: Washington, DC : American Educational Research Association, [2017] | Includes bibliographical references and index.
Identifiers: LCCN 2017009982 (print) | LCCN 2017012278 (ebook) | ISBN 9780935302653 (E-book) | ISBN 9780935302639 (hardcover : alk. paper) | ISBN 9780935302646 (pbk. : alk. paper)
Subjects: LCSH: Citizenship–Study and teaching–Cross-cultural studies. | Multicultural education–Cross-cultural studies. | Globalization–Political aspects–Cross-cultural studies.
Classification: LCC LC1091 (ebook) | LCC LC1091 .C5243 2017 (print) | DDC 370.116–dc23
LC record available at https://lccn.loc.gov/2017009982

Contents

**Part 7 Diversity and Citizenship Education: Implications of
Theory and Research for Teaching**

Preface

Global migration and the increasing racial, ethnic, cultural, linguistic, and religious diversity in nation-states around the world—and the growing recognition and legitimization of diversity—are causing educators to rethink citizenship education (Banks, 2008; Malin, Ballard, Attai, Colby, & Damon, 2014; Osler, 2016). The world-wide ethnic revitalization movements are challenging assimilationist notions of citizenship education and insisting that diverse cultures be reflected in school, college, and university curricula. Although diversity is an important part of education in multicultural nation-states, every pluralistic nation-state must also be concerned about unity, social cohesion, and a set of shared values that will cement the commonwealth.

Balancing unity and diversity in multicultural nation-states was the focus of a conference that the Center for Multicultural Education at the University of Washington sponsored at the Rockefeller Foundation's Bellagio Center, a study and conference center in Bellagio, Italy. The Bellagio Citizenship Education and Diversity Conference, held in June 2002 with support from the Spencer and Rockefeller Foundations, included participants from 12 nations. The papers presented at the conference were published in *Diversity and Citizenship Education: Global Perspectives* (Banks, 2004). One of the conclusions of the Bellagio Conference was that world migration and the political and economic aspects of globalization are challenging nation-states and national borders. At the same time, national borders remain tenacious, and the number of nations in the world is increasing rather than decreasing. The number of United Nations member states increased from 80 in 1950 to 193 in 2011 (Castles & Davidson, 2000; United Nations, n.d.). Globalization and nationalism are coexisting and sometimes conflicting trends and forces in the world today (Banks et al., 2005). The passage of the Brexit referendum in 2016, which requires England to leave the European Union, was a cogent and startling manifestation of voters' perception of the clash of national and global interests.

The Bellagio Conference concluded that educators throughout the world need to rethink and redesign citizenship education courses and programs to help students acquire the knowledge, attitudes, and skills needed to function in their nations, as well as in a diverse world society that is experiencing rapid globalization and quests by diverse groups for recognition and structural inclusion. Citizenship education should also help students develop a commitment to act to change the world to make it more just and democratic. Another conclusion of the Bellagio Conference is that citizenship and citizenship education are defined and implemented differently in various nations and in different social, cultural, economic, and political contexts. They are also contested ideas in nations around the world. Nevertheless, nations have shared problems, concepts, and issues, such as the need to prepare students to function within, as well as across, national borders.

Momentous events that occurred in nations around the world after the Bellagio Conference through 2015 made it appropriate and timely to assemble another group of scholars and researchers in multicultural education and citizenship education to revisit and assess the status of the theory, research, and practice in these areas in different nations. Changes such as the Arab Spring in the Middle East, the rise of the Islamic State of Iraq and Syria (ISIS), terrorist attacks in Europe and the United States, the Syrian refugee crisis and the xenophobic responses to it in Europe, the Black Lives Matter movement in the United States, and the widening gap between the rich and the poor in many nations (Milanovic, 2016) are among the pivotal events that have significantly influenced citizenship and citizenship education in most nations since 2002. The follow-up conference from which this book originated was held in June 2015 at the Talaris Conference Center near the University of Washington campus in Seattle, Washington. Scholars from 16 nations presented papers at the Talaris conference. In this book, the researchers and scholars who participated in the Seattle conference describe perspectives, issues, theory, research, and strategies for implementing citizenship education courses and programs in schools that will facilitate the *structural inclusion* of students from diverse ethnic, cultural, racial, linguistic, and religious groups into their nation-states.

We define structural inclusion as a set of attitudes and beliefs among students that are characterized by a feeling of political efficacy, political empowerment, and a belief that they can influence political and economic decisions that affect their lives by participating in the political system of their nation. In other words, students who feel structurally included in their nation's civic culture have *political efficacy* and a belief that their participation in the polity can make a difference. People who are not structurally included within the political and cultural systems of their nation-state are politically alienated, lack political efficacy, and participate at low levels. They often do not vote because they believe that their votes do not make a difference and that politicians are not concerned about them (Cohen, 2010). They also have negative views of politicians.

Focus of This Book

Many students from ethnic, cultural, racial, linguistic, and religious minoritized groups have weak identifications with their nation-states because they feel structurally excluded and marginalized. Research by scholars such as Abu El-Haj (2007), Maira (2004), and Nguyen (2012) have empirically documented the feelings of marginalization, structural exclusion, and ambivalent identities that immigrant students experience within their nation-states. The chapters in this book explore how citizenship education courses and programs can be reconceptualized and changed so that they will help these students attain a sense of inclusion, political efficacy, and clarified national identities. Events around the world within the last decade indicate that many racial, ethnic, cultural, linguistic, and religious minoritized youth do not believe that they are structurally included and integrated into their nation-states and societies. When groups and individuals do not feel structurally included, they focus on particularistic ethnic, cultural, linguistic, and religious issues and concerns rather than on the overarching goals of the nation-state.

When they feel marginalized and structurally excluded and are treated as the "Other," these students—such as Mexican Americans in the United States and Muslim students in France and England—tend to emphasize their ethnic or religious identities and to have weak attachments to their nation-state (Banks, 2015a). The chapters in this book adduce theory, research, and practice that describe why an important goal of civic education should be to help students from marginalized groups attain a sense of structural integration and political efficacy within their nation-states as well as reflective cultural, national, and global identities. Research indicates that the content and methods of school-based civic and multicultural education can promote structural inclusion. Research by Callahan and Muller (2013) indicates that high levels in immigrant students' civic knowledge and social connection in schools increase their civic efficacy and political participation. Consequently, courses that teach civic knowledge in classrooms, and schools that promote high levels of social connection among students, can help them to develop a sense of structural inclusion. The research on culturally responsive teaching, by scholars such as Ladson-Billings (1994), Lee (2007), and Au (2011), indicates that students of color become more actively engaged in learning, acquire more knowledge, and are more likely to feel structurally included when the content and pedagogy of instruction reflect their histories, cultures, and identities (Steele & Cohn-Vargas, 2013). Culturally responsive teaching promotes structural inclusion because it gives students recognition and civic equality (Gutmann, 2004). Research indicates that the recognition and civic equality that students experience in culturally responsive classrooms help them to feel structurally included (Lee, 2007).

An important goal of the Talaris conference, from which this book originated, was for "educators in different parts of the world . . . (to) share perspectives, issues, theories, research, and strategies for implementing citizenship education courses and programs in schools" (Banks, 2015b, p. 2). This book describes promising practices in different nations and guidelines that will help educators in different parts of the world design and implement effective civic education programs that enhance structural inclusion while respecting the cultural, linguistic, and religious characteristics of diverse groups. This book describes theory, research, and practices that have been implemented in various nations that can help educational practitioners to design effective civic education programs. It also identifies research questions related to civic education and diversity that need to be further investigated.

This book is organized in seven parts. Part 1 discusses cross-cutting issues and concepts related to globalization, migration, diversity, citizenship, and citizenship education. Part 2 focuses on three industrialized nations that are representative democracies—the United States, Canada, and South Africa. Parts 3–6 are organized by region. The nations discussed in each of these parts are located on the same continent and share many historical, cultural, and geographical characteristics. Part 7 describes the practice implications of the theory and research discussed in the preceding parts.

This book differs in several significant ways from its predecessor (Banks, 2004). Balancing unity and diversity was the focus of the 2004 book; the pivotal theme of this book is how to facilitate the structural inclusion of diverse ethnic, cultural, linguistic, and religious groups into their societies and nation-states. Most of the chapters in Parts 2–6 contain a profile of an effective teacher of civic education who works with students from diverse groups and uses visionary and engaging instructional strategies and interventions to foster structural inclusion, civic efficacy, and civic engagement and participation. This book also has a more robust section on nations in the Middle East than its predecessor.

James A. Banks
University of Washington, Seattle

References

Abu El-Haj, T. R. (2007). "I was born here, but my home, it's not here": Educating for democratic citizenship in an era of transnational migration and global conflict. *Harvard Educational Review, 77*(3), 285–316.

Au, K. H. (2011). *Literacy achievement and diversity: Keys to success for students, teachers, and schools.* New York: Teachers College Press.

Banks, J. A. (Ed.). (2004). *Diversity and citizenship education: Global perspectives.* San Francisco: Jossey-Bass.

Banks, J. A. (2008). Diversity, group identity, and citizenship education in a global age. *Educational Researcher, 37*(3), 129–139.

Banks, J. A. (2015a). Failed citizenship, civic engagement, and education. *Kappa Delta Pi Record, 51,* 151–154.

Banks, J. A. (2015b). *Global migration, structural inclusion, and citizenship education across nations: A conference sponsored by the Center for Multicultural Education* [conference program]. Seattle, WA: University of Washington.

Banks, J. A., Banks, C. A. M., Cortés, C. E., Hahn. C. L., Merryfield, M. M., Moodley, K. A., . . . Parker, W. C. (2005). *Democracy and diversity: Principles and concepts for educating citizens in a global age.* Seattle, WA: University of Washington, Center for Multicultural Education.

Callahan, R. M., & Muller, C. (2013). *Coming of political age: American schools and the civic development of immigrant youth.* New York: Russell Sage Foundation.

Castles, S., & Davidson, A. (2000). *Citizenship and migration: Globalization and the politics of belonging.* New York: Routledge.

Cohen, C. J. (2010). *Democracy remixed: Black youth and the future of American politics.* New York: Oxford University Press.

Gutmann, A. (2004). Unity and diversity in democratic multicultural education: Creative and destructive tensions. In J. A. Banks (Ed.), *Diversity and citizenship education: Global perspectives* (pp. 71–96). San Francisco: Jossey-Bass.

Ladson-Billings, G. (1994). *The dreamkeepers: Successful teachers of African American children.* San Francisco: Jossey-Bass.

Lee, C. (2007). *Culture, literacy, and learning: Taking bloom in the midst of the whirlwind.* New York: Teachers College Press.

Malin, H., Ballard, P. J., Attai, M. L., Colby, A., & Damon, W. (2014). *Youth civic development and education: A conference consensus report.* Stanford, CA: Stanford University, Center on Adolescence; and Seattle, WA: University of Washington, Center for Multicultural Education.

Maira, S. (2004). Imperial feelings: Youth culture, citizenship, and globalization. In M. Suárez-Orozco & D. B. Qin-Hilliard (Eds.), *Globalization, culture, and education in the new millennium* (pp. 203–234). Berkeley: University of California Press.

Milanovic, B. (2016). *Global inequality: A new approach for the age of globalization.* Cambridge, MA: Harvard University Press.

Nguyen, D. T. (2012). *Vietnamese immigrant youth and citizenship: How race, ethnicity, and culture shape sense of belonging.* El Paso, TX: LFB Scholarly Publishing.

Osler, A. (2016). *Human rights and schooling: An ethical framework for teaching social justice.* New York: Teachers College Press.

Steele, D. M., & Cohn-Vargas, B. (2013). *Identity safe classrooms: Places to belong and learn.* Thousand Oaks, CA: Corwin.

United Nations. (n.d.). *Growth in United Nations membership, 1945–present.* Retrieved from http://www.un.org/en/members/growth.shtm

Acknowledgments

It takes a community of committed scholars and substantial financial resources to conceptualize and implement an international conference and to publish a book that originates from it. I would like to thank the individuals and institutions that made our Talaris conference in Seattle intellectually stimulating and productive. The Spencer Foundation and the American Educational Research Association funded the conference. The funding provided by these two organizations enabled our conference to be held at the beautiful, sylvan Talaris Conference Center, which provided a residential venue for our conference that facilitated rich intellectual interactions and dialogues. I am grateful to Diana Hess, who was senior vice-president of the Spencer Foundation when our conference was funded, and to Felice Levine, executive director of AERA, for the potential they saw in our project and for funding it. I would like to thank Kimberly Bergsma, planning manager at the Talaris Conference Center, for being a sensitive and caring host who helped to make our stay enjoyable and memorable. I would like to thank Russell W. Rumberger, chair of the AERA Books Editorial Board, and his colleagues on the Board for their incisive, helpful, and encouraging comments on the manuscript. I am grateful to the three anonymous scholars who reviewed our manuscript for the AERA Books Editorial Board for their reading and their invaluable and discerning comments that helped to strengthen the book. I would also like to thank John S. Neikirk, director of publications at AERA, Martha Yager, managing editor, and Jessica Sibold, publications associate, for their diligent and insightful work during the production and editing of the manuscript for this book.

I am indebted to the authors of the chapters in this book for writing their papers prior to their arrival at the Seattle conference and for revising them after the conference, using feedback from external reviewers and the editor. The external reviewers prepared perceptive and helpful comments that greatly enriched and strengthened the chapters. A list of the external reviewers follows these Acknowledgments. Will Kymlicka was unable to attend our conference because of a previous commitment. I am grateful that he graciously agreed to read the manuscript and to write the Foreword. I would like to thank John Linse, senior publications designer at Creative Publications, University of Washington, for the exquisite design of the cover of this book and for his work and collaboration with me and the Center for Multicultural Education for nearly two decades.

Tao Wang and Yiting Chu, who were research assistants at the Center for Multicultural Education when the Seattle conference took place, played indispensable roles in the logistic arrangements for the conference and in the preparation of the manuscript. I am deeply appreciative of their contributions to the conference and to this book. Cherry A. McGee Banks was the associate chair of the Seattle conference and played a pivotal role in its conceptualization and implementation. As with all of the research projects and publications that I have undertaken during our nearly five-decade odyssey, she gave me unfailing support and encouragement for this intellectually stimulating and rewarding but challenging project.

External Reviewers

Ayman Agbaria, Haifa University, Israel
Saif Al-Maamari, Sultan Qaboos University, Oman
Theresa Alviar-Martin, Hong Kong Institute of Education, Hong Kong
Schirin Amir-Moazami, Free University of Berlin, Germany
Monisha Bajaj, University of San Francisco, U.S.
Mukhlis Abu Bakar, Nanyang Technological University, Singapore
Cherry A. McGee Banks, University of Washington, Bothell, U.S.
Keith C. Barton, Indiana University, U.S.
Saouma BouJaoude, American University of Beirut, Lebanon
Rachel Busbridge, Free University of Berlin, Germany
Margaret Crocco, Michigan State University, U.S.
Gunther Dietz, University of Veracruz, Mexico
Muhammad Faour, Phoenicia University, Lebanon
Shibao Guo, University of Calgary, Canada
Emre Güvendir, Trakya University, Turkey
Carole Hahn, Emory University, U.S.
Jonathan Jansen, University of the Free State, South Africa
Lee Jerome, Middlesex University, U.K.
Daehoon Jho, Sungshin Women's University, Korea
Kevin Johnson, University of California, Davis, U.S.
İlhan Kaya, Yildiz Teknik University, Turkey
Elizabeth Keyes, University of Baltimore, U.S.
Nadim Khoury, Bjørknes University College, Norway
Edith King, University of Denver, U.S.
Joyce King, Georgia State University, U.S.
Stephen Lafer, University of Nevada, Reno, U.S.
Zeus Leonardo, University of California, Berkeley, U.S.
Meira Levinson, Harvard University, U.S.
Françoise Lorcerie, Aix-Marseille University, France
Sigrid Luchtenberg, University of Duisburg-Essen, Germany
Darren E. Lund, University of Calgary, Canada
Ruth Mandel, University College London, U.K.
Karla McKanders, University of Tennessee, U.S.
Nagwa Megahed, American University in Cairo, Egypt
Seungho Moon, Loyola University Chicago, U.S.
Dirk Moses, European University Institute, Florence, Italy

Gerard Postiglione, University of Hong Kong, China
Jonathan D. Rigg, National University of Singapore, Singapore
Tatiane Cosentino Rodrigues, Federal University of São Carlos, Brazil
Beth Rubin, Rutgers University, U.S.
Alan Sears, University of New Brunswick, Canada
Avner Segall, Michigan State University, U.S.
Özlem Sensoy, Simon Fraser University, Canada
Jasmine Sim, Nanyang Technological University, Singapore
Rhonda Sofer, Gordon College of Education, Haifa, Israel
Crain Soudien, University of Cape Town, South Africa
Yasemin Soysal, University of Essex, U.K.
Chuanbao Tan, Beijing Normal University, China
Stephen Thornton, University of South Florida, U.S.
Saloshna Vandeyar, University of Pretoria, South Africa
Robert Verhine, Federal University of Bahia, Brazil
Jonathan Warren, University of Washington, Seattle, U.S.
Joel Westheimer, University of Ottawa, Canada
Suk-Ying Wong, Chinese University of Hong Kong, China
Shuqin Xu, Sun Yat-sen University, China
Shu Zhu, Beijing Language and Culture University, China
Geneviève Zoïa, Montpellier University, France
Victor Zúñiga, University of Monterrey, Mexico
David Zyngier, Monash University, Australia

Foreword

WILL KYMLICKA
Queen's University

This book addresses how citizenship education should be reconceived in an age of global migration. Traditional conceptions of citizenship education, often tied to homogenizing narratives of nationhood, are increasingly inadequate to the realities of "superdiverse" 21st-century classrooms and societies.[1] The chapters in this book identify the many different ways that educators around the world have responded to the challenges and opportunities of global migration, both at the level of state policies and at the level of individual teachers who seek to implement (or to work around) state policies. Taken together, the chapters provide a fascinating overview of a moment of profound, perhaps epochal, changes in the way citizenship education is theorized and taught.

I will not attempt here to summarize or catalogue these changes, but one preliminary observation is that the impact of global migration on citizenship education depends in part on whether migrants become citizens: that is, whether they are able to naturalize and thereby gain rights of membership in the political community where they reside. In traditional countries of immigration, there is a relatively clear path enabling at least some immigrants to become citizens. These immigrants are admitted as permanent residents, and having made their life in a new country, they have a right to naturalize after a period of residency (e.g., 5 years) and thereby be included among "the people" in whose name the state governs.[2]

The challenge to citizenship education in this context seems relatively clear: We need to revise inherited conceptions of "the people" to recognize the full diversity of all those who are members of society. Conceptions of "the people" have historically been tied to exclusionary and homogenizing narratives of nationhood, privileging majority ways of belonging while denigrating or rendering invisible minority identities and contributions.[3] A central task of citizenship education is to replace older, exclusionary ideas of nationhood with a more inclusive or multicultural conception of citizenship, which challenges inherited hierarchies of belonging and insists that society belongs to all its members, minority as much as majority. All members have a right to shape society's future, without having to deny or hide their identities. In this view, permanently settled immigrants are not "guests," "visitors," "aliens," or "foreigners"; they are "members" of the society and "citizens" like all other citizens. This has been a long-standing goal of multicultural education, including multicultural conceptions of citizenship education.

Several of the chapters discuss the fate of multicultural education, which has been subject to alternating waves of enthusiasm and skepticism. I'll return to some of the skepticism below. But it is worth emphasizing that multicultural citizenship rests on the assumption that immigrants settle permanently, become citizens, and thereby become members of "the people." Contemporary states are grounded in ideas of popular sovereignty: It is "the people" who are the bearers of sovereignty, which they exercise through the state. Permanently settled immigrants should be seen as members of the people in this sense. But the same is not necessarily true of temporary migrants. We do not typically think that tourists, international students, temporary asylum seekers, business visitors, or seasonal workers have a legitimate claim to political membership. Tourists who visit for one month, or international students who come to study the local language for six months, do not typically have a right to naturalize or to vote in elections. They are, indeed, more like "guests" or "visitors" than "members" or "citizens." As such, they are not necessarily included in conceptions of "multicultural citizenship." This understanding is, indeed, quite explicit in the multiculturalism policies adopted in Canada and Australia, which restrict their programming to permanently settled immigrant-origin ethnic groups, and which exclude temporary workers (such as the seasonal agricultural workers who come to Canada from Mexico at harvest time).[4] Since these groups are not citizens and are not eligible to become citizens, they are not included under the rubric of multicultural citizenship.

To say that temporary migrants are excluded from multicultural citizenship is not to say that they lack legitimate claims of justice, however. They may be visitors, not members, but they are human beings and, as such, have fundamental rights. We cannot enslave visitors, or subject them to torture, or treat them in ways that violate their dignity. This idea is often expressed through the idiom of universal human rights, owed to all individuals by virtue of their intrinsic moral status. It is one of the central tasks of education to inculcate respect for human rights and human dignity. Hence the importance of improved human rights education, which is emphasized in several chapters of this book. Given the rapid rise in various forms of temporary, circular, forced, and irregular migration, it is more important than ever that students learn to respect the basic human rights of all people, including the temporary visitors in their midst, the asylum seekers at the border, and the displaced and oppressed halfway around the world.

So we might think of civics education in an age of global migration as having two broad strands. First, there is citizenship education in the narrow sense, which focuses on how members of "the people" exercise their popular sovereignty. This requires some account of how a society determines who qualifies for membership, including how long-settled immigrants become members. In the age of global migration, this arguably requires a distinctly multicultural conception of belonging. Second, there is human rights education, which focuses on an ethics of respect for human dignity, and which is inherently cosmopolitan. Human rights education is applicable regardless of whether people are members of a given society, are staying temporarily, or are even present in the country.[5]

As I read the chapters in this book, the combination of multicultural citizenship and cosmopolitan human rights represents a compelling ideal for many authors and for the educators they profile. From Jordan to Japan, from Kuwait to Korea, from Germany to Lebanon, many educators seek to expand the conception of national membership to acknowledge all people who have settled permanently and made their life in a given country (i.e., we need a multicultural ethic of political membership); at the same time, many educators seek to strengthen respect for the human rights of all, even those who are just temporarily resident or whose rights are at risk in neighboring or distant countries (i.e., we need a cosmopolitan ethic of human rights). The descriptions of these efforts in various case studies in this book are both inspiring and revealing.

However, not all of the chapters endorse this vision. Indeed, what is striking to me, at least in comparison with the predecessor book (Banks, 2004), is the skepticism that several authors express about this combination, or more specifically, about the multicultural citizenship part of the package. While support for cosmopolitan human rights education is virtually unanimous in the chapters, support for multicultural citizenship is more muted and contested.

Undoubtedly, several factors explain this difference. One is skepticism about whether national narratives of membership and belonging can ever be truly transformed in a multicultural direction. Several chapters in this book document cases where moments of openness to multiculturalism have quickly passed and more homogenizing national narratives have been reasserted (e.g., in France, the United Kingdom, Germany). This tendency is exacerbated by the increasing "securitization" of education in an era of "the war against terror," which frames diversity as an issue of friends and enemies (as discussed in Osler's chapter).[6] So an earlier enthusiasm about the possibility of generating a compelling multicultural conception of nationhood has waned.[7]

Moreover, global migration has changed in a way that makes it more difficult to distinguish "permanent" migrants who are owed multicultural citizenship from "temporary" migrants owed cosmopolitan human rights. As Castles discusses, the very distinction between permanent and temporary migration is being challenged by scholars, who argue that we are living in a world of "superdiversity," with a multitude of legal statuses that are neither wholly temporary nor wholly permanent, but rather have varying degrees and levels of conditionality and precariousness (Vertovec, 2007). This development is reflected in calls to replace the old term "age of migration" (and "migration studies") with the new term "age of mobility" (and "mobility studies"). People no longer migrate permanently from country X to country Y; rather, they move repeatedly. They may become domiciled, but they do not "settle." As a result, in the view of many commentators, the multicultural conception of national citizenship is increasingly obsolete. People can no longer be neatly divided into permanent "members" and temporary "visitors": We are all just human beings who find themselves in a particular place at a particular moment, all subject to the risks of dislocation and global economic and environmental trends, all in various states of mobility.

In different ways, both of these observations challenge the view that the best response to global migration is to combine multicultural citizenship (for members) with cosmopolitan human rights (for nonmembers). If multicultural citizenship requires being able to identify which newcomers have settled permanently and thereby become members, then the proliferation of conditional and precarious legal statuses, and the realities of circular and temporary mobility, mean that fewer and fewer newcomers will be able to secure the protections of citizenship.[8] And even those fortunate few who secure legal citizenship through naturalization may find that they achieve only a second-class citizenship, constantly at risk of being judged alien or inadequate according to exclusionary and securitized narratives of nationhood.

Given these facts, skepticism about multicultural citizenship is understandable. But what is the alternative? The main alternative suggested in several chapters is to give more weight to cosmopolitan human rights and to reduce the importance of membership rights. States may continue to restrict national citizenship to newcomers who settle and integrate, but the political significance of that membership status can be minimized. In the case of Kuwait or the United Arab Emirates, for example, we might argue that even if migrant laborers are not eligible for national citizenship, this should not affect their labor rights, their access to health care, or the education rights of their children. These should be seen as fundamental human rights, regardless of one's membership status. In this way, we can shrink the importance of national citizenship, and expand the importance of universal human rights. The goal is not to expand the Kuwaiti state's view of who is a member of the Kuwaiti nation or the Kuwaiti people, as advocates of the multicultural citizenship approach would seek, but rather to insist that national membership should not determine people's treatment across a range of important issues. So, too, with the Syrian refugees in Lebanon and Jordan, or with the Somali migrants in South Africa. The goal is not necessarily to enable them to become citizens, but rather to strengthen the rights they are owed as human beings—in effect, to reduce the price that nonmembers pay for their lack of political membership.

A more radical suggestion would be to get rid of ideas of membership entirely and to base civics education entirely on universal human rights. This is hinted at in Chapter 3, by Hugh Starkey, who suggests that citizenship education should teach students to make "judgments on the basis of the universal standards of human rights" (p. 45), and in chapter 20, by Walter C. Parker, who suggests that a focus on human rights education is the logical conclusion of the case studies in this book. On this more radical proposal, nation-states would not have a two-track model of civics education, in which cosmopolitan human rights operated alongside national membership rights. Rather, they would have only cosmopolitan rights, owed to human beings as such, without any attempt to distinguish members from nonmembers. Educators would not ask South African children to think about the human rights of nonmembers or encourage a more multicultural conception of who belonged to the South African nation; rather, they would encourage the children not to think in terms of membership at all.

I doubt that either Starkey or Parker intends to make this radical suggestion. But this sort of pure cosmopolitanism is a significant strand in contemporary social and political theory, precisely because of growing skepticism that multicultural citizenship can respond to the intransigencies of nationalism or to the realities of changing patterns of mobility. And so it is worth asking: Can cosmopolitan human rights education take the place of multicultural citizenship education? Can we do without a politics of membership and belonging, and rely instead on a cosmopolitan ethic of respect for humanity? Is this the only or best way to address the realities of global mobility?

To my mind, this is the big question that is ultimately raised by several of the chapters, although it is perhaps too big to be addressed within this book. And I can hardly hope to answer it here. But I would note that there are both pragmatic and principled objections to pure cosmopolitanism. Pragmatically, if it is difficult to ask national majorities to embrace more inclusive conceptions of national membership, it seems utopian to ask them to stop caring about membership at all. There are also pragmatic worries about political stability. A cosmopolitan commitment to universal human rights tells us nothing about where political boundaries should be drawn: The Universal Declaration of Human Rights provides no guidance on whether there should be two countries in the world—or 20, or 200, or 2,000—or where their internal and external boundaries should be drawn. A cosmopolitan might respond that any such boundaries should be seen as accidental and arbitrary, but it is not clear that a democracy can function if its members view their boundaries as accidental and arbitrary. A stable democratic community requires that people have a sense of belonging together: For example, Norwegians feel that it is right and proper that they form a single political community that governs its members and its national territory, and that it would be wrong and unjust if Norwegians were subdivided or annexed. If the residents of Norway did not have the sense of belonging together—if they felt that they were just a random group of individuals thrown together in a randomly drawn territory—there would likely be interminable disputes about the redrawing of boundaries.

And this, in turn, raises more principled questions about whether "nations" or "peoples" have rights to self-determination and territorial sovereignty. Cosmopolitans tend to be dismissive of ideas of rights of self-government, but we might think that it is perfectly legitimate for the Norwegians—or the Kurds, or the Navajo[9]—to think of themselves as peoples with rights to self-determination, including the right to govern themselves and their national homelands, which in turn includes the right to make choices about various streams of permanent and temporary migration. If so, then we are inevitably back to ideas of membership and belonging, and to distinguishing settled immigrants, who are owed membership rights, from visitors, who are owed universal human rights.

Of course this is a superficial analysis. Much more could be said about how democratic politics is inextricably bound up with ideas of membership and belonging, as well as with ideas of cosmopolitan human rights.[10] And, as I said, I doubt that any of the authors in this book really intend to suggest that cosmopolitan human rights can entirely replace national membership rights. But there is a potential disjunction between the problems diagnosed in these chapters and the remedies being offered. Two distinct problems continually arise in these chapters: First, some permanently settled groups are wrongly denied their membership rights because they do not fit into the received national narrative; and second, some temporarily settled immigrant groups are denied their basic human rights. The chapters in this book provide a clear description of these problems. But insofar as the proposed remedy is to emphasize cosmopolitan human rights education, it seems incomplete. Educating students to recognize and respect the basic rights of all people, regardless of their membership status, is indeed a fundamental task of civics education. But, for as long as democratic politics is tied up with ideas of membership and belonging, educators will also need to help students think about membership in an ethically responsible way, including learning how to critically evaluate the traditional criteria (de jure and de facto) by which membership has been recognized.

This, I would argue, is one of the central tasks of multicultural citizenship education. The task is not to transcend or evade the distinction between members and nonmembers, but to think in a critical and ethically responsible way about the diversity of people who belong to society, and the diversity of ways in which they legitimately express that belonging. Multicultural citizenship education has run into roadblocks over the past decade, as several of the chapters document. But I would argue that it remains an essential part of civics education, alongside calls for more cosmopolitan human rights education.

Notes

1. The concept of superdiversity, used in several of the chapters, was coined by Steve Vertovec (2007, 2015) to capture the fact that migrants come from an increasingly diverse range of source countries and are assigned a dizzying array of legal statuses, often with conditional or precarious rights to stay, to work, to receive social benefits, and so forth. Immigrants are increasingly diverse not only in their ethnic and religious backgrounds but also in their legal and political statuses.

2. For the idea that political citizenship should track social membership, and why this entails that long-settled immigrants have a right to naturalize, see Carens, 2013.

3. The presence of such hierarchies of belonging in traditional narratives of nationhood is a recurring theme in all of the chapters of this book, but Angela Banks's chapter on the United States provides a particularly lucid discussion, not just of which groups were excluded by this hierarchy, but also of the grounds of worth and respectability used to rationalize the exclusions.

4. On the exclusion of temporary migrants from multiculturalism in Australia, see Levey, in press.

5. I am not implying that civics education is, or should be, formally divided into these two streams, or even that it should use these labels. Some authors define multicultural citizenship in a sufficiently broad way to include ideas of cosmopolitan human rights; and some conceptions of human rights education are sufficiently broad to include ideas of multicultural citizenship. But even if the two streams are classified under a single label, I would suggest that there remains an important difference in their underlying normative logic. One strand focuses on rights that derive from membership in a bounded community; the other focuses on rights owed universally, regardless of membership.

6. Even where an official policy of commitment to multiculturalism remains, as in Canada, it arguably has been reoriented in a neoliberal direction, reducing its potential to contribute to social justice. See the discussion of neoliberal multiculturalism in the chapter by Joshee and Thomas.

7. I have argued elsewhere that pronouncements of the "death of multiculturalism" are overstated and that multicultural conceptions of nationhood remain resilient in many countries (Kymlicka, 2015). But there is no denying that pro-multiculturalists are on the defensive.

8. For the argument that global mobility renders national multiculturalism obsolete, see, for example, Baines and Sharma, 2002; Carruthers, 2013; Fleras, 2015; and Glick Schiller, 2016. I address this in more depth in Kymlicka, in press.

9. For the argument that cosmopolitan defenses of migrants' rights to freely settle anywhere have ignored indigenous peoples' rights to govern themselves and their territories, see Lawrence and Dua, 2005.

10. I develop some of these ideas in Kymlicka, 2015, in press.

References

Baines, D., & Sharma, N. (2002). Migrant workers as non-citizens: The case against citizenship as a social policy concept. *Studies in Political Economy, 69*(1), 75–107.

Banks, J. A. (Ed.). (2004). *Diversity and citizenship education: Global perspectives*. San Francisco: Jossey-Bass.

Carens, J. (2013). *The ethics of immigration*. Oxford, UK: Oxford University Press.

Carruthers, A. (2013). National multiculturalism, transnational identities. *Journal of Intercultural Studies, 34*(2), 214–228.

Fleras, A. (2015). Beyond multiculturalism: Managing complex diversities in a postmulticultural Canada. In S. Guo & L. Wong (Eds.), *Revisiting multiculturalism in Canada: Theories, policies and debates* (pp. 311–334). Rotterdam, NL: Sense.

Glick Schiller, N. (2016). The question of solidarity and society. *Comparative Migration Studies, 4*(6), 1–9.

Kymlicka, W. (2015). Solidarity in diverse societies: Beyond neoliberal multiculturalism and welfare chauvinism. *Comparative Migration Studies, 3*(1), 1–19.

Kymlicka, W. (in press). Multiculturalism without citizenship. In A. Triandafyllidou (Ed.), *Multicultural governance in a mobile world*. Edinburgh, UK: Edinburgh University Press.

Lawrence, B., & Dua, E. (2005). Decolonizing antiracism. *Social Justice, 32*(4), 120–143.

Levey, G. (in press). Multiculturalism on the move: An Australian perspective. In A. Triandafyllidou (Ed.), *Multicultural governance in a mobile world*. Edinburgh, UK: Edinburgh University Press.

Vertovec, S. (2007). Super-diversity and its implications. *Ethnic and Racial Studies, 29*(6), 1024–1054.

Vertovec, S. (2015). *Super-diversity*. London, UK: Routledge.

Introduction

Global Migration and Citizenship Education

James A. Banks
University of Washington, Seattle

Migration within and across nation-states is a worldwide phenomenon. The movement of people across national boundaries is as old as the nation-state itself. However, never before in the history of the world has the movement of diverse racial, cultural, ethnic, religious, and linguistic groups within and across nation-states been as large-scale and rapid or raised such complex and difficult questions about citizenship, human rights, democracy, and education. Many worldwide trends and developments are challenging the notion of educating students to function in one nation-state. These trends include the ways in which people are moving back and forth across national borders, the rights of movement permitted by the European Union, and the rights codified in the Universal Declaration of Human Rights (1948).

Assimilation, Diversity, and Global Migration

Prior to the ethnic revitalization movements of the 1960s and 1970s, the aim of schools in most nation-states was to develop citizens who internalized national values, venerated national heroes, and accepted glorified versions of national histories. These goals of citizenship education are obsolete today because many people have multiple national commitments, live in more than one nation, and practice "flexible citizenship" (Ong, 1999). However, the development of citizens who have global and cosmopolitan identities and commitments is contested in nation-states around the world because nationalism remains strong. Nationalism and globalization coexist in tension worldwide. Although nationalism remains strong and tenacious, globalization has a significant influence on migration. In 2015, there were approximately 244 million international migrants in the world (United Nations, 2016). Many of these migrants have ambiguous citizenship status and are victims of structural exclusion, racial microaggressions, cultural erasure, deculturalization (Spring, 2010)—and, sometimes, violence. The outcome of the U.K. Brexit referendum—voting to leave the European Union in 2016—as well as the rising power of right-wing political parties in European nations such as Austria, France, and Hungary—are partly rooted in xenophobia and racism toward immigrants (Aisch, Pearce, & Rousseau, 2016)

Nations with different kinds of political systems—for example, democratic republics such as the United States and South Korea, federal republics such as Germany and Brazil, and Communist nations such as China and Cuba—must deal with complex educational issues when trying to respond to the problems wrought by international migration in ways consistent with their ideologies and declarations. Researchers have amply documented the wide gap between democratic ideals and the school experiences of minoritized groups in nations around the world. Students such as the Maori in New Zealand (Penetito, 2010), Muslims in France (Fredette, 2014), Chechens in Russia (Froumin, 2004), and Mexican Americans in the United States (Valenzuela, 1999) experience discrimination in school because of their ethnic, racial, cultural, linguistic, and religious differences (Banks, 2009).

Nation-states and their schools—regardless of the type of political system—must grapple with a number of salient issues, paradigms, and ideologies as their populations become more diverse. The extent to which nation-states make multicultural citizenship possible (Kymlicka, 1995), the achievement gap between minoritized and majority groups (Ladson-Billings, 2006), and the language rights of immigrant and minoritized groups (Gándara & Hopkins, 2010) are among the unresolved and contentious issues with which diverse nations and schools must deal. Nations throughout the world are trying to determine whether they will perceive themselves as multicultural and allow immigrants to experience multicultural citizenship (Kymlicka, 1995), or continue to embrace an assimilationist ideology. In nation-states that embrace multicultural citizenship, immigrant and minority groups can retain important aspects of their languages and cultures and enjoy full citizenship rights as well.

Nations in various parts of the world have responded to the citizenship and cultural rights of immigrant and minoritized groups in different ways. Since the ethnic revitalization movements of the 1960s and 1970s that were stimulated by the Black civil right movement in the United States, many of the national leaders and citizens in the United States, Canada, and Australia have viewed their nations as multicultural democracies (Banks, 2009; Banks & Lynch, 1986). An ideal exists within these nations that minoritized groups can retain important elements of their community cultures and participate fully in the national civic community. However, as the chapters in this book indicate, there is a wide gap between the ideals within these nations and the experiences of minoritized groups. Minoritized groups in the United States (Nieto, 2009), Canada (Joshee, 2009), and Australia (Inglis, 2009) experience discrimination both in schools and in the wider society. A citizenship education dilemma exists when nation-states try to "teach students democratic ideals and values within social, economic, and educational contexts that contradict [those] ideals" (Banks, 2004, pp. 9–10).

Other nations, such as Japan (Hirasawa, 2009), Korea (Moon, 2012), and Germany (Eksner & Cheema, Chapter 8, this volume; Luchtenberg, 2009), have been reluctant to view themselves as multicultural. In the past, citizenship was closely linked to biological heritage and characteristics in these three nations. The biological conception of citizenship in Japan, Korea, and Germany has eroded significantly in the last decade, but it has left a tenacious legacy in those nations. A statement made by German Chancellor Angela Merkel at a meeting of the Christian Democratic Union party in October 2010 evoked Germany's troubled past of dealing with ethnic, racial, and religiously diverse groups and made headlines around the world. Merkel said, "We kidded ourselves a while. We said, 'They won't stay, [and after some time] they will be gone,' but this isn't reality. And of course, the approach [to building] a multicultural [society] and to liv[ing] side by side and to enjoy each other . . . has failed, utterly failed" (cited in Clark, 2010). Castles (2004) refers to Germany's response to immigrants as "differential exclusion," which is "partial and temporary integration of immigrant workers into society—that is, they are included in those subsystems of society necessary for their economic role: the labor market, basic accommodation, work-related health care, and welfare" (p. 32). However, immigrants and their descendants are often excluded from full social, economic, and civic participation.

The chapters in this book describe the challenges that marginalized and minoritized racial, ethnic, cultural, linguistic, and religious groups experience in their efforts to attain full citizenship rights and participation in 18 nations. They also describe how civic and multicultural educators are conceptualizing and implementing civic education programs that enable minoritized students to develop a sense of structural inclusion, political efficacy, and civic participation. The chapters detail how these challenges can be mitigated by school reform that enables students from diverse groups to experience structural inclusion, equity, and cultural recognition (Gutmann, 2004). Most of the chapters on specific nations include profiles of effective teachers enabling their students to acquire civic literacy, political efficacy, and civic engagement skills.

Overview of Chapters and Parts

Diversity and Citizenship Education: Cross-Cutting Issues and Concepts

Three chapters in Part 1 describe the cross-cutting issues and concepts related to global migration, citizenship, and citizenship education. In Chapter 1, Castles examines the influence of global migration on human security and human development. He also describes emerging forms of migration, with a focus on women and forced migrants. Many international migrants come from the less developed nations in the Global South and seek work in developed nations in the Global North. These migrants experience many problems when they arrive at their destinations, including the denial of full citizenship rights and equal educational opportunities. They are also victimized by discrimination and xenophobia. Castle describes how immigration changes both the migrants and the communities into which they settle. He also describes the myriad difficulties that migrants experience in attaining full citizenship rights.

Bashir, in Chapter 2, describes the serious limitations of conceptualizing citizenship within nation-state boundaries and constructs and illustrates a regional notion of citizenship. He contends that globalization makes a regional conception of citizenship essential, especially in deeply divided and conflict-ridden societies. He maintains that globalization weakens the tight association between territorial nation-states, rights, and citizenship but also creates the possibility of establishing a deterritorialized, regional notion of citizenship that allows regional integration and normalization. Khanna (2016) echoes Bashir's vision when he argues that socially and economically, the United States is reorganizing itself around "regional infrastructure lines that ignore state and even national borders."

Starkey (Chapter 3), too, believes that citizenship should be conceptualized beyond the nation-state, but his conception of civic education is global rather than regional. He thinks that civic education should foster "cosmopolitan citizenship," which enables students to view themselves as connected to people in nations around the world; cosmopolitan citizenship is supranational and is guided by ideals stated in documents such as the Universal Declaration of Human Rights. Starkey views human rights as an essential component of civic education programs and interventions that foster cosmopolitan citizenship. He describes practical examples of how human rights lessons can be taught within national contexts, such as by including content that focuses on Martin Luther King, Jr., and the civil right movement in the United States, and on Nelson Mandela and the struggle against apartheid in South Africa.

United States, Canada, and South Africa

Global migration has increased ethnic, cultural, linguistic, and religious diversity in nations around the world (Banks, 2009). Immigrant nations such as Canada and the United States have been diverse since their founding. The ethnic and cultural diversity among the native peoples of these lands was greatly increased by the myriad European groups that conquered and colonized them. The United States and Canada view themselves as immigrant nations and historically have developed citizenship and citizenship education policies and initiatives that enabled most European immigrants to attain structural inclusion and social mobility; historically they have had more restrictive policies for immigrants from non-European nations such as China, Japan, India, Pakistan, and Nigeria. At present, Canada, the United States, and South Africa are industrialized representative democracies. South Africa shares with the United States a history of institutionalized discrimination and structural racism (Adam & Moodley, 2015). However, it is not an immigrant nation in ways that parallel Canada or the United States because Indigenous Blacks from different ethnic groups make up a large part of its population (e.g., 80.5% in 2015; Statistics South Africa, 2015).

The chapters in Part 2 describe ways in which citizenship and citizenship education are complex, multifaceted, and changing in the United States, Canada, and South Africa. Angela Banks (Chapter 4) details a theoretical framework for conceptualizing citizenship and identifies the values, norms, and practices that were considered essential aspects of American culture and used in making legal decisions about granting U.S. citizenship between 1790 and 1952. Banks critically analyzes congressional hearings and debates, administrative records, and judicial opinions during this period and identifies five key aspects of American culture that immigrants were required to adopt for naturalization: commitment to democracy and the rule of law, belief in individualism, self-sufficiency, Christian beliefs and morals, and English language skills. She also describes how desirable values, norms, and practices for naturalization purposes were racialized. In the final part of her chapter, Banks describes strategies for effectively teaching about immigration and citizenship using legal concepts and principles.

Joshee and Thomas (Chapter 5) chronicle the historical context in which citizenship education developed in Canada. Although Canada introduced a federal multiculturalism policy in 1971, the implementation of this policy was limited and complicated by assimilationist policies and pressures for Anglo-conformity, as Joshee and Thomas describe. Since the 1990s, policies relating to multiculturalism and citizenship education in Canada have been socially cohesive, emphasizing integration, national harmony, economic progress, and neoliberalism. Joshee and Thomas recommend "slow peace" as a promising approach to citizenship education that will mitigate cultural and structural forms of violence—such as racism and forced assimilation—that cause ethnic and racial conflict in Canadian society.

Slow peace derives from an engagement with the concept of slow violence (Nixon, 2011) and the Gandhian ethic of peace (Gandhi, 1993). Monica, the teacher profiled in Chapter 5, used the slow peace approach to help her students construct a community that promoted harmony and kindness and encouraged them to take actions to alleviate injustices in their communities and to develop a commitment to civic engagement, peace, and social justice.

Moodley (Chapter 6) illuminates the contradictions within South African society that result from the democratic constitution that it adopted in 1996 and the xenophobia that is experienced there by immigrants from other African nations. She describes how the tensions between universal human rights and rights based on citizenship give rise to xenophobia and discrimination against immigrants in South Africa. Moodley details the results of a study she conducted with South African students in four township secondary schools. Most of the students (51%) had "an outlook of compassion, inclusiveness, and care for the people." However, Moodley characterizes 25% of the students as xenophobic and 25% as ambivalent. She maintains that the current political education in South Africa fails to counter xenophobia among students. Moodley contends that teaching political literacy should be the focus of citizenship education because it will enable students to attain a cosmopolitan identity that will help to mitigate discrimination and xenophobia.

England, Norway, Germany, and France

The historic diversity in Europe was increased when thousands of immigrants from colonial nations such as India, Pakistan, Algeria, Jamaica, and Indonesia migrated to nations such as England, France, and the Netherlands to improve their economic status in the years following World War II. Diversity in European nations continued to increase during the 1980s and 1990s. However, most European nations do not view themselves as immigrant nations and have consequently found it difficult to construct citizenship and citizenship education policies and programs that reflect civic equality and exemplify multicultural citizenship (Koopmans, Statham, Giugni, & Passy, 2005; Lucassen, 2005; Osler & Starkey, 2005).

The population of Muslims is increasing throughout Europe, especially in France, the United Kingdom, and Switzerland. The growth of the Muslim population and the rash of terrorist attacks by ISIS and Islamic extremists in Western nations have stimulated the rise of xenophobia and Islamophobia in Europe. In 2004 France banned the wearing of religious symbols in state schools—for example, the headscarf or *hijab* worn by Muslim female students. In 2009, a referendum was passed in Switzerland that prohibited the building of minarets on mosques. One of the most difficult challenges with which European nations are dealing is the growth of Muslims in their populations. Many Europeans believe that Muslims are threatening European civilization and culture (Bawer, 2006). Islam is the fastest growing religion in both Europe and the United States (Cesari, 2004). In 2010, Germany and France had the largest populations of Muslims in the European Union (4.8 million and 4.7 million, respectively); however, Russia had the largest population of Muslims in Europe (14 million; Pew Research Center, 2015).

Osler (Chapter 7) discusses three challenges associated with integrating minority groups and implementing policies to support human rights and social justice in Europe: (a) the large number of refugees and migrants arriving in Europe; (b) public debates about diversity, integration, and multiculturalism; and (c) the securitization of education policy. Osler profiles Veronica, a Ghanaian British teacher of high school students in London, describing how her experiences as a minoritized British citizen motivated her to teach democratic citizenship, human rights, and social justice. Veronica's teaching exemplifies professional and moral ethics. She tried to empower her students from minoritized communities and to help both mainstream White students and minoritized students experience human rights education and develop political efficacy.

In the final part of her chapter, Osler uses case studies in England and Norway to reflect on national educational policy initiatives. She states that although the two countries differ in their levels of demographic diversity and integration of minoritized population groups, they share an assimilationist orientation in education policies, which emphasizes national values and the "securitization" of education policy that targets Muslim students. Osler concludes that Norway is facing "a human rights education paradox": Human rights principles are deemed essential, yet human rights education in schools is weak.

Eksner and Cheema (Chapter 8) use a postcolonial perspective to examine the public debate in Germany about how secular society responds to the resurgence of religion in educational institutions and civil society. They describe how the "othering" and exclusion of minoritized groups—especially Muslim youth—occur in German schools. The authors provide an overview of the hegemonic narratives that construct and represent Muslims as civilizational, cultural, ethnic, and religious "others," as opposed to Germans who represent the culture and values of Judeo-Christian Western civilization. These narratives were exacerbated by the ideas of enlightenment and secularism in German society. The authors contend that the recent terrorist attacks in Europe and the rise of ISIS instantiated discourses that viewed Islam as anti-Western.

Eksner and Cheema describe German civic education that is designed to develop active, responsible citizens and point out the contrast between democratic values and the reality experienced by minoritized students. The authors present a profile of Almas Nur, a human rights educator, and describe how her human rights–oriented approach addressed anti-Muslim racism through the "(Un)Believable" workshops. In the workshops students were invited to analyze discriminatory discourses and human rights abuses against marginalized groups and were empowered to learn "about, through, and for human rights." Eksner and Cheema conclude Chapter 8 by recommending training and professional development opportunities for teachers and nondominant youths that empower them to exercise their civic and human rights as transformative agents for social change.

Bozec (Chapter 9) presents an overview of the "French model" of citizenship that is centered on the secular values of the Republic and a strict separation of religion and the state (*laïcité*). She discusses the tensions between the assimilationist model of French citizenship education, which focuses on national identity, and the increasing presence of students of immigrant descent in French schools. Accommodating the needs of immigrant heritage students in schools is viewed as a religious or Muslim issue that is considered "anti-Republican" under the restrictive conception of *laïcité*. After the terrorist attacks in 2015, citizenship education emphasized student civic engagement and a less restrictive conception of *laïcité*.

Bozec profiles Arnaud, an effective citizenship education teacher. She describes the difficulties he experienced teaching in a school context characterized by inequality and discrimination. Arnaud tried to "increase students' awareness about the situation of Muslim people in France [and] their multiple identities" through conversation with students, reflective activities, classroom debates about civic issues, and the use of photographs. He also presented a diversity of perspectives regarding freedom of expression after the Charlie Hebdo terrorist attack—which occurred in Paris on January 7, 2015—and the complex nature of the social context, to help his students become informed and critical thinkers. Bozec uses the profile of Arnaud's teaching to illustrate the possibilities, as well as the challenges, of effective citizenship education in French schools.

China, Korea, and Singapore

China, Korea, and Singapore are grappling with ways to reconceptualize citizenship and citizenship education to reflect their increasing diversity. Nations such as Japan and Korea do not view themselves as immigrant nations but are characterized by growing ethnic, cultural, linguistic, and religious diversity. China has 55 officially designated ethnic minority groups (Postiglione, 2009). It is experiencing massive waves of internal migration from rural to urban areas (Wang, 2015); China now has one of the world's largest internal migrations, which consisted of 236 million people in 2013. Rural inhabitants are settling in large waves in cities such as Beijing, Shanghai, Guangzhou, and Shenzhen (National Bureau of Statistics of China, 2013).

In 2015, almost two million (1,741,919) foreign residents lived in South Korea, comprising 3.4% of its population. The number of foreign nationals in Korea tripled in the 10 years preceding 2015 (Eum, 2015). Although Chinese immigrants and their descendants constitute the dominant and largest percentage of Singapore's population (about 74.2%), Singapore is ethnically and linguistically diverse. In 2014, the Malay ethnic group made up approximately 13.3% of the population, Indians 9%, and other ethnic groups about 3.3% (Department of Statistics Singapore, 2015).

In Chapter 10, Law examines the tensions between ethnic diversity and citizenship education for ethnic minority groups in China. He reviews policies related to ethnic minority issues and citizenship education for ethnic minority students. These policies reflect China's effort to maintain ethnic diversity as well as national integration and security. Law also describes the affirmative educational policies that China has implemented to accommodate the education of ethnic minority students. Law states that China's citizenship education and ethnic solidarity education for ethnic minority students focuses on "national identification, dialectical materialism, and atheism." After analyzing the curriculum and textbooks, Law concludes that ethnic solidarity education in China prioritizes national unity and security concerns over ethnic diversity and educational equality for ethnic groups. The education of ethnic groups in China is guided by a strong assimilationist policy, despite the stated policy of permitting ethnic minority groups to maintain components of their languages and cultures. Law's chapter also supports the observation that "multicultural education in China has been conceptualized primarily as a compensatory endeavor that is designed to benefit marginalized ethnic minority groups. It is rarely viewed as an intervention strategy for the Han majority" (Banks, 2014, p. xvi).

Cha, Ham, and Lim (Chapter 11) describe the ways in which the focus on high-stakes testing causes schools and teachers in Korea to focus on the core subject areas such as math and reading and to largely neglect citizenship education. This approach, the authors contend, has produced students who are near the top of international ratings such as the Programme for International Student Assessment (PISA) in subjects such as mathematics and reading, but whose ability to deliberate on social issues and to participate in civic action are low. A wide gap exists between the students' high level of civic knowledge and their low level of civic engagement. The authors also discuss the challenges caused by demographic diversity in Korean society, which is neither widely recognized nor accepted by the general public.

The authors propose an alternative approach to citizenship education: the *yungbokhap* model, which consists of four dimensions: autonomy, bridgeability, contextuality, and diversity. Ms. Kim, a Russian language teacher, is profiled in this chapter. She uses the *yungbokhap* model to integrate citizenship education into her teaching. The authors describe how Ms. Kim taught the idea of "fair travel" to help her students think critically and reflectively about social issues in the global society and to cultivate their global citizenship through active and participatory learning. Cha, Ham, and Lim conclude their chapter by describing the benefits of creating a learning environment that fosters and sustains the *yungbokhap* model.

Ismail (Chapter 12) describes Singapore's national narrative as that of an accidental small nation that has defied expectations and become immensely successful economically and socially in managing diversity. She discusses the role that citizenship education has played in building a multicultural, multiracial, multireligious, and multilingual nation. Ismail describes the national curriculum—especially the social studies curriculum—which was designed to respond to globalization and to reach a "delicate balance between the national and the global with the overriding mission of economic survival."

Ismail analyzes the highly stratified education system in Singapore that has produced what she called a "testocracy"—a nation in which the fate of students is determined largely by their performance on standardized tests. Cha, Ham, and Lim, in Chapter 11, describe a similar kind of testocracy. Malik, the teacher profiled in Chapter 12, tried to teach beyond the testocracy structure, bringing his students' experiences and backgrounds into the classroom by inviting questions from them and creating an inclusive learning environment for all students, especially immigrant students. Malik's teaching practices demonstrate the potential for the co-existence of a national education curriculum and an individual teacher's agency.

The Middle East

The rich ethnic, cultural, linguistic, and religious diversity in the nations of the Middle East has created complex problems of constructing nation-states with shared national and civic cultures that are viewed as legitimate and inclusive by the diverse groups within each nation. The majority of the populations in nations such as Qatar and the United Arab Emirates (UAE) are immigrants (Faour & Muasher, 2011). Immigrants are also a significant part of Kuwait's population. In addition to the problems wrought by large immigrant, expatriate, and refugee populations, there is massive political alienation and discontent in many of the Gulf states, resulting in part from autocratic political leadership and massive unemployment among young people.

Many of the divisive tensions within Middle East nations originated in the Sykes-Picot Agreement signed May 19, 1916. France and Britain divided up the territories of the former Ottoman Empire without consideration for the cultural, ethnic, linguistic, and religious boundaries that existed within and between nations, but primarily to fulfill the aims of European nations seeking to establish spheres of influence (Encyclopaedia Britannica, 2016). Since December 18, 2010, public protests have occurred in nations such as Egypt, Libya, Morocco, Algeria, Syria, Oman, Saudi Arabia, and Kuwait. Young people were involved in most of the protests (Al-Nakib, 2012), which became known as the "Arab Spring." The youth participating in those protests and demonstrations used social media to voice their discontent and to organize politically.

As indicated in several of the chapters in Part 5 of this book, it is challenging for educators to teach for political literacy and active citizenship in nations with autocratic political systems that provide few possibilities for rigorous discussion, debate, criticism of political leaders, or civic engagement and participation. The disappointment and disillusionment that resulted from the failure of the Arab Spring, the rise of the Islamic State (ISIS)—which many young people have joined—and the reestablishment of autocratic leaders in most of the nations in the Middle East severely complicate and limit the possibility of educating students for political literacy and civic engagement in most nations in the Middle East. Pfeffer (2016) describes the failure of the Arab Spring and the reestablishment of autocratic leaders in most Middle Eastern nations:

> Across the region the tide had been turned back. In Bahrain, where a Shia majority, encouraged by Iran, demanded civil rights, the Sunni regime increased repression. In Yemen the president went into exile; and in Libya, Muammar Gadaffi was gunned down on the street. But in their absence these countries are torn by internecine conflict and civil war. Bashar Assad has survived in Syria, at the price of drowning the country in the blood of 300,000 citizens, dislocating over half the population from their homes and exiling at least four million.

Israel is usually considered a democratic nation-state that was founded as a haven for Jews, who were victims of the Holocaust during World War II and had been persecuted in many nations. However, Arab citizens (Agbaria, 2016) and Jewish immigrants, such as Ethiopians (Ben-Peretz & Aderet-German, 2016), face serious challenges to attaining full citizenship rights in Israel. Smooha (as cited in Tatar, 2004) describes Israel as an ethnic democracy "driven by ethnic nationalism, . . . identified with a 'core ethnic nation', not with its citizens" (p. 382).

Faour (Chapter 13) describes the sociopolitical and educational contexts in the Arab world for three types of immigrants: displaced people, refugees, and temporary workers or expatriates. He explains the civic marginalization and educational exclusion of immigrant and expatriate students in Lebanon, Jordan, and the United Arab Emirates. All three countries face challenges related to cultural diversity from within and acceptance of immigrants, expatriates, and refugees from a variety of nation-states, most recently refugees from Syria. Although many programs have been implemented to provide quality education for immigrant and refugee children in Lebanon, Jordan, and the United Arab Emirates, Faour found that many policies related to immigration and education for immigrant students in these countries deny them access to public education and use an exclusionary approach to education that is a form of injustice. He sets forth proposals for rethinking education for immigrant and refugee students in Lebanon, Jordan, and the United Arab Emirates, based on principles of social justice and human rights, including providing equal educational opportunities for students regardless of citizenship status, inclusive learning environments, and global citizenship education.

Akar (Chapter 14) describes education for active citizenship in Lebanon. He defines *active citizenship* as "a desirable form of citizenship grounded in democratic and human rights principles" and *education for active citizenship* as "an educational experience whereby learners live the approaches to being active citizens." He profiles Nadine, a civics teacher whose classes consisted of students from religiously and politically diverse backgrounds. Akar describes how Nadine reimagined and redesigned her civics curriculum in ways that went beyond the narrow content of the required textbooks, and how she engaged her students in activities such as filmmaking, debate, and poster making that focused on human rights and social justice issues in Lebanon as well as in the rest of the Arab world. These activities helped Nadine's students to develop autonomy, collaboration, and critical thinking skills as well as opportunities to learn active citizenship.

Al-Nakib (Chapter 15) describes the concepts of transformative citizenship and human rights education that support active and visionary learning. She provides an overview of the education system in Kuwait and national education policies that perpetuate what she calls "differential segregation" in Kuwaiti society. Al-Nakib provides a detailed analysis of one document on national citizenship education issued by the Kuwaiti Ministry of Education, which focuses on national citizenship and Islamic hegemony. She profiles Amani, an effective teacher of civic education, who taught in a girls' school. Al-Nakib describes how Amani encouraged her students to engage in active and transformative learning through activities and a creative rearrangement of the classroom space in spite of political and administrative restraints. Amani's pedagogical approaches included helping her students to analyze human rights issues in Kuwait by using alternative learning materials and simulation activities. Amani also encouraged her students to take action on student rights issues that were related to their daily lives. Al-Nakib also describes how Amani encouraged an Iraqi girl to share the culture of her country with her classmates to give her recognition and a sense of inclusion.

In Chapter 16, Aydin and Koc-Damgaci provide an overview of how citizenship was developed and enacted in the Ottoman Empire and the Turkish Republic, with a focus on the citizenship duties and rights of religious and ethnically minoritized groups. In the Ottoman Empire, which consisted of many diverse groups, minoritized groups were able to speak their home languages, practice their religions, and maintain their cultures. The authors contend that a multicultural education focus in teacher education is essential to guarantee the citizenship rights and accommodate the need of minoritized students, including Kurdish students and the recently arrived Syrian refugee children and youth. The authors present a profile of Mr. Ozgur, a Kurdish teacher who taught a class of diverse students in Istanbul. Mr. Ozgur responded to the cultural and linguistic backgrounds of his students with empathy and helped them to overcome prejudices they held toward other ethnically minoritized and immigrant students. Aydin and Koc-Damgaci describe how Mr. Ozgur developed empathy for students from diverse groups after being exposed to multicultural education. He tried to build a cooperative relationship with his students from diverse backgrounds and used culturally responsive instructional and evaluative strategies.

In Chapter 17, Bekerman and Cohen critically discuss the limitations of traditional discourses of multiculturalism and provide an overview of the social, historical, and political contexts that shape the Palestinian and Jewish conflicts in Israel. They analyze the national civics curriculum in Israel and conclude that it fails to engage Israeli students from diverse backgrounds and consequently fails to promote multicultural citizenship; instead, it reinforces social and political injustices. The authors present excerpts from interviews with civics teachers in Israel that reveal the challenges of providing civic education to diverse cultural, ethnic, and religious groups in Israel. The challenges include the fragility of Israel's democracy, a lack of teacher efficacy, and a narrowly focused civics curriculum. Bekerman and Cohen conclude Chapter 17 with a call for a curriculum that is inclusive of the complex cultural and civic identities of students from diverse Israeli groups.

Mexico and Brazil

The populations of Mexico and Brazil consist of Indians who were native to those lands, people of African descent whose ancestors were forced to come in chains, and many peoples of European descent, such as the Spanish and Portuguese. Mestizos (people of Amerindian-Spanish heritage) make up 62% of Mexico's population. Twenty-one percent of the population was classified in 2012 as predominantly Amerindian, 7% as Amerindian, and 10% as mostly European (Central Intelligence Agency, 2016). People of African descent make up a small part of the population, about 1.4 million, or 1.2% (Fernandez de Castro, 2015). The country has a substantial Indigenous population.

Mexican teachers interviewed in 1977 indicated that the Mexican school curriculum devoted considerable attention to the cultures of ancient Mexican Indians but essentially neglected the histories and plight of contemporary Indigenous groups (Banks, 1978). Levinson and Luna Elizarrarás, in Chapter 18, also describe how Indigenous groups were glorified in the 20th century but were granted few differentiated citizenship rights. These authors describe how minoritized groups in Mexico other than the Indigenous groups—such as people of African descent and immigrants from Asia, the Middle East, and Central and South America—are largely invisible in Mexico and in the school curriculum. Consequently, the authors characterize diversity in Mexico as "stealth diversity."

Brazil's Black population, which was 97 million in 2010, is the world's largest outside Africa. However, race and racial categories are complex in Brazil. In 2010, the official census indicated that 47.7% of the population was White, 43.1% was Mulatto, 7.6% was Black, 1.1% was Asian, and 0.4% was Indigenous (Central Intelligence Agency, 2016). Because of the fluid and intricate nature of racial categories and options in Brazil (Telles, 2004), the percentage of the people who self-identify as Black varies over time. In 2011, the *Guardian* published a story with the headline "Brazil census shows African-Brazilians in the majority for the first time," quoted here:

> For the first time since records began black and mixed race people form the majority of Brazil's population, the country's latest census has confirmed. Preliminary results from the 2010 census, released on Wednesday, show that 97 million Brazilians, or 50.7% of the population, now define themselves as black or mixed race, compared with 91 million or 47.7% who label themselves white. The proportion of Brazilians declaring themselves white was down from 53.7% in 2000, when Brazil's last census was held. (Phillips, 2011)

Levinson and Luna Elizarrarás (Chapter 18) state that the policy of citizenship and citizenship education in 19th-century Mexico was intended to assimilate its Indigenous population into a mainstream Mestizo culture, and that the policy continued in the 20th century, after the Mexican Revolution. A more pluralistic and inclusive policy has emerged since the 1980s. The authors emphasize developments at the lower secondary level since 1993 because the national ministry of education has focused most of its efforts in citizenship education at this level. Levinson and Luna Elizarrarás conclude that Mexican citizenship education has shifted from an emphasis on national identity and assimilation to a multicultural focus on democratic membership and participation. However, these policies and curricula have been limited and sometimes contradictory and do not reflect the full range of diversity in Mexico. Teachers with limited experiences and limited training for teaching about diversity face challenges in implementing the curriculum.

The authors present a profile of Esteban, who taught Indigenous students and students of other minoritized ethnic groups. They describe how Esteban made adjustments to the national curriculum to reflect the cultures and communities of his students and how he encouraged them to speak Indigenous languages, tried to understand their communities, and engaged in activities that helped them to recognize and respect cultural diversity and differences. He did this despite receiving little training and support from authorities.

Verrangia and Silva (Chapter 19) describe a number of significant changes in educational policy and race relations that have occurred in Brazil since the 1990s, when citizenship education began to appear in government documents. The authors document the long history of institutionalized racism and discrimination that have victimized African Brazilians and Indigenous peoples since the arrival of the Portuguese in Brazil in 1500. They describe the contradictions between Brazil's view of itself as a "racial democracy" and the institutionalized racial inequality that exists in Brazilian society.

Within the past decade, the government has developed legislation and policies related to diversity that established affirmative action programs, and has issued mandates and guidelines for the inclusion of African and African Brazilian history and culture in the curriculum. Verrangia and Silva contend that the struggle by Indigenous peoples and

Blacks for citizenship identity and inclusion have been, and will continue to be, a major factor in their structural inclusion in Brazilian society and the attainment of educational equality. The authors describe the positive changes that have resulted from the new legislation and policies, as well as the challenges that remain for Blacks and Indigenous people to attain full citizenship. The last part of Chapter 19 consists of a short essay by Solange Bonifàcio, an elementary school teacher who describes how she teaches literacy skills using content related to African and African Brazilian culture.

Human Rights Education and Curriculum Reform

For Parker (Chapter 20), the major curriculum implications of the chapters in this book have to do with human rights education and the teaching of human rights. He constructs his recommendation in the context of the major goal of the conference from which this book was generated: for "educators in different parts of the world . . . [to] share perspectives, issues, theories, research, and strategies for implementing citizenship education courses and programs in schools"—courses and programs that facilitate the structural inclusion of minoritized groups in their societies and nation-states (Banks, 2015, p. 2). Parker analyzes whether human rights education is likely to be successful as a curriculum reform. He also examines whether it is powerful and liberatory and will enable students to think in ways they would not learn to think in other spaces, communities, and institutions. Parker draws on critical sociology of knowledge to determine what kind of human rights knowledge should be taught in schools. He describes the work that is still needed to make human rights education a more robust and powerful curriculum initiative.

Parker is keenly sensitive to and knowledgeable about the limitations of schools and describes how they are embedded within their social, economic, and political contexts. He thinks that most of the problems that prevent the structural inclusion of minoritized students in their nation-states are external to schools. However, he believes that schools can "do something" to facilitate the structural inclusion of marginalized and minoritized students in their nation-states. That "something" is to teach students robust knowledge about human rights education.

Most of the chapters in this book discuss multicultural citizenship education and how it can be implemented effectively in schools. However, human rights education is a pivotal theme in several of the chapters and is a major recommendation in the chapters by Starkey (Chapter 3), Osler (Chapter 7), Eksner and Cheema (Chapter 8), Akar (Chapter 14), and Parker (Chapter 20). Kymlicka, in the Foreword, maintains that multicultural citizenship and citizenship rights and responsibilities must be a central focus in citizenship education even when human rights is an important component, because citizens must and do function within nation-states. He explicates the limitations of human rights education and sets forth "pragmatic and principled objections" to an exclusive focus on human rights and cosmopolitanism in citizenship education. Although none of the authors of this book recommend an exclusive human rights approach to citizenship education, Kymlicka's cautions merit serious reflection.

Parker views human rights education as a major implication of the chapters in this book. However, he agrees with Kymlicka that citizenship education must occur within the contexts and limitations of nation-states. Parker writes (in Chapter 20 of this volume):

> ... Nation-states do exist; they do take their sovereignty seriously; they do expect their schools to serve national, not cosmopolitan, purposes; and they will not be loosening their grip on education anytime soon. Indeed, they are eager to beat other nations on the international tables. This is not to say there are no transnational initiatives under way in local places, but as emphasized earlier in this chapter, the local agencies (such as the teacher cases presented in this volume) cannot provide the structural conditions necessary for their institutionalization. (pp. 473–474)

Balancing Unity and Diversity

As the chapters in this book indicate, multicultural societies are faced with the problem of constructing nation-states that reflect and incorporate the diversity of their citizens and yet have an overarching set of shared values, ideals, and goals to which all of their citizens are committed (Banks, 2007, 2008). The chapters in this book describe theory, research, policies, and practices that illustrate how state schools and teachers in 18 different nations are trying to attain this goal.

Cultural, ethnic, racial, linguistic, and religious diversity exists in each of the nations discussed in this book, as well as in nations around the world (Banks, 2009). One of the challenges to multicultural nation-states is to provide opportunities for different groups to maintain aspects of their community cultures while they are being structurally included in the nation so that they will develop a clarified national identity. A delicate balance of diversity and unity is an essential goal of multicultural nations and of teaching and learning in societies in which equality and social justice are major aims (Banks et al., 2005). Unity must be an important aim when nation-states are responding to diversity within their populations. Nations can protect the rights of minoritized groups and enable them to participate fully in the polity only when the people are unified around a set of values such as justice, equality, and human rights (Gutmann, 2004; Osler, 2016).

As the chapters in this book document, most nations in the past have tried to create unity by forcing minoritized racial, cultural, ethnic, linguistic, and religious groups to give up their community languages and cultures in order to participate in an imagined and constructed national civic culture (Anderson, 1983). Spring (2010) refers to this process as "deculturalization"; Valenzuela (1999) calls it "subtractive schooling." In the United States, in the 1950s, Mexican American students in the Southwest were punished for speaking Spanish in school. In the 1870s, the federal government began sending American Indians to off-reservation boarding schools, where their cultures and languages were eradicated (Lomawaima & McCarty, 2006). In Australia, Aboriginal children were taken from their families and forced to live on state missions and reserves (Broome, 1982), a practice that lasted from 1869 to 1969. These children are called the Stolen Generation. Kevin Rudd, the Australian Prime Minister, issued a formal apology to the Stolen Generation on February 13, 2008. In order to embrace their national civic culture, students from diverse groups must feel that it reflects their experiences, hopes, and dreams (Banks, 2008). Theory and research described in the chapters of this book indicate that schools and nations cannot marginalize the cultures of groups and expect them to feel structurally included in the nation or to develop strong allegiances or robust identification with it.

Citizenship education needs to be transformed in the 21st century because of global migration, the deepening diversity in nations around the world, and the quests by minoritized groups for equality, social justice, and human rights. Citizens in multicultural nations should be able to maintain attachments to their cultural communities and, at the same time, participate effectively in the shared national culture and polity. Unity without diversity results in cultural repression and hegemony, as was the case in the Soviet Union and in China during the Cultural Revolution, from 1966 to 1976. Diversity without unity leads to Balkanization and the fracturing of the nation-state, as occurred during the Iraq war when sectarian conflict and violence threatened that fragile nation in the late 2000s. Diversity and unity must coexist in a delicate balance in multicultural nations that hope to foster structural inclusion and equality for diverse racial, ethnic, cultural, linguistic, and religious groups.

References

Adam, H., & Moodley, K. (2015). *Imagined liberation: Xenophobia, citizenship, and identity in South Africa, Germany, and Canada.* Philadelphia: Temple University Press.

Agbaria, A. K. (2016). Ethnonational politics of citizenship education in Israel and the counterknowledge of Palestinian teachers. In J. A. Banks, M. M. Suárez-Orozco, & M. Ben-Peretz (Eds.), *Global migration, diversity, and civic education: Improving policy and practice* (pp. 156–176). New York: Teachers College Press.

Aisch, G., Pearce, A., & Rousseau, B. (2016, May 22). How far is Europe swinging to the Right? *International New York Times.* Retrieved from http://www.nytimes.com/interactive/2016/05/22/world/europe/europe-right-wing-austria-hungary.html?_r=0

Al-Nakib, R. (2012). Human rights, education for democratic citizenship and organisations: Findings from a Kuwaiti UNESCO ASPnet school. *Cambridge Journal of Education, 42*(1), 97–112.

Anderson, B. (1983). *Imagined communities: Reflections on the origin and spread of nationalism.* New York: Verson.

Banks, J. A. (1978). Multiethnic education across cultures: United States, Mexico, Puerto Rico, France, and Great Britain. *Social Education, 42,* 177–185.

Banks, J. A. (2004). Introduction: Democratic citizenship education in multicultural societies. In J. A. Banks (Ed.), *Diversity and citizenship education: Global perspectives* (pp. 3–15). San Francisco: Jossey-Bass.

Banks, J. A. (2007). *Educating citizens in a multicultural society* (2nd ed.). New York: Teachers College Press.

Banks, J. A. (2008). Diversity, group identity, and citizenship education in a global age. *Educational Researcher, 17*(3), 129–139.

Banks, J. A. (Ed.). (2009). *The Routledge international companion to multicultural education.* New York: Routledge.

Banks, J. A. (2014). Foreword. In J. Leibold & C. Yangbin (Eds.), *Minority education in China: Balancing unity and diversity in an era of critical pluralism* (pp. xiii–xvii). Hong Kong: Hong Kong University Press.

Banks, J. A. (2015). *Global migration, structural inclusion, and citizenship education across nations: A conference sponsored by the Center for Multicultural Education* [conference program]. Seattle, WA: University of Washington, Center for Multicultural Education.

Banks, J. A., Banks, C. A. M., Cortés, C. E., Hahn. C. L., Merryfield, M. M., Moodley, K. A., . . . Parker, W. C. (2005). *Democracy and diversity: Principles and concepts for educating citizens in a global age*. Seattle, WA: University of Washington, Center for Multicultural Education.

Banks, J. A., & Lynch, J. (Eds.). (1986). *Multicultural education in Western societies*. London: Holt.

Bawer, B. (2006). *While Europe slept: How radical Islam is destroying the West from within*. New York: Anchor Books.

Ben-Peretz, M., & Aderet-German, T. (2016). Narratives of success of Ethiopian immigrants: Implications for civic education. In J. A. Banks, M. M. Suárez-Orozco, & M. Ben-Peretz (Eds.), *Global migration, diversity, and civic education: Improving policy and practice* (pp. 132–156). New York: Teachers College Press.

Broome, R. (1982). *Aboriginal Australians: Black response to White dominance, 1788–1980*. Sydney, Australia: George Allen & Unwin.

Castles, S. (2004). Migration, citizenship, and education. In J. A. Banks (Ed.), *Diversity and citizenship education: Global perspectives* (pp.17–4). San Francisco: Jossey-Bass.

Central Intelligence Agency. (2016). *The world factbook: Ethnic groups*. Retrieved from https://www.cia.gov/library/publications/the-world-factbook/fields/2075.html#mx

Cesari, J. (2004). *When Islam and democracy meet: Muslims in Europe and the United States*. New York: Pelgrave Macmillan.

Clark, C. (2010). Germany's Angela Merkel: Multiculturalism has "utterly failed." *Christian Science Monitor*. Retrieved from http://www.csmonitor.com/World/Global-News/2010/1017/Germany-s-Angela-Merkel-Multiculturalism-has-utterly-failed

Department of Statistics Singapore. (2015, July). *Yearbook of statistics Singapore, 2015*. Retrieved from http://www.singstat.gov.sg/docs/default-source/default-document-library/publications/publications_and_papers/reference/yearbook_2015/yos2015.pdf

Encyclopaedia Britannica. (2016). Sykes-Picot agreement. Retrieved from http://www.britannica.com/event/Sykes-Picot-Agreement

Eum, S. (2015, July 6). Number of foreign residents in S. Korea triples over ten years. *The Hankyoreh*. Retrieved from http://english.hani.co.kr/arti/english_edition/e_international/699034.html

Faour, M., & Muasher, M. (2011). *Education for citizenship in the Arab world: Key to the future*. Washington, DC: Carnegie Endowment for International Peace.

Fernandez de Castro, R. (2015, December 15). Mexico "discovers" 1.4 million black Mexicans—they just had to ask. *Fusion*. Retrieved from fusion.net/story/245192/mexico-discovers-1-4-million-black-mexicans-they-just-had-to-ask/

Fredette, J. (2014). *Constructing Muslims in France: Discourse, public identity, and the politics of citizenship*. Philadelphia: Temple University Press.

Froumin, I. D. (2004). Citizenship education and ethnic issues in Russia. In J. A. Banks (Ed.), *Diversity and citizenship education: Global perspectives* (pp. 273–298). San Francisco: Jossey-Bass.

Gándara, P., & Hopkins, M. (Eds.). (2010). *Forbidden language: English language learners and restrictive language policies*. New York: Teachers College Press.

Gandhi, M. (1993). *Gandhi: An autobiography* (M. H. Desai, Trans.). Boston: Beacon Press.

Gutmann, A. (2004). Unity and diversity in democratic multicultural education: Creative and destructive tensions. In J. A. Banks (Ed.), *Diversity and citizenship education: Global perspectives* (pp. 71–96). San Francisco: Jossey-Bass.

Hirasawa, Y. (2009). Multicultural education in Japan. In J. A. Banks (Ed.), *The Routledge international companion to multicultural education* (pp.159–169). New York: Routledge.

Inglis, C. (2009). Multicultural education in Australia: Two generations of evolution. In J. A. Banks (Ed.), *The Routledge international companion to multicultural education* (pp.109–120). New York: Routledge.

Joshee, R. (2009). Multicultural policy in Canada: Competing ideologies, interconnected discourses. In J. A. Banks (Ed.), *The Routledge international companion to multicultural education* (pp. 96–108). New York: Routledge.

Khanna, P. (2016, April 15). A new map for America. *New York Times*. Retrieved from http://www.nytimes.com/2016/04/17/opinion/sunday/a-new-map-for-america.html

Koopmans, R., Statham, P., Giugni, M., & Passy, F. (2005). *Contested citizenship: Immigration and cultural diversity in Europe*. Minneapolis: University of Minnesota Press.

Kymlicka, W. (1995). *Multicultural citizenship: A liberal theory of minority rights*. New York: Oxford University Press.

Ladson-Billings, G. (2006). From the achievement gap to the education debt: Understanding achievement in U. S. schools. *Educational Researcher, 15*(7), 3–12.

Lomawaima, K. T., & McCarty, T. L. (2006). *To remain an Indian: Lessons in democracy from a century of Native American education*. New York: Teachers College Press.

Lucassen, L. (2005). *The immigrant threat: The integration of old and new immigrants in Western Europe since 1850*. Urbana: University of Illinois Press.

Luchtenberg, S. (2009). Migrant minority groups in Germany: Success and failure in Germany. In J. A. Banks (Ed.), *The Routledge international companion to multicultural education* (pp. 463–473). New York: Routledge.

Moon, S. (2012). Korea, multicultural education in. In J. A. Banks (Ed.), *Encyclopedia of diversity in education* (Vol. 3, pp. 1307–1312). Thousand Oaks, CA: Sage.

National Bureau of Statistics of China. (2013). *Zhong hua ren min gong he guo 2012 guo min jing ji he she hui fa zhan tong ji gong bao*. [Statistical communiqué of the People's Republic of China on the 2012 economic and social development]. Retrieved from http://www.stats.gov.cn/tjgb/ndtjgb/qgndtjgb/t20130221_402874525.htm

Nieto, S. (2009). Multicultural education in the United States: Historical realities, ongoing challenges, and transformative possibilities. In J. A. Banks (Ed.), *The Routledge international companion to multicultural education* (pp. 79–95). New York: Routledge.

Nixon, R. (2011). *Slow violence and the environmentalism of the poor*. Cambridge, MA: Harvard University Press.

Ong, A. (1999). *Flexible citizenship: The cultural logics of transnationality*. Durham, NC: Duke University Press.

Osler, A. (2016). *Human rights and schooling: An ethical framework for teaching social justice*. New York: Teachers College Press.

Osler, A., & Starkey, H. (2005). *Changing citizenship and inclusion in education*. New York: Open University Press.

Penetito, W. (2010). *What's Maori about Maori education? The struggle for a meaningful context*. Wellington, New Zealand: Victoria University Press.

Pew Research Center. (2015, November 17). *5 facts about the Muslim population in Europe.* Retrieved from http://www.pewresearch.org/fact-tank/2015/11/17/5-facts-about-the-muslim-population-in-europe/

Pfeffer, A. (2016, January 20). Why the Arab spring failed: Choosing survival over chaos. *Haaretz Daily Newspaper.* Retrieved from http://www.haaretz.com/middle-east-news/1.698071

Phillips, T. P. (2011, November 17). Brazil census shows African-Brazilians in the majority for the first time. *The Guardian.* Retrieved from https://www.theguardian.com/world/2011/nov/17/brazil-census-african-brazilians-majority

Postiglione, G. A. (2009). The education of ethnic minority groups in China. In J. A. Banks (Ed.), *The Routledge international companion to multicultural education* (pp. 501–511). New York: Routledge.

Spring, J. (2010). *Deculturalization and the struggle for equality: A brief history of the education of dominated cultures in the United States* (7th ed.). New York: McGraw-Hill.

Statistics South Africa. (2015). *Mid-year population estimate, 2015.* Retrieved from https://www.statssa.gov.za/publications/P0302/P03022015.pdf

Tatar, M. (2004). Diversity and citizenship education in Israel. In J. A. Banks (Ed.), *Diversity and citizenship education: Global perspectives* (pp. 377–405). San Francisco: Jossey-Bass.

Telles, E. E. (2004). *Race in another America: The significance of skin color in Brazil.* Princeton, NJ: Princeton University Press.

United Nations. (2016, January 10). *International migration 2015.* Retrieved from http://www.un.org/en/development/desa/population/migration/publications/wallchart/docs/MigrationWallChart2015.pdf

Valenzuela, A. (1999). *Subtractive schooling: U.S.-Mexican youth and the politics of caring.* Albany: State University of New York Press.

Wang, T. (2015). Marginality of rural migrant students in eleven Chinese high schools. *Journal of Ethnic and Cultural Studies, 2*(2), 21–32.

Part 1

Diversity and Citizenship Education: Cross-Cutting Issues and Concepts

Chapter 1

The Challenges of International Migration in the 21st Century

STEPHEN CASTLES
University of Sydney

In 2015, about a million undocumented migrants arrived in Europe, most applying for refugee status. The European Commission forecast some 3 million arrivals altogether in 2015 and 2016. Most have been Syrians, fleeing the seemingly endless civil war, but many came from other countries experiencing generalized violence, such as Iraq, Afghanistan, Somalia, and other African nations. In many cases, people arriving in Europe have both protection and economic motivations; in some cases, the latter are predominant. That is why many European politicians speak of a "migration crisis" rather than a "refugee crisis." Perhaps surprisingly, it seems the situation developed unexpectedly, even though numbers of asylum-seekers had grown quite rapidly in 2014. The European response has been piecemeal, uncoordinated, and chaotic—leading to conflict between national governments within the European Union (EU), as well as to varying reactions, from great generosity to open hostility, on the part of European populations.

Europe is by no means the only region to experience new types of mass migration. As was pointed out in the newsletter of the Washington Migration Policy Institute,

> The year 2015 was punctuated by a series of migration crises, from the unrelenting flows of asylum seekers and migrants to Europe's shores and displacement from new and ongoing conflicts in places such as Yemen and Ukraine, to the Nepal earthquake. (December 18, 2015, p. 1)

To give just one example, the United States experienced a surge in entries of unaccompanied children from Central America. U.S. border authorities apprehended more than 100,000 children from Central America and Mexico between October 2013 and August 2015. The Mexicans were generally sent back, while 77,000 children from Central America were released for housing and schooling in communities throughout the United States. One can imagine the classroom challenges this has created for thousands of teachers.

My purpose in this chapter is not to describe these migration crises but to examine their significance in scholarly efforts to understand the causes of migration and the effects it has on the societies of origin and of destination. In the 21st century, the dilemmas of human mobility across international borders are more evident than ever before. The economic, demographic, and political drivers of migration remain powerful, yet the public hostility to migration in some receiving countries continues to gain in strength. International and intercontinental flows of labor at all skill levels are crucial to the global economy. Together with other cross-border flows—of commodities, capital, intellectual property, and culture—human mobility is an integral part of globalization. Yet states continue to regulate entry of foreigners as a symbol of national sovereignty. At a time when regulatory frameworks for finance, trade, and many other aspects of international cooperation have been adopted, global governance of migration remains conspicuous mainly for its absence.

Yet this is a time of change. The global economic crisis is disrupting established patterns of migration. At the same time, settler populations in rich countries have proved more resilient than many expected, and flows to new industrial areas in Asia, Latin America, and Africa have grown. Developed countries and newly industrializing countries are competing for scarce skills; even lower-skilled labor is in short supply in some areas, because of the demographic transitions taking place in China and elsewhere. The labor-importing countries—after many years of refusal—have begun to talk to governments of migrant-origin countries through mechanisms such as the UN High-Level Dialogue on Migration and Development in 2006 and 2013, and the Global Forum on Migration and Development, which has met annually since 2007. In September 2016, the UN held its first-ever summit of world leaders on refugees and migrants.

This is a good moment to take stock of some of the key issues in international migration. In this chapter, I first look at the significance of migration for human security and human development and link it to processes of globalization. I then examine some emerging forms of migration, with special attention to women's migration and forced migration. Issues of diversity and multiculturalism in destination societies are discussed. Finally, I discuss possible future trends and the "global governance deficit."

The Significance of Migration for Human Security and Human Development

Since the beginning of the 21st century, governments have increasingly portrayed migration as a threat to security. The New York terrorist attacks of September 11, 2001, followed by a string of attacks in Madrid, London, and Bali, and, most recently, the 2015 massacres in Paris, led to a widespread belief that Muslim migrants could constitute a danger to democratic societies. This belief ignores the fact that the overwhelming majority of Muslims oppose fundamentalism. Rather than excluding Muslims from western societies, it is important that public policies are based on full participation, which is the best way of preventing the radicalization of an alienated minority. The idea of immigrants as a potential "enemy within" is not new (Guild, 2009). Indeed, for centuries immigrants have been seen as a threat to state security and national identity. Before Muslims, a succession of other groups were cast in this role, for example, Catholics, Jews, or foreigners in general (Cohen, 1994). Such attitudes have been used to justify immigration restrictions and reductions in civil liberties—often not just for immigrants but for the population as a whole.

The securitization of migration and ethnic minorities is based on a perspective that emphasizes the security of rich Northern states and their populations, while ignoring the reality that migration and refugee flows are often the result of the fundamental lack of human security in poorer countries in Asia, Africa, and Latin America. This absence of human security—which finds its expression in poverty, hunger, violence, and lack of human rights—is not a natural condition but a result of past practices of colonization and more recent imbalances in economic and political power, which have created extreme inequality. For example, in many less-developed countries with natural endowments of oil and other minerals, much of the wealth is monopolized by local elites and multinational companies, leaving the majority of the population as poor as ever, or even poorer (the so-called "resource curse"). Internal conflicts about economic and political power often lead to warfare, persecution of civilian populations, and mass displacement. Thus the social transformations inherent in globalization not only affect economic well-being but also lead to increased violence and lack of human security. Growing numbers of people have to leave their homes in search of protection and better livelihoods.

Migration policies, too, can exacerbate human insecurity. Where states refuse to create legal migration systems despite strong employer demand for workers, migrants experience high levels of risk and exploitation. Smuggling, trafficking, bonded labor, and lack of human and worker rights are the fate of millions of migrants. Even legal migrants may have an insecure residence status and be vulnerable to economic exploitation, discrimination, and racist violence. Many governments around the world try to resolve the contradiction between strong labor needs and public hostility to migration by creating differentiated entry systems that encourage legal entry of highly skilled workers while excluding lower-skilled workers or admitting them only on a restricted and temporary basis. Because labor-market demand for the lower-skilled workers is strong, millions of migrants are pushed into irregularity (i.e., crossing borders or taking up employment without permission from the destination country authorities).

Irregular migration affects most countries. The statistics on irregular migration are unreliable, due to the nature of such movements and because estimates may be manipulated for political reasons. The most accurate data are for the United States: As of 2010, there were 10.8 million irregular migrants living in the United States, down from the peak of 11.8 million in 2007 (Hoefer, Rytina, & Baker, 2011). An estimated 7.8 million irregular migrant workers make up 5.1% of the U.S. workforce (Passel & Cohn, 2009). The best estimates for the European Union range from 1.8 to 3.3 million—less than 1% of the EU's total population (Clandestino, 2009). Irregular migration is thought to be widespread in Africa, Asia, the Middle East, and Latin America—but the data are poor, partly because many countries do not make clear distinctions between regular and irregular migration (Castles, Cubas, Kim, & Ozkul, 2012).

A fundamental change in attitudes is a necessary step toward fairer and more effective migration policies. It is important to see migration not as a threat to state security, but as a result of the human insecurity that arises through global inequality. Throughout human history, people have migrated to improve their livelihoods and to gain greater security. Migration is an important aspect of human development. This approach to migration corresponds with Amartya Sen's principle of "development as freedom" (2001). Mobility is a basic freedom and has the potential to lead to greater human capabilities. According to the 2009

Human Development Report of the UN Development Program (UNDP), reducing migration restrictions and ensuring that people can move safely and legally helps enhance human rights and also can lead to greater economic efficiency and social equality (UNDP, 2009).

Globalization and Migration

Human mobility is an integral part of globalization. As less-developed countries are drawn into global economic linkages, powerful processes of social transformation are unleashed. Neoliberal forms of international economic integration undermine traditional ways of working and living (Stiglitz, 2002). Increased agricultural productivity displaces people from the land. Environmental change compels many people to seek new livelihoods and places to live. People move to the cities, but there are not enough jobs there, and housing and social conditions are often very bad (Davis, 2006). Weak states and impoverishment lead to a lack of human security and often to violence and violations of human rights. All these factors encourage emigration.

At the same time, globalization leads to social transformation in the economically developed countries of the Organisation for Economic Co-operation and Development (OECD), where industrial restructuring since the late 1970s has meant deskilling and early retirement for many workers. The new service industries need very different types of labor. But, due to declining fertility, relatively few young nationals enter the labor market. Moreover, these young people have good educational opportunities and are not willing to do low-skilled work. Even at times of high youth unemployment—such as the Eurozone crisis—young nationals are often reluctant to accept low-status jobs in construction, catering, and care occupations. At the same time, population aging leads to increased dependency rates and demand for labor in the service sector—especially for health services and aged care. Developed countries have high demand for both high- and low-skilled workers, and they need migrants—whether legal or not.

Globalization also creates the cultural and technical conditions for mobility. Electronic communications provide knowledge of migration routes and work opportunities. Long-distance travel has become cheaper and more accessible. Once migratory flows are established, they generate "migration networks": Previous migrants help members of their families or communities with information on work, accommodation, and official rules. Facilitating migration has become a major international business, including travel agents, bankers, lawyers, and recruiters. The "migration industry" also has an illegal side—smuggling and trafficking—which governments try to restrict. Yet the more governments try to control borders, the greater the flows of undocumented migrants seem to be.

According to the United Nations Department of Economic and Social Affairs (UNDESA), the world total of international migrants (defined as people living outside their country of birth or citizenship for at least one year) grew from about 100 million in 1960 to 153 million in 2000, and 244 million in 2015. This sounds like a lot, but it is only 3.3% of the world's 7.3 billion people. Since 1960 the number of international migrants has grown only slightly more rapidly than the overall global population (UNDESA, 2013b, 2015; UN Population Division, 2009). Thus nearly 97% of people live in their countries of birth, and internal migration is far greater than international migration. However, the falling costs of travel and communications have rapidly increased nonmigratory forms of mobility, such as tourism, business trips, and commuting.

Many international migrants come from less-developed regions and seek work opportunities in the richer postindustrial countries of Europe, North America, and Oceania, or in the emerging economies of the Persian Gulf states, East and Southeast Asia, and parts of Latin America. In 2013, 136 million international migrants lived in developed regions, while 96 million resided in developing regions.[1] Since 1990, the share of international migrants living in the developed regions has increased: In 2013, 59% of all international migrants lived in developed regions; up from 53% in 1990 (see Figure 1).

Overall, 69% of international migrants originate in the Global South, that is, in Africa, Asia, and Latin America and the Caribbean. Migrants from the Global South are as likely to move to other countries in the South as to head north: In 2013, approximately 82 million migrants originating in the South remained in the South, while a roughly equal number moved to northern countries. South-South migration is growing: Since 2000, the number of migrants living in "developing regions" has increased more rapidly than in the North (UNDESA, 2013b). By contrast, most migrants (54 million) originating in the North moved to other highly developed countries, while only 14 million went to developing countries.

However, focusing on international migration in isolation can create a deceptive picture. Many people in poorer areas move within their own countries. Internal migration attracts far less political attention, but its volume in population giants like China, India, Indonesia,

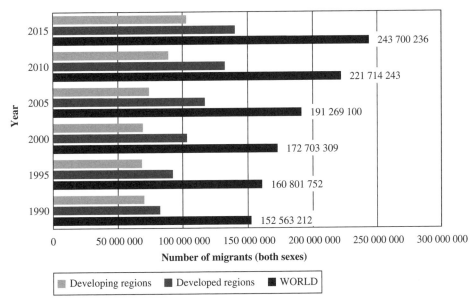

Figure 1. World migrant stock by major areas, 1990–2015. From S. Castles, 2016, p. 392. Copyright 2016 by Taylor & Francis. Reprinted with permission. Prepared from 2015 UNDESA Population Division data by Dr. Natascha Klocker, associate editor of *Australian Geographer*, and used here with her kind permission.

Brazil, and Nigeria is far greater than that of international movements; and the social and cultural consequences can be equally important. In China, the "floating population" of people moving from the agricultural central and western provinces to the new industrial areas of the east coast numbers at least 100 million, and many of these people experience legal disadvantage and economic marginalization very like international migrants elsewhere (Skeldon, 2006a).

Emerging Forms of Migration

This section discusses a few important trends in international migration. The "classical immigration countries," like Australia, Canada, and the United States, still base their ideologies on permanent immigration of mainly male heads of household, leading to permanent settlement and eventually to citizenship. But the realities of migration in the 21st century are rather different, with strong trends to temporary and circular migration, migration of women, and emergence of noneconomic types of migration.

Temporary and Circular Migration. Governments of migrant-destination countries have often preferred temporary migration to permanent, both because it is supposed to minimize integration costs and because it is seen as more acceptable to existing populations. Key examples are the European guest worker policies of the 1960s and early 1970s. Those policies had unintended consequences (many of the originally temporary workers became permanent settlers in the wake of the 1973 oil crisis), but temporary or contract labor systems have continued, especially in the Gulf oil states and emerging Asian industrial countries. Most European countries adopted zero immigration policies in the 1970s and 1980s, but more recently temporary migration policies have made a come-back under the new euphemism "circular migration."

Such policies were adopted by several countries, including Germany and Spain in the 1990s (Castles, 2006; Plewa & Miller, 2005). Their purpose was like that of the old guest worker policies: to recruit labor but not allow workers to bring in their families or to stay permanently—in other words, "to bring in workers but not people" (as the Swiss playwright Max Frisch put it). The new approaches were based on rigid limitations on duration of stay, job changing, and other worker rights. Such schemes became less significant in recent years, due to the Eurozone recession and the accession of Eastern and Central European countries to the European Union, which provided new labor reserves for Western and Southern Europe. Nonetheless, the principle of circular migration has been endorsed by the European Commission (2007, 2011) as the best approach to managing migration.

The desire for flexible temporary or circular migration schemes is, of course, not limited to Europe. In recent years, the United States has expanded temporary work-related visa schemes, which now bring in far more skilled workers than the green cards (which allow permanent residence). In 2010, 1.7 million temporary workers were admitted—mainly highly skilled personnel. The intake of seasonal agricultural workers (with H2A visas) also increased from 28,000 in 2000 to 139,000 in 2010 (Orrenius & Zavodny, 2010). The main countries of origin for temporary workers were Canada, Mexico, and India (UNDESA, 2009). This is a temporary rather than a circular scheme, even though workers may be allowed to reapply after returning home. By contrast, New Zealand's Recognized Seasonal Employer (RSE) scheme is based on circularity. It allows agricultural and horticultural employers to recruit seasonal workers under agreements with Kiribati, Tuvalu, Samoa, Tonga, the Solomon Islands, and Vanuatu. Workers are allowed to stay for a limited period of under one year, but can return in subsequent years (Ministry of Business Innovation and Employment, 2013). Temporary or circular migration schemes have also been adopted in Canada and Australia and are common in newly industrial countries such as South Korea, Malaysia, and Taiwan.

Women in Migration

A key development is the growth of female migration (International Organization for Migration [IOM], 2005, pp. 109–10). Although women have always played a major role in migration, their numbers have grown in recent years, and increasingly they move independently rather than as spouses of male migrants. Demand for female domestic workers surged from the 1980s in the Middle East and from the 1990s in Asia. The female share among first-time migrant workers from the Philippines rose from 50% in 1992 to 72% by 2006 (International Labour Office [ILO], 2007). Although some women migrate to take up professional and executive positions, most are concentrated in jobs regarded as low skilled and typically female: domestic workers, entertainers and hostesses, restaurant and hotel staff, and assembly-line workers in clothing and electronics. Often, these jobs offer poor working conditions and low pay and status. Female migration has considerable effects on family and community dynamics in the place of origin. Married women have to leave their children in the care of others, and long absences affect relationships and gender roles.

A rapidly increasing form of female migration is for marriage. Since the 1990s, foreign brides have been sought by farmers in rural areas of Japan, South Korea, and Taiwan due to the exodus of local women to more attractive urban settings (Lee, 2008). International marriages accounted for almost 14% of all marriages in South Korea in 2005, with even higher percentages in rural areas. Marriages are often arranged by agencies. This is one of the few forms of permanent immigration permitted in Asia. The young women involved (from the Philippines, Vietnam, and Thailand) can experience severe social isolation. China's one-child policy has led to severe gender imbalances, so that Chinese farmers are beginning to seek brides through agents in Vietnam, Laos, and Burma. By 2003, 32% of brides in Taiwan were from the Chinese mainland or other countries, and births to immigrant mothers made up 13% of all births (Skeldon, 2006b, p. 281). This has important cultural implications: The countryside is frequently seen as the cradle of traditional values, and the high proportion of foreign mothers is seen by some as a threat to national identity (Bélanger, Lee, & Wang, 2010).

Refugees and Forced Migration. Refugees and asylum seekers[2] are *forced migrants* who flee their home countries to escape persecution or conflict. The largest category of forced migrants is internally displaced persons (IDPs), who are forced to leave their homes but remain in their countries of origin. IDPs are often highly vulnerable, as they cannot access international protection. The number of forced migrants worldwide has risen sharply in recent years due to the increasing incidence of conflict and violence. By the end of 2014, 59.5 million individuals were forcibly displaced worldwide as a result of persecution, conflict, generalized violence, or human rights violations (19.5 million refugees, 38.2 million IDPs, and 1.8 million asylum seekers; United Nations High Commissioner for Refugees [UNHCR], 2015b). Displacement continued to increase sharply in 2015 due to conflicts in Syria, Iraq, Afghanistan, and several areas of Africa. By mid-2015, nearly half of Syria's total population of 23 million had been forced from their homes; 4.4 million were refugees (UNHCR, 2015a), mainly in the neighboring countries of Jordan, Turkey, and Lebanon, while 7.6 million were IDPs (Internal Displacement Monitoring Centre [IDMC], 2015).

The number of forced migrants has increased sharply over the last half century. Far from improving human security and reducing conflict, globalization has had the opposite effect. Situations of conflict, violence, and mass flight developed from the 1950s, in the context of struggles over decolonization and formation of new states. Local conflicts became proxy wars in the East-West conflict. Following the end of the Cold War, Northern economic interests—such as the trade in oil, diamonds, and weapons—continued to play an important part in starting or prolonging local wars. At a broader level, trade, investment, and intellectual property regimes that favor the industrialized countries maintain underdevelopment in the South. Conflict and forced migration are thus an integral part of the North-South division. This reveals the ambiguity of efforts by the "international community" (which essentially means the powerful Northern states and the intergovernmental agencies) to prevent forced migration.

As rich countries become less and less willing to admit asylum seekers, many seek refuge in new destinations, such as South Africa, Kenya, Egypt, Malaysia, and Thailand. Refugees and asylum seekers are the most disadvantaged of all in the new global migration hierarchy: In the past they were seen as worthy of international protection; now, entry rules have been tightened to the point where it is virtually impossible to enter most northern countries to make a protection claim. Refugees are forced to become irregular migrants and often experience long periods as irregular noncitizens.

Other Emerging Types of Migration. Improvements in transport and communications have made it possible for people to migrate for a wider range of reasons, and often to move temporarily and repeatedly. Indeed, some analysts now prefer to use the term *mobility* to stress the flexible nature of emerging types of movements, for purposes such as:

- *Education.* Students move internationally, especially for graduate studies, and some of them stay in the destination country to work for a period or permanently. Many students have to work part-time while at university, due to high student fees and living costs, providing a source of relatively cheap labor for retail, catering, and similar sectors.

- *Lifestyle.* Some people—especially young people of middle-class background—move in search of new experiences and different lifestyles. Such mobility is mainly temporary, but it can have significant impacts on destination areas.

- *Retirement.* People of retirement age, often from affluent backgrounds, move upon ceasing employment in search of better climates, lower living costs, and more attractive lifestyles. Examples include British people moving to Spain or Turkey, French people to Morocco, North Americans to Latin America or the Caribbean, and Japanese people to the Philippines, Australia, or New Zealand.

- *Climate-change-induced displacement.* Where climate change leads to major shifts in conditions of production or community life, some people may seek to move to seek new opportunities. In the case of sudden and catastrophic events, this movement may be seen as forced migration, while in the case of slow-onset change, migration may be one possible response strategy among others. However, most climate-change-induced displacement occurs within national borders (EACH-FOR Programme, 2009; Hugo, 2008; McAdam, 2010). Moreover, people are more likely to follow economic opportunities by migrating into areas of potential environmental stress—like the Asian mega-cities—than out of them (Foresight, 2011).

Immigrant Concentration

Immigrants are concentrated in the most developed countries, constituting between 5% and 23% of the population in the European Union (EU), North America, and Australia. The United States had an estimated 43 million overseas-born residents in 2010, 14% of the total population; Russia had 12 million; Germany, 11 million; and Saudi Arabia and Canada, 7 million each. In terms of share in the total population, the small oil states (e.g., Qatar and Kuwait) come first, with migrant workers and other expatriates accounting for over 70% of their populations. The share in Saudi Arabia is 28% and in Canada, 21% (UN Population Division, 2010). Australia had an immigrant population of 5.3 million at the 2011 Census, making up 25% of the total population. If children with at least one immigrant parent are added, about 45% of the Australian population consisted of immigrants or immediate descendants of immigrants. But European countries, which until recently aspired to be homogeneous nations, have also changed dramatically. Germany's foreign-born residents[3] make up 13% of the population—nearly as high as the United States. Other Western European countries host millions of immigrants, with population shares between 5% and 13% (OECD, 2007).

The mono-cultural nation seems to be a figment of an outdated nationalist imagination—in highly developed countries, at least. However, there are exceptions. Eastern European countries are in a state of economic and political transition and experience both emigration and immigration; as a result, immigrants constitute only 2% to 5% of their populations. In Japan, foreign residents make up only 1.7% of the population; in South Korea, only 2% (but the numbers are growing fast; OECD, 2012).

Many new industrial countries are experiencing large-scale immigration: Malaysia, Hong Kong, Singapore, Taiwan, and the Gulf oil states all rely heavily on migrant labor. The governments of such countries reject the idea of permanent settlement (as European states did in the 1970s) and therefore refuse to allow migrants to bring in their families or become citizens. Argentina and Chile attract many migrant workers; Mexico—still a major emigration country—is also a transit country for migrants from South and Central America, and increasingly also a destination for immigrants. As for Africa, although Europeans focus on migration northward across the Mediterranean, over 90% of African migration is actually within the continent, with both highly skilled and lower-skilled migrants moving to growth areas, for example in Libya, Gabon, Ghana, and South Africa (Bakewell & de Haas, 2007).

Migrants and their descendants settle mainly in large cities. For example, they make up 44% of the population of Toronto (Statistics Canada, 2007) and 25% in London (Office for National Statistics [ONS], 2002). Migrants go where the jobs are, and immigration can be used as a barometer of economic dynamism. Migrants also go where they can join compatriots, who help them to find jobs and accommodation—the "network effect." These mechanisms reinforce each other and lead to residential clustering, especially in the early settlement period of each group.

Concentration affects origin areas, too. In some countries and regions, it has become a normal part of young adulthood to spend a period working abroad—leading to a culture of emigration. Currently, about 10% of the populations of Mexico, Morocco, and the Philippines are living abroad (Castles, 2008). The Philippines has an official policy of being the "supplier of workers for the world"—and the majority of migrants are women who work as domestic helpers, teachers, nurses, and entertainers in Japan, the Middle East, Europe, and North America (Asis, 2005, 2008). Migrants often come from specific areas where working abroad has become part of the local political economy—for India, the state of Kerala is the prime example of labor migration to the Gulf. Often it is middle-income people with property and skills who have the resources to move; thus emigration can exacerbate skills shortages and inequality (for more detail on global migration and settlement see Castles, de Haas, & Miller, 2014).

Diversity, Integration and Multiculturalism

Migration changes communities and societies in complex ways. In areas of origin, returnees may import new ideas that unsettle traditional practices and hierarchies. Such influences have been called *social remittances* (Levitt, 1998), and they may be just as important as the better known *economic remittances* (money sent home by migrants, usually to their families). In destination areas, migration leads to unprecedented cultural and religious diversity. Migrants are often seen as symbols of threats to jobs, livelihoods, and cultural identities resulting from globalization. Campaigns against immigrants and asylum seekers have become powerful mobilizing tools for the extreme right.

Historically, nation-states have been based on ideas of common origins and culture. In the past, most migrants moved with the intention either of permanent settlement or of a temporary sojourn in one receiving country. Today, it is possible to go back and forth, or to move on to other countries. Increasingly, migrants see themselves as members of *transnational communities:* groups that live their lives across borders (Portes, Guarnizo, & Landolt, 1999). Many receiving countries have changed their nationality laws to help immigrants and their descendants become citizens (Bauböck, Ershøll, Groenendijk, & Waldrauch, 2006a, 2006b), for instance by recognizing dual citizenship (Faist, 2007). "Classical immigration countries," such as the United States, Canada, and Australia, built their populations and nations through immigration but were still largely unprepared for the increased cultural diversity resulting from the globalization of migration since the 1960s. European immigration countries have found it particularly hard to cope with the unexpected emergence of multicultural societies.

This helps to explain why there has been a backlash against multiculturalism. From the 1970s to the early 1990s, many countries moved toward policies designed to recognize the cultural identities and social rights of minorities and to reinforce the role of the state in combating discrimination and racism. In some cases, there were explicit multicultural policies (e.g., Canada, Australia, and the United Kingdom); in others, terms such as *immigrant policy* (Sweden) or *minorities policy* (Netherlands) were used; in yet others, the notion of *integration of foreign fellow citizens* (Germany) was applied. France was an apparent anomaly, with its republican model, which mandated rejection of ethnic monitoring and nonrecognition of immigrant cultures and communities. But even in France there were surrogate minority policies under the euphemistic label of *policy of the city*. In the United States, the prevailing view was that cultural affairs should not be the concern of the federal government and that integration was best left to the economy and the community. However, in the wake of the civil rights movement of the 1960s, federal and state governments did introduce measures to combat racial discrimination and to guarantee equal opportunities for all, while local authorities supported measures for minority education and participation.

Since the mid-1990s, such trends have been reversed. U.S. affirmative action measures have been removed, and there have been campaigns against use of minority languages. In Australia and Canada, multicultural policies still exist, but there is a new emphasis on citizenship and integration. In Europe, the official focus is no longer on recognition of minority cultures but rather on civic integration, social cohesion, and "national values." In Britain, for example, critics of multiculturalism argued that it had failed to provide a unifying national identity (Solomos, 2003). This was (explicitly or implicitly) linked to concerns about the integration and loyalty of Muslims, especially after the London bombings of July 2005. A citizenship test was introduced to promote knowledge of British society and values. Although government statements remained positive about the religious and cultural rights of minorities, a new pressure to conform with mainstream cultural and behavioral patterns was evident.

Similarly, in autumn 2005 the French government reacted to riots by ethnic minority youth not by trying to understand the social and economic causes of the unrest but by introducing tough new law-and-order measures (Body-Gendrot & Wihtol de Wenden, 2007). These were seen as discriminatory by people of migrant origin, but were popular with many French voters and helped Nicolas Sarkozy to become president in 2007. The Dutch government also made sharp changes in policy (Vasta, 2007), while Germany, Sweden, and other countries moved in similar directions. However, it is important to note that multicultural *discourses* have often declined more than actual multicultural *policies*: measures to recognize the social and cultural needs of immigrants and minorities have often changed little, even as public discourse has shifted (Banting & Kymlicka, 2012). The realities of diverse populations and their different lifestyles and social needs make special measures essential, especially at the local level.

The backlash against multiculturalism has been interpreted in various ways. A dominant approach in the media and politics is to acknowledge the social disadvantage and marginalization of many immigrant groups—especially those of non-European origin—but to claim that ethnic minorities are themselves to blame by clustering together and refusing to integrate. In this interpretation, recognition of cultural diversity has had the perverse effect of encouraging ethnic separatism and the development of "parallel lives" (Cantle, 2001). A model of individual integration—based if necessary on compulsory integration contracts and citizenship tests—is thus seen as a way of achieving greater equality for immigrants and their children.

By contrast, proponents of multicultural policies argue that the marginalization still experienced by members of ethnic minorities reflects the unwillingness of destination societies to deal with two issues. The first is the deep-seated cultures of racism that are a legacy of colonialism and imperialism. The second is the trend to greater inequality resulting from globalization and economic restructuring. Increased international competition puts pressure on employment, working conditions, and welfare systems. At the same time, neoliberal economic policies encourage greater pay differences and reduce the capacity of states to redistribute income to reduce poverty and social disadvantage. Taken together, these factors have led to a racialization of ethnic difference. Minorities often have poor employment situations, low incomes, and high rates of impoverishment. This, in turn, leads to their concentration in low-income neighborhoods and to growing residential segregation. The existence of separate and marginal communities is then taken as evidence of failure to integrate, and this in turn is perceived as a threat to the host society (Schierup, Hansen, & Castles, 2006).

Migration and International Relations: The Governance Deficit

Globalization led to the establishment of institutions of global governance, such as the International Monetary Fund (IMF) and the World Bank for finance, and the World Trade Organization (WTO) for trade. Migration, by contrast, has been seen as a preserve of national sovereignty. There is a serious governance deficit: The international community has failed to build institutions to ensure orderly migration, protect the human rights of migrants, and maximize development benefits (Bhagwati, 2003).

Elements of an international framework already exist in the International Labour Organization (ILO) Conventions No. 97 of 1949 and No. 143 of 1975, and in the 1990 UN International Convention on the Protection of the Rights of All Migrant Workers and Members of Their Families. However, relatively few countries have ratified these instruments, and there is little effective cooperation. In fact, by 2012 the most important international measure, the 1990 UN Convention, had only been ratified by 46 of the 193 UN member nations. Emigration countries have been concerned with reducing internal labor surpluses and maximizing remittances. Immigration countries have been reluctant to take steps that might increase labor costs.

Some regional bodies seek to cooperate on migration. The EU has gone furthest, by introducing free movement for citizens of member states and common policies regarding asylum and migration from nonmembers. Most regional bodies in Africa, Asia, and Latin America claim to be moving toward free movement of their citizens within the region, but few have actually achieved this. Both multilateral arrangements and bilateral cooperation between states could bring benefits. Migrants could gain through better protection and social security. Emigration countries could benefit from smoother transfer of remittances and from regulation of agents and recruiters. Immigration countries could gain a more stable and better trained migrant workforce.

In 2003, the Global Commission on International Migration (GCIM), mandated by the UN secretary general, took up its work. The GCIM Report (2005) argued that migration should be taken into account in national, regional, and global planning for economic growth, worldwide. The GCIM put forward proposals for maximizing the benefits of international migration, including measures to limit the "brain drain," to prevent smuggling and trafficking, to encourage the flow of remittances, and to enhance the role of diasporas as agents of development. A High-level Dialogue on International Migration and Development was held for ministers and senior officials at the UN General Assembly in September 2006. This led to the establishment of a Global Forum on Migration and Development, which has met annually since 2007 (Betts, 2011). A further High-level Dialogue took place at the UN in 2013.

Such meetings have no decision-making powers: They fulfill a merely advisory role, and powerful states have been unwilling to implement any measures that might lead to higher costs for migrant labor. But the difficulties experienced by developed states in managing migration may, in future, lead to more willingness to cooperate with origin states. Perhaps this might bring about greater North-South dialogue and cooperation on migration issues. However, this will only happen if all concerned are willing to move away from prioritizing short-term interests and look for new ways forward that will be of benefit to migrants, sending countries, and receiving countries alike.

The first-ever UN summit of heads of state on refugees and migrants took place in September 2019 (United Nations General Assembly, 2016). On the day of the summit, 193 member states signed a plan for addressing large movements of refugees and migrants: the New York Declaration. However, it is too early to evaluate the effectiveness of this plan.

Future Migration Trends

The experience of the global economic crisis from 2008 made it clear that short-term economic fluctuations do not alter the fundamental forces that bring about international flows of people in an increasingly interlinked world. Economic inequality and the demographic imbalances between the aging populations of the North and the large working-age cohorts in the South remain important factors in generating migration. At the same time, the improvements in transport and communications inherent in globalization make it easier for people to live in expanded social and cultural spaces, which have little to do with the borders of nation-states.

Yet, under the current global migration order, states still have the power to differentiate between those who are allowed to be mobile under conditions of safety and dignity (especially the privileged and highly skilled) and those who are forced to risk injury and exploitation in order to seek better livelihoods (mainly lower-skilled workers and asylum seekers). In the long run, this unequal migration may prove unsustainable. At present, policy makers in highly developed countries seem to believe that there is an inexhaustible supply of labor available in less-developed countries. This may be true for the next few decades, but it is unlikely to be so for much longer. The demographic transition to lower mortality and fertility is taking place everywhere. By the middle of this century, many areas in Latin America, South and Southeast Asia, and Africa may begin to experience their own labor shortages. They may no longer have reserves of young labor-market entrants willing to accept high levels of risk and exploitation in order to migrate to today's highly developed economies.

Demand for migrants is likely to remain strong in the North, but states may have to work toward a new migration order based on cooperation between origin and destination states and all the social groups affected. It will become crucial to reconceptualize migration not as a problem to be solved through strict control, but as a normal part of global change and development, in which decision makers should aim to minimize potential negative effects and help realize the potential benefits for the migrants as well as for the economies and the societies involved.

It is a mistake to see migration in isolation from wider issues of global power, wealth, and inequality. Mobility of people is an integral part of the major transformation currently affecting all regions of the world. Increasing economic and political integration means cross-border flows of capital, commodities, ideas, and people. In recent years, growing environmental challenges have made us realize that we live in one world and that national approaches on their own are inadequate. The same principle applies to migration: Global cooperation is essential, especially on human rights standards for migrants, and this requires approaches that abandon short-term national interests in favor of long-term cooperation between rich and poor nations. Fairer forms of migration should be an integral part of comprehensive development strategies designed to reduce global inequality.

Educational Challenges Caused by International Migration

Differing approaches to immigration and the incorporation of migrants and minorities have important consequences for education. Where politicians and the public perceive migrants as temporary sojourners, education may take two forms. First, in cases in which family reunion is prohibited (e.g., in many Middle Eastern and Asian countries), children who are brought in by their parents may have no right to education at all—the ultimate form of exclusion. However, teachers often make efforts to include migrant children in defiance of such rules. Second, in cases where schooling is provided for migrant children, educators may focus on maintaining the language and culture of the origin country, as a preparation for return. This approach implies different educational goals and segregated classes for migrant and local children, as was practiced in parts of Germany up to the 1980s (Castles, 2004). This too is an exclusionary approach, because migrant children receive a separate—and generally inferior—education, compared with local children. The German education policies of the "guest worker" period seem to be a reason for the persistence of disadvantage in today's second generation.

By contrast, countries following assimilation policies are very concerned to integrate migrant children into regular schools. In France and the United States, for example, the school has been seen as the key to achieving equal opportunities in society, because it offers a free and equal education to all. However, the claim to equality is often ideological, because the quality of schools varies considerably according to location, and educational quality is strongly influenced by class and race. Migrant children are often concentrated at the lower end of the social hierarchy, due to the disadvantaged position of many migrant parents. Equal chances in poor-quality schools do not generally offer a passport to social mobility.

Assimilationist schooling has another flaw: By ignoring children's cultural backgrounds it may isolate them and undermine the values and culture of their parents and communities. The result can be low self-esteem and failure. U.S. sociologists have pointed out that assimilation is not a general process of incorporation into society but actually means assimilation into a specific segment, defined according to class and race (Zhou, 1997). For instance, Hispanic children whose ties to their own ethnic culture are loosened may end up becoming members of violent gangs that draw them into drug use and criminality, while unassimilated youth who maintain traditional family values may actually be better equipped to succeed (Portes & Rumbaut, 2001; Rumbaut & Portes, 2001). Thus equal individual treatment in the school system can lead to unequal outcomes for children from disadvantaged and stigmatized groups.

Multicultural education was developed in response to the shortcomings of both exclusionary and assimilationist forms of schooling. By combining the principles of recognition of cultural difference and working for equality, it takes account of differing group backgrounds and seeks to develop the full potential of all students (Banks, 2012, 2016). Specific examples of multicultural education will be discussed in other chapters, but it is worth pointing to some general issues here.

First, as Black teachers and parents pointed out when it was introduced in Britain in the 1960s and 1970s, multicultural education can give the impression that the problems of migrant children are based on cultural dissonance rather than on racist exclusion. Many educators therefore called for antiracist education that stressed the need to address the attitudes of White students and their parents (Gillborn, 2008; Klein, 2012; Tomlinson, 2012).

Second, multicultural education faces a serious practical problem. If too much emphasis is placed on learning about cultural difference, it may take time away from working on the core subjects needed for later job success. Thus multicultural education risks producing graduates with lower levels of work-relevant cultural capabilities and skills. There is a potential contradiction between the goals of cultural recognition and equality, a contradiction that has to be carefully negotiated by educators.

Third, multicultural education is generally premised on the idea that children of migrants will settle permanently in the host country—an assumption that was largely justified until recently. But the increasing ease of travel and communication resulting from globalization undermines this assumption. As more and more people perceive themselves as members of transnational communities and maintain economic, social, political, and cultural relationships across borders, education needs to respond with new ways of conceptualizing citizenship and belonging.

Fourth, multicultural education models are still often focused almost exclusively on providing appropriate schooling for children of legal migrants, who have a right to send their children to school in the host country. The models rarely take account of the new political economy (described above) of distinct and exploitative work patterns, often characterized by informality and irregularity. Schools need to find ways of offering equal opportunities to children whose parents may lack legal residence rights and who are therefore in a precarious and irregular situation (Yoshikawa, 2011). The challenge for multicultural educators is to make the school into a tool of social inclusion—even for those marginalized by neoliberal economic policies.

Yet, despite such dilemmas, multicultural education is undoubtedly an important step forward compared with exclusionary or assimilationist approaches to schooling for children of migrants. Other chapters of this book provide detailed analyses of both the achievements and the challenges of multicultural education. But multicultural education is much more than a model for migrant education: To achieve its objectives, it must be an education for all children, whether of majority, minority, or migrant origin, and whatever their legal status. Multicultural education means helping to create a new awareness of the diversity of contemporary society for all young people. It can assist in overcoming histories of colonialism, racism, and xenophobia and is therefore a vital instrument for change. But to realize this potential, educationalists must address the very real problems still inherent in multicultural education models. Most important of all, they need to respond to the current powerful challenges to multiculturalism and the drift back toward assimilationism represented by the new discourses of social cohesion.

Notes

Parts of this chapter were adapted with permission from Castles, 2014. Copyright 2014 by Taylor & Francis.

1. UNDESA (2015) refers to the highly-developed countries of Europe, North America, East Asia, and Oceania as "developed regions" or "the North" and the less-developed regions of Africa, most of Asia, and Latin America as "developing regions" or "the South." This division is useful for broad comparisons but ignores emerging industrial countries, which have an intermediate position and attract many labor migrants. For many purposes, the World Bank (2015) classification of economies based on gross national income (GNI) per capita is more useful. As of July 1, 2015, low-income economies were defined as those with a GNI per capita of $1,045 or less in 2014; middle-income economies were those with a GNI per capita of more than $1,045 but less than $12,736; high-income economies were those with a GNI per capita of $12,736 or more. Lower-middle-income and upper-middle-income economies were separated at a GNI per capita of $4,125.

2. A *refugee* was defined in 1951 by the United Nations Convention Relating to the Status of Refugees as a person residing outside his or her country of nationality, who is unable or unwilling to return because of a "well-founded fear of persecution on account of race, religion, nationality, membership in a particular social group, or political opinion" (United Nations High Commissioner for Refugees, 2016). *Asylum seekers* are people who have crossed an international border in search of protection but whose claims for refugee status have not yet been decided.

3. About 7 million of Germany's foreign-born population are of non-German origin (the largest group being Turkish immigrants and their descendants), while about 4 million are ethnic Germans, most of whom came from the former Soviet Union and Eastern Europe after 1990.

References

Asis, M. (2005). Caring for the world: Filipino domestic workers gone global. In S. Huang, B. S. A. Yeoh, & N. Abdul Rahman (Eds.), *Asian women as transnational domestic workers* (pp. 21–53). Singapore: Marshall Cavendish Academic.

Asis, M. (2008). How international migration can support development: A challenge for the Philippines. In S. Castles & R. Delgado Wise (Eds.), *Migration and development: Perspectives from the South*. Geneva, Switzerland: International Organization for Migration.

Bakewell, O., & de Haas, H. (2007). African migrations: Continuities, discontinuities and recent transformations. In P. Chabal, U. Engel, & L. de Haan (Eds.), *African alternative* (pp. 95–117). Leiden, Netherlands: Brill.

Banks, J. A. (Ed.). (2012). *Encyclopedia of diversity in education* (4 vols.). Thousand Oaks, CA: Sage.

Banks, J. A. (2016). *Cultural diversity and education: Foundations, curriculum, and teaching* (6th ed.). New York and London: Routledge.

Banting, K., & Kymlicka, W. (2012). *Is there really a backlash against multiculturalism policies? New evidence from the multiculturalism policy index* (GRITIM Working Paper No. 12). Barcelona: Universitat Pompeu Fabra.

Bauböck, R., Ershøll, E., Groenendijk, K., & Waldrauch, H. (Eds.). (2006a). *Acquisition and loss of nationality: Policies and trends in 15 European states: Vol. 1. Comparative analyses* (IMISCOE Research). Amsterdam: Amsterdam University Press.

Bauböck, R., Ershøll, E., Groenendijk, K., & Waldrauch, H. (Eds.). (2006b). *Acquisition and loss of nationality: Policies and trends in 15 European states: Vol. 2. Country analyses* (IMISCOE Research). Amsterdam: Amsterdam University Press.

Bélanger, D., Lee, H.-K., & Wang, H.-Z. (2010). Ethnic diversity and statistics in East Asia: "Foreign brides" surveys in Taiwan and South Korea. *Ethnic and Racial Studies, 33*(6), 1108–1130.

Betts, A. (Ed.). (2011). *Global migration governance.* Oxford, UK: Oxford University Press.

Bhagwati, J. (2003). Borders beyond control. *Foreign Affairs, 82*(1), 98–104.

Body-Gendrot, S., & Wihtol de Wenden, C. (2007). *Sortir des banlieues: Pour en finir avec la tyrannie des territoires.* Paris: Autrement.

Cantle, T. (2001). *Community cohesion: A report of the Independent Review Team.* London: Home Office.

Castles, S. (2004). Migration, citizenship and education. In Banks, J. A. (Ed.), *Diversity and citizenship education: Global perspectives* (pp. 17–48). San Francisco: Jossey-Bass/Wiley.

Castles, S. (2006). Guestworkers in Europe: A resurrection? *International Migration Review, 40*(4), 741–766.

Castles, S. (2008). Comparing the experience of five major emigration countries. In S. Castles & R. Delgado Wise (Eds.), *Migration and development: Perspectives from the South* (pp. 255–284). Geneva, Switzerland: IOM.

Castles, S. (2014). International migration at a crossroads. *Citizenship Studies, 18*(2), 190–207.

Castles, S. (2016). Rethinking Australian migration. *Australian Geographer, 47*(4), 391–398.

Castles, S., Cubas, M. A., Kim, C., & Ozkul, D. (2012). Irregular migration: Causes, patterns, and strategies. In I. Omelaniuk (Ed.), *Global perspectives on migration and development: GFMD Puerto Vallarta and beyond* (pp. 117–151). Dordrecht, The Netherlands: Springer.

Castles, S., de Haas, H., & Miller, M. J. (2014). *The Age of Migration: International population movements in the modern world* (5th ed.). Basingstoke: Palgrave Macmillan.

Clandestino Research Project. (2009). *Comparative policy brief: Size of irregular population.* Hamburg, Germany: Author. Retrieved from http://clandestino.eliamep.gr

Cohen, R. (1994). *Frontiers of identity: The British and the others.* London: Longman.

Davis, M. (2006). *Planet of slums.* London: Verso.

EACH-FOR Programme. (2009). *Environmental change and forced migration scenarios* (EACH-FOR). Retrieved from http://www.each-for.eu/index.php?module=main

European Commission. (2007). *Circular migration and mobility partnerships between the European Union and third countries* (COM 2007, No. 248). Brussels: European Commission.

European Commission. (2011). *The global approach to migration and mobility: Communication from the Commission* (COM 2011, No. 743 final). Brussels: Commission of the European Communities.

Faist, T. (Ed.). (2007). *Dual citizenship in Europe.* Aldershot, UK: Ashgate.

Foresight. (2011). *Migration and global environmental change: Final project report.* London: The Government Office for Science.

Global Commission on International Migration. (2005). *Migration in an interconnected world: New directions for action: Report of the Global Commission on International Migration.* Geneva, Switzerland: Author. Retrieved from http://www.gcim.org/en/finalreport.html

Gillborn, D. (2008). *Race and education: Conincidence or conspiracy?* London: Rouledge.

Guild, E. (2009). *Security and migration in the 21st century.* Cambridge, MA: Polity.

Hoefer, M., Rytina, N., & Baker, B. (2011). *Estimates of the unauthorized immigrant population residing in the United States: January 2010.* Washington, DC: U.S. Department of Homeland Security.

Hugo, G. (2008). *Migration, development and environment* (IOM Migration Research Series No. 35). Washington, DC: International Organization for Migration.

Internal Displacement Monitoring Centre. (2015, December 18). *Syria IDP figures analysis.* Geneva, Switzerland: Author. Retrieved from http://www.internal-displacement.org/middle-east-and-north-africa/syria/figures-analysis

International Labour Office. (2007). *Labour and social trends in ASEAN 2007.* Bangkok: International Labour Office, Regional Office for Asia and the Pacific.

International Organization for Migration. (2005). *World migration 2005: Costs and benefits of international migration.* Geneva, Switzerland: Author.

Klein, G. (2012). United Kingdom: Race and education. In J. A. Banks (Ed.), *Encyclopedia of diveristy in education* (Vol. 4, pp. 2225–2231). Thousand Oaks, CA: Sage.

Lee, H.-K. (2008). International marriage and the state in South Korea: Focusing on governmental policy. *Citizenship Studies, 12*(1), 107–123.

Levitt, P. (1998). Social remittances: Migration driven local-level forms of cultural diffusion. *International Migration Review, 32*(4), 926–948.

McAdam, J. (Ed.). (2010). *Climate change and displacement: Multidisciplinary perspectives.* Oxford, UK: Hart.

Migration Policy Institute. (2015). *Top 10 migration issues of 2015* (Migration Information Source). Washington DC: Author. Retrieved from http://www.migrationpolicy.org/programs/migration-information-source/top-10-migration-issues-2015

Ministry of Business Innovation and Employment. (2013). *Recognised seasonal employer (RSE) Policy.* Wellington, New Zealand: NZ Government. Retrieved from http://www.dol.govt.nz/initiatives/strategy/rse/

Organisation for Economic Co-operation and Development. (2007). *International migration outlook: Annual report 2007.* Paris: Author.

Organisation for Economic Co-operation and Development. (2012). *International migration outlook: 2012.* Paris: Author.

Office for National Statistics. (2002). *Social focus in brief: Ethnicity 2002.* London: Author.

Orrenius, P., & Zavodny, M. (2010). *How immigration works for America* (Annual Report, Federal Reserve Bank of Dallas). Dallas, TX: Federal Reserve Bank of Dallas.

Passel, J. S., & Cohn, D. V. (2009). *A portrait of unauthorized immigrants in the United States.* Washington, DC: Pew Hispanic Center. Retrieved from http://pewhispanic.org/files/reports/107.pdf

Plewa, P., & Miller, M. J. (2005). Post-war and Post–Cold War generations of European temporary foreign worker policies: Implications from Spain. *Migraciones Internacionales, 3*(2), 58–83.

Portes, A., Guarnizo, L. E., & Landolt, P. (1999). The study of transnationalism: Pitfalls and promise of an emergent research field. *Ethnic and Racial Studies, 22*(2), 217–237.

Portes, A., & Rumbaut, R. G. (2001). *Legacies: The story of the immigrant second generation.* Berkeley, CA, and New York: University of California Press and Russell Sage Foundation.

Rumbaut, R. G., & Portes, A. (2001). *Ethnicities: Children of immigrants in America.* Berkeley, CA, and New York: University of California Press and Russell Sage Foundation.

Schierup, C.-U., Hansen, P., & Castles, S. (2006). *Migration, citizenship and the European welfare state: A European dilemma.* Oxford, UK: Oxford University Press.

Sen, A. (2001). *Development as freedom.* Oxford, UK: Oxford University Press.

Skeldon, R. (2006a). Interlinkages between internal and international migration and development in the Asian region. *Population, Space and Place, 12,* 15–30.

Skeldon, R. (2006b). Recent trends in migration in East and Southeast Asia. *Asian and Pacific Migration Journal, 15*(2), 277–293.

Solomos, J. (2003). *Race and racism in Britain* (3rd ed.). Basingstoke, UK: Palgrave-Macmillan.

Statistics Canada. (2007). *Immigration and citizenship: Highlight tables, 2001 Census.* Ottawa, Canada: Author. Retrieved from http://www.census2006.ca/english/census01/

Stiglitz, J. E. (2002). *Globalization and its discontents.* London: Penguin.

Tomlinson, S. (2012). United Kingdom, multicultural education in. In J. A. Banks (Ed.), *Encyclopedia of diveristy in education* (Vol. 4, pp. 2220–2225). Thousand Oaks, CA: Sage.

United Nations Development Program. (2009). *Human development report 2009: Overcoming barriers: Human mobility and development.* New York: Author. Retrieved from http://hdr.undp.org/en/reports/global/hdr2009/

United Nations Department of Economic and Social Affairs. (2009). *Trends in international migrant stock: The 2008 revision.* New York: Author. Retrieved from http://esa.un.org/migration/

United Nations Department of Economic and Social Affairs. (2013a). *International Migration Report 2013.* New York: Author, Population Division.

United Nations Department of Economic and Social Affairs. (2013b). *Population facts 2013/2: The number of international migrants worldwide reaches 232 million.* New York: Author.

United Nations Department of Economic and Social Affairs. Population Division. (2015). *Trends in international migrant stock: The 2015 revision.* New York: Author.

United Nations General Assembly. (2016). *UN Summit for Refugees and Migrants.* New York: United Nations. Retrieved from http://refugeesmigrants.un.org/summit

United Nations High Commissioner for Refugees. (2015a). *UN inter-agency sharing portal.* Geneva, Switzerland: Author. Retrieved from http://data.unhcr.org/syrianrefugees/regional.php

United Nations High Commissioner for Refugees. (2015b). *UNHCR global trends: Forced displacement in 2014.* Geneva, Switzerland: Author. Retrieved from http://www.unhcr.org/556725e69.html

United Nations High Commissioner for Refugees. (2016). *The 1951 Refugee Convention.* Geneva, Switzerland: Author. Retrieved from http://www.unhcr.org/en-au/1951-refugee-convention.html

United Nations Population Division. (2009). *International migrant stock: The 2008 revision.* New York: Author. Retrieved from http://esa.un.org/migration/p2k0data.asp

United Nations Population Division. (2010). *International migration 2009: Graphs and maps from the 2009 wallchart.* New York: Author. Retrieved from http://www.un.org/esa/population/publications/2009Migration_Chart/IttMig_maps.pdf

Vasta, E. (2007). From ethnic minorities to ethnic majority policy: Multiculturalism and the shift to assimilationism in the Netherlands. *Ethnic and Racial Studies, 30*(5), 713–740.

World Bank. (2015). *New country classifications.* Washington. DC: World Bank. Retrieved from http://data.worldbank.org/news/new-country-classifications-2015

Yoshikawa, H. (2011). *Immigrants raising citizens: Undocumented parents and their young children.* New York: Russell Sage Foundation.

Zhou, M. (1997). Segmented assimilation: Issues, controversies, and recent research on the new second generation. *International Migration Review, 31*(4), 975–1008.

Chapter 2

Beyond State Inclusion: On the Normalizing and Integrating Forces of Deterritorialized Citizenship and Civic Education

Bashir Bashir

Open University of Israel

Deeply divided societies, though they have their particular contexts, contents, and features, are generally pluralistic societies that are characterized by deep and persisting social cleavages and conflicts that considerably limit the possibility of having a common, stable, and functional political system. These cleavages and conflicts are organized along ethnic, religious, national, and cultural lines that are made salient and mobilized by leaders and parties for rival political reasons and purposes (Bar-Tal, 2000, 2013; Choudhry, 2008; Guelke, 2012). In their attempts to address conflicts in deeply divided societies, scholars (e.g., Choudhry, 2008; Horowitz, 2000; Lijphart, 2004; McGarry & O'Leary, 2004) have mainly resorted to traditional regimes of citizenship and consociational arrangements and constitutional designs. Consociational arrangements focus mainly on power sharing, collaboration, and consultation among the elites to address conflicts, and traditional regimes of citizenship chiefly emphasize the distribution of political, civil, and social rights to accommodate conflicts. However, the majority of these attempts viewed these conflicts as taking place exclusively within the boundaries of the nation-state while tending to overlook the regional dimensions of these conflicts and the impact of globalization on their accommodation and settlement. This chapter aims to contribute to filling this gap through specifically focusing on the contribution of democratic citizenship and civic education to accommodating and settling conflicts in deeply divided and intertwined societies where these conflicts are not purely intrasocietal or intrastate. These particular conflicts cannot be solved only through conventional and state-centered tools of conflict resolution and citizenship accommodation, for they have explicit continuities and traces in neighboring societies and thus spill over state borders. Examples of this particular type of deeply divided and intertwined societies include several cases in the Middle East, most prominently the Israeli-Palestinian conflict, as well as the cases of Bosnia and Herzegovina, Northern Ireland, Cyprus, and the Indo-Pakistani conflict. The contribution of democratic citizenship to mitigating and settling conflicts stems from its inclusionary potential. The inclusionary potential of democratic citizenship refers to the ability to extend the boundaries and structures of citizenship to accommodate new—often misrecognized, excluded, or underestimated—socioeconomic, cultural, and political claims and increase the feeling of belonging to the overarching political community and society of the nation-state. This notion of democratic citizenship, this chapter claims, is state-centered and premised on the tight association among the territorial nation-state, citizenship, and distribution of rights. Extensive processes of globalization have undermined this traditional and tight association and given support to the possible extension of citizenship beyond the sovereign borders of the nation-state.

This chapter argues that the structural disaggregation of citizenship redefines its inclusionary potential beyond sovereign state boundaries and equips this deterritorialized notion of citizenship with at least two additional potentials that are often ignored or underestimated in the debates on citizenship and civic education in deeply divided and intertwined societies. These two capacities are *normalization* and *regional integration*. The chapter concludes that these capacities considerably increase and strengthen the ability of democratic citizenship and civic education to contribute to mitigating, accommodating, and sometimes even solving lingering and protracted conflicts in deeply divided and intertwined societies.

This chapter is divided into three sections. The first section surveys major developments and shifts in the inclusionary potentials of democratic citizenship leading to one of the most recent developments in citizenship studies, namely, the decoupling or weakening of the tight traditional association among territorial nation-state, citizenship, and allocations of rights. The loosening of this association paves the way for deterritorialized and regional notions of citizenship and civic education. The second section argues that a deterritorialized regional citizenship is equipped with two additional inclusive powers, namely, normalization and regional integration, which contribute to the accommodation of intractable political conflicts in deeply divided and intertwined societies. The final section briefly outlines and examines the regional notion of civic education that emerges from a deterritorialized regional citizenship and explains its possible contribution to settling conflicts in deeply divided societies.

The Inclusionary Potential of Citizenship and Civic Education

Citizenship theories serve as the conceptual and theoretical source and reference for civic education. In other words, the moral and normative foundations and principles that inform the various notions of civic education hinge on theories of citizenship. These values and normative standards remarkably influence the exclusion and inclusion of citizens in the political community in general and in deeply divided and intertwined societies in particular. After briefly explaining this link between citizenship theories and civic education and presenting important developments in the inclusionary potentials of citizenship, this section shows that the majority of approaches that inform the inclusionary civic potentials of citizenship are state-centered and territorial. Profound processes of globalization that redefined some of the major roles of the nation-state brought to prominence the regional and intercommunal characters of conflicts in deeply divided societies. These conflicts have been unconvincingly viewed by dominant political players and academic quarters as intrastate or interstate conflicts in which the nation-state remains the main agent of arbitration and accommodation, when many of these conflicts are in fact intercommunal conflicts. *I argue that accommodating intercommunal conflicts that spill over state borders is better achieved through deterritorialized and regional conceptions of citizenship and civic education.* Furthermore, one should not deny the proposals of a few notions of citizenship and civic education that seek to transcend the conventional boundaries of the nation-state. However, these notions fall short, I argue at the end of this section, of specifying the new and additional inclusionary potentials of citizenship and civic education and their contribution to accommodating and settling conflicts.

A functioning, stable, and legitimate polity requires a minimal sense of common identity: "we"/"the nation"/"the people"/"the political community." This identity is supposedly based on solidarity, sympathy, and trust among the citizenry. These are civic dispositions that are necessary for social cohesion, integration, redistribution of resources, and mobilization. *Belonging to the political community/the "we" is determined by citizenship.* Citizenship entails rights and duties that stem from membership. The political community is built on and adheres to certain values and virtues. The "civic" is what determines the content, meanings, prioritization, and particularities of these values and virtues. Thus, the "civic" and its institutional and policy manifestations shape and establish the exclusion and inclusion of citizens in the political community (Lister, 2007). In its pedagogical form (i.e., civic education), the "civic" is traditionally concerned with transmitting these values and virtues to the members of the political community (Gur-Ze'ev, 2003), and schools and curricula are viewed as instruments of producing and reproducing collective identity and memory (Agbaria, Mustafa, & Jabareen, 2014; Al-Haj, 2005; Banks, 2008; Wertsch, 2002). Determining and grasping the meanings of "civic" considerably hinge on theories of citizenship (Bashir, 2015; Kymlicka & Norman, 1994). In order to better understand the alternative notion of civic education that I develop and offer in the third section of this chapter, one needs first to explore theories of citizenship and their inclusionary and exclusionary powers in more detail. This partly explains the renewed interest of political philosophers in civic education (e.g., Callan, 1997; Gutmann, 1987; Oldfield, 1990). This interest stems from the observation that in contemporary pluralistic societies and democracies citizens need to develop and acquire knowledge, skills, values, habits, and capabilities that are relevant to their membership in a community and crucial for developing public-minded and public-spirited responsibilities, attitudes, and dispositions (Galston, 1991; Macedo, 1990, 2003). These dispositions and attributes educate citizens to behave virtuously and responsibly. While the content (liberal, republican, multicultural, etc.), scope (limited/ thin or expansive/thick), and source (market, civil society, family, school, community) of these virtuous dispositions and attributions remain a controversial matter among scholars (e.g., McLaughlin, 1992), their importance for producing and reproducing citizens and common civic identity is widely acknowledged. My concern in this chapter, nevertheless, is with a specific set of criticisms of liberal democratic citizenship—namely, that it has failed to seriously accommodate deeply rooted and newly constructed social conflicts and cultural and ethnic diversities in acutely divided societies. The accommodation of diversities and conflicts is strongly linked (in addition to institutional and policy-related obstacles) to the inclusionary potentials of citizenship.

Inclusionary potential refers to the ability to redraw the boundaries and reform the structures of citizenship to accommodate socioeconomic, cultural, and political exclusions and strengthen the affiliation and attachment of the members to the political community and society. Traditionally, the inclusionary potential of liberal democratic citizenship was mainly associated with the expansion and extension of social rights for the purposes of social justice, integration, and cohesion (Lister, 2007). The most prominent advocate of the inclusionary potential of social citizenship was Thomas Humphrey Marshall (1950), who presented citizenship as an evolutionary concept that expands equality and increases social inclusion and integration. According to Marshall, the inclusionary potential of citizenship stems from viewing it as a framework for the social incorporation and accommodation of excluded individuals and groups (i.e., the working class) into society/state. Following Marshall, the dominant conception of citizenship viewed it as entailing the universal extension of a bundle of formal and equal rights (civil, political, and social) to all members of the polity (Turner, 2009). This unitary and universal notion of social citizenship became heavily affiliated with liberal and aggregative democracy in the postwar era. Citizens in this model are largely passive subjects: their role is reduced to voting at regular intervals for political parties and interest groups that bargain and make decisions on their behalf. Democracy, in this approach, is primarily a procedure, mechanism, or method rather than a substantive ethical value that embodies specific moral virtues such as civic freedom or social solidarity. Stated differently, classical liberals believed that liberal democracy could be secured even in the absence of virtuous citizenry. It can be secured by constitutional and institutional designs/state structures within which checks and balances that take the form of institutional and procedural devices and tools (such as federalism, two separate assemblies) guarantee the separation of powers and prevent oppression (Kymlicka & Norman, 1994).

Furthermore, underlying the dominate strand of liberal democracy was an assimilationist ideology of nationalism (Kymlicka, 2001; Miller, 1995, 2000; Tamir, 1993). National identity was viewed as the cement that brings the citizenry together and serves as a powerful and effective stabilizing, assimilating, and mobilizing force. Briefly, there has been a process of nationalization of citizenship where citizenship has become synonymous with nationality.

Warning against the exclusionary power of this equation, Hannah Arendt (1979) argued that the state was conquered by the nation during the interwar period in Europe and claimed that instead of being an instrument of the law, the state has become an instrument of the nation. In response to the exclusionary, procedural, and assimilationist notion of liberal citizenship, various political theorists have developed models of more inclusive forms of citizenship, including models of "multicultural" democracy, "participatory" democracy, "agonistic" democracy, and "deliberative" democracy. Participatory/republican democracy (e.g., Barber, 1984) has sought to enhance the inclusionary potential of citizenship through providing more opportunities for people to engage in intrinsically rewarding forms of political participation, as an opportunity for self-development, the exercise of civic virtue, and the achievement of common moral purpose and social cohesion. Deliberative democracy (e.g., Bohman, 1998; Dryzek, 2000; Habermas, 1994) has aimed to increase the inclusionary potential of citizenship through insisting that public deliberation in which citizens exchange reasons and evidence would lead to more rational, informed, and legitimate decisions and policies. Agonistic democracy (e.g., Deveaux, 1999; Honig, 1993; Mouffe, 2000) has aspired to improve the inclusionary potential of democratic citizenship through asserting that politics should be responsive to the fact that moral pluralism and disagreements are ineradicable dimensions of social relations and politics. *My concern in this chapter, however, is with a different type of criticism of liberal democratic citizenship—namely, that it has failed to seriously accommodate social conflicts and cultural and ethnic diversities in deeply divided societies.* Put differently, the inclusionary potential of citizenship is also directly linked to a wide range of claims and demands, such as cultural recognition, social dignity and worth, immigrant integration, social justice, redistribution of resources, care, visibility, and reparation (e.g., Bashir & Kymlicka, 2008; Fraser, 2000; Kershaw, 2005; Phillips, 1991; Taylor, 1994; Young, 1990, 2000). In light of the growing attention to the existence and persistence of internal ethnic, cultural, and moral heterogeneity and the diversity of contemporary democracies, the inclusionary potential of citizenship moved from focusing on struggles of social class for redistribution and political participation and deliberation to also focusing on the limits that other social structures such as race, ethnicity, disability, and gender impose on citizenship rights (e.g., Alexander, Pinson, & Yonah, 2011; Isin & Turner, 2007; Lister, 2007; Marks, 2001; Morris, 2005). It is largely in this context of failing to seriously take into account cultural and ethnic diversities and conflicts and deeply embedded social structures that we need to shift from assimilationist liberal and participatory and deliberative republican notions of citizenship to multicultural notions of citizenship and citizenship education (Banks, 2008; Kymlicka & Wayne, 2000).

In order to build a truly inclusive democratic citizenship, there is a need to challenge the fictitious cultural neutrality of liberal democracy and its homogenizing and assimilationist ideology of nationhood and move to a more multicultural conception of citizenship. Such a conception of citizenship attempts to replace or supplement nation-building policies with policies that explicitly recognize and accommodate groups whose cultural differences have been excluded from the national imaginary, whether these are indigenous peoples, national minorities, racial groups, religious minorities, immigrants and refugees, or stigmatized groups such as gays and lesbians (Bashir & Kymlicka, 2008).

To achieve greater cultural, socioeconomic, and political inclusion, multicultural citizenship should also address the challenges as well as the opportunities that have resulted from globalization (e.g., Banks, 2008; Osler & Starkey, 2005). In other words, under conditions of globalization that further strengthen various forms of interconnectedness and interdependence, local, national, regional, and global identifications are interactive, overlapping, evolving, and continually constructed. *However, many multiculturalists* (e.g., Banks, 2008; Kymlicka, 1999), *despite their acknowledgment of the impact of globalization, remain largely state-centered and view the distribution of rights associated with citizenship as one of the most important tasks of territorial and sovereign states.* They sustain the traditional tight association among the territorial state, citizenship, and rights. Prominent advocates of multicultural citizenship (e.g., Carens, 2000; Kymlicka, 1999) express serious doubts toward notions of citizenship that transcend the borders of nation-state because they argue that democratic citizenship requires a bounded territorial space in which citizens see themselves as part of a common *demos*. The process of globalization also brought to attention the regional and intercommunal dimensions of intractable political conflicts that exceed the conventional borders of nation-states. Instead of treating many of these conflicts as intrastate or interstate conflicts that could be settled either within the state through inclusive democratic citizenship or between states through bilateral agreements or treaties, processes of globalization have undermined the traditional role of the nation-state as an exclusive arbitrator of conflicts and grantor of citizenship. These processes have weakened and loosened the tight association among territorial nation-state, rights, and citizenship and thus structurally limited and compromised the inclusionary and accommodationist abilities of territorialized and state-centered notions of citizenship.

My claim in favor of attending to regional and global identities and the political, cultural, and socioeconomic entwinements that cut across state borders, in addition to conventional national identity and internal diversity, finds support in the claims of scholars who have argued that globalization and the human rights revolution since 1948 have given rise to new regimes of citizenship that exceed the paradigmatic Westphalian notion of the sovereign nation-state and have led to a reconfiguration of citizenship (e.g., de Koning, Jaffe, & Koster, 2015; Isin & Turner, 2007; Linklater, 1996; Osler & Vincent, 2002). The reconfigured notions of citizenship (e.g., Benhabib, 2007) place at their center, among other things, the disaggregation and uncoupling of territory, state, and citizenship and the presence of numerous locations below and above the traditional state institutions where civic experiences are encountered and registered. More specifically, scholars have proposed revised versions of citizenship such as "urban" (e.g., Holston & Appadurai, 1999), "global" (Linklater, 1998), "postcosmopolitan/ecological" (Dobson, 2003), "sustainable" (Bullen & Whitehead, 2005), "multilayered" (Yuval-Davis, 1999), and "intimate" (Plummer, 2001, 2003) citizenship. These versions, though seriously different on several issues (e.g., Habermas, 2001; Held, 1995; Nussbaum, 1996; Pogge, 1992; Young, 2000), stretched the inclusionary potential of citizenship beyond its conventional boundaries associated with the nation-state and its institutions and sites of operation. Indeed, these revised notions paid attention to the deterritorialization of certain rights; the weakening of the classical and tight association among territorial nation-state, rights, and citizenship; and the existence of multiple sites beyond (below or above) the state within which citizenship is articulated and exercised (de Koning et al., 2015). However, many of these notions either remained largely silent on the contribution of these new inclusive regimes of citizenships to accommodating and settling conflicts in deeply divided societies or failed to specify and explain the new capabilities and forces that boost the inclusionary potentials of citizenship. The following section is devoted to identifying and examining these additional inclusionary features of citizenship and their contribution to mitigating and settling intercommunal conflicts in deeply divided and intertwined societies.

The Normalizing and Integrating Powers of
Regional Citizenship

How can the disaggregation of citizenship, rights, and territory be valuable for strengthening the ability of citizenship and civic education to negotiate intractable conflicts? This disaggregation gives rise to normalization and regional integration as the main additional inclusionary powers of reconfigured and deterritorialized notions of citizenship. These powers foster the ability of citizenship to settle and accommodate conflicts in deeply divided and intertwined societies and regions. Normalization refers to a robust notion of peace that promotes mutual recognition and legitimacy, and regional integration focuses on usually underestimated cross-cutting cultural, civilizational, societal, and geographic interlinks to stimulate and foster multilayered and deep interactions and cooperation in the fields of culture, politics, economics, and security. Let me now further elaborate these inclusionary potentials and explain their contribution to accommodating conflicts. In the context of deeply divided and intertwined societies and polities, it is likely that the "internal" diversities that generate conflicts and exclusions have cultural and ethnic continuity and intimate links with groups that reside on the other sides of the state borders. Many modern nation-states were created on territories that are culturally, religiously, and ethnically heterogeneous. Nation-states dealt with these heterogeneities through various methods, which included oppressive assimilation, ethnic cleansing, exclusion, (forced) migration, or artificially separating groups by state borders. These cultural and ethnic heterogeneities and their overlapping regional dimensions are coming back to prominence not only because of the failures of exclusionary and assimilationist state policies to manage and settle "internal" conflicts but also because of the drastic intensification of regional and global contacts, interactions, and entwinements (Miodownik & Barak, 2014). The combination of the rise of cultural and ethnic diversities that cut across borders and societies and the loosening of the tight traditional links among citizenship, state, and rights reconfigures citizenship and poses new challenges to its traditional inclusive potentials. Most important among these challenges are issues pertaining to historical injustices and cultural and ethnic differences that transcend the sovereign boundaries of the state. It is in this context of reconfiguration that citizenship becomes concerned with the regional extension and distribution of rights and obligations.

As I indicated earlier in the chapter, this reconfiguration also substantively redefines political conflicts from being international conflicts articulated in terms of interference and violation of state sovereignty into intercommunal conflicts. This reconfigured regional citizenship contributes to settling these intercommunal conflicts through normalizing the relationships between the communities and peoples of the region. Normalization is the move from a state of enmity, contestation, and estrangement and alienation to a positive peace. In other words, normalization requires more than just a modus vivendi or negative/cold peace that seeks coexistence, stability, and lack of war. Normalization entails positive peace premised on mutual respect and legitimacy. Thus, normalization in the context of entwinements not only is between political institutions and entities but also transcends formal political and legal relationships and involves extensive economic and cultural cooperation and exchange in multiple sites below and above the conventional boundaries of the territorial nation-state.

Through its promotion of positive peace, normalization also entails historical reconciliation. One of the main and unique contributions of the reconciliation idea is its insistence on coming to terms with past injustices as an enabling condition for achieving mutual legitimacy and robust peace (Verdeja, 2009). Debates on inclusive citizenship in the past two decades have been influenced by the rising significance of the politics of reconciliation. Scholars (e.g., Bashir & Kymlicka, 2008; Schaap, 2005) have argued that there is a clear and direct link between the inclusionary potential of democratic citizenship and reconciliation in established democracies that have legacies of historical injustices. The politics of reconciliation is considerably concerned with addressing past injustices and linking these injustices to existing inequalities and exclusion. Thus, scholars (e.g., Balfour, 2005; Bashir, 2008, 2012; Rouhana, 2008) have argued that reconciliation's insistence on addressing past injustices strengthens and empowers the inclusionary potential of citizenship in consolidated democracies. While reconciliation has contributed to debates of democratic inclusion through its insistence on coming to terms with past injustices, it has mainly remained a state-centered enterprise. Reconciliation within the frame of a normalizing citizenship corresponds with the fact that many historical injustices and grievances cut across sovereign boundaries: sometimes the creation of these state borders is itself a main source of past and present injustices. Thus, normalizing citizenship enables the politics of reconciliation and its restorative justice to go beyond the traditional territorial and sovereign state borders in order to effectively address and settle conflicts and injustices in deeply divided and intertwined societies and regions.

One further unique inclusionary capability of reconfigured citizenship is regional integration. Regional integration traditionally refers to a process in which entwined neighboring states voluntarily seek greater levels of interactions and exchange, mostly in the fields of economics, development, and security (Mattli, 1999; Schiff & Winters, 2003). In other words, regional integration aims typically to promote and maximize economic growth and trade between two or more sovereign states through expanding regional cooperation and interaction and consolidating stability and security. While the orthodox and state-centered frame of citizenship did not relate to regional integration as one of its defining features or even as a consequence of citizenship, the uncoupling of the tight association among state, citizenship, and rights paves the way for regional integration to be intimately linked to and associated with citizenship that cuts across sovereign borders. Yet regional integration as a core component of a deterritorialized citizenship not only seeks to foster and strengthen interactions for purposes of trade, economic growth, and security but also aspires to achieve the integration of various communities and groups where social and cultural interactions are intensified and various exclusions, conflicts, and inequalities are addressed and restored. This notion of "deep integration" contributes to accommodating exclusions and mitigating conflicts through the extension and regionalizing of citizenship rights that include freedom of movement, residence, and marriage. These rights not only facilitate movements and interactions between culturally, religiously, and ethnically related communities that were disconnected and fragmented under the conventional national and state order but also foster a regional sense of belonging that consolidates local and regional stability and security.

Transnational Civic Education

Since the theoretical makeup and the normative principles of civic education largely depend on theories of citizenship, the reconfiguration of democratic citizenship and the expansion of its inclusionary potentials by normalization and integration give rise to a reconfigured notion of civic education. Civic education in regions and populations with diverse and interconnected histories, geographies, and identities goes beyond the essentialist and confining boundaries of the national order and categorization. Within the confines of the national order, civic education is trapped by a Westphalian paradigm of sovereignty and divisions according to which the boundaries of the political communities are distinct and separable and the site in which citizenship and civic education are granted and exercised is the sovereign, territorial, and ethnonational state. The national order overlooks the interconnections between communities and regions; risks ignoring internal contradictions, including groups that fall outside or between categories; and overshadows long histories of coexistence and tolerance. Notions of civic education that adequately capture and address the structural changes in citizenship and its normalizing and integrating capacities are largely transnational in their character. They question the dominant and conventional division of the modern world into separate nation-states and compartmentalized geographic regions. They stress long-term transnational political, cultural, and economic dynamics—connections and processes that have historically affected many regions—and interrogate the assumption that views the nation-state as the natural political form that shapes and frames our modern realities. They emphasize and celebrate diverse cultural, ethnic, and religious overlaps and interlinks. I briefly and sketchily outline and explore some of the main features of these notions of transnational civic education.

Decolonized Epistemologies

Transnational civic education aspires to expose students to and familiarize them with a critical and transnational perspective on the histories, traditions, and cultures of their region that seeks to transcend the confining limits of the hegemonic nation and state-building narratives (e.g., Cooper, 2014). By attending to the cultural and social histories of the societies and communities of a region prior to the emergence of nationalism, it promotes a decolonized epistemology that destabilizes ontological and discursive categories and notions that were installed and reproduced by colonial and national regimes. Decolonized epistemology teaches students that complex webs of cultural, social, religious, and economic interrelations and cooperation existed in their region for hundreds of years that transcended the inflexible and rigid borders of contemporary nation-states. Decolonized epistemology (e.g., Said, 2003) challenges, for example, the colonial and national approach of partition that views the Hindus and Muslims of the Indian subcontinent as inevitably oppositional identities. The colonial paradigm of partition in the subcontinent overlooks centuries-long fluid and flexible relationships and interactions and fuzzy identities (e.g., Kaviraj, 2010). Decolonized epistemology also interrogates the Eurocentric paradigm that categorizes and labels Arab and Jewish cultures and identities as necessarily dichotomous and belonging to two strikingly different and rival civilizations (e.g., Alcalay, 1992; Shohat, 1992). This Eurocentric identitarian and cultural classification, which believes in the superiority of so-called Western civilization, undermines and ignores the complex interactions and exchanges that existed between Semitic and non-Semitic cultures in the Levantine. The various cultures of the Levantine (e.g., Arab, Jewish, Turkish, and Romance cultures) were closely interconnected, intertwined, and overlapping. Decolonized epistemology not only exposes students to linguistic diversities but also helps them to become more aware and critical of the risks that underlie the contemporary reductionist, rigid, and essentialist discourse of identity politics and cultural and national belonging. This transnational approach that cuts across boundaries and borderlines educates for Levantine and subcontinent identities and politics, which requires shifting from pursuing partition, tribalism, and separation to promoting integration, intercultural diversity, and regionalism (Bashir, 2015).

Regional Integration

Transnational civic education views the various political entities/states as belonging to a larger region where regional integration is necessary and feasible. The purpose here is to cultivate awareness of the need to revive, develop, and foster a multilayered web of regional and transnational relations and connections. This transnational perspective goes hand in hand with decolonized epistemology. Decolonized epistemology will not only expose students to the existence of multiple loyalties and overlapping identities in a region and the world but also endow students with knowledge about potential alternative forms of political arrangements and aggregations (e.g., federative, confederative, regional unions, etc.) that either are substatist or go beyond the confining frame of the nation-state. Against the backdrop of cultural, religious, and ethnic diversities in multinational and multicultural empires and territories, the advent of the homogenizing national order at the end of the 19th and early 20th centuries dealt with these diversities through the horrors of ethnic cleansing and forced migration (Muslims in the Balkans), genocide (Armenians in Turkey), and the exchange of populations (Muslims in Greece and Greek Roman Orthodox in Turkey). While this national order that championed separation and sovereign borders managed to create more homogeneity in certain areas, it also produced regional fragmentation, intractable conflicts, and haunting legacies of historical injustices. Transnational civic education focuses on legacies of diversity and the productive potential implicit in regional integration and identifies more hospitable ways to accommodate diversities. For example, transitional education brings to attention the remarkable diversities and intercommunal relationships that existed in the ex-Ottoman territories such as the Balkans, Turkey, Armenia, Greece, and Syria, where one could find Greek-speaking Muslims, Turkish-speaking Orthodox Christians, Kurdish-speaking Armenians, and Arabic-speaking Jews (Doumanis, 2012). This is not to mention Armenians, Assyrians, Berbers, Copts, Syriacs, Turkmen, and Kurds in "Arab" or "Arab-majority" societies (Al-Rustom, 2015). Teaching about these diversities is not for the sake of romanticizing lost regional ethnic and linguistic diversities and interconnectedness. Rather, it is a refreshing reminder about the flexibility and malleability of identities and the considerable potential inherent in regional integration and normalization as powerful instruments of mitigating and settling modern conflicts that continue to haunt these regions today.

Revised Curricula

Unlike conventional notions of civic education that seek reproduction, depoliticization, or grant skills (Frazer, 2007), transnational civic education is constitutively transformative and critical in its orientation. Transnational civic education not only embraces and promotes multiple identifications and belongings to regional and global dimensions but also requires critical pedagogy (DeJaeghere, 2007; Freire, 1970) that profoundly rethinks and reforms the dominant and national curricula. Besides endowing citizens with critical and investigative tools, these reformed curricula demonstrate sensitivity to the particularities and histories of various groups through exposing citizens to the richness of cultural and religious interconnectedness and diversities of a region. For example, students will learn about several classics of Jewish thought written in Judeo-Arabic (Arabic written in Hebrew characters) by philosophers such as Moses Ibn Ezra, Saadia Gaon, Bahya Ibn Paquda, Solomon Ibn Gabirol, Yehuda Halevi, and Musa Ibn Maymun (Maimonides). Familiarizing students with Judeo-Arabic thought not only exposes them to linguistic diversity but also helps them to become more aware and critical of the risks that underlie the modern dichotomous and essentialist discourse of identity politics and cultural and national belonging. Furthermore, the revised curricula of a transnational civic education will teach students critical social and cultural histories that interrogate nationalistic master narratives and incorporate additional philosophical, cultural, and theological resources (e.g., Arabic, Persian, and Turkish) into the hegemonic and classical canon. Challenging the colonial and nationalist order lends support to questioning the reinvention and reimagination of dominant and reductionist concepts such as Judeo-Christian civilization. This so-called Judeo-Christian narrative selectively reimagines a very complex, largely anti-Semitic, relationship between Europe and its European Jewry and ignores centuries-long interactions with Islamic and Levantine civilizations. The revised curricula of a transnational civic education critically assess the exclusionary enterprise of Judeo-Christian civilization through incorporating the Islamic dimension as well as exploring Mizrahi Jews' historical and intellectual links to Islamic and Arab cultures. This critical assessment serves as a facilitating and enabling component for the promotion of regional integration and normalization in the region (Bashir, 2015).

Coming to Terms With Historical Injustices

Integration and normalization under the auspices of transnational civic education offer a wider, embedded, and contextualized analysis without romanticizing the history of a region and its groups. They call for critical reading of and engagement with the modern and contemporary histories of a region and the world. This critical reading pays attention not only to legacies of tolerance and coexistence but also to the horrors of colonialism, genocide, slavery, dispossession, and ethnic cleansing. Transnational civic education helps students to view these injustices not as singular events in a regional and global void but as part of larger processes of colonialism, imperialism, and nationalism that need to be addressed and repaired. Historical injustices often transcend and spill over the sovereign borders of the nation-state. In many cases the formation of these state borders is itself one of the main foundations of past and present injustices. Engaging with these conflicts and their generated historical and contemporary injustices requires placing acknowledgment of past injustices at the core of civic education (e.g., Ben-Porath, 2006). Acknowledgment of past injustices, within the frame of transnational civic education, is intimately linked to other related central requirements such as responsibility, reparation, and apology. I have argued elsewhere (Bashir, 2012) that these requirements, put together, give rise to a politics of reconciliation. The politics of reconciliation not only entails coming to terms with past injustices through revealing them, taking responsibility for causing them, and offering reparations and apology but also, and equally, demands normalization and integration through granting mutual recognition and legitimacy. Furthermore, the normalizing force of transnational civic education enables the politics of reconciliation to seriously consider the increasing interdependence of the lives of people in culturally, demographically, and economically interconnected regions, where the traditional territorial separation along sovereign borders no longer seems to effectively and peacefully address and settle conflicts and past and present injustices in deeply divided and intertwined societies.

For example, a transnational civic education frames coming to terms with the legacy of slavery in the United States, the Armenian Medz Yeghern, the Jewish Holocaust, the Assyrian Seyfo, and the Palestinian Nakba, to name a few major historical injustices, in a wider context of regional and global politics where coming to terms with these injustice is tied, among other things, to normalizing relationships, deeply integrating excluded groups, and achieving mutual legitimacy and positive peace. While transnational civic education requires showing sensitivity to the particularities and histories of these people and recognizing their national and cultural identities and rights, it insists that respecting these identities and rights institutionally cannot be accomplished sufficiently within the national frame of nation-states. It should take into account the intertwined realities and inseparability of the histories, rights, and identities of these peoples and regions and thus promote and embrace innovative multilayered regional institutional arrangements and constellations such as federation, confederation, and unions. Thus, transnational civic education is a dispersed enterprise in the sense that it simultaneously operates in several sites, including below and above the conventional structures of the state.

To sum up, transnational civic education in deeply divided and intertwined societies pursues a decolonized epistemology that recognizes and cultivates multiple and overlapping identities and connections, promotes deep regional integration and normalization, advances radically revised curricula, and insists on coming to terms with past injustices.

Conclusion

This chapter has argued that the stubborn persistence of cultural diversities and differences and the disaggregation and uncoupling of citizenship, state, and rights have led to a reconfiguration of democratic citizenship and civic education. This reconfiguration, the chapter argued, increases the capabilities of democratic citizenship and civic education to settle and accommodate conflicts in deeply divided and intertwined societies. More specifically, it empowers the inclusionary potential of citizenship with two more components, namely, normalization and regional integration. Normalization and regional integration are vital for settling intractable conflicts in regions that are ethnically, culturally, economically, and demographically heterogeneous and interconnected. Thus, under this reconfiguration, citizenship is not exclusively a state-centered institution, and it implies memberships in regional political communities and institutions. Since regional democratic citizenship is exercised in multiple sites, above and below the state, this requires and gives rise to hybrid forms of governance and institutions with enforceable legal authorities that involve nonstate actors.

Indeed, there might be diverging assessments of the empirical plausibility and feasibility of these dispersed notions of citizenship and civic education. Nevertheless, while the primary focus of this chapter is on the conceptual level, some of the proposed theoretical ideas are in line with existing conditions and nascent trends in certain regions or propose promising and inspiring possibilities for accommodating intractable conflicts in deeply divided and intertwined societies. While the European Union is the most prominent and discussed example of the disaggregation of rights from sovereign and territorial states and the possible development of regional citizenship, this chapter showed sketchily that transnational citizenship and civic education can be relevant for other parts of the world where intractable conflicts are married with deep regional intertwinements and diversities of various forms. The examples of the Indian subcontinent, the Balkans, and the Levant were very briefly discussed. The relevance of the proposed conceptual frame in this chapter, or at least some of its main components, is likely to be valid in other deeply intertwined, yet divided, regions and territories, such as the Korean peninsula, Latin America, and Africa. Surely, the specificities of regions vary substantively. Thus, the concrete institutional shape and the prioritization and ranking of the content of transnational democratic citizenship and civic education depend, among other things, on these particularities.

Some might argue (e.g., Joppke, 2007) that heterodox and reconfigured notions of citizenship and civic education cannot escape the state, because the demands and requirements (negatively or positively) that are raised are inevitably linked to the state. According to this view, citizenship remains an "intrinsically state-related" concept. Furthermore, one should not deny or underestimate the recent resurgence of the sovereign nation-state and the huge challenges and potential resistance facing the theorization and implementation of these proposals and their exact pedagogical and institutional articulations and policies in various regions. This critique, however, mistakenly assumes that all the revised and heterodox notions of citizenship seek to replace the modern nation-state with a global state without paying enough attention to the reasonable feasibility of other shared sovereign constellations such as regional entities and unions. In the absence and the unlikelihood of a global state with a sovereign and effective power to enforce law, regional bodies and unions are more feasible and equipped to assume this task of legitimate enforcement. Thus, transnational citizenship and civic education do not necessarily suggest that political borders are entirely diminishing. Rather, they propose multilayered and complex notions that partly transcend territorial and political boundaries and can be accommodated within the frames of several institutional and political constellations, such as confederation, condominium, and regional unions.

Acknowledgments

For constructive criticism on earlier versions of the chapter, my thanks go to Dirk Moses, Nadim Khoury, Rachel Busbridge, Azar Dakwar, Gal Levy, and the participants in the conference "Global Migration, Structural Inclusion, and Citizenship Education Across Nations" at the University of Washington, Seattle, June 22–26, 2015. They are responsible for neither the views expressed nor any error committed here.

References

Agbaria, A. K., Mustafa, M., & Jabareen, Y. T. (2014). "In your face" democracy: Education for belonging and its challenges in Israel. *British Educational Research Journal, 41*(1), 143–175.

Alcalay, A. (1992). *After Jews and Arabs: Remaking Levantine culture.* Minneapolis, MN: University of Minnesota Press.

Alexander, H., Pinson, H., & Yonah, Y. (Eds.). (2011). *Citizenship, education and conflict: Israeli political education in global perspective.* London: Routledge.

Al-Haj, M. (2005). National ethos, multicultural education, and the new history books in Israel. *Curriculum Inquiry, 35*(1), 47–71.

Al-Rustom, H. (2015). Rethinking the "post-Ottoman": Anatolian Armenians as an ethnographic perspective. In S. Altorki (Ed.), *A companion to the anthropology of the Middle East* (pp. 452–479). Hoboken, NJ: Wiley-Blackwell.

Arendt, H. (1979). *The origins of totalitarianism.* New York: Harcourt Brace.

Balfour, L. (2005). Reparations after identity politics. *Political Theory, 33*(6), 786–811.

Banks, J. (2008). Diversity, group identity, and citizenship education in a global age. *Educational Researcher, 37*(3), 129–139.

Barber, B. (1984). *Strong democracy: Participatory politics for a new age.* Berkeley, CA: University of California Press.

Bar-Tal, D. (2000). From intractable conflict through conflict resolution to reconciliation: Psychological analysis. *Political Psychology, 21*(2), 351–365.

Bar-Tal, D. (2013). *Intractable conflicts: Socio-psychological foundations and dynamics.* Cambridge, UK: Cambridge University Press.

Bashir, B. (2008). Accommodating historically oppressed social groups: Deliberative democracy and the politics of reconciliation. In W. Kymlicka & B. Bashir (Eds.), *The politics of reconciliation in multicultural societies* (pp. 48–69). Oxford, UK: Oxford University Press.

Bashir, B. (2012). Reconciling historical injustices: Deliberative democracy and the politics of reconciliation. *Res Publica, 18*(2), 127–143.

Bashir, B. (2015). On citizenship and citizenship education: A Levantine approach and reimagining Israel/Palestine. *Citizenship Studies, 19*(6–7), 802–819.

Bashir, B., & Kymlicka, W. (2008). Introduction: Struggles for inclusion and reconciliation in modern democracies. In W. Kymlicka & B. Bashir (Eds.), *The politics of reconciliation in multicultural societies* (pp. 1–24). Oxford, UK: Oxford University Press.

Benhabib, S. (2007). Twilight of sovereignty or the emergence of cosmopolitan norms? Rethinking citizenship in volatile times. *Citizenship Studies, 11*(1), 19–36.

Ben-Porath, S. R. (2006). *Citizenship under fire: Democratic education in times of conflict.* Princeton, NJ: Princeton University Press.

Bohman, J. (1998). Survey article: The coming of age of deliberative democracy. *Journal of Political Philosophy, 6*(4), 400–425.

Bullen, A., & Whitehead, M. (2005). Negotiating the networks of space, time and substance: A geographical perspective on the sustainable citizen. *Citizenship Studies, 9*(5), 499–516.

Callan, E. (1997). *Creating citizens: Political education and liberal democracy.* Oxford, UK: Oxford University Press.

Carens, J. H. (2000). *Culture, citizenship, and community. A contextual exploration of justice as evenhandedness.* Oxford, UK: Oxford University Press.

Choudhry, S. (2008). Bridging comparative politics and comparative constitutional law: Constitutional design in divided societies. In S. Choudhry (Ed.), *Constitutional design for divided societies: Integration or accommodation?* (pp. 3–40). Oxford, UK: Oxford University Press.

Cooper, F. (2014). *Citizenship between empire and nation: Remaking France and French Africa, 1945–1960.* Princeton, NJ: Princeton University Press.

DeJaeghere, J. (2007). Intercultural and global meanings of citizenship education in the Australian secondary curriculum: Between critical contestations and minimal construction. In D. Stevick & B. Levinson (Eds.), *Reimagining civic education: How diverse societies form democratic citizens* (pp. 293–316). Lanham, MD: Rowman and Littlefield.

de Koning, A., Jaffe, R., & Koster, M. (2015). Citizenship agendas in and beyond the nation-state: (en)Countering framings of the good citizen. *Citizenship Studies, 19*(2), 121–127.

Deveaux, M. (1999). Agonism and pluralism. *Philosophy and Social Criticism, 25*(4), 1–22.

Dobson, A. (2003). *Citizenship and the environment.* Oxford, UK: Oxford University Press.

Doumanis, N. (2012). *Before the nation: Muslim-Christian co-existence and its destruction in late Ottoman Anatolia.* Oxford, UK: Oxford University Press.

Dryzek, J. (2000). *Deliberative democracy and beyond: Liberals, critics, contestations.* Oxford, UK: Oxford University Press.

Fraser, N. (2000). Rethinking recognition. *New Left Review, 3*, 107–120.

Frazer, E. (2007). Depoliticising citizenship. *British Journal of Educational Studies, 55*(3), 249–263.

Freire, P. (1970). *Pedagogy of the oppressed.* New York: Herder and Herder.

Galston, W. (1991). *Liberal purposes: Goods, virtues, and duties in the liberal state.* Cambridge, UK: Cambridge University Press.

Guelke, A. (2012). *Politics in deeply divided societies.* Cambridge, UK: Polity Press.

Gur-Ze'ev, I. (2003). *Destroying the other's collective memory.* New York: Peter Lang.

Gutmann, A. (1987). *Democratic education.* Princeton, NJ: Princeton University Press.

Habermas, J. (1994). Three normative models of democracy. *Constellations, 1*(1), 1–10.

Habermas, J. (2001). The postnational constellation and the future of democracy. In *The postnational constellation: Political essays* (pp. 58–112). Cambridge, MA: MIT Press.

Held, D. (1995). *Democracy and the global order.* Cambridge, UK: Polity Press.

Holston, J., & Appadurai, A. (1999). Introduction: Cities and citizenship. In J. Holston (Ed.), *Cities and citizenship* (pp. 1–18). Durham, NC: Duke University Press.

Honig, B. (1993). *Political theory and the displacement of politics.* Ithaca, NY: Cornell University Press.

Horowitz, D. (2000). Constitutional design: An oxymoron? In I. Shapiro & S. Macedo (Eds.), *Designing democratic institutions* (pp. 117–147). New York: New York University Press.

Isin, E., & Turner, B. (2007). Investigating citizenship: An agenda for citizenship studies. *Citizenship Studies, 11*(1), 5–17.

Joppke, C. (2007). Transformation of citizenship: Status, rights, identity. *Citizenship Studies, 11*(1), 37–48.

Kaviraj, S. (2010). *The imaginary institution of India: Politics and ideas.* New York: Columbia University Press.

Kershaw, P. (2005). *Carefair: Rethinking the responsibilities and rights of citizenship.* Vancouver, Canada: UBC Press.

Kymlicka, W. (1999). Citizenship in an era of globalization: A commentary on Held. In I. Shapiro & C. Hacker-Cordon (Eds.), *Democracy's edges* (pp. 112–127). London: Cambridge University Press.

Kymlicka, W. (2001). *The politics in the vernacular: Nationalism, multicultural, and citizenship.* Oxford, UK: Oxford University Press.

Kymlicka, W., & Norman, W. (1994). Return of the citizen: A survey of recent work on citizenship theory. *Ethics, 104*(2), 352–381.

Kymlicka, W., & Wayne N. (2000). Citizenship in culturally diverse societies: Issues, contexts, concepts. In W. Kymlicka & W. Norman (Eds.), *Citizenship in diverse societies* (pp. 1–41). Oxford, UK: Oxford University Press.

Lijphart, A. (2004). Constitutional design for divided societies. *Journal of Democracy, 15*(2), 96–109.

Linklater, A. (1996). Citizenship and sovereignty in the post-Westphalian state. *European Journal of International Relations, 2*(1), 77–103.

Linklater, A. (1998). Cosmopolitan citizenship. *Citizenship Studies, 2*(1), 23–41.

Lister, R. (2007). Inclusive citizenship: Realizing the potential. *Citizenship Studies, 11*(1), 49–61.

Macedo, S. (1990). *Liberal virtues: Citizenship, virtues, and community.* Oxford, UK: Oxford University Press.

Macedo, S. (2003). *Diversity and distrust: Civic education in a multicultural democracy.* Cambridge, MA: Harvard University Press.

Marks, D. (2001). Disability and cultural citizenship. In N. Stevenson (Ed.), *Culture and citizenship* (pp. 167–179). London: SAGE.

Marshall, T. H. (1950). *Citizenship and social class and other essays.* Cambridge, UK: Cambridge University Press.

Mattli, W. (1999). *The logic of regional integration: Europe and beyond.* Cambridge, UK: Cambridge University Press.

McGarry, J., & O'Leary, B. (2004). *The Northern Ireland conflict: Consociational engagements.* Oxford, UK: Oxford University Press.

McLaughlin, T. (1992). Citizenship, diversity, and education: A philosophical perspective. *Journal of Moral Education, 21*(3), 235–250.

Miller, D. (1995). *On nationality.* Oxford, UK: Oxford University Press.

Miller, D. (2000). *Citizenship and national identity.* Oxford, UK: Polity Press.

Miodownik, D., & Barak, O. (2014). *Nonstate actors in intrastate conflicts.* Philadelphia, PA: University of Pennsylvania Press.

Morris, J. (2005). *Citizenship and disabled people.* London: Disability Rights Commission.

Mouffe, C. (2000). *The democratic paradox.* London: Verso.

Nussbaum, M. (1996). Cosmopolitanism and patriotism. In J. Cohen (Ed.), *For love of country* (pp. 3–17). Boston: Beacon Press.

Oldfield, A. (1990). *Citizenship and community: Civic republicanism and the modern world.* London: Routledge.

Osler, A., & Starkey, H. (2005). *Changing citizenship: Democracy and inclusion in education.* Maidenhead, UK: Open University Press.

Osler, A., & Vincent, K. (2002). *Citizenship and the challenge of global education.* Stoke-on-Trent, UK: Trentham Books.

Phillips, A. (1991). *Engendering democracy.* Cambridge, UK: Polity Press.

Plummer, K. (2001). The square of intimate citizenship: Some preliminary proposals. *Citizenship Studies, 5*(3), 237–253.

Plummer, K. (2003). *Intimate citizenship: Private decisions and public dialogues*. Seattle, WA: University of Washington Press.

Pogge, T. W. (1992). Cosmopolitanism and sovereignty. *Ethics, 103*(1), 58–75.

Rouhana, N. (2008). Reconciling history and equal citizenship in Israel: Democracy and the politics of historical denial. In W. Kymlicka & B. Bashir (Eds.), *The politics of reconciliation in multicultural societies* (pp. 70–93). Oxford, UK: Oxford University Press.

Said, E. (2003). *Freud and the non-European*. London: Verso.

Schaap, A. (2005). *Political reconciliation*. New York: Routledge.

Schiff, M., & Winters, L. A. (2003). *Regional integration and development*. Washington, DC: World Bank–Oxford University Press.

Shohat, E. (1992, September–October). Rethinking Jews and Muslims: Quincentennial reflections. *Middle East Report*, 25–29.

Tamir, Y. (1993). *Liberal nationalism*. Princeton, NJ: Princeton University Press.

Taylor, C. (1994). The politics of recognition. In C. Taylor & A. Gutmann (Eds.), *Multiculturalism: Examining the politics of recognition* (pp. 25–73). Princeton, NJ: Princeton University Press.

Turner, B. (2009). T. H. Marshall, social rights and English national identity. *Citizenship Studies, 13*(1), 65–73.

Verdeja, E. (2009). *Unchopping a tree: Reconciliation in the aftermath of political violence*. Philadelphia, PA: Temple University Press.

Wertsch, J. (2002). *Voices of collective remembering*. Cambridge, UK: Cambridge University Press.

Young, I. (1990). *Justice and the politics of difference*. Princeton, NJ: Princeton University Press.

Young, I. (2000). *Inclusion and democracy*. Oxford, UK: Oxford University Press.

Yuval-Davis, N. (1999). The multi-layered citizens: Citizenship in the age of globalization. *International Feminist Journal of Politics, 1*(1), 119–136.

Chapter 3

Globalization and Education for Cosmopolitan Citizenship

Hugh Starkey
University College London

The conferences organized by the Center for Multicultural Education at the University of Washington in Bellagio, Italy, in 2002 (Banks, 2004a) and in Seattle, Washington in 2015 (Banks, 2015) are part of a strategy by the center's leadership to bring scholars of citizenship education into dialogue with scholars of multicultural education. The aim is to challenge researchers to mediate the views of marginalized students, teachers, and parents and to develop frameworks of theory that can enable schools and education systems to offer access to an inclusive sense of citizenship (Banks, 1997, 1998, 2004b). This is a major task because citizenship education and multicultural education have developed as independent strands within the field of education. In the United States the National Association for Multicultural Education (NAME) and the National Council for the Social Studies (NCSS) have different origins and memberships. Although individual members have overlapping interests and concerns, at a formal level there is scope for greater dialogue. For example, a major NCSS initiative to provide detailed guidance for social studies standards involving collaboration between 15 organizations and consultation with 24 additional stakeholders did not include NAME in the writing or reviewing process (NCSS, 2013).

Implicit in the framing of the two conferences is the concern that democracy is being undermined in many national contexts, including the United States. While global migration has increased diversity in nations across the world, the school curriculum has often ignored or marginalized the perceptions and experiences of minoritized groups, who have to struggle for recognition as equal citizens.

This chapter reviews a number of theories or lenses that can help to inform the complex challenge of providing education in contexts of diversity in a way that recognizes the citizenship of minoritized groups and promotes, rather than threatens, democracy. Concepts such as citizenship, human rights, utopia, cosmopolitanism, and democracy provide different but complementary perspectives that interact, often in perhaps distracting creative tension. All these perspectives are continuously debated, defined, redefined, challenged, appropriated, and misappropriated. Nevertheless, I attempt to focus them all on a single challenge, namely, the challenge of learning to live together in societies characterized by superdiversity (Castles, Chapter 1, this volume; Vertovec, 2007). By so doing I suggest that there is a powerful underlying logic that can bolster discourses of equalities, freedoms, and capabilities that are required in struggles for social justice.

The concept of *education for cosmopolitan citizenship* draws on this range of perspectives and enables educators to embrace both unity and diversity in national contexts (Osler & Starkey, 2003, 2005; Osler & Vincent, 2002). It is based on a definition of citizenship as comprising feeling, status, practice, and explicit commitments to human rights. Cosmopolitan citizenship recognizes diversity at all levels, from the local to the global. However, this recognition requires scholars and educators to lead and promote a wide-ranging dialogue. If the nation-state is an imagined community (Anderson, 1991), then this dialogue constitutes a process of reimagining the nation-state as cosmopolitan (Osler, 2008). Such a debate involves contributions from political science, law, international relations, philosophy, sociology, social policy, social psychology, theology, geography, education, and other disciplines.

In a context of globalization, citizenship education inevitably engages with the realities of multicultural schools and communities. Theoretical perspectives and practical insights from multicultural education can facilitate the adaptation of citizenship education to these new contexts of diversity. This process requires that citizenship educators, whose role is often framed in narrowly nationalistic terms, recognize and embrace multicultural diversity. A dialogue with citizenship educators may encourage multicultural specialists to reemphasize the political dimension of struggles for rights that are so enriching for democracy.

Multicultural education is defined by the NAME as a philosophical concept that provides the basis for preparing students for living together in an interdependent world. It has its roots in "ideals of freedom, justice, equality, equity, and human dignity" (NAME, 2003). As the NAME definitional statement notes, these ideals are clearly articulated in constitutions such as those of the United States and South Africa and by the United Nations (UN), particularly in the Universal Declaration of Human Rights (UDHR; United Nations General Assembly, 1948). There is recognition both of the importance of a national and constitutional dimension and of the transnational dimension of human rights. The foundational ideals of a multicultural education that are valued both nationally and transnationally provide a vision that guides the project to reform citizenship education.

Cosmopolitanism

The Democracy and Diversity International Consensus Panel introduced the concept of cosmopolitanism to the Center for Multicultural Education's project of uniting multicultural education and citizenship education following Osler (2000a). The guidelines published by the panel suggest, but do not explicitly reference, cosmopolitan citizenship as a concept able to reconcile the goals of advancing both unity and diversity in a globalizing age (Banks et al., 2005). My contribution to the present book is to attempt to define and illustrate both *cosmopolitan citizenship* and *education for cosmopolitan citizenship*.

Cosmopolitanism derives from a perspective already present in ancient Greek philosophy and many religious traditions. It was developed in the European Enlightenment, notably by Immanuel Kant (Heater, 2002; Nussbaum, 2012; Nussbaum & Cohen, 1996; Osler & Starkey, 2005). It is based on a liberal conception of human beings as a single community in which all have equal entitlement to dignity and to fundamental freedoms. The cosmopolitan perspective has much to offer educators in multicultural societies in a globalized age, since it is an ideal that "combines a commitment to humanist principles and norms, an assumption of human equality, with a recognition of difference, and indeed a celebration of diversity" (Kaldor, 2003, p. 19).

Cosmopolitanism is a philosophy that has profound legal and moral implications. Since the end of World War II in 1945, it has found concrete expression in a view of human rights as based on the concept that all human beings are equal in dignity and that they belong together as members of the "human family," an expression used in the UDHR proclaimed by the United Nations General Asseumbly in 1948. The moral force of this international declaration that all human beings have equal entitlement to human rights and fundamental freedoms leads to a political obligation of states to ensure equal treatment and access to services and democratic structures for all, irrespective of origins or background, including ethnicity, religion, and nationality (Held, 2010).

The UDHR enunciates standards and principles that underpin international law, which is a system based on treaties between sovereign nation-states. Contemporary nation-states operate in a cosmopolitan world (Beck, 2002; Held, 1995). They voluntarily cede some sovereignty through their commitments to a range of human rights treaties and instruments that are effectively requirements of membership of the UN. These treaties provide a normative and international legal framework that member states of the UN are expected to observe. Whatever the actual extent of compliance with human rights norms, the legitimacy of states is no longer defined solely by reference to the nation but also by reference to the international human rights regime (Levy, 2010). Within and between states, cultures of human rights develop where there is a respectful approach to all individuals and recognition of the importance of self-defined, as well as ascribed, identities (Gutmann, 2003).

Citizenship

The concept of cosmopolitan citizenship brings together two ideas, cosmopolitanism and citizenship, each indicative of a worldview. The evolution of the nation-state from self-contained entity to international actor has influenced concepts of citizenship. A restrictive but common definition of citizenship refers to people in relationship to the nation-state as a sovereign polity (Stoker, 2011). This derives from the fact that the development of nationalism was premised on the concept of nationality as a "founding principle" (Isin & Wood, 1999, p. 93).

However, defining citizenship exclusively in terms of nationality fails to include understandings of the complex relationships in multicultural societies (Banks, 2009b; Osler 2011).

Nationalized citizenship is used to suppress an earlier tradition of citizenship as forged in struggle and representing the aspirations of people to exercise agency in the face of despotism and autocratic structures (see, for example, Knight, 2005, and Schama, 1989).

This tradition challenges any claim by the governments of nation-states that they alone have the moral and legal power to determine claims of citizenship. It has informed struggles for racial justice and civil rights as I will illustrate in a later section.

Global migratory movements have brought about a situation where national citizenship is often exclusionary. Although citizenship as nationality was at one point usually accorded by right to those born within the jurisdiction of the nation-state, the political salience of global migration has led governments to make the acquisition of nationality more difficult. It may be conditional on lengthy periods of residence, good conduct, and passing a citizenship test.

However, as Dewey noted, the identification of citizenship with the powerful discourse of nationality occurred at a specific point in history, the late 19th century, when imperialism flourished and democracy was reserved for a minority. He observed that newly established national education systems aimed to eliminate cosmopolitan perspectives and transnational identities. At this particular time,

> education became a civic function and the civic function was identified with the realization of the ideal of the national state. The "state" was substituted for humanity; cosmopolitanism gave way to nationalism. To form the citizen, not the "man," became the aim of education. (Dewey, 1916/2002, p. 108)

Dewey recognized that cosmopolitanism is a learned perspective. Education can develop the capacity of people to identify with fellow human beings irrespective of national boundaries and develop what Appiah calls "concern for strangers" (2006, p. 82). However, the promotion of cosmopolitan perspectives ceased to be a function of education when formal national education systems instead focused on promoting a concept of citizenship restricted to an unthinking and patriotic adherence to the nation-state. It may not be surprising that governments wish to define citizenship in their own terms as nationality, but the nationalization of citizenship is a political act that excludes many residents of nation-states who do not meet legal requirements for this status. The education of the national citizen relies on promoting "national boundaries as morally salient." It constrains learners' perspectives by irrationally glorifying and naturalizing nationhood as defined by borders that are essentially "an accident of history" (Nussbaum & Cohen, 1996, p. 11).

While Dewey (1916/2002) informs our current understanding of education as a cosmopolitan project, he also powerfully influences our understandings of the meaning of democracy and, particularly, of what democracy means in an educational context. Dewey's vision is of a cosmopolitan democracy in which the horizons of all members are constantly extended by opportunities to learn from those from other backgrounds. He concludes that

> a democracy is more than a form of government; it is primarily a mode of associated living, of conjoint communicated experience . . . each has to refer his own action to that of others, and to consider the action of others to give point and direction to his own. . . . [This] is equivalent to the breaking down of those barriers of class, race, and national territory which kept men from perceiving the full import of their activity. (p. 101)

In other words, in a democracy, the principle of reciprocity is fundamental. A citizen is required both to "refer his own action to that of others" and to "consider the action of others." Citizens are aware both of the impact of their own actions and of ways in which the behavior and lifestyle of others may enrich their own. Democracy requires "the breaking down of . . . barriers of class, race, and national territory." The idea of cosmopolitan democracy needs to be nurtured in school. Dewey recognized that this would require teachers to engage with controversial issues, but he stressed that "the emphasis must be on whatever binds people together in cooperative human pursuits" (Dewey, 1916/2002, p. 114).

In the current century, migrants may live in a particular nation-state for years without access to nationality. Consequently, urban schools in many countries include children who may not have attained or acquired the nationality shared by the politically dominant population but who will nonetheless have aspirations to be able to participate fully in political, social, and economic life (Pace & Bixby, 2008). The education and rights of these children are compromised if what is offered is a limited and limiting nationalistic perspective.

Educational movements promoting "global citizenship" have gained considerable traction in the 21st century. This recognizes the cosmopolitan perspective of citizenship in a globalized multicultural world of migratory flows. However, global citizens are perhaps framed in an international or diplomatic perspective in which a national identity continues to be salient. Cosmopolitan citizens have a commitment to people rather than governments. They are likely to challenge any actions or discourses of governments that fail to respect, protect, and fulfill human rights.

The realities of global migration and the demographic diversity of cities provide the opportunity to redefine citizenship in order to decouple it from a narrow focus on nationality. In so doing, we can follow Dewey in attempting to reclaim the aims of education from the powerful grasp of the nationalists.

One rearticulation of citizenship conceptualizes it as a feeling of belonging and a practice, as much as a status (Osler & Starkey, 2005). Education for cosmopolitan citizenship encourages feelings of solidarity and collective impulses to freedom that are not necessarily grounded in or dependent on a commitment to the nation (Osler & Starkey, 2003). Instead, education for cosmopolitan citizenship provides a way of looking at the world and making judgments on the basis of the universal standards of human rights. Cosmopolitan citizens, aware of their human rights and the entitlement of all human beings to these rights, look both backward and forward. The backward gaze brings into view abuses of human rights, including racial discrimination as well as political and social struggles for justice and equality. The forward gaze is to a utopian vision of justice and peace in the world (Osler & Starkey, 2010).

Nation-states depend on bureaucracies that derive from an Enlightenment tradition of modernity, based on rationality and imposing structure and order on society. Diversity challenges the preference for uniformity and the imposition of neat categories defined by boundaries and borders (Bauman, 1989). Cosmopolitan citizenship involves reimagining the nation as cosmopolitan (Osler, 2008). This is theorized by Beck (2012) as *cosmopolitanization,* that is, a process of "'encounter' or 'enmeshment' with the excluded Other" (p. 8). One of Beck's examples of cosmopolitanization is the political invisibility of migrant domestic workers, who are forced to give up their own family life and travel to distant countries to provide caregiving, cooking, and cleaning in institutions and private homes, sometimes living virtually as members of the employer's family. They are recruited on the basis of being exploitable for low wages, replacing local workers and creating new inequalities of nationality, color, and ethnicity (Beck, 2012).

Cosmopolitanism is also a trope featuring a wealthy elite with homes in tax havens and no sense of solidarity or moral obligation to a particular nation-state. This elite cosmopolitanism contrasts with the reality of an everyday and mundane cosmopolitanism, epitomized by the experience of migrants and their families who retain links across the world while contributing to local communities. Although globalization is often experienced as pressure on the nation-state from without, nations increasingly develop "*internal* globalization, globalization *from within* the national societies" in a process of cosmopolitanization (Beck, 2002, p. 17). This social theory underpins the task of reimagining the nation as cosmopolitan.

Conceptually, cosmopolitan citizenship recognizes that local struggles for justice have national and international dimensions and ramifications, to the extent that distinctions between national and international or local and global cease to be meaningful (Beck, 2012). Physically crossing borders may still require passports and permissions, but ideas, information, and culture, like cash, can be transmitted across borders instantaneously through the Internet, and solidarities are developed and sustained through social media. The cosmopolitan nation is a microcosm of global society, and living together requires bridge figures—individuals who straddle cultures and help to mediate when there are tensions, as well as help to expand the horizons of those who are culturally more limited (Zuckerman, 2013).

Human Rights as Utopia

A precursor to the conceptualization of education for cosmopolitan citizenship is found in a widely cited report from a UNESCO commission that identified four pillars of education in the 21st century (Delors, 1996). The report emphasizes that "learning to live together" in a multicultural, multifaith globalized world is one of the key challenges for education. Education based on "recognition of our growing interdependence" may help humanity "to manage the inevitable conflicts in an intelligent and peaceful way." Learning to live together in multicultural societies requires a vision based on the acceptance of the legitimacy of multiple points of view. Delors (1996) calls this vision a "necessary Utopia" (p. 11).

Human rights are the common standards that provide a basis on which governments and people can negotiate political and cultural differences. The common ground is that the same standards apply to all. This principle underpins both multicultural and citizenship education. The Universal Declaration of Human Rights (United Nations General Assembly, 1948) affirms that all the carefully defined rights and freedoms set out in its articles are the entitlement of all human beings "without distinction of any kind, such as race, colour, sex, language, religion, political or other opinion, national or social origin, property, birth or other status" (Article 2). It asserts the moral and political proposition that education "shall promote understanding, tolerance and friendship among all nations, racial or religious groups" (Article 26).

The vision of peace and equality expressed in the UDHR may be characterized as utopian. Human rights are concerned with the world as it should be rather than the world as it is. One important role of citizenship education is to highlight the gaps between "is" and "ought" and suggest strategies and actions for promoting social and economic justice. In principle, the inhabitants and citizens of any nation can demand of their government that their rights be upheld. The rights are the same across all nations, irrespective of local and regional political, social, and economic conditions and traditions. This international and transnational rights regime provides a philosophical, moral, and legal superstructure that interacts with the other political and economic superstructural elements of globalization (Spring, 2015).

Human rights provide a way of looking at the world. They are set out formally and definitively in various human rights instruments. The modern conception of human rights dates from the 1940s. The Allied Powers created the United Nations at the end of World War II, with a commitment to justice and peace in the world. The UN charter was signed in 1945; it proclaims respect for human rights as the means for achieving world peace. The International Human Rights Commission was established to draft the Universal Declaration of Human Rights, which was proclaimed by the United Nations General Assembly on December 10, 1948.

The preamble to the UDHR first sets out a fundamental principle of human rights, declaring that "recognition of the inherent dignity and of the equal and inalienable rights of all members of the human family is the foundation of freedom, justice and peace in the world. . ." (United Nations General Assembly, 1948, p. 1). The main innovation of the UDHR was in recognizing, for the first time, a *universal* entitlement to rights applying to "all members of the human family." Previously, because of a concern for national sovereignty, states were immune from external control or moral pressure when they enacted discriminatory legislation or allowed their agents freedom to undertake extrajudicial killings or torture.

The preamble to the UDHR also sets out a vision of a possible future that can be seen as utopian, saying that "the advent of a world in which human beings shall enjoy freedom of speech and belief and freedom from fear and want has been proclaimed as the highest aspiration of the common people" (United Nations General Assembly, 1948, p. 1). This section incorporates ideas set out in a speech by President Franklin D. Roosevelt in 1941. Roosevelt's four freedoms came in pairs: two kinds of freedom "to" and two kinds of freedom "from."

The first pair, freedom of speech and belief, are sometimes described as negative freedoms because they require only inaction by government. Asserted in opposition to interference from authority, they are among the civil and political rights essential to any form of democracy and political activity. Freedom of belief is frequently associated with religious persecution, but it applies equally to political beliefs.

The second pair (freedoms "from") are freedom from fear and freedom from want. Psychological freedom from fear is the right to security of citizens and others living in a given country or state, guaranteed through a system of policing and laws. Freedom from want is the right of access to basic standards of nutrition, health care, income, and shelter. Without these, human beings are deprived of their capacity to develop their capabilities (Sen, 2009) and thus effectively robbed of their dignity and personal liberty.

Following the preamble, human rights are then precisely defined in 30 articles. René Cassin, a member of the drafting committee of the UDHR, summarized the content as:

- personal rights (life, freedom, security, justice) in Articles 2–11;

- rights regulating relationships between people (freedom of movement, rights to found a family, asylum, nationality, property) in Articles 12–17;

- public freedoms and political rights (thought, religion, conscience, opinion, assembly, participation, democracy) in Articles 18–21;

- economic, social, and cultural rights (social security in the event of unemployment, sickness, or disability; work; equal wages for equal work; trade unions; rest and leisure; adequate standard of living; education; cultural life) in Articles 22–27 (cited in Osler & Starkey, 1996, p. 4).

Freedoms are not absolute. Where there are no constraints but an imbalance of power, the advantage is always with the powerful. The power relation is of the essence. A human rights perspective balances freedoms with a concern for equality of access to rights. Freedoms are exercised *in society,* and claiming them is constrained by the acceptance of the principle that all other human beings can claim the same right.

The vision in the UDHR of freedom, justice, and peace in the world is utopian. Utopia can be an inspiration and a driving force motivating humans to exercise agency and shape history (Mannheim, 1929/1991). Utopia as possibility has been theorized by Giddens as "utopian realism" (1990, p. 156) and by Rawls as "realistic utopia" (1999, p. 128). Looking at ideal solutions but relating them to actual social trends and developments may help address specific social and political problems.

That said, utopian visions characterized some of the most appalling political regimes of the 20th century (Moyn, 2010). Hitler, Stalin, Mao, and Pol Pot all governed on the basis of claims that they had a vision of a better world. The UDHR is proposed on an entirely different basis from "failed utopias" (Klug, 2000, p. 189) that are based on superiority of a race, class, or nationality. The failed utopias respond to the issue of living together by eliminating from the discourse of "us" those individuals and groups that challenge the authority or the authenticity of the single story vision (Adichie, 2009; Bauman, 1989). Contemporary authoritarian regimes continue to depict dissidents as enemies of the regime, who can be outlawed—that is to say, denied the protection of the law. Opponents were, and are, vulnerable to arbitrary arrest, detention, exile, and genocide. A human rights perspective on cosmopolitan citizenship emphasizes that all must be included in the "us," and it is this vision that drives political action.

Utopia requires and encourages imagination; it is this process of imagining utopia that has the capacity to challenge dominant discourses and assumptions that are taken for granted. Imagining that we can live differently from the way we presently do encourages us to question the premises on which our societies are organized. The concept of utopia serves to introduce "a sense of doubt that shatters the obvious" (Ricoeur, 1978, p. 21). In other words, by providing a positive vision of ideals for living together, we can encourage young people to be skeptical of curriculum content and school routines where they may serve to perpetuate injustices and discrimination.

In approaching the challenge of living together in increasingly diverse societies, a number of scholars and educators have drawn inspiration from the UN Convention on the Rights of the Child (United Nations, 1989). The internationally recognized legitimacy of claims of equality and justice inspired by the Convention provides a powerful tool for children and young people. It can encourage them as they explore and develop their political identities and understandings of rights-based citizenship. The Convention also provides a set of guidelines and an agenda for action for educators. It defines for children and young people the claims that they can make to ensure that their human rights are respected (Covell, Howe, & Polegato, 2011; Jerome, 2012; Osler & Starkey, 1998, 2005; Verhellen, 2000).

Human Rights as Struggle

In reality, there is always a struggle to achieve the ideals of freedom and justice that motivate education for cosmopolitan citizenship (Bowring, 2008; Osler, 2015, 2016). In every society, oppression and discrimination are likely to be experienced by young people, even when they also have scope for freedom and access to justice. Although all young people are likely to experience discrimination because they are considered less capable than adults, young people from minority groups and those with disabilities, as well as young women, may suffer a double or treble disadvantage. They are at an intersection of several discriminatory structures and practices. Among the most common manifestations of discrimination is the practice of ascribing identities to young people on the basis of their appearance or accent. Banks (2004a) notes that a "citizen's racial, cultural, language, and religious characteristics often significantly influence whether she is viewed as a citizen within her society" (p. 5). In other words, teachers or adults may make assumptions about young people or, indeed, about their parents that can lead to discrimination.

A commitment by teachers and other adults to promoting, protecting and defending internationally defined children's rights is a commitment to foreground the intrinsic universal qualities of individuals such as dignity and subjectivity. Such a perspective challenges ascriptive identities such as nationality, race, ethnicity, age, and gender (Soysal, 2012). On a practical level, citizenship education potentially supports struggles by citizen students to overcome prejudice and to challenge ascribed and limiting identities such as "child," "immigrant," or "less able." Such struggles contribute to an empowering education and may help to close what Levinson (2012) calls the civic empowerment gap, namely the difference between the facility that members of the majority community may have in achieving their demands and the struggles that minorities have, even in making their demands heard.

School curricula for history and social studies in many countries include major struggles for racial and social justice, such as the American civil rights movement and the ending of Apartheid in South Africa. I will draw lessons from the following narratives, parts of which are likely to be familiar to teachers and young people across the world and which illustrate the essence of cosmopolitan citizenship. In this case, the leaders of momentous campaigns call both for equal citizenship at home and for international solidarity in their pursuit of justice.

Struggle Against Apartheid

Nelson Mandela's speech when standing trial in South Africa resonates with educators today who aspire to the same ideals. His vision of the goal of his political struggle is a utopia that drives his actions.

> I have cherished the ideal of a democratic and free society in which all persons live together in harmony and with equal opportunities. It is an ideal which I hope to live for and to achieve. (Mandela, 1964)

Mandela was studying for a law degree and was committed to the rule of law, but his commitment to justice caused him to challenge the Apartheid laws. The principles of human rights inspired his struggle for the repeal of the Apartheid system that denied any form of meaningful citizenship to the majority Black population in South Africa.

In his autobiography, Mandela recalls the sense of global solidarity with the African National Congress (ANC) struggle at the time of his trial: "Night-long vigils were held for us at St. Paul's Cathedral in London. The students of the University of London elected me president of their students' union in absentia . . . (Mandela, 1994, p. 443). The trial was followed by 27 years in prison, after which Mandela led the transition of his country to a multicultural democracy based on a new constitution. This case illustrates several key points. First, there is the distinction between the law and justice. Second, struggles are led by dreams or visions of a better future. Finally, international solidarity, in this case by students and young people, provides much-needed support and encouragement for those struggling.

Civil Rights, Human Rights, and Citizenship

On his way to Oslo to receive the Nobel Peace Prize, Martin Luther King Jr. made a brief speech in London, where he linked the struggles for freedom and racial justice in the United States with those of Mandela and the ANC: "In our struggle for freedom and justice in the United States, which has also been so long and arduous, we feel a powerful sense of identification with those in the far more deadly struggle for freedom in South Africa" (1964, para. 1). King explicitly referred to "the great mass of South Africans denied their humanity, their dignity, denied opportunity, denied all human rights" (para. 5). And in the name of the struggle for human rights, he argued passionately for citizens in the United Kingdom and the United States to campaign and pressure their governments to implement economic sanctions against the apartheid regime, since it was "the one form of non-violent action that could bring freedom and justice to South Africa" (para. 6).

This is an example of a transnational action linking the United States, the United Kingdom, and South Africa in a common concern and struggle. The struggle was described as being against the denial of human rights. It identified a particular set of actions that citizens could promote from a sense of citizenship and solidarity, namely individual and collective sanctions.

Another example from this period involved teachers making a stand on the issue of voter registration. In January 1965, teachers' leader Frederick Reese persuaded virtually every Black teacher in Selma to march to the courthouse to demand to be registered to vote. Reese had forewarned the chair of the board of registrars in a polite letter requesting that the board be open on the Friday of the march. He pointed out that the courthouse was open for citizens to pay taxes any day of the week, but voter registration was restricted to the first and third Mondays of the month. As the teachers arrived, Reese recalled that Sheriff Jim Clark and his deputies formed a line across the door:

> I reminded him that the courthouse did not belong to him, it belonged to us also, and we were there as citizens . . . we had a right to go in the courthouse and I would not back down from that right. (quoted in Hampton & Fayer, 1990, p. 218)

In spite of their polite and measured request, as citizens, the response came in the form of billy clubs, as the sheriff and his men knocked the teachers down the steps.

The teachers had shown moral and political leadership in the cause of racial justice that stirred up the community. On February 1, Martin Luther King Jr. arrived and led 250 marchers to the courthouse, where they were all arrested and put in jail. Two days later, 800 schoolchildren marched, and they too were taken into custody. Citizenship, in this tradition, requires moral courage and a clear sense of the distinction between the law and justice. The standard by which the law and its enforcers should be judged is fair treatment, due process, and respect for human dignity. These principles are enshrined in the Universal Declaration of Human Rights, Articles 1–11 (United Nations General Assembly, 1948).

Bringing Together Local and Global Dimensions

Malcolm X traveled extensively in Africa in 1964. He became very much aware of the parallels between the anticolonial and postcolonial struggles and domestic struggles, including the voter registration campaign in the U.S. South. In his final speeches, he stressed the importance of human rights and the role of the United Nations. In a speech in Selma he accused the U.S. government under President Lyndon Johnson of dereliction of its duty to protect the 22 million Black citizens of the United States:

> In their failure to protect our human rights, they are violating the United Nations Charter and they are not qualified to continue to sit in that international body and talk about what human rights should be done in other countries of this earth. (quoted in Clark, 1992, p. 27)

Whereas accusations of hypocrisy in not respecting human rights were usually made against other countries, Malcolm X here used knowledge of international law to frame a domestic struggle. By bringing together the local and global dimensions, he put pressure on the government of his own country.

In a key speech to students in London, Malcolm X argued that the civil rights movement needed to rethink and focus instead on human rights. Civil rights imply a merely domestic struggle, whereas naming a struggle for human rights raises it to the level of "a problem of humanity, a problem of the world." He evoked the possibilities of people from Africa, Asia, Latin America, and Europe acting in solidarity with the U.S. civil rights struggle. Individuals and groups could "step into the picture and do whatever [was] necessary to help us see that our rights are guaranteed us—not sometime in the long future but almost immediately" (quoted in Clark, 1992, p. 63). This line of argument is an example of what Levy (2010) calls "recursive cosmopolitization," namely, that "local problems are resolved with recourse to global prescriptions while local solutions are inscribed in international institutions" (p. 579). The resolution of racial discrimination in the state of Alabama required the problem to be viewed from a wider perspective. First there was recourse to the federal government with a demand to uphold the U.S. Constitution, and then, when this proved slow, an appeal for global solidarity in the name of the moral authority of human rights. The success of the campaign then reinforced the status of the international human rights regime.

Citizenship Education in Multicultural Societies

The above examples of approaches to the struggle for citizenship and human rights can inform classroom discussions of current issues. Teachers may be wary of initiating such discussions because they can sometimes lead to clashes with school authorities or parents that schools find difficult to handle. However, it is precisely such controversial discussions that provide real learning opportunities (Hess, 2009; Hess & McAvoy, 2015). Rizvi (2009), taking a cosmopolitan perspective, argued that

> Our approach to teaching about global connectivity should begin with the local, but must move quickly to address issues of how our local communities are becoming socially transformed through their links with communities around the world and with what consequences. (p. 263)

To transpose Simone de Beauvoir's (1949/1972) famous assertion that one is not born a woman but becomes one, I would assert that, unless we confine the definition of citizen to nationality, citizens are not born, they are made. People learn to be citizens. This process starts with a realization that there is such a thing as a citizen and that citizens have choices and agency (Hudson, 2005). They have to acquire an identity as citizens, alongside many other identities. The construction of identities is a life-long process, but it is often most dramatically enacted at the time of adolescence. Wearing clothes and hairstyles designed to attract attention and subverting expectations in school uniforms or conventional dress may provoke daily conflicts with parents and school authorities. In this way young people develop their identities through an essentially political process of struggle for emancipation in the development of a personal lifestyle.

For some young people, participating in or organizing antiwar protests is a symbolic and accessible political activity. Local protests express global connectivity. Participation is a manifestation of cosmopolitan citizenship. A classic instance made legal history in the U.S. Supreme Court case *Tinker v. Des Moines School District* (1969). In 1965, Mary Beth Tinker, her brother, and a friend were excluded from school for wearing black armbands as a protest against the Vietnam War. Although the school allowed students to wear certain political symbols, this freedom of expression did not extend to the wearing of antiwar armbands. The parents took the case through the courts ending with vindication in the Supreme Court. In his judgment, Justice Abe Fortas made a now-famous assertion: "It can hardly be argued that either students or teachers shed their constitutional rights to freedom of speech or expression at the schoolhouse gate" (O'Brien, 2006, p. 8). While accepting that schools have the right to regulate dress and appearance and ban aggressive and disruptive actions, the judge argued that the armbands did not interfere in any way with the work of the school and the rights of other students.

A more recent example of students struggling to find adequate expression for their views was reported in an ethnically diverse school in northern California. Senior students in a class in government that encouraged discussion of current issues decided to start a Social Justice and Peace Club, with the support of their teacher. The name of the club is itself interesting, carrying echoes of the preamble to the UDHR. The students planned a lunchtime rally in school to mark the second anniversary of the invasion of Iraq. They submitted advance copies of their speeches and even toned them down in response to reaction from the principal. After a discussion with school authorities, the students were given permission to stage the event, but not to use any form of amplified sound. Just before the event, the two student organizers were told that they would be excluded from school for two days on the grounds, which they strongly denied, that they had harassed a visiting military recruiter. If they entered school premises they would be barred from graduating. The students organized a protest outside the school and subsequently found support from a civil liberties group as well as from their parents. After some months of negotiations, the students were finally allowed to hold a rally on the school premises and with amplification (Pace, 2008).

Another example of students using resistance and persuasion comes from a case study of a demographically mixed high school in London. In line with many instances of change in schools, inspired by neoliberal economic theories, the school leadership provided a new computer-based, individualized virtual science class for students preparing for important exams. The students found it hard to concentrate without the support of a teacher and felt they were learning nothing. Their resistance, informed by what they had learned about their rights in citizenship education classes, initially took the form of a letter to the head teacher. It attempted persuasion rather than threats, but expressed profound discontent. It legitimized the claim on the basis of the responsibility of the school to provide adequate preparation for the exam. Getting no response, the students organized a petition, involving a wider group of students. This led to a meeting with the head teacher, who insisted that the experiment of learning with computers had been a success. The students would not accept this and argued that the real reason for the virtual class was to save money. In this case there was no resolution of the issue, but the refusal of the head teacher to compromise eventually led to a full-scale strike of students and the departure of the head teacher (Mejias, 2012).

In these cases, students in demographically mixed schools learned to struggle for their rights and freedoms, using knowledge acquired in citizenship classes. Such practical learning may be of greater benefit to the students than classes based on reified notions of culture or situations where racism is denied or minimized. Multicultural education that starts from explorations of identities, rights, and struggles for justice looks very different from the approach implicit in the International Food Fair example below. The very real struggles for recognition and appropriate educational provision may involve parents, civil rights groups, the media, and in some cases the law.

In France, where the state is committed through its constitution and legislation to a radical separation of public and private spheres in the name of secular neutrality, struggles over school dress codes have been a live issue since 1989, when a school principal, associated with a right-wing party, suspended three girls from school for wearing headscarves (Lorcerie, 2005). A total ban on headscarves and other outward and visible signs of religious affiliation in schools was implemented in 2004, but the climate of intolerance toward religious symbols that was created by the legislation led in 2015 to two cases of young women being asked not to wear long black skirts in school. This is a clear case of school authorities' ascribing a particular meaning to a dress code that is not exclusively identifiable with any single religious tradition (Languille, 2015).

When the hijab was banned from French schools, Muslim families were forced to accept that if they were to access French state schools they had no choice but to conform to the national legislation. In a further development, the French government in October 2010 banned the concealing of the face in public spaces. The intention was clearly to outlaw the wearing of the *burqa* or the *niqab* in public, but since such a ban would be discriminatory on grounds of gender and religion, the more general interdiction of face covering was preferred. On human rights grounds, the ban restricts freedom of expression (in the sense of choosing what to wear in public) and also freedom of religion. It is also discriminatory because there are many exemptions to the ban. It does not apply to sports, drama, and medicine, for example. In fact, the only face covering likely to be systematically targeted is the *niqab* (Nussbaum, 2012). However, the European Court of Human Rights in 2014 upheld the ban on the grounds that the national government had the right to determine, on the basis of its own interpretation of national culture, the best way of preserving public order in order to promote peaceful coexistence (Languille, 2015).

The case of the French ban on concealing the face shows how cosmopolitan and national perspectives interact when it comes to interpreting the law. This case illustrates the uneasy interaction between politics, human rights law, and cosmopolitan human rights principles. Struggles for freedom of expression are essentially political. Young people are inevitably aware of power dimensions in their interactions with adults and with structures such as those imposed by school dress codes, timetables, examinations, and routines. Attempts by students to exercise agency in the context of these structures quickly reveal where power lies. Students have options such as resistance, which may be confrontational. However, where schools create real opportunities for participation, students may be persuaded of the rationale for the constraints or even be persuasive in making a case for change (Pérez-Expósito, 2012, 2015).

Struggles for self-expression and resistance to structures in place sometimes result in conflicts and confrontations with authority that may lead to punishments, including exclusion from school. Citizenship education can help young people to recognize the language and culture of the powerful and further help them to learn to communicate using appropriate linguistic and cultural registers, such as Standard English in the United States or the United Kingdom. The intention of such support is not, as perhaps in previous generations, to attempt to replace or cover up the language of the home or the street, because the young people need to be able to interact in those contexts as well. Rather it is to facilitate dialogue with a range of interlocutors, including administrators, employers, and elected representatives. The aim is therefore to help young people become adept at what linguists call "code switching" (Levinson, 2012). The ability to code switch is the capacity to change rapidly between language and cultural registers according to context. In linguistic terms it may require shifting between the language used between friends to a form of address more readily acceptable to a teacher or other authority figure. In cultural terms, it may require awareness, for example, that it is usual to wear formal clothes to attend or visit a place of worship. Tourists may be expected to cover their heads or remove their shoes. Understanding these codes is a useful skill that facilitates what social psychologists refer to as *identity management* (Adachi, 2014).

In multicultural contexts, given that people do not occupy single, static identity positions but have multiple identifications, all of which are undergoing constant change, identity management may be important (Ellemers & Van Rijswijk, 1997). It involves developing self-awareness to call upon when representing oneself to others, whether in terms of gender, sexuality, class, culture, or ethnicity, all of which complicate unilinear readings of race (Raby, 2004).

Evidence from empirical studies of schools practicing multicultural education suggests that, at a classroom level, the focus is not necessarily on the civic empowerment of students. For example, Chan (2007) conducted fieldwork in a school in Canada, located in a multicultural inner city area where students were said to speak 31 languages and have family links to 38 countries. The school attempted to provide a culturally sensitive curriculum. She focused on students' identities and ways in which the students' own narratives and cultural practices were challenged as they interacted with school activities, including, but not exclusively, the curriculum. Chan's underlying question was the extent to which these young people felt included (identified with the activity and with the school) or excluded (potentially felt rejected and therefore did not identify with the activity or the school).

Chan (2007) presented vignettes or stories. In each case, although the teachers intended to be inclusive, the outcomes were somewhat ambiguous. One example shows how a teacher prepared for and delivered a learning sequence that culminated in the school's International Food Fair. The starting point was a request from the teacher to name foods that the students ate at home and to identify different ways those foods were cooked. Students suggested pizza (baked), spaghetti (boiled), and fries. The teacher appeared to be frustrated by the responses of the students and was the only one to name "ethnic foods."

Although the teacher intended to be inclusive and to value the cultural backgrounds of the students, he was misguided because he was not prepared to accept the genuine answers the students gave. The students resisted this approach and declined what was effectively an invitation to assert their cultural difference, preferring to assert their common culture. Projects of nation building encourage people to "see likeness where, before, they might have seen difference" (Nussbaum, 2012, p. 14). The emphasis on difference in multicultural education provides ammunition for conservative political leaders in Europe who claim that multiculturalism has failed (Group of Eminent Persons, 2011).

The International Food Fair is an example of the contributions approach to multicultural education (Banks, 2006). This approach celebrates diversity and either ignores racism or treats it in terms of individual prejudice. However, the term "International" invites a diplomatic framing. Teachers may start to see students as representatives of nations or cultures. In a separate study, Levinson (2007) noted teachers turning to "the Filipino students for the 'Filipino perspective' on a topic, or to the African American child for the 'Black perspective'" (p. 632).

An identification of children in school with their countries of origin or parental origin can lead children and teachers to ascribe unwanted identities. In a study of a primary school in Cyprus, where attempts had been made to introduce intercultural education, Papamichael (2011) observed teasing directed at Paula, a high-achieving girl of Romanian origin. After media reports about a supermarket burglary by a Romanian man, one teacher described how some children in her class addressed Paula by making funny sounds with the word Romania and her name the next day. Although the incident was clearly upsetting to Paula, the teacher declined to react or respond, wishing to minimize the effects of the name calling. The teacher missed an opportunity to engage in dialogue with all the students and explore issues of exclusionary teasing.

Multicultural Education and Citizenship Education

The implementation of multicultural education in public schools may involve teachers of all disciplines, and it requires a climate, ethos, and organizational structure that reinforce rather than contradict the key messages. It involves content integration, knowledge construction, prejudice reduction, an empowering organizational culture, and equity pedagogy (Banks, 1997). It is "a process that permeates all aspects of school practices, policies and organization" (NAME, 2003). In this permeation model, all teachers have a role in promoting the cosmopolitan ideals of human rights and understandings of national constitutional guarantees of equality. The whole school community should ensure that minority perspectives are not ignored when decisions on curriculum content, allocation of resources, and staffing are made (NAME, 2003). However, without a dedicated, scheduled time for helping students explore these key concepts and ideas, a school's commitment to standards and to measurable indicators, such as examination success rates, may overwhelm good intentions (Mejias & Starkey, 2012). Hence the close alliance of multicultural education with citizenship education was endorsed by the Democracy and Diversity International Consensus Panel (Banks et al., 2005).

Since the beginning of the 21st century, governments and non-governmental organizations across the world have shown an interest in and commitment to citizenship education. Such interest stems from concerns about the effects of globalization and migration; an awareness of global inequalities; concerns about young people's lack of engagement with formal democratic processes and their perceived tendency toward antisocial behavior; and the rise of racist, ultranationalist, and sectarian political groups prepared to use violence to drive out or eliminate those defined by them as unworthy of protection (Osler & Starkey, 2006).

Citizenship education, which can also be known as social studies or civic education, has achieved a status in many parts of the world as a curriculum subject with scheduled time and specialized teachers. Even in its most anodyne form of civic education, where the focus is on national institutions of government, citizenship education has a political dimension. At least implicitly, it considers issues of power. It also, in principle, addresses the ideals of freedom, justice, equality, equity, and human dignity that underpin multicultural education.

That said, the political dimension of multicultural education remains somewhat undeveloped. The index of the *Routledge International Companion to Multicultural Education* (Banks, 2009a) directs those seeking information on "political literacy" or "racism and citizenship education" to just one of the 40 chapters in this volume (Starkey & Osler, 2009). Even in the context of antiracist education, which may highlight the privileges of dominant groups, it has been noted that political literacy and sociological understandings of racism are "frequently neglected" (Moodley, 2012, p. 1671). Another book intended to contribute to multicultural education by providing case studies of good practice omits key political concepts such as citizenship, democracy, human rights, and struggle from its index (Au, 2009).

In Canada, where a policy of multiculturalism, in place since 1971, has been widely taken up by schools, the emphasis still tends to be on tolerance, understanding, and celebration of difference—on acceptance of diversity and empathy for minorities rather than on economic and political realities (Joshee & Sinfield, 2010). Teachers may feel they have little opportunity to engage with sociological and political readings of school and society, including consideration of the role of the schools in the perpetuation of inequalities. Consequently, they "tend to de-politicize questions of race and racism" (Raby, 2004, p. 379).

In parallel, when the context is citizenship education, racial diversity is frequently an "invisible issue" (Pace, 2008, p. 32). The conceptualization of citizenship education as political education overlooks diversity as an issue (Crick, 1998; Osler, 2000b, 2008). Empirical studies of political discussions in schools reveal that they rarely focus on issues of diversity and racial justice (Hess & McAvoy, 2015). In this case, citizenship education avoids one of the major political realities that is salient in virtually any national context across the world.

Multicultural education and citizenship education can be brought together as education for cosmopolitan citizenship (Osler & Starkey, 2003; Osler & Vincent, 2002). Citizenship education as mandated and conceptualized by national education authorities is likely to have a limited and limiting "nation-bound perspective" (Sleeter, 2010, p. 1). Citizenship education informed by multicultural education can challenge that perspective, or at least challenge reductionist conceptions of the nation as representing and being represented in terms of the reified culture of a dominant group (Osler, 2008).

Conclusion

Cosmopolitanism is a perspective that conceptually unites multicultural education and citizenship education. This is implicitly recognized by Kymlicka (2004) in his contribution to the edited collection that came out of the Bellagio 2002 international conference hosted by the Center for Multicultural Education. Drawing on the contributions of Castles and Ong, Kymlicka noted that "the logic of multiculturalism can be seen as pushing the boundaries of the nation state" (p. xv). This was also picked up by Parker (2004) in the concluding chapter of *Diversity and Citizenship Education: Global Perspectives*, where he argues for cosmopolitan values to underpin his multinational curriculum for diversity and democracy.

One further development of the work of the 2002 Bellagio conference was the Democracy and Diversity International Consensus Panel (Banks et al., 2005), which explicitly advocated developing students' knowledge of human rights and of the tension between patriotism and cosmopolitanism. In the decade since the consensus panel, its framework and program of action have been widely used across the world. Globalization and social media have brought awareness of the world as an interdependent system more fully into the consciousness of citizens, including young people.

Nussbaum, in a classic dialogue with leading scholars of cosmopolitanism, asserted that "through cosmopolitan education we learn more about ourselves" (Nussbaum & Cohen, 1996, p. 11). In other words, by learning about and with other people from a diversity of traditions and cultures, we are able to relativize our own practices and beliefs. This feature of cosmopolitan education provides an argument in favor of the cosmopolitan approach based on self-interest, because individuals benefit from the capacity to be self-reflective. That approach is also likely to strengthen democracy, as it recognizes diversity as a democratic asset. In practical terms, education for cosmopolitan citizenship combines multicultural education with traditions of citizenship based on rights and struggle. In implementing this agenda, multicultural education might need to become more political, and citizenship education more multicultural.

References

Adachi, S. (2014, April). *Faith and social integration of young British Muslims in changing society: Identity management and knowledge of resources.* Paper presented at the British Sociological Association Conference, University of Leeds.

Adichie, C. N. (2009). The danger of a single story. Retrieved from www.ted.com/talks/chimamanda_adichie_the_danger_of_a_single_story/transcript?language=en

Anderson, B. (1991). *Imagined communities: Reflections on the origin and spread of nationalism.* London: Verso.

Appiah, K. A. (2006). *Cosmopolitanism: Ethics in a world of strangers.* London: Allen Lane.

Au, W. (Ed.). (2009). *Rethinking multicultural education: Teaching for racial and cultural justice.* Milwaukee, WI: Rethinking Schools.

Banks, J. A. (1997). *Educating citizens in a multicultural society.* New York: Teachers College Press.

Banks, J. A. (1998). The lives and values of researchers: Implications for educating citizens in a multicultural society. *Educational Researcher, 27*(7), 4–17.

Banks, J. A. (Ed.). (2004a). *Diversity and citizenship education: Global perspectives*. San Francisco: Jossey-Bass.

Banks, J. A. (2004b). Preface. In J. Banks (Ed.), *Diversity and citizenship education: Global perspectives* (pp. xix–xxv). San Francisco: Jossey-Bass.

Banks, J. A. (2006). *Race, culture and education: The selected works of James A. Banks*. New York: Routledge.

Banks, J. A. (Ed.). (2009a). *The Routledge international companion to multicultural education*. London: Routledge.

Banks, J. A. (2009b). Diversity and citizenship education in multicultural nations. *Multicultural Education Review, 1*(1), 1–28.

Banks, J. A. (2015). *Global migration, structural inclusion, and citizenship education across nations: A conference sponsored by the Center for Multicultural Education* [Conference program]. Seattle, WA: University of Washington, Center for Multicultural Education.

Banks, J. A., McGee Banks, C. A., Cortes, C. E., Hahn, C., Merryfield, M., Moodley, K. A., et al. (2005). *Democracy and diversity: Principles and concepts for educating citizens in a global age*. Seattle, WA: Center for Multicultural Education, University of Washington.

Bauman, Z. (1989). *Modernity and the Holocaust*. Cambridge, UK: Polity.

Beck, U. (2002). The cosmopolitan society and its enemies. *Theory, Culture & Society, 19*(1–2), 17–44.

Beck, U. (2012). Redefining the sociological project: The cosmopolitan challenge. *Sociology, 46*(1), 7–12.

Bowring, B. (2008). Misunderstanding MacIntyre on human rights. In K. Knight & P. Blackledge (Eds.), *Revolutionary Aristotelianism* (pp. 205–214). Stuttgart, Germany: Lucius & Lucius.

Chan, E. (2007). Student experiences of a culturally sensitive curriculum: Ethnic identity development amid conflicting stories to live by. *Journal of Curriculum Studies, 39*(2), 177–194.

Clark, S. (Ed.). (1992). *Malcolm X February 1965: The final speeches*. New York: Pathfinder.

Covell, K., Howe, R. B., & Polegato, J. L. (2011). Children's human rights education as a counter to social disadvantage: A case study from England. *Educational Research, 53*(2), 193–206.

Crick, B. (1998). *Education for citizenship and the teaching of democracy in schools*. London: Qualifications and Curriculum Authority.

De Beauvoir, S. (1972). *The second sex*. Harmondsworth, UK: Penguin. (Original work published 1949)

Delors, J. (1996). *Learning: The treasure within*. Paris: UNESCO.

Dewey, J. (2002). Democracy and education: An introduction to the philosophy of education. In S. J. Maxcy (Ed.), *John Dewey and American Education* (Vol. 3). Bristol, UK: Thoemmes. (Original work published 1916)

Ellemers, N., & Van Rijswijk, W. (1997). Identity needs versus social opportunities: The use of group-level and individual-level identity management strategies. *Social Psychology Quarterly, 60*(1), 52–65.

Giddens, A. (1990). *The consequences of modernity*. Cambridge, UK: Polity.

Group of Eminent Persons. (2011). *Living together: Combining diversity and freedom in 21st-century Europe*. Strasbourg, France: Council of Europe.

Gutmann, A. (2003). *Identity in democracy*. Woodstock, UK: Princeton University Press.

Hampton, H., & Fayer, S. (1990) *Voices of freedom: An oral history of the civil rights movement from the 1950s through the 1980s*. New York: Bantam.

Heater, D. (2002). *World citizenship: Cosmopolitan thinking and its opponents*. London: Continuum.

Held, D. (1995). Democracy and the new international order. In D. Archibugi & D. Held (Eds.), *Cosmopolitan democracy* (pp. 96–120). London: Polity.

Held, D. (2010). Cosmopolitanism after 9/11. *International Politics 47*, 52–61.

Hess, D. (2009). *Controversy in the classroom: The democratic power of discussion.* New York: Routledge.

Hess, D., & McAvoy, P. (2015). *The political classroom: Evidence and ethics in democratic education.* New York: Routledge.

Hudson, A. (2005). Citizenship education and students' identities: A school-based action research project. In A. Osler (Ed.), *Teachers, human rights and diversity: Educating citizens in multicultural societies* (pp. 115–132). Stoke on Trent, UK: Trentham.

Isin, E., & Wood, P. (1999). *Citizenship and identity.* London: Sage.

Jerome, L. (2012). Children's rights and teachers' responsibilities. In R. Mitchell & S. Moore (Eds.), *Politics, participation & power relations: Transdisciplinary approaches to critical citizenship in the classroom and community* (pp. 101–117). Rotterdam, The Netherlands: Sense.

Joshee, R., & Sinfield, I. (2010). The Canadian multicultural education policy web: Lessons to learn, pitfalls to avoid. *Multicultural Education Review, 2*(1), 55–75.

Kaldor, M. (2003). American power: From 'compellance' to cosmopolitanism? *International Affairs, 79*(1), 1–22.

King, M. L. (1964). Speech on South Africa at City Temple, London, December 1964. Retrieved from www.rfksafilm.org/html/speeches/africaking.php

Klug, F. (2000). Values for a godless age: The story of the UK's new Bill of Rights. Harmondsworth, UK: Penguin.

Knight, L. W. (2005). *Citizen: Jane Addams and the struggle for democracy.* Chicago: University of Chicago Press.

Kymlicka, W. (2004). Foreword. In J. Banks (Ed.), *Diversity and citizenship education: Global perspectives.* San Francisco: Jossey-Bass.

Languille, C. (2015). *La possibilité du cosmopolitisme: Burqa, droits de l'homme et vivre-ensemble* [The possibility of cosmopolitanism: Burqa, human rights and living together]. Paris: Gallimard.

Levinson, M. (2007). Common schools and multicultural education. *Journal of Philosophy of Education, 41*(4), 625–642.

Levinson, M. (2012). *No citizen left behind.* Cambridge, MA: Harvard University Press.

Levy, D. (2010). Recursive cosmopolitization: Argentina and the global human rights regime. *British Journal of Sociology, 61*(3), 579–596.

Lorcerie, F. (Ed.). (2005). *La politisation du voile en France, en Europe et dans le monde arabe* [The politicization of the headscarf in France, in Europe and in the Arab world]. Paris: L'Harmattan.

Mandela, N. (1964). *I am prepared to die.* London: Christian Action. Retrieved from https://www.bl.uk/collection-items/nelson-mandelas-speech-i-am-prepared-to-die-at-the-rivonia-trial

Mandela, N. (1994). *Long walk to freedom.* London: Abacus.

Mannheim, K. (1991). *Ideology and Utopia: An introduction to the sociology of knowledge.* London: Routledge. (Original work published 1929)

Mejias, S. (2012). *NGOs and human rights education in the neoliberal age: A case study of an NGO-secondary school partnership in London.* Unpublished doctoral dissertation, Institute of Education, University of London.

Mejias, S., & Starkey, H. (2012). Critical citizens or neoliberal consumers? Utopian visions and pragmatic uses of human rights education in a secondary school in England. In R. C. Mitchell

& S. A. Moore (Eds.), *Politics, participation and power relations: Transdisciplinary approaches to critical citizenship in the classroom and community.* (pp. 119–136). Rotterdam, The Netherlands: Sense.

Moodley, K. (2012). Political literacy and education. In J. Banks (Ed.), *Encyclopedia of diversity in education* (pp. 1670–1673). Thousand Oaks, CA: Sage.

Moyn, S. (2010). *The last utopia: Human rights in history.* Cambridge, MA: Belknap.

National Association for Multicultural Education. (2003). *Definition of multicultural education.* Retrieved from http://www.nameorg.org/definitions_of_multicultural_e.php

National Council for the Social Studies. (2013). *The college, career, and civic life (C3) framework for social studies state standards: Guidance for enhancing the rigor of K–12 civics, economics, geography, and history.* Silver Spring, MD: Author.

Nussbaum, M. C. (2012). *The new religious intolerance: Overcoming the politics of fear in an anxious age.* Cambridge, MA: Belknap.

Nussbaum, M. C., & Cohen, J. (1996). *For love of country: Debating the limits of patriotism.* Boston: Beacon.

O'Brien, E. (2006). *The many ways of student voice. An examination of student participation in decision-making in United States schools.* Unpublished master's dissertation, Faculty of Law, University of Fribourg.

Osler, A. (2000a). The Crick report: Difference, equality and racial justice. *Curriculum Journal, 11*(1), 25–37.

Osler, A. (Ed.). (2000b). *Citizenship and democracy in schools: Diversity, identity, equality.* Stoke on Trent, UK: Trentham Books.

Osler, A. (2008). Citizenship education and the Ajegbo report: Re-imagining a cosmopolitan nation. *London Review of Education, 6*(1), 9–23.

Osler, A. (2011). Teacher interpretations of citizenship education: National identity, cosmopolitan ideals, and political realities. *Journal of Curriculum Studies, 43*(1), 1–24.

Osler, A. (2015). Human rights education, postcolonial scholarship and action for social justice. *Theory and Research in Social Education, 43*(2), 244–274.

Osler, A. (2016). *Human rights and schooling: An ethical framework for teaching social justice.* New York: Teachers College Press.

Osler, A., & Starkey, H. (1996). *Teacher education and human rights.* London: Fulton.

Osler, A., & Starkey, H. (1998). Children's rights and citizenship: Some implications for the management of schools. *International Journal of Children's Rights, 6*(3), 313–333.

Osler, A., & Starkey, H. (2003). Learning for cosmopolitan citizenship: Theoretical debates and young people's experiences. *Educational Review, 55*(3), 243–254.

Osler, A., & Starkey, H. (2005). *Changing citizenship: Democracy and inclusion in education.* Maidenhead, UK: Open University Press.

Osler, A., & Starkey, H. (2006). Education for democratic citizenship: A review of research, policy and practice, 1995–2005. *Research Papers in Education, 24*(4), 433–466.

Osler, A., & Starkey, H. (2010). *Teachers and human rights education.* Stoke-on-Trent, UK: Trentham.

Osler, A., & Vincent, K. (2002). *Citizenship and the challenge of global education.* Stoke on Trent, UK: Trentham.

Pace, J. (2008). Teaching for citizenship in 12th grade government classes. In J. Bixby & J. Pace (Eds.), *Educating democratic citizens in troubled times: Qualitative studies of current efforts* (pp. 25–57). Albany: State University of New York Press.

Pace, J., & Bixby, J. (2008). Introduction: Studying citizenship education in troubled times. In J. Bixby & J. Pace (Eds.), *Educating democratic citizens in troubled times: Qualitative studies of current efforts* (pp. 3–24). Albany: State University of New York Press.

Papamichael, E. (2011). *Exploring intercultural education discourses and everyday practices in a Greek-Cypriot primary school.* Unpublished doctoral dissertation, Institute of Education, University of London.

Parker, W. C. (2004). Diversity, globalization, and democratic education: Curriculum possibilities. In J. Banks (Ed.), *Diversity and citizenship education: Global perspectives.* San Francisco: Jossey-Bass.

Pérez-Expósito, L. (2012). *Students' representations of political participation: Implications for citizenship education in Mexico City's secondary schools.* Unpublished doctoral dissertation, Institute of Education, University of London.

Pérez-Expósito, L. (2015). Scope and quality of student participation in school: Towards an analytical framework for adolescents. *International Journal of Adolescence and Youth, 20*(3), 1–29.

Raby, R. (2004). "There's no racism at my school, it's just joking around": Ramifications for anti-racist education. *Race Ethnicity and Education, 7*(4), 367–383.

Rawls, J. (1999). *The law of peoples.* Cambridge, MA: Harvard University Press.

Ricoeur, P. (1978). Imagination in discourse and action. In A.-T. Tymieniecka (Ed.), *The human being in action: The irreducible element in man: Part 2. Investigations at the intersection of philosophy and psychiatry* (pp. 3–22). Dordrecht, The Netherlands: Reidel.

Rizvi, F. (2009). Towards cosmopolitan learning. *Discourse: Studies in the cultural politics of education, 30*(3), 253–268.

Schama, S. (1989). *Citizens: A chronicle of the French Revolution.* London: Penguin.

Sen, A. (2009). *The idea of justice.* London: Allen Lane.

Sleeter, C. (2010). Probing beneath meanings of multicultural education. *Multicultural Education Review, 2*(1), 1–24.

Soysal, Y. (2012). Citizenship, immigration, and the European social project: Rights and obligations of individuality. *British Journal of Sociology, 63*(1), 1–21.

Spring, J. (2015). *Globalization of education: An introduction.* New York: Routledge.

Starkey, H., & Osler, A. (2009). Antiracism, citizenship, and education: European ideals and political complacency. In J. A. Banks (Ed.), *Routledge international companion to multicultural education.* New York: Routledge.

Stoker, G. (2011). *Prospects for citizenship.* London: Bloomsbury Academic.

United Nations. (1989). *Convention on the Rights of the Child.* New York: UNICEF.

United Nations General Assembly. (1948). *Universal declaration of human rights.* New York: United Nations.

Verhellen, E. (2000). Children's rights and education. In A. Osler (Ed.), *Citizenship and democracy in schools: Diversity, identity, equality* (pp. 33–43). Stoke-on-Trent, UK: Trentham.

Vertovec, S. (2007). Super-diversity and its implications. *Ethnic and Racial Studies, 30*(6), 1024–1054.

Zuckerman, E. (2013). *Digital cosmopolitans: Why we think the Internet connects us, why it doesn't and how to rewire it.* New York: Norton.

Part 2

The United States, Canada, and South Africa

Chapter 4

Citizenship, Culture, and Race in the United States

ANGELA M. BANKS
William & Mary Law School

Citizenship is a legal category that provides unique access to legal rights and material resources in the United States. Access to U.S. citizenship status has varied greatly throughout U.S. history. In 1790 naturalization was only available to noncitizens who were "free white persons" who had resided in the United States for two years, were persons of "good moral character," and "support[ed] the constitution of the United States" (Naturalization Act of 1790). By 1870 the racial requirements were expanded to include individuals of African nativity or descent (Naturalization Act of 1870). It was 1952 before all racial requirements were eliminated from U.S. naturalization law. Immigration scholars have written extensively about the reasons the racial restrictions existed, how they were enforced, how such restrictions shaped conceptions of race and belonging in the United States, and why these restrictions were eliminated.[1] Yet less attention has been given to how racially ineligible groups became eligible for citizenship.

In other work I have addressed this gap in the literature by examining the use of *respectability narratives* to counter justifications for excluding individuals of certain racial backgrounds from naturalization (Banks, 2016). Respectability narratives seek to alter the social meaning of the immigrant groups that have been constructed as a problem. Naming them respectability narratives builds on Elizabeth Brooks Higginbotham's (1994) work on "the politics of respectability" (p. 186). Higginbotham first coined this term in her study of the Women's Convention of the National Baptist Convention. During the late 19th and early 20th centuries, members of this organization worked to improve African American women's social status and legal rights by demonstrating African American women's adherence to mainstream middle-class values and practices. This was an explicit attempt to counter widespread claims that African American women were disreputable, and these claims were used to justify African American women's lower social status and limited legal rights. The legalist strand of the politics of respectability, as described by legal historian Kenneth Mack (2005), makes claims for legal rights based on arguments that the marginalized group has the same values, norms, and practices as mainstream society and therefore deserves the requested legal rights. Advocates seeking citizenship and legal immigration reform have used respectability narratives historically and continue to do so today (Banks, 2016).[2]

The analysis provided in this chapter provides the foundation upon which respectability narratives are built. Based on an analysis of congressional hearings and debates, administrative records, and judicial opinions regarding naturalization and racial requirements, this chapter identifies the values, norms, and practices that legal decision makers have deemed essential aspects of American culture for the purpose of naturalization. This analysis reveals that the fundamental aspects of American culture for citizenship purposes are a commitment to democracy and the rule of law, a belief in individualism, self-sufficiency, Christian beliefs and morals, and English language skills.

Race was an explicit naturalization requirement between 1790 and 1952, yet this chapter does not treat race as a distinct aspect of American culture for naturalization purposes. An analysis of congressional hearings and debates, administrative records, and judicial opinions reveals that race was viewed as a proxy for specific values, norms, and practices. Certain races were viewed as sharing American culture, and other races were seen as having values, norms, and practices that threatened American culture. Thus race was used to measure the existence of desirable values, norms, and practices. This chapter focuses on identifying the aspects of American culture that were deemed necessary for naturalization while acknowledging that the desirable values, norms, and practices were racialized. The racialization of values, norms, and practices was possible because race is a social construct that is "highly malleable and historically-bounded" (Bonilla-Silva, 1999, p. 899).[3] Racial categories are "created, inhabited, transformed, and destroyed" (Omi & Winant, 1994, p. 55). The existence of specific racial categories has changed over time, who is within each racial category has changed over time, and most important for this project, the meaning of racial categories has changed over time.[4] This chapter demonstrates that there is a specific set of values, norms, and practices that citizenship decision makers have relied upon to determine which immigrants are worthy of citizenship. Advocates for expanding access to naturalization have relied on this conception of American identity to change the social meaning of the racial categories of excluded immigrants.

Between 1790 and 1952 Congress debated naturalization requirements, administrative agencies implemented the enacted requirements, and courts reviewed agency naturalization decisions. In each of these contexts the legislative, executive, and judicial branches of government offered opinions about the values, norms, and practices necessary for American citizens. An analysis of congressional hearings and debates, administrative records, and judicial opinions between 1870 and 1943 reveals that citizenship decision makers viewed a commitment to democracy and the rule of law, a belief in individualism, self-sufficiency, Christian beliefs and morals, and English language skills as necessary values, norms, and practices for American citizenship.

This chapter proceeds in three parts. Utilizing the work of Bosniak (2000), Part I introduces a theoretical framework for conceptualizing citizenship. This framework provides a basis for understanding why culture and identity play a role in determining who will have access to citizenship status. Part II identifies five key aspects of American culture for citizenship purposes through an analysis of congressional hearings and debates, administrative records, and judicial opinions. Part III discusses specific techniques that teachers can use to bring ideas about culture and citizenship into their classrooms.

I. The Meaning of Citizenship

Citizenship is a concept that means different things to different people and groups. Bosniak (2000) has identified four different conceptions of citizenship within citizenship-related discourse. Citizenship is viewed as a *legal status*, an *identity*, *legal rights*, and *political engagement*. These conceptions are not mutually exclusive and are interrelated. For example, if legal rights are dependent upon having the formal status of citizen, then participation within the society will likely vary based on citizenship status. A key argument in this chapter is that access to citizenship status in the United States has depended on legal decision makers concluding that future citizens are culturally indistinguishable from mainstream American citizens. The relationship between citizenship status and culture is the relationship between citizenship as status and citizenship as identity. This is yet another example of the ways in which various conceptions of citizenship are interrelated.

Status

The legal status of citizenship is the means by which states designate formal membership within the state (Joppke, 2005). Joppke has referred to this as "citizenship as passport-holding" (p. 28). The legal status of citizen is granted by a state, and the state alone determines the criteria for determining who is or can become a citizen and what rights, benefits, and privileges are extended to citizens.

Individuals can acquire the legal status of citizen at birth or through naturalization. States grant citizenship to individuals at birth based on the *jus sanguinis* principle, the *jus soli* principle, or both. The *jus sanguinis* principle dictates that those with a blood connection to the state are citizens. Therefore if an individual's father or grandfather is or was a citizen, then the individual would be a citizen as well. Until the year 2000, citizenship at birth in Germany was exclusively available based on the *jus sanguinis* principle (Kirkland, 2006).[5] Pursuant to the *jus soli* principle, individuals born on the soil of a country are citizens of that country. The Fourteenth Amendment of the U.S. Constitution provides an example of citizenship at birth based on the *jus soli* principle. This amendment states that "all persons born or naturalized in the United States and subject to the jurisdiction thereof, are citizens of the United States and of the State wherein they reside" (U.S. Const. amend. xiv).

Naturalization is another means by which individuals can obtain the legal status of citizen. Naturalization requirements differ by state. Generally states require a certain period of residence, a specific immigration status, language skills, and other evidence of cultural assimilation. For example, the United States currently requires an individual to be at least 18 years old, have been admitted as a lawful permanent resident, have resided in the United States continuously for five years, be a person of good moral character, be "attached to the principles of the Constitution of the United States, and well disposed to the good order and happiness of the United States," "able to read, write, and speak English," and "knowledgeable about U.S. history and government" (Immigration and Nationality Act § 316; Immigration and Nationality Act § 319). Naturalization requirements often reflect a desire for new citizens to be culturally indistinguishable from mainstream citizens—with similar values, norms, and practices. In the United States this is reflected in the requirements that successful applicants speak English and be knowledgeable about U.S. history and government. The desire for this cultural connection is related to another conception of citizenship—identity.

Identity

Citizenship as an identity refers to a means by which people experience a sense of "solidarity . . . with others in the wider world" (Bosniak, 2006, pp. 19–20). One basis for a sense of solidarity is shared values, norms, and practices—shared culture. States extend citizenship status based on a variety of criteria as noted above, but a persistent criterion in the United States has been identity. Historically the United States has only granted citizenship status to individuals who were perceived as sharing a common cultural identity. The quest for citizenship status for African Americans, Native Americans, and Asian immigrants was very challenging because legal decision makers did not believe that these groups shared a common cultural identity with mainstream White citizens.

Citizenship as an identity is also distinct and separate from citizenship as a status. Individuals can have an American identity even if they lack the legal status of citizen. "DREAMers" provide an excellent example of the complex relationship between these conceptions of citizenship. DREAMers are individuals "who would benefit from the Development, Relief, and Education for Alien Minors Act" (Banks, 2013a, pp. 78).[6] These young people are not citizens and do not have lawful immigration status, yet they have been raised in the United States. These students are "coming out of the shadows to reveal their unauthorized immigration status and to seek legislative reform that will grant them equal access to higher education and jobs in the United States" (Banks, 2013a, pp. 78–79). They are engaging in political activism despite their lack of citizenship status and the risk that such activism may result in their deportation.

One DREAMer, Uriel, described his identity as an American as being rooted in a commitment to democratic values. He said,

> When we fail to speak up, when we fail to criticize, when we fail to stand up for our ideals, and when we fail to improve the lives of those around us; it is a far greater blow to the freedom, the decency, and to the justice which truly represents this nation we call home. (21 Reasons Why We Should Support the Dream Act— LEGAL IMMIGRATION!, 2010)

Despite lacking the status and the full rights of a citizen, Uriel is exhibiting a commitment to the growth and development of the United States based on the American beliefs of justice, equality, and individualism through nonviolent protest, a quintessentially American practice for social change. DREAMers and other unauthorized migrants are making claims to citizenship status based on their identity as Americans. They seek greater connection between these two conceptions of citizenship.

Ideas about which noncitizens have developed, or are capable of developing, a shared identity with mainstream American citizens have shaped access to citizenship status in the United States. Bosniak's citizenship typology helps explain why such a connection would exist. Citizenship is not merely a legal status that determines an individual's rights, benefits, and privileges within a state. Citizenship is also the basis for a sense of solidarity, and that solidarity is often based on shared values, norms, and practices. The following section identifies the key aspects of American culture that citizenship decision makers have deemed critical for citizenship acquisition via naturalization.

II. The Cultural Substance of American Citizenship

Concerns about the cultural assimilation of immigrants date back to the founding of the United States. As legal scholar Hiroshi Motomura (2006) has noted, "The immigrant experience in America has traditionally included some expectation of conformity to a white, Anglo-Saxon, Protestant majority" (p. 168). Today when people think about what makes an individual culturally American, many will say a commitment to the American Creed—liberty, justice, equality, and the fair treatment of all people (Myrdal, 1962).[7] Yet between 1790 and 1952, Congress, administrative officials, and the judiciary had a more specific idea about what made an individual an American. Congressional hearings and debates, administrative records, and judicial opinions demonstrate that being an American was dependent upon adopting specific values, norms, and practices. Individuals needed to show a commitment to democracy and the rule of law, a belief in individualism, self-sufficiency, Christian beliefs and morals, and English language skills. Between 1790 and 1952 Congress debated naturalization requirements, administrative agencies implemented the enacted requirements, and courts reviewed agency naturalization decisions. Through these contexts each branch of government offered opinions about who the law actually viewed as American and who the law ought to view as American. This part analyzes these resources and identifies what legal decision makers deemed essential aspects of American identity for the purpose of naturalization.

The racial requirements for naturalization provide a rich resource regarding the values, norms, and practices deemed necessary for American citizenship. Congressional hearings and debates provide insight on the meaning that was attached to certain racial and ethnic groups and how that meaning conformed to or contradicted the desired values, norms, and practices. Internal administrative memorandums identify specific norms and practices as necessary for American citizenship and debate the reliability of race as a proxy to measure them. Finally, a number of judicial opinions similarly identify the values, norms, and practices necessary for American citizenship and determine whether or not the applicants before the court possessed them regardless of their race or ethnicity. Additionally, in the Native American naturalization context federal law specified certain norms and practices as perquisites for naturalization, but they were stated at a high level of generalization. Internal administrative memorandums and policies along with judicial opinions operationalized these general requirements and offer a more detailed picture of the desired values, norms, and practices.

Democracy

Congressional debates in the 1790s reveal concerns that foreign residents' values, norms, and practices could pose a threat to America's democratic experiment. As noted by historian

James H. Kettner (1978), "Suspicion of the foreign-born and a belief that citizenship conferred political rights combined to shape the development of a federal naturalization policy in the 1790s" (pp. 241–242). The naturalization requirements adopted in the 1790s sought to limit access to citizenship to those noncitizens who were least likely to threaten America's political experiment (Kettner, 1978, pp. 241–242; 1790 Naturalization Act). A residence requirement was one tool used to accomplish this goal because it was viewed as useful for ensuring that future citizens had the time necessary to learn and adopt American political norms and values.[8] Kettner contends that in 1795 there was a shared assumption within Congress that a residence longer than two years should be required so that

> prejudices which the aliens had imbibed under the Government from whence they came might be effaced, and that they might, by communication and observance of our laws and government, have just ideas of our Constitution and the excellence of its institutions before they were admitted to the rights of citizen. (Kettner, 1978, p. 242)

Residence requirements existed when state law governed naturalization, and they were based on the assumption that "the exercise of political rights required a clear and conscious attachment to and familiarity with republican principles" (Kettner, 1978, p. 218). Time in the United States was thought to ensure "that those imbued with 'foreign principles' had the opportunity to assimilate the habits, values, and modes of thought necessary for responsible participation in a virtuous, self-governing republican community" (p. 219). These ideas remained prevalent when Congress became responsible for the naturalization laws. During congressional debates in the 1790s residence was viewed as an important requirement to ensure that immigrants had "a firm attachment to the Government" (quoted at p. 237). For example, Michael Stone of Maryland wanted a residence term long enough to guarantee

> . . .First, that he should have an opportunity of knowing the circumstances of our Government, and in consequence thereof, shall have admitted the truth of the principles we hold. Second, that he shall have acquired a taste for this kind of Government. (p. 237)

By the mid-1790s the French Revolution had sparked a European crisis, and Europeans were migrating to the United States in significant numbers. Those coming to the United States were viewed as "disenchanted Englishmen, aristocratic Frenchmen, German Pietists fleeing forced military service, French planters escaping from West Indian uprisings led by Toussaint l'Ouverture, and Irishmen in flight from British repression" (quoted in Kettner, 1978, pp. 239–240). Kettner contends that "the massive influx of foreign immigrants might have increased fears of alien intermeddling in politics in any case; however, the large number of refugees with passionate political beliefs made all newcomers doubly suspect" (p. 240). Such concerns led to the residence requirement increasing from two years to five years in 1795 and to 14 years in 1798.[9] The 14-year residence requirement was repealed in 1802 and returned to five years after Thomas Jefferson was elected president.[10]

Congressional suspicion of foreign residents shaped the naturalization requirements in the 1790s. Members of Congress were doubtful that "the subjects of all Governments,

Despotic, Monarchical, and Aristocratical, are, as soon as they set foot on American ground, qualified to participate in administering the sovereignty of our country" (quoted in Kettner, 1978, p. 240). Congress adopted naturalization requirements that would limit the ability of those without the desired political character to become U.S. citizens. This was primarily addressed through residence requirements because there was a sense that time in the United States would allow immigrants to develop the desired political character.

Yet residence was not viewed as a tool for politically assimilating non-White foreign residents and those who had a servitude status—indentured servants or slaves.[11] During the debates regarding the 1870 naturalization law members of Congress raised concerns about Chinese immigrants' lack of experience with democracy. Rather than accept that time spent in the United States would enable Chinese immigrants to adopt democratic values, norms, and practices, Congress concluded that this immigrant population was unassimilable. Senator George H. Williams expressed concern that Chinese immigrants were imperialist and that

> Mongolians, no matter how long they may stay in the United States, will never lose their identity as a peculiar and separate people. They will never amalgamate with persons of European descent; and so, as their numbers multiply, as thousands are added to thousands, until they may be counted by millions, we shall have in the United States a separate and distinct people, empire of China within the North American Republic. (Congressional Globe, 1870, p. 5157)

Senator Henry W. Corbett expressed concern about Chinese immigrants' ability to conform to American practices related to democratic governance. For example, he stated that Chinese immigrants were "not only interfering with the family relations, but in every conceivable way, are introducing the most corrupt practices into our community, which has heretofore been moral, religious, and not surpassed by any of the New England States" (Congressional Globe, 1870, p. 5163). One of the corrupt practices he was concerned about was election fraud. He predicted that "frauds upon the ballot-box will increase and become greater than they are now" (p. 5163). He went on to explain that in his own city

> there are two houses engaged in the importation of Chinese, and all that will be neces-sary will be for one party to go to one house and purchase the votes of the adherents of that house, and for the other party to go to the other house and purchase the votes of its adherents. (p. 5163)

Senator William M. Stewart also doubted Chinese immigrants' capacity for responsi-ble democratic engagement. He explained his opposition, stating that it was because he was "opposed to pagan imperialists, Chinese who do not understand the obligation of a Christian oath being incorporated in the body-politic" (p. 5155).

The congressional discussion of Chinese immigrants and democracy was markedly different from the discussion of Africans and West Indians and democracy. This immigrant population was presented as "wholly Americanized" and capable of responsible democratic governance (Congressional Globe, 1870, p. 5163). African and West Indian immigrants were also viewed as potentially beneficial for the Republican Party. Senator Charles Sumner received letters from individuals in Florida, Virginia, and California requesting that the naturalization laws allow Africans and West Indians to naturalize (p. 5155).[12] One letter from a Florida state senator explained that allowing such naturalization would "make the party stronger by adding at least two thousand to the number" (p. 5155). This was because the majority of African and West Indian immigrants in areas such as Key West were Republicans who had lived in the United States for many years (p. 5155).

Chinese immigrants' access to U.S. citizenship changed in 1943 in the midst of World War II. While repealing Chinese naturalization ineligibility was tied to the war effort, advocates for the repeal argued that Chinese immigrants were experienced democrats and held democratic values, norms, and practices. For example, the Reverend Bishop Yu Pin testified that the great friendship between the United States and China was rooted in "that great, human document the American Constitution" (*Hearing on H.R. 1882 and H.R. 2309 Before H. Comm. on Immigration and Naturalization*, 1943, p. 13). He explained that the American Constitution inspired the founder of the Chinese Republic, Sun Yat-Sen. Based on this model, "equality of race, religion, and class, and liberty for all is the law of the land in China today" (p. 13). The Reverend Bishop Yu Pin explained that children in classrooms across China "can quote the grand, human principles enunciated by the American Constitution. They have been taught that it stands for liberty and equality of all peoples. They know that it champions the personal rights and personal dignity of the individual" (p. 13).

Representative Frances P. Bolton similarly noted that in "the present Chinese Constitution, you will see that they have followed, in almost every respect, the principles of our own Constitution" (*Hearing on H.R. 1882 and H.R. 2309 Before H. Comm. on Immigration and Naturalization*, 1943, p. 61). Arthur Hummel, chief of the Asiatic Division of the Library of Congress, Washington, D.C., also supported the assessment of China as a democratic country. He said,

> I am in favor of this bill because I know that the Chinese people are, like ourselves, a democratic people—socially democratic people. They do not have now, nor have they yet worked out, all the techniques of democracy which we have, but I have no doubt that they will do so very soon after the war is over. But they have what is more important than that. They have a fundamentally democratic approach to life. (p. 25)[13]

Pearl Buck, a Pulitzer Prize–winning author who was raised in China by her missionary parents, had a similar assessment:

> The Chinese people are democratic throughout their history, and I cannot agree with that gentleman today who said China is in a state of chaos. I have lived in the most interesting period of Chinese life, when she was changing from the Old Empire into the modern form. The people are democratic people from the Old Empire. The center of rule was in the people of the villages. They are trained and ready because they have had for centuries the democratic idea. (p. 74)

This sentiment was repeated during the floor debates in the House. Representative John W. McCormack explained that

> our Constitution has been her governmental inspiration. Her children quote with pride our constitutional guaranties of liberty and equality. . . . The principles of the Government of China of today flow from their understanding of the principles of American Government. China is essentially a democratic people. (*Repeal of the Chinese Exclusion Laws*, 1943, p. 8580)[14]

Representative John W. Vorys described the Chinese as having "a democratic spirit which is simply magnificent" (*Repeal of the Chinese Exclusion Laws*, 1943, p. 8628). Representative Thomas F. Ford highlighted the belief in liberty as a commonality between the Chinese and Americans. He explained, "They have demonstrated that as a nation they possess qualities that we as a nation prize most—a love of liberty—a love so intense that they are willing to sacrifice blood and treasure immeasurably to sustain that principle" (*Repeal of the Chinese Exclusion Laws*, 1943, p. 8628). These types of statements from members of the public and members of Congress alike reassured Congress that repealing the Chinese Exclusion Act and allowing Chinese citizens to naturalize and become U.S. citizens would not threaten American democracy.

Supporters of the repeal of the Chinese Exclusion Act argued that Chinese immigrants were individuals who were experienced with democracy and supported democratic values, norms, and practices. Chinese immigrants were not to be feared as a group that would threaten American political life, because they had already adopted the desired values, norms, and practices. This argument was important because Chinese immigrants had historically been depicted as incapable of being responsible democrats. These arguments along with the foreign affairs concerns convinced Congress to repeal the Chinese Exclusion Act in 1943 (Banks, 2016).

Individualism and Self-Sufficiency

Another value that congressional and administrative agency records indicate was important for American citizenship is individualism, which was deeply connected to the self-sufficiency norm. For both Native Americans and Chinese immigrants the issues of individualism and self-sufficiency were raised.

A key goal of federal Indian policy in the late 19th and early 20th centuries was to make Native Americans "independent, self-sufficient citizens" (McDonnell, 1982, p. 399). Policy makers and members of Congress believed that this could only happen if Native Americans severed their ties to their tribal communities and stopped living communally. Administrative officials, in particular, believed that communal living undermined individual self-sufficiency. Self-sufficiency was not evaluated abstractly. Native Americans had been self-sufficient before their internal displacement in the mid-1800s, and many remained so afterward.[15] Yet the federal government viewed the means by which Native Americans were able to be self-sufficient as tribal communities as problematic. Government officials referred to their beliefs and practices as uncivilized and in need of reform. Thus self-sufficiency in and of itself was not the problem; rather, Native Americans had to become self-sufficient in White American society based on White American cultural norms. For Native American access to citizenship, individualism and self-sufficiency were inextricably linked.

Between the 1860s and 1924 Native American access to U.S. citizenship required demonstrating self-sufficiency. This requirement was present in treaties between the United States and Native American nations and in the 1887 Dawes Act and its amendments. For example, several treaties stated that before individuals could become U.S. citizens they had to demonstrate that they were "sufficiently intelligent and prudent to control their affairs and interests."[16] Other treaties required an applicant to appear in court and satisfy the court that the individual had "adopted the habits of civilized life" and "maintained himself and his family by his own industry."[17] The 1887 Dawes Act provided for tribal land to be divided into allotments granted to individual Native Americans. With an allotment came U.S. citizenship. By accepting an individual allotment within a reservation an individual formally ended his or her tribal relationship. Building on the treaty-based approach to U.S. citizenship, the Dawes Act extended U.S. citizenship to Native Americans born within the territorial limits of the United States who accepted an allotment. The U.S. government held the land allotted to individual Native Americans in trust for 25 years (Dawes Act). During the trust period the allottees were unable to sell or lease their land without the permission of the federal government (McDonnell, 1982). At the end of the 25-year trust period the individual would obtain a fee patent for the allotment free of any restrictions (Dawes Act).

The Dawes Act was amended in 1906 by the Burke Act in response to a Supreme Court decision holding that allottees became U.S. citizens at the time they received their allotment, not when they received their patent in fee (*Matter of Heff*, 1905). Members of Congress amended the Dawes Act because they did not want Native Americans to obtain U.S. citizenship until the trust period ended and it was evident that the allottees were self-sufficient. However, it was acknowledged that some allottees might become self-sufficient before the end of the trust period and allowances should be made for them to receive fee patents and citizenship in a timely fashion. Thus the Burke Act allowed the Secretary of the Interior to issue a patent in fee before the trust period concluded if the secretary was "satisfied that any Indian allottee [was] competent and capable of managing his or her affairs" (An Act to amend section six of an Act approved February eighth, eighteen hundred and eighty-seven, entitled "An Act to provide for the allotment of lands in severalty to Indians on the various reservations, and to extend the protection of the laws of the United States and the Territories over the Indians, and for other purposes," 34 Statutes at Large 182, 183 [1906]). These provisions in the Burke Act facilitated accomplishing a significant federal Indian policy goal—making Native Americans "independent, self-sufficient citizens" (McDonnell, 1982, p. 399).

Pursuant to both treaty provisions and federal statutory law, Native American access to U.S. citizenship depended on demonstrating self-sufficiency. Ideas about self-sufficiency and individualism were also present in arguments supporting Chinese immigrants' access to citizenship in 1943. Witnesses and members of Congress highlighted Chinese immigrants' ability to provide for themselves without government assistance.[18]

The idea that Chinese immigrants were self-sufficient not only fed into conceptions of the ideal American but also suggested that Chinese immigrants would not be a drain on American resources. The idea of self-sufficiency is related to the idea of individualism. This belief was also mentioned as one held by Chinese immigrants. Hummel concurred that Chinese immigrants were "rugged individualists" (*Hearing on H.R. 1882 and H.R. 2309 Before H. Comm. on Immigration and Naturalization*, 1943, p. 26). Representative Frances P. Bolton, Ohio, recalled earlier testimony "that the Chinese are the most individualistic race of the world" (p. 61). This characteristic was deemed beneficial for democratic governance (p. 61).[19]

Self-sufficiency has remained an important aspect of American culture for citizenship purposes. In order to obtain lawful permanent residence status, which is a prerequisite for naturalizing in the United States, an individual must demonstrate that he or she is not likely to become a public charge.[20] Current public discourse regarding the citizenship future of unauthorized migrants often raises the concern that unauthorized migrants are not self-sufficient. A frequent debate within American society has been whether or not unauthorized migrants are a net gain or net drain on society based on taxes paid and public resources utilized. For example,

> the Internal Revenue Service estimates that six million unauthorized migrants file individual tax returns each year. "Other researchers estimate that between 50 percent and 75 percent of unauthorized [migrants] pay federal, state, and local taxes." Unauthorized migrants also pay sales taxes. For example the Iowa Legislative Services Agency estimates that approximately 70,000 unauthorized migrants in the state paid between $45.5 million and $70.9 million in state income and sales taxes in 2004. The state of Colorado estimated that state and local taxes from unauthorized migrants were between $159 and $194 million annually.
>
> Despite these financial contributions, a number of studies conclude that the tax revenue generated by unauthorized migrants does not offset the total cost of services provided to them. Other studies conclude that unauthorized migrants pay more in taxes than they use in services. (Banks, 2013b, pp. 1448–1449; note citations removed)

These concerns about unauthorized migrants' economic contributions and self-sufficiency play a prominent role in public discourse about a pathway to citizenship for unauthorized migrants.

Christianity

While the U.S. Constitution mandates a separation of church and state, Christianity played an important role in the founding of the United States. Christianity was never a formal naturalization requirement, but a lack of Christian beliefs was used to justify prohibiting certain immigrants from being eligible to naturalize. Additionally arguments about the adoption of Christian beliefs and morals have been used to justify access to citizenship.

In 1870 one of the most strident justifications for prohibiting Chinese immigrants from naturalizing was that they were not Christians. Senators described this immigrant population as pagans whose lack of Christian beliefs posed a threat to the United States. For example, Senator George H. Williams explained that the Chinese immigrant's "traditions and teachings handed down by ancestors for thousands of years have made him an imperialist and a pagan" (Congressional Globe, 1870, p. 5155). He went on to note that it would be dangerous to put "political power and control . . . into the hands of eighty thousand Chinamen; men who know nothing of our Constitution, laws, customs, language, or religion, and whose idolatrous temples are crowding aside the churches of the Christian faith" (p. 5158). Senator William M. Stewart doubted Chinese immigrants' ability to engage in responsible democratic engagement. As noted above, he was "opposed to pagan imperialists . . . who do not understand the obligation of a Christian oath being incorporated in the body-politic" (p. 5155).

The first restrictive federal immigration statute was the Page Law, which prohibited the immigration of Chinese prostitutes.[21] The targeting of Chinese prostitutes reflected an attempt to respond to a threat to "Christian, monogamous marriage" (Abrams, 2005, p. 661). By 1943 a very different narrative had developed regarding Chinese immigrants and Christianity. Witnesses before the House Committee on Immigration and Citizenship testified that a significant number of Chinese people were Christian—or at least did not deny the existence of God.

The centrality of Christianity to American culture is also evident in the arguments made by Asian immigrants when the naturalization laws only allowed "white persons" or "persons of African nativity or descent" to naturalize (1790 Naturalization Act; 1870 Naturalization Act). During this time period one way Asian immigrants argued for access to naturalization was by arguing that they were "white persons." Asian immigrants sought to demonstrate their adoption of American culture as evidence of being a "white person" (López, 2006).[22] Takao Ozawa's case is a revealing example of using Christianity to demonstrate adoption of American culture.

Takao Ozawa came to the United States in 1894 as a child. Ozawa applied for naturalization in 1914. His application was denied after the U.S. attorney opposed the application, contending that Ozawa was not a "white person" (*Ozawa v. United States*, 1922, p. 189). Ozawa wrote his own legal brief and argued that he had adopted American values and practices (López, 2006; Ngai, 2004). He wrote, "In name, General Benedict Arnold was an American, but at heart he was a traitor. In name, I am not an American, but at heart I am a true American" (quoted in López, 2006, p. 80). He then proceeded to detail the various ways in which he had adhered to American norms and practices (emphasis added):

(1) I did not report my name, my marriage, or the names of my children to the Japanese Consulate in Honolulu; notwithstanding all Japanese subjects are requested to do so. These matters were reported to the American government. *(2) I do not have any connection with any Japanese churches or schools, or any Japanese organizations here or elsewhere. (3) I am sending my children to an American church and American school in place of a Japanese one.* (4) Most of the time I use the American (English) language at home, so that my children cannot speak the Japanese language. (5) I educated myself in American schools for nearly eleven years by supporting myself. (6) I have lived continuously within the United States for over twenty-eight years. (7) I chose as my wife one educated in American schools . . . instead of one educated in Japan. (8) I have steadily prepared to return the kindness which our Uncle Sam has

extended me . . . so it is my honest hope to do something good to the United States before I bid a farewell to this world. (quoted at p. 80)

The Supreme Court recognized Ozawa's adoption of American culture, noting that it was conceded that he "was well qualified by character and education for citizenship" (*Ozawa v. United States*, 1922, p. 189), but concluded that he was ineligible to naturalize.

Christianity has long been an aspect of American culture deemed relevant for naturalization decisions. Specific religious beliefs have never been a formal naturalization requirement, but perceptions of and assumptions about immigrants' religious beliefs have been an obstacle to obtaining access to naturalization.

Law Abiding

Congressional records also demonstrate that a commitment to the rule of law and being a law-abiding person has been an important aspect of American culture for the purpose of naturalization.[23] Concerns about criminality were rampant in the early 20th century, despite a lack of evidence supporting the idea that increased immigration led to increased crime.[24] These concerns supported the adoption of restrictive immigration policy in 1917, which limited the pool of immigrants that would be eligible for naturalization.[25] In particular the 1917 immigration reforms made a significant number of would-be immigrants inadmissible due to criminal activity. Consequently, the pool of immigrants eligible for naturalization shrank (1917 Immigration Act).[26]

In 1943 witnesses before the House Committee on Immigration and Naturalization and members of Congress described Chinese immigrants as "desirable residents" because of their commitment to the rule of law (*Repeal of the Chinese Exclusion Laws*, 1943, p. 8629 [statement of Rep. Gearhart]). This image of Chinese immigrants did not go unchallenged. On two occasions statements were offered suggesting that Chinese immigrants were not law-abiding residents. In the House of Representatives, Representative Compton I. White expressed his concern about the use of opium among Chinese immigrants. He explained that he knew "the habits of the Chinese. They are inveterate opium smokers most of the day. They brought that hideous opium habit to this country. These Chinese coolies provide a means of spreading it out among our boys and girls" (*Repeal of the Chinese Exclusion Laws*, 1943, p. 8626).[27] Concerns about opium were also mentioned in the Senate. Senator Robert Rice Reynolds submitted a letter from James R. Wilmeth, the national secretary of the National Council, Junior Order of United American Mechanics, as part of his remarks. This letter states that the "use of opium was introduced into this country by the Chinese. They established dens of vice and opium joints" (*Repeal of the Chinese Exclusion Laws*, 1943, p. 100015 [statement of Sen. Reynolds]).[28] Representative White identified other moral failures in Chinese immigrants, such as gambling and their "devious ways" (*Repeal of the Chinese Exclusion Laws*, 1943, p. 8626). He described them as

inveterate gamblers. . . . [T]he fan-tan games were run by the company, and the coolie losses were taken out of their pay with the result that most of the coolies were never free of debt. Talk about peonage and American standards of living! (*Repeal of the Chinese Exclusion Laws*, 1943, p. 8626)

Finally, he asked the House, "How many of you Members know anything of the devious ways of the 'wily Chinese'?" (*Repeal of the Chinese Exclusion Laws*, 1943, p. 8626).

Despite these statements, the overwhelming majority of statements regarding Chinese immigrants' commitment to the rule of law suggested a law-abiding population. However, the fact that criminality was discussed in the context of access to naturalization demonstrates how both those for and those against the repeal of the Chinese Exclusion Acts viewed it as a relevant aspect of American culture.

Citizenship decision makers have also raised concerns about Latino immigrants' respect for the rule of law. In the 20th and 21st centuries the rule of law issue has been raised in the context of unauthorized migrants and "criminal aliens." Unauthorized migrants are individuals who are without lawful immigration status either because they entered the United States without authorization or because they entered with authorization to stay for a specified period of time and they did not leave when required. Consequently, unauthorized migrants have been described as "illegal." These immigrants' failure to abide by U.S. immigration law is used to construct the group as lacking respect for the rule of law and having a willingness to engage in criminal activity.[29]

Latino immigrants are viewed as criminal not only because of immigration status but also because of the ways in which this population has been constructed as violent criminals. For example, in 1996 when Congress was revising the Immigration and Nationality Act, congressional discourse focused on violent criminals who entered the United States without authorization (Banks, 2013c). Latino immigrants were described not only as unauthorized but also as drug dealers who were involved in serious drug-related crime (Banks, 2013c). Members of Congress saw it as their duty to make it easier to deport immigrants with criminal records and to make the process quicker (Banks, 2013c). These perceptions cause the categories "Latino" and "unauthorized migrant" to be conflated. Latinos (citizens and immigrants) are constructed as individuals who are not committed to the rule of law (Banks, 2012). This construction creates significant hurdles for a pathway to citizenship for unauthorized migrants to become a reality.

A key aspect of American culture for the purpose of U.S. citizenship is a commitment to the rule of law. This view encompasses the idea that the U.S. government is accountable under the law and that all persons are as well. As such, engaging in unlawful activity is viewed as violating a key American value, norm, and practice.

English Language Skills

Language has an interesting history as a key aspect of American culture for the purposes of U.S. citizenship. Language did not become an explicit naturalization requirement until 1906. That year Congress decided that "no alien shall hereinafter be naturalized or admitted as a citizen of the United States who can not speak the English language" (1906 Naturalization Act, p. 599, sec. 8). The adoption of the English language requirement corresponded with significant hostility toward the growing number of Southern and Eastern European immigrants arriving in the United States. A frequent concern raised about this immigrant population was their inability or failure to assimilate. Yet prior to 1906 English language skills had been used to evaluate Native American candidates for U.S. citizenship and to determine whether returning Chinese Americans were in fact U.S. citizens (Lee, 2003). Both of these examples demonstrate that English language skills were viewed as an important aspect of American culture prior to 1906.

Treaty provisions governing Native American naturalization required either that individuals demonstrate that they "could read and speak . . . the English language" or that they had "adopted the habits of civilized life."[30] The Dawes Act of 1887 similarly extended U.S. citizenship to Native Americans who had "adopted the habits of civilized life." Courts and agency officials considered English language skills as evidence of adoption of "the habits of civilized life."

As early as 1909 Commissioner of Indian Affairs Robert Valentine created competency commissions to determine which Native American noncitizens were eligible for fee patents and U.S. citizenship pursuant to the 1906 Burke Act (McDonnell, 1982). The first commission worked on the Omaha Reservation in Nebraska.[31] The commissioners would personally meet with the residents of the reservation and determine their competency (p. 400).[32] As early as 1909 the Department of the Interior issued a circular detailing a set of questions to assist agents and superintendents in their decision-making process (Land Cir. #261 [Dep't of Interior, 1909]). By 1916 the department had developed a "Patent in Fee Report" for competency boards to utilize. The substance of this report and that of the 1909 circular are quite similar, but the circular requests significantly more information. Both the circular and the report required general information about the allottee and the land: for example, the name of the allottee, the agency, the allotment number, a description of the land, the value of the land, the act pursuant to which the allotment was made, the age of the applicant, the degree of Native American blood, and marital status. The degree of Native American blood an applicant had was used as a proxy for competence.

Competency commissions working throughout the Midwest consistently commented on the English language skills of Native Americans for whom fee patents were recommended. While English language skills were not listed in either the 1909 circular or the "Patent in Fee Report," competency commissions ascertained the English language skills of the applicants.[33] For example, the commission with the Yankton Sioux described the population as "unusually bright Indians, nearly all of them understand English and a large majority of them speak the English language very well" (McLaughlin, McPherson, & Leech, 1916). The commission working with the residents of the Ponca Reservation in Nebraska similarly noted that all of the applicants understood English and most were fluent speakers (McLaughlin et al., 1916).

The ability to speak English was also used to evaluate whether returning Chinese Americans were in fact U.S. citizens during the Chinese exclusion era (Lee, 2003). In 1898 the U.S. Supreme Court held that the children of Chinese immigrants born in the United States were U.S. citizens pursuant to the Fourteenth Amendment (*United States v. Wong Kim Ark*, 1898). When such individuals left the United States and returned they would be subject to the Chinese exclusion laws if not for their U.S. citizenship.[34] Proving U.S. citizenship based on birth in the United States was challenging because few had birth certificates for two reasons. First, "Chinese women often delivered their children at home" (Lee, 2003, p. 106). Second, a large percentage of the Chinese American population was born in

San Francisco, and the 1906 earthquake and fire destroyed all birth records (Lee, 2003). Consequently, immigration officials had to rely on applicant and witness testimony to determine birthplace (Lee, 2003). In addition to testimony, immigration applicants were "judged according to how well they could speak English, how much they conformed to American customs and dress, and how well they could identify local landmarks and recite basic facts about U.S. history" (p. 107).

English language skills were viewed as a reliable proxy for birth in the United States. For example, historian Erika Lee (2003) has explained that "it was not uncommon for immigration officials to note favorably that an applicant claiming citizenship dressed in American-style clothing and could speak English fluently" (p. 107). For example, immigrant inspector Alfred W. Parker evaluated Moy Good in 1905. Parker concluded that Moy was "an extraordinarily bright, intelligent Chinaman, dresses in American clothes, and speaks good English. By appearances and conduct, I should say that his claim to American birth is quite reasonable" (p. 107). Applicants who were unable to successfully complete a test in spoken English were denied entry based on being noncitizens subject to the Chinese exclusion laws. Lee Toy Mock, a U.S. citizen, was declared a noncitizen by immigration inspector P. J. Farrelly because Mock was an "alien [who] has not the slightest knowledge of the English language" (p. 107). Heavy reliance on English language skills was not an accurate proxy for birth within the United States. As Lee explained,

> Well into the mid-twentieth century, most Chinese immigrants and their American-born children still resided in segregated urban enclaves and had little contact with non-Chinese. Although many American-born children did attend public school and learned English, not all of them learned to speak the language fluently. (p. 108)

English language skills continue to be an important aspect of American culture for citizenship purposes. Current federal law requires successful naturalization applicants to "read, write, and speak English" (Immigration and Nationality Act § 316; 8 Code of Federal Register § 312). In the same way that Chinese immigrants and Native Americans were viewed as problematic because of limited English language skills, Latino immigrants have been viewed similarly. Anthropologist Leo Chavez (2008) has argued that a Latino Threat Narrative exists in the United States. This narrative contends that "Latinos are not like previous immigrant groups, who ultimately became part of the nation" (p. 2). Rather, Latino immigrants "are unwilling or incapable of integrating, of becoming part of the national community" (p. 2). One aspect of the Latino Threat Narrative is that Latinos are unable or unwilling to learn English. Political scientist Samuel P. Huntington (2004) has raised similar concerns about Mexican immigrants. While acknowledging that second- and third-generation Mexican Americans' English fluency matches that of past immigrant groups, he expressed uneasiness at the high levels of bilingualism within these generations.

Concerns about Latino immigrants' language skills have translated into judgments about this immigrant groups' respectability and worthiness for lawful immigration status and U.S. citizenship (Keyes, 2013, 2014). Opponents of a pathway to citizenship for unauthorized migrants often argue that the failure to speak English demonstrates a failure to adopt American values, norms, and practices. This leads these individuals to conclude that unauthorized migrants do not deserve legal status in the United States and a pathway to citizenship (Chavez, 2008; Federation for American Immigration Reform, 2002; Huntington, 2004; Johnson, 1997; Nicholls, 2013). Advocates for a pathway to citizenship are acutely aware of this narrative and corresponding argument. To counter it, advocates have focused on DREAMers and emphasized their English fluency and lack of fluency in any other language (Nicholls, 2013). Education scholar William Pérez (2009) captured this image of DREAMers when he described them as young people who

> having been educated in our schools, . . . speak English (often with more ease than they do Spanish), envision their futures here, and have internalized U.S. values and expectations of merit; yet they have no available paths for formal legal integration. (p. xxiv)

English language skills have been an important proxy for assimilation in the United States. Throughout U.S. history English language skills have been used to determine who ought to become a U.S. citizen and as evidence of who actually is a U.S. citizen. Language continues to play an important role in public opinion regarding immigrants' respectability—willingness to adopt mainstream American values, norms, and practices—and worthiness of lawful immigration status and access to U.S. citizenship.

Citizenship decision makers have identified a number of values, norms, and practices that are important aspects of American culture. In determining whether specific noncitizen groups should have access to U.S. citizenship via naturalization, five factors have been critical. Those five substantive aspects of American culture are a commitment to democracy, individualism and self-sufficiency, Christianity, a commitment to the rule of law, and English language skills. These aspects of American culture were relevant in the 19th century, and they remain relevant today.

III. Teaching

Students studying immigration and citizenship should be made aware of the cultural norms embedded within the legal rules governing citizenship. As a law professor I seek to do this by not simply teaching the legal rules regarding citizenship acquisition but also teaching the history of naturalization laws and the sociopolitical context in which those rules were adopted and changed. This approach to citizenship allows students to see the role that cultural norms play in the creation, interpretation, and enforcement of legal rules. It also enables students to see continuity in the way that culture is used to evaluate immigrant groups. For example, when reading congressional floor debates and congressional hearing transcripts about the 1870 Naturalization Act, students are confronted with explicit anti-Chinese bias within Congress. The anti-Chinese bias expressed by members of Congress focused on Chinese immigrants' religion, language skills, work ethic, and morality. I have students compare the arguments against Chinese immigrant access to naturalization in the 1800s with those against a pathway to citizenship for unauthorized migrants today. Students are able to see that the arguments focus on the same aspects of culture—language, criminality, and work ethic. Teachers of high school and college students could utilize similar teaching techniques by having students read and evaluate historical Supreme Court opinions and congressional records and compare them with current newspapers, blog posts, and congressional records.

Immigration and citizenship is a "hot" political issue today. As a result students often come to class with distinct opinions and perspectives on immigration and citizenship policy issues. A particular challenge is to help students see the legitimacy in opposing policy choices. Strategies I use to address this challenge include the following three examples. First, I assign readings that provide students with information about the technical process of migrating to the United States and becoming a citizen. Students are often shocked at how complicated the process is and the various factors involved in creating immigration rules. Second, I often do role-playing exercises in class in which students are required to take positions and make arguments that do not align with their personal beliefs. Finally, I give students a deportation survey. This survey includes descriptions of eight individuals living in the United States with different immigration statuses, length of residence in the United States, family ties in the United States, and criminal histories. The students are required to state whether they would or would not deport each individual. After completing the survey, the students discuss their answers in small groups and see whether they can develop consensus within the group about whom to deport. I then conduct a whole-class discussion in which the students are asked to identify which factors were decisive for them and why. This gives rise to wonderfully rich discussions about values and norms and how they should shape immigration policy.

This type of exercise is also useful when teaching about the relationship between immigration and national security. After September 11, 2001, the United States adopted additional registration requirements for nonimmigrants from specific countries, most of which are in the Middle East. In November 2015 the House of Representatives passed an act to require Syrian refugee applicants to undergo additional security screening by the Federal Bureau of Investigation. While these are current examples of the relationship between immigration and national security, this is not a new concern. Using Supreme Court cases addressing Cold War security threats and current policy and legislation, I ask students to identify the various state interests involved in addressing national security concerns in immigration. State interests that come up are public safety, maintaining the state's commitment to being a country of immigrants, and providing refuge to persecuted individuals. I also have students brainstorm important factors about the perceived threat. Examples include the type of threat an immigrant population is viewed as presenting, the seriousness of the threat, and the state's confidence in its ability to accurately identify the threat. This leads to a discussion about the level of proof and type of evidence needed to legitimately limit immigrants' access to the United States, to impose new requirements for admission, and to impose additional monitoring requirements on immigrants present in the United States. Through these types of discussions students develop the analytical skills needed to think critically about the values and norms at stake when confronted with the issue of immigration and national security.

Conclusion

Citizenship is a valuable resource in the United States because it provides a basis for specific rights and benefits. Access to citizenship via naturalization was subject to racial prerequisites between 1790 and 1952. Throughout this time period the racial requirements were expanded to include more and more racial groups. Members of Congress, judges, and administrative officials identified key aspects of American culture for citizenship purposes. Through an examination of congressional, administrative, and judicial records this chapter has identified five substantive aspects of American culture that have been important for the allocation of U.S. citizenship. Government actors have viewed a commitment to democracy, individualism and self-sufficiency, Christianity, a commitment to the rule of law, and English language skills as cultural prerequisites for American citizenship via naturalization. Noncitizens ineligible for naturalization have constructed narratives of their lives that highlight a commitment to these specific values, norms, and practices. The success of these narratives has varied over time, but citizenship and legal immigration reform advocates continue to use such narratives to change the social meaning of the immigrant groups seeking reform.

Notes

1. See, e.g., FitzGerald & Cook-Martín, 2014; Freeman, 1995; Horton, 2005; Joppke, 2005; Lee, 2003; López, 2006; Mills, 1997; Ngai, 2004; Ringer, 1983; Román, 2010; Salyer, 1995; Stokes & Meléndez, 2003.

2. Whether advocates utilize these narratives based on a normative commitment to the values, norms, and practices advanced or, rather, based on a strategic rhetorical move is not always clear. For the purposes of this chapter the motive behind the use of respectability narratives does not matter. What matters is that such narratives are deployed and that they draw on a very specific set of values, norms, and practices.

3. See also Jacobson, 1998, p. 4: "[r]aces are invented categories—designations coined for the sake of grouping and separating people along lines of presumed difference"; Omi & Winant, 1994, p. 55: "[t]here is no biological basis for distinguishing among human groups along the lines of race."

4. See, e.g., Jacobson, 1998, p. 2: "Entire races have disappeared from view, from public discussion, and from modern memory, though their flesh-and-blood members still walk the earth."

5. Germany now provides for citizenship at birth based on the *jus soli* principle when certain conditions are satisfied (Kirkland, 2006).

6. "This act creates a pathway to lawful immigration status for individuals who entered the United States under the age of 16, have been physically present for at least five years, earned a high school diploma or a GED, have good moral character, and are not inadmissible or deportable based on criminal activity or national security concerns. The DREAM Act would grant these individuals . . . [lawful immigration] status . . . for 10 years. If within that 10-year period the individual completed two years of college or military service and maintained good moral character, then he or she" would be eligible to naturalize and become a citizen (Banks, 2013a, p. 78).

7. See, e.g., "Jeff Hawkins shares," 2011; "Julia Duperrault shares," 2011; "Mayor Paul Bridges shares," 2011; Newmark, 2011.

8. Pursuant to the 1790 naturalization law, noncitizens were eligible to naturalize if they had been in the United States for two years (1790 Naturalization Act, § 1; see Kettner, 1978, pp. 241–242). In 1795 the residence requirement was extended to five years (1795 Naturalization Act, § 1).

9. 1795 Naturalization Act, § 1; 1798 Naturalization Act, § 1.

10. 1802 Naturalization Act, § 1; Kettner, 1978, p. 245.

11. Prohibiting enslaved persons from becoming citizens was necessary for the continuation of slavery in the United States. If enslaved persons became citizens and utilized the right to vote, they could repeal the legal foundation of slavery in the South.

12. One of the three letters read was from a Republican Party official, and another was from a Republican senator in Florida. In both instances the individuals explained the harm done by not allowing Africans and West Indians to naturalize.

13. See also Rev. John J. O'Farrell, associate editor of *Jesuit Mission*, New York, describing Chinese citizens as "being democratic in spirit" (*Hearing on H.R. 1882 and H.R. 2309 Before H. Comm. on Immigration and Naturalization*, 1943, p. 31).

14. Rep. McCormack also described China's leaders, Madam and Generalissimo Chiang Kai-shek, as "great, democratic, Christian leaders of a new and awakened China" (*Repeal of the Chinese Exclusion Laws*, 1943, p. 8580).

15. See, e.g., the Indian Removal Act of 1830. The Cherokee Nation refers to the forced migration of Native Americans pursuant to the Indian Removal Act as the Trail of Tears because of the devastating toll it took. Forced migrants faced hunger, disease, and exhaustion during their forced march west of the Mississippi. The government did not provide adequate supplies as promised, and death was common. Approximately 4,000 of the 15,000 Cherokee removed died during the Trail of Tears. See PBS, 1999.

16. See, e.g., Treaty with the Potawatomi, 1861 (1904, p. 825); Treaty with the Kickapoo, 1862 (1904, p. 836); Treaty with the Delawares, 1866 (1904, p. 940).

17. Treaty with the Kickapoo, 1862 (1904, p. 836); An Act making Appropriations for the current and contingent Expenses of the Indian Department, and for filling Treaty Stipulations with various Indian Tribes for the Year ending thirtieth June, eighteen hundred and sixty-six, and for other Purposes, 13 Statutes at Large 541, 562 (1865) (sec. 4); Treaty with the Delawares, 1866 (1904, p. 940).

18. See, e.g., *Hearing on H.R. 1882 and H.R. 2309 Before H. Comm. on Immigration and Naturalization*, 1943, pp. 69–70 (statement of Rep. Carl T. Curtis, Nebraska). During the hearings before the House Committee on Immigration and Naturalization Miss Pearl Buck explained that Chinese immigrants did not "go on relief" (pp. 69–70). See also *Repeal of the Chinese Exclusion Laws*, 1943, p. 8583 (statement of Rep. Dondero).

19. Representative Bolton also noted "that they are best fitted to what we interpret as democracy" (*Hearing on H.R. 1882 and H.R. 2309 Before H. Comm. on Immigration and Naturalization*, 1943, p. 61).

20. See Immigration and Nationality Act, § 212(a)(4): "Any alien who . . . is likely at any time to become a public charge is inadmissible." A public charge is a person who is unable to take care of him- or herself without government assistance. See Aleinikoff, Martin, & Motomura, 2012.

21. Page Law, 1875. See Abrams, 2005, for a detailed discussion regarding the assumptions made about Chinese immigrant women and the application of inadmissibility grounds based on polygamy and prostitution.

22. While none of the plaintiffs were successful, judges commented on the excellent character of the plaintiffs but said that based on either scientific evidence or common conceptions of race, Asians simply were not White persons and were thus ineligible to naturalize.

23. Concerns about adherence to the rule of law are somewhat captured by the naturalization requirement that an individual have "good moral character." This has been a naturalization requirement since 1790, when the first naturalization law was enacted. See the 1790 Naturalization Act, § 1. Historically this requirement did not automatically bar individuals with criminal convictions from becoming citizens. Courts and the administrative agency responsible for naturalization used a "flexible standard that recognized reform" (Lapp, 2012, p. 1574). If applicants with a criminal past could show reformation, courts were likely to conclude that they satisfied the good moral character requirement. The focus was

on the applicant's present moral character. As Lapp (2012) notes, a "backward-focused . . . conception of good moral character would result in the archaic and uncompromising view that people are beyond redemption or change" (p. 1589). During this time period citizenship decision makers often concluded that racially ineligible applicants were not committed to the rule of law. Citizenship decision makers were not concerned about applicants' past conduct but, rather, their present and future conduct. An outright ban on their eligibility for naturalization eliminated the need to establish specific violations of law.

24. The Dillingham Commission was a government commission organized to "make full inquiry, examination, and investigation, by subcommittee or otherwise, into the subject of immigration" (U.S. Immigration Comm'n, Immigration and Crime, 1910, volume 1, p. ii). The commission was deemed necessary after Congress was unable to adopt a comprehensive legislative scheme to address immigration in 1907. The commission became known for legitimating restrictionist policies that would later be enacted in the 1917 Immigration Act. In 1910 the commission concluded: "No satisfactory evidence has yet been produced to show that immigration has resulted in an increase in crime disproportionate to the increase in adult population. Such comparable statistics of crime and population as it has been possible to obtain indicate that immigrants are less prone to commit crime than are native Americans" (U.S. Immigration Comm'n, Immigration and Crime, 1910, volume 36, p. 1).

25. The Dillingham Commission reported that, when considering future immigration legislation, "care should be taken that immigration be such both in quality and quantity as not to make too difficult the process of assimilation" (U.S. Immigration Comm'n, Immigration and Crime, 1910, volume 1, p. 45). Many of the recommendations offered by the commission were aimed at limiting immigration and increasing governmental authority to remove immigrants.

26. 1917 Naturalization Act, § 3, prohibiting the admission of "persons who have been convicted of or admit having committed a felony or other crime or misdemeanor involving moral turpitude."

27. Representative Magnuson challenged this historical narrative by asking whether Representative White was "familiar with what country brought the opium habit to China." Representative White responded that he did "know something about that, too," but said no more (*Repeal of the Chinese Exclusion Laws*, 1943, p. 8626).

28. Mr. Wilmeth also raised concerns about Chinese organized crime and the wars that took place between the criminal organizations.

29. See, e.g., Banks, 2013b, pp. 1444–1445; Republicans on Immigration, 2014.

30. See, e.g., Treaty with the Kickapoo, 1862 (1904, p. 836); An Act making Appropriations for the current and contingent Expenses of the Indian Department, and for filling Treaty Stipulations with various Indian Tribes for the Year ending thirtieth June, eighteen hundred and sixty-six, and for other Purposes, 13 Statutes at Large 541, 562 (1865) (sec. 4); Treaty with the Delawares, 1866 (1904, p. 940).

31. The location of these commissions is important for the analysis in this chapter because "every Indian in Indian Territory" was declared a U.S. citizen by the 1901 Citizenship Act. An Act to amend section six, chapter one hundred and nineteen, United States Statutes at Large numbered twenty-four, 31 Statutes at Large 1447 (1901). Consequently, the issuance of a fee patent only offered citizenship to Native Americans residing outside of Indian Territory.

32. Individuals who were interested in obtaining a fee patent were to submit an application to the reservation superintendent, who would forward the application to the Indian Office along with his report regarding the applicant's competency. McDonnell, 1982, pp. 399–400. While the Burke Act did not explicitly require allottees to consent to the acceptance of a fee patent, it was implied (p. 400). Yet the competency commissions regularly recommended fee patents for allottees who did not want them, and they were often issued. See, e.g., *Indians of the United States: Investigation of the Field Service*, 1920 (congressional testimony of John R. Wise, Special Supervisor, Indian Service); LaFave, 1984.

33. The 1909 circular did ask whether the application was "in the hand-writing of the applicant," which could be viewed as an implicit inquiry into English language skills.

34. The first Chinese Exclusion Act was enacted in 1882 (Chinese Exclusion Act of 1882). By 1888 Congress prohibited all Chinese laborers from entering the United States, even if they were returning with a government-issued certificate (Chinese Exclusion Act of 1888).

References

Abrams, K. (2005). Polygamy, prostitution, and the federalization of immigration law. *Columbia Law Review, 105*(3), 641–716.

Aleinikoff, T., Martin, D. A., & Motomura, H. (2003). *Immigration and citizenship: Process and policy* (5th ed.). St. Paul, MN: Thomson/West.

An Act making Appropriations for the current and contingent Expenses of the Indian Department, and for filling Treaty Stipulations with various Indian Tribes for the Year ending thirtieth June, eighteen hundred and sixty-six, and for other Purposes, 13 Statutes at Large 541 (1865).

An Act to amend section six, chapter one hundred and nineteen, United States Statutes at Large numbered twenty-four, 31 Statutes at Large 1447 (1901).

Banks, A. M. (2012). The curious relationship between "self-deportation" policies and naturalization rates. *Lewis and Clark Law Review, 16*(4), 1149–1213.

Banks, A. M. (2013a). Closing the schoolhouse doors: State efforts to limit K–12 education for unauthorized migrant school children. In J. K. Donor & A. D. Dixon (Eds.), *The resegregation of schools: Race and education in the twenty-first century* (pp. 63–81). New York: Routledge.

Banks, A. M. (2013b). Members only: Undocumented students and in-state tuition. *Brigham Young University Law Review, 6*, 1425–1455.

Banks, A. M. (2013c). The normative and historical cases for proportional deportation. *Emory Law Journal, 62*(5), 1243–1307.

Banks, A. M. (2016). *Immigrants—They're just like us! Respectability and the quest for citizenship.* Unpublished paper, William & Mary Law School, Williamsburg, VA.

Bonilla-Silva, E. (1999). The essential social fact of race. *American Sociological Review, 64*(6), 899–906.

Bosniak, L. (2000). Citizenship denationalized. *Indiana Journal of Global Legal Studies*, 7, 447-509.

Bosniak, L. (2006). The citizen and the alien: Dilemmas of contemporary membership. Princeton, NJ: Princeton University Press.

Chavez, L. (2008). *The Latino threat: Constructing immigrants, citizens, and the nation.* Stanford, CA: Stanford University Press.

Chinese Exclusion Act of 1882, An Act to execute certain treaty stipulations relating to Chinese, ch. 126, 22 Statutes at Large 58 (1882) (amended 1884).

Chinese Exclusion Act of 1888, A Supplement to an Act entitled "An Act to execute certain treaty stipulations relating to Chinese," approved the sixth day of May eighteen hundred and eighty-two, ch. 1064, 25 Statutes at Large 504 (1888).

Congressional Globe, 41st Cong., 2d Sess. (1870).

Dawes Act, The Act of Feb. 8, 1887, 24 Statutes at Large 388 (1887).

Dep't of Interior, Land Cir. #261 (January 9, 1909), National Archives Records Administration, M21, Roll 76.

Federation for American Immigration Reform. (2002, October). *Assimilation.* Retrieved from http://www.fairus.org/issue/Assimilation

FitzGerald, D., & Cook-Martín, D. (2014). *Culling the masses: The democratic origins of racist immigration policy in the Americas.* Cambridge, MA: Harvard University Press.

Freeman, G. (1995). Modes of immigration politics in liberal democratic states. *International Migration Review, 29*(4), 881–913.

Hearing on H.R. 1882 and H.R. 2309 Before H. Comm. on Immigration and Naturalization, 78th Cong. (1943).

Horton, C. (2005). *Race and the making of American liberalism.* Oxford, UK: Oxford University Press.

Higginbotham, E. B. (1994). *Righteous discontent: The women's movement in the black Baptist church, 1880–1920.* Cambridge, MA: Harvard University Press.

Huntington, S. P. (2004). *Who are we? The challenges to America's national identity.* New York: Simon & Schuster.

Immigration Act of 1917, An Act to regulate the immigration of aliens to, and the residence of aliens in, the United States, 39 Statutes at Large 874 (1917).

Immigration and Nationality Act, An Act to revise the laws relating to immigration, naturalization, and nationality; and for other purposes, 66 Statutes at Large 163 (1952).

Indian Removal Act of 1830, An Act to provide for an exchange of lands with the Indians residing in any of the States or territories, and for their removal west of the river Mississippi, 4 Statutes at Large 411 (1830).

Indians of the United States: Investigation of the Field Service: Hearings Before H. Subcomm. of the Comm. on Indian Affairs, 66th Congress, Vol. 3 (1920) (congressional testimony of John R. Wise, Special Supervisor, Indian Service).

Jacobson, M. (1998). *Whiteness of a different color: European immigrants and the alchemy of race.* Cambridge, MA: Harvard University Press.

Jeff Hawkins shares his definition of "American." (2011, November 1). Retrieved from https://perma.cc/GDJ4-RBDF

Johnson, K. R. (1997). "Aliens" and the U.S. immigration laws: The social and legal construction of nonpersons. *University of Miami Inter-American Law Review, 28*(2), 263–292.

Joppke, C. (2005). *Selecting by origin: Ethnic migration in the liberal state.* Cambridge, MA: Harvard University Press.

Julia Duperrault shares her definition of "American." (2011, October 31). Retrieved from https://www.youtube.com/watch?v=CVFS8cOsUn0

Kettner, J. (1978). *The development of American citizenship, 1608–1870.* Chapel Hill, NC: University of North Carolina Press.

Keyes, E. (2013). Defining American: The DREAM Act, immigration reform and citizenship. *Nevada Law Journal, 14*(1), 101–155.

Keyes, E. (2014). Race and immigration, then and now: How the shift to "worthiness" undermines the 1965 Immigration Law's civil rights goals. *Howard Law Journal, 57,* 899–1071.

Kirkland, B. (2006). Limiting the application of jus soli: The resulting status of undocumented children in the United States. *Buffalo Human Rights Law Review, 12,* 197–221.

LaFave, L. L. (1984). South Dakota's forced fee Indian land claims: Will landowners be liable for government's wrongdoing? *South Dakota Law Review, 30*(1), 59–102.

Lapp, K. (2012). Reforming the good moral character requirement for U.S. citizenship. *Indiana Law Journal, 87*(4), 1571–1637.

Lee, E. (2003). *At America's gates: Chinese immigration during the exclusion era, 1882–1943.* Chapel Hill, NC: University of North Carolina Press

López, I. (2006). *White by law: The legal construction of race.* New York: New York University Press.

Mack, K. (2005). Rethinking civil rights lawyering and politics in the era before *Brown. Yale Law Journal, 115*(2), 256–354.

Matter of Heff, 197 U.S. 488, 505 (1905).

Mayor Paul Bridges shares his definition of "American." (2011, October 31). Retrieved from https://www.youtube.com/watch?v=JWuj0stI-w8

McDonnell, J. (1982). Land policy on the Omaha Reservation: Competency commissions and forced fee patents. *Nebraska History, 63*, 399–412.

McLaughlin, J., McPherson, C. M., & Leech, A. W. (1916, March 8). Letter to the Secretary of the Interior. McLaughlin Papers, Roll 6. Assumption Abbey Archives, Richardton, N.D.

Mills, C. (1997). *The racial contract.* Ithaca, NY: Cornell University Press.

Motomura, H. (2006). *Americans in waiting: The lost story of immigration and citizenship in the United States.* Oxford: Oxford University Press.

Myrdal, G. (1962). *An American dilemma: The Negro problem and modern democracy* (20th anniversary ed.). New York: Harper & Row.

Naturalization Act of 1790, An Act to establish a uniform rules of Naturalization, 1 Statutes at Large 103 (1790).

Naturalization Act of 1795, An Act to establish an uniform rule of Naturalization, 1 Statutes at Large 414 (1795).

Naturalization Act of 1798, An Act supplementary to and to amend the act, intituled [*sic*] An act to establish an uniform rule of naturalization; and to repeal the act heretofore passed on that subject, 1 Statutes at Large 566 (1798).

Naturalization Act of 1802, An Act to establish an uniform rule of Naturalization, and to repeal the acts heretofore passed on that subject, 2 Statutes at Large 153 (1802).

Naturalization Act of 1870, An Act to amend the Naturalization Laws and to punish Crime against the same, and for other purposes, 16 Statutes at Large 254 (1870).

Naturalization Act of 1906, An Act To establish a Bureau of Immigration and Naturalization, and to provide for a uniform rule of naturalization of aliens throughout the United States, 34 Statutes at Large 596 (1906).

Newmark, C. What it means to be American. *The Huffington Post* (2012, July 6). Retrieved from https://perma.cc/A9DY-QZVM

Ngai, M. (2004). *Impossible subjects: Illegal aliens and the making of modern America.* Princeton, NJ: Princeton University Press.

Nicholls, W. (2013). *The DREAMers: How the undocumented youth movement transformed the immigrant rights debate.* Palo Alto, CA: Stanford University Press.

Omi, M., & Winant, H. (1994, 2d ed.). *Racial formation in the United States from the 1960s to the 1990s.* New York: Routledge.

Ozawa v. United States, 260 U.S. 178, 189 (1922).

Page Law, Act of Mar. 3, 1875, 18 Statutes at Large 477 (repealed 1974).

PBS. (1999). *People and events: Indian removal 1814–1858.* Retrieved from http://www.pbs.org/wgbh/aia/part4/4p2959.html

Pérez, W. (2009). *We ARE Americans: Undocumented students pursuing the American dream.* Sterling, VA: Styles.

Repeal of the Chinese Exclusion Laws, 89 Cong. Rec. 8572–8606 (1943).

Republicans on Immigration. (2014). *Here's what Republicans really think about comprehensive immigration reform.* Retrieved from http://www.republicansintheirownwords.com/quotes.html

Ringer, B. (1983). *"We the people" and others: Duality and America's treatment of its racial minorities.* New York: Tavistock Publications.

Román, E. (2010). *Citizenship and its exclusions: A classical, constitutional, and critical race critique.* New York: New York University Press.

Salyer, L. (1995). *Laws harsh as tigers: Chinese immigrants and the shaping of modern immigration law.* Chapel Hill, NC: University of North Carolina Press.

Stokes, C., & Meléndez, T. (2003). *Racial liberalism and the politics of urban America.* East Lansing, MI: Michigan State University Press.

The Burke Act, An Act to amend section six of an Act approved February eighth, eighteen hundred and eighty-seven, entitled "An Act to provide for the allotment of lands in severalty to Indians on the various reservations, and to extend the protection of the laws of the United States and the Territories over the Indians, and for other purposes," 34 Statutes at Large 182, 183 (1906).

Treaty with the Delawares, 1866. (1904). Reprinted in C. J. Kappler (Ed.), *Indian affairs: Laws and treaties* (Vol. 2, pp. 937–942). Washington, DC: Government Printing Office.

Treaty with the Kickapoo, 1862. (1904). Reprinted in C. J. Kappler (Ed.), *Indian affairs: Laws and treaties* (Vol. 2, pp. 835–839). Washington, DC: Government Printing Office.

Treaty with the Potawatomi, 1861. (1904). Reprinted in C. J. Kappler (Ed.), *Indian affairs: Laws and treaties* (Vol. 2, pp. 824–828). Washington, DC: Government Printing Office.

21 Reasons why we should support the Dream Act—LEGAL IMMIGRATION! (2010, July 22). *Illegal in America: A San Francisco Blog on Civil Rights Issues.* Retrieved from https://perma.cc/L8B2-M8VV

United States v. Wong Kim Ark, 169 U.S. 649 (1898).

U.S. Const. amend. XIV.

U.S. Immigration Comm'n, Immigration and Crime, Senate Document No. 61-750 (3d Sess. 1910).

Chapter 5

Multicultural and Citizenship Education in Canada: Slow Peace as an Alternative to Social Cohesion

REVA JOSHEE
University of Toronto

MONICA THOMAS
Edmonton Public Schools

The stories of multicultural and citizenship education have been intertwined since the beginning of Canadian history. Over the course of time, both terms have taken on various meanings. Citizenship education has focused on loyalty to the crown, patriotism to Canada, naturalization, incorporation into Canada society, and active democratic engagement. Multicultural education has addressed immigrant integration, intercultural understanding, development of particular ethnocultural identities, and social justice. Currently, social cohesion presents itself as the policy focus that encompasses both multiculturalism and citizenship at the national level. This has had some significant implications for citizenship and multicultural education across all 13 provinces and territories. Social cohesion, as manifest in Canada, has focused on promoting harmony above all else and thus has minimized attention to social justice and active democratic engagement (Bickmore, 2006; Joshee & Sinfield, 2010). While we do not disagree with the importance of harmony within a society, we believe it does not have to come at the price of silencing dissent or neglecting social injustice. As an alternative to social cohesion we propose "slow peace," an approach based on an engagement with Nixon's (2011) notion of slow violence and a Gandhian ethic of peace.

The History of Multiculturalism and Citizenship in Canada

As in many other nation-states, one of the initial purposes of public education in Canada was to promote citizenship. At the outset, Canada was part of the British Empire, and the focus of citizenship education was promoting loyalty and patriotism to the Empire as well as an appreciation for British traditions. The dominant attitude toward people who were not of British origin was that of Anglo-conformity. This had several implications in regard to citizenship. For Francophones, it was a recanting of the original pact between British and French Canadians, whereby Canada was meant to be a nation based on cultural and linguistic duality. It led French Canadians across the country to develop an attitude of protectionism toward their identity (McLean, 2007). For the First Nations, Inuit, and Metis, it meant a continuation of policies and programs meant to "civilize" all aboriginal peoples. There is a growing recognition in Canada that this approach led to cultural genocide (Truth and Reconciliation Commission of Canada, 2015). For immigrants, the policy focus was assimilation, and both multiculturalism policy and multicultural education originated in the efforts to assimilate immigrants (Joshee, 2004).

Through the 1950s and early 1960s, citizenship education for adults was largely associated with what would now be called equity-focused work in immigrant integration and intergroup relations (Schugurensky, 2006). Notably, the one group whose education fell outside of this general trend was adults of First Nations origin. As Bohaker and Iacovetta (2009) have noted, "There were also critical differences between the immigrant and Aboriginal [citizenship] campaigns, including the virtual absence of any explicit discourse of cultural pluralism or unity-in-diversity in the Aboriginal programs for the period under review. Instead, these programs were characterized by a more marked policy of racial assimilation into white society" (p. 443).

Meanwhile, citizenship education in schools continued to focus on a more limited civics and patriotism curriculum. Tountas (1998) has noted that a textbook called *Canada and the Commonwealth*, published in 1953 and used widely in Ontario, "openly speaks of the White Man's Burden in a positive light. Here the coming of European powers to less developed nations to dominate them was described as a great benefit to the less civilized people of the world." At the same time, there were some initiatives designed to introduce K–12 students to issues of intergroup relations such as the Springfield Plan, which was imported from the United States in the late 1940s (Joshee & Johnson, 2007).

With the work of the Royal Commission on Bilingualism and Biculturalism (established in 1963)—known as the B&B Commission—from the mid-1960s to the early 1970s, there was a new focus on education, identity, and diversity in relation to ethnic groups of immigrant origin. The B&B Commission, which was established partly in response to unrest among Francophones in Quebec, made recommendations that created more cultural and linguistic security for Francophone communities outside of Quebec, especially because of the provisions that pledged to support increased efforts in bilingual education (in French and English; Cardinal, 2013; Hayday, 2013). But the fact that the mandate of the B&B Commission had been expanded to include "the contribution of other ethnic groups" (the title of book four of the B&B Commission Report), was seen by many Francophones, particularly in Quebec, as a direct threat to the status of their culture.

The introduction of the federal multiculturalism policy in 1971 focused attention on two areas: teaching of nonofficial or heritage languages and the sharing of culture. The first resulted in programs both within and outside of formal schooling. The second created renewed interest in multicultural concerts and food fairs, events that had first been promoted across the country by the railway companies in the 1930s (Burnaby, 2008; Joshee, 2004). Meanwhile, the same government that was promoting diversity had in 1969 introduced a white paper to dismantle the Indian Act and "afford First Nations people complete citizenship through total assimilation" (Druick, 2007, p. 151). The white paper was an attempt to dismantle all previous legislation regarding the Indigenous populations of Canada and would have resulted in negating the status of Indigenous peoples as the First Peoples of Canada. In particular, it was seen as an attempt to remove the possibility that First Nations might pursue land claims.

Two influential reports on Canadian studies (Hodgett, 1968; Symons, 1975) created interest in promoting citizenship and knowledge of Canada in schools. Osborne (1996, 2001) has argued that this era also signaled a growing awareness that students needed to develop the skills to become activists in order to become productive citizens. Consequently, teachers across the country were developing programs that gave their students a "guided experience of political activity" (Osborne, 1996, p. 52). While Osborne (1996) contended that there was considerable support for this approach, Hughes and Sears (2008) noted that there was little evidence that this activist orientation actually reached classrooms.

Following the adoption of the Canadian Charter of Rights and Freedoms in 1982, educators began to use this document as the basis for discussions of human rights and multiculturalism within citizenship education (Bromley, 2011). Alan Sears and his colleagues (1998) have noted that, through the 1990s, curriculum documents across the country defined citizenship in terms of "freedoms, justice, due process, dissent, the rule of law, equality, diversity, and loyalty" (p. 4). There is some evidence that this emphasis helped to create a "rights-based consciousness" among Canadian students (Lévesque, 2003, p. 110). Despite the broader lens of diversity, however, Lévesque (2003) notes that the work in the schools he studied did little to enhance understanding of Francophone or First Nations claims.

Social Cohesion, Diversity, and Citizenship Education

Notwithstanding the curriculum documents discussed above, since the 1990s, social cohesion has been increasingly linked to citizenship and multicultural education (Joshee & Sinfield, 2010). As Shuayb (2012) has noted, "The theory underpinning the social cohesion agenda in neoliberal states is market and economic driven. Its main objective is economic prosperity and the maintenance of the status quo through increased distribution of social goods, which should help address the inequalities" (p. 13). Shuayb argues that social justice is absent from the conversations on social cohesion in education and that the focus of citizenship education within this frame is on "promoting trust and solidarity and creating 'imagined communities'" (2012, p. 16).

Social cohesion has continued to gain traction since it was first introduced into public policy discussions. Jenson and her colleagues (Beauvais & Jenson, 2002; Jenson & Saint-Martin, 2003) have argued that it is now a large policy basket that has fundamentally altered the notion of citizenship in Canada and elsewhere. They argue that citizenship has ceased to be a simple question of the relationship between a state and its population. Instead there are now four partners in what they call the "welfare diamond" (Jenson & Saint-Martin, 2003, p. 80). The state is the first partner, and the other three partners are the business sector, the voluntary sector, and families. In this new configuration, the role of the state is to help prepare workers and to ensure a safe (read: conflict-free) environment in which the economy can thrive. Thus the role of the state shifts from supporting civic engagement and providing social security to supporting labor market participation and defending against real or perceived threats to the economy.

Three versions of social cohesion have emerged in relation to discussions of multiculturalism and citizenship. One views social cohesion as built on common values and a sense of shared identity. A second, which draws heavily on the work of Robert Putnam (2001), sees social cohesion as built on trust between the diverse groups and individuals in a society. In this view it is less important to develop a shared sense of identity than to invest in creating bonds between individuals and bridges between different communities. The third view emphasizes civic participation and focuses on how citizens engage with each other. Even though all three have been part of the policy conversation in Canada, the first two have been most influential (Joshee & Sinfield, 2010).

The common values approach draws on the neoconservative "we/they" discourse. The "we" in this case is the (Northern and Western) European group, which, politicians explain, has always shown tolerance and acceptance of others. The implication is that any problems or conflict, past or current, exist because "the others" were not or are not open, tolerant, and accepting (for a more complete discussion, see Joshee and Sinfield, 2010). The focus of multiculturalism has changed over the past few years so that its primary goal is now integration and social cohesion (Citizenship and Immigration Canada, 2012). The Minister of Defense, who was also the Minister Responsible for Multiculturalism[1] in the last cabinet of the Conservative Government (2013–2015), explained that this focus is necessary "to help young kids who are perhaps in at-risk situations to avoid getting into trouble, and to build bridges between communities" (Kenney, 2009a). The minister drew on the "we/they" discourse to establish that Canadians already accept diversity in our country because "We have this tradition, as I mentioned, of embracing diversity, grounded in our historic, I would say British liberal imperial tradition of pluralism" (Kenney, 2009b). But Kenney believes this tradition is at risk because of our growing diversity; in other words, increasing numbers of "them" entering "our" country. "They," according to Kenney, are establishing "ethnic enclaves" and increasingly "undermining the very strengths and underpinnings that have made Canada a great country" (Kenney, 2009b). Kenney singles out youth as a particular concern because he posits that this phenomenon of "ethnic enclaves" leads to "radicalization" and puts youth "at risk either to criminality or to extremism" (Kenney, 2009b). Thus the social cohesion discourse is extended beyond the economic realm, and immigrants (and others who are not part of the dominant "us" group) are seen as threats to safety and security.

The second version of social cohesion, which relates to Putnam's (1993) notion of social capital, is more evident in Canadian citizenship policy than in multicultural policy. In this version of social cohesion, the belief is that "People and groups with extensive social connections linking them to people with diverse resources tend to be more hired, housed, healthy, and happy" (Policy Research Initiative [PRI], 2005, p. 1). This view focuses on investing in citizens to ensure they can participate in the economy as an important first step toward involvement in public life more generally. Moreover, participation in public life should be geared toward those phenomena that promote harmony, meaning that conflict or dissent of any kind is to be avoided. Thus we see the emphasis on duty and responsibility in citizenship education for adult immigrants. These duties and responsibilities include obeying the law, getting a job, performing jury duty, voting in elections, and volunteering in the community (Citizenship and Immigration Canada, 2012). As Michel Dorais, former Deputy Minister of Citizenship and Immigration, noted in 2002, "In a socially cohesive society, both the individual and society recognize the value of building a sense of acceptance and belonging among people based on trust, shared values, and common experiences that bridge social, cultural, linguistic, and religious differences" (p. 4). The differences themselves may and probably will persist, but citizens must follow rules and participate in common activities that show others that they can be trusted.

The third version of social cohesion has elsewhere been called "social inclusion" (Joshee & Sinfield, 2010) or "democratic social cohesion" (Bickmore, 2006). With its focus on how people interact rather than on shared values or bonds of trust, some believe this version has the potential to support a justice-oriented approach to citizenship and multiculturalism (see, for example, Bickmore, 2006; Kymlicka, 2013; Soroka, Johnston, & Banting, 2006). In this view, "Social cohesion requires economic and social equity, peace, security, inclusion and access. Diversity and differences are conducive to social cohesion because they contribute to a vibrant political and social life" (PRI, 2002, p. 5). The definition of social cohesion that emerges from this perspective includes three components: (a) participation in political and civil society (including dissent), (b) bonds of trust between individuals, institutions, and policies (like bilingualism and multiculturalism) that would bridge differences and promote mutual respect, and (c) an inclusive society built on the principles of income distribution, equity, and access for all (Joshee & Sinfield, 2010). While this approach does allow for dissent and conflict, diversity remains something to be endured and bridged rather than an asset in and of itself. This leads to a new version of multiculturalism that Kymlicka has called "neoliberal multiculturalism," noting, "The goal of neoliberal multiculturalism is not a tolerant national citizen who is concerned for the disadvantaged in her own society but a cosmopolitan market actor who can compete effectively across state boundaries" (2013, p. 111).

As we can see, the three different versions of social cohesion are closely related. Collectively they have informed several aspects of education. In relation to multicultural and citizenship education, social cohesion discourses are most evident in the work on safe schools, character development, and citizenship across the country. The logic underlying policy statements on safe schools is that safety is a prerequisite for fulfilling the academic mandate of schools. The focus of the safe schools legislation, which came into the landscape in 2000, has been primarily reactive, that is, addressing violence after it occurs through lockdown procedures, suspensions, and expulsions. Although this area of policy was not initially identified as relating to multiculturalism or diversity, in many jurisdictions it is now seen as a primary policy addressing diversity. In Ontario, for example, the current policy framework for safe schools makes explicit reference to the Ministry of Education's Policy and Program Memorandum 119, Equity and Inclusive Education Policy. It focuses on violence prevention, but true to the logic of social cohesion, the focus of intervention is on specific individual behaviors, particularly bullying (Safe Schools Action Team, 2006).

As Policy and Program Memorandum 144, Bullying Prevention and Intervention, makes clear, bullying is seen as an act of one individual (or a group of individuals) against another individual and thus should be addressed by teaching students how to behave appropriately. Although there is an acknowledgement that bullying may be linked to issues of social diversity, there is no discussion of addressing systemic issues such as racism or sexism (Bickmore, 2005; Smith & Carson, 1998).

In a similar vein, the character development policies, which have either replaced or augmented citizenship education policies across the country, focus on teaching students behaviors and attitudes that will contribute to "safe, healthy, and orderly school environments" (Ontario Ministry of Education, 2006, p. iii). A particular focus is helping students "to develop self-discipline and the personal management skills that will make their communities, workplaces, and lives the best that they can be" (Ontario Ministry of Education, 2006, p. 2). In the Ontario character education program, for example, it is recognized that communities are culturally diverse and, therefore, that the mission of character development must be to "find common ground" and build consensus (Ontario Ministry of Education, 2006, p. 4). The message with regard to diversity is clear: It is a source of conflict, so we must move beyond it by focusing on commonalities. In addition, the focus on social cohesion supposedly ensures there is no conflict and thus helps to create a safe environment within which students will be able to concentrate on academic success.

Even where there is an attempt to put more emphasis on a social inclusion version of citizenship, as Kennelly and Llewellyn (2011) have argued, the result is not an active citizen in the sense of someone engaged in the betterment of social conditions for all. Instead, "civic learning rooted in neoliberalism imagines active youth as law-abiding persons who make individualized choices for success (Mitchell, 2003) and reduce their claims on the state (Brown, 2005; Rose, 1999)" (Kennelly & Llewellyn, 2011, p. 910). Further, as Karen Pashby (2013) pointed out in her detailed analysis of the Alberta curriculum related to citizenship education, even where there is significant attention to active citizenship, diversity, and human rights, because of the neoliberal framing, diversity becomes synonymous with individual difference. A significant social identity like race, for example, becomes conflated with differences based on individual characteristics such as height or eye color, and thus the notion of diversity becomes depoliticized and to a large extent meaningless. In short, regardless of the particular version of social cohesion, the concept itself is contrary to progressive or equity-seeking versions of citizenship and multiculturalism.

Slow Peace: An Alternate Future

Since at least the 1990s, there has been a widespread concern among Canadians about violence in society generally and in schools specifically. This has led to a proliferation of programs to address violence and conflict. These programs have been based on a limited notion of peace that links peace to the absence of direct violence and conflict. Since the early 1990s, peace researchers in Canada and elsewhere (e.g., Galtung & Ikeda, 1995; Smith & Carson, 1998; Toh & Floresca-Cawagas, 2000) have advanced a broader and more proactive view of peace. In this view, educators are called upon to understand and address the underlying causes of direct violence, namely, cultural and structural violence. Social injustice of any kind is a form of structural violence. Smith and Carson (1998) have argued that cultural violence includes the denial of the traditions and culture of a people. In other words, racism and state-sponsored assimilation are both forms of structural and cultural violence. Canadian educators have also made connections between education for peace and education for citizenship and social justice (Bickmore, 2006; Evans & Hundey, 2000; Smith & Carson, 1998; Toh & Floresca-Cawagas, 2000). As Bickmore has concisely stated, "To contribute to citizenship education for democratic agency, explicit curriculum can and must delve into the unsafe but real world of social and political conflicts and injustices that defy simple negotiated settlement, including the roots and human costs of current local and global injustices" (2006, p. 383).

We propose an approach that we call "slow peace." It grows out of an engagement with Gandhian principles[2] and Nixon's (2011) understanding of slow violence. We begin with key Gandhian concepts such as equality, *ahimsa*, nonpossession, nonexploitation, trustee-ship, violence, and nonviolence. Equality for Gandhi was understood in terms of dignity and status. In particular, as Dugger has explained, "struggle for status is predatory because one person acquires it only by taking it from someone else" (1982, p. 442). *Ahimsa* speaks to the interconnectedness of all living things and the imperative not to do harm in thought, word, or deed. Nonpossession, or *aparigraha*, is an idea by which Gandhi meant that we should learn to live simply and to limit our need for material goods (Patel, 2014). Gandhi believed that exploitation occurred because a set of integrated privileges existed for those at the top of the hierarchy in society. Diwan (1987) has identified these privileges as nonac-countability (or the reality that those in positions of power rarely have to account to those lower in the hierarchy), ease of opportunities (the reality that those who have more wealth and power are able to translate this into opportunities to extend or sustain their wealth and power), and higher levels of income and consumption. Non-exploitation, therefore, is dependent on recognizing these privileges and working to eradicate them. Trusteeship refers to the idea that all material resources we have should be used for the betterment of the society as a whole (Joshee, 2006). Violence is understood as any structure or action that does harm to individuals, animals, or the environment. To understand violence and nonvi-olence more completely, we pay particular attention to the work of Galtung and Ikeda, who said:

> Some cultures are very dangerous because they consider themselves select or chosen above all others. . . . Some structures are either highly repressive or exploitative— or both. Structures of this kind readily elicit revolutionary violence from below or counter-revolutionary violence from above. The combination of so-called chosen cultures and repressive social structures almost invariably and fairly speedily results in direct violence; from below in order to liberate, and from above in order to prevent liberation. (1995, p. 69)

Nonviolence, then, is not simply the absence of direct violence, but an active approach to building a society free of structural and cultural violence.

In his work on slow violence, Nixon (2011) also acknowledges his debt to Galtung (1969). Both Nixon and Galtung are concerned with expanding our everyday understanding of violence. Galtung spoke of structural and cultural violence as types of indirect violence that could potentially lead to physical or direct violence. He causes us to think more deeply about notions of agency as they pertain to violence. For example, if a young person grows up as a member of a marginalized community and is consequently denied opportunities because of her social location, and if that same young person is then set up to fail in school, who is to blame for her failure? Is this young person a dropout, or is she a pushout? In Galtung's view, structural and cultural violence are silent and unchanging (1969).

Nixon's slow violence differs from Galtung's structural violence in two important ways: first, it is more concerned with time than agency, and second, it is not viewed as indirect violence. Nixon's notion of slow violence is best explained as "a violence that grows gradually and out of sight, a violence of delayed destruction that is dispersed across time and space, an attritional violence that is typically not viewed as violence at all" (2011, p. 2). In other words, slow violence takes place at a rate that is typically outside our attention span. He argues that we generally only understand violence in terms of the spectacular—bombs being dropped, mass shootings, and explosions. Slow violence, on the other hand, happens over the course of years or even decades—what is called in France the *longue durée*. Nixon, for example, is particularly concerned with environmental degradation. He notes that slow violence generally happens to people and places that most of the world (read: the elites) see as unimportant or expendable. The violence also goes "unnoticed" because those to whom it happens are not seen as credible witnesses; their stories are not listened to or heard.

Building on Nixon's work, Robins developed a notion of slow activism, which he defined as including "patient modes of grassroots mobilisation, human rights–based pedagogies of active citizenship, litigation, and a 'critical engagement' with the modern, bureaucratic state" (2014, p. 93). This was the starting point of our notion of slow peace, but as we investigated slow violence and slow activism, we also examined the literature pertaining to the "slow" movements and began to think of some of the main principles associated with them, especially the notion of slowness as a stepping back to deliberately rethink how we engage in the world in ways that challenge dominant neoliberal discourses of speed and efficiency (see, for example, Hartman & Darab, 2012; Pink & Lewis, 2014).

From these inspirations, we have begun to articulate slow peace as proceeding from the following principles:

- Much of the violence in the world is slow violence that goes largely unnoticed because it happens over extended periods of time, is not necessarily contained to one geographic space, continues through practices and processes that are normalized and sanctioned, and largely affects the most marginalized and dispossessed people of the world;

- Attention to any form of violence necessitates concomitant attention to a practice of nonviolence that would address it;

- Our particular approach to peace and nonviolence follows from Gandhian principles;

- Slow peace necessitates stepping back to understand the taken-for-granted practices that contribute to various forms of slow violence, with particular attention to the ways in which those practices are embodied in the work we do as educators and researchers;

- It is important to focus on a specific form of violence writ large and to proceed by thinking about day-to-day practices that sustain this type of violence; and

- To be effective, slow peace requires a commitment to sustained action through a variety of forms and practices.

Slow Peace in One Classroom

The example of slow peace we will describe below comes from the classroom of the second author of this chapter. Monica was a Grade 3 teacher in the Edmonton Public School Board (school district). As part of her studies for her masters in educational studies, she participated in three iterations of a summer program called the Mahatma Gandhi Summer Institute for Building Peaceful Communities, at the University of Alberta. Through her participation in the summer institute, Monica learned about Gandhian principles and undertook work that allowed her to develop a pedagogy that would address peace, social justice, and citizenship through a relational approach to teaching. Consequently, she developed and refined her approach to slow peace over the last several years.

Initially, Monica focused on special activities that would highlight different aspects of the key principles she wanted to teach. Those principles included supporting the children's engagement with each other and the community in ways that reflected peace and kindness.

One of the first activities her students participated in was a "random act of kindness day/week" during which each student was to perform a random kindness for someone, not a friend, and report back to the class. The children's reports about their random acts revealed creative minds at work; more profound, however, was the children's enthusiasm for what they had done.

They also engaged in other activities to get them to think about people they might not otherwise notice in the school community. Before writing letters of appreciation to their school custodian, for example, they had a class discussion about the different people needed to make a school run smoothly, and the role of the school custodian was discussed. Then the conversation took off in an unanticipated direction. Everyone knew about some individually wrapped chocolate-covered cookies in the teacher's desk. A student suggested that Monica give one of her six cookies to the custodian and she agreed. Another student who had recently learned how to sew added excitedly that she could sew a pocket for the cookie; another student suggested she could bring in a gift bag for the pocket; and the students continued to build on each other's ideas to think of better and better ways to acknowledge the custodian.

Monica was profoundly moved by both the content and the diversity of the content in the students' letters. One particular student, who often had trouble following classroom rules, wrote about his appreciation for the custodian, who made "sakrifises" by risking his safety "to clean our school when it is dark outside." Other students included information that was not discussed, such as how wonderful it was to come into a clean classroom in the morning. Some of the students apologized for often leaving the classroom in such a messy state. One student suggested that the custodian might give the class the "Golden Garbage Can Award" at the next assembly, which triggered a discussion about giving without expectations. As a result, another student suggested that if they were awarded the "Golden Garbage Can Award," they should give it to another class.

Over a period of three years, Monica reflected more about what she truly wanted to communicate to her class. She determined that her goals stemmed from her beliefs about the meaning of education:

- Every student deserves a top-quality education;

- To be meaningful, curriculum must relate directly to the lives of students;

- Education should develop in all students an awareness of social injustice in all its forms; and

- Education must build the confidence of students so that they may speak up for themselves and speak out against injustice.

Monica stopped focusing on special activities to teach about peace and justice. In reflecting on this practice, she felt that it conveyed to students that working for peace was something that happened only on special occasions. Instead, she began weaving slow peace into the everyday practice of the classroom. For example, she talked with the students about the need to notice what was happening around them in their community and in the world. They talked about noticing if other students were alone at recess or lunch and about homelessness in their community. They also talked about how children live in other parts of the world. Part of the social studies curriculum in Grade 3 directed the instructor to teach about India. Monica used that opportunity to talk with the students about child slavery. Monica stressed that each individual has a responsibility to act in a way that will help to change a situation that he or she realizes is not right. Her students played with other children who were alone at recess and they participated in school-wide events that educated the community about homelessness in Edmonton. At the end of the study, they were still contemplating what they could do to address child slavery.

Monica also believed that she must model the kind of behavior she wished her students to acquire. To that end, she tried to reflect her commitment to Gandhian principles in her professional as well as her personal life. Professionally, for example, she found ways to publicly acknowledge those who supported her work. Personally, she and her three young daughters engaged together in initiatives that addressed injustice. Just as she did with her students, Monica talked with her daughters about noticing what is wrong and then taking responsibility for addressing the situation. She believed this helped her to stay true to her values in all circumstances. When one of her daughters was a Grade 6 student in the school where Monica taught, she volunteered for morning recess for one full year to assist a student who was an English language learner and was having difficulty with reading. Monica's daughter had not been asked to do this; she noticed someone who needed help and decided to do what she could.

Another issue Monica talked with the students about was how to address conflict in productive ways. For example, when Reva went to visit Monica's classroom, she observed an incident that took place when the students were returning from recess and Monica was not in the room. There were four or five students in the room, and one child said a second child had hit him. A third child asked the second child if he had indeed hit the first child. The second child looked down at the floor, then looked up again and said, "I did and I'm sorry." He then approached the first child, put his arm around the first child's shoulders and apologized to him. The first child accepted the apology. No one said anything about the incident to Monica. When Reva mentioned it to Monica after the students had gone, Monica noted that before she began her slow peace approach, she would hear about such events and the students would typically characterize them as bullying. She said that after the students learned the slow peace approach, she almost never heard the word "bullying" from them, except when there was something happening that they could not deal with themselves. Generally, conflict was resolved among the students using the principles of caring, empathy, and personal responsibility.

Monica was concerned with issues of rampant consumerism and the egocentrism we have tended to inculcate in our students through a culture of competition and self-interest. When the students asked for more when they were given a special treat, as they often did, she used those occasions to talk with them about the need to be thankful rather than greedy. She wanted the students to understand the importance of being satisfied rather than always wanting more material goods, and she wanted them to become aware of their own privilege. She also addressed these issues through her attention to noticing and responsibility. When the students were discussing child slavery in India with a guest in the classroom, one of the students asked if there were rich people in India. This led to a question about why those rich people did not help the children who were forced to work. After the guest had tried to answer the question, Monica intervened. She pointed out that some people might think the students in the classroom were rich because they had houses, clothes, televisions, computers, and toys. She asked the students, "Do you share what you have to address issues of poverty in your community?" She asked them not to answer the question out loud but to think about it. In this way she directed the students to notice their own relative wealth and to begin to think about their responsibility to use what they had to address inequality rather than to focus on acquiring more things.

Returning to the postulates of slow peace, we see that Monica identified consumerism, egoism, self-interest, and exploitation as key elements of slow violence that she wished to address in her classroom. She worked to ensure that her students understood the connections they had to each other, to others in the community, and to others in the world. Beyond seeing injustices that exist, she wanted them to understand that they had a role to play and they could make a difference. She used her understanding of Gandhian principles such as *ahimsa*, *aparigraha*, and nonexploitation to think about what she was doing in the classroom and how those actions connected to larger issues in the community and the world. As the examples above illustrate, these commitments were evident in Monica's work with her students.

Concluding Comments

Canadian education has always been concerned with issues of diversity and citizenship. Since the 1950s, there has been an impetus to move that work in the direction of creating an equitable and inclusive society. While there have always been forces that worked against the development of a progressive multiculturalism and active citizenship agenda since the neoliberal onslaught, those forces have recently become stronger. Current official approaches to citizenship and multiculturalism are developed within the dominant frame of neoliberalism and respond to the goal of social cohesion. Although there are three different variants of social cohesion in the Canadian policy web, all of them ultimately conceive of the ideal citizen as a self-interested individual who only focuses on getting a good job and contributing to the economy. This person is not concerned with social justice or equity.

Many scholars in Canada have rejected this view of citizenship and are trying to interrupt it in different ways. Some have done this by calling for a critical approach to teaching history that would create a foundation for a deep understanding of the current fissures in Canadian society (e.g., Clark, 2011). Others have focused on a rethinking of our approaches to understanding the relationship between the First Nations, Inuit, Metis, and Canadians of immigrant origins (e.g., Donald, 2012; Tupper, 2013). Still others have advocated for a productive engagement with the enormous diversity embedded in Canadian thought and policy (e.g., Sears, 2013). Finally, there has been considerable focus on thinking about citizenship through a global lens (e.g., Evans, Ingram, MacDonald, & Weber, 2009; Pike, 2008). We applaud all of these initiatives and add our own: the approach that we call slow peace.

Slow peace focuses on addressing everyday actions that contribute to maintaining the inequality and injustice that exist in the world. It makes a link between how we live on a day-to-day basis and the larger questions of citizen agency and community engagement. It does not accept the traditional understanding of Francophone and First Nations issues as outside the purview of a vision of multicultural and citizenship education. It proceeds from an understanding that violence exists in many forms and that addressing all forms of violence is necessary, while acknowledging that it is important to start small and commit oneself to action over the long term. As individuals we cannot address every form of violence, but we can instill in our students the habits of mind and practice that would allow them to grow and engage in larger movements.

If one of the hallmarks of slow violence is that it is diffused across time and space and is therefore unseen by most people, this is also the case for slow peace. Slow peace might go unnoticed because it does not seek to announce itself; as we see in the examples above, slow peace is a process that starts with the proverbial small steps and contains a commitment to constant rethinking and continued action. It requires moments of stepping back as much as it recognizes the necessity to move forward. It is not one activity or an easily discernible series of actions. It demands patience, humility, compassion, and critique. Shuayb (2012) argued that social cohesion is meant to be part of a peace and reconciliation agenda, yet that agenda has not been achieved because of being rooted in a neoliberal agenda. We believe slow peace rooted in *ahimsa* can take us forward in our educational work for engaged citizenship, social justice, and peace.

Notes

1. Jason Kenney was the minister responsible for multiculturalism for most of the 10 years that the Conservatives formed the government.

2. While we acknowledge that some critiques of Gandhi have emerged (e.g., Arundhati Roy's [2014] claim that Gandhi was a racist), many of these are critiques of Gandhi as an individual, as someone he himself might have called an "imperfect practitioner" of his own principles. It is beyond the scope of this chapter to engage with those critiques except to say that they take nothing away from the value of the ideas Gandhi developed through his practice and writings.

References

Beauvais, C., & Jenson, J. (2002). *Social cohesion: Updating the state of the research* (Canadian Policy Research Networks Discussion Paper). Ottawa, ON: Canadian Policy Research Networks.

Bickmore, K. (2005). Foundations for peacebuilding and discursive peacekeeping: Infusion and exclusion of conflict in Canadian public school curricula. *Journal of Peace Education, 2*(2), 161–181.

Bickmore, K. (2006). Democratic social cohesion (assimilation)? Representations of social conflict in Canadian public school curriculum. *Canadian Journal of Education/Revue canadienne de l'éducation, 29*(2), 359–386.

Bohaker, H., & Iacovetta, F. (2009). Making Aboriginal people 'immigrants too': A comparison of citizenship programs for newcomers and Indigenous peoples in postwar Canada, 1940s–1960s. *Canadian Historical Review, 90*(3), 427–462.

Bromley, P. (2011). Multiculturalism and human rights in civic education: The case of British Columbia, Canada. *Educational Research, 53*(2), 151–164.

Burnaby, B. (2008). Language policy and education in Canada. In R. Wodak & D. Corson (Eds.), *Encyclopedia of language and education: Language policy and political issues in education* (pp. 331–341). Rotterdam, The Netherlands: Springer.

Cardinal, L. (2013). The impact of the Commission on Bilingualism and Biculturalism on Francophone minority communities in Canada. *Canadian Issues,* Fall 2013, 18–25.

Citizenship and Immigration Canada. (2012). *Evaluation of multiculturalism program.* Ottawa, ON: Government of Canada. Retrieved from http://www.cic.gc.ca/english/resources/evaluation/multi/index.asp

Clark, P. (Ed.). (2011). *New possibilities for the past: Shaping history education in Canada.* Vancouver: University of British Columbia Press.

Diwan, R. (1987). Mahatma Gandhi and the economics of non-exploitation. *International Journal of Social Economics, 14*(2), 39–52.

Donald, D. (2012). Forts, curriculum, and ethical relationality. In N. Ng-A-Fook & J. Rottmann (Eds.), *Reconsidering Canadian curriculum studies* (pp. 39–46). New York: Palgrave Macmillan.

Dorais, M. (2002). Immigration and integration through a social cohesion perspective. *Horizons, 5*(2), 4–5.

Druick, Z. (2007). *Projecting Canada: Government policy and documentary film at the National Film Board* (Vol. 1). Montreal, QC: McGill-Queen's University Press.

Dugger, W. M. (1982). An Ayresian view of Gandhian economics. *Journal of Economic Issues, 16*(2), 441–444.

Evans, M., & Hundey, I. (2000). Educating for citizenship in Canada: New meanings in a changing world. In T. Goldstein & D. Selby (Eds.), *Weaving connections: Educating for peace, social and environmental justice* (pp. 120–145). Toronto, ON: Sumach Press.

Evans, M., Ingram, L. A., MacDonald, A., & Weber, N. (2009). Mapping the "global dimension" of citizenship education in Canada: The complex interplay of theory, practice and context. *Citizenship Teaching and Learning, 5*(2), 17–34.

Galtung, J. (1969). Violence, peace, and peace research. *Journal of Peace Research, 6*(3), 167–191.

Galtung, J., & Ikeda, D. (1995). *Choose peace: A dialogue between Johan Galtung and Daisaku Ikeda.* Chicago, IL: Pluto Press.

Hartman, Y., & Darab, S. (2012). A call for slow scholarship: A case study on the intensification of academic life and its implications for pedagogy. *Review of Education, Pedagogy, and Cultural Studies, 34*(1–2), 49–60.

Hayday, M. (2013). Canada's bilingual education revolution: The B&B Commission and official languages in education. *Canadian Issues,* Fall 2013, 29–34.

Hodgett, A. B. (1968). *What culture? What heritage?* Toronto, ON: Ontario Institute for Studies in Education.

Hughes, A. S., & Sears, A. (2008). The struggle for citizenship education in Canada: The centre cannot hold. In J. Arthur, I. Davies, & C. Hahn (Eds.), *SAGE handbook of education for citizenship and democracy* (pp. 124–138). Thousand Oaks, CA: SAGE.

Jenson, J., & Saint-Martin, D. (2003). New routes to social cohesion? Citizenship and the social investment state. *Canadian Journal of Sociology/Cahiers canadiens de sociologie, 28*(1), 77–99.

Joshee, R. (2004). Citizenship and multicultural education in Canada: From assimilation to social cohesion. In J. A. Banks (Ed.), *Diversity and citizenship education: Global perspectives* (pp. 127–156). San Francisco: Jossey-Bass.

Joshee, R. (2006). Ahimsa and teaching. *Connections, 29*(1), 6–13.

Joshee, R., & Johnson, L. (2007). Historic diversity and equity policies in Canada. In K. Tolley (Ed.), *Transformations in schooling: Historical and comparative perspectives* (pp. 111–122). New York: Palgrave.

Joshee, R., & Sinfield, I. (2010). The Canadian multicultural education policy web: Lessons to learn, pitfalls to avoid. *Multicultural Education Review, 2*(1), 55–75.

Kennelly, J., & Llewellyn, K. R. (2011). Educating for active compliance: Discursive constructions in citizenship education. *Citizenship Studies, 15*(6–7), 897–914.

Kenney, J. (2009a, February 20). *Speaking notes for the Honourable Jason Kenney, P.C., M.P. Minister of Citizenship, Immigration and Multiculturalism at the 6th Annual Internationally Educated Professionals' Conference.* Retrieved from http://www.cic.gc.ca/english/department/media/speeches/2009/2009-02-20.asp

Kenney, J. (2009b, March 18). *Speaking notes for the Honourable Jason Kenney, P.C., M.P. Minister of Citizenship, Immigration and Multiculturalism "Good Citizenship: The Duty to Integrate" at Huron University College's Canadian Leaders Speakers' Series.* Retrieved from http://www.cic.gc.ca/english/department/media/speeches/2009/2009-03-18.asp

Kymlicka, W. (2013). Neoliberal multiculturalism. In P. A. Hall & M. Lamont (Eds.), *Social resilience in the neoliberal era* (pp. 99–125). Cambridge, UK: Cambridge University Press.

Lévesque, S. (2003). Becoming citizens: High school students and citizenship in British Columbia and Québec. *Encounters in Theory and History of Education, 4,* 107–126.

McLean, L. R. (2007). Education, identity, and citizenship in early modern Canada. *Journal of Canadian Studies/Revue d'études canadiennes, 41*(1), 5–30.

Nixon, R. (2011). *Slow violence and the environmentalism of the poor.* Cambridge, MA: Harvard University Press.

Ontario Ministry of Education. (2006). Finding common ground: Character development in Ontario schools, K–12 (discussion paper). Toronto, ON: Ministry of Education.

Osborne, K. (1996). Education is the best national insurance: Citizenship education in Canadian schools, past and present. *Canadian and International Education 25*(2), 31–58.

Osborne, K. (2001). Democracy, democratic citizenship, and education. In J. P. Portelli & R. P. Solomon (Eds.), *The erosion of democracy in education* (pp. 29–61). Calgary, AB: Detselig Enterprises.

Pashby, K. (2013). *Related and conflated: A theoretical and discursive framing of multiculturalism and global citizenship education in the Canadian context* (Unpublished doctoral dissertation). University of Toronto, Toronto, ON, Canada.

Patel, N. A. (2014). Mindful use: Gandhi's non-possessive property theory. *Seattle Journal for Social Justice, 13*(2), 289–318.

Pike, G. (2008). Citizenship education in global context. *Brock Education, 17*(1), 38–49.

Pink, S., & Lewis, T. (2014). Making resilience: Everyday affect and global affiliation in Australian Slow Cities. *Cultural Geographies, 21*(4), 695–710.

Policy Research Initiative. (2002). *Inclusion for all: A Canadian roadmap to social cohesion: Insights from structured conversations.* Ottawa, ON: Government of Canada.

Policy Research Initiative. (2005). *Measurement of social capital.* Ottawa, ON: Government of Canada.

Putnam, R. D. (1993). *Making democracy work: Civic traditions in modern Italy.* Princeton, NJ: Princeton University Press.

Putnam, R. D. (2001). *Bowling alone: The collapse and revival of American community.* New York: Simon and Schuster.

Robins, S. (2014). The 2011 toilet wars in South Africa: Justice and transition between the exceptional and the everyday after apartheid. *Development and Change, 45*(3), 479–501.

Roy, A. (2014). Debunking the Gandhi myth [Appearance on the Laura Flanders Show, YouTube video]. Retrieved from https://www.youtube.com/watch?v=4-yMiBGBOe0

Safe Schools Action Team. (2006). *Safe schools policy and practice: An agenda for action.* Toronto, ON: Ontario Ministry of Education.

Schugurensky, D. (2006). Adult citizenship education: An overview of the field. In T. Fenwick & T. Nesbit (Eds.), *Contexts of adult education: Canadian perspectives* (pp. 68–80). Toronto, ON: Thompson Educational Publishing, Inc.

Sears, A. (2013). Possibilities and problems: Citizenship education in a multinational state: The case of Canada. In A. Reid, J. Gill, & A. Sears (Eds.), *Globalization, the nation-state and the citizen: Dilemmas and directions for civics and citizenship education* (pp. 296–318). New York: Routledge.

Sears, A., Clarke, G. M., & Hughes, A. S. (1998). *Learning democracy in a pluralist society: Building a research base for citizenship education in Canada.* Ottawa, ON: Council of Ministers of Education.

Shuayb, M. (2012). From social cohesion to social justice and care in education: Revisiting the theory and practice. In M. Shuayb (Ed.), *Rethinking education for social cohesion* (pp. 11–36). Basingstoke, UK: Palgrave Macmillan.

Smith, D., & Carson, T. R. (1998). *Educating for a peaceful future.* Toronto, ON: Kagan and Woo Limited.

Soroka, S. N., Johnston, R., & Banting, K. G. (2006). *Ties that bind? Social cohesion and diversity in Canada.* Montréal, QC: Institute for Research on Public Policy.

Symons, T. H. B. (1975). *To know ourselves*: *The Report of the Commission on Canadian Studies* (Vol. 1). Ottawa, ON: Association of Universities and Colleges of Canada.

Toh, S. H., & Floresca-Cawagas, V. (2000). Educating towards a culture of peace. In T. Goldstein & D. Selby (Eds.), *Weaving connections: Educating for peace, social and environmental justice* (pp. 365–388). Toronto, ON: Sumach Press.

Tountas, J. (1998). *The changes in teaching history in Ontario, 1945–1998.* Retrieved from http://instruct.uwo.ca/edu/500-001/history/b/

Truth and Reconciliation Commission of Canada. (2015). *Truth and Reconciliation Commission of Canada: Calls to action.* Retrieved from http://www.trc.ca/websites/trcinstitution/File/2015/Findings/Calls_to_Action_English2.pdf

Tupper, J. A. (2013). Disrupting ignorance and settler identities: The challenges of preparing beginning teachers for treaty education. *in education*, *17*(3), 38–55. Retrieved from http://ineducation.ca/ineducation/article/view/71/409

Chapter 6

Citizenship, Identity, and Human Rights in South Africa: Viewed Through the Lens of Xenophobia

Kogila Moodley

University of British Columbia

Worldwide xenophobia expresses itself in each country with specific rationalizations against different outsiders. In post-apartheid South Africa, xenophobia is characterized by a high degree of violence (particularly in 2008 and 2015). Xenophobia was denied by the African National Congress (ANC) government and labeled criminal. In South Africa the antagonism originates from below, among marginalized township dwellers, rather than from above, among right-wing demagogues, as in Europe or the United States. South African xenophobia is directed against fellow Africans, not Whites. Those who liberated themselves from apartheid in the name of human rights now strike out against migrants who have escaped violations of human rights or unlivable conditions in their home countries.

This chapter probes the attitudes of students in four Western Cape all-Black[1] township high schools, based on a written survey of open-ended questions and subsequent focus groups. In the context of deprivation and pervasive racialization, the potential for a critical, cosmopolitan political literacy is discussed.

A society that liberated itself in the name of universal human rights nevertheless demonstrates extreme hostility toward persons who have moved to South Africa because they lacked human rights at home. The conditions they have escaped range from restricted life-chances without jobs, to civil wars, to environmental disasters. The liberal democracy that replaced apartheid ushered in guaranteed rights for all South African residents, regardless of citizenship. But these inclusive human rights jar with the exclusive entitlements of citizens that underlie the legitimacy of a liberal democracy. With relatively porous borders, post-apartheid South Africa has admitted the most refugees of any African country, about 300,000 annually. Is there a limit, dictated by a state's resources and the hospitality of citizens? This so-called liberal paradox characterizes most Western democracies that have enshrined rights of refugees and asylum seekers, as the refugee crisis in the European Union vividly demonstrates.

Migrants pose the classic dilemma between universalist human rights and the individualist rights of citizens. The French revolutionaries of the Enlightenment tradition, in their Declaration of the Rights of Man and of the Citizen (1789), introduced the two distinct concepts. Both are intended to achieve equality, eliminate unmerited discrimination, and ensure justice. Global human rights have advanced with economic globalization. Even birthright citizenship is now considered, like inherited property, an unmerited advantage. Human rights relate to equality among all human beings, as well as between richer and poorer states. Human rights universalize the rights of "men" and women, regardless of national origin. The use of immigration quotas by national origin or religion was abolished in most democratic states during the 1960s, although tightened admission by selected national origins has been reintroduced in North America and Europe since September 11, 2001, the day of the Al-Qaeda terrorist attacks in New York City and Washington, D.C.

Citizenship rights, on the other hand, are bounded by the nation-states in which they apply. Advocates of citizenship rights argue that human rights can be realized only within and through nation-states. In his compelling book *A Man of Good Hope*, Steinberg (2014) wrote: "Perversely, xenophobia is a product of citizenship, the claiming of a new birthright [in South Africa]. Finally, we belong here, and that means that you do not" (p. 270). In this view, solidarity cannot be extended to everyone without limits but is grounded in identity, trust, and loyalty to fellow citizens. But does that mean that belonging together and communal identity require closure? Is connectedness, what Max Weber calls "Zusammengehörigkeitsgefühl" (cited in Lichtblau, 2000), a precondition for social rights? People from all over the world can live together harmoniously in the same democratic welfare state with subnational identities, as the Canadian model shows. Similarly, South Africa's parallel ethnic enclaves may not be the "imagined community" of solidarity but rather, "less a nation than an agglomeration of disparate tribes, riven by collective envies and rivalries," as Owen (2012, p. 49) argues, but the people do coexist relatively peacefully and freely with equal citizenship rights. Many even embrace the Habermasian "constitutional patriotism" (Habermas, 1992).

The problem with a high number of immigrants arises from a labor market from which locals feel shut out by too many newcomers. Does the South African state have the resources to accommodate refugees from the rest of the continent, given the high number of unemployed indigenes? Does South Africa have a special obligation toward a less developed continent? Many convincingly argue that if South Africa's substantial resources of human and material capital were more effectively deployed and not wasted by foolish policies, the state would soar in an expanding economy with less inequality and a more just distribution, which would also minimize the "immigration problem."

Whether migrants are a net benefit or a liability to the economies of the receiving countries is hotly debated. In most settings, "illegals" provide an exploitable, low-wage labor force, particularly for unskilled jobs that locals reject. Immigrants mostly supplement but do not replace indigenes. In South Africa and California, newcomers frequently are concentrated in economic niches, such as child and elder care, food processing, low-skilled construction jobs, farm labor, waitressing, and gardening. They also remit earnings to kin in their country of origin, which amounts to small-scale global redistribution. If big capital had an exclusive say, immigration restrictions would be relaxed, particularly for skilled migrants, such as Internet technology professionals. Migrants add to the industrial reserve army of labor. As unorganized cheap labor, migrants drive wages down. Therefore unions everywhere are generally opposed to open borders and unregulated free immigration, unless a "split labour market" (Bonacich, 1972) can be prevented through state regulations, as was the case with the state contracts for Turkish "guestworkers" in West Germany in the 1970s.

The pretence of the universality of human rights is not easily shed. The former apartheid state cannot openly violate its liberal constitution and evict asylum seekers in the same way that the White minority expelled Blacks to the rural hinterland. All nominally liberal states, including the United States, face the conundrum of principles of universal justice juxtaposed with communitarian injustice toward nonnationals.

Theorizing Xenophobia in the South African Context

How can universal human rights be reconciled with closed rights of citizens? Can hostility toward strangers be considered a universal phenomenon, perhaps an evolutionary conditioning for maximizing survival, as sociobiologists assert? Is the antagonism toward perceived foreigners an issue of an insecure identity? Can xenophobia be unlearned and corrected through appropriate political education? How can empathy with refugees be nurtured? The strangers in this case are not visibly different but share the same phenotype: they are sisters and brothers who assisted South African liberation, as the story goes. Therefore, are the "dangerous strangers" invented or constructed, just as European anti-Semitism once construed "Jews" as having all kinds of imaginary attributes? In a similar vein, in the Western world Islamophobia now ostracizes Muslims and predicts an Islamic "tide" that is "swamping" a region, turning it into "Eurabia" after emptying its welfare budgets.

Is xenophobia a collective paranoid delusion? Mental health textbooks define delusions as beliefs held with great convictions in spite of having little empirical evidence. Beliefs that foreigners are swamping, flooding, drowning, polluting a nation, introducing diseases, peddling drugs, defrauding the locals, and seducing women conjure up fear of imagined threats. Spreading fear of the stranger, lurking to invade and undermine a virtuous people, is an age-old tactic for constructing an enemy. Anti-Semitism under Nazi rule had perfected such a mobilization, projecting a worldwide Jewish conspiracy. Xenophobia resembles this fictitious logic but differs from the paranoid delusions of anti-Semitism.

In economic terms, newcomers may compete with locals for scarce resources, especially jobs. Migrants are a real threat under conditions of scarcity. This gives xenophobia a rationality that anti-Semitism lacks. Therefore, xenophobia should not be pathologized. A similar caution applies to the conflation of xenophobia with racism. The "figment of the pigment" lacks a scientific basis. It was invented to rationalize colonial domination with the "civilizing mission" as "the White man's burden." In contrast, the "othering" of strangers rests on the nepotism of the locals. Citizenship legitimizes excluding noncitizens from the rights of natives. Yet xenophobia cannot be reduced to problems of a labor market alone. One has to question whether an impoverished township life suffices to explain scapegoating. The neglect of the shantytowns was embedded in the overall political development of the country, where an urban elite paid only lip service to the fate of the poor. This reality compels the revisiting of a once-glorified liberation movement that is still politically strong but morally weak.

The unexpected xenophobic violence in South Africa is important, not only because xenophobia runs counter to all the ideals of pan-African solidarity, unity, and cosmopolitan identities that African leaders usually espouse, but also because the violent rage could spread to other targets. Jonathan Jansen, the respected vice-chancellor of the Free State University, has already warned, "Make no mistake, the people who are now pursuing foreigners will sooner or later turn on the rest of us" (Jansen, 2010). The popular rage against foreigners disproves the Mandela-Tutu vision of an inclusive "rainbow" nation (Nevitt, n.d.) or a glorious "African Renaissance" (William, 1999, p. 11). It makes a mockery of the much-heralded African Ubuntu[2] philosophy that self-development depends on the well-being and care for all other community members. Instead, the ongoing hostility could well be seen as a forerunner to an impending civil war between a growing underclass and an indifferent, self-enriching state elite.

As is well known, South African decolonization was achieved not by military means and departure of the colonizers—as happened in other African settler societies (Algeria, Rhodesia, Kenya, Mozambique, and Angola)—but with the cooperation of power holders who could have delayed their ultimate demise for some time. This unprecedented "negotiated revolution" (Adam & Moodley, 1993) has forced compromises on both antagonists that constrained implementation of the initial visions of the new regime. Transforming a colonial economy, capturing its "commanding heights," redistributing wealth and land or nationalizing the mines, proved impossible when the compromise essentially rested on the replacement of the political class in return for maintenance of the old property relations and neoliberal market order. What needs clarification is how much of the current malaise should be attributed to the apartheid past and how much to the shortsightedness of the new leadership. The legacy of racial oppression obviously is not wiped out by new nonracial legislation. Internalized habits of domination and submission last, often even unrecognized by well-intentioned progressive forces. However, blaming the apartheid legacy for most of the current political deficiencies has too easily exempted the inept, self-indulgent, greedy, and corrupt new rulers.

In Europe and the United States, anti-immigration sentiment is instigated from above by ultraconservative political leaders, while in South Africa, xenophobia originates from below and, with the exception of the Zulu king, is condemned by the political elite as "shameful" yet condoned through long denial. Theoretically, it would also seem problematic to view xenophobia as an "irrational" fear of strangers, as defined in the dictionary, when the "insiders" clearly benefit from excluding "outsiders" from scarce employment. Giving preference to kin over nonkin—however imagined and constructed such fluid boundaries of communities may be—is explained by sociobiologists (Van den Berghe, 1981) as bestowing an evolutionary advantage. If this explanation of mobilized ethnicity as nepotism is correct, then one solution would be to broaden in-group membership. In the case of xenophobia, this would mean redefining citizenship to include a more cosmopolitan notion, embracing diverse members in a state in place of an imagined homogeneity. Authors who view the nation-state as outdated in light of global migration propose extending citizenship rights and blurring the lines between citizens and noncitizens. In this vein, Soysal (1994), in her book *Limits of Citizenship*, suggests "a model of post-national membership that derives its legitimacy from universal personhood, rather than national belonging" (p. 15). Migrants are characterized by multiple belongings and multiple identities that need to be recognized and accommodated, rather than erased by an enforced nationality. Multiculturalism in a multi-ethnic state fits this need. Still, legal citizenship cannot include all of humanity, but in reality is tied to the restrictions of existing states. Yet, once "indigeneity" has been exalted, even those "foreigners" who have acquired citizenship but do not fit the image of "natives" become targets. The mob that chases assumed foreigners does not ask the victims about their immigration status.

At least the domestic interethnic tensions that have destroyed many an African state have been relatively contained in South Africa. One has to applaud the African National Congress for a long-standing "anti-tribalist" vision that embraces a "land for all the people who live in it," as the Freedom Charter states (ANC, 1955). So far, the ANC has held the fragile line on interethnic strife, although rivalries simmer under the surface. Mutual resentment between Africans and Coloureds or envy of more affluent Indians is seldom expressed publicly. These taboos may be viewed as mere political correctness, but they also prevent incitement. Compared with the rest of Africa, with its artificial borders, one of the great achievements of the ANC lies in establishing an expanded, broader "ideological border" (Balibar, 2002, p. 71). Ideological "borders of the mind" are ill defined; they can become deadly when stirred by communal rivalry or stay inclusive when based on a common supranational identity. The concept of a borderless world contrasts with the real geographical borders of all 200 sovereign states, both the outer, national borders and the subnational, often secessionist, borders within.

The insecure newcomers usually work harder at lower pay and are therefore preferred by employers. Can one expect the locals to adapt to the competition, utilizing the skills of immigrants, instead of discriminating against them? It is necessary to return to the question, Is xenophobia racism? Should the term "autochthony" (Geschiere, 2009, p. 21) be used instead? The concept, as defined by Geschiere (2009), denotes a nativist obsession with land and belonging, to which only genuine locals are entitled. With their sense of entitlement, locals feel compelled to expose "fake" claimants. Are such nativist claims justified, or must they be rejected as exclusionary "othering," or even racism?

Some exclusionary rules and "othering" can be justified. Most democratic settler societies, such as the United States, Australia, and Canada, have recognized "aboriginal rights" of "First Nations," from which later immigrants are legitimately excluded. It would be absurd, for example, to label the differential rights of citizens and noncitizens "racialization." If everything is racism or fascism, then nothing is racism or fascism. The amplification of analytical concepts occurs at the expense of specificity. This applies in particular to the institutionalized racism of the apartheid state. Surely the exploitative racism of a White minority toward a subordinate Black majority during apartheid must be distinguished from the hostility of a disempowered Black underclass toward Black newcomers. The demand for exclusion originating in the underclass aims at improving the survival and life chances of the poor. In contrast, apartheid's exclusionary policies reinforced the privileges of the already privileged. Therefore, some analysts (Mngxitama, 2016; Mzwakali, 2015) doubt that one can talk about Black racism altogether. They argue that such a reversal ignores the power relationship that is embedded in all racialization. Powerless people, in this view, cannot be racist.

Yet racism and xenophobia are universal, in different guises. Without asserting an essentialist definition, predominant supremacist attitudes of Japanese toward Koreans, Chinese Han toward minorities such as Tibetans, or Arabs toward Black Africans resemble the racialization of colonized people by Europeans. However, only Europeans developed an elaborate ideology of genetic and cultural differences to justify their conquest with a "civilizing mission." Xenophobia lacks the systematic ideological rationalization that characterizes Europe's old biological and new cultural racism. Xenophobia assumes national entitlement on the basis of indigeneity as a "natural" defense against "intruders" who want to partake in the entitlements of the insiders without their consent. The insiders resent sharing their space with outsiders, not because they feel superior, as in settler colonial racialization, but because newcomers are perceived as threatening their accustomed sense of belonging and entitlements. In short, colonial racism was aggressive and therefore needed rationalization; xenophobia is construed as self-defence and hardly needs justification in the view of the perpetrators. What justification does exist takes the form of a moral panic about intruders who cut into the native's rightful space.

In addition to being portrayed as an "economic threat," migrants are also labeled as a security risk. There seems to be a widespread consensus among most South Africans, without supportive evidence, that foreigners are overrepresented among criminals, just as some American politicians label all Muslims potential terrorists. With this protectionist worldview, the South African government taps into a national consensus. Inveighing against "too many foreigners" is not confined to the urban poor. Blacks and Whites, regardless of class position, share this skepticism. One can already hear informally that Zimbabweans dominate the management of too many South African companies and Nigerians hold too many professional jobs. Soon, indigenization of corporate executives could become the next demand of South African nationalists.

Aim and Methodology of Research About Student Attitudes in the Context of Townships

The face of xenophobia in South Africa was researched with the aim of gauging empirically whether the massive attacks on foreigners in May 2008 could recur (as they did in 2015 and on a smaller scale in between), whether the efforts of public education affected attitudes, and how the relationship of township dwellers with foreign migrants manifested itself. All the empirical data were collected in the Western Cape, because it is a high influx area for new foreign migrants. The mining industry in Gauteng (Johannesburg) historically employed large numbers of workers from neighboring countries; locals were accustomed to seeing migrants from Mozambique, Malawi, or Lesotho on the streets. In the Western Cape, with its majority of so-called Coloureds still in highly segregated residential areas and with the only provincial government not controlled by the ANC, the rapid change of the ethnic composition of whole areas on the Cape flats made for an explosive mix.

Apart from a content analysis of various local newspapers and radio discussions, this study is based on a variety of data, including personal face-to-face interviews with (a) teachers and school principals in four township schools on the Cape; (b) police personnel in Stellenbosch and Cape Town; (c) several foreign migrants in various settings; and (d) academics, journalists, judges, and a few politicians, including the deputy minister of home affairs, with expertise and interest in the topic. Space does not allow the reporting of their different perspectives, if student attitudes are to be adequately portrayed.

The most important source for the findings is a written survey with five open-ended questions, conducted in four secondary schools with students in Grades 11 and 12, followed by focus group discussions with the same students after they had filled out a questionnaire. Open-ended questions and free-flowing, semistructured discussions yield richer and more nuanced insights than the usual tick beside preformulated answers. Such closed questions merely describe, measure, and categorize xenophobia. They often contain replies that would not have emerged spontaneously. In contrast to preformulated items to be tested, open-ended questions allow the reasons for an opinion to be spelled out. To combat hostility, the rationalization and specific logic for an opinion must be known.

Altogether, 150 respondents participated in the survey and focus groups at the beginning of 2012. The 150 students in Grades 11 and 12, all Xhosa-speaking "learners" in the four township schools, ranged in age between 17 and 21, with an even gender ratio among the groups. It was assumed that if there were any potential recurrence of xenophobic violence, it would show in the attitudes toward foreigners among adolescents. Our theoretical aim was to gain deeper insights into the specific rationalizations and characters of potential xenophobic perpetrators, rather than to describe the suffering of victims, which has has been well covered in much of the literature (Desai, 2008; Dodson, 2010; Hassim, Twana, & Worby, 2008; Vandeyar & Vandeyar, 2015).

The Context of Township Schools

It is important to understand the environment in which learning and teaching take place in the majority of South African schools. There are undoubtedly pitfalls in presenting township life and schools as the opposite of "normal," as being uniformly a world of deficits and suffering. As Dlamini (2009) wrote in his rich memoir of Katlehong, "To define townships in terms of their problems is to reduce township residents themselves to problems—instead of seeing them as people with problems, some of which are personal and others collective: just like every human being on earth, in fact" (p. 118). This perspective does not mean normalizing poverty, or pathologizing students, but interpreting their complexity and uniqueness with as much accuracy as an outside observer can muster.

In South Africa as a whole, an estimated 9 million children (43% of the total) are growing up in single-parent households (Robinson, 2014), often without maintenance benefits despite court orders. In the Cape Flats the overwhelming majority of Black students live without the support of stable family structures. Most are born to single mothers or have fathers who live elsewhere and do not partake in family life. This trend was initiated by the migrant labor system of the past that split families. Many migrants from rural South Africa established a second family or informal relationship at their urban workplace and, in the process, neglected and alienated both. This trend continues even today, in part because opportunities for employment and the cost of housing often become structural impediments to "normal" family life. Extended families of women, grandparents, siblings, and neighbors raise children under the most trying conditions. In essence, the learners have to fend for themselves in a materially and spiritually impoverished environment, sometimes in child-managed homes.

Soudien (2012), among many South African educators, has drawn attention to "the absence of emotional intimacy," in addition to the sheer scale of physical deprivation: "Hungry children cannot learn. Emotionally alone children have difficulty in seeing in the school a source of hope. The physical realities that surround children hound them. . . . They do not have access to the kind of intimacy in their lives which makes experimentation with their potentialities reasonably safe" (p. 238). At their most vulnerable age, they are at risk of exploitation from drug dealers and criminal elements. Another local observer (Silber, 2012), familiar with township life, remarked:

> Children sent to schools with the hope of securing a better future find not a place of learning and security, but rather a gang war zone where young "gangsters" fight with screwdrivers, pangas, knives and guns. During the past month thousands of children have stayed home from school for fear of being caught in the crossfire, while others had to flee to the Eastern Cape. When children are not at school, they must play in overcrowded and under-served slums amongst heaps of uncollected rotting waste in pools of excrement and wastewater. (para. 7)

Despite these hardships, it is moving to see how women launder clothing by hand after a full day's work and children emerge in neat school uniforms. Little credit is usually given to the networks of women's cooperation and the ingenuity of the most disadvantaged, who are more pathologized than recognized for their skills in surviving.

Comparing the schools in the townships with the dozen former Model C schools 10 miles away in Rondebosch and Newlands is literally like facing day and night. Dedicated, punctual teachers, scrutinized by watchful parents, work an average of seven hours a day in whitewashed buildings, set in sprawling lawns with expansive rugby and cricket fields. A motivated, multiracial student population is already conditioned by class status to "naturally" continue in this role. The relatively high fees of these semiprivate schools ensure a class selection that perpetuates itself by outpacing the all-Black schools at every level. The leading Cape anti-apartheid activists always had their children enrolled in these private institutions of privilege, even during the apartheid era, when the slogan "Liberation before Education" was propagated. In contrast, teachers in the no-fee township schools work alone with little parental support. Most mothers, working long hours away from home as sole breadwinners, can barely afford to feed their families or purchase the schools' required items for their children, let alone have the time for involvement in school activities.

Waghid and Davids (2013) point to what seems to be a paradox:

> In our native country, South Africa, there is a tremendous distrust in the school, primarily as a consequence of what is considered the poor academic performance of students in reading, writing and arithmetic. Since government, homes, neighbourhoods and religious institutions are no longer performing their educational functions adequately, schools are expected to take them on. (p. 17)

When the two vital educational institutions of home and school disintegrate in a society, the repercussions go much deeper than is currently visible.

Banks (2015) has coined the intriguing term "failed citizenship" in opposition to "successful citizenship," which is defined in terms of "structural inclusion" and recognition of identity in "culturally responsive classrooms" that reflect the history of marginalized, "minoritized groups" (pp. 152–153). In the all-African schools we researched, with all-African teachers, the desired civic engagement of successful citizens had nevertheless failed. The neglect of the townships by the state has resulted in alienated *nominal* citizens. These second-class citizens are periodically mobilized as voters by the ruling ANC but are only rhetorically recognized. Despite an unsustainable, meager social assistance program, low-income communities are better labeled "no income groups," with most of the youth unemployed. Fifty percent of high school students in these communities drop out after Grade 10. The community responses are weekly "service delivery protests," blockades of highways, and increasing support for the populist Economic Freedom Front party. The scapegoating and looting of foreign-owned shops should not surprise under these conditions. Without material improvement of everyday life in all respects, civic commitment and belonging cannot be expected. Even the most imaginative and gifted social studies teacher would fail under these adverse, objective conditions of deprivation. And yet political literacy cannot be abandoned, and even small-scale, incremental improvements are worthwhile goals to be attempted, as will be discussed later.

How Students View Foreigners

Prior to the classroom visits, we introduced ourselves to the busy principals who were appreciative of the significance of our study. One principal commented at length on the problematic practice by Somalis of setting up shops close to the school in competition with existing local *spazas* (informal convenience stores usually operated from people's homes). Informal discussions with teachers also revealed awareness of the prevalence of xenophobia; some teachers were sensitive to the positive aspects of the presence of migrants, while others avoided direct expressions of their own views. Instead, conversations veered into the tremendous odds that township teachers have to overcome, as many do with remarkable resilience and success. South African teachers are heavily unionized in the South African Democratic Teachers Union, a militant and powerful self-declared Marxist-Leninist organization. Discussions focused mostly on ANC factions and personalities, and poor working conditions in and out of school that explained teachers' resistance to performance assessments. After introducing us to their class, two of the four social studies teachers left the room (which we preferred), and two stayed quietly without interfering in our discussions. Their presence may have influenced some student expressions in the focus groups but should not have impacted the anonymous questionnaires that we collected.

In gauging attitudes toward "foreigners" and focusing minds on the subsequent group discussions, five open-ended questions were posed. The first question that aimed at capturing the general attitude toward foreigners was, "Should foreigners be allowed to settle in South Africa? If 'yes,' under which conditions? If 'no,' why not?" The term "settle" left open the location and duration of foreigners' presence, to be specified under "conditions." The surprising positive feature of the responses was that only a minority in our sample objected to foreigners settling in South Africa. A clear majority of 69% affirmed the right of foreigners to settle there and listed a variety of reasons for welcoming or tolerating foreigners, though most respondents insisted that the foreigners should have papers and not be "here illegally." In this category of "conditional presence," some respondents mentioned employment: "They should be here only for work; if somebody is not working [the person] should hit the road; the working ones should have a contract of 5 years." Similarly, "qualifications" were cited by a few as conditions for entry. Other respondents pointed to conditions that were common for immigration permits anywhere: "Before they enter they should be checked for any criminal offences that they might have made in their country"; "Yes, as long as they will not contribute to the increasing crime rate of the country"; "Yes, but they should be told to pay tax." The underlying suspicion of migrants as potential deviants was clearly evident, even among the majority, who would not oppose their admission.

Only a small minority of our respondents favored unconditional acceptance of foreigners. Moral, religious, and humanitarian considerations were cited, together with historical gratitude for exiles' acceptance and utilitarian aspects of benefits from foreigners. In view of this predominant humanitarian predisposition, a common humanity overrode everything else: "Yes, they should be treated as citizens of South Africa; by doing that we would be building humanity in our country. This will help us when visiting other countries also"; "Yes, because they are also human beings like us who have needs and responsibilities"; "Yes, they should settle in South Africa without any conditions, because we are all people of God." Frequently, the impoverished conditions in the countries of origin were cited in support of immigration as a right of all Africans. For example, one respondent said: "Everyone has a right to stay wherever she/he wants to stay and most of all we are all Africans."

A minority of respondents invoked the African assistance to South African exiles as reasons for solidarity: "Yes, these people are our brothers and sisters. If they are running from poverty and war in their country we should help them, because they also did the same during the time of apartheid"; "During apartheid people from here went to different countries; they were welcomed there, treated with love and care." Sometimes historical ignorance was also revealed: "Yes, because when Dr. Mandela was in exile and he was a foreigner and they did not say he must go away."

A second question allowed respondents to amplify: "What do foreigners contribute to South Africa (good or bad)?" Again, a high number of respondents (61%) emphasized the good contributions, usually together with various negative features, which dominated in 39% of answers. Given the image of Black Africa in the media as a backward, "dark" continent, a negative image reinforced by apartheid indoctrination (as opposed to the reality of a modern, civilized, industrialized South), one would expect the South African respondents to display a similar arrogant, supremacist view. However, many expressed the opposite sentiment—that South Africans could learn and benefit from the skills foreigners brought with them. Little of the South African exceptionalism of an older generation—the idea that South Africa, as an industrial powerhouse, was not of Africa—could be found in this younger group. Some respondents said, about foreigners from other African countries: "They fix our phones and television with a good price"; "They have knowledge of everything"; "They are good in technology and they are highly educated and responsible." The opening of shops by foreigners was viewed by many respondents as "good" because "they are cheap and we can afford what they sell." Moreover, "Foreigners are also showing us their skills of doing business"; "Most foreigners are educated, so it boosts our economy."

Self-deprecation shone through when students consistently loathed dissenting voices in their own group: "It's not that they came here to take the jobs away. Black people can't do a thing for themselves; they just don't want to work. So they expect that other people from another country must not work too." There is repeated evidence of low self-image and a fatalistic acceptance of self-defined inability. For example, one respondent said: "They [migrants] are hard working. They open businesses and don't wait on government to give them something." A 17-year-old female said in a group discussion, "they are not liked because South Africans can't open spazas for themselves, because foreigners who come from poor countries open supermarkets and spazas competing with Black people." Self-diminishing comments reiterate a similar self- perception. An 18-year-old male respondent wrote: ". . . but what I can say is that there is nothing wrong with them and Xhosas are lazy; they don't wanna work and they expect to be paid big, while the foreigners accept what they are given." These replies echo the students' sense of their own shortcomings in navigating the routes to survival in a competitive, changing world.

Among the hardcore xenophobes who answered "No" to any admission of foreigners and emphasized insurmountable differences, a clear disbelief in any advantage was stated: "I belief they can't benefit us with anything, especially economically." Among the bad features of migrants, a clear ranking emerged in terms of frequency of mentions: Selling drugs ranked number one, followed by robbery; rape and prostitution; faking goods, money, and ID books; practicing witchcraft; and, not least, "taking jobs." One respondent quoted "the propaganda belief that they are witches, human traffickers, drug dealers, alcoholics and people with no manners." Cheating with witchcraft ranks prominently among the bad characteristics named. For example: "They come here with no houses. Then you offer a house to rent, maybe for about two years. When you come back, the house is in their name; they are dangerous, they use *muti* [traditional medicine of South Africa] and they are crooks." "Some pretend as if they are doctors whereas they do not have experience at all."

We did not expect that accusations of witchcraft would figure so prominently in many narratives. We were skeptical when we read about the emphasis on superstition in other similar studies, for example, in the analysis by du Toit and Kotze (2011), based on the World Values Survey. Usually, witchcraft is associated with rural unenlightenment, not with a modern city such as Cape Town, where even many shacks have multiple-channel TV and most youngsters own a cell phone. Perhaps more recently arrived students from rural Transkei were particularly prone to blaming the magic of witchcraft for what they could not explain rationally. Could it be that dismal living conditions required the belief in magic that explained the inexplicable?

People who refer to witchcraft have clearly grown up outside any Enlightenment tradition. Superstition still prevails in some sections, as is evident in the number of uncontrolled *muti* shops (African traditional healing stores selling plant- and animal-based products, which are advertised as cures for all ailments). While the obsession with witchcraft may be common in some sectors of South African society—even some ANC leaders participate in rituals to kill a bull in order to communicate with the ancestors—the paranoia about outsiders stealing, molesting, and raping local women features in xenophobia worldwide. It probably originates from the historical experience of conquering armies abducting the young women of the vanquished, from Alexander the Great in India to the Russians in Berlin in 1945. In the Bosnian war, Serbian men were officially encouraged to rape Muslim women in order to shame and ostracize them from their community and make Serbians out of their offspring. In both world wars, German armies were successfully mobilized with the imagery of protecting the virginity of the maidens from the dirty designs of the enemy.

Similarly, in South Africa, romantic contact between local women and foreign men is deeply resented, particularly given the traditional African patriarchal belief that the outsider ignores local customs, such as paying *lobola* (bride price). One respondent said: "They do traffic and sell our sisters to other countries." In the minds of several respondents, foreigners invaded the space and exploited not only resources but also bodies, because they "know us and understand how we think and do things . . . ; they pollute our place, and when they come here they always come with their family invading our space. They don't see us as people like them. . . . [T]hey see [us] as filthy and strippers, prostitutes." With regard to sexual offenses, a 17-year-old male asserted, "They have a tendency of dating 14, 15, 16 years old which is wrong." Others said, "Some of them took our sisters, girlfriends and left them with nothing"; or "They marry [our] daughters and make them pregnant. After they got the ID they dump them. So all in all they are opportunists."

A few hold foreigners responsible for all the maladies in the country: "The price of food in SA is too high; it increases every day, because we have the people who do not belong to South Africa." In the misery, insecurity, and inequality of township life, the basic enabling conditions for xenophobia are found. The foreigner serves as the ready scapegoat, even though the causes lie elsewhere. Scapegoating absorbs frustrations and empowers disempowered people by providing explanations for their misery.

A third question directly targeted xenophobic attitudes in the guise of asking about other people's hostility: "Some people do not like *amakwerekwere* [foreigners]. Why do you think they are not liked?" Using the derisory term *amakwerekwere* signaled that respondents should be free to express their negative feelings. There were a few respondents who critically reflected on the manipulation of negative images that they did not share: "I think it has something to do with myths that are being spread around our communities. Most of us end up being brainwashed by all sorts of these gossips, e.g., that they brought HIV and drugs to our people." However, many more respondents listed obvious differences (language, color, hair) and stereotypes as reasons for dislike: "stinking under their arms"; "Somalis in SA own businesses, but they do not wash and sleep on the top of their groceries." A few respondents pointed to jealousy: "*Amakwerekwere* have skills and they work harder than the Xhosa people. It is all about jealousy." Or, "They don't like them, because they say that they take their jobs and wives." In the group discussions, we asked specifically why Whites were not singled out for hostility. The students had never thought about why *mlungus* (Whites) were not considered *kwerekwere*. It was obvious, several respondents said: Whites spoke English or Afrikaans and were part of the country. The discussants readily supplied more answers: Whites ensured investments and thereby provided jobs; Whites had knowledge and skills needed for development; as tourists they brought in money; Whites did not live in the townships and crowd out the space.

South Africa successfully decolonized in 1994, but only politically and legally. Mental colonization continues. Historically conditioned habits and worldviews do not readily change with the color of the government, although it democratically represents the majority for the first time in the country's history. Afrophobia is only one manifestation of an internalized value system that despises the local but subconsciously glorifies European ways. Biko's Black Consciousness Movement attempted to change this and instill pride in the colonized, but succeeded in only a limited way. Biko (1978) focused primarily on "freeing minds" and strengthening self-esteem, in addition to abolishing structural oppression. Mental colonization revealed itself among our subjects in another way that can be termed "consumer colonialism." Many were incensed that *kwerekwere* sold fake commodities, such as CDs, DVDs, and brand-name clothing. They longed for the authentic, genuine clothes and watches, not the cheap imitations offered by the foreigners. In South Africa, equality is measured by how Whites live, not how African traditions would suggest. Gandhian austerity and a return to self-reliant simplicity are rejected by those with a colonial mindset.

A fourth question was intended to gauge perceptions of difference among foreigners as well as between foreigners and locals: "Based on your experience with foreigners in your area, are there any differences between the nationalities you have met or heard of? If yes, what are the differences? " We wanted to know whether respondents tended to generalize and lump outsiders together or to differentiate between the dozens of nationalities in the townships.

Despite being in the minority, most of those who answered with "No differences" did not do so in order to generalize and lump all foreigners together, but meant it in a positive sense, by emphasizing the unity of Africans: " No, I do not think that there is any difference between nationalities, because we are of the same colour and race." Others lauded qualities of foreigners that South Africans were said to lack: "I haven't seen a foreigner starting a fight." Among all the nationalities, Somalis were viewed most favorably and were frequently described as kind and as providing cheap goods. Some respondents identified with Somalis, citing similarities with their own poverty and even exempting them from being foreigners: "The Somalis are not selling us drugs; they came here because they are poor too, so they came here to make money and feed their family. That is the difference between foreigners and Somalians." "In our area there is a difference between Somalis and *amakwerekwere*, who have more experience about any business than Somalis, especially electrical things." "Somalians at my village if we asking for a donation they giving us anything." "Yes, we are very different the way we preach god, the way we dress, the way we talk, also the way we handle things." Obviously no comparative religion has ever been taught, as other comments about different gods reveal: "The god that we worship isn't the same"; "They don't believe in one god and their traditions are not the same." One has to keep in mind that South Africans in general consider themselves to be a very religious people, with multiple denominations represented. Many respondents asserted the usual stereotypes about the different qualities of outsiders. For example, "They speak too loud and like to shout and you think that they are fighting." Foreigners are contradictorily portrayed as both poor and rich: "They make money that South Africans never do. They are living in hotels and fancy houses and South Africans are living in shacks, so that is what's make them dislike."

Hygiene always figures prominently in designating outsiders and supposedly protects insiders from infection. The depiction of the outsider as unhygienic derives from a universal repulsion against dirt, disease, and contamination and is used to justify the social distance that goes with "othering." Education in multicultural understanding of different traditions of eating and cleaning is clearly lacking when one considers comments such as the following: "When they [Somalis] go to the toilet they don't use toilet paper, they are using water as a form of toilet paper." And, "Yes, in their shops, they smell very bad. They are dirty." "Some wash their children outside." "Their food is different. Some eat things that we South Africans see as a taboo to eat."

Among the different nationalities, Nigerians have the worst image and are mostly associated with drug peddling and other crimes. While Zimbabweans, Ethiopians, and Somalis are perceived as poor, "Nigerians are not poor, they come here to make fraud and take over." A teacher corroborated this image of Nigerians as able to reprogram cell phones so that they could use other people's account numbers to make long-distance calls back home, landing locals with huge bills. Typical is the contrasting picture by a 20-year-old female: "Yes, Somalis are very friendly and they even opened a shop near my house and they are not here to stay, they are here to work for their families in Somalia. Zimbabweans are also doing business going around risking their lives because they want their families to eat every night." But "The Nigerians and the Ghanas [sic] are the violent ones in my experience."

A final question was about assuming responsibility and personal intervention in xenophobic incidents: "Sometimes foreigners are attacked. If you saw such an incident what would you do? " Again, a majority of students indicated that they would not passively stand by, let alone cheer, but that they would call the police and try to help the foreign victim. For example, " People that are attacked also have rights." Even some of those who disliked foreigners said they would summon intervention because of a common humanity or an aversion to violence: "I would call the police because they are not animals, they are human beings just like us, but they must stop what they are doing, because it is not good to our people." "I would report the matter because nobody deserves to be attacked, no matter what conditions." Others sympathized but admitted that they feared being attacked, themselves: "So in my heart I would be willing to save them, but also scared of being attacked. It will all depend on how many people are attacking them."

Civic courage remained a rare virtue, given the nature of the violence that the respondents encountered: "Personally speaking, I wouldn't do anything, not because I hate them; I just would be fearing for my own safety and it is very violent in the township." "I'd do nothing in fear of me getting tortured for trying to stop the locals beating the foreigners." Other bystanders stated, "I don't do anything. I just stay in my home watching TV." Other residents distinguished between "good" and "bad" foreigners: "I would stop them if they are attacking the good foreigners because foreigners are not the same." A total lack of principle and moral judgment was evident in comments like this one: "I believe everyone is entitled to his or her opinion and if some people think that attacking is the way to go then they should go with what they believe in, but I wouldn't be part of it though."

A substantial minority (20%) admitted that their reponse would be not only passive bystanding but active aggressive support: "Talking from my heart I think I would attack too because seriously I don't like those people." "Honestly, I would just watch or attack them too, because people cannot tolerate what they do to our country and I think they have overpowered the government." "I would just ignore and hope they beat him/her to death. I don't like them and they make me sick. They should just pack their bags and go to their countries; we could do much better without them."

Those with a general outlook of compassion, inclusiveness, and care for people in need may be characterized, using a Weberian ideal type of construct, as representing a *humanitarian character*. Taking answers to all five questions together, 51% of our sample fell into this category. Humanitarians are able to differentiate between people in a category and generally have a realistic understanding of the plight that motivates migration. This leads to empathy.

An opposite attitude of overt hostility, hate, and prejudice toward foreigners may be dubbed a *xenophobic character*. Respondents in this class generally stressed the negative features of foreigners, refused to assist, and displayed various degrees of paranoia about outsiders who would "intrude," "swamp," "overcrowd." The written comments identified 24% in this class.

A middle group showed an attitude that may be termed *ambivalent character*. Students with this syndrome were not consistent in their attitudes; they considered foreigners as brothers in need of assistance but were hesitant to help, or else made their help contingent on circumstances. They showed understanding as well as hostility: "I like them, but not their behavior." Students in this category constituted 25% in our sample. They could be expected to behave in a number of different ways: They might participate in a xenophobic riot or act as bystanders, but also might come to the rescue of victims.

It was beyond the scope of this survey to establish to what extent the respondents' alleged experiences and the features they attributed to migrants were based on fact, fantasy, or projection. In short, the respondents displayed classical prejudices of in-groups against members of constructed out-groups, as described in a vast social science literature (Rex & Mason, 1986).

No major differences could be discerned between male and female respondents, who were evenly represented in our sample. Only an overrepresentation of female respondents among the ambivalent characters could be detected. From all the photographs of xenophobic rampages over the past decade, it appears that the perpetrators were exclusively young males. No empirical data are available as to whether female locals exhorted or restrained their male counterparts, as confirmed by Loren Landau (personal correspondence, November 8, 2012). In contrast, there were some clear differences in the response patterns among the four schools surveyed. Given that all other variables in the sample were identical, clearly some prior teaching about xenophobia or political education in general seems to have influenced the attitudes of students in some schools. If this assumption can be substantiated in further research, important lessons can be drawn about best practice in political education.

Our research shows that previous efforts in political education have not been particularly successful among a substantial minority of learners. That conclusion invites reflection on the state's responsibility for better learning conditions and teacher education. In light of our findings, the 2008 and 2015 episodes of xenophobic violence were not the first and most likely will not be the last incidents of this nature in South Africa. Indeed, several observers testified to the ongoing, daily harassment and often unpublicized killings of migrants. The very ambivalence of most respondents in our sample suggests space, opportunity, and a need for meaningful discussions. However, a wide-ranging conversation about integrating difference is not taking place. Neither the classroom nor the public sphere has clarified the role of migrants, except in creating moral panic about being "swamped," "flooded," and "crowded out" by "aliens." Repeated official communications associating foreigners with crime have exacerbated distrust and aggression.

The survey agency futurefact (Kock, 2014) reported that "64% of South Africans believe that, in general, people from South Africa are superior to those from other parts of Africa." Half of the 3,050 adults sampled by futurefact also thought "that most criminals in South Africa are foreigners" (Kock, 2014). Local ethnocentrism trumps continental identity because a majority do not view themselves as Africans but South Africans, akin to the thinking in Europe and the United States. Ethnocentrism by far outweighs solidarity, as almost three quarters stated "that South Africa should look after itself and its own people and not worry about the rest of Africa."

Conclusions About Citizenship Education in South Africa

Weinstein, Freedman, and Hughson (2007) have conducted intriguing research in the former Yugoslavia and in Rwanda on the role of education in the reconstruction of transitional societies after mass conflicts. They described the common practices of peace education and textbook reform as insufficient. Weinstein and his colleagues treated schooling as merely part of a necessary wider intervention for confronting the stereotypes, and contended "that without sustained contact in learning and social interaction, the youth will be unable to create any bridges to 'the other'; that in itself is a recipe for disaster" (p. 66). Similarly, South Africa lacks bridges of social interaction for the majority of youngsters. Most live in and are educated in mono-ethnic environments and racial separateness. Despite the official proclamation of nonracialism and a common civic identity, race recognition is everpresent. It is reinforced beyond visibility and different cultural traditions through a variety of objective conditions: Most names easily identify members of a group and so does accent, less obviously. With 11 official languages and some dozens of unofficial mother tongues, ancestry is frozen in daily communications, despite widespread multilingualism and the use of English as a medium of instruction. Affirmative action programs for "historically disadvantaged groups," regardless of current status, attach material benefits, preferential employment, or university admission to the old apartheid categories. The only difference lies in the previously imposed group identities, which now are voluntarily embraced. Blacks feel justified in claiming rights, while Whites mostly perceive themselves as excluded victims. The continued economic power and better education of the former ruling minority contrasts with the frustrations of a marginalized majority. The agitators of the underclass inveigh against privileged Whites and the new Black elite, alike.

In summary, the ideology of color blindness in a unified "rainbow nation" propagated by both the African National Congress and the liberal opposition—though for different reasons—is contradicted by the continuing racialization of everyday life, from racial segregation and schooling on the basis of poverty, to elite-privileging "Black Empowerment," to ill-conceived, noninclusive affirmative action quotas that neglect class background. These footprints of difference are imprinted much larger into the minds of people than the noble dreams of a blended rainbow nation. Racial identity may be the "figment of the pigment" for liberal academics, but as the famous Thomas theorem states, "things that are perceived as real are real in their consequences" (Merton, 1995, p. 401). When everybody's opportunities and life chances hinge on their place on a scale of "nativeness," the foreigners obviously occupy the lowest rung. To teach learners such constellations of reality rather than preach the official doctrine would be a crucial first step to understanding and combating xenophobia.

However, the state not only passively stands by but indirectly encourages xenophobia. The state, indeed, bears major responsibility for nudging people into xenophobic action, which state agencies themselves have legitimized. The South African Aliens Control Act of 1991 "allows officials to make random arrests on the basis of skin colour, vaccination marks, pronunciation of words, or understanding of local dialects" (Everatt, 2011, p. 13). Equipped with such arbitrary discretion, together with physical and verbal abuse of illegalized persons, it is no wonder that the township dwellers merely emulate illegally the hints they receive from the legal authority. What immigration controllers cannot achieve, the locals undertake on their behalf. Given that the police were perceived as not only ineffective but also in cahoots with foreigners by accepting bribes from them, the local xenophobes, in their minds, merely rectified a rotten situation for the benefit of the community.

The official denial of the existence of xenophobia adds to this dilemma. The 2014 *World Report* by the New York–based Human Rights Watch pointed out that the national government's "denial that the attacks were xenophobic had undermined the development of an effective long-term strategy by the police to prevent xenophobic crimes" (Fabricius, 2014, para. 4). Still, the question remains, why is it so obviously painful for ANC leaders to admit the prevalence of xenophobia among those who valiantly fought against colonial racism? The columnist Aubrey Matshiqi provides one answer: "If we were to concede that we are xenophobic, we run the risk of being dislodged from the moral position that apartheid bestowed on us as black people, and it's a risk that we are not willing to take" (Helen Suzman Foundation, 2010, p. 25).

The legacy of apartheid with similar practices in the post-apartheid state cannot be denied. People are products of their upbringing and conditions of socialization, even if they have fought against them. However, they can also overcome such legacies by understanding and reflecting on questionable roots. Such political literacy has not come about in South African townships, where the reasons for poverty and inequality are poorly understood. Almost all South African analysts of xenophobia vividly describe these connections with the past, but they fail to explain why such legacies were so readily internalized—in the case of our sample, by a generation that was not even born during apartheid.

In this study we posit, simply put, that a failed liberation can be held responsible for the high level of xenophobia in a society that was supposed to turn out differently. Therefore, we argue, only increased political literacy can create a cosmopolitan identity that immunizes against a violent citizenship of exclusion. The core of such an attempt lies in making people understand why they hate. It implies not only more information about the other, but basic knowledge about nation, patriotism, ethnicity, race, identity, ethnocentrism, tribalism, communalism, sectarianism, and other concepts with which we explain our world and construct meaning. Political literacy focuses on the process of deconstructing the causes of social conflict, the way in which diversity works, and the nature of dissent in society. The underlying goal is to engage in transformative action by shaping democracy through the use of well-formulated, reasoned argument, which requires, in turn, that individuals acquire habits of staying critically informed on current events. However, has a complacent ruling group a real interest in such nuanced, critical political education, when it is better served by uncritical conformity?

International comparative research has shown that civic education impacts nationalistic and xenophobic sentiment in different ways. Some authors (Weinstein et al., 2007) argue that education as an antidote to xenophobia is overrated. In some cases education may even reinforce divisions between "us" and "them," because education operates within the boundaries of society and all the myths and symbols of national images. However, a consensus has emerged that the right type of political literacy combats xenophobia effectively. Hjerm (2001), who surveyed eight European countries plus Australia and Canada, concludes, "Levels of nationalist sentiment as well as of xenophobia decrease with increasing levels of education in all the countries examined, despite substantial differences between the educational systems in the countries" (p. 37).

The students' responses, on the whole, seemed to regurgitate some popular themes learned as part of their "Life Skills" courses, in which citizenship education was left to the discretion of the teachers. In many ways, the students expressed positive aspects of the migrants in their midst. However, the frequent assertions about "essential" differences of the "others," their religious practices, their approaches to personal hygiene, and assumptions about their sexual and economic predatory predispositions indicated a need for multifaceted educational approaches.

Ironically, in a society that is so culturally diverse, there is little nonjudgmental understanding of cultural or religious differences. What is striking is the binary depictions of the "other" as capable, innovative, entrepreneurial, economically savvy, and serving the community by offering affordable goods, yet also unclean, wily, sexually exploitative, conniving, and dishonest. On the whole, students showed little understanding of their own human condition vis-à-vis the rest of the country, let alone any similarities with the condition of migrants and refugees in search of safety from other parts of the continent. Also noticeable was the negative self-reflection of themselves as "lacking" skills, initiative, courage, and trust in each other, and as reliant on handouts from the government.

When one considers that the parents of these "born-free" students were opponents of apartheid, the words of anti-apartheid activist Suttner (2015) speak volumes: "Freedom is not a single moment. It is an ongoing process, which must be deepened and defended even from those who fought for freedom yesterday" (para. 21). How to defend this hard-won freedom?

Educators can help to preserve freedom by teaching cosmopolitan understanding of citizenship, identity, and human rights:

- Students need to understand their own situation and condition through effective political literacy. Social conditions often deprive people of the security and self-confidence that would militate against the need to stigmatize others.

- As a basic requirement, students need to acquire a broader cosmopolitan understanding of the societal and global context in which they live and of the needs of "others."

- Students need to be taught respect for differences in lifestyle, religious observances, and linguistic preferences.

What this amounts to is a combination of education for a cosmopolitan political literacy and some essential understanding of fundamental skills for living with diversity in a multicultural society.

Above all, political literacy not only informs a person about contested ideas but enables the person to distinguish and make sense of competing values. Crick has rightly described politics as "a lively contest between differing ideals and interests, not a conventional set of stuffed rules" (Citizenship Foundation, 2012, para. 3). Teaching political literacy as consisting merely of lawmaking, or constitutional prescriptions of how conflicts between government agencies are settled, or how scarce goods are distributed, or what constitutes good and bad governance, misses the moral and ethical issues that always underlie political debates. Such a focus on political institutions is likely to stifle political interest among students. Students are motivated when they are invited to solve political problems, rather than being lectured on how a political system functions. Exposing young learners to moral controversies encourages autonomous, critical thinking. If such disputes are derived from current affairs and country-specific debates, they will stimulate rather than bore learners.

A salient challenge for educators, then, is how these concepts can be translated in the classroom. What would be some of the moral predicaments in which students could become engaged, in light of recent South African history? For example, is torture illegitimate under any circumstances? Or is it to be tolerated if lives can be saved? Should all politicians be forced to resign if they have intentionally lied to their constituents, and if so, how can such a rule be enforced? How can whistleblowers—workers who report rampant corruption in their employer's company—be encouraged and protected? Or should they be ostracized for betraying colleagues? Does the international community have a responsibility to protect citizens of tyrannical states? Or does such intervention constitute illegitimate imperialism? Should a country like South Africa welcome refugees and asylum-seekers or send them back to their countries of origin? Should prejudices and extremist views about other groups be tolerated in accordance with freedom-of-speech values? Or should they be prohibited and criminalized as hate speech?

Political literacy, to some extent, immunizes against racist temptations. Political literacy differs from the political education that is usually considered central to the participation of citizens in government. The aim of political literacy is to nurture the ability to read critically and deconstruct issues, events, and debates. It is a way of making sense of how inequality works, how institutional racism works, how racial binaries become entrenched, and how to challenge that kind of system. Specific counteracting policies flow from such an understanding, which is a precondition for successful practice.

Policies, procedures, consequences, and accountability for racist incidents need to be in place in all schools. So, too, should compulsory education in the skills to deal with a multiethnic clientele for teachers, police personnel, social workers, and hospital staff. With few exceptions, these conditions do not prevail, despite supposed commitments to cross-cultural communication. Deterrence and communication skills, as necessary as they are, are no substitute for political literacy. It is this wider context of understanding racist behavior that is missing in most current attempts to fight an obvious evil. Instead of demonizing racism or espousing the moral superiority of the "unprejudiced," it is necessary to understand the need to adopt a racist mentality. Social conditions increasingly deprive people of the security and self-confidence that ward off the impulse to stigmatize others. With the decline of self-realization in a political economy where more and more people are declared superfluous, scapegoating and other artificial forms of self-realization increase.

Racism may manifest itself in individual psychology, but it also needs to be understood in relation to the social structure at large, in which character development is always embedded. In this deeper sense, successful antiracism is predicated upon societal transformation. An apolitical consumerism that prioritizes the private realm while denigrating the public sphere cannot grasp the political significance of racism, let alone envisage the alternative that would eliminate the need for racial stigmatization. In short, the best job educators can do to combat racism is to ensure global political literacy.

Such a global political literacy would be based on a sound education to provide a *historical* understanding of the nature of prejudice, discrimination, and racism. This historical knowledge would draw upon a *comparative* and *international* perspective, cosmopolitan in nature. The underlying questions would be: How do local specifics differ from discrimination elsewhere? Why do particular manifestations of inequality and exclusion develop the way they do? What role did the state, public compliance, and specific group interests play in allowing unique characteristics to unfold? Critical analytical skills constitute the motivating force to decode mythologies and demystify popular ideologies. Students are encouraged to question conventional wisdom and to develop analytical skills in distinguishing, for instance, apartheid from fascism, old from new forms of racism, as well as racial, cultural, and gender-based essentialisms. Racism as an explanatory concept itself becomes the focus of critical inquiry.

In the past, South African political education, if pursued at all seriously, has focused mainly on voter education around electoral procedures and processes. It has regurgitated the history of the liberation movement and celebrated heroes of the struggle. It has neglected critical analysis and moral education enabling citizens to arrive at mature and informed judgments in ethical predicaments. Mathebula (2009) argues in her unpublished doctoral thesis that the recently proposed compulsory citizenship education programs in South Africa fail to promote "active, critical and inquiring citizens. These value-based education documents promote obedience, if not unquestioning loyalty to the South African government" (p. 97). In Mathebula's view, "the goals of citizenship education in South Africa would be better served by cosmopolitan ideals, that is, preparing South African learners to act in a local, natural and global scale" (p. 97).

How education for active, participatory citizenship can transform a historical reality of inequality into a better life for liberated people has defied solutions thus far. Increasing evidence suggests that new, nonracial injustices are even harder to combat than the more overt, morally discredited, previous racial system.

Acknowledgment

Much of the analysis in this chapter draws upon a book that I coauthored with Heribert Adam (2015), *Imagined Liberation: Xenophobia, Citizenship and Identity in South Africa, Germany and Canada.* Copyright 2015 by Temple University Press, adapted with permission. This research was conducted during a Fellowship at the Stellenbosch Institute of Advanced Study (STIAS).

Notes

1. In apartheid South Africa, the term *non-White* was used to refer to African, Coloured, and Indian South Africans. In resisting this negative labeling, these groups' preferred, inclusive term was *Black,* to describe all three groups. In this chapter, the terms *African, Black,* and *Black South African* are used interchangeably to refer to South Africans with African ancestry. At the same time, it needs to be mentioned that many immigrants also refer to themselves as African because they originate from the continent.

2. For further reference to Ubuntu, see Praeg and Magadla, 2014.

References

Adam, H., & Moodley, K. (1993). *The negotiated revolution: Society and politics in post-apartheid South Africa.* Johannesburg, South Africa: Jonathan Ball.

Adam, H., & Moodley, K. (2015). *Imagined liberation: Xenophobia, citizenship and identity in South Africa, Germany and Canada.* Philadelphia: Temple University Press.

African National Congress. (1955). *The freedom charter.* Retrieved from http://www.anc.org.za/show.php?id=72

Balibar, E. (2002). *Politics and the other scene.* London: Verso.

Banks, J. A. (2015). Failed citizenship, civic engagement, and education. *Kappa Delta Pi Record, 51,* 151–154.

Biko, S. (1978). *I write what I like: Selected writings* (A. Stubbs, Ed.). London: Bowerdean.

Bonacich, E. (1972). A theory of ethnic antagonism: The split labor market. *American Sociological Review, 37*(5), 547–549.

Citizenship Foundation. (2012). *Political literacy explained*. Retrieved from http://www.citizenship-foundation.org.uk/ main/ page.php?12

Desai, A. (2008). Xenophobia and the place of the refugee in the rainbow nation of human rights. *African Sociological Review, 12*(2), 49–68.

Dlamini, J. (2009). *Native nostalgia*. Johannesburg, South Africa: Jacana Media.

Dodson, B. (2010). Locating xenophobia: Debate, discourse and everyday experience in Cape Town. *Africa Today, 56*(3), 4–22.

Du Toit, P., & Kotze, H. (2011). *Liberal democracy and peace in South Africa*. Johannesburg, South Africa: Palgrave Macmillan.

Everatt, D. (2011). Xenophobia, state and society in South Africa, 2008–2010. *Politikon, 38*(1), 7–36.

Fabricius, P. (2014, January 22). Report criticises SA for human rights shortcomings. *Cape Times*, p. 4.

Geschiere, P. (2009). *The perils of belonging: Autochthony, citizenship and exclusion in Africa and Europe*. Chicago: University of Chicago Press.

Habermas, J. (1992) *Staatsbürgerschaft und nationale Identität* [Citizenship and national identity]. Frankfurt, Germany: Suhrkamp.

Hassim, S., Twana, K., & Worby, E. (Eds.). (2008). *South Africa: Go home or die here. Violence, xenophobia and the reinvention of difference*. Johannesburg, South Africa: Wits University Press.

Helen Suzman Foundation. (2010, August 18). *Roundtable discussion on strangers and outsiders: Overcoming xenophobia*. Johannesburg. Retrieved from http://hsf.org.za/resource-centre/ roundtable-series

Hjerm, M. (2001). Education, xenophobia and nationalism: A comparative analysis. *Journal of Ethnic and Migration Studies, 27*(1), 37–60.

Jansen, J. (2010, July 14). Jonathan Jansen: I am a foreigner—to hatred. *Times LIVE*.

Kock, C. D. (2014). 2013/14 crime stats: How is the SAPS really doing? Retrieved from http://www.politicsweb.co.za/politics/201314-crime-stats-how-is-the-saps-really-doing

Lichtblau, K. (2000). Vergemeinschaftung und Vergesellschaftung bei Max Weber: Eine Reconstruction seines Sprachgebrauchs [Communitarisation and socialization in Max Weber: A reconstruction of his use of language]. *Zeitschrift für Soziologie* [Journal of Sociology], *29*(6), 423–443.

Mathebula, P. T. (2009). *Citizenship education in South Africa: A critique of post-apartheid citizenship education policy*. Unpublished doctoral thesis, University of Witwatersrand, Johannesburg.

Merton, R. K. (1995, December). The Thomas theorem and the Matthew effect. *Social Forces, 74*(2), 379–424.

Mngxitama, A. (2016, January 12). *Black people can't be racist, says Mngxitama*. Retrieved from http://www.enca.com/south-africa/justice-department-finalising-hate-crimes-legislation

Mzwakali, S. (2015, October 13). Black people can't be racist. *Pambazuka News*. Retrieved from http://www.pambazuka.org/governance/black-people-can%E2%80%99t-be-racist

Nevitt, L. (n.d.). . . . Rainbow nation? *Cape Town Magazine*. Retrieved from http://www.capetown-magazine.com/whats-the-deal-with/rainbow-nation/125_22_17853

Owen, K. (2012). The sound we hear. In *Under the baobab: Essays in honour of Stuart Saunders on his eightieth birthday: Africa Yearbook of Rhetoric, 2*(2), 47–60. Cape Town, South Africa: Africa Rhetoric.

Praeg, L., & Magadla, S. (Eds.). (2014). *Ubuntu: Curating the archive*. Pietermaritzburg, South Africa: University of KwaZulu-Natal Press.

Rex, J., & Mason, D. (Eds.). (1986). *Theories of race and ethnic relations*. Cambridge, UK: Cambridge University Press.

Robinson, D. (2014, November 20). *Justice Department follows the DA's lead on maintenance defaulters*. Retrieved from https://www.da.org.za/2014/11/justice-department-follows-das-lead -maintenance-defaulters/

Silber, G. (2012, August 17). Why Cape Town has erupted and what we can do about it. *Ground Up*. Retrieved from http://www.groundup.org.za/article/why-cape-town-has-erupted-and -what-we-can-do-about-it/

Soudien, C. (2012). *Realising the dream: Unlearning the logic of race in the South African school*. Pretoria, South Africa: Social Sciences and Humanities Research Council.

Soysal, Y. (1994). *Limits of citizenship: Migrants and postnational membership in Europe*. Chicago: University of Chicago Press.

Steinberg, J. (2014). *A man of good hope*. Johannesburg, South Africa: Jonathan Ball.

Suttner, R. (2015). Naming xenophobia, Retrieved from http://suttner76.rssing.com/browser. php?indx=31795902&item=84

Van den Berghe, P. L. (1981). *The ethnic phenomenon*. New York: Elsevier.

Vandeyar, S., & Vandeyar, T. (2015). *Immigrant student identities in South African schools*, Charlotte, NC: Information Age.

Waghid, Y., & Davids, N. (2013). *Citizenship, education and violence: On disrupted potentialities and becoming*. Rotterdam, Netherlands: Sense.

Weinstein, H. M., Freedman, S. W., & Hughson, H. (2007). School voices: Challenges facing education systems after identity-based conflicts. *Education, Citizenship and Social Justice, 2*(1), 41–71.

William, M. (Ed.). (1999). *African renaissance*. Cape Town, South Africa: Tafelberg.

Part 3

England, Norway, Germany, and France

Chapter 7

Citizenship Education, Inclusion, and Belonging in Europe: Rhetoric and Reality in England and Norway

AUDREY OSLER

University College of Southeast Norway and University of Leeds

European nations face three key challenges in the second decade of the 21st century in enabling the integration of minorities and the implementation of educational initiatives to support human rights and social justice. The first relates to the unprecedented number of refugees and migrants arriving in Europe, which means that the continent as a whole now faces the reality of "super-diversity" (Vertovec, 2007). Migrants are no longer connected primarily to former colonial territories, as they once were for certain nations (for example, France, The Netherlands, the United Kingdom), but are drawn from a much wider geographic range and include significant numbers moving from Eastern and Central Europe to Western Europe. This situation impels a Europe-wide review of social and political policy responses, in particular moving from seeing migrants as a problem to recognizing them as an asset, particularly in a region with an aging demographic.

The second challenge relates to public debates about diversity, integration, and multiculturalism in different European contexts, including the role of education in promoting national identity and citizenship, on the one hand, and solidarity between people within and beyond the nation, on the other. In these debates, Islam has been presented as the limiting case for multiculturalism (Osler, 2009). Public debates and anxieties are fueled by neoconservative and cultural conservative voices from within political and cultural elites. Such sources do not support the notion of a conspiracy to Islamize Europe, but their arguments are used by conspiracy theorists to justify their stance and sometimes violent actions (Feteke, 2012). Within this climate it is sometimes difficult to secure recognition of Islamophobia as a form of cultural racism, posing a threat to a secure, inclusive, and human rights–oriented Europe. The challenge of addressing multiculturalism and national identity in education is further complicated by political debate about the future of the European Union, provoked in part by the growing influence of far-right political parties in mainstream European politics and, since 2015, by the decision of the British Conservative government to hold a referendum on whether the United Kingdom should remain within the European Union.

Populist ideas caught the imagination of voters in the United Kingdom referendum campaign. The referendum was instituted by a prime minister who hoped to appease the right wing of his party, and who fully expected the electorate to vote "Remain." The campaign took place with a prevailing anti-European Union message—"Take back control"—and in a much longer-term period of press hostility to the European Union. The result, requiring only a simple majority to vote "Leave," was 48% voting to remain and 52% to leave.[1] Populist, xenophobic, and Islamophobic messages, initiated by the United Kingdom Independence Party, were prominent in the "Leave" campaign. Immigration reporting was extremely negative: There were constant stories about immigrants "sponging" off the welfare state, "bleeding" the National Health Service dry, and of criminality (Berry, 2016). It would seem that the effects of the 2008 financial crisis, coupled with the impact of government-imposed austerity measures, were effectively linked in the popular imagination to "them." The longer-term impact of the Brexit vote on the European Union and on the United Kingdom remains unclear, yet the election result triggered an increase in reported hate crimes in the United Kingdom, in which minoritized groups, and notably Muslims, were targeted. The fear is that far-right parties may win upcoming elections in France and Germany in 2017.

The third and emerging challenge relates to the securitization of education policy, which has led to educational initiatives addressing radicalization and the targeting of Europe's Muslim populations. This chapter considers the degree to which such policies may operate to undermine civic equality and efforts to address ongoing inequalities and discrimination.

Each of these challenges intersects with education policy, with both similar and contrasting outcomes in different European sociocultural contexts. This chapter examines the broader policy context and reflects on national policy initiatives in two jurisdictions: England and Norway. On an international scale measuring the effectiveness of integration policies for minorities in education, the United Kingdom ranks 11th out of 38 countries; this score is described as "halfway favourable" (Migration Integration Policy Index [MIPEX], 2015). The United Kingdom's history of immigration in the second half of the 20th century, coupled with struggles by minority communities for civic and legal equality, meant that at the time of the 2012 London Olympics, the nation was apparently proud to assert a multicultural identity. Yet this identity is expressed in rather different terms compared to nations such as the United States and Canada and may serve to mask what education policy researchers have identified as an increasingly assimilationist agenda (Gillborn, 2008; Law & Swann, 2011). In Norway, by contrast, education policy has consistently asserted and constructed a homogeneous nation, in which formal political equality and legal equality are emphasized and cultural differences are overlooked (Osler & Lybæk, 2014). The nation has a strong human rights architecture, with human rights stressed as a national characteristic (Osler, 2015). Norway is ranked fourth, "favourable," in terms of education policies for minority integration (MIPEX, 2015).[2]

England and Norway together present an interesting comparison and one that might deepen understandings of education for democratic citizenship and human rights and allow for pointers that might inform policy and practice in a wider European context. In their responses to refugees from beyond Europe; country-specific yet parallel debates about diversity, multiculturalism, and Islamophobia; and state policies aimed at procuring security, Norway and England together raise questions of crucial importance to human rights, social justice, and, indeed, Europe's future.

Nevertheless, education policy does not consist solely of formal statements, laws, or guidelines but includes the interpretation and application of such documents by teachers. For this reason, the next section presents the perspectives, motivations, and beliefs of an experienced teacher of citizenship. Following this, I examine education policies in each jurisdiction, first addressing diversity, national identity, and the social inclusion of minorities and then emerging securitization.

Veronica's Story

This section focuses on a teacher whom I call Veronica. My aim, as in previous life history research, is "to focus on the meanings which the teachers themselves attach to actions, events and choices in their lives and work" (Osler, 1997b, p. 55) and relate these to the teaching of citizenship. Veronica has worked as a teacher for 20 years and taught Citizenship for the last 13, having originally trained to teach English. By exploring her understandings of her role, I aim to highlight some fundamental issues concerning education for citizenship, focusing on *political efficacy* and the *realization of greater social justice.*

Although born in Britain, Veronica identifies as Ghanaian. The vast majority of teachers in state-funded schools in England are recorded as White British (88%), and a further 5.2% are from Irish and other White backgrounds (Department for Education [DFE], 2014). The next largest groupings are Indian (1.6%) and Black Caribbean (1.0%). Veronica is part of the remaining 4% (which includes a number of teachers of Pakistani and African descent).

I have consciously chosen to portray a teacher from a visible minority. I sought the perspective of someone who might reflect critically on questions at the intersection of education for citizenship and diversity by drawing on her *professional* and *lived* experiences. I anticipated that, as a woman of color working in a predominately White school with fast-changing demographics, she would have important insights into the education of diverse young people for citizenship, political efficacy, and social justice. In particular, I am interested in how teachers empower students from minoritized communities. At the time of the interview,[3] Veronica was studying part-time for a doctoral degree and was obliged to reflect on her professional practice, so I anticipated that this would inform our conversation.

The voices of teachers from minoritized groups are underrepresented in schools and in accounts of citizenship learning. Such teachers remain less likely to achieve senior positions in schools than their White British peers, with 93.9% of head teachers recorded as White British (5.9 percentage points higher than in the teaching force as a whole; DFE, 2014). White British people make up 80.5% of the total population of England and Wales. London is the most ethnically diverse area, with White residents making up 59.8% of the population (Office for National Statistics, 2012). This teacher portrait makes a small contribution to addressing the underrepresentation of minority voices, drawing attention to asymmetrical power relations in the wider society and education community.

Veronica is not presented as an exemplary teacher or in any way typical of teachers in Europe or in England or Norway—the two jurisdictions on which this chapter focuses. Despite this, her experiences are in some ways reflective of a wider community of citizenship teachers. In summer 2015, when I invited her to talk, she was working in a large secondary school in an outer East London borough. She was in her 50s and a mature entrant into teaching, having gained her teaching qualification in 1993, when she was in her mid-30s. The demographic profile of teachers across England is predominantly female: three out of four teachers in publicly funded schools are women. Teachers aged 50 and over make up 19.5% of all secondary school teachers (DFE, 2014).

I wish to explore the *political and moral responsibilities* of the teacher. It is perhaps a commonplace assumption that many teachers do not see their work as political. More, I posit, see teaching as a moral endeavor, subscribing to different degrees to "an ethic of care" (Noddings, 2013), particularly when engaging with justice and human rights. Life history and the individual's life experiences provide fertile material in enabling a deeper understanding of how teachers define professional responsibilities and ethics.

This teacher portrait aims to explore one teacher's influences and motivations in teaching for citizenship and social justice, by situating them within a *specific social, cultural, and historical context*. It is this context that shapes upbringing, career opportunities, values, and teaching practices. Veronica talked about her career and family, later sending me additional information by e-mail, to give, as she put it "a sense of the early influences on my life."[4] The complex ways in which she makes sense of her work shed fresh light on schooling for citizenship, inclusion, and belonging. With these factors in mind, I turn to her portrait.

School Environment

Over a decade, Veronica's school and neighborhood have seen substantial demographic change. The school originally served a predominately White British working-class community. While White British students remain the largest ethnic group, today's population is much more diverse, including students of Bangladeshi, Pakistani, sub-Saharan African, and Eastern and Central European heritage. While many are British-born, a growing number are themselves migrants. Around a quarter of the students speak English as an additional language, and around half are entitled to support through the "pupil premium," extra funds to improve the achievement of children considered educationally disadvantaged.[5]

Over one third (37%) of London residents are recorded as born overseas; the city is eighth worldwide in terms of nonnative residents, second in Europe only to Brussels (62%; International Organization for Migration, 2015). Like Toronto, Sydney, Los Angeles, and New York, London is recognized as a global gateway city (Çağlar, 2014). The suburban neighborhood where Veronica works has come to reflect the super-diversity that characterizes early 21st-century London as a global city, at the heart of the international economy (Sassen, 1991).

When I met Veronica, she was working as a head of department, responsible for Religious Education, Citizenship, and Personal, Social and Health Education (PSHE). She was one of the pioneering teachers to introduce citizenship education in 2002 when it became a statutory subject in secondary schools across England. Over the years her role has evolved. This is not surprising, since this curriculum innovation marked a significant change from previous practice. Many schools were obliged to recruit nonspecialists to take a lead, as trained specialists were newly qualified and in extremely short supply (Figueroa, 2004). As Veronica explained:

> When I was appointed head of Citizenship [at my current school], it was an external appointment, having been second in charge of Citizenship and PSHE at a previous school. And then I fell into this role. I was the first to introduce Citizenship/PSHE into the borough.

At the beginning, Veronica herself was a nonspecialist leading a volunteer team of nonspecialists.

Early Life and Education

Veronica draws heavily on her family heritage to explain her interest in citizenship. Early in our conversation she told me: "I'm very proud of being a Ghanaian—born here [in London] but brought up in Ghana." Her parents came to London as students in the late 1950s, and her father studied at the London School of Economics, where he strengthened his lifelong commitment to social justice. Before this he had been the head teacher of a small school in Ghana, while her mother had worked as a pupil-teacher.[6]

Veronica made frequent references to ways in which each parent had influenced her outlook, particularly in relation to politics and political engagement. Her father she describes as "curious about different cultures and lifestyles," encouraging his daughter to share this curiosity. About her mother, Veronica emphasized how she "always encouraged a thirst for learning. She would always say: 'An educated person is someone who has traveled the world and met different people.'"

Veronica left Britain as a small child in 1962, when her parents finished their studies and returned home "to be part of the new independent Ghana." Both parents stressed the importance of being aware of news and political developments. As a young girl, Veronica experienced the political upheaval of the 1966 coup when the army displaced Ghana's first president, Kwame Nkrumah. The family was living in Burma Camp, the Ghana armed forces headquarters, as Veronica's father was then a captain and education officer in charge of army schools in Accra. Although they were not directly involved in the coup, Veronica vividly recalls that day: "We were just going home from school, and we had to run home—a really frightening experience."

Veronica's mother has always emphasized the importance of listening to the news, so that her children are conversant with local, national, and world affairs. To underline the importance of this message, she would tell her children, "You've got to know when you've got to run," reminding them of the political ferment they experienced as young children. As an old lady, she continues to keep in touch with current events. Veronica explained:

> She lives in Ghana but still rings us to tell us what is happening here in the U.K. and the U.S., and if we haven't heard about an event, we are reminded of the importance

to keep abreast with news events! If you were to ask anyone who knows her what she constantly listens to or reads, apart from her Bible, they will tell you her radio and newspapers. These days she says that she is not reading as much, but she always gets us to get her portable radio sets. Our constant discussions about current affairs as a family had a great influence on my life as a child and in the subjects that I studied. Growing up, I was very aware of both mum and dad being instrumental in ensuring that they financially supported relatives who could not [otherwise] afford their secondary education. They instilled in us the importance of education and said that it was the one thing that no one could ever take away from us.

From early childhood Veronica's parents stressed the importance of education, as well as political awareness and moral responsibility. Supporting others to continue their schooling reflects a family practice of an "ethic of care" (Noddings, 2013).

An Economic Migrant

One reason that Veronica is able to empathize with many of her students is her early childhood experiences in Ghana and, perhaps equally significantly, her experiences of migration in search of work as a young adult, first to Nigeria and then the United Kingdom. She graduated from the University of Ghana in 1981 and, as the result of economic uncertainty and limited graduate opportunities, soon felt the need to seek employment abroad: "Between 1982 and 1984, I lived in Nigeria for almost two years with my husband, at a time when so many Ghanaian graduates migrated to Nigeria, which at the time was booming." The couple eventually decided to leave the region and try their luck in the United Kingdom. This was an opportunity to secure a comfortable future and for Veronica to further her education, but it presented some emotional challenges in that the Ghanaian authorities required her to give up Ghanaian citizenship upon settling in the United Kingdom. Veronica explains:

> One reason I came back to the U.K. in 1984 with my husband was because of the poor economic situation in Ghana. I took advantage of the fact that, because I had been born here and was therefore a British citizen, it was "easier" for us to come back to the U.K. I had to relinquish my Ghanaian citizenship because we were not allowed dual citizenship during Rawlings's time. We now can have dual citizenship. I always say that I am Ghanaian.

For Veronica, the concept of flexible citizenship (Ong, 1999) and citizenship education that fosters flexible and multiple identities in education (Mitchell & Parker, 2008; Osler, 2011b) is not innovative but commonplace, rooted in her life experience.

Once settled in London, Veronica eventually found work in a bank and later worked for a teachers' union. Four years after arriving in London she had completed a diploma for personal assistants, but her experience of working for the union convinced her that she wished to train as a teacher because, as she put it, "I wanted to make a difference to young people's lives. I still do!" So in 1993 she completed her postgraduate teaching qualification in

English, following this in 1997 with an MA in educational management, in the expectation that this might progress her career: "I thought that the more educational qualifications I had, the chances of getting senior positions would be easier—a very sub-Sahara African perspective about the link between educational qualifications and a 'good' job." In fact, this assumption about the link between educational qualifications and career progression is not confined to U.K. teachers from the sub-Saharan region. Many U.K. teachers from minoritized groups believe that they will be better positioned in the job market if they improve their formal qualifications, with a number suggesting that to succeed, they need to be "better than" their White colleagues in both skills and qualifications. Somewhat problematic is the channeling of minoritized teachers away from mainstream education, into specific fields of employment associated with the management of minoritized students (Ghuman, 1995; Osler, 1997a, 1997b). This means that mainstream White students are less likely to encounter teachers like Veronica, who bring transnational and peripheral experiences to the mainstream.

Yet Veronica does not simply draw on her past to shape her approaches to teaching. She also draws on her experience of parenting, conscious that her children's experiences, and those of her students, can inform her practice. She believes that she can learn from young people, in an ongoing process of self-development as a teacher and citizen.

Motherhood, Schooling, and Racism

In discussing teaching, Veronica made frequent references to her role as a daughter and mother and to the challenges of bringing up two sons in Britain, seeking to reconcile their experiences of growing up in London with events and values that shaped her early life in Ghana. As she put it: "Family experience, experience with my own sons, influences how I do things in school." Veronica explained that when meeting new students entering secondary school (Year 7),[7] she shares her experiences and tells them about her family background:

> It breaks down barriers. With Year 7 I tell them where I come from and how I'm interested in them. I let them know that I don't know everything. I am telling a lot about me, but I can still be a professional. I want them to connect with "Miss"—they do ask. I tell them my parents were like that, that they were interested in people and ready to learn from different people and cultures.

She explained how this connection and what Noddings (2013) has characterized as an "ethic of care" create a constructive learning environment, not detracting from professional duties but enhancing them. When encountering students who do not respond, Veronica sometimes seeks her sons' advice, both as older teens and as young adults:

> This young White boy, cheeky chappie,[8] was always disrupting class. I'm quite friendly to students, but I am a disciplinarian, I would send him out. Sometimes, I ask my sons for advice. One day I was having no success and thinking, What is good for the child? My son said, "Look at him as an individual and find out what he likes." I noticed his clothes weren't clean. One day, I found him with his head on the table.

I asked, "Are you all right?" He had his head on the table. He was surprised: "I haven't eaten." I thought, No wonder you can't work. I gave him something to eat, and then I encouraged the children to share what they had with each other.

Recognizing the negative impact of poverty on educational achievement (Blanden & Gregg, 2004), Veronica's solution extends beyond the pedagogical, finding a concrete caring solution to an immediate problem—a child's hunger. But this connection leads to a further pedagogical step, consistent with the human rights orientation of Veronica's classroom, namely, supporting and enabling students, many of whom are also encountering poverty and hardship, to express everyday solidarity by sharing food.

Veronica explained that, for her, "often the most challenging students are White working-class British boys, in Year 8." Since she focused on boys, I asked whether they took up a disproportionate amount of her time. She responded:

Girls at our school, girls see me as a role model—they are glad they have got a Black teacher, someone they can aspire to. I tell them I am still studying, they know, young Black girls see their mother as role models. They say, This boy is not going about this the right way. They know that the only way to get out of poverty is to be educated. But nevertheless, they know that you still meet these challenges because of their color. Girls are generally very focused.

By contrast, Veronica was concerned that young Black British boys, including her sons, risk fulfilling negative societal expectations: "I have some really articulate young Black boys. [Yet] there are times when I see a Black boy just fulfilling a stereotype. You need to give support, to back them in what they *can* do." One of Veronica's greatest challenges was supporting boys and young men who were responding to perceived racism:

One of the things I always say to my sons, I won't give them the platform to [simply] say, "It is racism." I ask: "Are you sure? What did you do?" If I find out the teacher is still giving aggravation, then I will go in [to school] and talk about it. I don't want them to say, "I can't do this because I'm Black." I don't want them to feel they can't achieve because of racism.

Nevertheless, Veronica acknowledged that in seeking to instill the belief that racism can be surmounted, she had underestimated the difficulties that young Black people educated in Britain, particularly young Black men, face (Law, Finney, & Swann, 2014). Her Ghanaian upbringing protected her from this injustice, and now that her sons are young adults, she has come to realize, in conversation with others, that she has perhaps on occasion been somewhat naïve. She recognizes that in Britain the issue of negative expectations and negative stereotypes can weigh heavily on young Black boys.

Although she tried to present her sons as role models to certain students, she spoke of the tension between encouraging young people (her sons and her students) and the hostile climate in which they were growing up and being schooled: "I've got two sons, and

I use them [as examples to my students], as young Black men—both are educated, went to university. But the issue of [low] expectations that they have here [in Britain]. . . ." Veronica went on to describe an incident at her younger son's school:

> He has never restricted his friendships to young Black boys, but the school had an issue they were investigating, and the police brought all the young Black boys together; and my son had been with his White friends, and they [his friends] said he was with them and asked: "Why are you bringing all the Black students together to be interviewed?" The police were called, and the police came into school, and the teachers—what shocked me was that the teachers didn't say, "Stop, don't segregate by color!" It made him [my son] angry—he could have gone the other way. . . . I had to say: "What would your grandpa have wanted you to do? Not come down to their level. Enunciate your rights. You know your rights." Now they are older, I've stopped worrying.

After this experience, Veronica came to recognize that teachers, instead of protecting students from disadvantage and discrimination, may uphold and maintain prevailing discriminatory attitudes by failing to speak out.[9] She saw how such events might alienate students.

Despite her claim that she had "stopped worrying," Veronica expressed further anxieties about what could happen to her sons away from home. She stressed that, as young Black men, they had to "know where not to go." The same son had attended a barbeque in Romford. When he came home and reported, "We've just been chased by White kids" upon leaving the party, she warned him "not to go to that area again." Romford town center was the scene of a notorious racially aggravated knife attack by seven men on two teenagers in 2002, in which one, Darren Bagalo, suffered near-fatal stab wounds (Branigan, 2003). The attack was in a number of ways reminiscent of the murder of Stephen Lawrence in 1993. Lawrence's murder eventually led to the setting up of the Macpherson Inquiry, which concluded that institutional racism not only had severely hampered the police investigation but extended beyond into all areas of British public life (Macpherson, 1999). In the Bagalo case, one of the gang avoided capture and imprisonment until 2012 ("Man jailed for 2002 racially aggravated attack," 2012), so the crime, and the fear it created, must have resonated locally when Veronica's children were growing up.

Veronica told another story of her older son's encounter with the police, soon after he bought a car:

> He doesn't drink, he likes dancing. A police officer stopped him and asked him to step out, checked his papers, his insurance, and breathalyzed him. He wasn't speeding, he just had a flashy car and he's a young Black man! He was breathalyzed; the officer found no trace of alcohol. So he breathalyzed him a second time. Ebo didn't get angry—you know the statistics. So instead of fulfilling stereotypes, [remember] you're not a Black boy, you are just you.

As the earlier story of police officers intervening in a school incident illustrates, both Veronica's sons have faced police officers in highly racialized contexts and have been stopped and questioned without due cause. These events, together with other life experiences, have led Veronica to reassess the earlier approach she had adopted as a mother of young children and more readily recognize "everyday racism" (Essed, 1991). On this issue, Veronica explicitly acknowledges learning from her children's experiences:

> My sons, they've given me a different perspective. My son, coming from the library, the *library*, he was stopped—you know the figures about stop and search. . . . Now I've been living in England for a longer time—there are lots of incidents at my level. I have this friend; she came from the West Indies when she was 13. She'd say I was in denial. Lots of things she said [about racism and inequalities in British society] were true.

Veronica went on to observe that many Black teachers in London are employed as substitute teachers and take on a particularly challenging task, working with little job security and sometimes struggling to secure students' respect. She recalled one of these teachers telling her: "Do you know that you get more respect because of your [London] accent? Because I've got an African accent they don't listen."

Veronica sees one of her responsibilities as a teacher to equip all students, and specifically students from marginalized and minoritized groups, to achieve a greater feeling of inclusion and belonging. For her, citizenship learning is essentially about participation. Like other teachers from minoritized backgrounds, she built upon her life experiences when thinking about how she should achieve this goal. In a sense, her professional practice is founded as much on lived experience as it is on formal education or training. She has developed a specific *political consciousness*, or what Freire (1973/2002) refers to as "critical consciousness," responding as an educator, to a greater or lesser degree, to the specific economic, social, cultural, and political context in which she finds herself. One respondent in a previous study of the life histories of Black professionals in education, working as a senior school inspector responsible for multicultural education, felt that he had achieved career seniority largely through developing a political consciousness directly related to his life experiences:

> None of it [my expertise] is in the area in which I would say I am academically quali-fied. . . . [I]t is by virtue of my racial experience and cultural experience more than my formal study. My credibility is built on my capacity to articulate and analyse who I am. (Ken, in Osler, 1997b, p. 135)

Veronica, having trained as an English teacher, was educating her students for citizenship and taking a Citizenship leadership role by drawing on her life experiences, particularly on her experiences as a mother of two Black boys rather than her formal training. She sought to support both her own children and her students in knowing and claiming their rights. As she stated: "I always enjoy teaching citizenship and the human rights aspect. It's one of those subjects where you can discuss on a range of levels." Effectively, she recognized both a political and a moral or caring dimension to her professional role as well as to her role as a mother.

Practicing Citizenship Education in and Beyond the Classroom

In autumn 2015, a few weeks after my conversation with Veronica, secondary schools across England were obliged to begin the process of introducing the English Baccalaureate (EBacc). This award requires students to secure pass grades on the examinations called the General Certificate of Secondary Education (GCSE) taken at age 16 in five core subjects: English, mathematics, a science, a foreign language, and either history or geography. Students who began secondary school in September 2015 will be required to secure a pass grade in all five areas in order to gain the EBacc award when they take their GCSE examinations in 2020 (DFE, 2015). This development implies a downgrading of the Citizenship GCSE, since many students who might otherwise have elected to study citizenship in Years 10 and 11 may be obliged to focus on reaching the required level in the core subjects.

Veronica explained how her school, under pressure from school inspectors to demonstrate improved standards, had further reduced opportunities for students to study Citizenship at the same time as official policy undermined the standing of this area of learning:

> I'm not just interested in [teaching] class, but active citizenship, student voice, and a project Question Time, which I organized at borough level. It involved public debating, and . . . it gave the school a high profile. But it's been marginalized—both by the EBacc and by the curriculum [being] swept aside, shoving children aside. I enjoyed the political aspects, [developing] political literacy. We entered everyone for GCSE [examinations] in Citizenship. The results, they were good. . . . Sixty percent passed, but compared with other subjects, for example, Sociology, which was an option [elective], the hierarchy [school leadership] thought these results were not good.

Consequently, at Veronica's school, Citizenship, which had previously been taken by all students as an examination course, became an elective, taken by a minority of students, with reduced timetable hours.

A further policy change is that GCSE coursework has been reduced in favor of final examinations. All coursework that takes place is now "controlled assessment," that is to say, written up and completed under timed conditions in class. From Veronica's perspective, this means that individual initiative and creativity is denied her students in their project work:

> With citizenship at GCSE, you [now] have to do controlled assessment. It's a move away from course work; students could [originally] do some project which was 60% of the GCSE criteria. With controlled assessment, it is still course work, but with a prescribed time for the write-up, in the teacher's presence. It's very prescribed.

For her, these developments not only imply denial of the active learning methods she advocates but also reduce opportunities for education for human rights and social justice (United Nations, 2011) beyond the classroom, since students cannot pursue a theme about which they care but, rather, are required by hard-pressed teachers to opt as a class to explore the same topic:

> Most teachers, they want to get the whole class to do one project. If your literacy skills [are poor,] . . . then you do badly. It's really now just a judgment of their literacy skills. I'm interested in political literacy, voting, children's rights. . . .

Veronica feels constrained by government-promoted "outcomes-based learning," which she believes restricts student-led learning:

> I don't believe in what the government is doing. I don't think it is right at all. I have very high expectations of the students, and I've been doing negotiated learning . . . in an ethnically, culturally, and linguistically diverse school.

The new curriculum guidelines, which emphasize standards, are, for Veronica, a denial both of student diversity and of student interests.

Two topics that Veronica feels are particularly interesting and relevant to students at her school are child rights and refugees. She believes that learning about the U.N. Convention on the Rights of the Child (CRC; United Nations, 1989) "was especially beneficial to kids from minority ethnic groups—we have a lot from sub-Saharan Africa." She noted that students made observations such as: "Oh Miss, my mum needs to know . . . we have a right to privacy." Veronica stressed the importance of young people knowing their rights but claiming them without undermining their parents. She argued: "You've got to be aware of the [home] context. I was very aware . . . of the need for them to contextualize the CRC."

Likewise, Veronica argued that the topic of refugees was particularly important for students who remain predominantly White British working class, for whom terms such as *refugee* and *asylum-seeker* may carry negative connotations, largely due to the way in which such groups are portrayed in sections of the popular press. Veronica explained:

> Even though I am Black they [White British students] would still talk about refugees in a critical way. [Consequently,] [s]ome of the students, they wouldn't necessarily say they were refugees, but economic immigrants. I would explain why there are refugees, using Jill Rutter's work.[10] I would use Refugee Week [as a vehicle to introduce the topic of refugees and asylum-seekers to students].

Veronica's observation that "even though I am Black" she encounters students' hostile views about refugees relates to a widespread confusion in the United Kingdom concerning everyday usage of the terms *refugee*, *asylum-seeker*, and *migrant*. These terms are sometimes used synonymously and applied generally to persons of color. Veronica had anticipated (wrongly as it turns out) that students would avoid repeating commonly used negative media stereotypes about refugees (Rutter, 2005) in the presence of a Black teacher because they were familiar with the word *refugee* used as a racist slur. Veronica gave the example of a White British student who, after he had had a chance to study the subject and learned about the migration experiences of his peers, explained that he had not meant to express antagonism to classmates. She concluded: "Definitely citizenship is related to community cohesion."[11]

One further way in which Veronica sought to involve the whole school in celebrating diversity was through "multicultural events" such as an annual fashion show, which were popular among students and their families and which brought good local press coverage. She noted, "I love entertainment," and she wanted students to take responsibility for the organization of the event and have fun. However, Veronica was upset that the school had redesigned the show, making it more professional, with students having to audition. She observed: "It's not a talent show! I went along with it. But the kids were very disappointed; it's normally in July—they start talking about it from January. It's now very structured. But I still insisted the kids lead."

Finally, Veronica reflected on her responsibility for meeting the needs of students from specific communities, giving, first, the example of students of African heritage:

> I work with young people in Year 10 on the Speak Out Challenge.[12] There are lots of kids of African heritage, and I want them to learn, to be politically aware, and to develop skills. And so, I use Martin Luther King as a role model and draw on his oratory.

Veronica draws this particular group of students into the competition and into developing such skills by choosing an individual (Martin Luther King, Jr.) and subject matter (racial justice) from which she hopes they will draw inspiration.

Veronica is also conscious of the growing phenomenon of Islamophobia (Halliday, 1999) and its impact on students. She described how some students who wore hijabs had been subject to abuse from adult drivers while traveling to school. She had consequently decided to include Islam within the Religious Education curriculum. Religious education content is determined at a local level, and in the area where Veronica worked there was a provision that Christianity and one other world religion be included. But Veronica remained concerned about the government's Prevent agenda, designed to safeguard young people from radicalization and extremism.[13] She felt that police officers who were working with schools to tackle terrorism and extremism were "dealing with it the wrong way. . . . You can't just talk at kids. The best way is through citizenship education, but it's being manipulated and downgraded." Moreover, she was highly critical of the role of school inspectors:

> [Concerning] radicalization, OFSTED [Office for Standards in Education, Children's Services and Skills] are just ticking boxes. Citizenship education, where real discussion is possible, has become the most marginalized subject, and not just at our school. [Anti][r]adicalization education is not [treated as] a school-level thing, it's seen as

an issue of child protection. Whereas in A level Sociology [an examination course taken at age 16+] there is an opportunity to examine globalization, terrorism, and also immediate questions like stop and search. I'm able to say, in relation to what is going on now [referring to the Prevent agenda], how ridiculous.

Finally, Veronica identified a language hierarchy among students. She observed that, generally speaking, students from Central and Eastern Europe were proud of their home languages, whereas African students often refused to acknowledge or use their home languages at school. She commented:

> I rarely make assumptions about them—we've got children who are EAL [English as an Additional Language] in low-ability groups because of language. For example, there's a student right now from Afghanistan in a SEN [special educational needs] group who I am sure is misplaced.

Here Veronica is referring to a student placement in a "low-ability" track and the labeling of that student as "special needs," referring to an unspecified learning difficulty. The student in question actually needs an environment in which students' multilingualism is recognized and built on (Kenner & Hickey, 2008).

Veronica's observations on citizenship learning, student participation, and political efficacy, as they relate to her own teaching, school practices, and national policy developments, are wide-ranging. To conclude this portrait I reflect on her orientation to teaching for social justice, drawing on a model from earlier life history research.

To Challenge or Transform?

In previous research on British teachers' lives and careers (Osler, 1994, 1997a, 1997b, 1999), I examined the life histories of 48 individuals of Caribbean and South Asian heritage.[14] From this study, undertaken when Veronica was embarking on her teaching career, I proposed a model of six orientations to schooling: rejecting, conforming, reforming, affirming, challenging, and transforming (Osler, 1997b, pp. 192–193). I draw on this model to discuss Veronica's approach to her professional role and her understandings of citizenship teaching and learning.

Of these orientations, Veronica appears to operate broadly within two: *challenging* and *transforming*. Within a *challenging* orientation, she diagnoses that Black and minority students are highlighting inequalities in the education system. These inequalities are not confined to one ethnic group, although she sees male students as particularly vulnerable to inequitable treatment and likely to protest directly. She responds by encouraging collaboration between students and teacher, and between students, through cooperative group work and attempts to promote solidarity between students. She uses her curriculum leadership role to challenge some management decisions, encouraging the school community to be self-critical, although she is a pragmatist and goes along with some things. At the same time, she occasionally adopts a *reforming* stance, as when she acts as a role model to young Black women, without necessarily looking deeper into their educational needs and the skills and support they may later need to address injustice and inequality, for example, in the labor market.

A *transforming* orientation diagnoses the problem as one of injustice and racism, including deeply ingrained structures and attitudes inherited from the past. Earlier in her career, and when she was new to the United Kingdom, Veronica avoided a transforming orientation. Yet then, as now, she adopted a vision of human experience based on human rights principles, compatible with a transforming orientation.

Her upbringing and her parents' ideals encourage Veronica to value diversity and hybridity. Similarly, her experiences of migration and a transnational lifestyle encourage her to promote multiple identities and include multiple perspectives. She leans toward a transforming orientation in her commitment to the empowerment of all students and their engagement in decision making.

Perhaps one of the greatest hindrances facing Veronica in adopting a transforming perspective is her slow recognition of the extent of racism in the United Kingdom and the ways in which it acts as a barrier to full participation, even among highly motivated students. However, it is her lived experience, and particularly that as a mother bringing up two Black sons in an institutionally racist society, that has caused her to rethink. Veronica's continued energy and her critical approach to her own self-development appear to have supported her in moving more fully toward a transforming orientation as her career develops.

Citizenship Education Policy in England

As Veronica's account suggests, despite the introduction of citizenship education as a statutory subject in secondary schools in England in 2002, many gains made from this time appear to have been lost. This section considers why teachers such as Veronica might then have been hopeful as to the opening up of new possibilities for political literacy and the inclusion of minorities through education. It examines policy developments over the past 15 years, giving attention to social inclusion and students' political efficacy, the needs of visible minorities, and the education of all students for a society characterized by diversity.

Social Cohesion and the Alleged Migrant Threat

Official justifications for citizenship education supported a climate in which migrants and minorities could be blamed for societal problems by presenting a deficit model of these groups. The foundational document, the Crick report (Qualifications and Curriculum Authority, 1998), followed this trend, implying, for example, that minorities were a constituency more likely to flout national laws and conventions (Osler, 2000). The Crick report failed to recognize gender differences or discuss unity and diversity in a multicultural democracy. Instead it stressed unity or cohesion (Osler, 2005, 2011a). The new school Citizenship curriculum was introduced in the wake of disturbances in certain northern towns, which a government-commissioned review blamed on minorities' lack of integration (Cantle, 2001).

In his review of citizenship education policy developments in England at the turn of the century, Figueroa (2004) lent weight to the thesis that the official multiculturalism of this period was somewhat cynical. He noted that citizenship education was promoted to support a Labour government policy of "community cohesion," introducing an oath of allegiance and provisions for testing knowledge of life in the United Kingdom and English, Welsh, or Scottish Gaelic language skills, provisions that were implemented from November 2005. Minority communities were seen as a threat to community cohesion and in particular need of citizenship education. The Green Paper that followed introduced new and problematic terms for aspirant citizens, including *earned citizenship* and *probationary citizenship* (Home Office, 2008). A focus on "our values" implied distinct and superior British values separately positioned from those recognized by the international community and founded on shared human rights principles. Citizenship thus became conditional, something that can be withheld. Indeed, the message is that to achieve social cohesion, those seeking naturalization need to pass a number of tests of their commitment, tests not applied to citizens by birth (Osler, 2009). As Figueroa (2004) observed, there was, in fact, no evidence that a lack of English language skills or of loyalty to the United Kingdom was responsible for riots in northern towns in 2001, any more than such factors might lead to terrorism. Instead he observed that "social and economic deprivation, discrimination, Islamophobia, resentment between White and Asian communities, and activity by the far right all seem likely contributing factors" (p. 222).

Nevertheless, the Crick report was embraced by scholars and teachers who, like Veronica, hoped that Citizenship would create a curriculum space in which political literacy might be developed. This reform was the first effective attempt to enable political literacy and efficacy through the curriculum in the post–World War II era. The new curriculum enabled social science graduates to follow professional courses in education. Until the introduction of Citizenship as a subject in 2002, such graduates had been ineligible for teacher training since their subject knowledge was not deemed relevant. It is this social science knowledge that Veronica sees as benefiting students, helping them to understand social realities, and enhancing community cohesion. For many teachers working for racial justice, citizenship education is not about disciplining minorities, as some official curriculum statements imply, but a means through which all students might learn to live together.

National Identity and the Other

Despite a deficit view of minorities in official citizenship discourses, it was not until after the July 7, 2005, London suicide bombings that there was significant political leadership in favor of teaching about diversity as an aspect of citizenship learning in English schools. The resultant government-commissioned Ajegbo report (Department for Education and Skills, 2007) proposed that the Citizenship curriculum should include a strand on "Identity and Diversity: Living Together in the UK" (p. 97). This development came directly from official concerns about terrorism and a desire to promote Britishness, shared values, and patriotism through the teaching of citizenship and history (Osler, 2008, 2009a, 2009b).

Following Ajegbo, a second version of the Citizenship curriculum, enacted from 2009, reasserted the role of history in promoting national identity and cohesion and making learners familiar with British values and culture. In this respect it drew directly from Crick, assuming that minorities need to learn how "we" behave and understand "our" (apparently singular) way of doing things (Osler, 2011a). Integration was presented as a one-way process, reflecting the official government understanding of integration (Department for Communities and Local Government, 2008), which might more accurately be characterized as assimilation.

The revised curriculum was built on an approach advocated by then–prime minister Gordon Brown, emphasizing Britishness and British history. Brown (2006) stressed a loss of national confidence coinciding with the end of empire and argued for a new emphasis on patriotism:

> To address almost every one of the major challenges facing our country—[including], of course, our community relations and multiculturalism and, since July 7th, the balance between diversity and integration; even the shape of our public services—you must have a clear view of what being British means, what you value about being British and what gives us purpose as a nation.

Although Brown did not present cosmopolitanism and patriotism as incompatible, he echoed concerns about "diversity and integration," linking these to terrorism. His vision addressed local and global dimensions, but these aspects vanished when he focused on schools. He argued that British history, presented as a grand narrative progressing to liberty and democracy, be central to citizenship education. His political rhetoric overlooked the realities of 21st-century U.K. history education, with its emphasis on critical thinking. Instead, his model of school history emphasized national cohesion (Osler, 2009, 2011a). Seven years after the introduction of the Citizenship curriculum, the framework appeared to be shrinking, with history education proposed as a means of teaching about national identity and "Britishness."

But in 2010, following a general election, a new Conservative-led coalition government announced that it wished to review the entire national curriculum. The 2014 national curriculum retains a Citizenship program of study in secondary schools, with aims and attainment targets that all local authority-maintained schools are obliged to follow. However, various governments have, since 2000, followed a policy of promoting schools known as academies, which are free from local authority control and not obliged to follow this curriculum. The government advocates academies as a means of improving standards.[15] The number of academies has increased rapidly, so that by 2012 a third of all secondary schools were designated academies (Gorard, 2014).[16]

Furthermore, the aims of the Citizenship curriculum have changed significantly. The purpose of Citizenship is to

> foster pupils' keen awareness and understanding of democracy, government and how laws are made and upheld. Teaching should equip pupils with the skills and knowledge to explore political and social issues critically, to weigh evidence, debate and make reasoned arguments. It should also prepare pupils to take their place in society as responsible citizens, manage their money well and make sound financial decisions. (DFE, 2013)

In this, democracy is interpreted as a system of government, with little weight given to citizen participation. The emphasis is on "responsible citizens" rather than citizens' rights. Money management takes on a prominent role. Many of the gains in citizenship education, related to learning to live together in a society characterized by diversity and founded in human rights, have disappeared from official discourse. The potential of citizenship education, introduced in 2002, to contribute to strengthening young people's political efficacy and empowering students, particularly those from minoritized groups, has not been realized. As Veronica observes, there is a shrinking space for Citizenship in schools in England, and the subject has largely fallen off the agenda of all but the most committed schools.

Learning for Democracy in Norway

Democracy and Diversity

In contrast to England, Norway, like other Scandinavian countries, has a strong tradition of democracy education. Education is concerned with democratic skills for living together, and the emphasis is on *processes* more than content. Important among these processes is consensus-building.

Over 30 years, Norway has seen substantial and fast demographic change: between 1995 and 2001 the number of immigrants and their descendants grew significantly (Eriksen, 2013). Within a total population of 5 million there are around 848,200 migrants and children born to migrant parents (16.3%; Statistics Norway, 2016). In Oslo, migrants and their children constitute 33% of the population.

In the face of diversity and growing global complexity, Norwegian education policy reasserts the importance of a singular national identity as a means by which loyalty to the nation is realized. National identity is understood as founded in a common history, language, and culture. A study of documents from 1994 to 2008 constituting the legal curriculum framework confirms that adherence to "Christian and humanist" values remains a central policy goal (Osler & Lybæk, 2014). The curriculum emphasizes the national canon and subject knowledge judged as essential in building a common national identity. Some documents seem more concerned with establishing an educational framework that preserves children's right to participation than with what students should learn or how they will experience participation, equality, and justice.

Although diversity is recognized as a prerequisite for democracy (Banks et al., 2005; Osler, 2012; Parker, 2003), there is evidence that Norwegian teachers do not necessarily feel confident in preparing students for living in a multicultural society, having lacked this focus in their professional training (Vedvik, 2011). Minority students report racism and discrimination at school (Øia & Vestel, 2006). There is also evidence to suggest that teachers may hold a deficit view of minority students, assuming that they need more help than their White peers in understanding democracy (Biseth, 2011).

Norway has a long history of institutional and state discrimination against the Sami and national minorities. Research on young people's knowledge of Sami history suggests that the curriculum fails to meet learners' entitlements under the CRC (Lile, 2011; Vedvik, 2011). Osler and Lybæk (2014) have reported that before 2013, subject curricula were silent with regard to issues of past discrimination toward indigenous people. A new learning outcome requires students to be able to outline Sami history; consider the consequences of the Norwegianification from the mid-19th century to the present day; and study the Sami struggle for rights. (p. 558)

Despite this amendment, there is a continuing curriculum silence concerning the 1942 deportation of Jewish Norwegians and their murder at Auschwitz and anti-Semitism today (Osler & Lybæk, 2014). Failure to address the recent past, fully recognize past diversity and discrimination, and properly address inequalities persisting in today's multicultural society constitutes a miseducation of today's students, from both minority and mainstream populations. One difficulty concerns a reluctance to address race and racism within the social science and education research (Bangstad, 2015; Lindquist & Osler, 2016; Osler, 2015). A constructed myth of national homogeneity serves to silence multiperspectivity and denies full recognition of diversity in schools.

A Human Rights Education Paradox

In Norway, as across the Nordic societies, a commitment to human rights is seen as part of national identity. These societies are frequently characterized as deeply democratic and homogeneous, following a model whereby differences are resolved through consensus. Intuitively, we might expect nations where human rights are closely associated with national identity to be ideal places for human rights education (HRE). Norway is widely recognized as having a strong human rights architecture. Yet Langford and Schaffer (2015) have referred to the "Nordic human rights paradox" (p. 1) whereby the Nordic countries take pride in promoting human rights abroad while policymakers are increasingly opposed to the expansion and application of international human rights mechanisms at home, citing practices such as the extradition of foreign nationals to countries where they risk torture, restrictions on immigrants, and the criminalization of homelessness.

In education and research, the Nordic countries cooperate politically through the Nordic Council of Ministers. The objective of regional cooperation in the field of children and youth is to create "the right to good living conditions" and to improve children's and young people's opportunities for influence. Explicitly, these "should be promoted for all children and young people on equal terms, regardless of gender, ethnic, cultural or socio-economic background, age domicile, sexual orientation and disability. *This work is based on a rights-based perspective* " (Nordic Council of Minsiters, 2010, p. 7; my emphasis). In the case of Norway and Denmark, this rhetoric, which attaches significance both to school democracy (learner participation) and to the foundational importance of human rights, is apparently not well matched by HRE *content*, in either the school curriculum or teacher education. There are no national data available for Norwegian schools, but a 2012 study in neighboring Denmark, by the Danish Institute for Human Rights, found that only one in four teachers agreed with the statement "In Denmark, human rights are so universal that it is not a topic I need to give special attention to in my teaching." Most teachers recognized that explicit human rights teaching was essential but reported that their own teaching was "indirect" or "implicit." They tended to address human rights spontaneously or as a dimension of another topic, often without mentioning "human rights" or "rights" (Decara, 2013). As in Norway, there is no substantial practical guidance on human rights teaching. The study concluded that although respect for human rights is central to all democratic societies, HRE has a weak status within Danish schools. The Danish Institute for Human Rights recommends that what is needed to guarantee a healthy democracy is a national action plan for HRE that includes professional support for teachers.

The revised 2014 Norwegian constitution makes human rights education a *constitutional* entitlement (Osler, 2014), proclaiming that "education shall promote respect for democracy, the rule of law and human rights." There is no parallel Norwegian HRE study, but qualitative research with high school teachers found that where human rights education was taking place, it tended to focus more or less exclusively on human rights problems internationally, rather than at home (Vesterdal, 2016). Teachers focused on violations rather than on human rights as principles for living together, judging violations within Norway to be insignificant in relation to those encountered in other countries and, therefore, of little interest.

Within Norwegian teacher education different institutions are free to give greater emphasis to diversity and human rights, so that, for example, at the University College of Southeast Norway, Drammen campus, there is a specific focus on intercultural education.[17] Nevertheless, there appears to be a tendency in Norway to treat "democracy" and "human rights" as interchangeable concepts in everyday discourse. Consequently, human rights may also be taught as in Danish schools, with no explicit reference to "rights" or "human rights." Although the Norwegian constitutional amendment gives legitimacy to HRE, and to those working to promote it, it remains to be seen whether it will directly impact schools and teacher education.

The concept of consensus may also have significant implications for HRE. As Bowring (2012) has emphasized, conflict, struggle, and challenge of the status quo are essential for the realization of human rights. Recognition of conflicting worldviews is a prerequisite in realizing a democratic classroom, as is engagement with viewpoints of minoritized and marginalized groups. Imposed consensus is antidemocratic. Rather than teaching so as to subdue dissent, democratic classrooms need spaces in which competing values and worldviews can be confronted.

The Nordic countries characterize themselves as traditionally homogeneous in ethnic and political terms. Yet this can mask significant political and constitutional differences both within and between the Nordic nations (Langford & Schaffer, 2015) as well as disguising past ethnic diversity (Osler & Lybæk, 2014). In the case of Norway, an apparent historical homogeneity has been constructed through policies that have attempted to restrict immigrants judged to be different and by a curriculum that has marginalized the role of indigenous people and national minorities in the national story (Osler & Lybæk, 2014).

A societal emphasis on consensus may reflect deep democratic processes of consultation and deliberation, but combined with a self-characterization as a human rights–friendly society, there is a risk of moral superiority, in which the newcomer must be inducted into "our" human rights framework. Minority viewpoints become difficult to accommodate, since consensus implies conformity to the majority way of doing things. When consensus is combined with an understanding of the nation as a "moral superpower" (Langford & Schaffer, 2015), minority perspectives may be excluded.

The Nordic nations have traditionally welcomed refugees fleeing human rights violations in other parts of the world. Refugees might reasonably be expected to enrich Norwegian understandings of human rights through engagement and dialogue. But if human rights are understood to belong, first and foremost, to "us" rather than "them," then the first step in a process of societal integration is to induct the newcomer into "our" (already strong) democracy. Achieving consensus may mean first conforming to "our" national values, rather than a genuine process of democratic deliberation in which all learn from each other. Newcomers may feel pressure to abandon aspects of their identity in order to integrate. Dual citizenship, for example, is not generally permitted. By varied means, the myth of national homogeneity is strengthened and maintained. Effectively, there is a human rights education paradox.

Why, then, does Norway score well on the MIPEX international scale of education policies to enable integration? This appears to stem, in large part, from the importance given to Norwegian language education for newcomers. While access to Norwegian is critical for integration and political efficacy, Norwegian language proficiency is often equated with equal access. There is little recognition of other barriers to participation that newcomers encounter. Multicultural education is equated with language education. Thus when asked to measure the effectiveness of multicultural education, experts may consider only language provision, overlooking a broader package of needs for both mainstream and minoritized students in learning to live together.

Securitization of Education Policy

In Norway and the United Kingdom, as in other northern European countries, education policy discourses, directly or indirectly, have begun to address education, and specifically the schooling of Muslim children and youth, with reference to security, radicalization, and extremism (Coppock, 2014). Concerns about achievement gaps between minoritized youth and the mainstream, and discrimination in the wider society, are overlooked as policies and the media focus on the need to protect young people from the dangers of radicalization. Processes of othering, which Eriksen (2013) has identified, mean that educational efforts to combat politically motivated violence are likely to target Muslim-heritage students.

Where security services or police are involved in such programs, there is a real risk that educational goals take second place to security concerns. Such initiatives may be ill-conceived and undermine, rather than strengthen, social cohesion. In Britain, where six major antiterrorism acts were passed between 2000 and 2011, governments have focused almost exclusively on threats from Islamist terrorism and neglected far-right racist and xenophobic agendas in favor of a concentration on Muslims (Osler, 2011a). In Norway, too, Muslim students appear to be the target of such initiatives, despite the fact that in 2011 the nation saw a major act of terror by far-right gunman Anders Behring Brevik in which 77 died, which he asserted was an attack on the then Labor government's multicultural policies.[18]

An Oslo news article illustrates how such processes play out. It reports on the municipality's efforts to counter radicalism. Entitled "The Threat From Radical Islam Is 'Largely Created by the Media,'" it describes how schools are collaborating with police to address potential radicalization. The headline quotes an educator to suggest that the threat is not as grave as political and media discourses suggest. However, the article explains that the purpose of the initiative is not simply to counter radicalism but "to allow the teacher *to capture evidence of harmful radicalization*" (Slettholm, 2015; my translation and emphasis). This dual purpose places teachers in the role of security agents. Despite official acknowledgment that "various forms" of extremism exist, the article reinforces public concern about Islamist extremism.

In the United Kingdom, the government's Prevent program, presented initially as a community-led approach to tackling violent extremism (Department for Communities and Local Government, 2007), has come to define relationships between government and Muslim communities (Kundnani, 2009). In 2011, Prevent changed from funding local initiatives to imposing a centralized agenda. The Prevent duty requires schools and day care providers to promote "fundamental British values" about which there appears to be limited agreement. In 2015, in the wake of revelations that a number of British schoolchildren and families had left Britain to travel to Syria, the Counter-Terrorism and Security Act 2015, Sec. 26, imposed on specified authorities, including local authorities, schools, and social services, a duty to give due regard to the need to prevent people from being drawn into terrorism.

Schools and other bodies must refer those they believe to be vulnerable to the police, who decide whether to refer them to a panel ("Channel," on which representatives of the local authority and police sit) to prepare "support packages" to reduce their vulnerability. The criteria for the referral of children and young people are extremely broad and vague: Panels have a long list of indicators focusing on "engagement with a group, cause or ideology," "intent to cause harm," and "capability to cause harm" (HM Government, 2015, p. 11). Indicators of engagement include feelings of grievance and injustice; feeling under threat; a need for identity, meaning, and belonging; a desire for status; susceptibility to indoctrination; and a desire for political or moral change. Indicators of "intent to cause harm" include overidentification with a group or ideology, "them and us" thinking, dehumanization of the enemy, and harmful objectives. Finally there are indicators of "capability to cause harm": individual knowledge, skills, and competencies; access to networks, funding, or equipment; and criminal capability (p. 28). There is no legal duty to seek the consent of parents or guardians before a child comes before the panel, but if parents refuse, this may be grounds for judging the child at risk, leading to the potential removal of the child from the family.

Many of these indicators reflect common child and adolescent behaviors. The effect of both Prevent and the Oslo antiradicalization initiative is likely to inhibit children's and young people's freedom of speech at an age when they are developing their thinking. There is a real danger that school, a place where learners should have opportunities to discuss ideas and explore opinions, will become a place where students, particularly those of Muslim heritage, may be reluctant to express themselves.

The Institute for Race Relations provides numerous documented examples of how child referrals have been made (Webber, 2016). Some 900 child referrals took place from 2012 to 2015. Of 796 referrals in June–August 2015, 312 (39%) were children. Three cases of schools' and local authorities' efforts to implement the Prevent duty are outlined here.

Case A. Primary School Questionnaire

In one outer-London borough, officials circulated a questionnaire to primary schools for completion by children as young as 9, profiling their religious views to record potentially "extremist" attitudes. At one primary school, seven children aged 9–10 were identified as "vulnerable to radicalization" and selected for "targeted intervention." The children's names were subsequently made public.

Case B. Learning About Extremism in Personal, Social, and Health Education

In one all-White rural Norfolk school, in the context of PSHE, teachers were told to show Year 9 children videos of "Jihadi John" boasting of ISIS (Islamic State of Iraq and Syria) beheadings and victims being prepared for beheading.

Case C. A Peaceful Protest: Boycotting Israeli Products

A 15-year-old boy was referred to police under the Prevent program after he brought leaflets to school promoting a boycott of Israel. A police officer said that the boy's views on sanctions against Israel were "terrorist-like beliefs." A cafeteria employee reported him to teachers for asking whether lunches were prepared with ingredients from Israel (Webber, 2016).

It is clear, from these and other examples, that Prevent threatens to deny children's freedom of belief, thought, and expression, contravening CRC entitlements. Some teachers are ill-prepared to implement the duty to protect young people, while others are concerned that the program risks alienating those it purports to support. For students with little or no contact with Muslims, watching a video of an ISIS fighter talking about beheadings is likely to fuel Islamophobia and mistrust.

Conclusions

Education for citizenship, democracy, and human rights is essentially about enabling young people to develop political efficacy and learn to live together in societies characterized by diversity and complexity. Minoritized communities have long served to highlight European societies' existent challenges, bringing these into sharper focus. What is commonly labeled as Europe's "refugee crisis" reflects a widening gap between Europe's ideals—human rights and security for all—and the harsh realities of ongoing cultural racism and Islamophobia, coupled with growing hostility to migrants. Ironically, at a time when explicit education for human rights is most needed, both Norway and the United Kingdom have reemphasized "national" values and the assimilation of minorities, rather than the creation of strong programs for learning to live together based on cosmopolitan, human rights principles.

Governments have a duty both to protect their populations from terrorist threats and to ensure that all students have access to human rights education relevant to their everyday lives. Yet, rather than strengthen education for living together, authorities in both nations have taken steps toward the securitization of education, which undermines Europe's avowed commitment to human rights standards.

Education policy is, however, interpreted and enacted by teachers and never applied in a technical or neutral fashion. In the field of education for democratic citizenship and human rights, this is perhaps more critical than in other curricular areas. Teachers, working with students, their families, communities, and civil society, may still find spaces to enable students to develop greater political efficacy. Just as minoritized communities often highlight societies' existent problems, so they remain particularly vulnerable to denials of rights. It is when teachers, like Veronica, acknowledge their political as well as their moral responsibilities to their students that spaces of hope for students' greater political efficacy are created and strengthened.

Notes

1. Younger voters elected overwhelming to remain: 73 percent of 18–24 year olds; 62 percent of 25–34 year olds; and 52 percent of 35–44 year olds made this choice. Yet among older citizens (who are more likely to vote) these patterns were reversed, so that among the over 65s the percentage voting to remain was just 40 percent (BBC, 2016).

2. Germany is ranked 16th ("halfway favourable"), and France, 21st ("slightly unfavourable") (MIPEX, 2015). The MIPEX methodology can be critiqued, but MIPEX provides a comparative overview of national policies.

3. The interview took place at a hotel in central London on June 14, 2015.

4. I sent her a draft portrait for verification.

5. The pupil premium is additional per capita funding, allocated to students entitled to free school meals, in the care of the local authority (e.g., in foster homes), and from military families.

6. Pupil-teachers were untrained teachers. Typically, a pupil-teacher underwent some secondary schooling and then taught primary school grades. A shortage of qualified teachers meant that this system persisted in Ghana until 2014 (Frimpong, 2014).

7. Year 7 students are aged 11–12 years.

8. *Cheeky chappie* is colloquial U.K. English, generally meaning a boy or young man who is mischievous but likable, with a happy-go-lucky attitude.

9. Multicultural education courses within teacher education programs were largely discontinued from the 1990s. Tomlinson (2008) has highlighted how government prescriptions on teacher education content mean that they have effectively been disallowed, leaving teachers ill-prepared to challenge racial injustice.

10. Jill Rutter has produced a number of publications on refugee children that are accessible to teachers. See Rutter, 2005, for ways in which teachers can challenge negative discourses about refugees through citizenship education.

11. The concept of community cohesion is discussed below in relation to British government policy.

12. The Speak Out Challenge is a public speaking competition run in schools in London and Essex organized by the Jack Petchey Foundation. Participating students receive up to six hours of training in public speaking skills; see http://www.jackpetcheyfoundation.org.uk/speak-out-challenge.

13. Prevent, a U.K. government policy, is discussed below.

14. These 28 women and 20 men included university students, mid-career teachers, and those in senior positions, such as principals, administrators, and inspectors.

15. Gorard (2014) has found no evidence to suggest that such schools are more (or less) effective than those they replace.

16. In 2016 the Conservative government announced plans to force all schools to become academies (Asthana & Stewart, 2016), further undermining citizenship education entitlements.

17. Since 2013, there has been a national project on democracy and diversity in teacher education.

18. Public debate following the massacre focused primarily on security, not education, as a means of tackling violent extremism.

References

Asthana, A., & Stewart, H. (2016, March 15). Every English school to become an academy, ministers to announce. *The Guardian.* Retrieved from http://www.theguardian.com/education/2016/mar/15/every-english-school-to-become-an-academy-ministers-to-announce

Bangstad, S. (2015). The racism that dares not speak its name: Rethinking neonationalism and neo-racism. *Intersections: East European Journal of Society and Politics, 1*(1), 49–65.

Banks, J. A., McGee Banks, C. A., Cortes, C. E., Hahn, C. L., Merryfield, M. M., Moodley, K. A., . . . Parker, W. C. (2005). *Democracy and diversity: Principles and concepts for educating citizens in a global age.* Seattle, WA: University of Washington, Center for Multicultural Education.

Berry, M. (2016). Understanding the role of the mass media in the EU referendum. *EU referendum analysis.* Political Studies Association/ Loughborough University/ Centre for the Study of Journalism, Culture & Community Bournemouth University. Retrieved from http://www.referendumanalysis.eu/eu-referendum-analysis-2016/section-1-context/understanding-the-role-of-the-mass-media-in-the-eu-referendum/

Biseth, H. (2011). Citizenship education in Scandinavian multicultural schools. *Citizenship Teaching and Learning, 7*(1), 71–88.

Blanden, J., & Gregg, P. (2004). Family income and educational attainment: A review of approaches and evidence for Britain. *Oxford Review of Economic Policy, 20*(2), 245–263.

Bowring, B. (2012). Human rights and public education. *Cambridge Journal of Education, 42*(1), 53–65.

Branigan, T. (2003, April 23). Stephen's legacy. *The Guardian.*

British Broadcasting Corporation. (2016, June 24). *EU referendum: The result in maps and charts.* Retrieved from http://www.bbc.co.uk/news/uk-politics-36616028

Brown, G. (2006, January 16). Who do we want to be? The future of Britishness. *Fabian Society.*

Çağlar, A. (2014). *Urban migration trends, challenges and opportunities* [Background paper]. Geneva, Switzerland: International Organization for Migration.

Cantle, T. (2001). *Community cohesion: A report of the independent review team.* London: Home Office. Retrieved from http://dera.ioe.ac.uk/14146/1/communitycohesionreport.pdf

Coppock, V. (2014). "Can you spot a terrorist in your classroom?" Problematizing the recruitment of schools to the "war on terror" in the United Kingdom. *Global Studies of Childhood, 4*(2), 115–125.

Decara, C. (2013). *Mapping of human rights education in Danish schools.* Copenhagen, Denmark: Danish Institute for Human Rights. Retrieved from http://www.humanrights.dk/files/media/dokumenter/udgivelser/mapping_of_hre_in_danish_schools.pdf

Department for Communities and Local Government. (2007, April). *Preventing violent extremism: Winning hearts and minds.* London: Author.

Department for Communities and Local Government. (2008). *The government's response to the Commission on Integration and Cohesion.* London: Author. Retrieved from http://www.communities.gov.uk/documents/communities/pdf/681624.pdf

Department for Education (DFE). (2013, September). *Citizenship programmes of study: Key stages 3 and 4. National curriculum in England*. London: Author. Retrieved from https://www.gov.uk/government/uploads/system/uploads/attachment_data/file/239060/SECONDARY_national_curriculum_-_Citizenship.pdf

Department for Education (DFE). (2014, April 10). *School workforce in England: November 2013. Statistical first release* (SFR 11/2014). London: Author.

Department for Education (DFE). (2015, June 22). *Policy paper: English Baccalaureate*. London: Author. Retrieved from https://www.gov.uk/government/publications/english-baccalaureate-ebacc/english-baccalaureate-ebacc

Department for Education and Skills. (2007). *Curriculum review: Diversity and citizenship (Ajegbo report)* (PPSLS/D35/0107/14). London: Author.

Eriksen, T. H. (2013). *Immigration and national identity in Norway*. Washington, DC: Migration Policy Institute.

Essed, P. (1991). *Understanding everyday racism: An interdisciplinary theory*. Newbury Park, CA: Sage.

Feteke, L. (2012). The Muslim conspiracy theory and the Oslo massacre. *Race and Class, 53*(3), 30–47.

Figueroa, P. (2004). Diversity and citizenship education in England. In J. A. Banks (Ed.), *Diversity and citizenship education: Global perspectives* (pp. 219–244). San Francisco: Jossey-Bass.

Freire, P. (2002). *Education for critical consciousness*. New York: Continuum. (original work published 1973)

Frimpong, E. D. (2014, September 10). GES terminates appointment of all pupil teachers. *Graphic Online*. Retrieved from http://www.graphic.com.gh/news/general-news/30415-ges-terminates-appointment-of-pupil-teachers.html

Ghuman, P. A. S. (1995). *Asian teachers in British schools*. Cleveden, UK: Multilingual Matters.

Gillborn, D. (2008). *Racism and education: Coincidence or conspiracy?* London: Routledge.

Gorard, S. (2014). The link between academies in England, pupil outcomes and local patterns of socio-economic segregation between schools. *Research Papers in Education, 29*(3), 268–284.

Halliday, F. (1999). "Islamophobia" reconsidered. *Racial and Ethnic Studies, 22*(5), 892–902.

HM Government. (2015). *Protecting vulnerable people from being drawn into terrorism. Statutory guidance for Channel panel members and partners of local panels*. London: Author. Retrieved from https://www.gov.uk/government/uploads/system/uploads/attachment_data/file/425189/Channel_Duty_Guidance_April_2015.pdf

Home Office. (2008, February) *The path to citizenship: Next steps in reforming the immigration system*. London: Home Office Border and Immigration Agency.

International Organization for Migration. (2015). *World migration report: Migrants and cities: New partnerships to manage mobility*. Geneva, Switzerland: Author.

Kenner, C., & Hickey, T. (2008). *Multilingual Europe: Diversity and learning*. Stoke-on-Trent, UK: Trentham.

Kundnani, A. (2009). *Spooked! How not to prevent violent extremism*. London: Institute for Race Relations.

Langford, M., & Schaffer, J. K. (2015). *The Nordic human rights paradox: Moving beyond exceptionalism* (University of Oslo Faculty of Law Research Paper 2013-25). Oslo, Norway.

Law, I., Finney, S., & Swann, S. J. (2014). Searching for autonomy: Young Black men, schooling and aspirations. *Race Ethnicity and Education, 17*(4), 569–590.

Law, I., & Swann, S. (2011). *Ethnicity and education in England and Europe: Gangstas, geeks and gorjas*. Farnham, UK: Ashgate.

Lile, H. K. (2011). *FNs barnekonvensjon artikkel 29(1). Om formålet med opplæring: En rettssosiologisk studie om hva barn lærer om det samiske folk* [U.N. Convention on the Rights of the Child

Article 29(1). The purpose of education: A sociological study of what children learn about the Sami people]. Unpublished doctoral dissertation, University of Oslo, Norway. Retrieved from http://www.jus.uio.no/smr/forskning/arrangementer/disputaser/hadi_lile.html

Lindquist, H., & Osler, A. (2016). Navigating race and ethnicity in research: Reflections on working with Norwegian schools. *Race Equality Teaching, 33*(3), 12–18.

Macpherson, W. (1999). *The Stephen Lawrence inquiry.* London: Stationery Office.

Man jailed for 2002 racially aggravated attack on teens. (2012, December 19). *The Voice.* Retrieved from http://www.voice-online.co.uk/article/man-jailed-2002-racially-aggravated-attack-teens

Migration Integration Policy Index (MIPEX). (2015). *Education: Key findings.* Retrieved from http://www.mipex.eu/education

Mitchell, K., & Parker, W. (2008). I pledge allegiance to . . . flexible citizenship and shifting scales of belonging. *Teachers College Record, 110*(4), 775–804.

Noddings, N. (2013). *Caring: An ethical approach to ethics and moral education* (2nd ed.). Berkeley, CA: University of California Press.

Nordic Council of Ministers. (2010). *Strategy for children and young adults in the Nordic region.* Copenhagen, Denmark: Nordic Council of Ministers Secretariat. Retrieved from http://gaztematika.gipuzkoangazte.eus/documents/74494/461412/Strategy+for+children+and+young+people/8bbef82c-5a94-4c0e-9c14-c3ef00cd6551

Office for National Statistics. (2012, December 11). *Ethnicity and national identity in England and Wales.* Retrieved from https://www.ons.gov.uk/peoplepopulationandcommunity/culturalidentity/ethnicity/articles/ethnicityandnationalidentityinenglandandwales/2012-12-11?

Øia, V., & Vestel, T. (2006). *Møter i det Flerkulturelle* [Multicultural meetings] (Rapport 21/7). Oslo, Norway: NOVA.

Ong, A. (1999). *Flexible citizenship: The cultural logics of transnationality.* Durham, NC: Duke University Press.

Osler, A. (1994). Education for democracy and equality: The experiences, values and attitudes of ethnic minority student teachers. *European Journal of Intercultural Studies, 5*(1), 23–37.

Osler, A. (1997a). Black teachers and citizenship: Researching differing identities. *Teachers and Teaching: Theory and Practice, 3*(1), 47–60.

Osler, A. (1997b). *The education and careers of Black teachers: Changing identities, changing lives.* Buckingham, UK; and Bristol, PA: Open University Press.

Osler, A. (1999). The educational experiences and career aspirations of Black and ethnic minority undergraduates. *Race Ethnicity and Education, 2*(1), 39–58.

Osler, A. (2000). The Crick Report: Difference, equality and racial justice. *Curriculum Journal, 11*(1), 25–37.

Osler, A. (2005). Looking to the future: Democracy, diversity and citizenship education. In A. Osler (Ed.), *Teachers, human rights and diversity* (pp. 3–22). Stoke-on-Trent, UK: Trentham.

Osler, A. (2008). Citizenship education and the Ajegbo report: Re-imagining a cosmopolitan nation. *London Review of Education, 6*(1), 9–23.

Osler, A. (2009a). Testing citizenship and allegiance: Policy, politics and the education of adult migrants in the UK. *Education, Citizenship and Social Justice, 4*(1), 63–79.

Osler, A. (2009b). Patriotism, multiculturalism and belonging: Political discourse and the teaching of history. *Educational Review, 61*(1), 85–100.

Osler, A. (2011a). Education policy, social cohesion and citizenship. In P. Ratcliffe & I. Newman (Eds.), *Promoting social cohesion: Implications for policy and frameworks for evaluation* (pp. 185–205). Bristol, UK: Polity Press.

Osler, A. (2011b). Teacher interpretations of citizenship education: National identity, cosmopolitan ideals, and political realities. *Journal of Curriculum Studies, 43*(1), 1–24.

Osler, A. (2012). Citizenship education and diversity. In J. A. Banks (Ed.), *Encyclopedia of diversity in education* (Vol. 1, pp. 353–361). Thousand Oaks, CA: Sage.

Osler, A. (2014, July 17). Norway's quiet revolution. *Times Higher Education*. Retrieved from http:// www.timeshighereducation.co.uk/comment/opinion/norways-quiet-revolution/2014481 .article

Osler, A. (2015). Human rights education, postcolonial scholarship, and action for social justice. *Theory and Research in Social Education, 43*(2), 244–274.

Osler, A., & Lybæk, L. (2014). Educating "the new Norwegian we": An examination of national and cosmopolitan education policy discourses in the context of extremism and Islamophobia. *Oxford Review of Education, 40*(5), 543–566.

Parker, W. C. (2003). *Teaching democracy: Unity and diversity in public life*. New York: Teachers College Press.

Qualifications and Curriculum Authority. (1998). *Education for citizenship and the teaching of democracy in schools (Crick report)*. London: Author.

Rutter, J. (2005). Understanding the alien in our midst: Using citizenship education to challenge popular discourses about refugees. In A. Osler (Ed.), *Teachers, human rights and diversity* (pp. 133–153). Stoke-on-Trent, UK: Trentham.

Sassen, S. (1991). *Global cities: New York, London, Tokyo*. Princeton, NJ: Princeton University Press.

Slettholm, A. (2015, February 23). Oslo Kommune: Trusselen fra radikal islam er "i stor grad medieskapt" [Oslo municipality: The threat from radical Islam is "largely created by the media"]. *Aftenposten Osloby*. Retrieved from http://www.osloby.no/nyheter/Oslo-kommune-Trusselen -fra-radikal-islam-er-i-stor-grad-medieskapt-7912041.html

Statistics Norway. (2016, January 1). *Immigrants and Norwegian-born to immigrant parents*. Retrieved from https://www.ssb.no/en/befolkning/statistikker/innvbef

Tomlinson, S. (2008). *Race and education: Policy and politics in Britain*. Maidenhead, UK: Open University Press.

United Nations. (1989, November 20). Convention on the Rights of the Child. Adopted and opened for signature, ratification and accession by General Assembly resolution 44/25. Retrieved from http://www.ohchr.org/en/professionalinterest/pages/crc.aspx

United Nations. (2011, December 19). *United Nations Declaration on Human Rights Education and Training. Final adoption by the General Assembly*. Retrieved from http://www.ohchr.org/EN/ Issues/Education/Training/Pages/UNDHREducationTraining.aspx

Vedvik, K. O. (2011). Begredelig kunnskap om samer. Den norske stat viser liten vilje til å passe på at barn lærer om det samiske folk, til tross for at det er lovfestet [Lamentable knowledge of the Sami. The Norwegian government shows little willingness to ensure that children learn about the Sami people, despite the fact that it is statutory]. *Forskning.no*. Retrieved from http://www.forskning.no/artikler/2011/desember/306997

Vertovec, S. (2007). Super-diversity and its implications. *Ethnic and Racial Studies, 30*(6), 1024–1054.

Vesterdal, K. (2016). *The roles of human rights education in Norway. A qualitative study of purposes and approaches in policy and in upper secondary schools* (Unpublished doctoral dissertation). Faculty of Social Sciences and Technology Management, Norwegian University of Science and Technology, Trondheim, Norway.

Webber, F. (2016). *Prevent and the children's rights convention* [Report submitted to the Council of Europe Human Rights Commissioner]. London: Institute for Race Relations.

Chapter 8

"Who Here Is a Real German?"
German Muslim Youths, Othering, and Education

H. Julia Eksner

Frankfurt University of Applied Sciences

Saba Nur Cheema

Anne Frank Educational Centre

A teacher, who wanted to demonstrate how diverse her classroom was, asked her class of students: "Who here is German?" Most students raised their hands, presumably because they had citizenship. The teacher then laughed and repeated the question but phrased it differently: "No, no, no. You *know* what I mean! Who here is a *real* German?"

—Almas Nur, human rights educator

In this chapter, taking a postcolonial perspective, we examine the frames of reference that shape German conceptions of citizenship and belonging. We look at the intersection of religion and racialization by outlining the processes of ascription and exclusion with which youths marked as Muslim grow up in Germany.[1] At the center of the investigation is the question of how "othering" and the exclusion of religious minorities—especially youths to whom a Muslim identity has been ascribed by dominant society—are enacted in contemporary school practices in Germany. Postcolonial studies provide valuable concepts for describing ethnocentric hegemonies that maintain global and local inequalities and exclusive practices (de Oliveira Andreotti & de Souza, 2012; Meer, 2014). We identify long-standing narratives of ethnic citizenship, secularism, and ethnicity that define who is of the German state and who is not, and we argue that the experiences of youths marked as Muslim in Germany are structured by intertwining narratives about Europe and its Muslim "others." Scholars need to examine how these global hegemonies find their way into education settings and practices in Germany today—via narratives about "the Orient" versus "the West," "Enlightenment," "Christian values," and secularism—so that German educational settings and practices can become places of inclusion, participation, and equity.

In this chapter we explore how youths marked as Muslim who grow up in Germany but who are not "of" Germany navigate their identities as both religious and ethnic others and as German citizens. For years, there has been heated public debate in Germany about how "secular" society should respond to the resurgence of religion in educational institutions and the civil sphere. The debate was triggered by the rising numbers of students and teachers who are Muslim and who wish to publicly practice their religious beliefs—their constitutional right. We trace how this fundamental constitutional right translates into multiple embattled locations and discourses that define which practices are considered as belonging and which as other. Drawing on case studies, we discuss the prolonged legal battle for female teachers' right to wear the Muslim headscarf (*hijab*), as well as the exclusionary ways in which belonging and nonbelonging of Muslims are practiced and ascribed in German discourse. To illustrate educational openings in this situation, we discuss the efforts of Almas Nur, a young human rights educator, to develop and conduct student workshops to address anti-Muslim exclusion. We detail the objectives and methods of the curriculum and how it is experienced by various participants. We close by highlighting the unresolved contradictions that emerge in interventions of this kind for educators, and we reflect on possible steps to address such contradictions in the future.

Growing up Muslim in Germany

About one third of youths in Germany today come from immigrant communities. Until 2000, an ethnic conception of citizenship grouped Germany's population into "Germans" and "foreigners" (Brubaker, 1994; Smooha, 2002) and restricted access to German citizenship to those born to ethnically German parents (*jus sanguinis*, or "right of blood").[2] In 2000, the citizenship law was reformed to allow access to "non-ethnics." The reform responded to an ongoing demographic shift in Germany in which 18.6% of the population—and 33% of the population under the age of 5—were born to parents who were not both ethnic Germans (Statistisches Bundesamt, 2007).[3]

In today's civic democracy, old and new conceptions of citizenship coexist, and the work of transformation is being done on a daily basis. Currently, 20% of the population—and 35% of the population under the age of 5—have immigration histories. The context of Germany's transitional ethnic democracy defines the ongoing negotiation of civic inclusion and participation by religious minority youths in Germany. We suggest that, although de facto citizens who are marked as Muslim may be accepted "in" Germany to varying degrees, they are in many ways not recognized as "of" Germany, or, in other words, as citizens and political subjects (Asad, 2003; Özyürek, 2005).

Over the last decade, Germany's largest immigrant populations have been primarily defined by their religio-cultural membership.[4] In 2015, about 5.5% of the population in Germany—4.4 to 4.7 million people—were estimated to be members of ethno-cultural communities who are marked as Muslim (Bundesamt für Migration und Flüchtlinge (BAMF), 2016).[5] Muslims in Germany come from 49 countries with a wide variety of religious affiliations. Although across Western countries Muslim immigrant communities are subsumed into a single pan-ethnic category of "Muslim" (Dwyer, 1998; Modood, 1997; Vertovec & Rogers, 1998), the generic term "Muslim" ignores the reality that Muslims in Germany have diverse ethnic backgrounds (e.g., immigrants from Turkey, Arab countries, Iran, Bosnia, Pakistan), as well as diverse religious and political orientations (Haug, Müssig, & Stichs, 2009).[6] There is a wide variety of Muslim religious practices in Germany's diverse Muslim communities, including those of conservative-orthodox orientations, liberal orientations of "Euro-Islam," Islamic mysticism, and Islamist fundamentalism (AlSayyad & Castells, 2002). At the same time, the "silent majority" of "cultural Muslims," liberal and largely nonreligious members of Muslim immigrant communities, are co-opted by mainstream coverage about the minorities of orthodox religious or fundamentalist Muslims (Akbarzadeh & Roose, 2011).

Youths make up a large and growing proportion of those marked as Muslim: In 2009, 41% of Muslims in Germany were under the age of 24, and 25% were under the age of 15 (Haug, Müssig, & Stichs, 2009).

In the context of the ongoing discursive construction of "Islam" and "Muslims" in Germany, public discourse portrays Muslims as not "integrated" and places particular demands on Muslims to demonstrate compliance with German culture and values. Gendered accounts depict young Muslim males as deviant and aggressive, whereas women—especially those wearing headscarves—are conceived as passive or oppressed. The heated debate around Muslim religious and gender practices (e.g., the right of female teachers to wear headscarves and the right of Muslim girls to be exempt from gym class)—as well as the politicization of Islam in the context of global political developments—are instantiations of these discourses (Brettfeld & Wetzels, 2007; Caglar, 1995, 1997; Ewing, 2008; Özyürek, 2014; Vertovec & Rogers, 1998; Zick, Küpper, & Hövermann, 2011).

Opinion polls have found that 57% of the population in Germany perceives Islam as a threat, whereas 6% don't think Islamic principles fit into Western society. Forty percent of ethnic Germans report feeling like strangers in their own country, even in regions of Germany where immigration is as low as 2%. Twenty-five percent of the population believes that immigration for Muslims should cease (Bertelsmann, 2015).[7] These attitudes are also expressed by actions: Muslims in Germany report more experiences of discrimination and victimization than other immigrant groups. In the year 2007, two thirds of Muslim respondents reported incidents of victimization or discrimination. In the same year, severe victimization experiences and physical attacks, as well as damage to property, were reported by 22% of the Muslim population in Germany (Brettfeld & Wetzels, 2007, p. 240).

With societal opinion polarized around the question of the role of Islam and the place of Muslims in Germany, a global crisis in 2015 displaced millions of refugees and led approximately 500,000 refugees—many from countries with predominantly Muslim communities—to seek asylum in Germany.[8] The ongoing discussion about whether Germany could and should allow these refugees to make Germany their permanent home, and what such acceptance would mean for Germany as a society, has amplified the volume of the public debate about Muslims and Islam to screeching levels. It has also led to an increase in public physical altercations against children, youths, and adults who are marked as Muslims.

Even before these recent developments, however, youths marked as Muslims were very aware of these stigmatizing discourses and their effects. More than 30% of high school students who identified as Muslim reported that they experienced German society as disadvantageous for Muslims (among respondents of all ages, 50% reported this experience; Brettfeld & Wetzels, 2007, p. 240). Other studies have found that many Muslims in Germany perceive that Germans have a negative image of Islam and that media reporting about Islam and Muslims is one-sided. Young people from Arab and Muslim immigrant communities frequently report experiences of stigmatization as "terrorists" and "fundamentalists." In one study, almost 85% of Muslim youths agreed that they were upset about the fact that after a terrorist attack, the first suspected subjects are Muslims, a fact that they took to reflect a global prejudice against Muslims (Brettfeld & Wetzels, 2007, p. 240).

In sum, the positioning of most youths from Muslim communities in Germany is characterized by disadvantage, even as ongoing demographic change is eroding the formerly clear-cut majority-minority relationship. Because most Muslim youths in Germany are socially positioned as both working-class and ethno-culturally marginalized, they find themselves on the weaker side of a deep social antagonism within German society. Ethnicized and marginalized youths experience a particular set of exclusionary processes as they are marked and excluded as "foreigners," "immigrants," and "Muslims"—and they reflect on, and react to, these ascriptions and exclusions. Muslim youths who grow up in this social and discursive context face the challenge of coming to a positive understanding of themselves and of formulating and sustaining positive identities as Muslim Germans.

Religion and Racialization in Germany

The German headscarf debate serves as a specific example of how long-standing master narratives referencing religion, ethnicity, culture, and political orientation are interwoven in the debate over belonging and citizenship. Along with other authors, we understand the heated public debate about the "religious other" versus the "secular civil sphere" as one instantiation of the ongoing process of defining citizenship and belonging in Germany (Amir-Moazami, 2007; Dalsheim, 2010; Habermas, 2006; Heimbach-Steins, Wielandt, & Zintl, 2006; Karakaşoğlu & Luchtenberg, 2004; Salvatore, 2006; Schiffauer, 2002; Wiese, 2011; Windandy, 2011; Yalcin-Heckmann, 1998).

At the center of contestation in the headscarf debate is the right of female Muslim teachers to wear headscarves in German state schools. The debate started in 1997, when a young teacher of Afghan background, Fereshta Ludin, was banned from teaching in a state school in the federal state of Baden-Württemberg because she insisted on wearing a headscarf. The state's ministry of culture reasoned that the Islamic headscarf, as a sign of "cultural segregation," was not appropriate for a teacher to wear in school. The ministry of culture considered the wearing of a headscarf by Muslim female teachers in public schools—which is a constitutional right in Germany (i.e., freedom of religious expression)—as a violation of the constitutional neutrality of state institutions. The argument that was presented against the wearing of the headscarf was that teachers represent the state in their role as civil servants and must remain "neutral." They therefore were not allowed to express religious or political affiliations while teaching (Amir-Moazami, 2005). A teacher with her head covered was seen as a threat to the role of civil servants in Germany, who—in taking an oath—are regarded as representatives of the state and of its norms and values (Amir-Moazami, 2005). The state of Baden-Württemberg ended up passing a law that explicitly prohibited the Islamic headscarf from being worn by teachers. The public debate around the ruling was picked up by the national media, where it stayed a top-priority news item for years. The case was taken to the German Supreme Court, which in 2003 supported the headscarf ban and declared it a state matter. The Supreme Court ruling led to a resurgence of the nationwide debate as other states followed in prohibiting headscarves. Fereshta Ludin gave up her legal struggle for her right of religious expression as a teacher. At the same time, Christian symbols were still displayed in many German schools.[9]

More than ten years later the headscarf dispute was picked up again when a similar case was brought to court. In March 2015, the Supreme Court, in a landmark decision, revised its ruling on the headscarf ban. The Supreme Court's decision now states that headscarves can be banned by federal states only if the scarves cause "imminent and concrete danger" to a particular school's atmosphere and state neutrality. A regulation in the state of North Rhine-Westphalia, in which the display of Christian-Occidental cultural symbols had been explicitly exempted from the previous ruling, was also declared in violation of the constitution. The privileging of Christian symbols was found to violate the principle of equality of religions. The Supreme Court stated that teachers as citizens have a right to religious freedom. Neither students nor their parents have a right not to be confronted with teachers who are wearing headscarves for religious reasons. The court ruling specified that "headscarves by themselves do not have an advertising or missionizing effect" and that the visible religious affiliation of teachers does not violate the neutrality of the state because the state does not affiliate with a particular belief. The implication of this ruling is that teachers in the state of North Rhine-Westphalia are free to wear a Muslim headscarf, a Jewish *kippah* (skullcap), a Christian cross, or a nun's habit. This decision can be reversed, however, if "serious conflicts" are the result of this practice (German Constitutional Court, 2015). The reference to a potential for "threat" and "conflict" was interpreted by the press to imply cases such as Muslim students pressuring younger Muslim students to wear headscarves (Rath & Bax, 2015). The ruling was binding only for the state of North Rhine-Westphalia, however, as it confirmed the verdict issued by the state. Since then, only a few of the other states have followed with legally binding rulings.

The embattled history of the headscarf legislation speaks strongly to the symbolic meaning of the Islamic headscarf in German institutions. Whether teachers in German schools are allowed to profess religious allegiance is clearly not the only issue at hand. The debate was phrased in the terms and concepts of constitutional rights that give religious freedom to Germany's citizens, on the one hand, and require the neutrality of the state, on the other. However, many critics voiced a concern that schools held Muslim religious practices to a standard to which widespread Christian religious practices were not held. Most important, perhaps, the debate was carried out in a language couched in strongly ethnicizing and culturalizing terms.

Master Narratives of Belonging

This section draws on the concept of *hegemony* to describe the ways in which notions of who belongs as a citizen are created by practices, narratives, and discourses that create "others" (Bourdieu, 1976; Gramsci, 1971; Lears, 1985; Sayer, 1994). Hegemonic formations represent ensembles of relatively stable social forms and relations (Mouffe, 1988); they are the "winning" formations of public representation in the struggle over power between antagonistic social groups. Although hegemony is never conclusively established and is continually contested (Bakhtin, 1981; Gramsci, 1971), analyses of discourse and institutional practices indicate that the hegemonic formations established in and across Europe erase the ethnic, cultural, and religious diversity of citizens. The formations subsume heterogeneous citizenries and their various worldviews to narratives that distinguish between "us" and "them." Although hegemonic discourses overtly use secular and rationalist rhetoric, they are barely disguised in their civilizational, racialized, and religious content. As such, the narratives of European countries today are built on and synthesize intersecting discourses about the civilizational, cultural, religious, ethnic, and political differences between "Europeans" and those marked as Muslims (Asad, 2003; Lemish, 2010; Mignolo, 1995).

The most deep-rooted European hegemonic formations engender a civilizational narrative in which the West and its history are portrayed in continuity with Judeo-Christian traditions and Occidental civilization. In Germany, the civilizational master narrative is further expressed in a cultural narrative. Since the 19th century, there has been an established culturalizing discourse about the West that identifies specific "culture areas" (*Kulturkreise;* Frobenius, 1897–1898) and asserts the importance of a local (i.e., German) "guiding culture" (*Leitkultur*). Entailed in the civilizational-cultural narrative is an implicit religio-cultural dimension that is based on the alleged Judeo-Christian civilizational roots of society. The positioning of Western and Judeo-Christian culture as opposed to Muslim-Oriental culture represents one variation of a pan-European cultural-civilizational discourse specified and customized to various national and regional contexts (Dumont, 1986; Grosfoguel & Mielants, 2006; Hüttermann, 2011).

In the headscarf debate, "German" cultural norms and values were continually cited. References to the implicit "orientation of values" in the German constitution and guiding culture (*Leitkultur*) were ubiquitous, and German values were explicated to be those of the "Christian Occident," the Enlightenment, the French Revolution, Greek antiquity, and humanism (Amir-Moazami, 2005). The norms and values of the state (i.e., secular, enlightened, Western, progressive) were contrasted with norms and values associated with wearing a headscarf (i.e., religious, non-Western, traditionalist). The discursive shift from state neutrality to Christian-Occidental values of German society was a recurring pattern in the headscarf debate. Although the debate is commonly understood as an instantiation of the contestation of the religious in the "secular" realm of educational institutions in Germany, it is indicative of how nondominant religious markers have become a stand-in for multiple dimensions of difference, including civilizational, ethnic, and cultural differences.

Postcolonial scholars have deconstructed the civilizational narrative of European Judeo-Christian tradition as a "fictitious amalgam" that came into being only after the moral shock of the Holocaust beckoned a public repositioning of the historical relationship and intertwining of Germany and its Jewish minority. The notion of "Occidental/Western/ modern" civilization is vague because its discursive content continuously shifts. The discursive construction of Western civilization as rational, secular, humanistic, and progress oriented is less rooted in social reality than is it used to differentiate the "West" from "the rest." It prominently entails an othering of Oriental cultures as irrational, religious, nondemocratic, and reactionary (Salvatore, 2006).

Modern instantiations of the civilizational discourse are stigmatizing portrayals of Muslims that have been spread by global media since the 1980s. Since the 2001 attacks on the World Trade Center in New York City, these portrayals have coalesced into a public image of Muslims and Islam as the West's antithesis (Abbas, 2004; Brown, 2006; Mandel, 2008). Europe's "others" are marked by archaic gender practices, conflict, political extremism, and religious fundamentalism (Abbas, 2004; Schiffauer, 2007); Western and Christian civilization versus Oriental and Islamic civilization are presented as essential and opposed entities (Featherstone, 2009; Goody, 2006; Said, 1979). The entities are inscribed with essential political values that are conferred to their respective populations: Democratic values are categorized as Western, and fundamentalist religious values are categorized as Oriental or Muslim (Huntington, 1996). Central to this construction is the impossibility of value consensus and the inevitability of conflict between those entities. Because competing narratives are not mutually exclusive, the construction of the West as Christian coexists with a narrative of the West as secular, which is another hegemonic formation of citizenship in European countries today.

The secular narrative portrays the West as the heir of Enlightenment and as such, secular and rationalist (Asad, 2003). Building on the civilizational narrative, secularity is portrayed as a logical and modern continuation of Judeo-Christian traditions and Occidental civilization (Mignolo, 1995). This modern and secular self-representation, a guardian against the threat of a backlash into the religious, is the primary mode in which the media and the public in Germany today represent themselves. The religious and the secular are hierarchically construed across a linear progression in historical time, in which secularization is the necessary product of modernity in society (Habermas, 2006, 2008; Mignolo, 1995).

The headscarf debate instantiates this discursive landscape, which has shifted from fear of minority segregation—as expressed in the 1997 decision—to fear of Islamic religious extremism. The 2005 Muhammad cartoon protests, the 2010 Florida Koran-burning protests, and the global uproar over an amateur video defiling Muhammad and Islam—covered by *Newsweek* under the sensationalist title "Muslim Rage" (Ali, 2012)—helped establish a view of Islam as not only other but also religiously extremist. As a result of the *Charlie Hebdo* murders, and of fears about the Islamic extremist rebel group ISIS (Islamic State of Iraq and the Levant; Cockburn, 2014), German concern about radical Islam reached an all-time high. At the writing of this chapter, global Islam as archaic, anti-Western, and extremist is portrayed as a threat to Western states and societies (Beck, 2015).

At the same time that the West is portrayed as the secular antithesis to radical Islam, the nominally secular societies, such as Germany, do not in fact show an absence of religious culture or practices (Fischer, Hotam, & Wexler, 2012). The endurance of religious ideas, tacit acceptance of them, and hence the intertwining of religion and democracy in European societies has been amply documented (Asad, 2003; Özyürek, 2005). Secularist policies at the level of the European Union and the German state demonstrate that the Euro-Christian roots of European secularism today often discriminate against religious minorities and privilege Christians (Özyürek, 2005). Christian practices (e.g., the Christian calendar, Christian holidays, Christian symbolism) continue to be sustained in Germany's secular institutions, as they are across Europe. In German schools, for instance, the display of Christian crosses—which violates the constitutional neutrality of state institutions—was for many years standard practice and continues to be legal in many states. In sum, the secularist claim of Germany's government and institutions is contradicted by the reality of a postsecular society (Habermas, 2008), in which hegemonic Christian, secular, and nondominant religious practices are negotiated.

In addition to referencing civilizational and ethnocultural values, the debate raises the question of what it means to be German today. The German ethnic narrative sees an ethnic nation sharing a common descent (*jus sanguinis*), and it is the ethnic nation—not the citizenry—that shapes the symbols, laws, and policies of the state.[10] The German model of citizenship has historically revolved around an ethnocultural "community of descent" that has been resistant to the absorption of new members. The conception of the nation not as a nation of citizens but as a *Volk* nation, bound together by blood and culture, was challenged by the 2000 reform of citizenship law that grants the right of citizenship to non-ethnics (van Krieken, 2000). Although the children of immigrants born in Germany have the right to acquire German citizenship, naturalization is not automatic and there are barriers to acquiring it (e.g., one cannot become a citizen if one relies on social security, has a criminal record, or drops out of high school). The notion of civic Germanness is still very much evolving.

Anti-Muslim Racism and Civic Participation

This section draws on the concept of anti-Muslim racism to explore the ways in which ethnicized—and racialized—notions of citizenship manifest in the practices and ideologies that structure belonging in Germany. The racialization and exclusion of Germany's ethnocultural others, such as Muslims as nondominant European communities, have been discussed under the terms *Islamophobia* and, more recently, *anti-Muslim racism* (Hafez, 2014; Klug, 2013, 2014; Meer, 2014; Modood, 1997; Shooman, 2014). Although there is no fully agreed-upon definition of what the concept of Islamophobia entails, most authors conceive of it as a form of racialization: "Religion is 'raced' and Muslims are racialized" (Sayyid, 2011, p. 276). In the discourse about Islam, the words "Islam" and "Muslim" are "superimposed" on each other, and "jihad, fatwa, umma, sharia, and so on—[are] routinely quoted against Muslims" (Klug, 2013, p. 677). Because "neither Muslims nor Islam exist without the other . . . it is not really possible to separate hatred of Muslims from a hatred of Islam" (Miles & Brown, 2003, p. 166).

Islamophobia is best conceptualized as a form of cultural racism. In this view, Islamophobia includes racialized phenomena exactly because racism is not only about biology. Visible markers—whether ethnic markers (e.g., phenotype, name) or ethnocultural styles of clothing—are seen as markers of group membership to which cultural traits (i.e., trait-like religious and political beliefs, as well as values and norms) are assigned as inherent. In this move, cultural traits that are ascribed based on a "Muslim" appearance are essentialized. In a separate step of devaluation, these traits, and the person carrying them, are stigmatized. Islamophobia is thus perceived through a broader concept of racism, one that breaks out of the mold of biological determinism (Klug, 2013, p. 677).

Although "anti-Muslim racism" describes a structure of exclusion and oppression, this chapter focuses on its underlying mechanism: othering. Youths marked as Muslim experience othering along several lines of difference: first as immigrants, second as ethnocultural others, and third as religious others (based on their assumed religious membership). Othering of youths marked as Muslim is based on certain visible markers (e.g., phenotype, name, clothing) and occurs via the ascription of both religious membership (i.e., being born into a Muslim family) and religious orientation (i.e., de facto beliefs), both of which are discursively connected to radical and jihadist political and cultural beliefs thought to be shared by "Muslims." Practices of othering include overt structures of exclusion as well as sometimes subtle moments of microaggression (Perez Huber & Solorzano, 2015), in which dominant speakers point out the "difference" of a nondominant person or group. Othering via microaggression may also include "innocent" questions and unquestioned assumptions about the others' practices and creeds.

How, then, can young people who are marked as Muslim truly be citizens in a context that—although granting constitutional participation and access—continues to other and exclude them through institutional structures and practices? Education programs against anti-Muslim racism and for the inclusion and participation of Muslim Germans in civil society are evidently needed in German civil society. And yet it is a topic hardly present in the civic education landscape. On the contrary, although most civics curricula indicate a general allegiance to inclusive notions of citizenship, schools and classrooms are infused with more or less subtle ideas of who is a citizen and who is not, which perpetuate the othering and exclusion of youths marked as Muslims in Germany today.

Diversity and Citizenship Education in Germany

Germany's transitional ethnic democracy sets the context for the difficult negotiation of civic inclusion and participation of religious minority youths in Germany. Civics curricula and classroom practices in diverse settings have been shown to reflect local narratives of citizenship; that is, they address who is considered to be of the state and who is not. However, as some of the chapters in this book demonstrate, schools, classrooms, and informal education settings that do not offer explicit civics instruction also transmit implicit notions of citizenship and belonging. As such, both overt and nonovert curricula and practices reproduce the values and norms of society at large (Al-Haj, 2005; Bloemraad, Korteweg, & Yurdakul, 2008; Lemish, 2010; Mandel, 2008; Pinson, 2007). The "latent" or "hidden" curricula entailed in classroom practices and discourse include a variety of messages and tools of communication and they supplement standard curriculum during activities such as field trips, annual topics, holiday celebrations, memorial days, and home room or "educator" time set aside in the classroom for weekly discussion of current events (Anyon, 1979; Lemish, 2010). It is these informal mechanisms of civic education (Lemish, 2010) that, in concert with other social arenas of socialization—including the family, the community, and the military—are the primary ways in which notions of citizenship and civic mindedness are transmitted and acquired.

In Germany, civic education is part of various school subjects and runs under a range of different names (e.g., political education, citizenship education, social studies, political studies) (Luchtenberg, 2004). Civic education curricula are designed with an active dimension as expressed in the concept of "responsible citizenship." The concept of citizenship that emphasizes the substantive, active dimension of citizenship has replaced the formal conceptualization of citizenship based on a rights model (Delanty, 1997). The concept of responsible citizenship addresses topics such as awareness and knowledge of rights and duties, as well as civic values such as democracy and human rights, equality, participation, partnership, social cohesion, solidarity, tolerance of diversity, and social justice.[11] The framework of responsible citizenship is widespread in European countries and has become a priority area for the member states of the Council of Europe (Council of Europe & O'Shea, 2003).

Firmly implemented in the civics curriculum of Germany's schools, education promoting responsible citizenship is meant to guide students toward political literacy, democratic attitudes and values, and active participation in civil society. As part of the development of political literacy, students are supposed to learn about theories of human rights and democracy, become familiar with how political and social institutions function, and learn to appreciate cultural and historical diversity. The attitudes and values needed to become responsible citizens include learning self-respect and respect for others, listening and resolving conflicts peacefully, contributing to harmonious coexistence among people, developing values consistent with a pluralist society, and building a positive self-image as citizen. The goals of active civic participation are typically implemented by enabling students to become involved in the life of the school and the local community, where students are supposed to acquire the skills needed to make a responsible and constructively critical contribution to public life. Students are given the opportunity to experiment practically with democratic principles (e.g., by voting for student representatives). In addition, their capacity to act on each other's behalf and engage in appropriate initiatives is encouraged.

The categories of objectives are interdependent. Whereas one category relates to the formal acquisition of theoretical knowledge, another category requires greater involvement by students in terms of opinions and attitudes, and in another, students are expected to mobilize for action and play a full part in the political, social, and cultural life of the community. In Germany, curricula corresponding to the "political literacy" category are more in evidence than those concerned with active participation and development of the values and attitudes needed for good practical citizenship (European Commission, 2005, pp. 24–25). As in other European states, there is a gap between "knowing" democratic principles and "practicing" them. Empirical studies in Germany show that although youths and young adults agree with abstract and generalized democratic values, they show less agreement on concrete examples of how such democratic values would be enacted in real-life situations. Democracy as a model of government thus finds widespread acceptance, whereas the practices that are necessarily linked to this model are less accepted (Gaiser, Gille, Krüger, & de Rijke, 2011). The questions arise: How deep is youths' understanding entailed in these professed democratic values? How inclusive and exclusive are their notions of citizenship?

Although civic education is an uncontested part of school curriculum, educators in German schools face a variety of challenges, including the challenge to mold students into active citizens and to assure that democratic principles are not only known by students but also practiced. Furthermore, and at the center of the argument of this chapter, educators are faced with the challenge to adapt their civics curricula and the way they view their students to the changing legal definition of citizenship that came about with citizenship reform in 2000.

Thus, civics education is distributed across the entire school curriculum and includes time spent outside of "study time." Therefore, although official civics curricula might teach liberal and secular notions of citizenship, in-built assumptions often contradict these notions; although democratic principles and processes may be taught, nondominant social groups are still engaged in an ongoing contestation over their civic rights (Al-Haj, 2005; Derricott, 1998; Levy, 2005; Pinson, 2007).

Students from nondominant groups face particular challenges. Although nondominant students in German schools might learn about the liberal and secular narratives that confirm the constitutional rights of religious minorities and the neutrality of the state in class, they may have experiences that reveal how their rights are regularly violated in interactions in school and in the public sphere. They may also be aware that there are competing and ambivalent conceptions about who is "of" the state—ethnically, culturally, and religiously (Asad, 2003; McLaughlin, 1992)—and that nondominant groups are not typically included in these conceptions. Finally, classroom discourses and practices bear on whom members of dominant society declare fit to govern themselves and who lacks such capacity. For students from nondominant groups and those from dominant groups, practices and narratives become effective elements of the formation of political subjects and their subjectivities (Isin, 2012). For educators, it is important to address how nondominant youths—among them those ascribed as Muslim—negotiate their identities and subjectivities as political subjects and citizens of Germany.

The development of interventions that are effective against the othering of religious minorities requires curriculum that empowers young people to know the constitutional rights of religious minorities and to become active on their behalf. This is beginning to happen in informal civics education. The remainder of this chapter is devoted to a discussion of a curriculum that addresses anti-Muslim exclusion that was developed and implemented by the human rights educator Almas Nur. It details the objectives and methods of her curriculum and portrays how students and teachers engage in reflecting on anti-Muslim racism in their own lives and in their experiences in school.

"(Un)Believable": Connecting Human Rights and Civic Education

Almas Nur, a human rights educator with Pakistani roots born in Germany but not "of" Germany, and a coworker started developing the program "(Un)Believable: Religions on the Agenda" in 2011.[12] When Nur was growing up, she herself faced the challenge of how to be a German citizen while her civic belonging to Germany was constantly being questioned. Nur's intersectional positioning is characterized by her identities as Ahmadi Muslim, ethnicized (and racialized) immigrant, and young woman. She became a facilitator working in the field of civic education at the age of 16. In the summer of 2012, Nur and a few colleagues started facilitating their own workshops with youths and teachers.

The workshop focuses on the intersection of religion, human rights, and discrimination by addressing anti-Muslim racism and its consequences. Students participate in a four-hour session that incorporates inclusive and participative methods to discuss and analyze discourses and stereotypes about Muslims and other religious minorities. The teacher trainings address teachers working with heterogeneous student groups. The overall program aims to deconstruct explicitly or implicitly racist and biased views as of Muslims and other nondominant religious groups in Germany.

At the heart of the work conducted by Nur and her colleagues is a human rights-based approach that aims to raise awareness for those who are affected by human rights abuses in everyday life. The approach focuses on those who are most marginalized, excluded, or discriminated against. These people suffer in several contexts and levels: interpersonally, structurally, and institutionally. Learning about the experiences and disadvantage of persons who are affected by discriminatory practices is an essential condition for any action toward a more inclusive society.

In her workshops, Nur invites participants to explore the experiences of affected groups. Students analyze public discourses, media coverage, and news in order to determine where and how abuses and discrimination take place. The goal is to make students more sensitive to and critical about various aspects and types of discrimination. Nur's methods and exercises incorporate the perspectives of marginalized groups by presenting initiatives, organizations, and specific cases. By naming nondominant groups, citing their views, and letting students explore situations in which representatives share their experiences and their actions in order to challenge positions, nondominant students get to know people with whom they share experiences of exclusion. Students meet people with whom they might identify and they learn about kinds of activism and organizations that they may have not been exposed to previously. The ultimate goal of human rights education is empowerment: giving youths the knowledge and skills to take control of their lives and other's lives and to stand up against human rights abuses. Nur and her colleagues try to empower, motivate, and support ideas for actions on how to tackle discrimination.

To Nur and the other educators, human rights education means more than just learning and talking about human rights. There are three dimensions to human rights education: learning *about, through,* and *for* human rights. Learning about human rights implies being aware of the existence of human rights. It involves learning about the history and development of human rights and the fact that human rights are perpetually embattled and acquired and are constantly evolving and progressing. It may also include learning about different kinds of human rights or different sets of rights for marginalized groups: women, children, and persons with disabilities, for example.

Learning through human rights plays a crucial role in Nur's perception of civic education, especially when working with teachers. She views teachers in Germany—state representatives—as obligated to respect, protect, and fulfill human rights. Teachers should position themselves in the context of human rights (education) and thus embody human rights—the recognition of inclusion and participation—in their behavior, language, and conduct. For Nur, this paradigm means being sensitive to visible and nonvisible forms of stigmatization (e.g., skin color, LGBTQ issues). It is paramount that students experience respect, fairness, and equality in their learning settings—even if they don't necessarily know about the concept of human rights. Nur says: "Students do not necessarily need to know about human rights to experience human rights (Almas Nur, interview with authors, February 2, 2015).

Finally, learning in a human rights context for Nur is often associated with empowerment: to motivate and support youths' energies for activism in achieving the realization of human rights. Human rights education teaches human rights and the need for their realization, and consequently aims at empowering people to fight and engage for human rights, to become active, and to speak up when human rights are being violated (Flowers, 2000; Lohrenscheit, 2006; United Nations Office of the High Commissioner for Human Rights, 2000).

The Workshop for Youths: "Questions of Faith? Religion(s) Together"

The workshop with students from Grade 9 and up is typically conducted in the education center at which Nur works, rather than at school. The workshop is designed to take four hours, and students and teachers dedicate a whole school day to the experience. This timing is very important: "Students who come to our program should enjoy it fully and experience a setting different from school."

Nur starts the student workshops with several short exercises to warm up the students and introduce the topics. Three sequential activities follow: the barometer of opinion, religion and media, and radio reality.

In the barometer of opinion activity, students are asked to position themselves around the room according to how much they agree or don't agree with some statements that are read aloud about religion. The exercise offers students the opportunity to think about publicly debated issues that may affect them. There is no right or wrong answer, and participants are not allowed to comment on their peers' positioning. These parameters create a climate in which others' opinions are respected and listened to. Statements include "Religion is a private matter"; "The media coverage about religion is neutral and objective"; and "Freedom of religion is a right every religious community in Germany has." When on the topic of media coverage about religion, lively discussion usually ensues. Typically, most students don't agree that the media are neutral. Comments include: "When the media show terrorists, they say Islamists, not terrorists," "If a Muslim commits a crime, they say it was a radical Muslim. When a Christian commits a crime, they say he is insane or something like that." "When a Muslim kills someone, he is called Islamist." "Half of what they show in the media is a lie . . . everything is a lie. Everybody tells a different story, you don't know whom to believe."

Students likely have heard of the concept of freedom of religion before the workshop. Nur elaborates the idea of the right of freedom of religion: Freedom of religion does not mean solely that every human being has the freedom to choose, change, or give up his or her religious belief. The right of freedom of religion also means protection and equality: Every person's belief is protected, and no matter which religious belief someone has, that person has the same rights as any other person. In the discussion that follows, students—many of whom are from religious minority groups, especially Muslims—often discover that this principle is not a reality in Germany: "Yes, that sounds good, but only in theory. Reality is different."

Building on this discussion, the next activity, on religion and media, focuses on media coverage about religion and religiosity. Students are shown covers of leading German magazines (e.g., *Der Spiegel, Stern, Focus, Geo*) and asked to discuss the images on the covers in small groups. Groups discuss how religion is presented and the possible consequences and impact of these images on public debate. Students typically note that, except for articles about Buddhism, religions are mostly negatively connoted in the German press. Religion is represented as backwards and antimodern. Most of the images show stereotypical representations of Islam and/or Muslims. The students typically discuss and reflect on the narrow and predominantly negative coverage of Islam and Muslims, highlighting the effects of this coverage on people who are marked as Muslims in Germany.

One of the cover images shows women wearing headscarves; the title identifies Muslim women as oppressed and weak ("Allah's Disempowered Daughters," *Der Spiegel*, 2004). In the context of the public debate about headscarves, the discussion of this cover often becomes emotional and sometimes aggressive. Nur believes that when Muslim students who wear a headscarf respond to these images, they feel empowered: "This image is totally wrong! Muslim women are not oppressed. I am not oppressed." "I am happy to finally talk about this in my class. I think a lot of classmates think I have been forced to wear the headscarf—but let me tell you, no. This is not the case. These pictures and the media are wrong."

Controversial images of the Pope are discussed as well, and many students realize that not only Islam is represented negatively. Students start analyzing the images in more detail and find that media coverage about Islam shows "Muslim people," whereas those about Christianity show the Pope as an individual, not groups of "Christian people." They also notice that articles about Christianity do not criticize Christianity as much as they do the crimes of individuals, while in articles covering Islam, Islam itself is under suspicion.

Nur and her colleagues refer often to human rights and antidiscrimination during the discussion. Keeping in mind that media reports are an important source of information for students, Nur and her colleagues do not declare "the media" to be a problem, but rather support students in being critical about what they see and read. They encourage students to read different kinds of news sources in order to find out about different views on public issues. Nevertheless, many of the students Nur works with come into the classroom already disenchanted with, and largely disengaged from, a mainstream media in which they do not find themselves represented accurately or fairly.

Discrimination is inherent not only in public discourse but also in institutional structures, regulations, and practices. The radio reality exercise seeks to analyze social inequalities and redress discriminatory practices in the school setting. Nur hands out short stories that describe various dilemmas that are likely close to the students' own experiences. For instance, one narrative, "Gym or Mosque?" tells a story about a boy, Mo, and his best friend, both among the best basketball players at their school. In the story, a teacher announces that everyone who is interested can participate in basketball practice after school. The teacher organizes a vote to decide which weekday to hold practice on. The majority of students vote for Friday afternoon, a time slot that is a problem for Mo, who regularly attends the Friday afternoon prayer in his mosque. The teacher is now in a dilemma because he (and Mo's best friend) want Mo to attend practice but cannot change the decision because the group decided on the date based on the democratic principle of voting.

Students are invited to discuss the case and think about possible solutions: What could be done to satisfy everyone? The students find this task hard, but it leads to a critical examination of basic practices and regulations that are part of their reality. "There is no possibility to satisfy everyone!" a student explained. He further stated, "That is the problem when you live somewhere as minority: You are not considered in decisions." Students are asked to prepare a short radio broadcast in which—as a role-play—Mo, his friend, the teacher, and other students all discuss the problem. Assuming the perspective of the person affected by discrimination creates and teaches empathy among the students. In the last step, Nur asks the students to think about possible courses of actions for creating a better situation for the people affected in the various scenarios. Students come up with possibilities for action and discuss them: "I would create awareness by posting articles and other information on Facebook." "I would mention the case in class so we can discuss it with our teacher." "I would search for activist groups who support people who are discriminated against and find about their activities." Students leave the workshop feeling empowered to initiate constructive debate and become agents for social change.

Reflections

This chapter discussed the ways in which the ongoing negotiation of who is included and who is excluded from German notions of citizenship impacts the civic subjectivities of youths marked as Muslim in Germany. It depicted several ways in which the practices and regulations of German education institutions are a battleground in the negotiation of full civic participation for Muslim German youths. It presented two specifics situations (i.e., the headscarf debate and Nur's curriculum to address anti-Muslim racism) in order to make the point that classrooms and schools are where practices of inclusion and exclusion should be addressed. It provided a specific example of integrating a curriculum that supports understanding exclusionary practices and developing empowered responses to all youths—both those interpellated and those witnessing the interpellation, that is, the process where individuals are addressed *through* ideology *and* recognize themselves *by it,* thus illustrating how subjects can be complicit in their own domination (Althusser, 1972).

Nur's civic education program was developed and implemented by a nonprofit organization and implemented in informal settings outside of school. Informal education settings are spaces that allow the piloting of innovative, and at times perhaps inconvenient, approaches and programs that might meet more resistance in institutional settings. As these kinds of programs are beginning to reveal their effectiveness, the hope is that they will be replicated in more schools and in formal teacher trainings.

Perhaps the most important target group in combating anti-Muslim racism in Germany are those who directly work with youths: educators and teachers. Current teaching practices range from ignoring Muslim youths who contradict stereotypes to verbalizing stigmatizing beliefs about youths marked as Muslim that ascribe to them particular political and cultural worldviews.

A layer of complexity is added by the fact that many educators in Germany have a strongly antireligious stance based in ideas of enlightenment and secularism. Their views about Muslims often mix stereotypes that stigmatize and racialize immigrant "others" with a more general rejection of religious views and practices. It is important to develop methods that allow teachers to explore these distinctions and reflect critically on them.

In order to be able to meet all their students at eye-level, educators who are not from nondominant groups need particular awareness and sensitivity in how they use language and loaded terms that create exclusion. Thus, educators need time to reflect on their attitudes and practices to become aware of how they themselves may unintentionally perpetuate exclusion. It is crucial for educators to realize that heterogeneity is the norm in German classrooms. Instruction and coursework to address these issues is practically nonexistent in formal teacher training programs at German universities. Clearly, it needs to be provided. In the meantime, mandatory continuing education programs addressing these themes should be obligatory for teachers in German schools.

Another important group that needs to be supported is that of youths themselves, both those interpellated by anti-Muslim racism and those who are witnesses. In many ways, youths are similar to their teachers: Students as well as teachers make exclusionary statements that are mainstays of public opinion in Germany. Many youths and teachers are surprised once they start to understand the onslaught of anti-Muslim imagery in the media and reflect on what it means for the lives of Muslims in Germany.

There are important differences between students and educators, however. Although the vast majority of teachers in Germany do not have an immigrant, or specifically Muslim, background, a large number of the students do. Hence, students are positioned as the ones to whom traits are ascribed by discourse, and teachers often as those who ascribe. Youths marked as Muslim are in the process of constructing their identities as adult citizens of German society while being othered. The challenge posed to German society is how to address these youths' experiences and how to provide them with tools to make sense of them. Nur and her team address these experiences, engaging the "silenced dialogue" (Delpit, 1995) and pointing out stereotypes in order to deconstruct them. Although Nur prefers to name practices of exclusion rather than ignore them, it is not entirely clear whether identifying stereotypes and prejudice dismantles them in the long run.

Nur's work supports youths in developing a critical lens and awareness about what it means to be a citizen and have citizenship rights in Germany. Such work is the stepping-stone that allows minority youths to align their multiple social identities into a shared notion of "transversal" citizens. The idea of transversal citizenship needs to be implemented in the German education system and in society at large in order to achieve shared civic identities and full participation in civil society (Yuval-Davis, 1999).

In order to get to this point, nondominant youths need to be empowered to demand their civic and human rights within the education system and within society. Because hegemony does not yield without being challenged, those who are ascribed and marginalized must be part of the change. Youths—both those interpellated and those who are witnesses—need to be informed citizens who can correct injustice and demand a level playing field. It is they who must call out educators on discriminatory language. Youths—as the adults of the future—are therefore the most important agents of social change and they need to learn about and develop opportunities for action within the structures and practices they encounter.

Here we end with the words of Almas Nur: "If I am not the one in power, and I can't change policies, I can still do a lot through symbolic work. It is important to not use certain terms. Symbolic work can change a lot for the ones who are affected by these words. Human rights talk is not cheap."

Notes

1. The expression "youths marked as Muslim" is used here to make explicit that experiences of being Muslim in the public sphere are defined primarily by ascription processes and have less to do with religious membership or personal religious practice.

2. The German nation as "a prepolitical community of individuals who are bound to each other by the commonness of either their 'nature' (their blood) or their culture (their language, literature, religion, and history)" (Preuß, 1996, p. 542) was expressed in its citizenship law, which from 1913 to 2000 conferred citizenship exclusively according to the *jus sanguinis* principle of kinship ties and descent.

3. The German annual census did not begin to assess *immigrant background* as an indicator until 2005. Before that, only *German citizenship* and *foreign citizenship* were used as indicators (Statistisches Bundesamt, 2007).

4. Overall, religious membership and religious orientation in Germany are characterized by heterogeneity: Two thirds of the population belong to Catholic or Protestant Christian churches, and about one third have no religious affiliation.

5. Muslims in Germany are estimated to break down into Sunnites (74%), Alevites (13%), Shiites (7%), Ahmadiyya (2%), as well as other small communities.

6. The official construction of who counts as Muslim is part of the problematic construction of religio-cultural minorities in Germany. Accurate statistics on religious membership and orientation do not exist, and in the absence of appropriate census measures, religious membership of Muslims is inferred from a family's country of origin. Religious membership in the "Muslim" community is thus ascribed, and who "counts" as Muslim is not based on actual membership in a religious community, nor it is based on an individual's self-identification as Muslim in terms of personal religious orientation (Spielhaus, 2013).

7. Although these polls paint a troubling picture of the anti-Muslim climate in Germany, an opening may be exist in reviewing the opinions of the generation aged 16–25. In this age group, the perception of threat by Islam, as well as the idea that Islam does not fit into Western society, is significantly less expressed. A possible explanation for this finding is that the younger generation is growing up in more diverse schools, with 25% of youth coming from Muslim communities (Bertelsmann, 2015).

8. In 2015, the German Federal Agency for Migration and Refugees received 476,649 formal asylum requests (of these, approximately 30,000 were unaccompanied minors). This number is 273,815 more than in 2014; 162,510 of these asylum seekers came from Syria.

9. Institutionalized religion plays a strong role in contemporary Germany: Christian churches are guaranteed privileges such as the collection of church taxes by the state and for the church, and the organization of religious instruction in state schools (Robbers, 1995). Church and state separation in Germany is thus incomplete (Daiber, 1995). Religious plurality in the public sphere is in many ways dominated by the role that institutionalized religion plays.

10. Ethnic democracies distinguish strongly between members of the ethnic nation and non-members. Therefore, closure to new members characterizes ethnic nations (Goldstein, 1997; Herzog, 1997; James, 1989; Sabean, 1984).

11. The concept of responsible citizenship is part of the German constitution (*Grundgesetz*): Article 33 specifies that "every German in every federal state has the same civil rights and duties." The ethnic phrasing of this constitutional law ("German" instead of "citizen") foreshadows some of the problems that arise in its implementation, although it embodies the notion that citizens have both rights and the duty to be active as citizens.

12. The program was initiated by the director of the Anne Frank Education Centre in Frankfurt, who believed that the center's mainstay of civic and Holocaust education programs should be expanded to address his concerns about the growing anti-Muslim discourse in the German public. The center is a nongovernmental organization that since 1997 has offered a wide range of programs for students and teachers. Combining historic-political education with human rights education, it promotes democratic principles based on the notion of human rights and examines human rights issues without bias and from diverse perspectives through a variety of educational practices.

References

Abbas, T. (2004). After 9/11: British South Asian Muslims, Islamophobia, multiculturalism, and the state. *American Journal of Islamic Social Sciences, 21*(3), 26–37.

Akbarzadeh, S., & Roose, J. M. (2011). Muslims, multiculturalism and the question of the silent majority. *Journal of Muslim Minority Affairs, 31*(3), 309–325.

Ali, A. H. (2012, September 17). Newsweek goes for broke with "Muslim rage." *Atlantic Wire.*

Al-Haj, M. (2005). National ethos, multicultural education, and the new history textbooks in Israel. *Curriculum Inquiry, 35*(1), 47–71

AlSayyad, N., & Castells, M. (Eds.). (2002). *Muslim Europe or Euro-Islam: Politics, culture, and citizenship in the age of globalization.* Lanham, MD: Lexington Books.

Althusser, L. (1972). *Lenin and philosophy and other essays.* New York: Monthly Review Press.

Amir-Moazami, S. (2005). Muslim challenges to the secular consensus: A German case study. *Journal of Contemporary European Studies, 13*(3), 267–286.

Amir-Moazami, S. (2007). *Politisierte Religion. Der Kopftuchstreit in Deutschland und Frankreich* [Politicized religion: The headscarf conflict in Germany and France]. Bielefeld, Germany: Transcript Verlag.

Anyon, J. (1980). Social class and the hidden curriculum of work. *Journal of Education, 162*(1), 67–89.

Asad, T. (2003). *Formations of the secular: Christianity, Islam, modernity.* Stanford, CA: Stanford University Press.

Bakhtin, M. M. (1996). Discourse in the novel (C. E. a. M. Holquist, Trans.). In M. Holquist (Ed.), *The dialogic imagination: Four essays* (pp. 259–422). Austin: University of Texas Press. (Original work published 1981)

Beck, G. (2015). *It is about Islam: Exposing the truth about ISIS, Al Qaeda, Iran, and the Caliphate.* New York: Treshold.

Bertelsmann Stiftung. (2015). *Religionsmonitor 2015—Sonderauswertung Islam* [Religions Monitor 2015—Special Analysis of Islam]. Retrieved from http://www.bertelsmann-stiftung.de/fileadmin/files/Projekte/51_Religionsmonitor/Religionmonitor_Specialstudy_Islam_2014_Overview_20150108.pdf

Bloemraad, I., Korteweg, A., & Yurdakul, G. (2008). Citizenship and immigration: Multiculturalism, assimilation, and challenges to the nation-state. *Annual Review of Sociology, 34*(1), 153–179.

Bourdieu, P. (1976). Les modes de domination [The modes of domination]. *Actes de la Recherche en Sciences Sociales, 2*(2–3), 122–132.

Brettfeld, K., & Wetzels, P. (2007). *Muslime in Deutschland: Integration, integrationsbarrieren, Religion sowie Einstellungen zu Demokratie, Rechtsstaat und politisch-religiös motivierter Gewalt: Ergebnisse von Befragungen im Rahmen einer multizentrischen Studie in städtischen Lebensräumen* [Muslims in Germany: Integration, barriers to integration, religion as well as attitudes towards democracy, the state, and political-religious violence—Findings from a multicentric study in urban milieus]. Hamburg, Germany: Bundesministerium des Inneren.

Brown, M. D. (2006). Comparative analysis of mainstream discourses, media narratives and representations of Islam in Britain and France prior to 9/11. *Journal of Muslim Minority Affairs, 26*(3), 297–312.

Brubaker, R. (1994). *Citizenship and nationhood in France and Germany.* Cambridge, MA: Harvard University Press.

Bundesamt für Migration und Flüchtlinge. (2016). *Wie viele Muslime leben in Deutschland? Eine Hochrechnung über die Anzahl der Muslime in Deutschland zum Stand 31. Dezember 2015* [How many refugees live in Germany? A projection about the number of Muslims in Germany on December 31, 2015]. (Working Paper 71). Nürnberg, Germany: Bundesamt für Migration und Flüchtlinge.

Caglar, A. S. (1995). McDöner: Döner Kebap and the social positioning struggle of German Turks. In J. A. Costa & G. Bamossy (Eds.), *Marketing in a multicultural world* (pp. 209–230). London: Sage.

Caglar, A. S. (1997). Hyphenated identities and the limits of "culture." In T. Modood & P. Werbner (Eds.), *The politics of multiculturalism in the new Europe: Racism, identity and community* (pp. 169–185). London: Zed Books.

Cockburn, P. (2014). *The Jihadis return: ISIS and the new Sunni uprising.* New York: OR Books.

Council of Europe & O'Shea, K. (2003). *Developing a shared understanding: A glossary of terms for education for democratic citizenship.* Strasbourg, France: Council of Europe.

Daiber, K.-F. (1995). *Religion unter den Bedingungen der Moderne. Die Situation in der Bundesrepublik Deutschland* [Religion under conditions of modernity. The situation in the Federal Republic of Germany]. Marburg, Germany: Diagonal Verlag.

Dalsheim, J. (2010). On demonized Muslims and vilified Jews: Between theory and politics. *Comparative Studies in Society and History, 52*(3), 581–603.

De Oliveira Andreotti, V., & de Souza, L. M. T. M. (2012). (Towards) global citizenship education "otherwise." In V. de Oliveira Andreotti & L. M. T. M. de Souza (Eds.), *Postcolonial perspectives on global citizenship education* (pp. 1–8). New York: Routledge.

Delanty, G. (1997). Models of citizenship: Defining European identity and citizenship. *Citizenship Studies, 1*(3), 285–303.

Delpit, L. (1995). The silenced dialogue. In L. Delpit (Ed.), *Other people's children: Cultural conflict in the classroom* (pp. 21–47). New York: New Press.

Derricott, R. (1998). National case studies of citizenship education. In J. J. Cogan & R. Derricott (Eds.), *Citizenship for the 21st century* (pp. 23–92). London: Kogan Page.

Dumont, L. (1986). Are cultures living beings? German identity in interaction. *Man, 21*(4), 587–604.

Dwyer, C. (1998). Contested identities: Challenging dominant representations of young British Muslim women. In T. Skelton & G Valentine (Eds.), *Cool places: Geographies of youth cultures* (pp. 50–65). London: Routledge.

European Commission. (2005). *Citizenship education at school in Europe.* Brussels: Eurydice/European Commission.

Ewing, K. P. (2008). *Stolen honor: Stigmatizing Muslim men in Berlin*. Stanford, CA: Stanford University Press.

Featherstone, M. (2009). Occidentalism: Jack Goody and comparative history. *Theory Culture & Society, 26*(7–8), 1–15.

Fischer, S., Hotam, Y., & Wexler, P. (2012). Democracy and education in postsecular society. *Review of Research in Education, 36*, 261.

Flowers, N. (2000). *Human rights education handbook: Effective practices for learning, action, and change*. Minneapolis: University of Minnesota.

Frobenius, L. (1897–1898). Der westafrikanische Kulturkreis [The West African culture area]. *Petermanns Mitteilungen, 43/44*.

Gaiser, W., Gille, M., Krüger, W., & de Rijke, J. (2011). Jugend und Demokratie [Youth and democracy]. In Friedrich Ebert Stiftung (Ed.), *Demokratie in Deutschland 2011: Ein report der Friedrich-Ebert-Stiftung* [Democracy in Germany 2011: A report of the Friedrich Ebert Foundation]. Berlin, Germany: Friedrich-Ebert-Stiftung.

German Constitutional Court (BVERFG). (2015, January 27). *Ein pauschales Kopftuchverbot für Lehrkräfte in öffentlichen Schulen ist mit der Verfassung nicht vereinbar* [A general headscarf ban for teachers in public school is not in agreement with the constitution] [Press release].

Goldstein, E. L. (1997). "Different blood flows in our veins": Race and Jewish self-definition in late nineteenth century America. *American Jewish History, 85*(1), 29.

Goody, J. (2006). *The theft of history*. Cambridge, UK: Cambridge University Press.

Gramsci, A. (1971). *Selections from the prison notebooks of Antonio Gramsci* (G. S. Q. Hoare, Trans.). London: Lawrence & Wishart.

Grosfoguel, R., & Mielants, E. (2006). The long-durée entanglement between Islamophobia and racism in the modern/colonial capitalist/patriarchal world-system: An introduction. *Human Architecture: Journal of the Sociology of Self-Knowledge, 1*, 1–12.

Habermas, J. (2006). Religion in the public sphere. *European Journal of Philosophy, 14*(1), 1–25.

Habermas, J. (2008). Die Dialektik der Säkularisierung [The dialectic of secularization]. *Blätter für deutsche und internationale Politik* [Pages for German and International Politics] (4), 1–13.

Hafez, F. (2014). Shifting borders: Islamophobia as common ground for building pan-European right-wing unity. *Patterns of Prejudice, 48*(5), 479–499.

Haug, S., Müssig, S., & Stichs, A. (2009). *Muslimisches leben in Deutschland* [Muslim life in Germany]. Hamburg: Bundesministerium des Inneren.

Heimbach-Steins, M., Wielandt, R., & Zintl, R. (Eds.). (2006). Religiöse identität(en) und gemeinsame Religionsfreiheit. Politische und religiöse Voraussetzungen des Zusammenlebens in "postsäkularer" Gesellschaft- eine Einführung [Religious identities and shared religious freedom: Political and religious conditions for co-existence in post-secular society]. In M. Heimbach-Steins, R. Wielandt, & R. Zintl (Eds.), *Religiöse Identität(en) und gemeinsame Religionsfreiheit. Eine Herausforderung pluraler Gesellschaften* [Religious identities and shared religious freedom] (pp. 9–24). Würzburg, Germany: Ergon-Verlag.

Herzog, T. (1997). Hybrids and *Mischlinge:* Translating Anglo-American cultural theory into Germany. *German Quarterly, 70*(1), 1–17.

Huntington, S. P. (1996). *The clash of civilizations and the remaking of world order*. New York: Simon & Schuster.

Hüttermann, J. (2011). Moscheekonflikte im Figurationsprozess der Einwanderungsgesellschaft: Eine soziologische Analyse [Conflicts about mosques during the development of immigration society: A sociological analysis]. In M. Krüger-Potratz & W. Schiffauer (Eds.), *Migrationsreport 2010: Fakten—Analysen—Perspektiven* [Migration report 2010: Facts—Analysis—Perspectives]. Frankfurt, Germany: Campus Verlag.

Isin, E. F. (2012). Citizenship after Orientalism: An unfinished project. *Citizenship Studies, 16*(5–6), 563–572.

James, H. (1989). *A German identity: 1770–1990.* New York: Routledge.

Karakaşoğlu, Y., & Luchtenberg, S. (2004). Islamophobia in German educational settings: Actions and reactions. In B. van Driel (Ed.), *Confronting Islamophobia in educational practice.* Stoke-on-Trent, UK: Trentham.

Klug, B. (2013). Islamophobia: A concept comes of age. *Ethnicities, 12*(5), 665–681.

Klug, B. (2014). The limits of analogy: Comparing Islamophobia and antisemitism. *Patterns of Prejudice, 48*(5), 442–459.

Lears, T. J. J. (1985). The concept of cultural hegemony: Problems and possibilities. *American Historical Review*, 567–593.

Lemish, P. (2010). Civic and citizenship education in Israel. *Cambridge Journal of Education, 33*(1), 53–72.

Levy, G. (2005). From subjects to citizens: On educational reforms and the demarcations of the "Israeli-Arab." *Citizenship Studies, 9*, 271–291.

Lohrenscheit, C. (2006). A human rights based approach in education. In M. Brown, A.-M. Eekhout, & Y. Baleva (Eds.), *Dare in action: Vision and practice for democracy and human rights education in Europe.* Berlin, Germany: Partners Pulgaria Foundation.

Luchtenberg, S. (2004). Ethnic diversity and citizenship education in Germany. In J. A. Banks (Ed.), *Diversity and citizenship educaiton: Global perspectives* (pp. 252–272). San Francisco: Jossey-Bass.

Mandel, R. (2008). *Cosmopolitan anxieties: Turkish challenges to citizenship and belonging in Germany.* London: Duke University Press.

McLaughlin, T. H. (1992). Citizenship, diversity and education: A philosophical perspective. *Journal of Moral Education, 22*, 235–250.

Meer, N. (2014). Islamophobia and postcolonialism: Continuity, Orientalism and Muslim consciousness. *Patterns of Prejudice, 48*(5), 500–515.

Mignolo, W. D. (1995). *The darker side of the Renaissance: Literacy, territoriality, and colonization.* Ann Arbor: University of Michigan Press.

Miles, R., & Brown, M. (2003). *Racism* (2nd ed.). London: Routledge.

Modood, T. (1997). "Difference": Cultural racism and anti-racism. In P. Werbner & T. Modood (Eds.), *Debating cultural hybridity: Multi-cultural identities and the politics of anti-racism* (pp. 154–172). London: Zed Books.

Mouffe, C. (1988). Hegemony and new political subjects: Toward a new concept of democracy. In C. Nelson & L. Grossberg (Eds.), *Marxism and the interpretation of culture* (pp. 89–101). Urbana: University of Illinois Press.

Muslimische Frauen in Deutschland: Allahs rechtlose Töchter [Muslim women in Germany: Allah's disempowered daughters]. (2004). *Der Spiegel*, [German Weekly], front cover.

Özyürek, E. (2005). The politics of cultural unification, secularism, and the place of Islam in the new Europe: Commentary. *American Ethnologist, 32*(4), 509–512.

Özyürek, E. (2014). *Being German, becoming Muslims: Race, religion, and conversion in the new Europe.* Princeton, NJ: Princeton University Press.

Perez Huber, L., & Solorzano, D. G. (2015). Racial microaggressions as a tool for critical race research. *Race, Ethnicity and Education, 18*(3), 297–320.

Pinson, H. (2007). Inclusive curriculum? Challenges to the role of civic education in a Jewish and democratic state. *Curriculum Inquiry, 37*(4), 351–382.

Preuß, U. K. (1996). Two challenges to European citizenship. *Political Studies, 44*(3), 534–552.

Rath, C., & Bax, D. (2015, March 13). Religionssymbole an Schulen: Das Kopftuch ist frei [Religious symbols in school: The head scarf is free]. *taz.de.* Retrieved from http://www.taz.de/!5016688

Robbers, G. (1995). Staat und Kirche in der Bundesrepublik Deutschland [State and church in the Federal Republic of Germany]. In G. Robbers (Ed.), *Staat und Kirche in der Europäischen Union* [State and church in the European Union] (pp. 61–78). Baden-Baden, Germany: Nomos.

Rothman, L. (2012, November 1). A cultural history of mansplaining. *The Atlantic*. Retrieved from https://www.theatlantic.com/sexes/archive/2012/11/a-cultural-history-of-mansplaining/264380/

Sabean, D. W. (1984). *Power in the blood: Popular culture and village discourse in early modern Germany*. Cambridge, UK: Cambridge University Press

Said, E. W. (1979). *Orientalism*. London: Penguin.

Salvatore, A. (2006). Public religion, ethics of participation, and cultural dialogue. In A. Aziz Said, M. Abu-Nimer, & M. Sharify-Funk (Eds.), *Contemporary Islam: Dynamic, not static* (pp. 83–100). London: Routledge.

Sayer, D. (1994). Everyday forms of state formation: Some dissident remarks on "hegemony." In G. M. Joseph & D. Nugent (Eds.), *Everyday forms of state formation: Revolution and the negotiation of rule in modern Mexico* (pp. 367–378). Durham, NC: Duke University Press.

Sayyid, S. (2011). Thinking through Islamophobia. In S. Sayyid & A. Vakil (Eds.), *Thinking through Islamophobia: Global perspectives* (pp. 1–4). New York: Columbia University Press.

Schiffauer, W. (2002). Die Debatten um den islamischen Religionsunterricht: Zur Rolle von Religion in der deutschen politischen Kultur [The debates about Islamic education: On the role of religion in German political culture]. In H. Lehmann (Ed.), *Multireligiösität im vereinigten Europa: Historische und juristische Aspekte* [Multireligiosity in unified Europe: Historical and legal aspects] (p. 115–134). Göttingen, Germany: Wallstein Verlag.

Schiffauer, W. (2007). Der unheimliche Muslim: Staatsbürgerschaft und zivigesellschaftliche Ängste [The scary Muslim: Citizenship and fears of civil society]. In L. Tezcan & M. Wohlrab-Sahr (Eds.), *Konfliktfeld Islam in Europa* [Islam as conflicted field in Europe] (pp. 111–134). Baden-Baden, Germany: Nomos-Verlag.

Shooman, Y. (2014). "*. . . weil ihre Kultur so ist*": Narrative des antimuslimischen Rassismus [". . . Because this is their culture": Narratives of antimuslim racism]. Bielefeld, Germany: Transcript Verlag.

Smooha, S. (2002). The model of ethnic democracy: Israel as Jewish and democratic state. *Nations and Nationalism, 8*(4), 475–503.

Spielhaus, R. (2013). *Muslime in der Statistik. Wer ist Muslim und wenn ja wie viele?* [Muslims in the Census: Who is Muslim and if yes, how many?]. Berlin: Mediendienst Integration.

Statistisches Bundesamt. (2007). *Bevölkerung und Erwerbstätigkeit. Bevölkerung mit Migrationshintergrund—Ergebnisse des Mikrozensus 2005.* [Population and employment: Population with immigrant background—Results of the microcensus 2005]. Wiesbaden, Germany: Author.

Statistisches Bundesamt [Federal Census Bureau]. (2011). *Bevölkerung mit Migrationshintergrund: Mikrozensus* [Population with immigrant background: Micro-census]. Wiesbaden, Germany: Author.

United Nations Office of the High Commissioner for Human Rights. (2000). *Human rights training: A manual on human rights training methodology*. New York: United Nations.

Van Krieken, R. (2000). Citizenship and democracy in Germany: Implications for understanding globalization. In A. Vandenberg (Ed.), *Citizenship and democracy in a global era* (pp. 123–137). London: Macmillan.

Vertovec, S., & Rogers, A. (Eds.). (1998). *Muslim European youth: Reproducing ethnicity, religion, culture*. Aldershot, UK: Ashgate.

Wiese, K. (2011). Grenzen der Religionsfreiheit ausloten. Zur Diskussion um Kopftuch- und Burka-Verbote [Interrogating the borders of religious freedom on the debate about headscarf and burka]. In H. K. Elke Ariëns & Manfred Sicking (Eds.), *Glaubensfragen in Europa* [Religious questions in Europe] (pp. 87–126). Bielefeld, Germany: Transcript Verlag.

Windandy, J. (2011). Religiöse und säkulare Argumente im Konflikt? Kritik einer irreführenden Dichotomie. [Conflict of religious and secular arguments? Critique of a misleading dichotomy]. In H. K. Elke Ariëns & M. Sicking (Ed.), *Glaubensfragen in Europa* [Religious questions in Europe] (pp. 175–196). Bielefeld, Germany: Transcript Verlag.

Yalcin-Heckmann, L. (1998). Growing up as a Muslim in Germany: Religious socialization among Turkish migrant families. In S. Vertovec & A. Rogers (Eds.), *Muslim European youth: Reproducing ethnicity, religion, culture* (pp. 167–191). Aldershot, UK: Ashgate.

Yuval-Davis, N. (1999). The multi-layered citizen: Citizenship in the age of globalization. *International Feminist Journal of Politics, 1,* 119–136.

Zick, A., Küpper, B., & Hövermann, A. (2011). *Die Abwertung der Anderen: Eine europäische Zustandsbeschreibung zu Intoleranz, Vorurteilen und Diskriminierung* [The devaluation of others: A description of the European status quo on intolerance, prejudice and discrimination]. Berlin, Germany: Friedrich Ebert Stiftung.

Chapter 9

Citizenship and Diversity in Education in France: Public Controversies, Local Adaptations, and Commitments

GÉRALDINE BOZEC

University of Nice Sophia Antipolis

Public education has traditionally been conceived in France as a central institution to build citizenship, a sense of common belonging, and shared values (Déloye, 1994). The political and media reactions to the 2015 terrorist attacks conducted in the name of Islam emphasized, once again, this role attributed to the school (Lorcerie, 2016). It was argued that schools must reinforce their role in educating citizens, enabling them to reject violence, to internalize secular values, and to cherish the importance of freedom of expression and of common belonging (Vallaud-Belkacem, 2015a, 2015b). The so-called French model of citizenship appeared to be questioned by the terrorist attacks that occurred in France in January and in November 2015.

The idea of the *republic* is at the core of this model. Basically, the republican conception of the political community defines it as a neutral, individualistic, and universalistic sphere. In the civic sphere, citizens are recognized not as members of groups and communities (such as religion, social class, and ethnicity) but as individuals sharing the same attachment to the nation and to democratic values. The republican conception of citizenship, which is linked to a long history of power struggles between the state and the Catholic Church, makes it difficult to recognize pluralism as a core public value (Birnbaum, 1998; Duchesne, 1997; Zoïa, 2010).

This republican pattern has not been the only way of conceiving citizenship in France. Different and often contradictory versions of it have existed, depending on actors and contexts, and several types of contestation of such a pattern developed, for example, through the labor movement, feminism, and the anticolonialist current. But since its formulation and entrenchment in the 19th century, it has represented a powerful symbolic reference, which shapes the perceptions, the discursive strategies, and the practices of actors at different levels, from governmental actors to grassroots teachers.

Over the last three decades, new challenges have contributed to the debates about the meanings of citizenship and the role of the school in citizenship education. In a context of economic and social difficulties, a feeling of crisis has spread across French society, and growing concerns have been expressed about social cohesion and the conditions for living together. Decolonization, the acceleration of globalization, and European integration have put into question the prevalent role of the nation-state, the place of France in the global scene, and the self-image of the French nation as a "model" (Schissler & Soysal, 2005). Increasing concerns have also been expressed about immigration, which is most often described as a "problem," and about the place of Islam in French society (Noiriel, 2007; Simon, 2013; Tiberj, 2014).

This chapter focuses on the place and conceptions of citizenship education and diversity in the French public school system. The first section describes recent developments in education policies and practices. The second section presents a case study of a teacher, which allows for the identification of both current limitations and opportunities for more effective citizenship education at school.

Public Education, Citizenship, and Diversity in France: Toward a New Pattern After the 2015 Terrorist Attacks?

Historical Legacies: National Citizenship and Laïcité *as Core Elements of Public Education*

The French Revolution at the end of the 18th century represented a first attempt to break with the ancient divisions of the *Ancien Régime*, characterized by a hierarchical social and political order (with the division into three groups: the nobility, the clergy, and the "Third Estate"). The revolutionary forces tried to create a new political order in which citizens were equal individuals without intermediary bodies between them and the state. Throughout the 19th century and the beginning of the 20th century, competitive conceptions of the political community existed. The conflict between republican forces and the Catholic monarchists was the most important one. Republicans wanted to emancipate the sphere of citizenship from the control of the Catholic Church. One particularity of the French context—captured by the French-specific term *laïcité*—is the proactive and highly conflictive dimension of the process of secularization that occurred in the 19th and 20th centuries: The separation of state and religion was enforced in France intentionally by republican state elites, and at different moments in a rather radical manner. This resulted in a high degree of separation between the religious and the public spaces (Hervieu-Léger 2003). Secularity in France means more than the principles of freedom of conscience, neutrality of the state, and equality between all religions. It often implies that religions are excluded from the public sphere and from public institutions, as in the case of religious education, which is not allowed in public schools. Public education was indeed historically the most central battlefield of this opposition between the republican camp and the Catholic one. The creation of a public, free, "laic," and compulsory primary school in the 1880s under the Third Republic aimed to entrench republican principles by teaching them to children. Religious education was replaced by moral and civic education. This education was conceived as a way to convey to pupils a basic knowledge of republican political institutions, to make them "love" the republic, and to emancipate them from religious dogmatism. The public school was asked to foster a civic identity disconnected from traditional and primary affiliations (religion but also family and social class) and to rebuild a united and peaceful nation, capable of going beyond its former divisions.

The school of the Third Republic is said to have played a decisive role in building the French nation and fostering national homogeneity. It conveyed national culture and language to pupils in a rural France where local belongings and a diversity of local languages predominated (Weber, 1983). This movement of nationalization was linked to economic processes—the development of capitalism requiring common and homogenized culture and language (Gellner, 1989)—but also to political reasons: School education aimed to turn people into loyal national citizens (Déloye, 1994; Rokkan, 1999), capable—in a context of military rivalries—of sacrificing their lives for the motherland.

While the setting up of public education under the Third Republic contributed to more political equality by handing down basic political knowledge to pupils as future citizens, it was not conceived at that time as a means of fighting against socioeconomic inequalities. Public education was internally segregated into separated structures, dividing the school population according to gender and socioeconomic lines. Girls received for decades a specific education, more focused on their future domestic role (Mayeur, 1979). Over time, school curricula for girls and boys became progressively similar, and in 1975 a law made coeducation compulsory, recognizing a development that was already in progress. The socioeconomic divisions were also progressively reduced, at least formally. The primary classes located in high schools, which required the payment of tuition and were attended by pupils of upper social classes, progressively disappeared between the 1930s and the 1950s, which led to the unification of the first level of the French school system. The barriers to access to lower secondary education and its internal divisions into different and hierarchical streams were also gradually eliminated from the 1950s to the 1970s. This resulted in a mass secondary education system, more unified formally and gathering most of the students of the same generation, even if strong social inequalities continued to exist in education.[1]

Immigration and Diversity Over the Last Decades

The plurality of French society, related to the successive waves of immigration, was a nonissue in the field of education until the 1970s. The school education of the children of immigrant parents, similar to that of children in rural families, was supposed to enable them to embrace French national culture and national language and to identify with the French nation while abandoning their previous cultural identities. This monistic and assimilationist conception of national identity is particularly illustrated by the way history was conceptualized and taught (Citron, 2008). Told from the point of view of the nation-state, the school narrative of French history had a strong unifying aim: it highlighted the supposed original unity of the "Gallic people" and the administrative, territorial, and cultural unification carried out by Romans, Frank chiefs, royal dynasties, and republics (Bozec, 2010). It overlooked dark parts of French history such as conflicts and oppression related to colonization, as well as immigration and diversity (De Cock & Picard, 2009).

Questions related to nation and national identification lost some importance in the decades following World War II. This period was marked by economic prosperity, and the political ideologies of that time—liberal, revolutionary, or reformist—did not make national and cultural identities a central issue. From the 1970s onward, the situation changed. In a context of economic difficulties, legal labor immigration flows were stopped, followed by family reunification policies. Growing debates about the so-called integration of immigrants and their descendants and the meaning of national belonging emerged. Since the 1980s, the rise of far-right National Front party has contributed to the politicization of the issues related to immigration and Islam in a negative way, and such a framing has tended to spread in other segments of the political spectrum over time.

Education was, again, one of the major arenas for these debates about diversity and unity. During a very short period, from the mid-1970s to the first half of the 1980s, the value of cultural differences and the promotion at school of the so-called "cultures of origin" of children of immigrants were explicitly asserted. Schools—particularly those receiving significant proportions of children of immigrants—were invited to develop "intercultural" activities. However, intercultural education remained poorly defined and not proactively defended by the Ministry of Education through detailed guidelines and teacher training (Lorcerie, 2002). Against this background, intercultural education actually often came to focus on the children of immigrants only, rather than addressing the multiple identities of all the students, and despite positive intentions, to develop culturalist approaches by assigning them to a fixed, homogeneous, and often folklorist "culture of origin."

Different actors (intellectuals, educational nongovernmental organizations such as the Ligue de l'Enseignement, other nongovernmental organizations, and some political actors) have been advocating for a better recognition of plurality within education for three decades, but most often in a specific manner, distant from the more common versions of the multiculturalist approach. Indeed, probably due to the weight of universalism and individualism in French political culture, there is a widespread distrust toward the "groupist" dimension of the multiculturalist credo, which puts the emphasis on the cultural specificities of communities and groups instead of common belonging and individuality (Boucher, 2000; Laborde, 2010). The advocates of cultural diversity in education in France are thus mostly in line with the republican ideal while also paying attention to the risks of a too-narrow and assimilationist version of it, which would reject plurality. In their conception, identity stems from the diverse background of each individual, is multiple, and evolves over time and according to situations. The dangers of ethnocultural assignments are thus pointed out—considering some groups as holding cultural differences, even with positive intentions, not only relies on a poor understanding of the complexity of individual identity but contributes to processes of stigmatization and discrimination by confining these groups to otherness and difference. The promoters of cultural diversity in education see plurality as a characteristic of the whole society, which gathers diverse individuals. They advocate for a more inclusive narrative of French history and contemporary society, which does not overlook the plurality of individuals, the longtime presence in France of diverse immigrants, and the conflictive parts of French history, such as the colonial past and slavery (Dhume & Hamdani, 2013).

Despite the existence of some French actors defending the recognition of plurality in education, actual education policies have not gone far in this direction during the last several decades. The only existing scheme that may relate to cultural diversity currently consists of courses about cultures and languages "of origin" (*enseignements de langues et de cultures d'origine*), which are taught outside normal school hours to students on a voluntary basis. The *enseignements de langues et de cultures d'origine* scheme was recently opened to all families who requested it, even though they might not have the nationality of the related country of origin. It is noteworthy that this scheme remains isolated from the rest of the school activities and does not address the diversity of all the students present at school. In such a scheme, plurality tends to be confined to people with immigrant backgrounds. Instead of plurality, there is a growing emphasis on a restrictive conception of *laïcité* and on an assimilationist view of national identity that has been observable during the last decade.

The Growing Emphasis on National Identity From 2002 to 2012

At the end of the 1990s, under the left government, a few measures promoted a better recognition of the heritages and memories related to immigrants and minorities in France. A law adopted in 2001 (known as the Taubira law, from the name of M.P. Guyana Christiane Taubira) labeled the Black slave trade and slavery as a crime against humanity and promoted teaching about slavery in public schools. The government also commissioned a report on the creation of a cultural center dedicated to the history of immigration, which was to work in close partnership with schools. Following the impetus of the European Union, which adopted a racial equality directive in 2000, a comprehensive legal framework and policies to fight ethnic discrimination were also adopted in the late 1990s and early 2000s by the left government. However, the education sector remained apart from that trend. Ethnic discrimination in schools has hardly been addressed, and it remains to a great extent a taboo subject (Dhume & Hamdani, 2013).

The subsequent period, between 2002 and 2012, was characterized by a growing emphasis on national identity and national unity, despite a few measures that continued to relate to the fight against discrimination and the promotion of diversity. The Right, which came into power in 2002, did not abandon the initiative launched by the former left government: the National Center for the History of Immigration (Cité Nationale de l'histoire de l'immigration) was opened in 2007. This public cultural center promotes the contribution of immigrants to French history and memory and cooperates with schools in educational activities related to these issues. Changes in school curricula were also adopted in 2008–2010, which gave slightly more emphasis to the themes of colonialism, decolonization, and the history of immigration within the history curriculum of secondary schools (Legris, 2010).

However, in the same period, the right majority also put the emphasis on a monistic conception of society and national identity. Between 2002 and 2012, national belonging was asserted as the prevalent identity and as antithetical to minority ethnic and religious affiliations, evoked through the pervasive reference to the fight against *communautarismes* (Bozec, 2015; Dhume, 2007). This vague and never-defined term had been used in political speeches since the 1990s to cast doubt on the national loyalty of some segments of minority groups, implicitly accused of preferring their particular subgroup and of rejecting national belonging and "republican" values. The themes of the necessary "respect" and "love" of the nation (and of its symbols) were put at the forefront of the political agenda (Bozec, 2015;

Simon, 2013), including in education. Public education was described in governmental speeches as a central institution to reinforce national unity and pride (Chirac, 2003; Ferry, Darcos, & Haigneré, 2003; Ministère de l'Education nationale [MEN], 2004). In November 2003, President Jacques Chirac declared that students should learn at school "the values, the originality, the strength of the French message," "the history, the one of the nation, of its institutions," and "to respect its anthem and flag."[2] Different measures were taken to reinforce national loyalty through education: the 2005 law on education made the teaching of "republican values" an official mission of public schools. The right government was even caught off-guard by its political majority on those issues. The compulsory learning of the national anthem ("La Marseillaise") by primary education pupils was introduced by some right-wing M.P.s through an amendment to the 2005 law on education. An article introduced by amendment into another law in 2005 on the recognition of French repatriates from North Africa recommended that "school curricula recognize in particular the positive role of the French presence overseas, especially in North Africa. . . ."[3] This measure was denounced by historians, teachers, left activists, and education organizations throughout 2005 and was finally repealed in February 2006. These two initiatives reveal the importance given to the positive value of the French past and of the French "model" by a significant part of the French right wing since the 2000s.

The French assimilationist model gained even more importance when Nicolas Sarkozy came to power in 2007. While the setting up of a "Ministry of Integration, National Identity, and Immigration" represented an institutional novelty, the speeches and measures adopted in the field of education exacerbated (rather than gave birth to) trends that had already been apparent since 2002. The theme of "respect" for the nation and its symbols gained even more visibility in declarations and policies related to education. The authoritarian dimension of nationalism was also accentuated. National symbols should not only be understood and learned by students; they should foster an attitude of submission and deference, as clearly apparent in this speech by President Sarkozy in 2008 on the new curricula for civic and moral education in primary schools:

> This civic and moral education notably contains the learning of the rules of politeness or courtesy, the knowledge and the respect of values and emblems of the French Republic: the tricolor flag, it's not nationalism to teach our children to respect the national anthem, the nation that is theirs, Marianne, the national anthem—when listening to it our children must stand up.

In 2009–2010, the government launched what it called a "debate on national identity": this public debate, carried out at different levels of society (on a dedicated website for citizens, in public schools, in prefectures, etc.), was supposed to identify the main features of French national identity in order to foster a sense of unity within the nation. The debate on national unity brought about a bitter controversy in the media and in political spheres. Left-wing actors and antiracist organizations firmly criticized the initiative and considered it a dangerous attempt to define national identity in a rigid way and as stigmatizing to immigrants and ethnic minorities.

The governmental focus on national identity led to some shifts in the required curricula of primary schools. History and civic education curricula for primary education, reformed in 2008, focused even more than in the past on the national level. According to the 2008 curricula, during civic education classes, for example, "pupils study particularly the following issues: . . . 'the constitutive features of the French nation: the characteristics of its territory (in relation with the geography curriculum) and the steps of its national unification (in relation with the history curriculum), the rules to access to nationality, the national language . . .'" (MEN, 2008, pp. 85–86). Young pupils aged 8–9 years old "learn to recognize and respect the emblems and symbols of the republic (La Marseillaise, the tricolor flag, the bust of Marianne, the anthem 'Liberté, Egalité, Fraternité')" (MEN, 2008, p. 48). Being able to identify the national symbols was already mentioned in the former curricula, but in 2008 the idea of "respect" for the nation, which was present in some governmental speeches of the period, was added as a teaching objective.

The Evolving Meanings of Laïcité

French debates about the place of religion in education had been centered for a long time on the relationship between Catholic private-owned schools, most of them publicly funded since the end of the 1950s, and state schools. In the 1980s this debate became less contentious because state funding of these schools became increasingly accepted as a "given" situation. From that period, the place of Islam in French society and in public education became the most important point of controversy. Debates on the meaning of *laïcité* have often been restricted to this dimension. The question of the integration of immigrants and their descendants has been increasingly seen through a "Muslim" framing and defined in religious terms (Tiberj, 2014). In the field of education, this was apparent through recurrent controversies about the presence of Muslim religious symbols and practices in public schools, in particular the wearing of the Muslim head scarf, or hijab.

This religious symbol was often depicted negatively in the French national press as a symbol of women's inequality, cultural backwardness, and family and community pressure (Molokotos-Liederman, 2000). Its fundamentalist nature and the question of whether it is a real religious prescription according to the Koran were also intensively discussed. The first "head scarf affair" occurred in 1989, when three young Muslim girls were expelled from their public school because they refused to remove their head scarves. The Council of the State, the highest French court in France, consulted by the minister of education at that time, Lionel Jospin, published a recommendation that came to a rather liberal conception of the French principle of *laïcité:* It stated that the expression of religious beliefs by students was not contrary to the principle of *laïcité* provided that it was not religious proselytizing, did not infringe on other students' freedom of conscience, and did not threaten public order in schools. Despite this rather liberal conception of *laïcité,* the left government recommended that, through dialogue, families and girls should be convinced to remove religious symbols when entering school. A few years later, right-wing Minister of Education François Bayrou criticized the risk of "break-up of the nation into separated communities" and issued a circular inviting schools to prohibit "ostentatious" religious symbols at school (MEN, 1994, p. 8). In practice, the issue was dealt with locally and on a case-by-case basis, leading to a variety of practices regarding toleration of the head scarf in public schools.

The debate was launched again in the early 2000s, with high media coverage of a new case. Yet the situation proved to be somewhat calmed since, according to the mediator specifically in charge of dealing with conflictive cases, only 150 difficult cases were recorded each year (compared with 450 five years before). Most of them were resolved by dialogue—expulsions did not exceed 10 per year (Hafiz & Devers, 2005, p. 202). But political and state actors appeared firmly committed to pushing for a stricter conception of *laïcité*, presented as requiring the invisibility of religion in public spaces such as schools and as a central component of French national identity that all individuals must "respect." The law of March 2004 and the related circular of May 2004 banned any symbol that clearly revealed a religious identity—the circular explicitly referred to the "Islamic head scarf, however it is called, the skullcap and a cross whose size is obviously excessive." [4] Actually, these regulations still have not resolved the problems of interpretation school actors may have: Head teachers still have to assess whether the dress has an obvious religious dimension, for example, bandannas or long dark dresses hiding the female body, and in some schools these situations still lead to conflicts with students and families (Bozec, 2016a). The 2004 law was justified by state actors and other supporters by the alleged singularity of relationships and roles at school—children and teenagers' freedom of conscience has to be protected from the potential intrusion of other pupils (and adults) with different beliefs and from family and community pressure. This approach demonstrates a rather paternalist state's approach to the autonomy of children and teenagers—their emancipation from the influence of others has to be enforced by state regulations (Laborde, 2010; Maurer, 2006); and the mere visibility of a religious symbol is seen as potentially sufficient to encourage changes in their beliefs. Increasingly, *laïcité* is used as a way to ensure the exclusion of the "religious" from school space, leading to more uniformity (at least visible) among students.

Some forms of accommodation of Muslim pupils' religious needs do exist in practice, such as meals without pork or without meat in school canteens, but these remain controversial issues—there have been recurrent controversies in the media and political debates regarding school menus at the national and local levels. The danger of creating visible religious divisions (according to what children eat at the canteen) is pointed out. The possible introduction of halal meals in some schools—although there is no evidence that they exist—has also brought up recurrent criticisms.

Conceptions of national identity and *laïcité* that leave little room for diversity have been central in political speeches and school policies since the mid-1980s and particularly between 2002 and 2012, a decade marked by increasing assimilationist trends. As noted above, it is above all the primary education curriculum that was impacted, with citizenship education and history curricula being recentered in 2008 on the French nation and a unitary view of it. Such a tendency is not so predominant in secondary education curricula: At this level, citizenship and history education also promote European citizenship and understanding of global issues. They also contain some elements related to the history of immigration.

Citizenship Education, Knowledge, and Political Discussions

Citizenship education is also a matter of political knowledge and democratic values. The citizenship education curriculum has proposed since the 1980s a comprehensive approach to political principles and institutions. It is implemented from primary education through high school. Students learn about the French and E.U. political institutions. They also learn about major political concepts such as public liberties, equality, and democratic participation.

Different types of obstacles, however, hinder the development of an effective citizenship education. First, there is a gap between the formal curriculum and the actual practices of citizenship education. If France is the country in Europe with the highest number of school hours specifically dedicated to citizenship education according to the official curriculum (Eurydice, 2012), the provision of citizenship education in practice is not developed to the same extent and varies according to teacher (Bozec, 2016b). Indeed, some teachers tend to use these hours to complete their coverage of the curriculum for other subjects, which are seen as more important and/or have greater weight in the assessment of pupils in secondary education national examinations.[5]

In other respects, one can observe that the place granted to debates and to the expression of students' opinions and experiences is often very limited in citizenship education (as in other parts of the school curricula). As underlined in the analyses of Program for International Student Assessment survey results, French students have good performance when they have to find information and give an account about it but underperform when they are required to build a free argument and express their opinions (Grenet, 2008). The school curriculum provides for "argumentative debates" to be organized in the classroom during citizenship education classes, particularly in secondary education. However, these debates are not always implemented. They occur more frequently in high schools than in lower secondary schools (Bozec, 2016a; MEN, 2013) but do not occur often there. This teaching method focuses on the quality of argumentation, and very often these arguments are constructed intellectually only, not making significant allocations for the actual experiences of students. Moreover, students may have difficulties recognizing issues as properly political, since controversy hardly enters school discussions (Bozec, 2008, 2010). In accordance with the principle of *laïcité*, the political neutrality of teachers is a strong norm in education. However, it is mainly interpreted as involving the silence of school actors, including students, on political issues.

Regarding students' participation, local practices vary according to individual teachers and schools (Barrère & Martuccelli, 1998; Bozec, 2014). Although different measures contribute to increase students' rights at school (through the setting up of participative councils, mainly in secondary schools), students often report that they are not being listened to enough at school and hardly consider their school as a space for participation (Ballion, 1998; Becquet, 2009; Condette-Castelain, 2009; MEN, 2013; Rayou, 1998; Roudet, 2005). Their engagement outside schools in humanitarian or political activities is not often recognized inside school.

The dominant conception of schools in France—as a place for providing knowledge, with the conception of knowledge itself defined by science and intellectual elites and then handed down in schools in a vertical way—plays a large role in accounting for the limited room made for participative practices and for students' experiences and opinions in French schools. The decisive role played by the experience of political discussions and participation at school in political efficacy and political interest is hardly found in French schools (Ehman, 1972; Geboers, Geijsel, Admiraal, & ten Dam, 2013; Hahn, 1998; McDevitt & Kiousis 2006; Schulz, Ainley, Fraillon, Kerr, & Losito, 2010; Torney-Purta, Lehmann, Oswald, & Schulz, 2001).

The Gap With Taught Civic Values: Social Inequalities and Ethnic Discrimination in School Space

A "citizenship education dilemma" (Banks, 2004, p. 9) does exist in the French case, as in other nations: Educators are supposed to teach about the value of democracy and equality in order to make students willing to make democracy progress; at the same time, they cannot ignore the gaps between these democratic ideals and social reality. The most problematic reality, in this respect, is the gap between the asserted values in citizenship education and inequalities that continue to be strong in schools. Program for International Student Assessment surveys reveal that France has one of the highest levels of social inequalities in education among developed democracies (Baudelot & Establet, 2009; Dubet, Duru-Bellat, & Vérétout, 2010; Felouzis & Charmillot, 2012). Ethnic inequalities are also strong. Children of immigrant parents are a significant proportion of the school population, particularly in public education. Most studies stress that they underperform compared with students from the majority population (Brinbaum & Kieffer, 2009). The interpretation of these differentials is still debated between scholars who argue that they are mainly related to social class inequalities—because the majority of immigrants are of lower social classes—and those who also point out the role played by ethnic discrimination in schools. A number of studies emphasize the importance of processes of ethnicization in the school space: School practitioners' representations and practices are based on ethnic categorizations, which equate ethnic minority background to lower school achievement and cultural traits (Bozec, 2010; Lorcerie, 2003, 2005; Zéphir, 2010, 2013), including a dogmatic practice of Islam within families and values that infringe on gender equality (Bozec, 2016b). The Ministry of Education's approach to differentials in educational outcomes is mainly framed in terms of social and gender inequalities. But ethnic segregation between schools (Felouzis, Liot, & Perroton, 2007) and within them between classes (Payet, 1995), as well as ethnic discrimination in school guidance practices (Dhume, 2014), are also important phenomena. Ethnic minority students perceive this discrimination—compared with other students, they are more critical of the school system, which they often consider unfair (Brinbaum & Kieffer, 2009; Zirotti, 2003).

The gaps between civic values taught at school—among them equality—and social processes of selection and discrimination occurring in the school system may have important consequences for students' citizenship education. A seminal work by Langton and Jennings (1968) showed that citizenship education courses could reinforce a distance toward politics and participation among Black students from the middle class because of the contradiction between the content of the teaching and the reality of exclusion these students knew about through the contacts they had because of their social background with the White mainstream society. This issue is not easy to tackle for educators. A possible way of going beyond this dilemma is to continue to teach about democratic principles while not hiding their incompletion in social reality.

It seems important for teachers to provide a realistic citizenship education that does not present France as the "human rights country" par excellence and French public institutions as necessarily turned toward the common good. If the picture of French society and institutions that is given in the classroom is too far from reality, most students will probably not adhere to citizenship education and not trust their teachers. And why should they engage themselves to make democracy progress, if the way democracy works is already so positive? Therefore, citizenship education should provide students opportunities to reflect on actual issues and challenges for democracy. Yet it should not lead students to discouragement and political cynicism. Thus it should also help them to identify the resources they can rely on and encourage them to mobilize for social change. Civic action can be promoted by helping students to attain knowledge and reflect on examples of political action and social movements, which may increase students' awareness of the possibility to act in favor of democratic progress, but also by giving value, inside the classroom, to present students' engagements in organizations and actions within and outside the school.

Toward a New Agenda for Citizenship Education After the 2015 Terrorist Attacks?

The terrorist attacks of January 2015, conducted on behalf of Islam against the *Charlie Hebdo* newspaper and a kosher minimarket, caused a real shock in France. Once again, public education was put at the forefront of debates. In the aftermath of the attacks, public education was blamed for not having been able to ensure social integration and educate students to be full citizens and to identify with republican values (which include the core principle of freedom of expression). To some extent, however, these terrorist attacks also provided state actors with an opportunity to legitimize and carry out the reform they were planning before the attacks regarding citizenship education (and the organization of lower secondary education, too).

When it assumed power in 2012, the left government announced its plan to reform the French policy of integration, but it has remained quite prudent on the issue—in order to avoid controversies, governmental actors have recurrently reasserted their adhesion to the "republican" model and their refusal of a so-called multicultural "Anglo-Saxon model" (actually poorly understood as a promotion of ethnoreligious communities instead of common belonging). After the terrorist attacks of January 2015, national unity was displayed around republican values, among which was the importance of the freedom of expression. This climate constituted a political window of opportunity for the government to assert its policy positions regarding education. On January 22, 2015, Minister of National Education Najat Vallaud-Belkacem announced a "broad mobilization of school for the values of the republic."[6] At the same time, the ministry submitted the curriculum of a new "moral and civic education" to teachers and teacher organizations—this curriculum was modified and implemented in September 2015. At first glance, these developments may appear as in line with previous policies that emphasized national unity. The campaign for the values of the republic and citizenship education at school, as now conceived, do not depart from traditional approaches when emphasizing the importance of passing on common republican values. But there has also been a slight shift toward a new approach of citizenship and diversity in education. A stronger emphasis is put on the need for changing teaching methods in citizenship education, for implementing debates inside the classroom more than before, and for valuing at school students' civic engagement. The new curricula of civic and moral education, as well as a booklet on *laïcité* issued in October 2015 and sent to all French schools, have developed a renewed view of *laïcité*, more agreeable and less centered on Islam and on the control of religious behaviors considered "anti-republican" (Lorcerie, 2016). Education policies now also make issues such as racism, equality, and discrimination more central—the need to teach about them but also to fight against them inside the school.

To go further in this direction, however, school itself will have to question more directly its own practices and invite professionals to set up collective reflection and concrete processes to prevent discrimination more effectively. In addition, the issue of France's religious diversity is still poorly emphasized in these policy discourses. Last, it should be noted that the Ministry of Education has not made these new orientations about equality and diversity very visible—this "aggiornamento" remains rather "quiet" (Lorcerie, 2016); it is mainly implemented in training sessions that do not target all education professionals and reaches the public even less. What is more, the attacks that took place in Paris on November 13, 2015, created a new context, not favorable to proactive policies combating discrimination and promoting diversity. The shock provoked by these attacks, which took place in the Stadium of France in Saint-Denis, on several streets in the northeast of Paris, and in a concert hall, the Bataclan, and led to 130 deaths, brought a new climate of fear. It has contributed to the rise of anti-Islam and anti-immigrant opinions, as indicated by the high vote for the National Front in the regional elections of December 2015 and in various opinion polls on attitudes toward Islam in 2015 and 2016. Against this background, it is doubtful that policies promoting a better image of immigration and Islam in French society can find real legitimacy.

Case Study: Citizenship Education Into Practice

The teacher case study was not chosen as an example that only illustrates "good" or "innovative" practices in the field of citizenship education. It mirrors the conditions, difficulties, and progress of effective citizenship education. The teacher, Arnaud, is very engaged in his mission of citizenship education. He is also committed to fighting against educational inequalities and tries to promote diversity and immigration as positive components of French society. Consequently, he is different in many ways from other teachers. However, a number of local and national influences have also influenced Arnaud's practices. This case study is conceived as a way to identify some of the existing limitations as well as opportunities for improving citizenship education in the French context.

The Teacher's Profile

Arnaud is 39 years old and has been a lower secondary teacher for 15 years. He teaches history, geography, and civic education. Like most young teachers, he started his career in a lower secondary school situated in a disadvantaged neighborhood. The school was located in a city in a Parisian suburb and was attended by mainly working-class students, most of whom were ethnic minorities and of diverse countries of origin. The city was known as a place of violent confrontations between inhabitants and the police in 2007, following the accidental death of two teenagers after their motorbike crashed with a police car.

Arnaud changed schools seven years ago. The school where he works now is more mixed in terms of social backgrounds compared with the previous one.[7] However, the majority of the students are still from working-class backgrounds, and ethnic minorities are a significant part of the school population. The school is located in the northeast of Paris. One of its two buildings is situated near the kosher minimarket that was the target of the terrorist attack of January 9, 2015. A measure of confinement of the school was set up the day of the attack, which strengthened the shock it provoked.

Contributing to the Fight Against School Inequalities

Arnaud is very sensitive to school inequalities and is engaged in trying to eliminate them. This is reflected by his career in disadvantaged areas and his commitment to work with the most marginalized students. It is also echoed through his different educational activities and engagements. Arnaud demonstrates much attention to his students' family backgrounds. He is convinced that his job is also to understand students' personal situations so that he is able to take them into account in their educational needs.

For five years, Arnaud has been the coordinator in his school of a specific local scheme developed by the Parisian educational authorities. This scheme, called *Dispositif de Socialisation et d'Apprentissages* (Socialization and Knowledge Scheme), is designed for voluntary students who have school difficulties or are at risk of dropping out of school. Three small groups of students are gathered in the same class for six weeks and benefit from specific school support. Cultural and art activities are also carried out with them. This system is seen by Arnaud and his colleagues as an efficient way to make these students progress and to establish a more positive relationship between them and the school. Cultural activities and projects bring these students together. The small size of the class permits a personalized relationship between teachers and students and makes a high consideration of each student's needs possible. Arnaud and his colleagues are aware that such a scheme may create stigmatization of the targeted students, who may be perceived by other students as needing special support because of their poor school performance. However, the school staff makes many efforts to present the arrangement in terms of support, and because it is temporary in the school year, the risk of stigmatization is reduced. Arnaud sees progress among the students involved in this scheme.

Despite these engagements, Arnaud feels rather discouraged by his institutional context. Like many other teachers, he believes that his efforts are not recognized by educational authorities. For example, he would have liked for *Dispositif de Socialisation et d'Apprentissages* to be assessed and the findings of the study to be disseminated among the stakeholders in order to help them improve their practices. But he was not informed about any assessment. He is also very critical about the recent reform of priority education zones, which reduced the number of schools that receive increased resources because they have the most difficulties. After a first announcement that his school would remain among the priority education zones, it was then removed from the list. With other colleagues, Arnaud took part in a protest to denounce the decision. Finally, it was decided that his school would continue to receive supplementary resources, but not to the same extent as the schools of the new defined priority education zones. Arnaud is disappointed by this development, which he views as a nonrecognition of his school staff's commitment.

Citizenship Education, Knowledge, and Controversial Issues

Like many other teachers, Arnaud had not dedicated much time to civic education for years. This part of the curricula is less central in the national assessment of the *brevet des collèges* (certificate for general education, which is given at the end of lower secondary education), compared with history and geography. Moreover, most French teachers lack training in civic education. Arnaud realized over time that civic education was very important and that it was crucial not to overlook it. He was contacted by a school publisher to take part in the conception of civic education textbooks for lower secondary education, and this experience gave him more knowledge and confidence to teach civic education effectively to his own students.

In Arnaud's opinion, citizenship education is greatly a matter of knowledge. Without basic knowledge about democracy, institutions, and topical issues, students may not be able to develop critical thinking and the skills needed to understand political debates, all the more so as this education is not given within most families. Arnaud's civic education classes consist of giving information to students about one issue (for example, justice and public liberties, which are some themes of the curriculum in lower secondary education) and making them reflect on and answer questions. Knowledge is also seen as a decisive element to deconstruct prejudices, in particular those against minority groups.

A few times, Arnaud also set up debates in his classroom about civic issues. During the first interview I had with him in April 2015, he expressed some doubts about the use of this teaching method. According to what he observed when he tried to have debates in the classroom, students often had difficulties discussing these issues because they lacked basic information about them—the debates may thus be quite poor or leave too much space for misconceptions or prejudices. Arnaud also admitted that he lacked the time and train- ing to make discussions in the classroom more effective. His teacher practices in citizen- ship education echoed to some extent the dominant conception of teaching in the French education system—it is centered on the teacher's passing on of knowledge to students, and knowledge is considered as something rather separate from students' experience. However, Arnaud's conceptions were evolving in the context of the implementation of the new civic and moral education curriculum in September 2015. This curriculum puts more empha- sis on implementing debates in the classroom and on the students carrying out projects and productions (such as exhibitions, writing articles in the school newspaper, and the implementation of civic actions in the school or in the local area). Arnaud was made more sensitive to those aspects, especially through discussions he had about the reform of civic education with the school inspector in charge of this subject. During our second interview, conducted in early 2016, he stressed that teaching methods in civic education should be more interactive.

Moreover, even before the implementation of the new curriculum, Arnaud was convinced that history and civic education should not avoid controversial issues. He refuses to convey an idealistic image of French history and national identity. In history, for example, he required his students to work on the Algerian decolonization war in 2004, although it is still a controversial topic. The use of the term *war* to describe France's conflict with Algeria was recognized officially in France only in 1999. The issue is part of the history curriculum, but some teachers are not comfortable teaching about it, in particular about the massacre of October 17, 1961, when a demonstration of Algerian people organized by the French section of the Front de Libération Nationale (liberation front during the Algerian War) was cracked down on by the police. With a colleague, a teacher of French, Arnaud required his students to write an account imagining the life of an ordinary French family during the war. This was part of a trilogy—one other account was written about World War I, and another, about World War II. Students encountered different witnesses of the Algerian War, French and Algerian people, and were made sensitive to the plurality of points of view about the war. They could also learn about the situation of people of Algerian origin in contemporary France. This type of project was conceived as a way to express value for students' work and to encourage them to consider history as their own. The accounts were edited and received several awards, and a few events were organized to promote them.

Importance of Diversity but Refusal of Ethnocultural Assignments

Through history and civic education classes, Arnaud describes diversity as an important feature of French society. Some topics of the official curricula are related to diversity, but Arnaud goes further in this direction. This is related to his educational and political values but also to his own family story. Arnaud's family has diverse origins, notably Italian and *pied-noir*.[8] He now lives in a multiethnic Parisian neighborhood and is very positive about the diversity that his own children can experience in the local school.

As a teacher, Arnaud is very attentive to the diversity of students and wishes to give a positive image of it in the classroom. However, he refuses to do this by inviting some particular students to talk about the country of origin of their parents or to identify to a given ethnocultural "group." This appears to him as risky because it may confine these students to otherness and difference, whereas they experience themselves as young people like other students and do not necessarily identify themselves with their parents' country of origin or with a particular cultural subgroup. Arnaud searches for alternative ways to promote diversity while avoiding assignation and ethnicization. He found several opportunities to teach about diversity by using the history, geography, and civic education curriculum. The theme of immigration, for example, is present in the history and geography curriculum. In 2014–2015, he chose to require his students to work on immigration through the same kind of narrative exercises he used for the Algerian War. One activity was to make students write a short essay on the experience and difficulties of an imagined immigrant who came to France. Through such an activity, which requires knowledge about immigration as well as an ability to identify with a human experience, Arnaud thinks that his students can better understand immigration processes (including, for some of them, the story of their own family) and can also better view France as a nation of immigration and diversity. Arnaud is also very enthusiastic about the teaching of Islam in the history curriculum. For students, these lessons are times when they learn many things because even Muslim students do not have a deep knowledge about the history of Islam. In the teacher's view, it is a way for all students to learn about a religion that is important in France today and to have a better idea of France as a religiously diverse nation.

Arnaud also chose to work with his students on Roma people. Themes of the civic education curriculum (present in both the former and the new curricula)—about "the diversity of individuals and human groups" and about "discrimination"—were used in this way. Students used different sources of information about Roma people. They could understand their diversity, whereas Roma people are often considered as a homogeneous group. Students also learned about the difficult social conditions and the discrimination that affect a number of Roma groups.

The Teacher's Reactions to the Terrorist Attacks of January 2015

Like many other teachers, Arnaud was profoundly shocked by the terrorist attacks that occurred in France in January 2015 and wondered how he might explain to his students these dramatic and searing events. Some teachers did not know how to react and preferred not to address the issue. Others, such as Arnaud, chose to discuss it immediately after the first attacks.[9] The evening of the *Charlie Hebdo* attack, he reflected on what he would say to students with his wife, who is also a history, geography, and civic education teacher in another school. In line with the dominant framing of the issue in the media and in the guidelines and material provided by the Ministry of Education, they decided to insist on freedom of expression and to give information on what *Charlie Hebdo* is. But this choice was also charged emotionally: "We had the impression that we lost everything. . . . So it was very important to say to students, 'No, there is still something, freedom of expression is still a fundamental basis of our democracy.'" Tackling the issue by emphasizing freedom of expression was a way of resolving, at least temporarily, the "citizenship education dilemma" (Banks, 2004, pp. 9–10) that was raised in that situation—it was a way of reassuring students and preserving in their minds the value of the political principles that had been infringed in such a violent way. The issue was not addressed only in that way. Arnaud also considered it very important to give students information about *Charlie Hebdo* and about the limitations of freedom of expression in the French democracy. He mentioned that mocking a religion is permitted because France is a "laic" country and blasphemy is not recognized as an offense. But he also told his students that mocking individuals because of their particular religion and infringing on the dignity of individuals through publications is prohibited by law.[10] He said that *Charlie Hebdo* was taken to court on several occasions after complaints from Catholic and Muslim organizations. This was considered a way to make students sensitive to the debates and conflicts that surround the principle of freedom of expression in France. Arnaud also took time to explain what *Charlie Hebdo* is because many students did not know that it is a newspaper and not a person. These reference points were considered pivotal in order to enable students to develop informed and critical thinking about the events.

In a number of French schools, the mandated minute of silence and the schools' actions to commemorate the victims of the terrorist attacks brought up controversies and negative reactions by some students, as reported by the media and by various scholars and practitioners. Arnaud was not confronted with reactions such as the legitimization of terrorism on behalf of Islam (presented as insulted by *Charlie Hebdo*) or conspiracy theories. But the day following the *Charlie Hebdo* attack, one of his students came to school for the first time with henna on her hands and arms and felt ill at ease during the activity he carried out on the attack. At the end of the class, she came and talked with Arnaud. She said that she was uncomfortable about the unanimous reactions of defense of the newspaper, whereas she felt that this newspaper regularly insulted Islam. Arnaud took some time to answer her, trying to address her questions, and advised her to continue to discuss the issue with her teachers and with the head teacher. Beyond this specific situation, Arnaud considered it very important to address the students' questions and to listen to their feelings about the attacks in the classroom. He was very shocked by some of the words of the minister of education, who recommended that dialogue be set up in the classroom after the attacks but also said that some opinions cannot be heard in a French republican public school and so would be sanctioned. To Arnaud, that was potentially dangerous because it could result in students becoming silent and also in the perpetuation of the misconceptions that students may have had about the attacks. In his view, the educational role of school makes it a space for dialogue. He also considered the use of the slogan "Je suis Charlie" ("I am Charlie") in the aftermath of the attacks a delicate issue. Some teachers even displayed posters with this slogan in their school to demonstrate their condemnation of the attack (Simon, 2015). To Arnaud, this slogan represents a false unanimity that prevents discussion instead of favoring it. He personally chose to explain to his students that this slogan has several meanings, from the defense of freedom of expression as such to the defense of the editorial policy of the newspaper, which are not equivalent stances.

His reaction to the minute of silence that the Ministry of Education requested was similar. As civil servants, public educators had to set it up, and it was organized in Arnaud's school. He recognized that it had positive aspects because it created a solemn moment that could help students become sensitive to the importance of freedom of expression and to the refusal of violence. Nevertheless, he regretted that it was organized so hastily, which made it difficult for many teachers to have time to explain what it meant to students.

Presenting the complexity of the current context was crucial to Arnaud. He thought that it was important to increase his students' awareness of the situation of Muslim people in France and of the stigmatization from which they suffer. Just after the January attacks, he presented a poster by the Collectif Contre l'Islamophobie en France (Collective Against Islamophobia in France) to one of his classes.[11] This poster represented a contemporary version of the Serment du Jeu de Paume (Tennis Court Oath), during which around 300 revolutionary deputies, on June 20, 1789, took the oath not to separate before a constitution was written. In the poster, the oath is taken by contemporary French people, including

Muslim ones (some of them wear religious clothes, such as women's head scarves); they solemnly affirm that they "also are the nation" ("*Nous aussi sommes la nation*"). At the bottom of the poster, an inscription states, "Islamophobia is not an opinion. It's a crime" (my translations). Arnaud showed this poster to his students to illustrate the feeling of exclusion many ordinary Muslim people feel in current French society, whereas they have a strong feeling of belonging to the French nation. This presentation was also a way to recall that freedom of expression does not mean having the right to mock or insult people because of their religion.

Arnaud's reactions to the November 13 attacks in Paris were similar. He disapproved of some of the guidelines issued by the Ministry of Education in order to help teachers tackle the issue in the classroom, which put the emphasis on the psychology of children and teenagers and also related the issue to *laïcité*, the refusal of violence, and other points that are in the civic education curriculum. As he noted in his own classes, students were shocked by the attacks because they took place near where they live and touched many young people. Arnaud believed that the event had both psychological and intellectual components. Consequently, a "psychological" approach was not sufficient. He reports that his students also had many factual questions about the attacks, such as "What is Daech?", "What is happening in Syria?", and "Why was the Bataclan chosen as a place for the attacks?" Arnaud regretted that those informational aspects were not sufficiently addressed in the ministry's guidelines. For him, dealing with an issue such as this needs time. Just after the attacks, he took some time to answer his students' questions with two other teachers before setting up the minute of silence. But he also told his students that he needed time to answer all of their questions properly. He then prepared himself and organized another moment in class—in January 2016—to discuss the attacks and give information on Daech (Islamic State of Iraq and the Levant), the situation in Syria, and the characteristics of terrorism today.

Consistent with what he did one year before, Arnaud also thought it crucial to increase students' awareness about the situation of Muslim people in France and their multiple identities (their attachment to France and to their city but also to their religion). He used the work by a photographer, France Keyser, who encountered Muslim people in Marseille just after the January attacks and then again in December 2015, after the Parisian attacks. The photographer took pictures of Muslim people and gathered letters they had written on their feelings and situation after the attacks in January. These texts reveal that these Muslim people were attached to France and to republican values but, because of their religion and origins, felt stigmatized and discriminated against in French society, even more so since the attacks. In the classroom, Arnaud showed the pictures and letters and read one of them by a young Muslim doctor who was 30 years old and wore the head scarf outside the hospital, who described herself as "more French than French" but also as increasingly becoming "a foreigner" for her "fellow citizens" since the attacks.[12] This moment was a way for Arnaud to deal with the theme of differences and discrimination (which is part of the civic curriculum) from a concrete and lively point of view and to deal with issues that are constantly debated in public discourse.

Conclusion

The case study of Arnaud's teaching reveals several aspects that are at stake when discussing citizenship education in France. The image of France as a land of immigration and of cultural and religious diversity has not been central in political speeches and in school curricula during the last several decades. However, some French teachers, such as Arnaud, are keen to promote this diversity, which is a daily reality in their student populations and cannot be denied. Given the weight of an individualistic and universalistic conception of citizenship in France, there is, however, widespread suspicion toward any form of group-oriented approach to diversity issues. Consequently, teachers who are committed to teaching about diversity usually promote it indirectly—they do not encourage students to talk about their religion or their origins in the classroom, because they fear that such a request would nourish ethnocultural ascriptions. They, rather, choose to use parts of the curricula and other material to illustrate the history of immigration to France and the diversity of religions and cultural references in France today.

In another respect, such an indirect way of approaching diversity issues shows, in civic education as in other subjects, the limited space made for students' experiences in French classrooms. Like other parts of the curriculum, citizenship education in practice has often been conceived primarily as a matter of knowledge and information. The new citizenship education curriculum, which found fresh legitimacy in the aftermath of the terrorist attacks of January 2015, might lead to a shift—it promotes a "culture of engagement" among students that educators have to foster, as well as the organization of debates in the classroom as a favored method. Such a reform is ambitious and will probably be difficult to put into practice—it will require a change in teaching methods in general (not only in citizenship education classes) and thus a transformation in the prevalent education culture in France. However, as illustrated by Arnaud's views of the new curriculum, it may encourage transformations, even limited ones, toward more interactions and discussions in citizenship education classes and projects.

Notes

1. See below for more details about inequalities in the French school system.

2. Here and below, all translations are mine.

3. *Loi n° 2005-158 du 23 février 2005 portant reconnaissance de la Nation et contribution nationale en faveur des Français rapatriés* [Law N°2005-158 of 23 February 2005 on the gratitude of the nation and national contribution toward French repatriates]. Retrieved from https://www.legifrance.gouv.fr/affichTexte.do?cidTexte=JORFTEXT000000444898&dateTexte=&categorieLien=id

4. Circulaire n°2004-084 du 18-5-2004. *Respect de la laïcité. Port de signes ou de tenues manifestant une appartenance religieuse dans les écoles, collèges et lycées publics* [Circular n°2004-084 of 18 May 2004. Respect of *laïcité*. Wearing of symbols and clothes expressing a religious belonging in primary, secondary, and high schools]. Retrieved from http://www.education.gouv.fr/bo/2004/21/MENG0401138C.htm

5. Civic education is part of the national examination at the end of lower secondary education (*brevet des collèges*), but with a low coefficient. It is not assessed for the high school diploma (*baccalauréat*).

6. *Onze mesures pour une grande mobilisation de l'école pour les valeurs de la République* [Eleven measures for a broad mobilization of school for the values of the republic]. Retrieved from http://

www.education.gouv.fr/cid85644/onze-mesures-pour-un-grande-mobilisation-de-l-ecole-pour-les-valeurs-de-la-republique.html

7. Ten years ago, there were two schools instead of one, a 10-minute walk from each other. The two schools differed in terms of students' social backgrounds, one receiving many more middle-class students than the other. The school authorities decided to bring the two schools together, with the first two grades in one school building and the two others in the other. This decision has made the situation sometimes not easy for teachers (who have had to move from one building to another to teach their courses) but has also made the school population of each school building more mixed, socially.

8. *Pied-noir* refers to the French population settled in the former colonies of North Africa.

9. The reactions to the attacks inside schools were actually very diverse, as was notably highlighted during the academic conference organized by the Réseau International Education et Diversité (Education and Diversity Network) in May 2015 on the theme "L'école: De la violence aux valeurs? Retour sur le traitement scolaire des attentats de janvier 2015 en France" ["School, from violence to values? Looking back at the way the January 2015 attacks were tackled at school in France"]. See the related publications in the *Diversité* journal (no. 182, 2016).

10. The French law imposes limits on freedom of expression in order to respect other fundamental principles: freedom of conscience (and consequently the right to have a religion and religious feelings and not to be insulted or attacked for that reason); "equality of all citizens without distinction of origin, race, and religion" (a principle stated in the French constitution that recognizes for all individuals an equal dignity regardless of their beliefs). The French law of 1881 on the freedom of the press prohibited insults and libels based on a person's belonging (or not belonging) to a religion. Moreover, the European Convention of Human Rights—which France signed—also recognizes freedom of conscience as a core principle and protects it.

11. The poster can be seen on the website of the Collectif Contre l'Islamophobie en France (http://www.islamophobie.net/articles/2012/10/31/ccif-nsln-campagne-communication-islamophobie-nous-sommes-la-nation).

12. See the content of this exhibition on French Muslims, with pictures and letters, on the *Nouvel Observateur* website (http://tempsreel.nouvelobs.com/galeries-photos/societe/20151210.OBS1141/photos-nous-musulmans-de-france.html).

References

Ballion, R. (1998). *La démocratie au lycée* [Democracy in high schools]. Paris: ESF éditeur.

Banks, J. (2004). Democratic citizenship education in multicultural societies. In J. A. Banks (Ed.), *Diversity and citizenship education: Global perspectives* (pp. 3–15). San Francisco: Jossey-Bass.

Barrère, A., & Martuccelli, D. (1998). La citoyenneté à l'école: Vers la définition d'une problématique sociologique [Citizenship at school: Toward the definition of a sociological question]. *Revue Française de sociologie, 39*(4), 651–672.

Baudelot, C., & Establet, R. (2009). *L'élitisme républicain: L'école française à l'épreuve des comparaisons internationales* [The republican elitism: The French school system questioned by international comparisons]. Paris: Seuil.

Becquet, V. (2009). Se saisir du conseil de la vie lycéenne: Des principes à l'exercice de la fonction de délégué [Using the council of high school life: From principles to the implementation of the role of delegate]. *Carrefours de l'education, 28,* 65–79.

Birnbaum, P. (1998). *La France imaginée* [Imagined France]. Paris: Gallimard.

Boucher, M. (2000). *Les théories de l'intégration entre universalisme et différencialisme. Des débats sociologiques et politiques en France: Analyse des textes contemporains* [Theories of integration between universalism and differentialism. Sociological and political debates in France: Analysis of contemporary texts]. Paris: L'Harmattan.

Bozec, G. (2008). Enfance et politique [Childhood and politics]. *La Pensée, 354*, 123–133.

Bozec, G. (2010). *Les héritiers de la Républiquepp. Éduquer à la citoyenneté à l'école dans la France d'aujourd'hui* [The heirs to the republic: Educating to citizenship at school in France today]. Unpublished doctoral dissertation, Political Science, Institut d'Etudes Politiques, Paris.

Bozec, G. (2014). Emanciper et conformer: Les tensions de la socialisation civique à l'école primaire [Emancipating and normalizing: The contradictions of civic socialization in primary schools]. *Recherches en education, 20*, 52–65.

Bozec, G. (2015). Apprendre la nation à l'école: Des politiques scolaires aux pratiques de classe [Learning the nation at school: From school policies to classroom practices]. In C. Husson-Rochcongar & L. Jourdain (Eds.), *L'identité nationale: Instruments et usages* [National identity: Instruments and uses] (pp. 81–105). Paris: PUF/CURAPP.

Bozec, G. (2016a). *Education à la citoyenneté à l'école. Politiques, pratiques scolaires et effets sur les élèves* [Citizenship education at school. Policies, school practices and effects on students]. Paris: CNESCO. Retrieved from http://www.cnesco.fr/wp-content/uploads/2016/04/Rapport_%C3%A9ducation_citoyennet%C3%A9.pdf

Bozec, G. (2016b). Une laïcité qui cherche sa voie. L'après-Charlie dans un lycée "mobilisé" de quartier populaire [Looking for its path. The post-*Charlie* laïcité in a "mobilized" high school of a working-class area]. *Diversité, 182*, 34–40.

Brinbaum, Y., & Kieffer, A. (2009). La scolarité des enfants d'immigrés de la sixième au baccalauréat: Différences et polarisations des parcours [School achievement of children of immigrants from the sixth grade to the 12th grade: Differences and polarization of school careers]. *Population, 3*(64), 561–610.

Chirac, J. (2003, November 20). *Allocution de M. Jacques Chirac, Président de la République, sur le renouvellement du rôle de l'école, les enjeux actuels de l'enseignement et l'amélioration du métier d'enseignant* [Speech by Mr. Jacques Chirac, President of the Republic, on the renewal of the role of school education, the current issues of teaching and the improvement of the teaching profession]. Paris. Retrieved from http://discours.vie-publique.fr/notices/037000363.html

Citron, S. (2008). *Le mythe national: L'histoire de France revisitée* [The national myth: French history revisited]. Paris: Les Editions de l'Atelier.

Condette-Castelain, S. (2009). L'implication des élèves dans la vie de l'établissement: Regards croisés des enseignants et des conseillers principaux d'éducation [Students' involvement in the school life: A comparison of views of teachers and education advisers]. *Carrefours de l'éducation, 28*, 53–64.

De Cock, L., & Picard, E. (2009). *La fabrique scolaire de l'histoire: Illusions et désillusions du roman national* [The building of history at school: Illusions and disillusionments of the national narrative]. Marseille, France: Agone.

Déloye, Y. (1994). *Ecole et citoyenneté: L'individualisme républicain de Jules Ferry à Vichy: Controverses* [School and citizenship: The republican individualism from Jules Ferry to Vichy: Controversies]. Paris: Presses de la Fondation Nationale de Sciences Politiques.

Dhume, F. (2007). *Racisme, antisémitisme et "communautarisme": L'école à l'épreuve des faits* [Racism, anti-Semitism and "communitarianism": The school put to the test of facts]. Paris: l'Harmattan.

Dhume, F. (2014). *Entre l'école et l'entreprise, la discrimination en stage: Une sociologie publique de l'ethnicisation des frontières scolaires* [Between school and job market, discrimination in internship: A public sociology of the ethnicization of school boundaries]. Aix-en-Provence, France: Presses universitaires de Provence/IREMAM.

Dhume, F., & Hamdani, K. (2013). *Vers une politique française de l'égalité. Rapport du groupe de travail "Mobilités sociales" dans le cadre de la "Refondation de la politique d'intégration"* [Toward a French policy of equality. Report by the "Social Mobility" group in the framework of the "Reform of the Integration Policy"]. Paris: La Documentation française.

Dubet, F., Duru-Bellat, M., & Vérétout, A. (2010). *Les sociétés et leur école: Emprise du diplôme et cohésion sociale* [Societies and their school system: Weight of diploma and social cohesion]. Paris: Seuil.

Duchesne, S. (1997). *Citoyenneté à la française* [French citizenship]. Paris: Presses de la Fondation Nationale des Sciences politiques.

Ehman, L. H. (1972). Political efficacy and the high school social studies curriculum. In B. G. Massialas (Ed.), *Political youth, traditional schools: National and international perspectives* (pp. 90–102). Englewood Cliffs, NJ: Prentice-Hall.

Eurydice. (2012). *L'éducation à la citoyenneté en Europe* [Citizenship education in Europe]. Brussels, Belgium: Agence exécutive "Education, audiovisuel et culture."

Felouzis, G., & Charmillot, S. (2012). *Les enquêtes PISA* [PISA surveys]. Paris: PUF.

Felouzis, G., Liot, F., & Perroton, J. (2007). *L'apartheid scolaire: Enquête sur la ségrégation ethnique dans les collèges* [School apartheid: Empirical study of ethnic segregation in lower secondary schools]. Paris: Seuil.

Ferry, L., Darcos, X., & Haigneré, C. (2003). *Lettre à tous ceux qui aiment l'école: Pour expliquer les réformes en cours* [Letter to all who like school: To explain ongoing reforms]. Paris: CNDP/Odile Jacob.

Geboers, E., Geijsel, F., Admiraal, W., & ten Dam, G. (2013). Review of the effects of citizenship education. *Education Research Review, 9,* 158–173.

Gellner, E. (1989). *Nations et nationalisme* [Nations and nationalism]. Paris: Payot.

Grenet, J. (2008, February 8). PISA: Une enquête bancale? [PISA: A shaky survey?]. *La vie des idées.fr.* Retrieved from http://www.laviedesidees.fr/PISA-une-enquete-bancale.html

Hafiz, C. E., & Devers, G. (2005). *Droit et religion musulmane* [Law and Muslim religion]. Paris: Dalloz.

Hahn, C. L. (1998). *Becoming political: Comparative perspectives on citizenship education.* Albany: State University of New York Press.

Hervieu-Léger, D. (2003). Pour une sociologie des "modernités religieuses multiples": Une autre approche de la "religion invisible" des sociétés européennes [Toward a sociology of "multiple religious modernities": A different approach to the "invisible religion" of European societies]. *Social Compass, 50*(3), 287–295.

Laborde, C. (2010). *Français, encore un effort pour être républicains!* [French people, you need a further effort to be republican!]. Paris: Seuil.

Langton, K., & Jennings, M. K. (1968). Political socialization and the high school civics curriculum in the United States. *American Political Science Review, 62*(3), 852–867.

Legris, P. (2010). Les programmes d'histoire en France: La construction progressive d'une citoyenneté plurielle, 1980–2010 [History curricula in France: The gradual building of a plural citizenship, 1980–2010]. *Histoire de l'éducation, 126,* 121–151.

Lorcerie, F. (2002). Education interculturelle: État des lieux [Intercultural education: An overview]. *Ville-Ecole-Intégration Enjeux, 129,* 170–189.

Lorcerie, F. (Ed.). (2003). *L'école et le défi ethnique: Éducation et integration* [The school and the ethnic challenge: Education and integration]. Paris: ESF éditeur/INRP.

Lorcerie, F. (Ed.). (2005). *La Politisation du voile. L'affaire en France et son écho à l'étranger* [The politicization of the head scarf. The issue in France and reactions abroad]. Paris: L'Harmattan.

Lorcerie, F. (2016). Laïcité 2015. Aggiornamento en sourdine [*Laïcité* 2015. A quiet aggiornamento]. *Diversité, 182,* 21–27.

Maurer, S. (2006). *Muslim worship in France: Practical stakes and response of public actors.* New York: International Center for Migration, Ethnicity and Citizenship.

Mayeur, F. (1979). *L'éducation des filles en France au XIX*^e *siècle* [The education of girls in France in the 19th century]. Paris: Hachette.

McDevitt, M., & Kiousis, S. (2006). Deliberative learning: An evaluative approach to interactive civic education. *Communication Education, 55*, 247–264.

Ministère de l'Education Nationale. (1994, September 29). Circulaire du 20 septembre 1994 relative au port de signes ostentatoires dans les établissements scolaires [Circular of 20 September 1994 on the wearing of ostentatious signs in schools]. *Bulletin Officiel de l'Education nationale, 35.*

Ministère de l'Education Nationale. (2004). *Guide républicain: L'idée républicaine aujourd'hui* [Republican guide: The republican idea today]. Paris: Scéren/Delagrave.

Ministère de l'Education nationale. (2008). *Qu'apprend-on à l'école élémentaire? Les nouveaux programmes 2008–2009* [What is learned at primary school? The new curricula 2008–2009]. Paris: CNDP.

Ministère de l'Education nationale. (2013). *Rapport Morale laïque—Pour un enseignement laïque de la morale* [Report on secular ethics—For a secular teaching of ethics]. Paris: Author.

Molokotos-Liederman, L. (2000). Pluralisme et éducation: L'expression de l'appartenance religieuse à l'école publique. Le cas des élèves d'origine musulmane en France et en Angleterre à travers la presse. [Pluralism and education: The expression of religious belonging in public schools. The case of students from Muslim origin in France and England through press]. *École pratique des hautes études, Section des sciences religieuses. Annuaire, 113*(109), 535–538.

Noiriel, G. (2007). *Immigration, antisémitisme et racisme en France (XIX*^e*–XX*^e *siècle): Discours publics, humiliations privées* [Immigration, anti-Semitism and racism in France (19th–20th centuries): Public speeches, private humiliations]. Paris: Fayard.

Payet, J.-P. (1995). *Collèges de banlieue* [Suburb middle schools]. Paris: Armand Colin/Masson.

Rayou, P. (1998). *La cité des lycéens* [The public life in high schools]. Paris: L'Harmattan.

Rokkan, S. (1999). *State formation, nation-building, and mass politics in Europe.* Oxford, UK: Oxford University Press.

Roudet, B. (2005). Les jeunes, les valeurs et la démocratie à l'école [Youth, values and democracy at school]. In V. Becquet & C. De Linares (Eds.), *Quand les jeunes s'engagent. Entre expérimentations et constructions identitaires* [When youth engage themselves. Between experimentations and identity constructions] (pp. 95–106). Paris: L'Harmattan.

Sarkozy, N. (2008, February 15). *Déclaration de M. Nicolas Sarkozy, Président de la République, sur les priorités et défis de la réforme de l'enseignement primaire* [Speech by Mr. Nicolas Sarkozy, President of the Republic, on priorities and challenges of the reform of primary education]. Périgueux, France. Retrieved from http://discours.vie-publique.fr/notices/087000571.html

Schissler, H., & Soysal, Y. N. (Eds.). (2005). *The nation, Europe and the world.* New York: Berghahn Books.

Schulz, W., Ainley, J., Fraillon, J., Kerr, D., & Losito, B. (2010). *ICCS 2009 international report: Civic knowledge, attitudes, and engagement among lower-secondary school students in 38 countries.* Amsterdam, The Netherlands: International Association for the Evaluation of Educational Achievement.

Simon, A. (2015, May 28). *Les attentats de Charlie Hebdo du point de vue des enfants: Quelle médiation de l'école?* [The *Charlie Hebdo* attacks from children's point of view: Which school mediation?]. Paper presented at "*L'école: De la violence aux valeurs? Retour sur le traitement scolaire des attentats de janvier 2015 en France*" [The school: From violence to values? Perspectives on the school approach to the January 2015 attacks in France], organized by the Réseau International Education et diversité, Aix-en-Provence, France.

Simon, P. (2013). Contested citizenship in France: The republican politics of identity and integration. In A. Cole, S. Meunier, & V. Tiberj (Eds.), *Development in French politics* 5 (pp. 203–217). Basingstoke, UK: Palgrave Macmillan.

Tiberj, V. (2014). L'Islam et les Français: Cadrage des élites, dynamiques et crispation de l'opinion [Islam and French people: Elites' framing, dynamics and tension among public opinion]. *Migrations Société, 26*(155), 165–181.

Torney-Purta, J., Lehmann, R., Oswald, H., & Schulz, W. (2001). *Citizenship and education in twenty-eight countries*. Amsterdam, The Netherlands: International Association for the Evaluation of Educational Achievement.

Vallaud-Belkacem, N. (2015a, January 13). *Déclaration de Mme Najat Vallaud-Belkacem, ministre de l'éducation nationale, de l'enseignement supérieur et de la recherche, sur la refondation de l'école, notamment la laïcité, la citoyenneté et la réussite educative* [Speech by Ms. Najat Vallaud-Belkacem, Minister of National Education, Higher Education and Research, on the rebuilding of the school, notably *laïcité*, citizenship and educational success]. Paris. Retrieved from http://discours.vie-publique.fr/notices/153000083.html

Vallaud-Belkacem, N. (2015b, January 22). *Déclaration de Mme Najat Vallaud-Belkacem, ministre de l'éducation nationale, de l'enseignement supérieur et de la recherche, sur la mobilisation de l'*école *pour les valeurs de la République* [Speech by Ms. Najat Vallaud-Belkacem, Minister of National Education, Higher Education and Research, on the mobilization of the school for the values of the republic]. Paris: IDEM. Retrieved from http://discours.vie-publique.fr/notices/153000153.html

Weber, E. (1983). *La fin des terroirs: La modernisation de la France rurale, 1870–1914* [Peasants into Frenchmen: The modernization of rural France, 1870–1914]. Paris: Fayard.

Zéphir, S. (2010). Usages professionnels de la catégorisation ethnique en zone d'éducation prioritaire [Professional uses of the ethnic categorization in priority education areas]. *Migrations société, 22*(132), 215–230.

Zéphir, S. (2013). Catégorisation ethnoraciale en milieu scolaire: Une analyse contrastive de conseil de discipline [Ethnoracial at school: A comparative analysis of discipline hearings]. *Revue Française de Pédagogie, 184*, 81–94.

Zirotti, J.-P. (2003). Les élèves maghrébins, des acteurs sociaux critiques [North African students as critical social actors]. In F. Lorcerie (Ed.), *L'école et le défi ethnique. Education et integration* [The school and the ethnic challenge: Education and integration] (pp. 209–218). Paris: ESF éditeur.

Zoïa, G. (2010). Faut-il avoir peur de l'ethnicité? Le cas français [Should one fear ethnicity? The French case]. *Anthropologie et Société, 34*(2), 199–223.

Part 4

China, South Korea, and Singapore

Chapter 10

Education and Citizenship Education of Ethnic Minority Groups in China: Struggles Between Ethnic Diversity and National Unity

Wing-Wah Law
University of Hong Kong

This chapter examines the struggles between ethnic diversity and national integration in education and citizenship education for ethnic minorities in China. It argues that despite the Communist Party of China's emphasis on ethnic pluralism, the state uses education and citizenship education for ethnic minorities as a hegemonic instrument to subordinate ethnic diversity into national unity and social stability and to assimilate ethnic minority cultures and identities into state-prescribed national ones. Social stability and national security concerns have long been used to balance ethnic diversity and national integration in China, and they are important considerations in handling ethnic relations and affairs and in providing education and citizenship education for ethnic minority students. To maintain social stability and strengthen national integration, the Communist Party of China solicits ethnic solidarity and ethnic minority support by implementing preferential ethnic minority policies to protect ethnic minority rights and ethnic distinctiveness and to facilitate minority participation in Han-dominated mainstream society. When social stability, ethnic solidarity, and territorial integrity appear threatened, the state uses national security concerns, particularly the self-perceived threat of foreign aggression, to justify increased control over ethnic minority relations and the assimilation of ethnic minority groups into mainstream society.

This chapter first presents the general background of China and then examines state strategies for maintaining ethnic plurality as well as policies on ethnic minority relations and affairs. It then discusses the citizenship education curriculum common to Han and ethnic minority students and specific curricula that foster students' ethnic solidarity and national unity. It examines contentious issues confronting China's efforts to maintain ethnic plurality within a national integration/national security framework. Finally, it explores the implications of China's understanding of ethnic diversity promotion and national unity in multiethnic countries.

The Context of Education and Citizenship Education for Ethnic Minorities

Since 1949, the Communist Party of China has been the ruling party of the People's Republic of China. China is one of the world's few self-proclaimed socialist countries in existence today. Its more than 1.3 billion people are spread over 9.6 million square kilometers divided into 34 administrative regions: four municipalities, 23 provinces, five autonomous ethnic regions, and two special administrative regions (Hong Kong and Macau, former British and Portuguese colonies, respectively). China is a multiethnic society. Chinese leaders have considered ethnic minorities strategically important to the nation's development, social stability, and territorial integrity at home, and to its international image in the world. To strengthen ethnic solidarity and national integration, the Chinese leadership has implemented preferential and coercive ethnic minority policies with a view to maintaining ethnic plurality within the framework for national integration.

The Strategic Importance of Ethnic Minorities to a Multiethnic China

China is ethnically, linguistically, culturally, and religiously diverse (Banks, 2014; Mackerras, 2003). Although it is overwhelmingly Han (91.5%), China encompasses 55 ethnic minority groups (8.5%; Population Census Office under the State Council & National Bureau of Statistics, 2011), the largest being Zhuang (17 million) and Manchu (10 million), and the smallest being Hezhen and Lhoba (less than 5,000 each). Simplified Chinese and Putonghua (developed mainly from the Han language) are China's common written and public-occasion oral languages, respectively. Although Hui and Manchu commonly use spoken and written Chinese languages, the other 53 ethnic minority groups have their own spoken languages (State Council, 2009b). Twenty-two ethnic minority groups have 28 scripts, 16 of which were created or improved with state help (e.g., Zhuang, Miao, and Buyei). About 60% of the ethnic minorities regularly use their own oral languages, and 30% use their own scripts. Most ethnic minority groups have their own religions, although seven groups (including in Tibet and Inner Mongolia) uphold mainly Tibetan Buddhism, whereas 10 (including Hui, Uygur, and Kazak) are Muslim.

Since 1949, the Communist Party of China has deemed ethnic solidarity important, with Mao Zedong opposing both Han chauvinism (i.e., Han superiority over ethnic minorities) and local ethnic chauvinism (placing ethnic minority interests above the nation's) as barriers to ethnic solidarity and to China's unification of and socialist undertakings in China, views enshrined in 1984's regional ethnic autonomy law (National People's Congress, 1984). Similar to his predecessors (e.g., Hu, 2009), in a 2014 national conference on ethnic work, President Xi Jinping urged ethnic groups to prioritize ethnic solidarity and national unification as the keys to China's long-term prosperity and stability and to China's global revitalization in the 21st century (Xinhua News Agency, 2014).

Ethnic minorities are of significant strategic importance to China for several reasons. First, ethnic minorities inhabit all administrative areas in China: about 70% of ethnic minorities live in western China and 30% in central and eastern China (State Council, 2009b). Ethnic harmony and coexistence are vital to China's national development and its social and political stability (Xinhua News Agency, 2014). An ethnic conflict in one part of the nation can have ripple effects elsewhere. In 2009, for example, massive ethnic riots erupted in Urumqi, Xinjiang (northwest China) following a fatal brawl between Uygur and Han factory workers more than 3,000 kilometers away in Guangdong (southeast China).

Second, ethnic minorities' shares of resources for and/or contributions to China's development are proportionately greater than that of the Han population. Their designated autonomous areas make up nearly 65% of China's territories and contain significant portions of China's natural resources, such as forestry (44%), water (42%), natural gas (45%), and rare earths minerals used in high-technology industries (State Ethnic Affairs Commission & State Statistical Bureau, 2013).

Third, China is bordered on the west and the north by 14 countries. These border areas are home to 60% of China's ethnic minority population (State Council, 2009b). In addition, more than 30 ethnic minority peoples share ethnic origins with people living on the other side of the borders, many of whom are relatives or friends (Wu, 2007). This situation, according to the Ministry of Education and State Ethnic Affairs Commission (2009), raises concerns about China's territorial integrity and national security.

Fourth, other (particularly Western) countries have criticized China's human rights record and ethnic issues, placing political pressure on Chinese leadership (Ma, 2008). To improve its international image, China has, since 1991, issued various white papers highlighting its policies on and progress in human rights (e.g., State Council, 2013), economic and social development in ethnic minority areas (particularly Tibet and Xinjiang), and ethnic minorities' rights to existence, development, education, health, culture, and religious freedom (State Council, 2009a, 2015b).

Major Ethnic Relations and Affairs Management Policies

Because of the strategic importance of ethnic minorities, the state has, since 1949, emphasized ethnic pluralism within national unity in its approaches (both coercive and cooperative) to ethnic relations and affairs. Following the Soviet model of multiethnic state building (Connor, 2009), the state has addressed China's vast ethnic heterogeneity by adopting five major policies guided by five constitutional principles: equality among ethnic groups; protection of ethnic minority people's rights and interests; ethnic groups' freedom to use their oral and written languages; regional autonomy and self-governance in high-ethnic minority-concentration areas; and prohibitions against activities undermining national unity or promoting ethnic discord (National People's Congress, 2004, Article 6). The first four policies are noncoercive, whereas the fifth involves the use of force to suppress ethnic minority activities that might threaten China's social stability and/or territorial integrity.

The first policy, begun in the 1950s, identified and classified ethnic groups (民族识别) and gave them official status in China's state governance. As a result of the policy, the number of recognized ethnic minority groups increased from 38 in 1958 to 55 in 1979. Ethnicities were recorded in people's identity documents to define ethnic boundaries, to consolidate and perpetuate ethnic identities, and to ensure ethnic minorities could legally benefit from preferentialism.

The second policy established various semi-autonomous, ethnically based areas for ethnic minorities living in concentrated communities, including, by 1990, five regions (Inner Mongolia, Xinjiang, Guangxi, Ningxia, and Tibet), 30 prefectures, and 120 counties that, combined, were home to about three-quarters of all Chinese ethnic minorities. To protect and regulate these ethnic autonomous areas, China enacted the Regional National

Autonomy Law (National People's Congress, 2001), which allows ethnic minorities in ethnic autonomous areas to be governed by people of their own ethnicity (Article 17) and to form government organs, enact laws and regulations to meet local ethnic needs, adopt their ethnic languages as common languages, preserve and develop their ethnic cultures, and distribute revenue (Articles 10, 11, 19, 21, and 32).

However, these powers do not allow self-determination, because ethnic autonomous areas are deemed inalienable parts of the People's Republic of China. Local governments, under the state leadership of the Communist Party of China, are required to defend national unification, prioritize national interests, and implement and accomplish state-assigned tasks (Articles 5 and 7). Despite constitutional guarantees of religious freedom, ethnic minorities must separate religion from education and prevent foreign control of their religious bodies and activities (Article 11). Moreover, the heads of ethnic autonomous areas are state-appointed; procuratorates and courts are under central authority; and police forces require the State Council's approval (National People's Congress, 2004). This system was criticized for being "top-down and directed by the state" (Guan, 2015, p. 22).

The third policy concerns affirmative action measures (social, economic, political, and educational) designed to enhance disadvantaged ethnic minority groups' equality and competitiveness. For example, ethnic minority families are exempted from the one-child family policy and may have two, three, or more children, depending on their group's overall population. As a result, ethnic minorities grew from 5.8% of the population in 1964 to 8.4% in 2010 (State Ethnic Affairs Commission & State Statistical Bureau, 2013). Other state policies foster autonomous areas' economic development by offering financial, taxation, and industrial development incentives and providing special funds and subsidies for economic, social, and cultural development (Guan, 2015). Despite being only 8.5% of the population, ethnic minorities made up roughly 14% of National People's Congress representatives from 1954 to 2008 (except between 1964 and the mid-1980s; State Council, 2009b).

The fourth policy addressed economic disparities between ethnic minority peoples and Hans due to the dramatic development of Han-dominated eastern and coastal China since 1978. In the 1990s, co-development and co-prosperity policies approved numerous infrastructure projects in ethnic autonomous areas to improve the economy and living standards of ethnic minority peoples. In the 2000s, these areas were incorporated into the western China development project. Subsequently, many Hans entered ethnic minority markets competing for employment and resources, which led to criticisms that co-development was a strategy for ethnic minority peoples' economic and political assimilation (Park, 2013).

The fifth policy involves suppression for social stability and territorial integrity purposes (e.g., the 1959 military crackdown on Tibetan independence activities). It exists because the first four policies did not prevent serious violent ethnic conflicts. In fact, interethnic conflicts have intensified since the 1990s. Large-scale, deadly riots between Tibetans and Hans in Tibet and Tibetan-inhabited areas of other provinces in 2008 and between Uyghur and Hans in Urumqi in 2009, for example, ended in suppression by force, closures of monasteries or mosques, mass arrests, and tighter political control by the state.

Ethnic Minority Education: Policy and Practice

Particularly since 1978, China has emphasized education for ethnic minority students, like other areas of ethnic affairs, as an important national security concern. In 2013, ethnic minorities accounted for about 10% of China's 240 million students (China Education Yearbook Editorial Board, 2014). Education for ethnic minorities is of strategic importance to China's "national unification, ethnic solidarity, national security," and global rejuvenation (Ministry of Education, 2014b). Ethnic minority education policies adopt the principles of other ethnic-based policies to protect ethnic minority students' right to education. To ensure basic equality, ethnic minority and Han children are given equal access to education and study the same national curriculum. However, because ethnic minority students are disadvantaged by geographical, financial, and language barriers, China has taken steps at different educational levels to address this problem.

Equal Opportunity for Educational Provision

As with their Han counterparts, ethnic minority students in China rely on education as a major means of upward social mobility. Ethnic minority and Han students compete within the same educational structure, comprising primary (Grades 1–6), junior secondary (Grades 7–9), senior secondary (Grades 10–12), and higher education. Primary and junior secondary education constitutes nine-year compulsory schooling, although ethnic autonomous areas may offer primary and junior secondary education over 10 to 13 years, depending on local conditions (Guo, 2011). Senior secondary education has two separate curriculum tracks: one track prepares students for university, whereas the vocational/technical track facilitates direct entry into the labor market. Public examinations are major means of screening and selecting Han and ethnic minority students for admission to senior secondary education, undergraduate education, and postgraduate studies.

To enhance its global competitiveness and facilitate domestic reforms, China has sought to turn its large population into a national resource and development asset by gradually expanding its education system. In 1986, it introduced nine-year compulsory education; it expanded senior secondary and higher education in the 1990s. Between 1991 and 2013, the percentages of age cohorts entering senior secondary and higher education rose from 25% to 86% and from 3.5% to 34.5% respectively (Ministry of Education, 2014a). Although this expansion of education has increased both Han and ethnic minority children's access to education, ethnic minority groups are over-represented in secondary education compared to their proportion of the population (8.5%), but under-represented in higher education. In 2013, 9.72% of all students and 8.55% of all full-time teachers were ethnic minorities (see Table 1).

Ethnic minority and Han students study the same highly centralized national school curriculum intended to ensure uniformity of knowledge, skills, and dispositions among all students. After 1978, China's national one-curriculum-one-textbook policy began to give way to the use of one curriculum with multiple textbook versions to accommodate different local conditions. In the early 2000s, the Ministry of Education (2001) began to divide the primary and junior-secondary education curriculum into three major tiers: national

Table 1. Numbers and Percentages of Students and Teachers at Different Education Levels, 2013

Education Level	Student Enrollment			Full-Time Teachers		
	All	Ethnic minorities		All	Ethnic minorities	
		Number	%		Number	%
Preschool	38,946,903	3,155,937	8.10	1,663,487	102,672	6.17
Primary	93,605,487	10,409,488	11.12	5,584,644	589,984	10.56
Junior Secondary	44,401,248	4,710,203	10.61	3,480,979	311,437	8.95
Regular Senior Secondary	24,358,817	2,109,133	8.40	1,639,459	121,459	7.41
Vocational/Technical	13,064,036	1,022,214	7.82	605,025	32,797	5.42
Universities/Colleges	24,680,726	1,844,503	7.47	1,496,865	79,439	5.31
Total	239,057,217	23,251,478	9.72	14,470,459	1,237,788	8.55

Source: China Education Yearbook Editorial Board (2014).

components for all students (80–85% of total class hours); components specific to local conditions and needs; and components catering to different schools' and students' needs.

Enforcing Affirmative Action for Ethnic Minorities' Greater Educational Opportunity

China also introduced affirmative action policies benefiting ethnic minority students, similar to U.S. preferential education policies addressing "inequalities arising from past practices or conditions" (Zhou & Hill, 2009, p. 1). In China, teacher quality and school conditions for the minority population lag behind that of the Han population. To increase ethnic minority students' representation in education and to protect their education rights, China implemented a series of ethnically oriented affirmative action policies, including establishing ethnic minority schools, allowing ethnic minority-language instruction, relaxing postcompulsory education admissions standards for ethnic minority students, and providing additional resources for ethnic minority education.

Providing education to sparsely distributed ethnic minority children presents some challenges. First, allocating ethnic minority students to Han schools would disadvantage them due to minority students' limited Chinese language proficiency. Second, most of China's widely distributed ethnic minority population lives in remote or difficult-to-access areas. Third, ethnic autonomous areas populated mainly by a specific ethnic minority group commonly accommodate other ethnic minority groups' languages and cultures. Fourth, very few ethnic autonomous areas have an ethnic minority majority population (e.g., Tibet, 92%, and Xinjiang, 60%; Population Census Office under the State Council & National Bureau of Statistics, 2011). Concentrating ethnic minority schools in certain areas would not universalize nine-year compulsory education among ethnic minority children from more remote areas whose families might not be able to afford the resulting travel and accommodation costs. Widely dispersed ethnic minority schools might recruit fewer students, however, and might have higher operation costs than local governments and ethnic minority families can afford.

To address these concerns, China established three main types of ethnic minority-designated primary and secondary schools, in and out of ethnic autonomous areas: mono-ethnic minority schools for children of a single ethnic minority group (where population concentrations allow); mixed-ethnic minority schools (mostly in areas with multiple ethnic minority groups); and mixed Han/ethnic minority schools (mostly in urban areas; Guo, 2011). In mixed-ethnic minority schools and Han/ethnic minority schools, children of different ethnicities learn their own ethnic languages in segregated classes. China also established ethnic minority schools with accommodations for children from sparsely populated areas. In 2011, ethnic minority students (roughly 25 million) were enrolled in 19.4% of China's 241,250 primary schools and 14.4% of its 67,750 secondary schools (State Ethnic Affairs Commission & State Statistical Bureau, 2012). Ethnic minority secondary vocational and technical schools prepare ethnic minority students for direct labor market entry, and 211 ethnic minority universities and colleges foster socioeconomic and political elites in ethnic autonomous areas by offering degree or subdegree programs to 16 million ethnic minority students (State Ethnic Affairs Commission & State Statistical Bureau, 2012).

Another affirmative action policy establishes ethnic minority languages as instructional media. In 1956, Putonghua became the official medium of instruction for the Han population, and local dialects (e.g., Cantonese or Shanghainese) may not be used in schools. However, ethnic minority students in ethnic autonomous areas were exempted from this policy and retained the legal right to learn using spoken and/or written ethnic minority languages, a policy later codified in China's constitution. Schools were, however, encouraged to offer ethnic minority students voluntary Chinese-language-learning opportunities.

To facilitate socioeconomic interconnectivity and ethnic interdependence, the State Council, in the early 1980s, implemented a bilingual teaching and learning policy (双语教学) intended to enhance ethnic minority students' Chinese proficiency. Ethnic minority peoples use their written and spoken ethnic languages as instructional media, but are encouraged to learn and use Chinese; ethnic minority peoples without written ethnic languages use Chinese as their main instructional medium, assisted by their spoken ethnic languages. This policy does not affect ethnic minority students with widely used Chinese mother tongues (e.g., Hui and Manchu) and who are in sparsely dispersed in Han areas.

As a result, ethnic minority schools today feature three broad bilingual instructional media modes, depending on the existence, concentration, and dispersion of ethnic minority languages and communities (Wang, 2007; Xia, 2007): (a) double-major mode, in which Chinese and ethnic minority language are communication media with equal status; (b) major-minor mode, in which Chinese is the main language and an ethnic minority language is the supplemental communication medium (or vice versa); and (c) Chinese language textbooks and teaching materials, with ethnic minority language oral communications. In other arrangements, Xinjiang, in the mid-2000s, separated primary and secondary schools' instructional media by subject: Chinese for English language, Chinese language, mathematics, science and information technology, and ethnic languages for citizenship education, history, geography, and other subjects (Ma, 2010).

A third policy involves special arrangements to improve ethnic minority students' access to postcompulsory education. The policy dates to China's first national college admission examination in the 1950s and was enshrined in 1984's Regional National Autonomy Law, which requires higher education institutions and senior secondary vocational/technical schools to set lower standards and requirements for admitting ethnic minority students (National People's Congress, 1984, Article 65). Revisions stipulate that special consideration be given to students from small-population ethnic minority groups (National People's Congress, 2001, Article 71). By the early 2000s, ethnic minority students could be admitted to higher education institutions with examination scores 10–80 marks lower than their Han counterparts, depending on geographic location and the higher education institution's type and competitiveness (Teng & Ma, 2009).

Unlike Han students, ethnic minority students who are not initially accepted by a higher education institution can attend remedial matriculation classes (预科班) at ethnic minority universities and colleges or designated universities in economically developed areas (e.g., Peking University) to improve their knowledge of key senior secondary subjects (Ministry of Education, 2005) and to gain a basic understanding of their preferred specialty. The policy began in the 1950s and was revitalized in the 1980s. Courses last for one year, with students who are weak in Chinese language attending a second year. Successful ethnic minority students are allowed to enroll in specialties or corresponding undergraduate courses at their higher education institutions. The state sets matriculation class admission quotas for different specialties according to ethnic areas' needs.

Tibetan and Uyghur students have enjoyed particularly good access to high-quality secondary schools and universities. In the mid-1980s, China began requiring cities' secondary schools and universities in 16 municipalities and provinces to offer Tibetan classes and admit Tibetan students; by 2008, 70,000 Tibetan students had enrolled (State Council, 2009b). In 2000, Uyghur students began to be offered Xinjiang classes in high-quality senior secondary schools in major cities; in 2008, 24,000 Uyghur students took Xinjiang classes in 50 senior secondary schools in 28 cities in 12 provinces and municipalities (State Council, 2009b).

The fourth affirmative action policy involves providing more education resources in ethnic autonomous areas than in Han areas. Despite holding large amounts of land and natural resources, ethnic autonomous areas' contribution to China's gross domestic product is low: less than 10% between 1995 and 2011 (State Ethnic Affairs Commission & State Statistical Bureau, 2012). Local government expenditures in these areas outstripped revenue by around 6% between 1990 and 2011. Ethnic minority education, particularly in ethnic autonomous areas with large ethnic minority populations (e.g., Tibet), relies heavily on state subsidies.

Beyond their regular budgetary appropriations, local governments have, since the 1950s, subsidized ethnic minority schools' facility improvements, teacher salaries, and student living expenses (Xia, 2007). Local governments and universities are required to help ethnic minority students experiencing financial difficulties complete their studies (National People's Congress, 2001, Article 71). In the 1990s, China established additional funds to improve the condition and quality of ethnic minority schools and to produce ethnic minority textbooks and teaching materials for bilingual education; by the late 2000s, 10 administrative regions had translated Chinese language textbooks into nearly 30 ethnic minority languages for 6 million students from 23 ethnic minority groups (Wu, 2011).

In sum, ethnic minority education has been challenged by ethnic minorities' geographic distribution and ethnic-related issues such as language, barriers that have largely been eased (but not eradicated) by China's equal education opportunity and affirmative action policies. Ethnic minorities' representation in primary and junior secondary education (about 11%) is higher than their proportion of the population (see Table 1), but more efforts are needed to increase ethnic minority students' representation at higher education institutions. Some studies (discussed later in this chapter) question the effectiveness of these affirmative action measures.

Citizenship Education for Minority Students

China's civic education for students, and ethnic minority students in particular, reveals an increasing tension between being open to a globalized world and ensuring ethnic solidarity and national security domestically. Since 1978, citizenship education has gradually traded its ideologically dualistic (socialist/capitalist) orientation for one more accommodating of multiple (local, national, global) citizenships, albeit with greater emphasis on the national. Because of their strategic importance to national security, ethnic minority students receive additional citizenship education to reinforce their belief in ethnic solidarity and foreign countries' conspiracy against China's peaceful evolution.

Providing a Common Citizenship Education Curriculum for Ethnic Minority and Han Students

Regardless of ethnicity, all students must successfully complete the same citizenship education curriculum to advance to the next education level: Moral Character and Life (Grades 1–2); Moral Character and Society (Grades 3–6); Ideological Thoughts and Moral Character (Grades 7–9); Ideological Thoughts and Politics (Grades 10–12); and two courses (两课) from various modules in higher education institutions. Before 1978, China's education institutions had the ideo-political task of preparing students for class struggle and fostering their identity as "new socialist persons" whose lives were commanded by politics in new socialist China (Chen, 1969). In citizenship education lessons, both Hans and ethnic minority students studied Mao's writings, the Communist Party of China's version of revolutionary history and its dualistic (capitalism/socialism, enemies/friends) worldview, and Marxism.

In response to domestic social changes and global challenges, China has revised its citizenship education curriculum several times since 1978. In the 1980s and 1990s, curriculum changes mainly reflected themes of reform and opening to the world (Law, 2011). To prepare students for the transition to a socialist market economy, China required all students to study Deng Xiaoping's reform theories, views on Chinese socialism, and major national development policies, including market principles and the rule of law. To increase exposure to and understanding of the world, all students were asked to learn from the best experiences and practices of other countries, to communicate with people from other cultures respectfully, and to study major religions and international organizations.

In the early 2000s, China revised primary and secondary curricula to strengthen students' cognitive and affective affiliation and identification with local, national, and global communities. The Ministry of Education (2002) explicitly defined a multilevel, multidimensional citizenship education framework similar to Kubow, Grossman, and Ninomiya's (2000) model. The Chinese framework fosters Han and ethnic minority students' multiple identities by affiliating them with five major life levels: self, family and school, community, nation, and the world. Each level covers three social dimensions: living context (including temporal and spatial features); activities (daily, economic, political, and cultural); and relations (personal, cultural, legal). Although the Ministry of Education (2012a) fine-tuned the primary and secondary citizenship education curriculum in the early 2010s, this accommodative framework still equips students to be contributing members of their family, school, community, nation, and world, and all political textbooks reflect these five levels and three dimensions.

An analysis of the Ministry of Education's (2012a, 2012b, 2012c) primary and junior secondary citizenship education curriculum standards shows that the global component fosters students' belief that all peoples share the world, face similar problems, and must collaborate on their future. The global component examines basic world geography; different peoples, cultures, and customs; the impacts of science and technology on economy and human life; shared global problems (e.g., pollution, scarcity of resources, terrorism); and world peace and cultural diversity.

The local component fosters students' different local identities by enhancing their cognitive understanding of and attachment to their communities. This component provides ethnic minority students an important opportunity to cultivate their ethnic minority identities. Both Han and ethnic minority students are taught about their communities' major developments, products, traffic and environmental conditions, and scenic places. They also learn the importance of participating in local activities, protecting public facilities, observing social norms, and respecting and preserving local cultures.

The national component helps students develop a common national identity by mastering basic knowledge about China and fostering their patriotism and love for China. Students study China's national symbols and rituals; China as a unified multiethnic country; China's geography, population, economic and political systems, culture, and history; pressing problems (e.g., natural disasters, regional disparities); China's history of resisting foreign invasion; how the Communist Party of China has rebuilt China since 1949; China's domestic and global achievements, particularly post-1978; citizens' rights and responsibilities; China's two centennial goals (i.e., becoming moderately prosperous by 2020 and reviving China globally by 2049, the centennial year of the foundings of the Communist Party of China and the People's Republic of China, respectively); the One-China Principle (i.e., Taiwan is an inalienable Chinese province); the link between Chinese people's fate and China's; and identification with and pride in China and Chinese culture.

Extracurricular activities, including flag-raising ceremonies, Young Pioneers and Communist Youth League activities, patriotic movies, and visiting patriotic education bases, promote the national citizenship education component among Han and ethnic minority students. In both Han and ethnic minority areas, hidden curriculum through, for example, sculptures and slogans displayed on campus helps students internalize Communist Party of China–prescribed ideologies and values and enhances their sense of patriotism (Zhu, 2007).

Although national citizenship education fosters students' identification with local, national, and global communities, it also emphasizes national identity (as prescribed by the Communist Party of China–led state) and ties it to local and global identities, that is, ethnic groups' and the world's relations to and with China (Law, 2014). Students study different Chinese communist leaders' versions of Chinese socialism and strategies for governance and nation (re)building, including Jiang Zemin's "three represents" theory from the 1990s, Hu Jintao's "eight graces and eight disgraces" from the mid-2000s, and Xi Jinping's "China's dream" from the early 2010s (Law, 2011).

Reinforcing Ethnic Solidarity Education for National Security

Ethnic minority students, particularly in ethnic autonomous areas, are taught ethnic minority-specific patriotic citizenship education emphasizing national identification, dialectical materialism, and atheism (to counter religious superstition; Cao, 2012; Meng, 2010), and are the main target of ethnic solidarity education (ESE). After 1978, China designated ESE as a high-level national security concern and made it a mandatory curriculum component. Students were encouraged to interpret ethnic minority problems using a Communist Party of China–led ethnic diversity/national unity framework, and using ad hoc events to further extracurricular ESE. Compared to national citizenship education, ESE is less politically and ideologically accommodating and targets ethnic minority students, not Hans.

Making ESE a High-Level National Security Concern. Despite removing class struggle from its party line, the state has retained its anti-Western Cold War mentality and has adopted a conspiracy-theory approach to justify ESE. Since 1949, ethnic minority problems, ethnic solidarity, and ESE have been important national concerns. In the 1950s, ESE was a part of citizenship education and focused on resisting the United States, supporting North Korea, resisting imperialist invasion, and eradicating imperialist/counter-revolutionary influences (China Education Yearbook Editorial Board, 1984). It portrayed China as an inclusive multiethnic family and reminded students of ethnic groups' struggles against imperialism and foreigners' attempts to make ethnic minorities independent of China. Despite China's increased openness since 1978, the Ministry of Education and State Ethnic Affairs Commission (2009) still accuses "international adversaries" of attempting to "Westernize and split" (西化和分化) China and use domestic separatist forces and ethnic, religious, and human rights issues to infiltrate, divide, sabotage, and subvert China. In addition to easing domestic interethnic conflicts, ESE is a long-term strategic plan for guarding against foreign infiltration. Although ESE is provided to ethnic minority and Han students, its contents and activities target ethnic minorities.

After the 1989 Tiananmen Square incident (perceived by the Communist Party of China as a Western attempt to overthrow its rule through peaceful revolution), the state reinforced ESE and patriotic education. In 1994, ESE was promoted in seven administrative regions (including Beijing, Liaoning, and Sichuan); it was extended to China's other areas in 2000. Beginning in 1999, the Ministry of Education and State Ethnic Affairs Commission (1999) required primary and junior secondary schools, respectively, to offer two ESE courses: Knowing Ethnic Groups in China and China's Policies on Ethnic Groups. The first course provided primary students with basic knowledge of China's 56 ethnic groups' features, lifestyles, customs, and cultures. The second course helped junior secondary students understand Marxist perspectives on ethnicity and religion and the Communist Party of China's ethnic and religious policies.

The upheavals in Tibet (2008) and Xinjiang (2009) reinforced the Communist Party of China's belief that hostile foreign forces were conspiring against China and threatening its national security. It condemned domestic and foreign "adversary forces" for organizing the riots and infiltrating Chinese schools (Publicity Department of the Communist Party of China Central Committee, Ministry of Education & State Ethnic Affairs Commission, 2009). These ethnic conflicts signaled to China that its ethnic solidarity efforts were ineffective and elevated ESE to a vital component of the ideo-political "battle" for the hearts and minds of China's children and youths; despite massive social unrest in Tibet, Xinjiang, and related ethnic minority areas, the state strengthened ESE across China.

Making ESE a Mandatory Curriculum Component Across the Nation. The Ministry of Education and State Ethnic Affairs Commission's (2008) revised curriculum guidelines made ESE an integral part of the local component of formal curricula and assigned 10–12 annual class hours in primary and junior secondary education, 8–10 hours in regular senior secondary education, and 12–14 hours in senior (vocational/technical) secondary education.

The ESE curriculum is a political socialization instrument used to develop students' Communist Party of China–prescribed ethnic knowledge and concepts and their passion for national unity and ethnic solidarity. The ESE curriculum gives Grades 3–4 students an elementary education in and awareness of ethnic solidarity; Grades 5–6 students a basic knowledge of ethnic groups and the necessity of "promoting ethnic solidarity, defending national unity, and opposing ethnic separatism"; Grades 7–8 students an understanding of China's ethnic policies and how to analyze practical ethnic issues; and Grades 10–12 students faith in the superiority of the Communist Party of China's ethnic policies and in China's global revival (Ministry of Education & State Ethnic Affairs Commission, 2008). The revised ESE curriculum comprises four courses: The Big Family of the Chinese Nation (Grades 3–4); General Knowledge about Ethnic Groups in China (Grades 5–6); Ethnic Policies (Grades 7–8); and Ethnic Theories (Grades 10–11). There are no specific ESE courses for Grade 9 and 12 students, due to public examination concerns.

To ensure political correctness, the Communist Party of China tightly controlled production of the four textbooks and related teaching materials used for ESE curriculum, with the Ministry of Education and State Ethnic Affairs Commission overseeing their writing, compilation, review, and approval (Publicity Department of the Communist Party of China, 2009). Using unapproved materials is not permitted. Since 2009, local governments have been required to report annually on ESE progress and achievements. Because ESE previously had not been vigorously promoted in schools (Postiglione, 2014), in the early 2010s, China amended political examinations for admission to senior secondary, college, and postgraduate education to include not less than 15% ESE-related examination content.

Subordinating Ethnic Diversity to National Unity under Communist Party of China Leadership. An analysis of ESE curriculum guidelines and textbooks suggests that the Communist Party of China uses ESE to consolidate and sustain its political leadership in China. Specifically, it rationalizes, in ESE, prioritizing national unity over ethnic diversity and assimilating ethnic minority groups into Han-dominated, Communist Party of China–governed China.

Although acknowledging individual ethnic groups' distinctiveness, textbooks teach students to subsume Han and ethnic minority groups' ethnic identities into a higher, ancient Chinese political and cultural identity. This subordination begins at the outset, with *The Big Family of the Chinese Nation*, for Grades 3–4 (Editorial and Compilation Team for Ethnic Solidarity Education Textbooks, 2009c). In one passage, the text subsumes Han and ethnic minority groups into a "unified, multiethnic socialist" China with many written and spoken languages, employs the "Chinese nation" (中华民族) as the "collective name" for all 56 ethnic groups, and describes Han and ethnic minority cultures as integral to "Chinese civilization" (中华文化) (p. 1).

A similar subordination can be found in *General Knowledge about Ethnic Groups in China* (Editorial and Compilation Team for Ethnic Solidarity Education Textbooks, 2013), which hints that today's Han and ethnic minority groups can be traced back to ancient China and that all Han and ethnic minority groups are now "national citizens" (国家公民) of China and "children of the Chinese nation" (中华儿女) (p. 1). The textbook calls students successors of socialist undertakings who should "always keep in mind" (时刻牢记) that they are members of the Chinese nation (p. 71).

The ESE textbooks teach the gradual convergence of ethnic identities into a commonly shared larger "common entity" (共同体), namely the Chinese nation, and later into a communist utopia. This message is most conspicuous in *Ethnic Theories* (Grades 10–11; Editorial and Compilation Team for Ethnic Solidarity Education Textbooks, 2009b), which predicts the trend of ethnic convergence in an international context by positing an increase in large ethnic groups due to mergers among small ones. It asserts that ethnic groups' formation and development are dynamic, and states that, although ethnic groups are stable entities based on shared ethnicity, inhabitation, language, customs, and identification, increasing exchanges and interactions have rendered the boundaries among ethnic groups less distinctive. The notion that ethnic groups' use of a common language is "an inevitable trend" in the world (p. 4) facilitates the adoption of Chinese spoken and written languages as common languages in China.

Using Marxist ideology, this textbook (Editorial and Compilation Team for Ethnic Solidarity Education Textbooks, 2009b) links ethnic groups' division, regrouping, and assimilation to their extinction, calling it the highest level of ethnic development, which will come only when social classes and countries become extinct, that is, when true world communism emerges. Until then, ethnic groups and countries will remain interdependent and must co-progress and co-develop; countries provide ethnic minorities with policies and conditions (e.g., a stable environment) important to their development and prosperity. The last passage (of the textbook and the entire ESE curriculum) concludes that, until the coming of the communist utopia, China is a "common entity" of 56 ethnic groups built on the foundation of Chinese history and bonded by Chinese culture (p. 79).

The four textbooks teach students about the primacy of Chinese socialism and Communist Party of China leadership and about the precedence of national interests when maintaining ethnic solidarity. *Ethnic Policies* emphasizes that the core and foundation of China's ethnic solidarity are, respectively, the Communist Party of China's "leadership and solidarity" and the "socialist system and national unity" (Editorial and Compilation Team for Ethnic Solidarity Education Textbooks, 2009a, p. 10). *Ethnic Theories* expands the propaganda slogan, "no Communist Party of China, no new socialist China" to include "no independence, no liberation, and no prosperous development for individual ethnic groups" (Editorial and Compilation Team for Ethnic Solidarity Education Textbooks, 2009b, p. 68). It stresses that the co-development and co-prosperity of ethnic groups must follow the path of China's socialist construction and the "great revival of the Chinese nation," the "political foundation" of which is the Communist Party of China's leadership and ideological persistence (pp. 48, 81). The textbook stresses the supremacy of national interests over the shared interests of all ethnic groups and the absolute importance of subordinating the latter to the former in any conflict (p. 28).

To increase students' faith in the leadership of the Communist Party of China during China's nation (re)building, the four textbooks repeatedly recount Communist Party of China achievements. Ethnic groups are introduced in ways that remind students of the Communist Party of China–led state's achievements in advancing their rights and living standards, particularly since 1978. This strategy is most obvious in *Ethnic Policies* (Editorial and Compilation Team for Ethnic Solidarity Education Textbooks, 2009a). After describing China's major ethnic minority policies, the textbook cites examples illustrating the benefits ethnic minorities derive from Communist Party of China policies, such as overrepresentation in the National People's Congress (due to the Communist Party of China's equality policy) and socioeconomic progress in Inner Mongolia and Tibet (due to its ethnic autonomous area policy).

The ESE textbooks warn students of threats to China's national unity and harmony among Han and ethnic minority groups, which the books present as a millennia-old political and cultural hallmark of Chinese civilization. Although admitting that problems in Tibet and Xinjiang are disturbing longstanding harmonious relations between Han and ethnic minority groups, the textbooks criticize hostile foreign forces and domestic ethnic separatists for using ethnic, religious, and human rights issues to incite interethnic hatred and unrest and of plotting to "Westernize . . . split . . . [and] subvert" the People's Republic of China (Editorial and Compilation Team for Ethnic Solidarity Education Textbooks, 2009b, pp. 59, 60). The curriculum exhorts students to actively defend ethnic solidarity and oppose schisms. In addition to stressing the Communist Party of China's approach to sustaining national unity, the textbooks repeatedly encourage students to develop "four identifications": with China as their homeland; with the Chinese nation as a collective entity; with Chinese culture; and with socialism with Chinese characteristics. The books repeat former-president Hu Jintao's warning that unrest and ethnic independence lead to disaster (祸), whereas national unity and solidarity bring "blessings" (福) to all ethnic groups (Editorial and Compilation Team for Ethnic Solidarity Education Textbooks, 2013, p. 71).

Using ad Hoc Events to Further ESE. In addition to lessons, the Communist Party of China–led state makes use of ad hoc events to further ESE, particularly in ethnic autonomous areas with longstanding ethnic problems. For example, one year after the 2008 Tibetan riots, the state implemented a series of propaganda activities aimed at Tibetan students in Tibet and Tibetan-inhabited areas celebrating the 50th anniversary of Tibet's liberation and emphasizing its Communist Party of China–led economic, social, and cultural achievements, particularly since 1978. Two months after the 2009 Xinjiang riots, the state organized pro-China and pro-ethnic-solidarity activities to assure Tibetan and Xinjiang students that China cares about their autonomous regions, to remind them of improvements in those regions, to strengthen support for unity and solidarity and opposition to separatism, and to urge the students to serve China in the future (Li, 2010). Local authorities organized similar activities for teachers, including talks and seminars to cultivate their awareness and support of the Communist Party of China's "three maintenances" position (maintaining ethnic solidarity, social stability, and national unification), resistance to illegal religious activities, and opposition to ethnic separatism.

Contentious Issues in Ethnic Minority Affairs and Education

Since 1949, the Communist Party of China–led state has implemented policies and measures to manage ethnic minority relations and affairs in domains ranging from politics to education. Yet, China's unity-based ethnic pluralism continues to face four important, interrelated challenges: the rise of ethnic conflicts and violence; the impact of preferentialism on ethnic equality; ethnic plurality in standardized curricula; and the supremacy of social stability and national integration in ethnic minority students' education and citizenship education.

Plurality in Unity as a Guiding Principle

The causes of ethnic conflict and social unrest in China are complicated and multifaceted, and simply advocating unity-based ethnic plurality or suppressing ethnic voices cannot eradicate either. In 1992, under President Jiang Zemin, China blamed increased ethnic conflicts on six factors, five domestic and one international. The domestic factors were economic and cultural disparities; disputes over economic interests; lack of mutual understanding and respect for one another's cultural traditions and languages; religious complications; and deliberate attacks on national unity and ethnic solidarity. To a large extent, these factors explain recent Tibetan- and Uyghur-related ethnic riots.

The sixth reason reflects the Communist Party of China's Cold War mentality and belief that foreign powers were conspiring against China and threatening its national security. Jiang (1992) attributed the rise in ethnic conflicts to overseas and domestic adversaries using ethnic problems to infiltrate China and support extremely small minorities' independence efforts. In 2009, President Hu Jintao blamed "three forces" (三股势力), both foreign and domestic, for planning and organizing widespread ethnic violence in Tibet and Xinjiang: terrorism of violence; religious extremism; and ethnic separatism. Hu (2009) singles out the Dalai Lama and Rebiya Kadeer of the World Uygur Congress as representatives of such foreign adversaries. To guard against foreign infiltration, in its medium-term (2014–2020) plan for developing ethnic minority groups, the Ministry of Education (2014b) designates Tibet, Xinjiang, and Tibetan-inhabited territories in four other provinces as areas for research on how to safeguard students from radical religious thought and how to teach general religious knowledge in ethnic autonomous areas.

To avoid interethnic conflicts and national security threats and solicit ethnic solidarity, China, under Hu (2009), made ethnic diversity within a unified Chinese nation (多元一体) its guiding principle for ethnic solidarity, social harmony, and stability. The concept was first proposed by Chinese sociologist and anthropologist Fei Xiaotong (1999), who expounded that China is one common political entity comprising 56 ethnic groups with different origins, languages, and cultures and that these groups are interconnected, interdependent, and supplementary to one another. He argued that national and ethnic identifications are not interchangeable, and that the former transcends identification with an ethnic group. Similarly, Hu (2009) argues that each ethnic group is indispensable to the Chinese nation, the harmony and organic unity of which is based on "three inseparables" (Han from ethnic minorities, ethnic minorities from Han, and ethnic minorities from ethnic minorities) and sustained by "three maintenances." In 2014, President Xi Jinping based his appeal for nationwide ethnic solidarity on Fei's plurality in unity concept and Hu's harmonious multiculturalism (Xinhua News Agency, 2014).

Although China's guiding principle of unity-based plurality rationalizes preferentialism, Ma Rong (2004) has attributed the intensification of ethnic conflicts in China to China's policies. Despite China's ideal of co-prosperity, interethnic economic gaps have widened since the 1990s. Some ethnic policies have triggered conflict between Hans and ethnic minorities, as in the 2009 Xinjiang riots. Postiglione (2014) suggests that China has entered a "critical pluralism" stage, in which increasing disparities and unequal opportunities in education, the economy, and elsewhere are exacerbating interethnic social tensions and cultural differences. Mackerras (1995, 2003) attributes ethnic conflicts to ethnic minority peoples' reaction to their coercive integration during the Cultural Revolution (1966–1976), increased diversification of commonalities among ethnic minority communities, and increased ethnic consciousness globally. These deep-seated causes are more than the Communist Party of China's harmonious multiculturalism strategy can handle.

Affirmative Action as a Balance Among Equality, Ethnic Pluralism, and National Unity

China faces the challenge of simultaneously ensuring interethnic equality, promoting ethnic pluralism through preferentialism, and pursuing national unity in a multiethnic country. In the United States, affirmative action is a subject of great debate. Although affirmative action can partially remedy or compensate for social inequality and injustice due to historical discrimination, integrate ethnic minorities into mainstream society, and foster diversity in schools and the workplace (Kennedy, 2013), opponents argue that its benefits cannot outweigh its costs and that it harms individuals and society at large by reinforcing, rather than weakening, discrimination against ethnic minorities and by discriminating against majority groups, defying meritocratic principles of equality (Schuck, 2014). Affirmative action measures are also debated in China, but the debate centers on whether ethnic preferentialism eases interethnic conflicts and balances ethnic pluralism with national unity, particularly considering social unrest in Tibet and Xinjiang.

This issue of preferentialism stems from proposals to depoliticize and deinstitutionalize ethnicity as an anti-inequality strategy for easing interethnic conflicts, advocated by Ma Rong, a leading critic of the Communist Party of China's ethnic minority policies. Like Fei (1999), Ma (2004) conceptualizes China as a multiethnic nation-state, a shared political community of 56 ethnicities. Unlike Fei, Ma proposes replacing ethnic minority groups' political identities with a common national cultural identity, arguing that, good intentions notwithstanding, preferentialism institutionalizes ethnic inequality, causes increased ethnic tensions, and deters ethnic integration by strengthening ethnic consciousness. He suggests that China should depoliticize and culturalize ethnic relations by treating ethnic minority groups as cultural rather than political entities; by treating ethnic minorities and Hans alike in regard to social welfare and education; by weakening ethnic consciousness by assimilating ethnic minorities into traditional Chinese culture; and by reinforcing ethnic minorities' identification with China.

Hu and Hu (2011) push the precedence of national over ethnic identity to an extreme: the deinstitutionalization of ethnicity. Arguing that all ethnic groups should be equal in all aspects before the law, Hu and Hu propose eliminating preferentialism from political and social institutions. Contending that trans-ethnic national unity and identification requires ethnic minorities' full assimilation into Chinese society and culture, they urge weakening ethnic minority groups' ethnic consciousness by stripping elites and autonomous areas of special rights and status and integrating ethnic minorities' unique ethnic elements into Chinese culture. Furthermore, ethnic minority people's national consciousness and pride should be strengthened by vigorously promoting Putonghua as China's common language; national symbols and rituals; interethnic marriages; and interethnic schooling. Unlike Hu and Hu, Ma (2013) recognizes the importance of protecting ethnic minority groups' historical, religious, and cultural traditions; ethnic diversity in consolidating and sustaining China as a nation-state; and interethnic co-development and co-prosperity to enhance political, economic, and cultural identification with China.

Opponents have criticized these theorists for disguising Han cultural chauvinism as ethnic equality and argue that the coexistence of ethnic and national identities among ethnic minorities balances the inevitable inequalities between ethnic majorities and minorities in multiethnic nations (Zheng, 2014). As a leading opponent, Wang Xien (2009) contends that national and ethnic problems are political in nature and that state responses are political behaviors. Wang accuses depoliticization and culturalization advocates of logical inconsistency because their proposals are not cultural but political in nature—that is, intended to maintain China's social and political stability. Wang asserts that, despite their political nature, ethnic-based identification and policies give necessary recognition to ethnic groups' existence and development as naturally formed communities in China's history and should therefore be retained. He argues that, although rising ethnic minority consciousness is socially destabilizing, it can enhance rather than prevent ethnic fusion; it should not be seen as "ethnic isolation" (民族隔绝), but as a means for ethnic groups to pursue their ethnic developments and thus contribute to national development (p. 4). Wang believes ethnic autonomous areas are vital to the preservation of ethnic identities, offer important institutional protection for ethnic minority groups' rights, and provide common territory for economic, political, and cultural development. He insists that abolishing ethnic minority policies would perpetuate gaps between ethnic minorities and Hans, as the former continue to face economic, employment, language, and educational disadvantages.

Similar equality issues have been raised regarding preferentialism in education. Leibold (2014) succinctly captures the academic debate and public discourse (particularly on the Internet) regarding Hans' reactions to lowering admission standards to give ethnic minority students greater access to higher education institutions. He finds increased online Han nationalism and resentment of affirmative action, with many Han students calling it "reverse discrimination" (p. 142).

China has adopted both of the above views. On the one hand, the state continues affirmative action and efforts at preserving ethnic languages and cultures and shows no sign of depoliticizing ethnicity in state governance. On the other hand, the state emphasizes national identity by condemning ethnic localism, uses ESE to posit China's ethnic groups' shared cultural origin, and promotes Chinese language and culture in ethnic minority area schools. It also emphasizes that ethnic minority groups, as Chinese citizens, have a responsibility to resist ethnic division and defend national unity and solidarity (State Council, 2009b), subsuming ethnic plurality and identities to a larger national identity.

Catering to Ethnic Plurality and Diversity in a Unified School Curriculum

Despite the Ministry of Education's (2001) rhetorical emphasis on the importance of ethnic diversity, its attention to individual ethnic minority students' or areas' needs is undermined by the close relationships among school curriculum, textbooks, and teachers.

China has long used a unified school curriculum to ensure equal scholastic opportunity for ethnic minority students and their Han counterparts. The curriculum levels the field for ethnic minority and Han students competing for higher education, employment opportunities, and social mobility. The multilevel, multidimensional citizenship education framework gives ethnic minority students equal opportunity to broaden their knowledge of China and the world and to foster multiple identities in a multilevel, multicultural world.

China began to allow multiple versions of textbooks in the 1980s in order to address different areas' and students' diverse needs. In the 2000s, it adopted a tripartite (national, local, school) framework for school curricula. To some extent, the local and school components of the curriculum offer ethnic minority and Han students' chances to learn about the features, developments, and needs of their ethnic communities, an opportunity that has been enhanced by the ESE introduced in the late 2000s.

However, these curriculum efforts are insufficient for ethnic minority students' diverse needs, because teaching and learning organization and content are highly uniform (Wan & Bai, 2008) and the national component commands 80% of the curriculum. Textbooks all reflect the same curriculum standards and are published by government-designated publishers.

The unified school curriculum can affect ethnic minority students' distinctive ethnic identities (Mackerras, 1995): Han-culture-dominated curriculum standards and teaching contents create gaps between what ethnic minority students are taught and their experiences at home and in the community (e.g., daily habits, religious beliefs, values, customs; Wan & Bai, 2008). Similarly, both the national and the revised citizenship education curricula have been criticized for being Han-centric, denying ethnic minority students' cultural rights and choices and reducing their attachment to and pride in their ethnicity (Du & Jin, 2005). It is unlikely that the dual educational tasks of preserving ethnic minority culture and identity and enhancing ethnic minority people's upward mobility in Han-dominated society and economy will be achieved in Tibet (Yi, 2006). All this suggests that a unified school curriculum and similar textbooks could prevent meeting students' diverse needs in the classroom.

Chinese Language as a Political Instrument for National Integration and Stability

Despite its emphasis on ethnic plurality and affirmation action for ethnic minority groups, China has repeatedly highlighted the supreme importance of maintaining national unity, keeping social stability, and overcoming ethnic separatism. After the social unrest in Tibet and Xinjiang, in addition to reinforcing ESE in ethnic minority areas, China began to emphasize the ideo-political role of learning Chinese language in socializing and assimilating ethnic minority students into Han-dominated Chinese society and culture.

In the 2000s, China's leadership increased its efforts to popularize Chinese language in ethnic minority areas, having previously stipulated its importance to China's sovereignty and dignity, national unity, and solidarity (National People's Congress, 2000). Against the background of domestic economic and social changes and the challenges of ethnic division and religious radicalism, the Communist Party of China Central Committee and State Council (2014) reiterated the importance of Putonghua and written Chinese as common languages, reaffirming their determination to establish Chinese language as a mandatory school subject nationally (including in ethnic autonomous areas), to promote the use of written Chinese and Putonghua in ethnic minority students' education and to ensure that students master basic Chinese language skills. To that end, in 2013, the Ministry of Education revised curriculum standards for Chinese language in ethnic minority schools; despite a rhetoric emphasis on learning Chinese as a second language, the curriculum establishes communicative and identity functions for ethnic minority students' Chinese language learning that are the same as those for (mainly Han) mainstream schools.

As in (mainly Han) mainstream schools, the ethnic minority school curriculum standards require students to achieve basic proficiency in reading, speaking, listening, and writing Chinese in order to enhance their ability to communicate with other people nationally (Ministry of Education, 2012d, 2013b). To reduce resistance, however, proficiency standards are lower: whereas mainstream primary school students are required to know about 3,000 commonly used Chinese words and to write about 2,500, students in ethnic minority schools must meet these levels by the end of their junior secondary education (i.e., after three more years). Within their nine-year compulsory schooling, students in mainstream schools read an additional four million words (excluding textbooks and classroom materials); ethnic minority students read 900,000.

Moreover, both mainstream and ethnic minority school students are required to learn the Chinese language for national identity formation. In its national curriculum standards, the Ministry of Education (2012d) states that learning the Chinese language can help students understand Chinese culture, love the Chinese language, and foster their patriotism. Similarly, in its specific curriculum standards for ethnic minority schools, the Ministry of Education (2013b) asserts that learning Chinese can help ethnic minority students strengthen their consciousness of national identity (祖国意识), fortify their solidarity with the Chinese nation, and inherit and promote Chinese cultures and traditions. Ethnic minority students must first cultivate their cultural consciousness and appreciation of Chinese traditions and customs, including Chinese festivals, idioms, and calligraphy. Then, ethnic minority students, through learning Chinese, are expected to develop their love for and pride in the Chinese nation and a willingness to defend its solidarity. Chinese language textbooks are required to foster ethnic minority students' patriotism and their sense of the Chinese nation's dignity and solidarity. Moreover, in line with Xi's China Dream of making China strong and reviving the Chinese nation in the world, the Ministry of Education (2013a) requires schools (in both Han and ethnic minority areas) to teach students Chinese calligraphy and how to use a Chinese writing brush to encourage students to treasure and preserve Chinese culture and to strengthen their confidence in Chinese culture and their passion for the nation.

It remains to be seen how popularizing learning Chinese among ethnic minority students will affect China's national security and students' affiliation and identification with the Chinese nation and Chinese culture. Most likely, it will enhance students' Chinese language proficiency, increase their competitiveness in the labor market, enable them to participate more fully in China's political system, and draw them closer to Han-dominated mainstream society.

Conclusion

The chapter has demonstrated that ethnic minority affairs are situated within the Communist Party of China–prescribed framework of national integration and solidarity. Education and civic education for ethnic minority groups is more important for imposing Communist Party of China–defined national culture and identity than for preserving ethnic minority cultures and identities. Social stability, ethnic solidarity, and territorial integrity have been driving forces behind China's efforts to balance ethnic plurality and national unity when managing ethnic relations and affairs and providing education and civic education for ethnic minority groups. Despite its efforts, China's leadership has yet to strike a balance among taming ethnic conflicts and violence, addressing issues of inequality between majority and ethnic minority groups, and easing tensions between local ethnic, national, and global identities.

It is never easy to balance ethnic plurality and national integration—in society or in education—in a multiethnic country, as the example of China attests. Despite the common interests shared by a country and its ethnic minority groups, national and ethnic identifications are intrinsically contradictory. Forcing all ethnic groups to share and live in the same unified culture is impossible, no matter how preferential the ethnic minority policies, how coercive the ethnic policies, or how intensive the ESE might be.

The case of China suggests that states can maneuver the balance between ethnic pluralism and national unity to their advantage by using social stability and national security concerns to tilt the balance toward various sides at various times and given different political considerations. An authoritarian state can use ethnic diversity to promote national unity in such a way that national integration takes precedence over or even subsumes ethnic plurality.

Striking a balance between ethnic diversity and national unity in society and education can be complicated by political motives underlying policies for sustaining political leadership, protecting territorial integrity, and maintaining social stability. In 2015, China revised the National Security Law, tying its territorial integrity and national security concerns to the Communist Party of China's political security and national leadership role and prohibiting divisive ethnic activities, "the interference in domestic religious affairs by foreign forces," and extremism (National People's Congress Standing Committee, 2015, Articles 26–28). The leadership also reinforced the promotion and education of Communist Party of China–prescribed socialist values and legitimated the role of Chinese culture in maintaining ethnic solidarity and national security (Article 23). The same year, the State Council (2015a) declared upholding Communist Party of China leadership a fundamental aspect of ethnic minority education and made ESE a regular curriculum item for all students at every educational level. All this suggests that the bottom line for balancing ethnic plurality, national integration, social stability, and national security in China is that no challenge to the leadership of the Communist Party of China or to China's national unity or territorial integrity is permissible. The revised law provides a strong legal justification for the Communist Party of China to prioritize national unity over ethnic pluralism when it feels its leadership is threatened by ethnic conflicts or divisions. As a result, education and civic education for ethnic minority students has become a device used more for enhancing national integration than for preserving and sustaining ethnic plurality.

Acknowledgments

I would like to express my gratitude to Ms. Qing Yuan and Dr. Min Li for their research assistance. This chapter would not have been possible without the financial support of the University of Hong Kong's Research Output Prize and Centre for Educational Leadership.

References

Banks, J. A. (2014). Foreword. In J. Leibold & Y. Chen (Eds.), *Minority education in China: Balancing unity and diversity in an era of critical pluralism* (pp. xiii–xvii). Hong Kong: Hong Kong University Press.

Cao, Y. (2012). Shaoshu minzu diqu gongmin yishi peiyang yanjiu [Citizenship awareness among ethnic minorities]. *Lanzhou Daxue Xuebao* [Journal of Lanzhou University (Social Sciences)], *40*(2), 100–104.

Chen, T. H.-E. (1969). The new socialist man. *Comparative Education Review, 13*(1), 88–95.

China Education Yearbook Editorial Board. (1984). *Zhongguo jiaoyu nianjian 1949–1981* [China education yearbook, 1949–1981]. Beijing: People's Education Press.

China Education Yearbook Editorial Board. (2014). *Zhongguo jiaoyu nianjian 2014* [China education yearbook, 2014]. Beijing: People's Education Press.

Communist Party of China Central Committee & State Council. (2014, December 23). Guanyu jiaqiang he gaijin xinxingshixia minzu gongzuo de yijian [Views on strengthening and improving ethnic works in the new context]. *Renmin Ribao* [People's Daily], pp. 1, 2.

Connor, W. (2009). Mandarins, Marxists, and minorities. In M. Zhou & A. M. Hill (Eds.), *Affirmative action in China and the U.S.: A dialogue on inequality and minority education* (pp. 27–46). New York: Palgrave Macmillan.

Du, Z., & Jin, Y. (2005). Minzu diqu duoyuan wenhua kecheng [Multicultural curriculum in ethnic minority areas: Problems and countermeasures]. *Zhongguo Jiaoyu Xuekan* [Journal of Chinese Society of Education], *9*, 38–40.

Editorial and Compilation Team for Ethnic Solidarity Education Textbooks. (2009a). *Minzu zhengce changshi* [Ethnic policies of China]. Beijing: Hongqi Press.

Editorial and Compilation Team for Ethnic Solidarity Education Textbooks. (2009b). *Minzu lilun changshi* [Ethnic theories]. Beijing: Central Radio and TV University Press.

Editorial and Compilation Team for Ethnic Solidarity Education Textbooks. (Ed.). (2009c). *Zhonghua dajiating* [The big family of the Chinese nation]. Beijing: People's Press.

Editorial and Compilation Team for Ethnic Solidarity Education Textbooks. (2013). *Minzu changshi* [General knowledge about ethnic groups in China]. Beijing: People's Press.

Fei, X. (1999). *Zhonghua minzu duoyuan yiti geju* [The pattern of diversity in unity of the Chinese nation] (Revised ed.). Beijing: Minzu University of China Press.

Guan, K. (2015). Nei yu wai: Minzu quyu zizhi shijian de zhongguo yujing [Interior versus exterior: The practice of ethnic regional autonomy under Chinese context]. *Qinghua Daxue Xuebao (Zhexue Shehui Kexue Ban)* [Journal of Tsinghua University (Philosophy and Social Sciences)], *1*, 16–25.

Guo, X. (2011). Minzu jiaoyu lilun yu zhengce shulun [The theory and policy of ethnic minority education]. Changsha, China: Hunan Normal University Press.

Hu, A., & Hu, L. (2011). Dierdai minzu zhengce: Cujin minzu jiaorong yiti he fanrong yiti [The second-generation ethnic policy: Toward integrated ethnic fusion and prosperity]. *Xinjiang Shifan Daxue Xuebao (Zhexue Shehui Kexue Ban)* [Journal of Xinjiang Normal University (Edition of Philosophy and Social Sciences)], *5*, 1–12.

Hu, J. T. (2009, 30 September). Zai guowuyuan diwuci quanguo minzu tuanjie jinbu biaozhang dahuishang de jianghui [Speech at the State Council's fifth national ceremony to commend ethnic solidarity]. *Renmin Ribao* [People's Daily], p. 2.

Jiang, Z. M. (1992). Lun minzu gongzuo [Review on work for ethnic minorities]. In Communist Party of China Central Committee Literature Editorial Board (Ed.), *Jiang Zemin Wenxuan* [Selected works of Jiang Zemin] (Vol. 1, pp. 177–194). Beijing: People's Press.

Kennedy, R. (2013). *For discrimination: Race, affirmative action, and the law*. New York: Pantheon.

Kubow, P., Grossman, D., & Ninomiya, A. (2000). Multidimensional citizenship: Educational policy for the 21st century. In J. J. Cogan & R. Derricott (Eds.), *Citizenship for the 21st century: An international perspective on education* (pp. 115–134). London: Kogan-Page.

Law, W.-W. (2011). *Citizenship and citizenship education in a global age: Politics, policies, and practices in China*. New York: Peter Lang.

Law, W.-W. (2014). Social change, citizenship, and citizenship education in China since the late 1970s. In S. Guo & Y. Guo (Eds.), *Spotlight on China: Changes in education under China's market economy* (pp. 19–36). Rotterdam: Sense.

Leibold, J. (2014). Han Chinese reactions to preferential minority education in the PRC. In J. Leibold & Y. Chen (Eds.), *Minority education in China: Balancing unity and diversity in an era of critical pluralism* (pp. 299–319). Hong Kong: Hong Kong University Press.

Li, B. (2010). Zhashi tuijin zhongxiaoxue minzu tuanjie jiaoyu [To make solid progress in education for ethnic solidarity]. In China Education Yearbook Editorial Board (Ed.), *Zhongguo jiaoyu nianjian 2010* [China education yearbook, 2010] (pp. 402–403). Beijing: People's Education Press.

Ma, R. (2004). Lijie minzu guanxi de xinxilu: Shaoshu zuqun wenti de "qu zhengzhihu" [New perspective to understand ethnic relations: Depoliticalization of ethnicity]. *Peking University Xuebao (Zhexue shehui kexue ban)* [Journal of Peking University (Humanities and Social Sciences)], 6, 122–133.

Ma, R. (2008). *Ethnic relations in China*. Beijing: China Tibetology Publishing.

Ma, R. (2010). Guanyu zhongguo shaoshu minzu jiaoyu de jidian sikao [On the issues of ethnic minority education in China]. *Xinjiang Shifan Daxue Xuebao (Zhexue Shehui Kexue Ban)* [Journal of Xinjiang Normal University (Edition of Philosophy and Social Sciences)], 31(1), 6–18.

Ma, R. (2013). Ruhe jinyibu sikao woguo xianshizhong de minzu wenti: Guanyu "dierdai minzu zhengce" de taolun [Further thinking on ethnic issues in China: On "the second-generation ethnic policy"]. *Zhongyang Minzu Daxue Xuebao (Zhexue Shehui Kexue Ban)* [Journal of the Central University for Nationalities (Philosophy and Social Sciences Edition)], 4, 5–10.

Mackerras, C. (1995). *China's minority cultures: Identities and integration since 1912*. Melbourne: Longman.

Mackerras, C. (2003). *China's ethnic minorities and globalisation*. Melbourne: Longman.

Meng, L. (2010). *Xin zhongguo minzu jiaoyu zhengce yanjiu* [Policy research on education for ethnic minorities in new China]. Beijing: Science Press.

Ministry of Education. (2001). *Jiaoyubu jichu jiaoyu kecheng gaige gangyao (Shixing)* [Guidelines on the curriculum reform of basic education: Pilot]. Beijing: Ministry of Education.

Ministry of Education. (2002). *Pinde yu shehui kecheng biaozhun (Shiyan gao)* [Curriculum standard for moral character and society: Pilot version]. Beijing: Beijing Normal University Press.

Ministry of Education. (2005). *Putong gaodeng xuexiao shaoshu minzu yukeban, minzuban guanli banfa (Shixing)* [Instruction concerning the management of ethnic matriculation classes and ethnic-oriented classes in higher education institutes (Provisional)]. Beijing: Ministry of Education.

Ministry of Education. (2012a). *Yiwu jiaoyu pinde yu shenghuo kecheng biaozhun* [Curriculum standards for primary education and junior secondary education: Moral character and life]. Beijing: Beijing Normal University Press.

Ministry of Education. (2012b). *Yiwu jiaoyu pinde yu shehui kecheng biaozhun* [Curriculum standards for primary education and junior secondary education: Moral character and society]. Beijing: Beijing Normal University Press.

Ministry of Education. (2012c). *Yiwu jiaoyu sixiang pinde kecheng biaozhun* [Curriculum standards for primary education and junior secondary education: Ideological thoughts and moral character]. Beijing: Beijing Normal University Press.

Ministry of Education. (2012d). *Yiwu jiaoyu yuwen kecheng biaozhun* [Curriculum standards for primary education and junior secondary education: Chinese language]. Beijing: Beijing Normal University Press.

Ministry of Education. (2013a). *Zhongxiaoxue shufa jiaoyu zhidao gangyao* [Guidelines for calligraphy education in primary and secondary education]. Beijing: Ministry of Education.

Ministry of Education. (2013b). *Minzu zhongxiaoxue hanyu kecheng biaozhun (Yiwu jiaoyu)* [Curriculum standards for primary and junior secondary schools for ethnic minorities: Chinese language]. Beijing: Ministry of Education.

Ministry of Education. (2014a). 2013 nian quanguo jiaoyu shiye fazhan tongji gongbao [Statistical report on educational achievements and developments in China in 2013]. *Zhongguo Jiaoyu Bao* [China Education Daily], p. 2.

Ministry of Education. (2014b). *Quanguo minzu jiaoyu keyan guihua (2014–2020)* [National plan for research in education for ethnic minorities, 2014–2020]. Beijing: Ministry of Education.

Ministry of Education & State Ethnic Affairs Commission. (1999). *Guanyu zai quanguo zhongxiaoxue kaizhan minzu tuanjie jiaoyu huodong de tongzhi* [Circular concerning activities to promote education ethnic solidarity in primary and secondary schools]. Beijing: Ministry of Education.

Ministry of Education & State Ethnic Affairs Commission. (2008). *Xuexiao minzu tuanjie jiaoyu zhidao gangyao (Shixing)* [Guideline on education for ethnic solidarity (Pilot)]. Beijing: Ministry of Education.

Ministry of Education & State Ethnic Affairs Commission. (2009). *Quanguo zhongxiaoxue minzu tuanjie jiaoyu gongzuo bushu shipin huiyi jiyao* [Summary notes of the national video conference on the organization of work on ethnic solidarity education in primary and secondary schools in China]. Beijing: Ministry of Education.

National People's Congress. (1984). *Zhonghua renmin gongheguo minzu quyu zizhi fa* [Law of the People's Republic of China on regional national autonomy]. Beijing: National People's Congress.

National People's Congress. (2000). *Zhonghua renmin gongheguo guojia tongyong yuyan wenzi fa* [Law of the People's Republic of China on the standard spoken and written Chinese language]. Beijing: National People's Congress.

National People's Congress. (2001). *Zhonghua renmin gongheguo quyu zizhi fa (2001 nian xiuzhengban)* [Law of the People's Republic of China on regional national autonomy (Revised in 2001)]. Beijing: National People's Congress.

National People's Congress. (2004). *Zhonghua renmin gongheguo xianfa* [The Constitution of the People's Republic of China]. Beijing: China Law Publishing.

National People's Congress Standing Committee. (2015). *Zhonghua renmin gongheguo guojia anquan fa* [National security law of the People's Republic of China]. Beijing: National People's Congress.

Park, B.-K. (2013). China's ethnic minority policy: Between assimilation and accommodation. *Review of Global Politics, 41*, 25–44.

Population Census Office under the State Council & National Bureau of Statistics. (2011). *2010 nian liliuci quanguo renkou pucha zhuyao shuju* [Major figures on 2010 population census of China]. Beijing: China Statistics Press.

Postiglione, G. A. (2014). Education and cultural diversity in multiethnic China. In J. Leibold & Y. Chen (Eds.), *Minority education in China: Balancing unity and diversity in an era of critical pluralism* (pp. 27–43). Hong Kong: Hong Kong University Press.

Publicity Department of the Communist Party of China Central Committee, Ministry of Education, & State Ethnic Affairs Commission. (2009). *Guanyu zai xuexiao kaizhan minzu tuanjie jiaoyu huodong de tongzhi* [Circular concerning the promotion of ethnic solidarity education activities in schools]. Beijing: Ministry of Education.

Schuck, P. H. (2014). Assessing affirmative action. *National Affairs, 20*, 76–96.

State Council. (2009a). *Development and progress in Xinjiang* (White paper). Beijing: State Council.

State Council. (2009b). *Zhongguo de minzu zhengce yu geminzu gongtong fanrong fazhan (Baipishu)* [China's ethnic policy and common prosperity and development of all ethnic groups] (White paper). Beijing: State Council.

State Council. (2013). *Progress in China's human rights in 2012*. Beijing: State Council.

State Council. (2015a). *Guanyu jiakuai fazhan minzu jiaoyu de jueding* [Decision concerning speeding up the development of ethnic minority education]. Beijing: Ministry of Education.

State Council. (2015b). *Xizang fazhan daolu de lishi xuanze (Baipishu)* [The development path and historical choice of Tibet]. Beijing: State Council.

State Ethnic Affairs Commission & State Statistical Bureau. (2012). *Zhongguo minzu tongji nianjian 2012* [China's ethnic statistical yearbook 2012]. Beijing: China Statistics Press.

State Ethnic Affairs Commission & State Statistical Bureau. (2013). *Zhongguo minzu tongji nianjian 2013* [China's ethnic statistial yearbook 2013]. Beijing: China Statistics Press.

Teng, X., & Ma, X. (2009). Zhongguo gaodeng jiaoyu de shaoshu minzu youhui zhengce yu jiaoyu pingdeng [Preferential policies for ethnic minorities and equality in China's higher education]. *Taiwan yuanzhumin yanjiu luncong* [Taiwan Indigenous People Studies], *5*, 191–208.

Wan, M., & Bai, L. (2008). Xifang duoyuan wenhua jiaoyu yu woguo shaoshu minzu jiaoyu zhi bijiao [A comparison between western multicultural education and Chinese ethnic education]. *Minzu Yanjiu* [Ethno-National Studies], *6*, 32–41.

Wang, X. (2009). Yetan zai woguo minzu wenti shang de "fansi" he "shishiqiushi"—Yu Ma Rong jiaoshou de jidian shangque [Discussion with Professor Ma Rong about ethnic problems in China]. *Xinan Minzu Daxue Xuebao (Renwen Sheke Bank)* [Journal of Southwest University for Nationalities (Humanities and Social Science)], *1*, 1–17.

Wang, Y. (2007). Fazhan zhong de zhongguo shaoshu minzu jiaoyu [Ethnic minority education of China in development]. *Minzu Jiaoyu Yanjiu* [Journal of Research on Education for Ethnic Minorities], *2*, 5–10.

Wu, D. (2011). *Zhongguo jiaoyu gaige fazhan yanjiu [Educational reform and development in China].* Beijing: Educational Science Publishing.

Wu, S. (Ed.). (2007). *Minzu wenti gailun* [Introduction to ethnic problems] (3rd ed.). Sichuan: Sichuan People's Press.

Xia, S. (2007). *Zhongguo shaoshu minzu jiaoyu* [Education for ethnic minorities in China]. Beijing: Wuzhou Chuanbo Publishing.

Xinhua News Agency. (2014, 29 September). Zhongyang minzu gongzuo huiyi ji guowuyuan diliuci quanguo minzu tuanjie jinbu biaozhang dahui zaijing junxing Xi Jinping zuo zhongyao jianghua [Xi Jinping made an important speech at the national ethnic work conference and the sixth award ceremony for national ethnic solidarity and progress]. Retrieved from http://news.xinhuanet.com/politics/2014-09/29/c_1112683008.htm

Yi, L. (2006). Choosing between ethnic and Chinese citizenship: The educational trajectories of Tibetan minority children in northwestern China. In V. Fong & R. Murphy (Eds.), *Chinese citizenship: Views from the margins* (pp. 41–67). London: Routledge.

Zheng, F. (2014). Zuqun wenti "fei zhengzhihua"? [Depoliticizing ethnic problems?]. *Xianggang Shehui Kexue Xuebao* [Hong Kong Journal of Social Sciences], *46*, 135–166.

Zhou, M., & Hill, A. M. (2009). Introduction. In M. Zhou & A. M. Hill (Eds.), *Affirmative action in China and the U.S.: A dialogue on inequality and minority education* (pp. 1–24). New York: Palgrave Macmillan.

Zhu, Z. (2007). *State schooling and ethnic identity: The politics of a Tibetan neidi secondary school in China.* Lanham, MD: Lexington.

Chapter 11

Citizenship Education in Korea: Challenges and New Possibilities

YUN-KYUNG CHA, SEUNG-HWAN HAM, *and* MI-EUN LIM
Hanyang University

South Korea, having risen from the rubble of four decades of oppression under colonial rule and a devastating war, has now become a role model whose success is considered worthy of being emulated by many developing countries across the world. In less than half a century, Korea has built one of the world's largest economies and has become a leading country of technological innovation. Furthermore, it has also made a successful transition from a military dictatorship to a dynamic democracy. Korean people's pride in their country as a civilized, modern industrial society seemed unquestionable when it joined the Organisation for Economic Co-operation and Development as a member state in 1996 and successfully hosted the 1988 Olympic Games and the 2002 World Cup soccer games. In recent years, the so-called *hanryu* phenomenon or the "Korean wave" has become a noticeable pop culture trend in many countries, showing the competence of Korea as a member of the leading developed countries.

The unforgettably tragic sinking of the *Sewol* ferry on April 16, 2014, which resulted in the death of more than 300 passengers, however, shattered Korean people's confidence and pride into pieces. The sinking of the *Sewol* ferry triggered a series of critical questions and reflections not only about the effectiveness of the disaster management system but also on the overall self-portrait of South Korea as a whole. Shocked and deeply ashamed, the entire nation was in wrenching agony. Serious doubt was raised concerning Korean people's single-minded pursuit of wealth and prestige with no attention to its unintended effects. Epitomized by the scene of the captain and crew members hurriedly escaping from the sinking ferry, leaving behind hundreds of passengers locked in cabins, was also the painful truth that the Korean educational system has not been very successful in producing public-minded, responsible, and caring citizens.

In any modern "schooled" society in the world, one can hardly question the legitimacy of the argument that the utmost concern of the public education system is to educate youth to become competent and participatory citizens. The future of society is widely believed to be determined by the quality of education that youth receive in school. Thus, schools throughout the world are expected to effectively function as primary social institutions that cultivate in students not only the core knowledge of subject matter but also solid civic virtues and ethical standards.

However, the effectiveness of citizenship education in today's educational environment in Korea seems to be, at best, questionable. As academic performance in the so-called core subject areas has been strongly emphasized in the context of the high-stakes testing regime, schools tend to devote a minimal amount of curricular time and resources to civic and citizenship education. Teachers, under the strong pressure of "accountability," are rarely motivated to encourage students to engage with challenging and controversial issues in an increasingly diversifying society. To most students, civic education is nothing more than another set of factual knowledge to be memorized for higher scores on the standardized achievement tests.

Regarding the promotion of appropriate civic values and skills and other important dimensions of citizenship development, the current status of civic education as it is treated in school settings is far from satisfying. In the context of ever-expanding neoliberal politico-economic governance and the resulting spread of a materialistic worldview, increasingly fewer students are inspired by pro-social virtues such as open-mindedness, tolerance of different opinions, willingness to prioritize civic duties over self-interests, readiness to engage in a critical and reflective manner, and collaboration for the common good. Few students actively seek opportunities through authentic engagement with public life to learn the civic knowledge and attitudes that are necessary to become responsible citizens.

The implication of such a gloomy diagnosis of the ineffectiveness of current citizenship education in Korea is quite clear. In spite of the urgency and importance of promoting a well-informed, empowered, and participatory citizenship in an increasingly interconnected and diversifying world, the mission is destined to fail without a systematic and drastic reform of the present educational system. In this chapter, we first discuss the current social change under way in South Korea and its challenges for citizenship education. We then present an instructional profile of a foreign language teacher who implemented an exceptional module of global citizenship education despite the meager systemic support she received. Finally, we propose an alternative model of education whereby citizenship education can be reimagined in a new educational ecology.

Challenges in Citizenship Education in Diversifying Korea

South Korea might appear to be a country with excellent citizenship education, according to the International Civic and Citizenship Education Study (ICCS) conducted by the International Association for the Evaluation of Educational Achievement in 2009 that assessed eighth grade students (14-year-olds) in 38 educational systems (Schulz, Ainley, Fraillon, Kerr, & Losito, 2010). As expected, there was considerable variation across the participating educational systems in terms of students' civic knowledge. South Korea was one of the top-performing countries, along with Finland, Denmark, and Taipei in Taiwan. Students from South Korea had an average test score far more than half of one international standard deviation above the ICCS average.

However, the very high score of South Korean students in civic knowledge contrasted sharply with the very low level of their participation in civic activities both inside and outside school. South Korea was significantly below the ICCS average in all seven out-of-school activities surveyed—participation in "a youth organization affiliated with a political party or union," "an environmental organization," "a human rights organization," "a voluntary group doing something to help the community," "an organization collecting money for a social cause," "a cultural organization based on ethnicity," and "a group of young people campaigning for an issue" (Schulz et al., 2010, p. 131). Almost the same pattern was observed regarding civic activities in school as well. South Korea showed a significantly lower level than the ICCS average in five of the six activities surveyed—"voluntary participation in school-based music or drama activities outside of regular lessons," "active participation in a debate," "taking part in decision-making about how the school is run," "taking part in discussions about a school assembly," and "becoming a candidate for class representative or school parliament." The only activity for which South Korea was not significantly different from the ICCS average was "voting for class representative or school parliament" (p. 138).

Such a drastic contrast between the high level of civic knowledge and the low level of civic engagement observed in South Korea is not very surprising. South Korea has long been a top-performing country in international assessments such as the Program for International Student Assessment and the Trends in International Mathematics and Science Study. Although such impressive performance has attracted international attention from around the world, inside observers of public education in South Korea have long been well aware of the dark side of the high academic performance of its students. For most students in South Korea, it is quite common to suffer from extreme competition in schools, as education is seen as a tool for status competition—a competition not only between students themselves but also between their parents. Although the students' performance is remarkably higher than in most countries in the world, their academic confidence and enjoyment have been reported to be very low—students seem to have enough knowledge to do well on tests, but they do not seem to understand the true value and meaning of such knowledge (Cha, Ahn, Ju, & Ham, 2016; Song & Jung, 2011). While students possess knowledge about what is right and desirable to do in a democratic society, they do not seem to internalize it to a degree that they can translate it into action. Citizenship education, as a part of the larger educational system of South Korea, is liable to be distorted due to the status competition logic that underlies the system.

The situation appears more complicated regarding multicultural citizenship education. Squeezed between powerful neighbors such as Japan and China, Korea has historically experienced innumerable episodes of invasion and aggression from other countries. Given such a geopolitical context, the Korean people have developed a strong sense of ethnic identity and defensive nationalism. Even today, bloodline purity and cultural homogeneity are widely seen as the primary basis of national membership. Hybridity or difference from the mainstream culture is often associated with evil and being socially stigmatized. Until recent years, school textbooks emphasized national solidarity based on ethnic and cultural homogeneity. Loyalty to the nation and moral obligations, rather than civic agency and empowerment, were the primary concerns of civic education in Korea. While Korea's civics textbooks started to discuss the rights of diverse groups of people in society and the need to empower them toward democratic equality in the 1990s, traditional citizenship narratives based on the ideology of national homogeneity still remain in such texts (Moon, 2013).

The increasing diversification of the demographic configuration of Korean society during the last two decades, however, has posed a new challenge to civic education. The rapid industrialization of Korean society, coupled with the acceleration of economic and cultural globalization processes, has precipitated migration both within and from abroad. The influx of marriage immigrants, migrant workers, and North Korean defectors has been reshaping Korea into a diverse society. As of January 2015, there were approximately 1.74 million foreign residents, constituting approximately 3.4% of the Korean population (Ministry of Government Administration and Home Affairs, 2015). This includes approximately 208,000 children with immigrant backgrounds, who have become the Korean government's most important target group for multicultural education policies and programs over the last decade.

The increasingly diversified classrooms in Korea require a broader conception of citizenship education that empowers individual students to become active and responsible members of the globalized, multicultural society—regardless of their ethnic, socioeconomic, and cultural backgrounds. Nonetheless, a huge disparity between the espoused vision and the actual practice of citizenship education in Korea seems almost inevitable because formal education is widely regarded as merely a means of status competition. Competitive culture dominates school life. Teachers, rather than being respectful professionals who help each student become "capable of leading a moral and social life" (Durkheim, 1956, p. 72), have now been demoted to the role of salespersons of knowledge and skills. Classmates become potential enemies. Apathy and an egoistic way of life permeate classrooms. The situation becomes even worse when the student body is increasingly diversified while the basic grammar of the education system remains unchanged and not truly ready to address the challenges of intensifying globalization and human migration.

The current education system of Korea, which is geared toward "achievement contests," systematically and inevitably produces a large number of "losers" at the expense of a small portion of "winners" in the zero-sum game of competition in public education. With the exception of those students who are doing relatively well on tests, the majority of the students are wasting their time. The accumulation of their wasted time throughout their school lives consequently leads to failure in their career building. Many of them suffer from low self-esteem and resentment and lack of confidence (Choi et al., 2013; Song & Jung, 2011). Even the high achievers are not winners: instead of becoming empowered and responsible citizens of a global, multicultural society, many of them become egoistic, narrow-minded, intolerant, and disrespectful persons (Cha, 2008; Kim et al., 2010). Segregation and polarization along ethnolinguistic, religious, and socioeconomic borders create tensions and conflicts among students in school (Kim et al., 2009; Lee, 2012). It is thus not that surprising to see that students from low-income families, students with special needs, and students with immigrant backgrounds encounter various forms of social exclusion in school.

An Alternative Possibility: *Yungbokhap* Education in Korea

The dominant model of schooling in the world today, which has lasted over the past two centuries with few drastic modifications, is currently undergoing substantial reform in many parts of the world. Such reform initiatives are typically rooted in reasonable doubt concerning the model's adequacy for educating competent and responsible members of today's changing world—a world in which we witness new social changes that are inter-twined with increased human mobility and rapid technological innovation, all on a global scale as well as at a local level. Today, the global and the local frequently intersect in every corner of society, constructing what may be called "glocal" social realities in which we continuously face new hopes and challenges in multiple layers of societal context. Although the dominant model of schooling that has survived until today was once quite successful in terms of its instrumental efficiency in teaching massive groups of future citizens a standard-ized set of knowledge, skills, and attitudes, the utility and legitimacy of such a traditional model of schooling is increasingly subject to doubts and criticisms.

In an effort to develop a conceptual framework for redesigning the traditional model of schooling, an alternative approach to schooling called the *yungbokhap* model of education is currently being envisioned in scholarly and policy circles in South Korea. The Korean term *yungbokhap*, roughly translated, means "holistic integration." This *yungbokhap* model has been conceptualized as an integrative and holistic approach to teaching and learning not only in terms of classroom practices but also in terms of administrative and policy arrange-ments at multiple layers of the education system (Cha et al., 2016). This alternative model of education emphasizes the centrality of the role of education in promoting all students' authentic and meaningful learning experiences. The central point where this alternative model drastically departs from the traditional model is that the alternative model prob-lematizes the practice of empowering some students at the expense of all others who are alienated from deep engagement in meaningful learning under the traditional model of schooling, which produces visible success stories at the cost of unheard stories of failure. If we understand education in a democracy as a futuristic public project, then education should be built and designed to contribute to the welfare of all students as future citizens.

This alternative model of education is based on a socioecological perspective that sheds light on the importance of nurturing a larger educational ecology in which sustainable school improvement is constantly fostered from inside schools rather than being imposed externally in a top-down manner. One of the possible directions in which the *yungbokhap* model can be developed is the ABCD criteria, where ABCD denotes *autonomy*, *bridgeability*, *contextuality*, and *diversity*. This framework has recently been under development in South Korea in an effort to provide a large yet realistic picture of how educational reform initia-tives may develop (Cha et al., 2015; Ham et al., 2015; Lee et al., 2013). Below, we briefly discuss citizenship education with reference to the *yungbokhap* model.

Autonomy

Citizenship education should support learner autonomy. In recent decades, educational discourse around the world has been problematizing the phenomenon that students are viewed as passive recipients of a standardized package of information and knowledge. Education policy priorities have shifted the focus from authoritative structures of knowledge ready for consumption to increased student empowerment and learner-centrism. Student learning is now understood as being facilitated and enriched through promoting inquiry-based and discovery-oriented approaches to curriculum and instruction. In light of the importance of individual students' active and self-directed engagement in learning, students are increasingly portrayed as capable individuals whose learning processes evolve toward greater autonomy and self-reflection in their growth. In accordance with such a discursive shift, the profession of teaching is understood as a highly difficult and complex job that involves numerous instances of classroom teaching where immediate professional decision making is required to foster student engagement in autonomous learning. As autonomous professionals, teachers are not only curriculum implementers but also curriculum theorists and designers. A high level of school autonomy is also needed so that teachers may be given wide latitude and professional discretion to make important decisions in curriculum development and implementation. School administrators and leaders should pay sustained attention to how to provide teachers the necessary administrative and professional support so that teachers can become professionally creative and autonomous in order to constantly improve their teaching.

Bridgeablility

Citizenship education should stretch over various subject areas. The changing model of schooling around the world sheds light on the importance of creating an educational environment where students are encouraged to become active and entrepreneurial learners who experience authentic intellectual achievement through interdisciplinary approaches of thinking and learning. In contrast to the traditional view of the school curriculum as a collection of segmented sets of knowledge to be consumed by students, today's students are expected to become active agents of learning and creative producers of knowledge. Most educational scholars and policy makers today would consider it problematic if students remain passive recipients of a standardized package of knowledge, even if they demonstrate high performance on tests. In line with this transition, the image of the learner is shifting toward an integrative knowledge designer who can contribute to knowledge building through creative methods of deconstructing and reassembling different bodies of knowledge. Student learning that involves such an interdisciplinary and inquiry-oriented model of education also requires a new image of teachers because such a model inevitably requires a high level of intraschool collaboration whereby teachers can learn from diverse experiences and perspectives and enrich their instructional practice. This accounts for why a range of educational reform ideas and policies in many countries commonly highlight the image of teachers as professionals who are empowered to actively develop curriculum models and instructional strategies both by themselves and in collaboration with colleagues. Schools are increasingly conceptualized as collaborative and dialogic communities of inquiry in which differences in knowledge, experiences, and perspectives may be creatively bridged using a variety of methods of interdisciplinary thinking and problem-solving skills.

Contextuality

Citizenship education should be contextualized. Educational reform movements around the world stress the importance of nurturing individual students' authentic and meaningful learning experiences (Newman, 1996; Robinson, 2015). Students are expected to grow as lifelong learners and creative problem solvers so that they can gain and produce the kinds of knowledge and skills they need as they move forward in their lives. Thus, learning is seen as more than a simple process of mastering a predetermined set of knowledge that is alien to individual students. Rather, learning is conceptualized as a process of students' active interaction with their social context. Such a conceptualization of learning recognizes students' own contextual positioning as an anchoring point from which learning can unfold in a variety of ways. What this kind of learning entails is students' active interpretation of and participation in multiple layers of social context of which they themselves are part, either physically or genealogically. Teaching strategies that are consistent with such authentic and meaningful learning are understood as processes of fostering individual learners' ability to creatively recontextualize knowledge so that it may be actively reinterpreted and given meaning from the learners' perspectives. In this respect, the importance of the curriculum is not restricted to the rich "text" of curricular content but also stems from the "context" the curriculum can evoke for students.

Diversity

Citizenship education should empower all learners. Students are diverse, and individual students' distinctiveness and uniqueness must be given special attention so that they can experience greater engagement with meaningful learning. Contemporary democratic values that valorize individual personhood as the fundamental basis of one's distinctive and special roles in society undergird various education policies for empowering all learners regardless of their sociocultural group memberships. The educational literature has persistently highlighted the importance of educators' keen awareness of student diversity and the effective use of such diversity as a valuable asset for teaching and learning (Banks & Banks, 2012; Gardner, 1983; Paris, 2012). Curricula around the world have been constantly, although slowly, revised to represent more diverse epistemic models (Ramirez, Bromley, & Russell, 2009). Furthermore, the entire educational system should be redesigned to cultivate and nurture the diversity of human talents rather than forcing all students to uniformly conform to a narrowly defined set of standards. Cultivating the diversity of human talents is very important in today's globalized world. Our future citizens will no longer live in isolated societies. In the globally interconnected world, human activities inevitably involve a greater degree of exchange of ideas and other human products (Castles & Miller, 2009; Lechner & Boli, 2008). Competent individuals are no longer those who understand how to conform but, rather, those who can challenge and innovate from different perspectives. The rise of such a new social reality makes it an important social priority to ensure that all students are given enough and equitable opportunities to grow as competent lifelong learners who can develop their own talents in unique ways. Such a diversity of talents is an essential condition for individual citizens to initiate collaborative and transformative engagement with their local, national, and transnational communities.

An Instructional Profile: Global Citizenship Education

In this next section, an instructional module is presented by Ms. Lim—a passionate teacher who developed and implemented the module for her own classroom teaching. Her instructional module gives us a sense of how the *yungbokhap* model of education described above may be effectively integrated into the practice of classroom teaching in the context of citizenship education.

A Foreign Language Teacher Thinks About Global Citizenship

I have been a Russian language teacher for the past 19 years. Ever since I was young, I was such an active girl when learning English, Japanese, and French. I also had overseas pen pals as a result of my interest in foreign countries and languages. In 1991, while I was a college student, I saw the Soviet Iron Curtain breaking down along with perestroika, and out of my curiosity about the unknown world, I decided to major in Russian. During my study in Moscow for three years, beginning in 1994, I was able to meet students and migrants of diverse races that I had not seen in Seoul. I suppose that my sensitivity to globalization and multiculturalism at that time, in the mid- to late 1990s, must have been above the average of that of Koreans in general. My interest in other countries continued to increase through my hobby of traveling overseas. I have gone backpacking in many countries of the world during my summer and winter vacations, making friends from diverse countries and experiencing local cultures.

Then, one day in 2009, I happened to encounter a book about "fair travel," which reinterpreted travel in relation to international issues of human rights, economy, politics, culture, environment, and education. Reading some concrete examples of "unfair travel" in the book made me critically ruminate on my past 10 years of travel experience. My interest in the "unfair world" that began with fair travel extended to an everyday life of fair trade and ethical consumerism. After I became aware of issues such as international poverty, human rights, and environment degradation, the stories of travel that I told to my students changed. Previously, I had told them my travel stories as a way of introducing them to cultural diversity with the hope of helping them acquire openness to multiculturalism and a receptive attitude toward diversity by getting rid of their prejudice against different countries in the world. However, after my perception changed, I began to place the emphasis of my travel stories on social responsibility as a global citizen open to multiculturalism. I can say that my changed view of travel has also changed my view of life and education. Since then, I have tried to provide my students with many opportunities to talk and think about various social issues. In my Russian classes, I have tried to create a culture where diverse values can coexist in the classroom and students can discuss social issues.

Five years after my first encounter with the notion of fair travel, a major disaster occurred in Korea. On April 16, 2014, a huge ferry sank in the sea, and it was regrettable and poignant that hundreds of 11th grade students and other passengers were onboard and not rescued. At that time, I was a homeroom teacher of 12th grade students. Regretfully, one of my students lost his younger brother in the accident. In Korea, 12th grade is considered a wearisome and vicious period during which students are required to focus solely on their studies for college admission by putting aside their personal ambitions. All 26 students in my 12th grade class were immersed in shock and deep sorrow after watching what happened to their classmate.

During the early days after the accident, when all the accusations were directed at the captain and the crew who deserted the passengers inside the sinking ship, professional ethics awareness was one of the main issues brought into the social spotlight. My students were agonizing over the situation with a feeling of helplessness and sharing in social indignation mixed with anger toward the ferry crew, distrust in elders, and disappointment in the government and the nation as a whole. The students, who had previously only cared about achievements in their studies and had no interest in social issues, now shared the grief of their classmates and began to critically consider social issues. A humane and natural exchange of feelings and a joint concern for social issues was something that I thought I needed to help the students to internalize. It was deeply painful for me as a teacher to see my students brokenhearted.

In April 2014, I could not tell my students to simply focus on their preparations for college admission. I thought that what I *could* do for them was to get them out of their absorption with the disaster and teach them to think widely and look objectively at reality in order to make good decisions. I wanted to help my students, who felt that their society was unjust, to widen their view of the problems of the world. I thought that this was a very teachable moment for global education.

Instruction Implemented: Cultivating Global Citizenship Through Reflective Thinking

The participants of the class were 44 senior high school students, aged 17 to 19, who attended the foreign language high school where I work. These students performed relatively well in their basic foreign language skills and tended to have more international exchange experiences than many other students attending ordinary public schools. I used "fair travel" as a concrete teaching-learning activity to conduct a model global citizenship education class. Fair travel is an extension of "fair trade" from the tourism industry, where producers and consumers ideally have an equal relationship (Tepelus, 2006). The main idea of fair travel or sustainable developmental travel is that economic and developmental benefits should be given back to the local community. Further, it is a form of travel that involves a deep meaning of the pursuit of fairness to make it possible to discuss and adjust the developmental process in the context of an equal relationship between travelers and local people.

The main purpose of the "fair travel" class activities I developed was to help students become acquainted with various problems of global society related to travel (the knowledge domain), experience attitudinal changes through reflective thinking (the value domain), and cultivate global citizenship through applying their changed attitudes in social participation (the function domain; Kim & Lim, 2014). The objective of the class was to cultivate global citizenship in my students through reflective thinking for 12 weeks. The class was based on the notion of the "scaffolded reading experience—a set of activities specifically designed to assist a particular group of students to successfully read, understand, learn from, and enjoy a particular selection" of text (Graves & Graves, 1995, p. 29). Students were not assumed to be passive but, rather, as having the potential to become creators of their own meaningful learning through active reading and reflective thinking processes.

My program in the class proceeded from April to July 2014. The first phase was the "before reading" phase, which was allotted five hours. It was an activity designed to increase the interest of the students through a discussion on the issues of global citizenship that were learned through various types of media, such as newspapers, films, and documentaries. Through this activity, learners could understand that many global issues are closely related to their own daily lives. In the second, "on reading" phase, each student was to spend his or her leisure time voluntarily reading for six weeks. Through these readings, the students could come to know and understand some unfair and irrational cases of world travel. Moreover, the necessity of being a responsibly behaved traveler who possesses global citizenship awareness was emphasized. The third phase was the "after reading" activity phase, which covered 10 hours. This phase was given much weight in the overall 12 weeks of the class design, and it took a lot of time and effort to plan and implement. The activities included self-reflective narrative sharing, self-reflective writing, meeting with the author of the "fair travel" book, and overall review. These four activities were not independent but, rather, were recursive and focused on reflective thinking.

At the end of the 12-week class, many students indicated that the self-reflective narrative sharing time was the most meaningful and memorable portion of the class. After sharing, many students opened the book again to actively revisit the shared narratives and relate them to what they read in the book:

> The time for sharing stories with friends was very meaningful, more than words can express. For those of us who had been locked inside the senior high school box and been insensitive to each other, focusing only on college admission, it became possible to share our perceptions and beliefs in detail more than ever before by listening to one another's own stories. I was very fortunate to have gained such precious memories, which were like an unforgettable oasis during my frustrating school days. (C. L., reflective writing assignment, June 13, 2014)[1]

Global citizenship education is not the same as education that produces global leaders who speak foreign languages fluently or who have a sense of etiquette. It involves transformative learning for critical and reflective thinking about the world and developing the ability to think about the intersection of the global and the local in the daily lives of students. Global citizenship, as an alternative to overcome country-centric exclusivism, is an integral part of civic and citizenship education that promotes respect for all human beings. Global citizenship education pursues and implements a new paradigm for human coexistence in a global multicultural society as it emphasizes learners' participation and practice beyond abstract knowledge.

After the end of my 12-week class, I analyzed the reflective narrative sharing activity and the students' reflective writings. I concluded that the students had experienced the following changes. First, I noticed *an increased awareness of global social problems*, which was a change in the *knowledge* domain. Until the students read the "fair travel" book, based on their previous knowledge, they did not doubt the fact that the development of a tourism industry results in job creation and economic benefits for the local tourist site areas. However, after completing the book, they could understand the real causes and structures of the problems that exist in the relationship between the strong and the weak within the political economy of an international society. They were able to understand the structural wealth disparity between the northern and southern hemispheres, as well as the victims (including the environment) of giant, profit-seeking capital enterprises in developing countries. They also became aware that socioeconomic disparities are often global issues:

> I had never thought of the fact that there were many people suffering in the places I passed by in my travels. There was no way for me to know about it. (J. K., reflective writing assignment, June 13, 2014)

> I have been naively thinking that the tourism industry is an activity that helps the local community. Why couldn't I realize the fact that throughout my travels I have been paying my money to big multinational companies? (H. L., reflective writing assignment, June 13, 2014)

Another important change, which was observed in the *value* domain, was the students' *understanding of "me" and "the world" reflectively*. Global citizenship education is an extension of a world perspective. In this respect, there were perception and value changes in the learners. The students explained that they had an unusual experience that made them feel embarrassed: they were stunned by the issues they read about fair travel, which they had never previously considered. Through the reading activities, the students came to realize the unfair realities of international society, which they had not previously recognized. They critically reflected on their own mind-set and attitudes toward life:

> Before reading the book, for me, money and status was all. However, now I have decided to become a person who works for a just world. I would like to express my gratitude to the author of this book and to other social activists. (J. H., reflective writing assignment, June 15, 2014)

> I now realize that I never questioned the expensive entrance fees of museums in Europe with stolen heritages of other nations. Perhaps, a sense of national and cultural

superiority has been inherent in our minds. (Y. L., reflective writing assignment, June 14, 2014)

Finally, the students' global citizenship was demonstrated through their *action and engagement*, which I recognized as a noticeable change in the *function* domain. Global citizenship education should not be just about knowledge acquisition but be designed organically to enhance the critical and reflective thinking of learners in practice. Through the reading activity, the students in my class learned that they all, as citizens of the world, should become responsible members of global society. Moreover, they realized that transforming their sense of global citizenship into responsible action is important for the development and sustainability of local communities. Most students emphasized the necessity of the social practice of fair travel beyond mere personal practice. Further, they understood that practicing responsibility as a global citizen is not difficult to accomplish. They stated that it is important to cooperate with a group of like-minded people:

> I can be considerate not only during my travel but also while I am at school. While using the restroom, though it's wastepaper for us, it is a huge burden for the janitors. I think that I need to practice considering others through small actions in my daily life. (H. K., reflective writing assignment, June 13, 2014)

I chose global citizenship education to console my students who were still struggling with social rage as a result of the great tragedy of the ferry accident. I wanted to broaden their view to objectively look at the community to which they belong within the greater realm of the global world. After the reflective reading activities and the process of sharing their views and reflections, they became more interested in social problems than before. I believe that the "fair travel" activity I developed may be applied in other classrooms as a useful teaching-learning activity for global citizenship education. Through the experience of this class, I was led to believe that global citizenship education may be integrated into classroom teaching, regardless of subject of study, if the teacher has the courage to provide students with the opportunity for critical and reflective thinking.

Making the Exception the Norm

Ms. Lim's global citizenship education module illustrated above is a nice example of the ways in which the ABCDs of the *yungbokhap* model of education were effectively integrated into classroom teaching. In terms of "A," autonomy, Ms. Lim successfully positioned herself as a curriculum designer with a fairly high degree of professional autonomy. Her motivation for the development and implementation of a global citizenship education module stemmed not from bureaucratic control or external pressures but from her own professional conviction and personal hope that she had as an educator. Effectively fostering students' active engagement in learning through "fair travel" activities, she found that their learning process evolved toward critical and self-reflective thinking, a form of learning outcome qualitatively different from the passive storage of knowledge. With respect to "B," bridgeability, Ms. Lim's instructional module was quite flexible in order to incorporate various social issues into the class in connection with the notion of global citizenship. Students in the class were both encouraged and empowered to bridge different bodies of knowledge and varying perspectives through interdisciplinary ways of thinking and learning. The "self-reflective narrative sharing" time provided students valuable opportunities to develop skills to share ideas and revisit their own thinking. Viewed from the "C," contextuality, of the class, Ms. Lim designed her module as a process of students' active interpretation of and participation in multiple layers of social context. The fair travel book not only served as a fixed "text" for curricular content but also set out a rich "context" in which all students could delve into various social issues at both global and local levels in relation to their daily lives. Assessed on the basis of the criterion of "D," diversity, Ms. Lim's class effectively took advantage of student diversity in terms of their varying perspectives on fair travel and related social issues by creatively converting such diversity into a valuable asset for teaching and learning.

However, Ms. Lim's excellent implementation of global citizenship education is, unfortunately, a rare exception rather than the norm in Korea. As a foreign language teacher, she implemented a global citizenship education module out of her personal conviction that she had to do something for her students after the great tragedy of the *Sewol* ferry disaster. Citizenship education in Korea in most cases, however, means little more than a fixed set of factual knowledge to be consumed and memorized to achieve a high score on standardized tests. The question then becomes: What should the new model of education entail to continuously foster constructive educational experiments as in Ms. Lim's case? How can we make the exceptional no longer exceptional but the standard?

We believe that the quality of citizenship education cannot be independent of the larger educational ecology within which citizenship education is implemented. An alternative model of schooling based on the ABCD criteria will be feasible only to the degree to which such a model can be supported and sustained within the larger socioecological environment. Although education changes society, education is also a product of society. In this dialectic relationship between education and society, any attempt to reform education would be only partially successful unless it is accompanied by sufficient effort to change the socioecological environment within which education is deeply embedded. The socioecological environment is a "social" environment in the sense that multiple actors and institutions play roles together to constitute the entire environment: No single group of actors can change the whole; only systemic effort works. It is also an "ecological" environment because it sustains itself and evolves like an ecosystem—creating and establishing a new environment is a challenging task, but once it is established, it becomes fairly sustainable. The success of a new model of education oriented toward the ABCDs will depend on how systemically and persistently a healthy socioecological environment, whose governing rules and values accord with what the ABCD model envisions, is nurtured, as illustrated in Figure 1. This is the responsibility not solely of teachers or schools but of all of us, as we are all part of the larger socioecological environment, whose norms, values, and visions are collectively embodied in important social institutions, including public education.

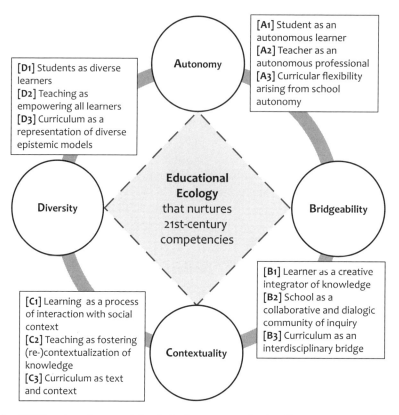

Figure 1. The ABCD-ecology framework for designing tomorrow's schooling.

Conclusion

To many outside observers, Korean education is a dazzling example of a success story. Political leaders, such as former U.S. President Barack Obama, have lauded South Korea for its rigorous education system, in which more than 85% of South Korean high school graduates go on to college. In addition to the close-to-universal enrollment rates for both elementary and secondary education, the quality of education, as measured by students' academic achievement, is also very impressive. Korean students consistently come out on top in cross-national comparisons, such as the Program for International Student Assessment and the Trends in International Mathematics and Science Study, that assess students' performance in core subject areas. Even in civic knowledge, South Korea ranked third in the world and first in Asia in a recent International Civic and Citizenship Education Study across 38 countries (Schulz et al., 2010). Coupled with rapid industrialization and modernization over the past half century, Korean education has been understood as the key agent of national development and social progress.

However, from an insider's perspective, Korean education is utterly failing to produce empowered and competent citizens for the 21st century. In school climates permeated by grueling competition, authentic and meaningful learning experiences fostered by caring and collaborative interaction among students are beyond imagination. Students often become ruthless adversaries, and the primary concern they have is how to defeat or dominate their competition by all means available. Rather than being a "great equalizer," education in Korea is currently being blamed for becoming a major mechanism of social inequality and class reproduction. The achievement gap between the haves and the have-nots has increased over time. The meritocratic belief that "a dragon may arise from a creek"—a Korean adage meaning that one may succeed out of a disadvantaged background—seems no longer quite valid in today's Korean society. Students from "marginalized families," who are more vulnerable to alienation and discrimination in schools, suffer the most in this educational "jungle." Even the "winners" of the competition do not seem to be that happy—while Korea has the largest proportion of top academic performers among Organisation for Economic Co-operation and Development member states, it has the least proportion of students who feel happy in school (Nyamkhuu, 2014).

Under these circumstances, citizenship education in Korea is facing tremendous challenges as the Korean social order rapidly transforms into a diverse society. The sudden influx of marriage migrants, guest workers, and North Korean defectors has raised serious questions about the taken-for-granted notion of Koreanness. Nationalist solidarity based on ethnic, linguistic, and cultural homogeneity is no longer possible or desirable. A more holistic and systemic approach to citizenship education, rather than a technical and limited reform effort, is called for to effectively address diversity issues in Korea. We believe that *yungbokhap* education, the alternative model of schooling that we have proposed, represents a new possibility for an effective and authentic form of citizenship education to overcome discrepancies between civic knowledge and civic engagement in our increasingly interconnected multicultural world.

Acknowledgment

This work was supported by a National Research Foundation of Korea grant funded by the Korean government (NRF-2014S1A3A2044609).

Note

1. All block quotations in this chapter are from students' own written reflections, translated by the chapter authors.

References

Banks, J. A., & Banks, C. A. M. (Eds.). (2012). *Multicultural education: Issues and perspectives* (8th ed.). Hoboken, NJ: Wiley.

Castles, S., & Miller, M. J. (2009). *The age of migration: International population movements in the modern world* (4th ed.). New York: Guilford Press.

Cha, Y.-K. (2008). Segyehwa sidaeui daeanjeog gyoyugmodelloseoui damunhwa gyoyug [Multicultural education as an alternative educational model in the era of globalization]. *Multicultural Education Studies, 1*(1), 1–23.

Cha, Y.-K., Ahn, S.-H. G., Ju, M.-K., & Ham, S.-H. (2016). Yungboghabgyoyugui hwagjangjeog jaegaenyeomhwa ganeungseong tamsaeg [*Yungbokhap* education: Toward an expansive (re) conceptualization]. *Multicultural Education Studies, 9*(1), 153–183.

Cha, Y.-K., Ju, M.-K., Ahn, S.-H. G., Ham, S.-H., Jung, J., Park, J.-H., . . . Lee, H.-J. (2015). *ABCD-based pre-service teacher education for creativity and character education.* Paper presented at the Ewha Womans University Teacher Education 100th Anniversary International Conference, Seoul, South Korea.

Choi, S. H., Ku, J., Kim, J., Park, S., Oh, E., Kim, J., & Baek, H. (2013). *PISAwa TIMSS gyeolgwae gibanhan ulinala hagsaengui jeonguijeog teugseong hamyang bangan* [Affective characteristics of Korean students and ways for fostering their affective development based on PISA and TIMSS results]. Seoul, South Korea: KICE.

Durkheim, E. (1956). *Education and sociology.* (S. D. Fox, Trans.). Glencoe, IL: Free Press.

Gardner, H. (1983). *Frames of mind: The theory of multiple intelligences.* New York: Basic Books.

Graves, M. F., & Graves, B. B. (1995). The scaffolded reading experience: A flexible framework for helping students get the most out of text. *Reading, 29*(1), 29–34.

Ham, S.-H., Choi, D.-S., Choi, S. B., Choi, Y. C., Jo, H. S., Kim, B., . . . Soh, R. N. (2015). *The ABCD's of the changing model of schooling: Toward nurturing integrative creativity.* Paper presented at the 2015 International Conference of the Korean Association for Multicultural Education, Seoul, South Korea.

Kim, J. H., & Lim, M. E. (2014). Gongjeongyeohaeng sueobhwaldonge natanan segyesimingyoyugui uimi tamsaeg [A study on global citizenship education based on scaffolded reading activities utilizing a "fair travel" book in a high school]. *Journal of Korean Education, 41*(3), 213–239.

Kim, T.-J., Jeon, I., Byon, J., Jang, H., Bahn, J., Jo, Y., . . . Han, M. (2010). *Hangug cheongsonyeonui siminyeoglyang gugjebigyo yeongu: Gugjesimingyoyugyeongu (ICCS) chamyeo* [International comparative study of Korean adolescents' civic competencies: Based on the International Civic and Citizenship Education Study (ICCS)]. Seoul, South Korea: KEDI.

Kim, Y. B., Kim, S. S., Park, H. J., Shin, H. S., Park, J. H., Kim, K. S., & Lee, K. J. (2009). *Hangug gyoyug hyeonhwang bunseog: Jiyeog gan haggyo gan gyoyug gyeogchaleul jungsimeulo* [An analysis of the status of school education: Focusing on differences across schools and locations]. Seoul, South Korea: KEDI.

Lechner, F. J., & Boli, J. (2008). *World culture: Origins and consequences.* Malden, MA: Blackwell.

Lee, J. (2012). Hangugui minjogjuuiwa damunhwajuui [Ethnic nationalism and multiculturalism in Korea]. *Multicultural Education Studies, 5*(1), 199–215.

Lee, S.-K., Ku, H., Kim, S., Kim, S.-J., Moon, J.-E., Ahn, S.-H. G., . . . Hwang, S. (2013). Yungboghabgyoyug peulogeulaem guseongeul wihan gicho yeongu: Hyeonjang salye bunseogeul tonghan guseongteul jeogyong ganeungseong tamsaeg [Developing *yungbokhap* education programs: A development framework and its applications]. *Journal of Learner-Centered Curriculum and Instruction, 13*(3), 483–513.

Ministry of Government Administration and Home Affairs. (2015). *2015 jibangjachidanche oegugin-juminhyeonhwang tonggye* [Statistics on foreign residents by local government in 2015]. Seoul, South Korea: Author.

Moon, R. (2013). Globalization and citizenship education: Diversity in South Korean civics textbooks. *Comparative Education, 49*(4), 424–439.

Newman, F. M. (1996). *Authentic achievement: Restructuring schools for intellectual quality.* San Francisco: Jossey-Bass.

Nyamkhuu, T. (2014). *PISA 2012: Happiness or performance?* Retrieved from http://www.unescobkk.org/education/news/article/pisa2012-happiness-or-performance/

Paris, D. (2012). Culturally sustaining pedagogy: A needed change in stance, terminology, and practice. *Educational Researcher, 41*(3), 93–97.

Ramirez, F. O., Bromley, P., & Russell, S. G. (2009). The valorization of humanity and diversity. *Multicultural Education Review, 1*(1), 29–54.

Robinson, K. (2015). *Creative schools: The grassroots revolution that's transforming education.* New York: Viking.

Schulz, W., Ainley, J., Fraillon, J., Kerr, D., & Losito, B. (2010). *ICCS 2009 international report: Civic knowledge, attitudes, and engagement among lower secondary school students in 38 countries.* Amsterdam, the Netherlands: International Association for the Evaluation of Educational Achievement.

Song, K.-O., & Jung, J. (2011). Gonggyoyug gaehyeogbanghyangui gugjebigyobunseog [International comparative analysis of directions for educational reform]. *Korean Journal of Educational Administration, 29*(4), 513–537.

Tepelus, C. (Ed.). (2006). *For a socially responsible tourism: Code of conduct for the protection of children from sexual exploitation in travel and tourism* (2nd ed.). New York: Steering Committee.

Chapter 12

Citizenship Education and Diversity in Singapore: Navigating Identity in This "Brave New World"

RAHIL ISMAIL

National Institute of Education, Nanyang Technological University

Singapore's geopolitical context is the legacy of British colonialism in a Malay-dominated region and subsequent migration, notably from China and the South Asian subcontinent. The widespread post–World War II independence movement brought Singapore first to a federation with Malaysia in 1963 and then to independence on August 9, 1965. Throughout Singapore's history, nation building has been framed by colonial influences and postcolonial nationalistic narratives of struggles and successes (Lee, 2000; Ooi & Shaw, 2004).

Singapore today encompasses a predominantly Chinese population with sizable minority communities of Malays (approximately 15%), Indians (7.4%), and "others" (1.4%; National Population and Talent Division, 2015). Singaporeans are administratively categorized into "neat quadrants" (Bokhorst-Heng, 2007, p. 637) of Chinese, Malays, Indians, and others (CMIO). The underlying principle of this categorization is "unity within diversity," but racial differences need "disciplining" (PuruShotam, 1998) toward nation building. The principle of "unity within diversity" is buttressed by an official commitment to meritocracy, bilingualism, incorruptibility, and a formal and informal recognition of out-of-bounds (OB) markers that signify offending behavior or language or views on race, language, and religion and are considered impermissible breaches of multiracial harmony and tolerance.

The People's Action Party has sustained political control over the last 50-plus years through a "prosperity consensus pact" (Ooi & Shaw, 2004) between the government and the governed, wherein strict government controls are tolerated as a means toward social and economic stability and prosperity. Prosperity consensus was a compelling incentive for citizens of the struggling nation to engage in a spectrum of economic, social, political, and moral nation-building programs.

The national "Singapore story" is one of a highly successful small nation-state that came to being unexpectedly, confounding ominous predictions (Hill & Lian, 1995). Michael Liefer describes Singapore's birth as one in which "statehood [was] rudely thrust upon it" (Hill & Lian, 1995, p. vii). This "accidental nation" was forged by the cultivation of the 4Ms: the multicultural, multiracial, multireligious, and multilingual components that ensure "equal representation and equal allocation of resources" (Ooi & Shaw, 2004, p. 54) without direct hegemonic, assimilative pressure on minority groups. The strategy has largely been successful: by 2015, U.S. President Barack Obama described Singapore as being able to "bring together people who may look different, but they all think of themselves as part of Singapore. And that has to be a strength, not a weakness, but that requires leadership and government being true to those principles" (NewsAsia, 2015).

Singapore is the little engine that could. It is a small island state with no natural resources, which became a first-world nation in one generation (Lee, 2000). Fiftieth-anniversary celebrations were underlined by impressive statistics measuring economic growth, material wealth, social governance, and education standards (Paleit & Hughes, 2015). The Organisation for Economic Co-operation and Development placed Singapore first in mathematics and science scores among 76 countries, concluding that this standard of education was "a powerful predictor of the wealth that countries will produce in the long run" (Goy, 2015). Singapore today is a proud "little red dot" with a mission to sustain its success well into the 21st century.[1]

Nation-building in Singapore was impelled by economic imperatives, and socialization policies were used as stabilizing measures to manage the fault lines of diversity, especially racial differences. A type of citizenship socialization evolved "in which the individual becomes a citizen through performing the duties of the practice of citizenship" (Hill & Lian, 1995, p. 32; see also Spring, 2004), coalescing into a unique Singapore identity of hard-fought multiracial co-existence. This identity was not forged just by the promise of prosperity but by the concept of a positive future achieved by a meritocratic education system as measured by national standardized examinations. As an education and, accordingly, as a citizenship approach, the basic framework was adaptable and sensitive to internal and external challenges. It has contributed to the overall national social and economic goals for more than 50 years (Gopinathan, 2007; Spring, 2004). Indubitably, recognizing this contribution of education raises the issue of the role, purpose, and ends of education as a socialization process toward an imagined community (Anderson, 1983; Sim & Print, 2005; Wang, 1968) or as a transformative conscience-raising process toward, for example, social justice (Banks, 2004; Banks 2007).

As a socialization process, citizenship education encompasses embedded socio-political power structures with their own (un)conscious biases and ideological neuroses (Allport, 1979; Goffman, 1986; Street, 2003) that seek to replicate rather than question the status quo. Singapore is no different from any sovereign entity upon achieving self-determination. In fact, the post-1965 journey has been a continual renegotiation, recrafting, and remaking of identity. Singapore, according to is harsher critics, is not just an "accidental nation" but also an efficient economic unit. The purpose of education there is to foster an "obedient citizenry who will provide a safe haven for multinational corporations" (Spring, 2004, p. 21).

In the pursuit of economic prosperity, complexities of multicultural principles of respecting and valuing diversity have been cloaked under the guise of the uneasy term "tolerance." The national policy of meritocracy has become an "aggressive" (Trocki, 2006, p. 158) pursuit of material wealth. Education based on assessing test-based knowledge has led to a range of indictments: the inflexibility of groupthink, a lack of creativity (Low, 2014), the misguided shunning of the humanities (Hoe, Samsudin, & Yeo, 2015), and the ineffectiveness of bilingualism with mastery in none (Linda Lim, 2014). Attending concerns include a possible sclerotic system of democratic, meritocratic elitism, with unquestioned entitlement embedded, producing implications for social mobility that education is supposed to facilitate (Ng, 2011).

The next 50 years will prove extremely challenging for Singapore: the processes of nation-building and citizenship education will require complex, authentic, and empathetic responses to the 4Ms. If citizenship, as a concept both in education and in society, is a matter of contestation among the different groups of stakeholders in a globalizing Singapore, a critical rather than passive form of citizenship should be the goal. Singapore education policy makers have taken steps in that direction; this chapter assesses those efforts.

Citizenship Education as Nation-Building

The Ministry of Education (MOE) describes the Singapore education system (Ministry of Education, 2015c, p. vi) thus:

> Singapore's education system aims to bring out the best in every child by enabling students to discover their talents, realise their full potential, and develop a passion for life-long learning. We seek to nurture the whole child, and help them develop an enduring core of competencies, values and character, to ensure that they have the capabilities and dispositions to thrive in the 21st century. Our multiple educational pathways cater to students with different strengths, interests and learning styles, developing each child to his fullest potential.

By 2015, education was "part of the Singapore success story" (Ministry of Education, 2015a, p. 2). MOE programs are tied to national policies: official citizenship and multicultural instruction are infused throughout the syllabus and related educational activities. The National Institute of Education, the only teaching institute in the country, functions concurrently with the MOE to promote these national principles (see Ministry of Education, 2017, for the Humanities syllabus).

In general, the system provides a pupil at least 10 years of general education: six years in primary school, which is compulsory, and four or five years in secondary school. Education may be continued another two years in a junior college in preparation for an institution of higher learning, with most pupils sitting for the Cambridge advanced level (A-level) examinations. An alternative path provides pupils with a polytechnic technical education with the possibility of continuing onto a university education. A MOE brochure describes the system as offering "diverse pathways" (2015a, p. 5): a diverse range of abilities is assessed through "transparent and meritocratic criteria" (2015a, p. 23) to become "many pathways, one mission" (Ministry of Education, 2007). Independent and autonomous schools offer academic paths and certifications and are generally perceived as elite institutions that provide advantageous paths toward advancement.[2]

Each stage of the education ladder is builds on the "previous stages and lays the foundation for subsequent ones":

> The person who is schooled in the Singapore Education system embodies the Desired Outcomes of Education. He has a good sense of self-awareness, a sound moral compass, and the necessary skills and knowledge to take on the challenges of the future. He is responsible to his family, community and nation. (Ministry of Education, 2015b, para. 2)

The emphasis is on developing a common national identity of "Singaporean": a neutral nonracial identifier with a common, shared identity; a national curriculum reinforces this overarching citizenship objective.

Citizenship education has existed in various forms and under different labels since Singapore became independent, with generations of Singaporeans schooled to understand, appreciate, and internalize, for example, racial harmony as a national good. Whether presented as national education, civics moral education, the Singapore story, shared values, or examinable academic subjects such as history, science, geography, economics, and social studies, citizenship values are infused in all subjects. Social studies in particular has tremendous potential as a tool for citizenship education.[3]

The 1979 Goh and Eng reports (Sim & Print, 2005) were early responses to globalization and attempts to strengthen Asian values against Westernization. Early responses to globalization and attempts to strengthen Western values were integrated with moral education in "Being and Becoming Good Citizens," the goal of which was to encourage a deliberative approach to globalization. Successive programs included "Religious Knowledge and Confucian Ethics" in 1982; the "Shared Values" program in 1991; civics moral education in 1992 (Sim & Print, 2005); and the "Singapore 21 Report" in 1995 (Hill & Lian, 1995).

In 1997, national education and nation-building education attained an indisputable place in the national consciousness, another layer in the process "aimed at deliberately developing and shaping positive knowledge, values, and attitudes of Singapore's younger citizenry" (Sim & Print, 2005, pp. 63–64). The goal of national education is "to develop national cohesion, cultivate the instinct for survival as a nation, and instill in our students confidence in our nation's future. It also emphasizes on [sic] cultivating a sense of belonging and emotional rootedness to Singapore" (Ministry of Education, 2015f, para. 1). In 1997, "Thinking Schools, Learning Nation" continued the initiative to groom critically trained citizens to meet the challenges of the 21st century. "Teach Less, Learn More" was introduced in 2004, with an emphasis on improving the quality of teacher-pupil interaction through a critical approach to learning, understanding, and application of knowledge: a content-reduction strategy. The goal was to teach "hearts and minds," not to focus exclusively on passing the mandated, high-stakes examinations.

In April 1998, the Teachers Network was formed "to promote the professional and general well-being of teachers . . . as a catalyst for teacher-initiated development" (Ministry of Education, 1998, para. 3). Resources are directed through professional development programs such as GROW (Growth-Recognition-Opportunities and Well-Being), with "professional opportunities for teachers through a system of incentives and rewards" (Ismail, 2010b, p. 13). In 2010, the Academy of Singapore Teachers, devoted to "professional excellence in education," was launched with a mission to "better prepare students for the 21st century. [T]eachers will be required to deliver education that is increasingly customised and collaborative, while being grounded in sound moral and social values" (Ministry of Education, 2010, para. 2). As part of the Singapore story, the symbiotic relationship between the government and the MOE has been fundamental, especially during challenging periods such as the "tiger" economy in the 1980s, the Asian economic crisis of 1997, and the current global "age of insecurity" (Judt, 2010) in combination with an unforgiving global market.

Since the general elections of 2011, in which the ruling People's Action Party lost a few parliamentary seats (Ismail & Shaw, 2011; Low & Vadaketh, 2014), reassessments of the seemingly intractable foundational myths surfaced. The country entered an era of a "new normal" or a "post-consensus" Singapore, where questions were being asked about the future by its people and leaders regarding the Singapore identity. Geoffrey Benjamin (1976) noted that multiracialism is one of Singapore's founding myths, and so, seemingly, is meritocracy. Meritocracy, allegedly a fair system of effort and reward, presupposes a level playing field which does not exist in a diverse society with different privileging and marginalizing identity markers. This merit paradox, which rewards not effort but unearned privilege, had until 2011 affected mostly minority and lower-income groups (Barr, 2006b; Chong, 2014). Now, it also affects "the managed, middle-class multiracial society" (Trocki, 2006, p. 137).

A multiracial nation proud of its multiracial curriculum has the potential to promote diversity education while simultaneously transmitting official citizenship values. Scholarly work on diversity education—its meaning, potentials, challenges, benefits, and (un)intended consequences—includes forays into social, political, economic, and historical contexts (Banks & Banks, 2016; Drum & Howard, 1989; Guinier, 2015; Spencer, 1998). The Singapore story has also been examined and subjected to critical discourse at multiple levels (Barr, 2006a; Benjamin, 1976; Chua, 2007; Clammer, 1998; Lai, 2004; Low & Vadaketh, 2014; Rahim, 1998), especially in an increasingly critical discourse on the impact of the meritocratic system on personal and national identities (Barr & Skrbiš, 2008; Low, 2014; Trocki, 2006).

In an era of intensified interconnectedness between the national and the global, Singaporeans are proud of the country's survival instinct (or, conversely, its siege mentality). Navigating the brave new world of interconnectedness demands the deconstruction of the complexities of relational power within and beyond this small nation-state's borders. A move toward critical thinking is not only realistic but necessary for Singapore's survival as an economic and sovereign entity.

Contemplating Implications

Diversity in a globalizing Singapore is seen as problematic, and the state-directed showcasing of the "other" as an exotic difference in national and educational narratives needs to be examined critically. Singapore's preparation for tomorrow's adults in a hyper-globalized world cannot continue to be a "diversity-lite" of superficial tolerance or official management of the "visibility" of differences. The critical deconstruction of the complexities and impacts of diversity cannot be limited or confined to officially approved boundaries (Ismail, 2014) given the impact of and opportunities presented by globalization. It is challenging to confine the "private frustrations" emanating from racism, exclusion, and marginalization by omnipresent "public cheer" of hegemonic narratives of racial harmony (Ismail, 2010b, p. 26). The realities of differences and diversity, including privilege and structural marginalization, cannot continue to be masked by Racial Harmony Days or other displays of "positive" tolerance, not only within the CMIO population but also among transient workers in an increasingly congested island state.

The effects of globalization can be seen in the changing demographic landscape of classrooms, which now include pupils from nontraditional areas such as the People's Republic of China. An increase in intercultural marriages has also put a strain on identification based on race and the associated ascribed cultural practices and aspirations. Socialization processes through education demand new approaches not based on citizenship issues of nation building but on the concept of a sustainable multiracial society. With a declining birth rate, approximately only 3.37 million people today are Singapore citizens, in a population of 5.53 million (National Population and Talent Division, 2015). The implications of these demographic trends go beyond national identity to sustainability as a viable sovereign state.

Globalization has sharpened the focus on the mechanics of embedded power within structured and unstructured socialization processes with concurrent demands for credible responses. New challenges with globalization mean that the old methods of managing diversity will no longer suffice. Singapore's "exceptionalism" is tested by the complex "hypermobile worlds of capital, commodities and communications which can in turn foster multiple, domestic labor inequities" (Ismail & Shaw, 2011, p. 1). Michael D. Barr (2016) contends that "the genie of scepticism and accountability has been released from its bottle, and it is hard to see how it can be put back in . . . the narrative of exceptionalism is dead and the Singapore elite finds itself struggling to cope in a new and critical political environment" (p. 1).

Singaporeans have suffered from an economic race to the bottom, with ethnic minorities bearing the brunt (Mutalib, 2012) with increasing costs of accessing public housing, a high cost of living, the perceived marginalization of Singaporeans for cheaper "foreign talent," the competitive education process, and the psychological and physical dislocation emerging from what some might consider a casual attitude toward migration (Chong, 2010; Velayutham, 2007). Critics cite Singapore as one of the most inequitable societies in the world, with a disturbing Gini coefficient score (Wilkinson & Pickett, 2010, p. 15); at the same time, it is one of the most expensive cities in the world (BBC, 2015).[4]

In 2002, Prime Minister Goh Chok Tong spoke at the National Day Rally of becoming a nation of "stayers" and "quitters" (Singapore Government Press Release, 2002). Educated, mobile, and globally oriented Singaporeans are "quitting" Singapore as part of the transnational expression of the global age.[5] ("More than half of S'poreans," 2012, October 9). The government response—importing new communities into Singapore—creates significant pressures not only on the existing infrastructure of housing, transportation, education, and employment but on all residents' psychological and emotional disconnections of identity and security. There is a need to reconsider and review polices, as the rules of life have been affected in palpable ways. The prosperity pact on which Singapore was founded is in jeopardy and with that the survival of the nation, with consequences for citizenship education.

National Education: Responding to Globalization

Education institutions have responded to globalization with efforts to review, innovate, adapt, and implement. As noted by Gopinathan (2007), "there is a need to reconsider some of the arguments and to review the policy responses, especially in education" (p. 53). Citizenship education has been recrafted but is still framed within a unique Singapore context and concept. Fundamentally, citizenship education is anchored territorially but controlled politically to promote Singapore values while actively engaging with external global influences and pressures. This trend reflects globalizing on its own terms: maintaining a delicate balance between the national and the global with the overriding mission of economic survival. In this effort, previously uncomplicated notions of citizenship in the national pledge, such as "one united people" and being a "good" citizen, have been revised.

The main vehicle of response to globalization is the social studies curriculum (Sim & Print, 2005). The 2012 secondary and primary syllabus outlines the philosophy:

> At the heart of the Singapore Social Studies (SS) curriculum is preparing students to be citizens of tomorrow. The curriculum helps them to understand the interconnectedness of Singapore and the world they live in and appreciate the complexities of the human experience. Drawing on the social life that is of meaning and interest to the learners, SS seeks to ignite students' curiosity to inquire into real-world issues that concern their lives. Through inquiry and authentic learning experiences, SS helps students to attain relevant knowledge and understandings about these issues, develop reflective and critical thinking skills, and appreciate multiple perspectives. (Ministry of Education, 2015d, p. 1)

Introduced as a compulsory component in upper secondary schools in 2001, this examined subject, within a national curriculum framework with a comprehensive syllabus and MOE-authored textbooks, fosters rooted Singaporeans with global sensitivity. Its interdisciplinary approach strives for "21st-century competencies." The primary school syllabus, implemented in 2012, introduces pupils to a history-based foundation for "belonging," with three main clusters consisting of six areas of focus implemented within a six-year program (Ministry of Education, 2015d, p. 3), excerpted here:

- *Cluster 1: Discovering Self and Immediate Environment*

. . .[P]upils would explore who they are in relation to the people and places around them. They would also explore the communities in Singapore. Pupils would not only come to appreciate the cultural diversity in Singapore but also learn about the cosmopolitan nature of the Singapore society as they study about countries where new migrant communities come from.

- *Cluster 2: Understanding Singapore in the Past and Present*

. . . [P]upils would develop an appreciation of the country they live in as they learn about the contributions of different groups of people to the growth of Singapore. Pupils would also come to value the resilience as well as resourcefulness of our forefathers and political leaders.

- *Cluster 3: Appreciating the World and Region We Live In*

. . . [P]upils would learn about the world and the various communities of people. Fostered in the pupils would be a deeper appreciation of the interconnectedness of the world and the legacy of human achievements of societies, past and present. The journey for the child culminates with an understanding of Southeast ties with the region.

The syllabus for the secondary school (technical) track develops these foundational narratives into contemporary "issues-based" familiar and new narratives. The familiar narratives focus on the importance of sustaining racial, cultural, and religious consensus; there is a heightened emphasis on cultivating awareness and resilience in navigating geopolitical shifts. Everything is anchored on embedding a nationalistic Singapore identity cognizant of the impact of an interdependent global world. It is a national curriculum with a global perspective and claims about the importance of patriotism (Ministry of Education, 2013, p. 4), planned as follows:

Lower Secondary

- Living in a multicultural society
- Responding to migration
- Resolving conflict and building peace
- Protecting our environment

Upper Secondary

- Managing our financial resources
- Caring for our society

The social studies program represents a carefully calibrated concentric layering of citizenship education. The program begins with the private individual, moves to the family unit, and widens to the immediate school, the local community, national-citizenship responsibilities, and the larger global society. This approach is not unlike that of Banks (2004) in taking into account national, historical, and cultural differences in engagement with the global community. The curriculum envisions "globalized" Singaporeans: citizens who are rooted to Singapore through shared values and cultures while taking full advantage of the economic opportunities of the global economy (Spring, 2004).

The remaking of a new national narrative in response to globalization has been strategic and predictable: to "create an imagined nation that would secure economic growth and harmonious ethnic ties . . . to define Singapore as a global city" (Kluver & Weber, 2003, p. 371; see also Ong, 2015).

Preliminary Assessments

The national curriculum progressively de-emphasizes "moral education, enhancement of thinking skills, and encouragement of participation for more active citizenship" (Sim & Print, 2005, p. 66). In the attempt to "change gears" (Hussain, 2014) to foster "informed, concerned and participative citizens" (Ministry of Education, 2016, p. 2), there are attempts within the education curriculum to critically interrogate complexities of the self, the nation, and the world. Although these objectives suggest positive possibilities, there are some structural limitations.

Social studies as citizenship education has a unique Singapore identity. It does not address directly the inherent weaknesses and contradictions on which this multiracial society has been institutionalized. The system has been impacted by a highly controlled, examinations-result-oriented culture, as well as by the structural, social, and political-economic frameworks of a racialized Singapore society. The reluctance to address effectively and officially some of the (un)intended outcomes of multiracial policies, the elusiveness of an equitable meritocracy, and discernible national inequities are disconcerting.

The education system offers differentiated economic destinations. Merit is measured by national standardized testing that is gamed by financial affluence and social influence and fueled by a thriving industry of expensive private tutoring after school hours. This education superstructure can be seen not as a tool for empowerment but as one that replicates societal economic power, thwarting social mobility with disquieting effects on groups increasingly marginalized by an increasingly uneven playing field (see Ng, 2014).

Singapore today is essentially a "testocracy" (Guinier, 2006, p. 136) in which everything can be lost or gained through examination results. Despite MOE's claim of "every school a good school" (Ministry of Education, 2015e), education has become a stratified phenomenon: the different pathways facilitate differences (Tan, 2010). These differences are not equitable, with pupils from minority and lower-income groups unable to compete or game the system due to their dissimilar social, cultural, and financial resources as compared to their dominant, hegemonic counterparts (Barr, 2006a, 2006b; Chong, 2014; Low, 2014; Ng, 2015). An over-representation of particular ethnic groups in differentiated streams hints at outcomes that are seemingly validated by the national examinations (see Chong, 2014).

Streaming into pathways at key points based on examination results marks pupils for paths carved from deceptive groupings of being "more" or "less" able. Secondary school pupils may be funnelled to paths marked as "express," "normal," or "normal technical" in heirarchical order. Students are then presented with a curriculum based on their ascribed abilities. This streaming (and separation) process co-exists alongside the "better" elite schools that offer different privileging opportunities, raising significant questions about equity and meritocracy. The stratified education hierarchy is reflected in the formulation and execution of nation-building education (Ho, Sim, & Alviar-Martin, 2011; Tan, 2010).

This stratification is bound by the primacy of allegiance to the state. Lee (2015) notes eight metaphoric themes that echo the theme of "Our People, Our Home." She describes the phenomenon as "ideational preoccupations of the government as the agent-organisation seeking to preserve its hegemonic leadership" (p. 99). This observation is similarly suggested by Sim and Print (2005):

> A more critical interpretation would suggest that National Education in general, and therefore social studies in particular, are more about attempts by governing elites to maintain power in increasingly challenged contexts (by forces of globalisation) than a more genuine concern for better educating young people. (p. 65; see also Sim & Ho, 2010)

An assessment of the "Inquiry Focus and Guided Questions" secondary school syllabus reveals that teachers consider the syllabus as part of national citizenship education and are not averse to following it as part of their professional responsibility. The syllabus content is consistent in the refrain of "unity within diversity"; it calls for a daily pledge pertaining to Singapore citizens' rights "regardless of race, language and religion." Teacher interaction with the syllabus and classroom practices runs along a continuum of "conservative" to "progressive" approaches, with the former providing more emphasis on transmission than interrogation (Sim & Print, 2009a, pp. 713–714). It is convenient to hail "socially concerned educators" (Sim & Print, 2009a, p. 714) as more effective than those pursuing a doctrinaire approach, but this argument is too simplistic to assign teachers progressive ("persuasive") or conservative ("didactic") labels because Singapore teachers must balance their personal and professional dispositions within structural limits.

There is an intrinsic dialectical tension in educating pupils for active citizenship within boundaries of what is permissible by OB-markers rules and state-directed philosophies and control of the national good (see Ho, Alviar-Martin, & Leviste, 2014; Leonel Lim, 2014). Some individually directed teachers are motivated to embrace the full potential of the inquiry process in directing pupils through active citizenship exercises. The confidence and luxury of following this path speaks to the core components of the secondary syllabus inquiry process of "sparking curiosity, gathering data, exercising reasoning, reflective thinking" (Ministry of Education, 2013, pp. 22–23) but within examinable considerations (Sim, 2008). For these teachers, the social studies syllabus is an opportunity to engage pupils in ways that may not have been available in the past (Ho, Sim, & Alviar-Martin, 2011; Sim & Print, 2009b, p. 380).

Most teachers, however, are pressured to complete the syllabus, to guide their pupils to the correct answers, and to support their schools in achieving the best results. This "teaching to the test" is not unanticipated. The national socialization process regarding the OB markers of race, language, and religion partly explains an inherent reluctance to guided inquiry with "teaching to learn" becoming a part of getting the "right answer." Examining uncomfortable and controversial subjects of racism, marginalization, social injustice, and structural and systemic contradictions can be daunting. The result can be self-censorship, resulting in "safe" approaches—conforming to rather than interrogating the status quo.

Placing pupils by race, accent, class, and test scores has also produced low expectations of these pupils' ability to process critical issues (Davie, 2015; Delpit & Dowdy, 2008; Ng, 2003). Student involvement tends to be passive, befitting these students' future roles as obedient factors of production in a globalized economy as part of a greater national good.

The potential of the inquiry process can be discerned in another context. Based on formal and informal conversations with Singapore teachers in 2015, a form of differentiated citizenship education has evolved borne by the meritocratic paradox of exacerbating rather than ameliorating inequities. A meritocratic elitism in the allegedly "better" elite schools reflects the advantages of embedded social, political, and economic privilege. Pupils in these schools do not suffer from low expectations but instead benefit from the entitlement to an active, critical citizenship education that should be the right of all pupils. These students are perceived as more able pupils, as validated by their examination results and other privileging markers of worth; teachers in these schools speak of their students' ability to deconstruct a range of issues, including gay rights, free speech on the Internet, and the rights of foreign workers. As noted by Han, this privileged treatment of allegedly "better" students (2000)

> seems to assume that students of different academic abilities will perform different social and political roles in society. . . . Among other things, there appears to be a policy to encourage a relatively small elite, comprising the most able to think independently about national issues and to arrive at their own conclusions about these issues. (p. 65)

Generally, the intent of national curriculum is not to reform an economically directed education structure but to produce generational change. Social studies as citizenship education continues the concept of citizenship as a social-economic integrative tool used by a ruling class. The modern environment of global movement, shared information, and generationally different aspirations demand a response, and the response seems to be managed recalibration. At worst, this response can also be considered an inadequate rear guard action or an unsustainable delicate balancing act. An alternative proposal for meeting current and future challenges would involve reframing and restructuring the national education philosophy and the ingrained national mind-set about the mythic power of grades.

Policy Imperatives

Globalization demands a major conceptual interrogation of more than just citizenship education—of the entire edifice of Singapore foundational pillars and the 4Ms, especially meritocracy. Singapore's national education policy makers need to reassess policy formulation, program implementation, and teacher education beyond the needs of building a multiracial society bonded by a prosperity consensus. Citizenship education today is markedly different than it was in 1965 and must go far beyond the single-minded pursuit of growth (Low & Vadaketh, 2014). Whether it is in the depiction of Singapore ethnic minorities, economically less privileged citizens, foreign workers, or designated "terrorists," the dominant narratives should not continue to include stereotypical representations, solipsistic interpretations, and racialized/racist subtexts corroborated by national examinations. The preparation of globally competent citizens demands a reassessment of relational power in terminological, definitional, and conceptual formulations and policy executions. The complexities of diversity include not just mutual respect and common dignity but also the pursuit of social justice through global citizenship. Ensuring the maturation of globally competent citizens is a reasonable aspiration for any sovereign state. The inexorable interconnectedness of the global community and the expanding chronicles of citizens' differences and their numerous impacts need to be incorporated for any critical understanding of the dangers of replicating the dominant and subordinate power status.

Singapore's informal and formal diversity education and socialization process should embrace a nuanced, authentic, and respectful understanding of difference and diversity. This calls for eschewing the superficial ornamentalism of the "3Fs" of food, fashion, and festival approach (Ismail, 2010b), in which CMIO groups are expected to "showcase" their cultures, with minority groups seen as the more exotic "other." The related "3Cs" of commodification—cuisines, costumes, and celebrations (Ismail, 2014)—are not restricted to minority groups but can perpetuate stereotypes of false harmony while embedding and signaling (in)visible power structures. Singapore's rich cultural diversity is currently presented through minimalist interactions, without substantial cultural exchanges on the challenges of living in a multiethnic society. This passive tolerance (Chua, 2005, p. 18) of the other, rather than cultivating a respectful understanding of difference, continues as migrants, new citizens, and foreign workers are seen as shallow "flags and folklores" extensions to the 3Fs.

Critical discourses have explored the intertwining political, social, and economic threads and their disparate (un)intended outcomes in terms of education, housing, and employment. In Singapore, opportunities as promised under a fair meritocratic system are affected by structural and informal forms of exclusion (see Yahya, 2015). The official commitment to meritocracy and some associated affirmative actions are largely aspirational, given disparate privileging and exclusionary realities. Race consciousness as framed by folk information, latent negative views, and entrenched notions of alleged racial superiority persists in the form of unexamined privileges, structural exclusion, and everyday racism facilitated by reductionist, essentialized, racial identifiers (Barr, 2006a; Goh, Gabrielpillai, Holden, & Khoo, 2009; Lee, Ismail, Ng, Sim, & Chee, 2004; Rahim, 1998; Trocki, 2006).

These marginalization processes have been further embedded with the impact of globalization on the most vulnerable. Differential treatment is meted to minority communities that now form a significant part of the national landscape. These communities include foreign workers from the People's Republic of China and south Asia, domestic workers from southeast Asia, and white "foreign talent." The racial and color-based hierarchy, evident in the automatic privileging and exclusion of groups with associated socioeconomic occupations, is not formally acknowledged.

Conversely, one can argue that there are promising signs in the "'reciprocal' relationships" (Chong, 2005, p. 273) between activists and government authorities. A spectrum of interest groups representing transient workers' rights, environmental protection, and citizens' rights has grown under even the watchful eye of government authorities. But this growth is facilitated as part of the overall calibration of managing the forces of globalization. If citizenship education is an extension of diversity education in a world marked by inequities (Banks & Banks, 2016), it can be a promising development.

The institutionalization of local and transnational volunteerism in the national education curriculum is a complementary development framed within the unequal power status between the privileged and the marginalized. Voluntary work can "be an avenue for and expression of one's solidarity with one's fellow citizens" (Han, 2000, p. 70), but it is marked by embedded power structures (Nadler, 2002). Volunteerism (or "voluntourism") enables individuals to respond in a calibrated manner to global engagement through a safe valve (or smug satisfaction) while simultaneously eschewing controversial global issues (Ismail, 2010a). Engagement is with a global economic, social, and ethnic "other," creating an imbalanced relationship replete with powerful suggestions of power and status. A key Singapore identity marker, voluntourism has the inherent danger of framing global engagement as a "curriculum of pity" (Bigelow & Peterson, 2002, p. 5), or ego tourism. A 19-year-old Singapore student lamented the local volunteering scene: "The mindset that only those 'less fortunate' than ourselves deserve our care is also depressing. Community service is about the Community, not about 'superior' volunteers 'doing good' for 'inferior beneficiaries' " (Yeo, 2015, "Volunteering: Quality more important"). Volunteering can be a means of participating in a democratic process, but "doing good" can be a distraction from questioning local and global inequities.

Citizenship education in a globalizing world needs to address the diverse global realities that are the legacies of geography, history, politics, economics, and contemporary machinations. Education policy makers must scrutinize the processes of diversity education itself and rethink education processes and objectives beyond what the Singapore social studies curriculum offers. Education can be assessed through the lens of competitive meritocracy's debilitating outcomes: "a society that is materialistic and unpleasantly aggressive. . . . It is a growth that may be the problem" (Trocki, 2006, p. 158). In criticism of Singaporean education, Linda Lim wrote that "the whole social development of the nation has led youth and their families to despise manual and menial jobs" (Linda Lim, 2014, p. 80). These criticisms of Singapore's education system in a globalizing world explain in part the real and psychological displacement of "core" Singaporeans as economic restructuring makes them expensive to hire while being simultaneously discombobulated by "uppity" non-Singaporean workers.

Questioning meritocracy might ameliorate the outcomes of a testocracy and the implications of the rise of an entrenched elite class. Attempts at tweaking meritocracy have included relabeling ("sustainable meritocracy" or "tempered meritocracy"; Institute of Southeast Asian Studies, 2015, p. 11) with alternative measures of success. The testocracy will continue to reign as long as the national culture puts overwhelming value on test scores and Singaporeans continue to value an individual's worth based on material and physical characteristics. Guinier's (2015) extensive deconstruction of the "tyranny of meritocracy" and recommendations regarding "democratic merit" (pp. 122–134) might have a place in addressing Singapore's meritocracy problem, although the concepts might not be compatible with Singapore's political philosophy and cultural aspirations.

Singapore is in the midst of comprehending, managing, and recrafting a fractured identity. The identity based on compartmentalization and reductionism does not reflect the more fluid nature of reality, especially in the current "age of migration" (Kymlicka, 1995, p. 193). The national founding myths, even revised, will be difficult to sustain because there is no real anchor for all communities in multiracial Singapore except in the unraveling prosperity pact. As Kluver and Weber (2003) note: "In this sense, and in spite of its greater economic and political clout, Singapore suffers from a severe disadvantage. . . . it has been unable to generate a self-sustaining national mythology that would tie its citizens to its shores" (p. 386).

Singapore was founded on the politics of economic pragmatism. The attending values were "internalized by Singaporeans through a variety of mechanisms of socialization" and "have contributed to the development of sovereignty and the sense of nationality in Singapore" (Hill & Lian, 1995, pp. 33–34). Singaporeans are grappling with the increasingly complex and challenging processes of forging nationhood while attempting to forge other connecting bonds among its citizens. Overall social and cultural patterns suggest that as the prosperity consensus frays, the nation will continue to be tested.

The current strategy is a "glocal" approach, one balancing central control with individual expressions to negotiate an interconnected web of changes and impact. Inclusion and exclusion, nationalism and internationalism, are not easy to balance as the vicissitudes of governance, education, diversity, environment, and identities have augmented global insecurities and national anxieties. There are limits to confronting globalization on one's own terms (Chong, 2006), and attempts at "civic rebalancing" (Modood, 2013, p. 145) demand authentic and complementary measures for both core and new Singaporeans. As there are limits to the efficacy of the National Integrative Council, for example, there are also limits on the national education curriculum on citizenship education.

Globalization can sustain national survival in complex ways that can include the notion of social justice if one ascribes to a conceptual framework of diversity education that goes beyond simply "knowing" information. A social justice curriculum can address issues of inclusiveness, tolerance, and equity based on a humane respect for an individual's unique identity. Diversity education can be a transformative reform process working toward dignity, equity, and social justice (Banks & Banks, 2016) framed by a respectful recognition of the individual (Taylor, 1994).

Classroom Teacher Case Study

Malik is relatively new to the teaching profession, having made a midcareer change. He is in his mid-30s with a young family and a wife in the teaching service. As a member of one of Singapore's minority groups, Malik is fluent in English, Malay, and Tamil. His experience in the security services industry combined with his background contributes to his teaching philosophy, which in turn influences his classroom interactions and teaching practices.

Malik acknowledges that his personal values and teaching philosophies have been shaped by an economically challenging childhood. His hardworking father stressed the importance of doing things "the right way." For Malik, to teach is to embrace the holistic nature of education with "respect," "empathy," and "social responsibility" as core components. First-hand experiences and the downside of the Singapore "success story" are prisms for his efforts to teach beyond the testocracy superstructure. For Malik, teaching in a government school with pupils and staff from diverse socioeconomic backgrounds is preferable to teaching in an elite monoethnic or independent school. Malik considers his approach in and beyond the classroom as opportunities for character building not necessarily incompatible with MOE's directive to create "informed, concerned, and participative citizens" (Ministry of Education, 2013, p. 3).

Malik is committed to balancing his professional responsibility toward the nation and his personal duty to his students. Although he supports government-directed measures on nation building, or "forced tolerance," he is equally committed to his pupils as unique individuals. In the classroom, Malik betrays none of the stricter personality traits one might expect of a former security officer. He has a natural gift of friendly ease while interacting with students, coupled with an empathetic and respectful tone. He is comfortable with and interacts well in a multiracial classroom of students with varied socioeconomic backgrounds.

When teaching social studies, Malik responds to pupils' opinion of the topics as being dry, irrelevant, and distant by focusing on their lives as future citizens of a changing Singapore. Teaching is a "tough process" where the lesson needs to be "sold" to the students. Malik wants his students to understand social studies in the context of their own experiences and backgrounds. This is not necessarily demographic profiling, but rather involves working with the "reality" of a highly stratified education system. Malik does not want to fall prey to the latent discrimination of students from certain socioeconomic backgrounds and academic labels.

A typical lesson starts with "why," such as why build many private condominiums in an area without public housing. The last 15 minutes of a lesson are dedicated to answering questions from students; if they ask Malik for his opinion, he attempts to give multiple perspectives rather than a singular view. His aim is to convey the message that "all perspectives are important." Such questioning is not incompatible with the demands of the social studies syllabus, but there is "terrible pressure" to contain the discussion within the time limit, within the syllabus, and in a large classroom. As a responsible professional, Malik wants his students to learn the social studies curriculum as part the core Singapore value of "one united people regardless of race, language, and religion." But he is also determined to trigger thoughts and model actions that question dominant, hegemonic narratives regarding his students' (in)abilities and worth.

With students at the lower end of the academic scale and suffering from endemic low expectations, Malik strives to make the classroom an inclusive learning space by listening to their stories and sharing motivational experiences. He recognizes that these efforts are "definitely not a one-lesson thing" but rather enduring opportunities to stress values that may be marginalized in a results-oriented society. For example, it is vital for Malik that the sports team he coaches learn the finer points of sportsmanship behavior in both victory and defeat. Similarly, compulsory visits to senior citizens home are predicated with reminders that these visits are about "respect" and not about teaching "pity."

Malik understands the impact of migration on Singapore's social-economic landscapes. However, his attention to new migrants underlines a sensitive understanding of their integration process as well as his responsibility as their teacher. In the classroom, he ensures that these students are integrated with nonimmigrants in group activities and paired with native students in a "buddy system" as he monitors their progress. He is determined to treat all students and groups of students equally, but he will not ignore students from migrant communities. In a self-directed initiative, Malik conducts a history lesson introducing students to Singapore history before colonialism took hold in 1819, giving historical context for the evolutionary nature of Singapore's CMIO construct.

Malik balances his confident convictions with the grim realism of teaching citizenship education through social studies. He makes genuine efforts to deconstruct hegemonic narratives, presenting authentic and respectful understanding of differences and rethinking education beyond the lens of competitive meritocracy. He is committed to multicultural principles relating to difference and diversity through inclusionary and respectful practices. He strives for equity education in which students are given opportunities to achieve their full potential. However, his aspirations are tempered with the realism of "accommodating the superstructure." According to Malik, the "government will tell us what to do," and citizens must accommodate the system. In other words, he is not blind to the realities of the embedded testocracy. Malik's teaching practice balances the national education curriculum with his personal convictions as a teacher and a citizen. He is committed to continuing to recognize the "value of the individual without demeaning him."

Final Thoughts

The Singapore story is a powerful narrative of resilience and adaption. The synergetic relationship between the national education system and the teacher training programs as geared to national economic development is palpable (Chen & Koay, 2010). A mixture of cautionary reminders and optimism, the exhortation by Prime Minister Lee Hsien Loong in October 2014 to "remember the past, be confident of the future" (Hussain, 2014) is a familiar reframing of the narrative as a bridge between the past and the present. The narrative thread of survival is being rewoven as a cooperative, united action between Singaporeans and their leaders. Are the foundational and contemporary national narratives still recognizable in the daily realities of ordinary Singaporeans? Are measures adequate to mollify national anxieties in an increasingly unpredictable world?

New global challenges demand new narrative myths and new heroic inspirations while retaining established social and economic power structures. The death of Singapore's first prime minister, Lee Kuan Yew, in March 2015 prompted this assessment:

> Looking forward towards the future, it remains to be seen how his legacy will be upheld. Mr. Lee's ideas still inform the policies of the People's Action Party, despite its adeptness to changing electoral and socioeconomic realities. Most recently, this adeptness has seen shifts towards more inclusiveness, a tempered meritocracy and an increase in welfare measures and in the social safety net that are likely to continue. (Institute of Southeast Asian Studies, 2015, p. 11)

A state conceived of and managed as an efficient economic unit requires more than solidarity sound bites and exhortations to strengthen the core (Ong, 2015). With the passing of Lee, an avenue to generate a contemporary nation-building narrative in a globalizing age has opened. The unprecedented wave of public emotion after his death morphed into the institutionalization of a founder's narrative. This reliance on the power of talismanic hagiography represents a conservative, hegemonic approach. Lee's son, the current prime minister, believes that Singapore will be tested as a nation as it transitions into the "next phase" (Hussain, 2014), with national survival as the main stake. This next phase will probably be characterized by a Singapore society and education system framed not by critical inquiry of an interconnected world but by a selected, controlled "understanding" of global and national diversity through socially and economically constructed privileged lenses.

Notes

1. Originally an insult allegedly uttered by the leader of a neighboring Southeast Asian nation, "little red dot" has become a proud identity marker.

2. For an overview of the education system, see Ministry of Education, 2015c.

3. In January 2016, MOE announced the launch of a refocused social studies syllabus (Ministry of Education, 2016) with a critical assessment format that rewards "well-argued answers" and an "issue investigation" project that will be a part of the school-based assessment but not a part of the national examinations (Goy & Seow, 2016).

4. Singapore's 2009 Gini coefficient score is 42.5; the richest 20% of households command nine times the wealth of the poorest 20%. See Wilkinson and Pickett (2010).

5. Much was made of a 2012 survey by a global media and marketing service that "56 per cent of the 2,000-odd polled agreed or strongly agreed that, 'given a choice, I would like to migrate'" (Hooi, 2012).

References

Allport, G. (1979). *The nature of prejudice*. New York: Perseus.

Anderson, B. (1983). *Imagined communities: Reflections on the origin and spread of nationalism*. London: Verso.

Banks, J. A. (2004). Teaching for social justice, diversity, and citizenship in a global age. *Educational Forum, 68*(4), 289–298.

Banks, J. A. (2007). *Educating citizens in a multicultural* society (2nd ed.). New York: Teachers College Press.

Banks, J. A., & Banks, C. A. (2016). *Multicultural education: Issues and perspectives* (9th ed.). Hoboken, NJ: John Wiley.

Barr, M. D. (2006a). Racialised education in Singapore. *Educational Research for Policy and Practice, 5*(1), 15–31.

Barr, M. D. (2006b). The charade of meritocracy. *Far Eastern Economic Review, 169*(8), 18.

Barr, M. D. (2016). Ordinary Singapore: The decline of Singapore exceptionalism. *Journal of Contemporary Asia, 46*(1), 1–17. Retrieved from http://www.tandfonline.com/doi/full/10.1080/00472336.2015.1051387.

Barr, M. D., & Skrbiš, Z. (2008). *Constructing Singapore: Elitism, ethnicity and the nation-building project.* Copenhagen: Nias.

BBC. (2015, March 2). *Singapore remains world's most expensive city.* Retrieved from http://www.bbc.com/news/business-31689124

Benjamin, G. (1976). The cultural logic of multiculturalism. In R. Hassan (Ed.), *Singapore: society in transition* (pp. 115–133). Oxford, UK: Oxford University Press.

Bigelow, B., & Peterson, B. (2002). *Rethinking globalization: Teaching for justice in an unjust world.* Milwaukee: Rethinking Schools.

Bokhorst-Heng, W. (2007). Multiculturalism's narratives in Singapore and Canada: Exploring a model for comparative multiculturalism and multicultural education. *Journal of Curriculum Studies, 39*(6) 629–658.

Chen, A. Y., & Koay, S. L. (2010). *Transforming teaching, inspiring learning.* Singapore: National Institute of Education.

Chong, T. (2005). Civil society in Singapore, popular discourses and concepts. *Sojourn, 20*(2), 273–301.

Chong, T. (2006). Singapore globalizing on its own terms. In D. Singh & L. C. Salazar (Eds.), *Southeast Asian Affairs* (pp. 265–282). Singapore: Institute of Southeast Asian Studies.

Chong, T. (Ed.). (2010). *Management of success: Singapore revisited.* Singapore: Institute of Southeast Asian Studies.

Chong, T. (2014). Vocational education in Singapore: Meritocracy and hidden narratives. *Discourse: Studies in the Cultural Politics of Education, 35*(5), 637–648.

Chua, B. H. (2005). *Taking group rights seriously: Multiracialism in Singapore.* Working Paper No. 124. Asia Research Centre, National University of Singapore. Retrieved from http://www.murdoch.edu.au/Research-capabilities/Asia-Research-Centre/_document/working-papers/wp124.pdf

Chua, B. H. (2007). Multiculturalism as official policy: A critique of the management of difference in Singapore. In N. Vasu (Ed.), *Social resilience in Singapore* (pp. 51–80). Singapore: Select.

Clammer, J. (1998). *Race and state in independent Singapore 1965–1990: Multiculturalism and the cultural politics of pluralism.* Aldershot, UK: Ashgate.

Davie, S. (2015, 31 December). Teachers' bias can limit students' future. *The Straits Times.*

Delpit, L., & Dowdy, J. K. (2008). *The skin that we speak: Thoughts on language and culture in the classroom.* New York: New Press.

Drum, J., & Howard, G. (January 1989). *Multicultural and global education: Seeking common ground.* Las Palomas de Taos, REACH Centre for Multicultural and Global Education, and the Stanley Foundation. Taos, NM: Author.

Goffman, E. (1986). *Stigma: Notes on the management of spoiled identity.* New York: Simon and Schuster.

Goh, D. P., Gabrielpillai, M., Holden, P., & Khoo, G. C. (Eds.). (2009). *Race and multiculturalism in Malaysia and Singapore.* London: Routledge.

Gopinathan, S. (2007). Globalisation, the Singapore developmental state and education policy: A thesis revisited. *Globalisation, Societies and Education, 5*(1) 53–70.

Goy, P. (2015, May 13). Singapore tops biggest global education rankings published by OECD. *The Straits Times*.

Goy, P., & Seow, J. (2016, 6 January). Revised social studies syllabus tackles hot-button issues. *The Straits Times*.

Guinier, L. (2006). Diversity and equality: Balancing the scales. In K. Holbrook, A. S. Kim, B Palmer, & A Portnoy (Eds.), *Global values 101* (pp. 123–144). Boston, MA: Beacon.

Guinier, L. (2015). *The tyranny of the meritocracy*. Boston, MA: Beacon.

Han, C. (2000). National education and "active citizenship": Implications for citizenship and citizenship education in Singapore. *Asia Pacific Journal of Education, 20*(1) 63–72.

Hill, M., & Lian, K. F. (1995). *The politics of nation building and citizenship in Singapore*. London: Routledge.

Ho, C. H., Sim, J. B.-Y., & Alviar-Martin, T. (2011). Interrogating differentiated citizenship education: Students' perceptions of democracy, rights and governance in two Singapore schools. *Education, Citizenship and Social Justice, 6*(3) 265–276.

Ho, L. C., Alviar-Martin, T., & Leviste, E. N. P. (2014). "There is space, and there are limits": The challenge of teaching controversial topics in an illiberal democracy. *Teachers College Record, 116*(5), 1–28.

Hoe, S. F., Samsudin, S. N., & Yeo, V. J. (2015, June 16). Roundtable on the state of literature education and its implications. *IPS-SAM Spotlight on Cultural Policy Series*. Singapore: Institute of Policy Studies.

Hooi, J. (2012, October 6). *Singapore's emigration conundrum*. Retrieved from http://forums.sgclub .com/singapore/singapores_emigration_conundrum_421474.html

Hussain, Z. (2014, October 4). PM calls on S'pore to look outwards and to the future. *The Straits Times*.

Institute of Southeast Asian Studies. (2015). *ISEAS Monitor, 3*. Singapore: Author.

Ismail, R. (2010a). "I get by with a little help from my friends?" Volunteerism as multicultural experiential education. *Multicultural Education Review, 2*(2), 32–56.

Ismail, R. (2010b). *International comparative study of multicultural education. The Singapore story: The response from education*. A paper presented in the 2010 International Conference of the International Alliance of Leading Education Institutes, Seoul.

Ismail, R. (2014). The "new" multiculturalism: National and educational perspectives. Retrieved from http://www.hsseonline.edu.sg/journal/volume-3-issue-2-2014/%E2%80%9Cnew% E2%80%9D-multiculturalism-national-and-educational-perspectives

Ismail, R. & Shaw, B. J. (2011, November). *Future proofing the intelligent island? Singapore resilience*. In Proceedings of the 1st World Sustainability Forum. Basel, Switzerland: Sciforum Electronic Conference Series. Retrieved from http://sciforum.net/conference/wsf/paper/614

Judt, T. (2010). *Ill fares the land*. London: Penguin.

Kluver, R., & Weber, I. (2003). Patriotism and the limits of globalization: Renegotiating citizenship in Singapore. *Journal of Communication Inquiry, 27*(4), 371–388.

Kymlicka, W. (1995). *Multicultural citizenship*. Oxford, UK: Oxford University Press.

Lai, A. E. (Ed.) (2004). *Beyond rituals and riots: Ethnic pluralism and social cohesion in Singapore*. Singapore: Eastern Universities Press, Marshall Cavendish.

Lee, C., Ismail, R., Ng, M., Sim, J., & Chee, M. F. (2004). Children's experiences of multiracial relationships in informal primary school settings. In A. E. Lai (Ed.), *Beyond rituals and riots: Ethnic pluralism and social cohesion in Singapore* (pp. 114–143). Singapore: Eastern Universities Press, Marshall Cavendish International.

Lee, K. Y. (2000). *From third world to first: The Singapore story 1965–2000*. New York: Harper.

Lee, M. (2015). Critical metaphor analysis of citizenship education discourse. *Public Relations Inquiry, 4*(1), 99–123.

Lim, L. [Leonel]. (2014). Critical thinking and the anti-liberal state: The politics of pedagogic recontextualization in Singapore. *Discourse: Studies in the Cultural Politics of Education, 35*(5), 692–704.

Lim, L. [Linda]. (2014). What's wrong with Singaporeans? In D. Low & S. T. Vadaketh (Eds.), *Hard choices: Challenging the Singapore consensus* (pp. 79–96). Singapore: NUS Press.

Low, D. (2014). Good meritocracy, bad meritocracy. In D. Low & S. T. Vadaketh (Eds.), *Hard choices: Challenging the Singapore consensus* (pp. 48–58). Singapore: NUS Press.

Low, D., & Vadaketh, S. T. (2014). *Hard choices: Challenging the Singapore consensus*. Singapore: NUS Press.

Ministry of Education. (1998, April 30). *Teachers' network*. Retrieved from http://www.moe.gov.sg/media/press/1998/980430a.htm

Ministry of Education (2007, December 13). *Own a piece of education history*. Retrieved from http://www.moe.gov.sg/media/press/2007/pr20071213.htm

Ministry of Education. (2010). *Academy of Singapore teachers*. Retrieved from https://www.moe.gov.sg/news/press-releases/academy-of-singapore-teachers

Ministry of Education. (2013 *Social Studies Syllabus Secondary One to Four Normal (Technical) Course)*. Retrieved from https://www.moe.gov.sg/docs/default-source/document/education/syllabuses/humanities/files/social-studies-normal-technical-2014.pdf

Ministry of Education. (2015a). *Bringing out the best in every child*. Retrieved from https://www.moe.gov.sg/docs/default-source/document/about/files/moe-corporate-brochure.pdf

Ministry of Education. (2015b). *Desired outcomes of education*. Retrieved from https://www.moe.gov.sg/education/education-system/desired-outcomes-of-education

Ministry of Education. (2015c). *Education statistics digest 2015*. Retrieved from https://www.moe.gov.sg/docs/default-source/document/publications/education-statistics-digest/esd-2015.pdf

Ministry of Education. (2015d). *Primary social studies syllabus*. Retrieved from https://www.moe.gov.sg/docs/default-source/document/education/syllabuses/humanities/files/social-studies-syllabus-2012-110615.pdf

Ministry of Education. (2015e). *Every school a good school*. Retrieved from https://www.moe.gov.sg/education/education-system/every-school-a-good-school

Ministry of Education. (2015f). *National Education*. Retrieved from http://ne.moe.edu.sg/ne/slot/u223/ne/index.html

Ministry of Education. (2016). *Social studies syllabus upper secondary express course normal course*. Retrieved from https://www.moe.gov.sg/docs/default-source/document/education/syllabuses/humanities/files/2016-social-studies-(upper-secondary-express-normal-(academic)-syllabus.pdf

Ministry of Education. (2017). *Subject syllabuses humanities*. Retrieved from http://www.moe.gov.sg/education/syllabuses/humanities/

Modood, T. (2013). *Multiculturalism*. Cambridge, UK: Polity Press.

More than half of S'poreans would migrate if given a choice: Survey. (2012, October 9). *AsiaOne*. Retrieved from http://news.asiaone.com/News/Latest+News/Singapore/Story/A1Story20121007-376116.html

Mutalib, H. (2012). *Singapore Malays: Being ethnic minority and Muslim in a global city state*. London: Routledge.

Nadler, A. (2002). Inter-group helping hand relations in power relations: Maintaining or challenging social dominance between groups through helping. *Journal of Social Issues, 58*(3), 487–502.

National Population and Talent Division. (2015, September). *Population in brief.* Retrieved from https://www.nptd.gov.sg/portals/0/homepage/highligh/populati.pdf

NewsAsia, C. (2015, June 3). *US President Obama praises Singapore's economic success, racial integration.* Retrieved from http://www.channelnewsasia.com/news/singapore/us-president-obama/1888428.html

Ng, I. (2015). Education and social mobility. In F. Yahya (Ed.), *Inequality in Singapore* (pp. 25–49). Singapore: World Scientific.

Ng, I. H. (2011, February 16). Growing worry of social immobility. *The Straits Times.*

Ng, I. Y. (2014). Education and intergenerational mobility in Singapore. *Educational Review, 66*(3), 362–376.

Ong, W. (2015, November 30). *Singapore story 2.0: Strengthening the core.* Retrieved from https://www.rsis.edu.sg/wp-content/uploads/2015/11/CO15260.pdf

Ooi, G. L., & Shaw, B. J. (2004). *Beyond the port city.* Singapore: Pearson.

Paleit, A., & Hughes, J. (2015, March 23). *From third world to first: Lee Kuan Yew's legacy in charts.* Retrieved from https://www.ft.com/content/f902856e-d126-11e4-86c8-00144feab7de

PuruShotam, N. S. (1998). *Negotiating language, constructing race: Disciplining difference in Singapore.* Berlin: Mouton de Gruyter.

Rahim, L. Z. (1998). *The Singapore dilemma: The political and educational marginality of the Malay community.* New York: Oxford University Press.

Sim, B. Y., & Ho, L. C. (2010). Transmitting social and national values through education in Singapore: Tensions in a globalized era. In T. Lovat, R. Toomey, & N. Clement (Eds.), *International research handbook on values education and student wellbeing* (pp. 897–917). Berlin, Germany: Springer.

Sim, B. Y., & Print, M. (2005). Citizenship education and social studies in Singapore: A national agenda. *International Journal of Citizenship and Teacher Education, 1*(1), 58–73.

Sim, B. Y., & Print, M. (2009a). Citizenship education in Singapore: Controlling or empowering teacher understanding and practice? *Oxford Review of Education, 35*(6), 705–723.

Sim, B. Y., & Print, M. (2009b). The state, teachers and citizenship education in Singapore. *British Journal of Educational Studies, 57*(4), 380–399.

Sim, J. B.-Y. (2008). What does citizenship mean? Social studies teachers' understanding of citizenship in Singapore schools. *Educational Review, 60*(3), 253–266.

Singapore Government Press Release. (2002, August 18). *National day rally address by Prime Minister Goh Chok Tong at the University Cultural Centre.* Retrieved from http://www.nas.gov.sg/archivesonline/speeches/view-html?filename=2002081805.htm

Spencer, M. S. (1998). Reducing racism in schools: Moving beyond rhetoric. *Social Work in Education, 7*(1), 25–36.

Spring, J. H. (2004). *How educational ideologies are shaping global society: Intergovernmental organizations, NGOs, and the decline of the nation state.* Mahwah, NJ: Lawrence Erlbaum.

Street, B. (2003). What's "new" in new literacy studies? Critical approaches to literacy in theory and practice. *Current Issues in Comparative Education, 5*(2), 77–91.

Tan, J. (2010). Education in Singapore: Sorting them out? In T. Chong (Ed.). *Management of success: Singapore revisited* (pp. 288–308). Singapore: Institute of Southeast Asian Studies.

Taylor, C. (1994). The politics of recognition. In D. T. Goldberg (Ed.), *Multiculturalism: A critical reader* (pp. 25–73). Oxford: Basil Blackwell.

Trocki, C. A. (2006). *Singapore wealth, power and the culture of control.* London: Routledge.

Velayutham, S. (2007). *Responding to globalization: Nation, culture and identity in Singapore.* Singapore: Institute of Southeast Asian Studies.

Wang, G. (1968). *The use of history.* Athens, OH: Centre for International Studies.

Wilkinson, R. G., & Pickett, K. (2010). *The spirit level: Why equality is better for everyone.* London: Penguin.

Yahya, F. (Ed.). (2015). *Inequality in Singapore.* Singapore: World Scientific.

Yeo, M. (2015, June 3). *Volunteering: Quality more important.* Youth forum. *The Straits Times.* Retrieved from http://www.straitstimes.com/forum/volunteering-quality-more-important

Part 5

The Middle East

Chapter 13

Citizenship Education, Immigrants, and the Quest for Justice in the Arab World

MUHAMMAD FAOUR
Phoenicia University

The Arab world is rich in religious, ethnic, and socioeconomic diversity among citizens and in national and cultural diversity among immigrants. This unique phenomenon poses challenging questions about citizenship, human rights, and social justice for educators in several Arab countries, particularly since their educational systems aim to raise graduates who will conform to the political regimes' ideologies by promoting national identity and patriotism.

This chapter addresses the marginalization of the children of immigrants in the education systems of Lebanon, Jordan, and the United Arab Emirates (UAE), where immigrants comprise substantial percentages of the population. It begins by describing the political, societal, and educational background in the Arab world and then discusses the concept of social justice in the Arab context. Issues of social justice and human rights for immigrants are presented in a separate case study for each of the three countries, with special relevance to education. The chapter concludes with suggestions for reducing educational injustice in the Arab countries.

Background

In addition to the Palestinian Authority and the Gaza Strip entity, there are 21 member states in the League of Arab States. Over 370 million people spanning parts of Asia and Africa live in the Arab world (World Bank, 2013), which abounds with religious and ethnic diversity. Most Arabs are Sunni Muslims, but Shiite Muslims make up a majority of citizens in Iraq and Bahrain and form large communities in Lebanon, Kuwait, Oman, Yemen, and Saudi Arabia. Religious minorities are numerous and dispersed in the Arab countries. Christian Arabs constitute significant proportions of citizens in individual states—particularly Lebanon. The ethnic composition of citizens in the Arab world is also diverse, including not only Arabs but also Kurds in Iraq and Syria, Berbers in Morocco and Algeria, and Armenians in Lebanon and Syria (Faour, 1993).

Most Arab political regimes are authoritarian and deprive their citizens of basic political rights and civil liberties. Assessing the status of freedom with regard to political rights and civil liberties in the world, Freedom House (2015) described the overwhelming majority of Arab countries (18 of 23) as "not free," four as "partly free," and only Tunisia as "free." During the past five years, civil liberties improved only in Tunisia, while deteriorating in other Arab countries. It is worth noting that among 12 countries in the world to which Freedom House gave its lowest rating for political rights and civil liberties, four were Arab countries (Saudi Arabia, Somalia, Sudan, and Syria).

Migration is a distinctive feature of the Arab region, with significant political, social, and economic implications. Immigrants may be classified into three categories: (a) *displaced people*, (b) *refugees*, and (c) *temporary workers* or *expatriates*. Immigrants to the oil-exporting countries are temporary workers, mainly from Southeast Asia, along with large numbers from other Arab countries and from many Western countries. These immigrants are characterized by national, ethnic, religious, linguistic, racial, and socioeconomic diversity. Two extreme cases of labor migration are the oil-exporting countries Qatar and the UAE, where more than 70% of the population is constituted by immigrants, also known as *nonnationals* or *expatriates* (United Nations [UN] Department of Economic and Social Affairs, 2013). Immigrants to non–oil-exporting countries are mainly people who have fled persecution, political turmoil, or civil wars in their countries.

Political unrest and military conflicts in the past decade have resulted in massive population displacement. Several millions of people have been displaced within their own countries—notably in Iraq and Syria. Today, about one million of the migrants in Jordan are displaced people from Syria and Iraq, and close to half the population of Lebanon were displaced from Syria, Palestine, and Iraq (UN High Commissioner for Refugees [UNHCR], 2015a; United Nations Relief and Works Agency for Palestine Refugees in the Near East [UNRWA], 2015). Displaced people and refugees are *forced migrants*. The term *displaced* is used to indicate an expected short duration of stay and unwillingness on the part of the host country to keep the forced immigrants as permanent residents. In the Arab world, the term *refugee* historically is reserved for Palestinians who are registered with UNRWA. Palestinians, many of them refugees, comprise the majority of the population in Jordan, but the Jordanian government has also used the term *refugees* to describe displaced Syrians.

All immigrants who have brought their families with them need schooling for their children. Governments are in charge of the educational systems and run public K–12 schools; individuals and private organizations own and operate private schools. Significant differences exist between public and private schools and within both categories of schools in their curricula, degree of authoritarianism, respect for diversity, and social justice. Many private schools follow the national curriculum and resemble public schools, but a good number of private schools that are run by Westerners or use international curricula tend to follow the international standards that are implemented in democratic societies.

In most of the Arab Gulf countries, public education is available only to citizens. In the other Arab countries, government policies differ by country. Some countries require immigrant or noncitizen children (expatriate, displaced, and refugee children) to obtain special permission from the ministries of education to attend public schools, thus pushing most of them to study in private schools that charge varying amounts of tuition. Other countries permit all immigrant children to study in public schools.

Social Justice: Contested Concept and Unfair Practices

Social justice means different things to different people. It is a concept that has evolved over time—taking on new meanings in response to legal, cultural, social, and political changes. Historically, Aristotle introduced the concept of "distributive justice" (Keyt, 1991). Before the advent of Islam, Arab tribes considered customs and traditions as a basis for justice. Monarchs claimed fairness in the treatment of subjects based on traditions and laws that bestowed the monarchs with absolute power. Theocratic regimes referred to certain interpretations of religious books and traditions for imposing justice. One interpretation of social justice in Islam is based on God's sovereignty, whereby the Muslim ruler is expected to be impartial to all citizens without discrimination by gender, race, class, religious belief, or physical disability. The Muslim ruler must be guided by the Quran and the *sunna* (authentic sayings and exemplary deeds of the prophet Muhammad), and must consult with the governed people, who in return must show obedience, unless he violates basic Islamic tenets (Asyraf, Wan Ibrahim, & Nooraihan, 2012).

Today, educators agree that social justice implies fairness (Hytten & Bettez, 2011). Young (1990) views injustice in terms of five forms of oppression: exploitation, marginalization, powerlessness, cultural imperialism, and violence. Multicultural education and education for diversity can produce social justice in schools in Western democratic societies through various means, including prejudice reduction and the creation of an empowering school culture (Banks, 2006, 2011). Such a school culture is essentially democratic, with diverse social groups experiencing equality and cultural empowerment. Education for social justice cannot be separated from education for citizenship with a human rights perspective. The Universal Declaration of Human Rights empowers marginalized groups with legal, political, social, cultural, and economic entitlements in their quest for social justice (Shultz & Abdi, 2008; Starkey, Chapter 3 in this volume).

In the present chapter, the notion of justice in education draws on Banks's (2014) concept of "structural inclusion" of students in the political and cultural system of their nation-state. But instead of limiting the relevance of justice in education to the nation-state of students, it is extended to the Arab state where immigrant students live. Although that state is not their nation-state, the fact that immigrant students reside on that state's territory entitles them, from a human rights perspective, to basic educational services, to be provided by the state or another designated agency such as the United Nations' refugee agency (the UN High Commissioner for Refugees, or UNHCR).

The questions of social justice, human rights, and citizenship are further addressed below in the cases of Lebanon, Jordan, and the UAE, with special emphasis on the civic marginalization of students from migrant families.

Lebanon: Divided Plural Society, Weak State, and Mass Migration

Lebanon's name has been linked to a host of descriptors that point to its perennial state of political instability and societal fragmentation or pluralism: "the precarious republic" (Hudson, 1985), "a house of many mansions" (Salibi, 1990), and "a house divided"

(Mackey, 2006). Major conflicts in Lebanon are often protracted and destructive, with repeated failures at resolution. They have multiple sources (demographic, economic, social, and religious) at various levels of society (individual, family, sect, community, political group, and state), many of them interdependent. The conflicts are quite dynamic. The issues associated with each conflict, for example, change over time, as do the parties, the demographics, the relative balance of power among sects and groups, and other contextual factors. Scholars attribute Lebanon's instability and conflicts to various factors—notably, a sectarian political structure originating in the colonial period, changing demographics, a disputed state identity, a weak state, and a heterogeneous society comprising 18 recognized religious sects. Freedom House (2015), based on its assessment of the status of civil liberties and political rights in Lebanon, describes the nation as "partly free."

Economically, Lebanon has a free-market, service-oriented economy dominated by the banking and tourism sectors. After years of civil war and political instability, the government has been burdened with a huge national debt, and economic growth has been slow. For two and a half years, Lebanese politicians failed to elect a new president, and the cabinet and parliament were paralyzed. However, the banking sector remains sturdy. Nongovernmental organizations (NGOs) are active. The national army and security forces are strong enough to shield the country from violent domestic conflict arising from political discord.

In Lebanon, students are exposed to citizenship education through a civics course titled "Civic Education and National Upbringing," which is taught in the public and private schools that follow the Lebanese official school curriculum. Of the nine main objectives of the course, three are directly relevant to citizenship, diversity, and social justice:

- Teach the learner how to critique, debate, accept the other, and solve problems with peers through a spirit of peace, justice, and equality.

- Develop the learner's social spirit, being an organic member of the society whose unity is enriched with diversity.

- Promote the learner's awareness of her/his humanity and close relationship with fellow humans regardless of gender, color, religion, language, culture, and other differences (Lebanon Ministry of Education and Higher Education, 1997).

These objectives clearly embrace education for democracy, human rights, and social justice—objectives that are aligned with the Lebanese constitution (Frayha, 2012).

Lebanese civics books provide a detailed discussion of universal human rights, including those of women, children, persons with special needs, and teachers—as well as the role of international organizations and the League of Arab States in defending human rights. Political rights and obligations, especially the right to vote, are also addressed. The Lebanese constitution adopts the rights incorporated in the Universal Declaration of Human Rights, which was proclaimed by the United Nations General Assembly in 1948 (UN, 1948). Social justice is also promoted in the civics textbooks, in general terms, with no special reference to the social and political status of immigrants, particularly Palestinians, Syrians, and Asian domestic workers.

Public schools also teach Islamic religion to Muslim students and Christianity to Christian students. Each of the two religions upholds absolute values and defends what, in the eyes of its followers, is "truth." Students learn that issues of personal status (marriage, divorce, inheritance) are governed by their religious authority, which favors them over adherents of other religions. Thus students receive inconsistent messages regarding what it means to be a contributing member of Lebanese society, as civics texts subscribe to the principles of pluralism, national unity, acceptance of other beliefs and cultures, and the equality of Muslims and non-Muslims.

Further complicating matters is the role of many teachers in imparting religious values and behaviors that convey intolerance toward other beliefs, a circumstance that is often overlooked despite its critical significance. Teachers impose their own thoughts and attitudes on their students in a process that is affected by the prevailing culture within schools and made easier through the dominant, teacher-directed methods of lecturing and rote learning, as well as the lack of open discourse and critical reasoning.

After many years of political turmoil and civil strife, each major religious sect in Lebanon has either built or expanded its own K–12 private schools. Many of these schools mainly attend to their religious constituencies, nurturing attitudes of distinction from members of other religious groups, thus widening the differences among religious groups in Lebanon. Within each category of sectarian schools, there are also schools that belong to various political parties directly or through supporting owners.

Close to two thirds of ninth-grade students in both public and private schools in 2008 believed that each religious sect should educate its own members. This statistic reflects the strong influence of religious sects and leaders and reveals that young students consider sects as their first choice for the provision of educational services and perhaps also for political guidance (El Amine & Abou Chedid, 2008).

Another small-scale study found that one third of civic education teachers in 16 secondary private schools in Lebanon were concerned about students' "blind commitments" to political parties or to a certain leader, family, or group (Akar, 2012). Almost all of the teachers indicated the absence of real-life situations in the civics books, which resulted in students' finding the topics "hypocritical and, thus, unimportant" (Akar, 2012, p. 474). All teachers expressed some difficulty in teaching civics, particularly when students mentioned in class how political confessional groups or individuals got away with breaking laws and how the culture of *wasta* (personal connections and networks) could be demotivating. Another difficulty for teachers arose when allowing students to practice freedom of expression during debates about controversial subjects such as religion and politics. As a result, many teachers avoided such debates in fear of disputes and emotional stress among students, thereby limiting students' opportunities to develop essential citizenship skills— notably, active listening and dialogue. These opportunities were further constrained by the teachers' self-conceptions as holders of the knowledge that students needed and their emphasis on memorization and rote learning (Akar, 2012).

Immigrants: A Grim Picture of Injustice

This section will focus on the two main groups of displaced and refugee populations in Lebanon: Palestinians since 1948 and Syrians since 2011. Not discussed in this section is a third, smaller group of displaced people from Iraq, including Assyrians, and a fourth group of home helpers from Asian and African countries.

Palestinians. A few years after becoming a sovereign state in 1943, Lebanon received tens of thousands of Palestinian refugees who had been forced out of their homeland. Now, Palestinian refugees number about half a million, comprising 10% of resident citizens, and live mostly in camps, receiving vital support from the United Nations Relief and Works Agency for Palestine Refugees in the Near East (UNRWA, 2015). UNRWA provides significant, yet insufficient, services, mainly in education and health. Palestinians in Lebanon have experienced injustice in various domains for the past 67 years: legal, economic, social, and political. Under the pretext of preventing temporary refugees from becoming permanent residents, Lebanon has deprived Palestinians of basic human rights. The Palestinians have limited access to free public schools and public health services, are not allowed to own property, and cannot legally be employed in 20 syndicated professions, such as engineering and medicine (UNRWA, 2015). As a result, most professional Palestinians who studied in private schools and universities in Lebanon had to emigrate, seeking employment and citizenship in other countries.

In 2010, 8% of refugees of school age (7–15 years) were not enrolled in any school; two thirds above the age of 15 did not complete ninth grade; and only half of Palestinian youths aged 16–18 years were enrolled in secondary schools or vocational training centers. Poverty was extreme: Two thirds of Palestinian refugees were poor, subsisting on less than six U.S. dollars per day. Unemployment was high. In 2010, 56% of the population was jobless and only 37% of the working-age population was employed. The employment rate among men was substantially higher than among women: 65% versus 13%. Those who had a job were often in low-status, casual employment, insufficient to lift them out of poverty (Chaaban et al., 2010). To further exacerbate the plight of the Palestinian refugees in Lebanon, thousands of Palestinian refugees from Syria joined them in search of safety.

Despite Palestinian refugees' physical presence in the country for over half a century, some scholars contend that the Palestinians do not seek assimilation through Lebanese citizenship and that they would be satisfied with civil and economic rights in return for paying taxes until the Palestine problem is resolved (Chaaban et al., 2010).

Syrians. The influx of displaced Syrians en masse starting in 2011 exacerbated the multitude of problems that Lebanon had been facing for several years. Over one million women, men, and children have crossed the Lebanese-Syrian borders since 2011, seeking any form of accommodation all over the country, which has already housed about half a million Syrian workers. The United Nations refugee agency expected the number of displaced Syrians to have exceeded 1.8 million by the end of 2015 (UNHCR, 2015a). Because influential political parties vehemently rejected the idea of building camps for them, poor Syrian refugees have had to settle in any available dwelling or set up tents and shacks on public land. Syrian resident and displaced populations are more than one third the size of the citizen population of Lebanon, which is close to five million. Most of the Syrians are living in abject poverty. The UN High Commissioner for Refugees, in his speech to the UN Security Council in December 2015, reported that 9 in 10 Syrians in Lebanon were living below the national poverty line, and only half of all children were in school (UNHCR, 2015b). Those who were better off managed to secure housing and jobs or start their own businesses. Syrian entrepreneurs have succeeded in competing with their Lebanese counterparts. Syrian workers in various types of skilled and unskilled jobs have also displaced their Lebanese counterparts as they accept lower wages and limited fringe benefits. The loss of jobs and businesses to Syrian competition has led many Lebanese to oppose the continued presence of Syrians in Lebanon.

The circumstances of Syrians in Lebanon are unique among those of other displaced migrants. First, Lebanon and Syria are neighboring countries whose citizens have shared special social and economic ties for generations. Second, in 1976 the Syrian regime sent armed troops to help end the civil war in Lebanon, but the troops soon turned into an occupying force, which took control of the state and the country's resources until the assassination of then-premier Rafiq Hariri in 2005. That occupation, which lasted for more than two decades, left deep feelings of hostility toward Syrians by many Lebanese. Even so, when the popular uprising began in Syria against the Assad regime, a large percentage of Lebanese sympathized with the rebels until the uprising turned into a protracted civil war that started to affect the security situation in Lebanon. Military encounters between Syrian rebels belonging to extreme Islamist groups and the Lebanese army provoked feelings of hatred among many Lebanese, triggering acts of violence against displaced Syrians living in shacks and camps. Over the years, local newspapers reported a general fear among people in various villages and cities that the Syrian migrants living among them harbored militants or sleeper cells that could undertake terrorist activities. Incidents of social deviance such as prostitution, robberies, and violent crimes have increased in areas that have high concentrations of Syrians. In response, vigilante groups have formed, pursuing surveillance and taking the law into their own hands when deemed necessary. Other groups only monitor the movements of the displaced Syrians and report suspected activities to the Lebanese authorities.

In the midst of this tense situation, thousands of Syrian children are out of school. The thousands that are accommodated in public schools may not be receiving the high-quality education that their Lebanese counterparts receive. Furthermore, thousands of other children are enrolled in private confessional schools—Muslim and Christian—where many are indoctrinated into the divisive values and politics of those schools while learning basic subjects.

According to the UNICEF Regional Director for the Middle East and North Africa, fewer than 25% of Syrian children in Lebanon study in public schools. Most Syrian children have been out of school for one to two years, thereby being subjected to higher risks of exploitation and abuse. Several reasons are cited: cost of transportation and tuition, concern for the safety of children, subjects taught in a foreign language, and crowded public schools with no space for more students (Azar, 2014). Another major hurdle is that parents must submit their child's report card prior to registration. This requires a risky trip to Syria and taking another risk of being denied reentry to Lebanon. Many have decided to avoid the risks by opting not to send their children to school (Parkinson, 2014).

Syrian refugee parents whose children are out of school describe their children as the "lost generation." They are concerned about their future, worrying that educational exclusion and discrimination in exile will have a lasting detrimental effect on their children's social behavior and attitudes toward others (Parkinson, 2014). A rise in the scale of discrimination, violence, and acculturation in classrooms is documented in an ongoing study of public, private, and UNRWA schools that enroll Syrian students (Shuayb, 2014). The Lebanon Migrant Center of Caritas, an NGO, has found numerous cases of discrimination against Syrian children in public schools. One troubling example was found in a school in the Bekaa province, where Syrian refugee children wore uniforms of a different color from those worn by the Lebanese children. School administrators, teachers, and members of parent-teacher associations voiced complaints that Syrian refugee children were being helped while the Lebanese children were getting nothing. A number of donors were increasingly concerned about rising tensions between Syrian refugees and their host communities. Many Lebanese were blaming the high inflation in the country on the presence of Syrian refugees (personal interview with Caritas officer Mirella Chekrallah, December 2013).

As hostilities toward the Syrian refugees increased, the Ministry of Education and Higher Education started implementing educational exclusion by not admitting new Syrian children into public schools. However, the ministry has pressured UN agencies to provide funds for opening afternoon shifts in public schools for Syrian students only (Shuayb, 2014).

Although the Ministry of Education and Higher Education, in collaboration with humanitarian agencies, has been able to admit over 100,000 Syrian children into the public school system, with support from the international community, there is still an acute need for alternative schooling. In 2014 it was estimated that some 500,000 Syrian children would need to access education outside the formal system, by means such as bringing nonformal education to tented settlements, where children could learn, play, and receive psychosocial support in a safe environment (Azar, 2014). *Nonformal education* offers a diversity of structured programs that cater to the special learning needs of students. The objective of these programs is to teach basic academic and social skills that would facilitate the students' transfer to regular schools. There is also need for *informal education,* which is less structured and does not form a bridge to a regular school. Instead, it aims at developing specific skills such as financial literacy and interpersonal social skills.

Educational Consequences for Immigrants. Although the sojourn of Palestinian refugees in Lebanon is indefinite, as their return to Palestine is uncertain, the Lebanese public and politicians consider them as temporary residents awaiting return to their home country. Successive governments have relegated the role of public schooling to UNRWA, whose quality of services is declining with shortage of funds. As noted by Castles (Chapter 1 in this volume), education for this type of immigrant student in Lebanon aims at safeguarding the culture of the home country while segregating the students from their Lebanese counterparts. This is an exclusionary approach to education and is thus a form of injustice as defined earlier.

Hundreds of thousands of Syrian children have been living in Lebanon for several years with no end date in sight. Thousands are out of school, and those who are in school do not all receive the same form or quality of education. In public schools, they study the Lebanese curriculum but are segregated from Lebanese children. In private schools, there is more variation by school. Islamic schools teach the Lebanese curriculum with an additional subject on Islamic religion, often with emphasis on a particular sect or school of thought. Christian schools teach either the Lebanese or the French curriculum, with an additional subject on Christian religion, often with emphasis on a particular denomination. Secular schools and schools run or funded by international agencies and regional NGOs may teach either the Lebanese or the Syrian curriculum to Syrian students. These examples imply different educational goals for Syrian and Lebanese children, as well as a wide variation in educational goals among Syrian students themselves. Again, this is an exclusionary approach to education and a practice of injustice.

Jordan: Challenges of National Identity and Social Justice

Jordan has limited natural resources and a services-oriented market economy that depends on workers' remittances and international aid to secure its survival. Jordan is a rent-seeking state whose main proceeds come from external grants and concessional loans as a result of its geopolitical position (Mansour, 2014).

Jordan is a hereditary monarchy, classified by Freedom House (2015) as "not free," in view of its restrictions on civil liberties and political rights. The country is strongly influenced by the Palestinian-Israeli conflict, as the majority of its population is Palestinian. But there are several categories of Palestinians in Jordan that can be distinguished through colored cards issued to them by the government.

Palestinians: Injustice for Many

Palestinians who hold yellow cards carry permanent Jordanian passports with national ID numbers. Green card holders are West Bankers allowed to visit Jordan and return to the West Bank. Blue card holders are Palestinians from Gaza, also allowed to visit Gaza and return to Jordan. Pink card holders are Palestinians from Gaza, allowed only a temporary stay in Jordan. Many people who have green cards have ambiguous status because the Palestinian National Authority, which granted their Palestinian passports, is not a sovereign state.

Access to all public services, including education and health care, is restricted to Palestinians who hold permanent passports and are thus considered citizens. Residents of the refugee camps generally go to UNRWA schools, though they have access to both public schools and UNRWA schools. According to UNRWA (2015), there were over two million registered Palestinian refugees in Jordan in 2015, including 117,000 who went to UNRWA schools. Pink card holders who opted to join Jordanian schools were treated as foreigners and thus had to pay their school tuition fees in foreign currency (Al-Abed, 2004.). They were also excluded from free health care, with no exceptions for children in this policy (Gabbay, 2014).

As for work, Palestinians without a national number have no right to public employment. Those who seek work in the private sector have to obtain a work permit. For professionals in medicine, law, or engineering, this requires membership in a professional organization, which is open only to Jordanians with a national number (Gabbay, 2014). Thus, a large percentage of Palestinian students in Jordan are not "structurally included" (Banks, 2014) within the Jordanian state and society and have no political efficacy, a circumstance that may lead to political alienation. These Palestinians clearly demonstrate a case of social injustice.

National Identity Challenges

Jordan has been active over the past decade in promoting a Jordanian national identity among citizens through various means. But a Jordanian citizen, as is the case with citizens of other Arab countries, has multiple identities, the most common of which are religious, tribal, ethnic, and national (Faour & Muasher, 2011). Empirical evidence for multiple identities in Jordan was obtained in a 2004 study of youth. Respondents ranked Islamic religion as their first affiliation (34%), followed by Jordanian identity (31%), tribe (15%), geographic location (8%), and the Arab nation (7%; Touq, 2012, p. 4).

Citizenship education in Jordan faces several key challenges. The first challenge is that among Jordanian citizens of Palestinian descent, who comprise the majority of the population, many show dual loyalties. They harbor deep feelings toward their Palestinian national identity, which can take precedence over their Jordanian identity. Whereas many in Jordan are concerned about the Palestinian identity, pluralists consider Palestinian Jordanians as part of their multicultural society (Kubow & Kreishan, 2014). The Jordanian schoolbooks downplay the debate about Palestinian identity when narrating the history of Palestinian refugees. These books decontextualize the phenomenon of an exodus of refugees from Palestine by discussing it under a general Arab societal experience (Brand, 2010).

A second challenge is the persistence of primordial loyalties—tribal and regional— which interfere with a civic identity based on rule of law and equality of citizens. A third is the challenge of the rising influence of Islamic extremist movements within a society that is deeply religious. These movements are intolerant of religious diversity and place loyalty to their political party above loyalty to the state (Touq, 2013). A fourth challenge is the prevalence of authoritarian culture and patriarchal relations in society. Such a culture is not hospitable to independent critical thinking, open discussions, or dissent (Touq, 2012). It has also contributed to widening the economic gap between the wealthy and the poor, as the already privileged elite continue to receive special privileges from the state (Identity Center, 2014). The fifth challenge is the restriction on political rights and civil liberties under an authoritarian monarchy with limited political participation. These challenges weaken the rule of law and interfere with implementation of social justice principles— notably those of universal human rights.

Whereas schoolbooks in Lebanon explicitly and uniformly adopt the Universal Declaration of Human Rights, Jordan's schoolbooks do not endorse all the rights in the Declaration. For example, the sixth-grade book for "civic and national education" contains a special unit on democracy and human rights. The unit covers most of the rights included in the Universal Declaration of Human Rights, and in other UN statements on women's rights and the rights of the child, as well as the rights and obligations addressed in the Jordanian constitution. But the unit neglects the right of citizens to political participation and the universality of human rights. Furthermore, an Islamic approach is adopted when the text elaborates on the rights, citing Islamic examples for illustration.

Middle and high school students in Jordan relate the concept of citizenship to civic engagement and obedience but not to political rights. A good citizen keeps her/his country clean and obeys the law. According to civics teachers, the school curriculum emphasizes loyalty to the king and belonging to the country, with increasing attention to family allegiance. However, the political grievances and the economic and social demands raised in the Arab Spring receive little attention (Kubow & Kreishan, 2014).

Nevertheless, there have been some significant achievements in teaching citizenship and social justice in Jordan. They include enhancing openness to world cultures, respect for the different "other," dialogue, critical thinking, innovation, and awareness of citizens' rights and responsibilities (Touq, 2013). Among the few examples from a governmental initiative to include students in citizenship-related activities, one that stands out is the student parliamentary councils project, which was initiated in 2010. Through this project, students in public and private schools learn democratic practices and develop basic citizenship skills such as negotiation, open discussion, respect for diversity, and the rules and procedures of civic participation, including voting and running for office. However, the efficacy of this project and its outcomes have not yet been assessed. Another promising project is the Democratic Empowerment Programme, dubbed "Demoqrati," which was launched in 2013 under the umbrella of the King Abdullah II Fund for Development. It seeks to promote among the youth the values of democracy and democratic practices such as respect for the rule of law, rejection of violence, acceptance of others, dialogue, and accountability. By 2014, Demoqrati had launched 90 debating clubs and stimulated volunteerism at schools and universities, promoting accountability, transparency, and the right of access to information, and supporting community service initiatives (Demoqrati, 2015).

While Jordan did not experience a popular upheaval similar to those in Egypt or Tunisia, domestic pressure convinced the king to initiate some reforms. Concerned about the prospect of devastating civil strife as in neighboring Syria, political activists became more modest in their reform expectations, much to the pleasure of the regime. New approaches to reform include awareness campaigns about selected topics, notably gender discrimination, human rights, and citizenship education (Harris, 2015). Gender discrimination exists in the case of the female citizen who marries an immigrant or a foreigner. She is unable to pass on her citizenship to her children (or her husband). The children of these marriages usually do not have access to basic public services such as health and education. To oppose this type of gender discrimination, a number of organizations and activists in Jordan have engaged parliamentarians, ministers, and journalists (Harris, 2015).

Immigrant Workers: Legislated Injustice. Immigrant workers of various nationalities, notably Egyptian, comprise one third to one half of the total Jordanian labor force. They are subject to nationality-specific legislation that specifies the occupations that each nationality may be employed in, the ability of these workers to bring their families to Jordan, and other reduced freedoms. There are reports about frequent abuses of these workers' legal rights by Jordanian employers, such as paying them minimum legal wages when citizens with similar skill sets would be paid more, delaying payment of salaries, and providing poor living accommodations. Furthermore, court cases on violation of migrants' rights were more likely to be settled in favor of the employers (Identity Center, 2014).

Iraqi and Syrian Refugees: A Heavy Burden

The military conflict in Iraq that began with the American military operations in 2003 led to the displacement of hundreds of thousands of Iraqis to Jordan. Many had sufficient financial means to settle down and open their own businesses while awaiting the end of hostilities in Iraq. Thousands, however, could not afford to support themselves and became a burden on the Jordanian economy. The number of Iraqis decreased as many returned to their home country or moved to third countries. In 2015, the total number of Iraqi refugees in Jordan was about 57,000 (UNHCR, 2015c).

The situation of Syrians is more problematic. Some 938,000 women, men, and children have fled to Jordan from the war in Syria since 2011 (UNHCR, 2015c). Jordan quickly settled the refugees in camps, the largest being the Zaatari Camp (80,000), which has been described as the fourth-largest city in Jordan. The camp was built in a desert. It has tents, makeshift shops, sports fields, and schools for children. The Azraq Camp opened in April 2014. It has steel caravans instead of tents, a supermarket, and organized "streets" and "villages." The aim of the design was to provide the Syrian dwellers with a sense of community and security (MercyCorps, 2015). Still, most Syrian refugees are poor. As noted previously, the UN High Commissioner for Refugees, in his speech to the UN Security Council in December 2015, reported that 9 in 10 Syrians in Jordan lived below the national poverty line, and only half of all Syrian children were in school (UNHCR, 2015b).

The UNESCO Amman Office is implementing a European-funded project to promote quality education and skills development in schools with mixed populations of Syrian and Jordanian children. The project is meant to address the challenges posed by the influx of Syrian refugees for the quality of education in Jordan and to improve the employment prospects of young Syrian refugees. The student activities are designed to (a) build the capacity of Jordanian teachers in pedagogical and mentoring strategies for emergency situations; (b) provide informal and nonformal education programs and vocational skills to Syrian youth inside the Zaatari refugee camp; and (c) provide informal and nonformal education programs and vocational skills to Jordanian and Syrian youth in urban areas, particularly those areas that have limited opportunities for schooling, recreation, and skills development (UNESCO, 2014).

The Save the Children Federation has three education programs for Syrian refugee children: (a) the Early Childhood Development program (for children 0–6 years old), which provides access to protective, inclusive, and participatory early childhood educational programs, including capacity building for local institutions to provide appropriate educational materials and support for Syrian children; (b) the Basic Education program (for children 6–14 years old), which builds a learning environment as well as the capacity of public school staff to apply a child-centered approach in geographic areas with high concentrations of Syrian refugees; and (c) the Informal Education program (for children 12–24 years old), offered to adolescents and youth, particularly those who have dropped out of school and cannot be readmitted. The Informal Education program provides friendly spaces where youth receive training in basic interpersonal skills, employability skills, and financial literacy. In addition, Save the Children is building the capacity of teachers, counselors, and directors of education at the Jordanian Ministry of Education to ensure the smooth integration of Syrian students into public education (Save the Children Federation, 2015).

Educational Consequences for Immigrants

Jordan does not usually allow immigrant workers from Africa and Asia to bring in their families. The few parents from those continents who succeed in bringing in their children find that the children have no access to public schools. Castles (Chapter 1 in this volume) describes such a situation as "the ultimate form of exclusion" (p. 14).

Palestinian immigrant children do not comprise one homogeneous group. Those who hold Jordanian citizenship are better integrated into Jordanian society than those who do not. However, providing citizenship education that does not consider the children's Palestinian national identity as distinct from the Jordanian identity is not a fair practice. A multicultural approach that recognizes both national identities in schools would be an appropriate response to the Palestinians' quest for justice in education.

A more pronounced case of social injustice applies to the Palestinians who are not Jordanian citizens and thus are not treated equally with regard to public educational services. Palestinian children who belong to this group are treated like foreigners who should pay school tuition in hard currency. Most children in refugee camps go to UNRWA schools, as in the case of Lebanon. This is one form of exclusion in education.

Syrian refugees constitute a new, large group of temporary sojourners who are receiving substantial support from international donors. Their case has highlighted serious weaknesses in Jordan's public services. Poor Jordanian families pay more than Syrian refugees do for educational services and have to compete with them for public educational services that are deteriorating (Francis, 2015). This has generated ill feelings among poor Jordanians toward Syrian refugees. Furthermore, most Syrian migrant children remain segregated from Jordanian children in schools, another example of exclusion in education.

United Arab Emirates: Citizenship Education in a Global City

The UAE is a federation of six emirates, two of which are widely known to the outside world: Abu Dhabi and Dubai. Abu Dhabi is the capital and the UAE's richest, main producer of oil, while Dubai is the center of regional business and the symbol of openness to the Western world. Dubai and Abu Dhabi together comprise a global hub of migrants from all walks of life and all occupations. However, the UAE is classified by Freedom House as "not free" because of the restrictions on civil liberties and political freedoms. The UAE society is tribal and Islamic, with citizens representing only 8% of the total resident population. Resident nonnationals come from all over the world; Asian nationalities comprise the largest group, followed by Arab nationalities (Al-Maamari, 2013).

Citizenship education in the UAE is shaped by the political, demographic, economic, and cultural features of the country. There is a federal Ministry of Education, but its policies may not be followed in each of the six emirates. Economically, the country is strongly linked to the global economy, thereby placing pressure on the local Islamic, Arab, tribal society to integrate into a global, liberal culture that embraces Western behaviors.

The UAE's strategic plan in public education for 2010–2020 aims to develop students' awareness of the importance of social and voluntary work and to enhance their moral standards. The primary goal of the curriculum on national education is to educate Emiratis who will (a) safeguard the Islamic, Arab culture; (b) show national allegiance through actions, notably defending the homeland physically and morally; (c) respect law and order, and (d) acquire knowledge of a variety of civic principles and of the UAE state structure (Al-Maamari, 2013).

A recent national document on the UAE civic education curriculum (United Arab Emirates, Ministry of Education, 2013) reiterated the general goals of education cited in the strategic plan, notably that the learner would (a) demonstrate her/his national identity and belonging to UAE as a Muslim Arab society and be aware of its traditions and customs, which she/he would observe in daily life; (b) recognize citizenship based on feelings of love for the homeland and obedience to UAE leaders; and (c) uphold commendable ethical values. These goals are reflected in the school books, which stress the cultural identity of the state and its Arab Islamic heritage without any notable reference to Western democracy (Faour, 2013).

Civic and citizenship education targets Emiratis only. It is offered in public schools from kindergarten to 12th grade and focuses on morals and patriotism. For example, one course is entitled "Emirates: My Homeland." The topics in social studies, history, geography, Arabic language, and Islamic education have titles such as "My Large Family," "My Lovely Emirates," "Let's Work Together," and "My Duties Toward Neighbors." Highlighted in these textbooks are the civic principles of social responsibility, self-reliance, ethical behavior, and volunteering and community service in social organizations (Al-Maamari, 2012).

Good citizens in the UAE are expected to demonstrate loyalty to the ruling family and the state through a variety of actions, such as conformity with customs and traditions in dress and social behavior, demonstrations of pride in the history of the country and the achievements of its rulers, and participation in the annual celebrations of national unity. They should also appreciate the benefits and rewards that the rulers hand to them (Al-Maamari, 2013).

Civic education books do not address the Universal Declaration of Human Rights. Rather, they introduce citizens' rights and obligations as stipulated in their constitutions or statutes, for example, the rights of the citizen; the rights of the family; the rights of siblings in Islam; the rights to residency, education, health, security, and work; and the obligation to show respect for others' opinions (Faour, 2013). In practice, basic human rights, such as freedom of expression, are frequently violated by the state (Freedom House, 2015). Human Rights Watch described how in March 2011 the UAE government cracked down on 132 Emirati critics who had requested full election by universal suffrage for the Federal National Council. They were accused of "insulting" the UAE rulers (Khaled, 2013). Recently, the

UAE has legislated against perceived cybercrime, limiting Internet activity and prohibiting criticism of government officials or advocacy for democratic reform (Khaled, 2013).

In public school classrooms, political and social issues, such as expatriate labor, are not discussed. Social studies teachers are ill-prepared to facilitate such discussions in civic education classes. This has contributed to deficiencies in the knowledge of UAE history and government among Emirati high school students. When asked about the reasons for their deficient knowledge in civics, students indicated their disinterest in the subject, which the education system considers to be less important than mathematics and sciences. Students also disliked the rote learning method used in civics, and they referred to the scarcity of co-curricular and extracurricular activities that would make the subject more interesting and relevant to their lives. Activities that accompany civic education aim to raise patriotic feelings and awareness of national identity such as celebrating the national unity day and participating in Emirati cultural expressions—folk dancing, local songs, and poetry (Al-Maamari, 2013).

The Arab uprisings did not reach the UAE, but the instability and violent strife that other countries experienced in the aftermath raised serious concerns in the UAE. Both political leaders and citizens were worried about the impact of the Arab Spring on their own country. In a recent survey of Emirati youth aged 18–24, one third believed that "democracy will not work in the region" (i.e., the Arab region), and 24% were unsure of their opinions. But the overwhelming majority of the youth (71%) had confidence in their government's ability to tackle the growing influence of the terrorist organization ISIS (Arab Youth Survey, 2015).

Segregation and Ranking of Immigrants

Thousands of immigrant workers enjoy a much higher standard of living than they had in their home countries, but a number of issues related to social justice cannot be overlooked. The plight of numerous immigrant workers in the UAE has been documented for many years. They are segregated and placed in a rigid system of social hierarchy. At the top are the locals, who own everything with their oil money. Except in the "free zones," only nationals can start a business without an Emirati partner, or get a work permit without a local sponsor. Next on the hierarchy come the Western foreigners who make double the salaries they made at home. Beneath them are the Arab immigrants—Egyptians, Palestinians, and Lebanese. The unskilled Asians and Africans—Pakistanis, Indians, Indonesians, Ethiopians—are at the base of the pyramid (Abdul-Ahad, 2008).

Many expatriate contract workers from Asia and Africa are subject to a wide range of injustices, including unpaid wages, confiscation of passports, physical abuse, and forced labor. An October 2014 Human Rights Watch report documented abuses against domestic workers in the UAE, including unpaid wages, excessive workloads, food deprivation, lack of rest periods, and confinement in the workplace. Domestic workers also reported physical or sexual abuse and forced labor, including in situations of trafficking. The *kafala* (local sponsor) system restricts most workers from moving to a new job before their contracts end unless they obtain their employer's consent, putting many workers in abusive situations. Many migrant workers feel intense financial pressure, not only to support their families at home but also to pay off huge debts to recruitment agencies (International Trade Union

Confederation, 2014). Labor strikes or complaints by expatriate workers are not welcome, and troublemakers are deported immediately. The view is that foreigners are supposed to be "polite" and respectful of these rules and otherwise should depart.

Citizenship Amid Multiple Nationalities and Cultures

The UAE government has been promoting national identity through various means, including education. This policy has been more forcefully pushed since the failures of the popular uprisings in other Arab countries. But pursuing such a policy when citizens comprise a tiny minority in a multinational society undergoing rapid social and economic transformation is a cause for concern. Inequality between citizens and immigrants with regard to several public services and civic rights and violation of some of the basic human rights of immigrants from the lower socioeconomic class pose a threat to political stability.

Educational Consequences for Immigrants. The concept of citizenship is based on the key principles of equality, freedom, social justice, and human rights. Educating young Emiratis to become zealous nationalist citizens who are attached only to their local culture and narrow national interests without caring about the other cultures in their society is a recipe for future conflict and instability. Further compounding this problem is the fact that about 40% of schools in the UAE are private, and they teach different international curricula with different approaches to citizenship. Thus students in private schools, both Emiratis and expatriates, are not exposed to the same notions of citizenship and social justice as the Emirati students in public schools (Al-Maamari, 2013).

Of course, immigrant workers who are prohibited from bringing their families to the UAE are thereby deprived of the option of educating their children there. This is a case of extreme exclusion in education. And the immigrants' children who are educated in separate schools rather than together with citizens' children, despite the likely higher quality of education in the schools for noncitizens, represent another example of exclusion in education. While immigrant children from affluent families go to high-quality private schools that provide a better education than the public schools, the immigrants' lack of access to public education is an example of social injustice.

Reconceptualization of Education to Redress Injustice

In Arab countries, the quest for social justice in education for immigrant students is a long and difficult journey. In countries such as Jordan and Lebanon, conceptualization of social justice in relation to migrants is constrained by rising dire economic problems and vulnerability of the political systems. This environment reduces the scope of social justice to the fulfillment of basic human needs—personal safety, housing, food, basic health care—in addition to education and employment. Provision of these needs is far beyond the means of these two countries, which are already desperately calling for increased external assistance. However, even if enough funds and qualified human resources were available to provide for these needs, the schism and daily disputes between citizens and forced migrants (displaced people and refugees) is likely to endure.

In the public schools of Jordan and Lebanon, the first and foremost challenge is to create space for the huge numbers of new students before offering them any kind of education, regardless of its quality. But these schools must also be innovative in offering equal opportunities to immigrant children regardless of their legal status and whether their parents are displaced people, refugees, or temporary workers. It is equally challenging for teachers to provide a positive, inclusive learning environment based on respect for different social classes and ethnic, national, and religious groups when these groups are hostile and resentful of each other in the larger society. Nevertheless, the educators' task is not impossible, because immigrants in both Jordan and Lebanon publicly state that they do not wish to be assimilated into their host nations and that their stays will end once they can return to their home countries.

The social justice path for the UAE is different. It is a rich country that is being built by expatriates who, in various domains, are not treated equally to citizens. Expatriate employees know that their relationship with Emirati employers is contractual, temporary, and conditional. To expatriates, the UAE is like a work site that one goes to for as long as the employer desires, with the main goal of saving as much as one can. Home and homeland, where expatriates' citizenship rights are respected, are external to that site. Rulers as well as citizens insist on maintaining the status quo, keeping a vigilant eye on any attempts by expatriates to change the nature of the relationship. Under these circumstances, there is no room for equality between citizens and residents and no opportunity for migrants to become integrated into the local society.

The UAE's population is one of multiple nations, yet segregated between citizens and resident migrants. Social injustice can be addressed by compensating the disadvantaged groups and by respecting their basic human rights in policy and practice—notably in schooling. From a social justice and human rights perspective, public schools should be accessible to both citizens and immigrants, and civic education should endorse an inclusive, multicultural approach.

In the Arab world in general, the emphasis on patriotism and national identity in citizenship education is not conducive to the promotion of social justice. In the aftermath of the Arab Spring, with its calls for freedom, equality, and justice—and in the presence of millions of immigrants in different Arab countries—the need for new concepts of citizenship that supersede short-term national interests becomes urgent. As increasing numbers of people engage in economic and cultural relationships across borders of sovereign states, concepts of transnational and global belonging become more relevant than local citizenship. One way that educators can respond to this change is by introducing global citizenship education, an approach that can redress some of the injustices found in each of the Arab countries. Global citizenship education is inclusive, targeting the development of the full potential of all students, citizens and migrants alike. Its aim is to empower learners to integrate local and global activities in order to tackle and solve national as well as global issues and partake proactively in making the world more just, safe, tolerant, and sustainable. Global citizenship education requires holistic education reform, which Arab governments have either avoided or not considered seriously.

Various stakeholders—teachers, principals, parents, students, private-sector organizations, NGOs, and community leaders—need to collaborate in pushing forward an agenda of global citizenship education that includes a social justice perspective. According to that perspective, schools should develop students' skills of independent and creative thinking, problem solving, self-confidence, effective communication, collaboration, dialogue, and analysis and monitoring of change processes. Schools should create an interactive, inclusive climate based on respect for universal values such as peace, human rights, democracy, justice, nondiscrimination, diversity, and tolerance. In such a school climate, both citizen and migrant students are exposed to vast opportunities to participate in decision-making processes at school and in the local community, and on national and global issues. This process generates globally responsible citizens who are able to take civic action to enhance social justice and influence unfolding events for the greater good.

Such a school climate requires good governance and qualified teachers—components that are uncommon in Arab public schools. Teachers strongly contribute to the development and nurturing of their students' skills and values, including those related to global citizenship and social justice. Transparent and accountable leaders in schools create a democratic culture that is conducive to fostering universal values such as social justice and diversity.

Equally important in the aftermath of the Arab Spring and the rise of Islamic militant extremism is the development of pro-democratic interpretations of Islam, which is a strong bond among the Arab societies. Such interpretations espouse universal human rights, including freedom of faith, respect for diversity, social justice, and equality of citizens and immigrants. Most Muslim Arabs believe in Islam's absolute truth and power to redeem them of their weaknesses and anomalies. Thus, they are vulnerable to various religious interpretations, including those that foster hatred and antagonism, not only toward other religions but also toward their fellow Muslims who are in disagreement. Advocates of pro-democratic interpretations of Islam have to be brave enough to withstand death threats while aggressively speaking out for their ideas in public. Such interpretations provide a necessary ideological umbrella for any serious reform of Islamic education, as well as for civics courses in Arab public schools. The road to social justice in education in the Arab world will be long and difficult, fraught with danger and serious risks of failure. But the effort will pay high dividends sooner or later for the welfare and prosperity of Arab societies.

Note

An earlier version of this chapter was presented in April 2015, at the annual meeting of the American Educational Research Association, in Chicago, Illinois.

References

Abdul-Ahad, G. (2008, October 8). We need slaves to build monuments. *The Guardian*. Retrieved from http://www.guardian.co.uk/world/2008/oct/08/middleeast.construction

Akar, B. (2012). Teaching for citizenship in Lebanon: Teachers talk about the civics classroom. *Teaching and Teacher Education, 28*(3), 470–480.

Al-Abed, O. (2004, February). *Palestinian refugees in Jordan*. Retrieved from http://www
.forcedmigration.org/research-resources/expert-guides/palestinian-refugees-in-jordan

Al-Maamari, S. (2012). *Tarbiyat Almuatana fi Dowlat Alimarat Alarabiya Almuttahida* [Education
for citizenship in the UAE]. Background paper commissioned by Carnegie Middle East Center,
Beirut, Lebanon.

Al-Maamari, S. (2013). Promoting national identity in a multicultural society: The case of UAE
citizenship education. In M. Faour & S. Abourjaili (Eds.), *Executive summaries of the commissioned background papers* (pp. 30–32). Beirut, Lebanon: Carnegie Middle East Center.

Arab Youth Survey. (2015). *Infographics*. Retrieved from http://www.arabyouthsurvey.com/media/

Asyraf, H. A. R., Wan Ibrahim, W. A., & Nooraihan, A. (2012). Islamic concept of social justice in the
twentieth century. *Advances in Natural and Applied Sciences, 6*(8), 1423–1427.

Azar, M. (2014). *Bringing learning to Syrian refugee children in Lebanon*. Retrieved from http://www
.unicef.org/infobycountry/lebanon_71753.html

Banks, J. A. (2006). *Race, culture and education: The selected works of James A. Banks*. London:
Routledge.

Banks, J. A. (2011). Educating citizens in diverse societies. *Intercultural Education, 22*(4), 243–251.

Banks, J. A. (2014). *The quest for justice through civic education in multicultural nations: A proposal for
an AERA presidential session*, p. 1.

Brand, L. A. (2010). National narratives and migration: Discursive strategies of inclusion and
exclusion in Jordan and Lebanon. *International Migration Review, 44*(1), 78–110.

Chaaban, J., Ghattas, H., Habib, R., Hanafi, S., Sahyoun, N, Salti, N. . . . Naamani, N. (2010). *Socioeconomic survey of Palestinian refugees in Lebanon*. Beirut, Lebanon: American University of
Beirut and United Nations Relief and Works Agency for Palestine Refugees in the Near East.

Demoqrati. (2015). ʻAn al-barnamaj [About the program]. Retrieved from http://www.demoqrati
.jo/about.aspx

El Amine, A., & Abou Chedid, K. (2008). Education and citizenship in Lebanon: An overview of
survey results. In *Education and citizenship: Concepts, attitudes, skills and actions* (pp. 23–42).
Beirut, Lebanon: United Nations Development Programme.

Faour, M. (1993). *The Arab world after Desert Storm*. Washington, DC: United States Institute of
Peace.

Faour, M. (2013, May). *A review of citizenship education in Arab nations* (The Carnegie Papers).
Washington, DC: Carnegie Middle East Center, Carnegie Endowment for International Peace.

Faour, M., & Muasher, M. (2011, October). *Education for citizenship in the Arab world: Key to
the future* (The Carnegie Papers). Washington, DC: Carnegie Middle East Center, Carnegie
Endowment for International Peace.

Francis, A. (2015, September 21). *Jordan's refugee crisis* (The Carnegie Papers). Washington, DC:
Carnegie Middle East Center, Carnegie Endowment for International Peace.

Frayha, N. (2012). *Alislah Attarbawi Wattarbiya Almuwatiniyya fil Alam Alarabi: Alhala Allubnaniya*
[Education reform and citizenship education in the Arab world: The case of Lebanon].
Background paper commissioned by Carnegie Middle East Center. Beirut, Lebanon.

Freedom House. (2015). *Freedom in the world 2015*. Retrieved from https://freedomhouse.org/sites/
default/files/01152015_FIW_2015_final.pdf

Gabbay, S. M. (2014). The status of Palestinians in Jordan and the anomaly of holding a
Jordanian passport. *Journal of Political Sciences and Public Affairs, 2*(1). Retrieved from
http://dx.doi.org/10.4172/2332-0761.1000113

Harris, M. (2015, February). *Jordan's youth after the Arab Spring*. Sidney, Australia: Lowy
Institute for International Policy. Retrieved from http://www.lowyinstitute.org/publications/
jordans-youth-after-arab-spring

Hudson, M. C. (1985). *The precarious republic: Political modernization in Lebanon.* Boulder, CO: Westview.

Human Rights Watch. (2014, October 22). *"I already bought you": Abuse and exploitation of female migrant domestic workers in the United Arab Emirates.* Retrieved from https://www .hrw.org/report/2014/10/22/i-already-bought-you/abuse-and-exploitation-female-migrant-domestic-workers-united

Hytten, K., & Bettez, S. C. (2011). Understanding education for social justice. *Educational Foundations, 25*(1–2), 7–24.

Identity Center. (2014). *Social justice in Jordan.* Retrieved from http://www.identity-center.org/sites/ default/files/Social%20Justice%20in%20Jordan_0.pdf

International Trade Union Confederation. (2014, November 23). *Gulf countries: Increase migrant worker protection* (Gulf, Asian labor ministers at 3rd Abu Dhabi dialogue). Brussels, Belgium: Author. Retrieved from http://www.ituc-csi.org/gulf-countries-increase-migrant?lang=en

Keyt, D. (1991). Aristotle's theory of distributive justice. In D. Keyt & F. D. Miller, Jr. (Eds.), *A companion to Aristotle's politics* (pp. 238–78). Oxford, UK: Blackwell.

Khaled, J. (2013, January 16). *The plight of migrant workers in the Gulf.* Retrieved from https://www .opencanada.org/features/the-plight-of-migrant-workers-in-the-gulf/

Kubow, P. K., & Kreishan, L. (2014). Citizenship in a hybrid state: Civic curriculum in Jordan's education reform for knowledge economy era. *Middle Eastern & African Journal of Educational Research, 13,* 4–20.

Lebanon Ministry of Education and Higher Education. (1997). *Manhaj Maddat Attarbiya Alwataniya Wattanshia Almadaniya* [Curriculum of the subject national education and civic upbringing]. Beirut, Lebanon: Educational Center for Research and Development.

Mackey, S. (2006). *Lebanon: A house divided.* New York: W. W. Norton.

Mansour, Y. (2014, December 22). Rentier states. *Jordan Times.* Retrieved from http://www .jordantimes.com/opinion/yusuf-mansur/rentier-states-0

MercyCorps. (2015). *Quick facts: What you need to know about the Syria crisis.* Retrieved from https://www.mercycorps.org/articles/turkey-iraq-jordan-lebanon-syria/quick-facts-what-you -need-know-about-syria-crisis

Parkinson, S. E. (2014, September 7). *Educational aftershocks for Syrian refugees in Lebanon.* Retrieved from http://www.merip.org/educational-aftershocks-syrian-refugees-lebanon

Salibi, K. (1990). *A house of many mansions: The history of Lebanon reconsidered.* Oakland, CA: University of California Press.

Save the Children Federation. (2015). *Jordan: What we do: Humanitarian response.* Retrieved from https://jordan.savethechildren.net/what-we-do/humanitarian-response

Shuayb, M. (2014, May 14). *A lost generation? Education opportunities for Syrian refugee children in Lebanon.* Retrieved from http://www.rsc.ox.ac.uk/events/a-lost-generation-education-opportunities-for-syrian-refugee-children-in-lebanon

Shultz, L., & Abdi, A. A. (2008). A human rights and global citizenship perspective. In *Education for social justice* (pp. 7–11). Ottawa: Canadian Teachers Federation.

Touq, M. (2012). *Attarbiya Almuwatiniya fi AlUrdun wa Filasteen* [Citizenship education in Jordan and Palestine]. Background paper commissioned by Carnegie Middle East Center, Beirut, Lebanon.

Touq, M. (2013). Citizenship education in Jordan: Harmony between curriculum and educational practices? In M. Faour & S. Abourjaili (Eds.), *Executive summaries of the commissioned background papers* (pp. 12–14). Beirut, Lebanon: Carnegie Middle East Center.

UNESCO. (2014). *Emergency education response to Syrian refugees in Jordan.* Retrieved from http://www.unesco.org/new/en/amman/education/technical-vocational-education-training/emergency-education-response-to-syrian-refugees-in-jordan/

UN High Commissioner for Refugees. (2015a). *2015 UNHCR country operations profile—Jordan.* Retrieved from http://www.unhcr.org/cgi-bin/texis/vtx/page?page=49e486566&submit=GO

UN High Commissioner for Refugees. (2015b). *United Nations Security Council (7592nd Meeting). Briefing on the humanitarian situation in Syria, Remarks by António Guterres, United Nations High Commissioner for Refugees, New York, 21 December 2015.* Retrieved from http://www.unhcr.org/567861459.html

UN High Commissioner for Refugees. (2015c). *2015 UNHCR country operations profile—Lebanon.* Retrieved from http://www.unhcr.org/cgi-bin/texis/vtx/page?page=49e486676&submit=GO

United Arab Emirates, Ministry of Education. (2013, January). *Alwathiqa alwataniya li manhaj attarbiya alwataniya littaaleem alaam walkhas* [The national document for the national education curriculum in public and private education in the United Arab Emirates]. Retrieved from https://www.moe.gov.ae/Arabic/Docs/Curriculum/tarbeya.pdf

United Nations. (1948). *The Universal Declaration of Human Rights.* Retrieved from www.un.org/en/documents/udhr/index.shtml

United Nations Department of Economic and Social Affairs, Population Division. (2013). *International migration wallchart 2013.* Retrieved from http://www.un.org/en/development/desa/population/migration/publications/wallchart/index.shtml

United Nations Relief and Works Agency for Palestine Refugees in the Near East. (2015). *Where we work.* Retrieved from http://www.unrwa.org/where-we-work

World Bank. (2013). *Data—Arab World.* Retrieved from http://data.worldbank.org/region/ARB

Young, I. M. (1990). *Justice and the politics of difference.* Princeton, NJ: Princeton University Press.

Chapter 14

Transforming the Civics Curriculum in Lebanon for Learning Active Citizenship

BASSEL AKAR

Notre Dame University, Louaize

Since its independence in 1943, the Republic of Lebanon's government officials have consistently turned to education for citizenship as a driver for social cohesion in a country with 18 official religious sects and scores of political parties. Social and political turning points in Lebanon triggered each of the three national education reforms in 1946, 1971, and 1997, respectively. Moreover, each of the reforms transformed the vision of the ideal citizen through the curricular subjects for citizenship—civics, history, and geography. Identity, for example, was formulated primarily as "Lebanese" for the first national curriculum after independence (1946), then nearly replaced with the Arab identity in 1971 during the rise of Arab nationalism, and later consolidated as Lebanese and Arab in the 1997 curriculum that followed the 1975–1990 civil war (Frayha, 2004).[1] In addition, the post–civil war 1997 national curriculum (Ministry of Education and Higher Education, 1997b) emphasizes a citizenship for social cohesion, democratic participation, and conflict transformation. However, studies examining the approaches of learning for active citizenship in schools consistently suggest that practices of classroom learning and teaching, curricular aims and activities, and assessment undermine an active citizenship grounded in dialogic engagement, critical thinking, and collaboration (Akar, 2012b, 2014; Lebanese Association for Educational Studies, 2003; Shuayb, 2012; U.N. Development Programme, Ministry of Education and Higher Education, & Council for Development and Reconstruction, 2008).

This chapter investigates how a civics teacher in Lebanon reimagined the civics national curriculum to transform the traditional didactic civics classroom into a dialogic, collaborative, and cosmopolitan learning experience. I first describe the type of citizenship envisioned for living in communities of growing diversity and outline pedagogies that best foster this type of citizenship. Two theoretical variables—citizenship and citizenship education—provide the analytical framework for investigating approaches to improving how children learn active citizenship. For the case of Lebanon, I present the aims of education for active citizenship and evidence that shows how practice (e.g., classroom learning) draws children away from any opportunity to behave as active citizens. I then introduce Nadine and her approaches in reformulating lesson plans and facilitating critical pedagogies for an active citizenship that is enhanced through diversity.

Active Citizenship and Citizenship Education

Understanding and developing citizenship—the relationship between individuals and surrounding communities—become increasingly critical as communities become more diverse. To date, the level of diversity of people in communities or, in this case, nation-states around the world is at its highest. At the level of crossing political borders, people have found migration or mobility the most desirable option for accessing better work and study opportunities and safety from war and persecution (Boswell & Geddes, 2011). Within political borders and among people of the same national citizenship status, we see a multitude of religious sects, languages, political parties, and other cultural elements. Unfortunately, differences in values and access among others result in conflicts, including armed conflict. The root of conflict, however, is neither the state of diversity (Banks, 2008) nor movements such as migration and mobility (Castles, 2010). Instead, conflicts and tensions result from the unpreparedness or unwillingness of people and government to celebrate and capitalize on the increasing diversity of cultural elements.

Citizenship education provides individuals and communities with the necessary approaches to enhance standards of living when their social ecology is enriched with a diversity of people from different cultural backgrounds. Through such an educational experience, students would work and learn with peers from different cultural backgrounds when proactively addressing social injustice, empowering vulnerable people, and promoting human rights standards (Banks et al., 2005). Effective learning for citizenship allows individuals "to feel unique as well as unified" (Akar, 2009, p. 47). Moreover, learning for citizenship enables individuals in diverse communities to live cohesively and nonviolently. In other words, citizenship education is about learning to live together (Delors, 1996).

When researching citizenship education, defining the intended form of citizenship provides an analytical framework for examining the effectiveness or at least directions of education policy and practice. In this section, I define "active citizenship" as a desirable form of citizenship grounded in democratic and human rights principles. Furthermore, formal and nonformal education for active citizenship demands an educational experience whereby learners live the approaches to being active citizens.

Active Citizenship

At a most basic level, we can understand citizenship as the relationship between the individual and surrounding communities. Citizenship research typically investigates two dimensions of this relationship: elements and dynamics. Elements of citizenship specify the particular variables that make up the relationship. For example, Marshall (1950) argued that civil, political, and social rights constituted the nature of an individual's freedom to participate and access to basic services. Despite its significant influence on citizenship studies (Hoxsey, 2011), this model has been critiqued as being narrow considering the growing diversity of communities and ongoing struggles of underrepresented groups (Lister, 1997). In an attempt to further develop a relationship based on rights and obligations, Isin and Turner (2002a) introduced three axes that illustrated the (1) extent of inclusion/exclusion, (2) content of stated rights and responsibilities, and (3) depth of thickness/thinness.

For this study, I examined citizenship based on an even broader framework of three interrelated elements: status, feelings, and practice (Osler & Starkey, 2005a). This model allows for a more holistic understanding of people's behaviors and levels of identity and the influences they have on each other. In Lebanon, legal status determines, to a great degree, one's sense of belonging and forms of participation. Lebanese nationals have far more access to civil rights (e.g., health care, education, and voting) than do non-Lebanese and the refugees who make up almost a quarter of the population. Legal status also includes gender status. Lebanese women married to non-Lebanese men cannot pass on their Lebanese citizenship status to their children, who are in turn excluded from access to civil rights.

Heated debates in citizenship studies emerge when defining the dynamics of an idealistic relationship between individuals and their surrounding communities. In traditional citizenship discourse, the community is interpreted as the nation-state, and so debates around who is in service of whom are framed within republican, communitarian, and liberal approaches (Beiner, 1995; Isin & Turner, 2002b, 2007). Extending beyond the political borders of a nation-state, global citizenship situates individuals as citizens of the world (Bîrzéa, 2000; Dill, 2013; Falk, 1993), while cosmopolitan citizenship extends even further to a cosmopolis of humankind grounded in human rights (Banks et al., 2005; Gunesch, 2007; Nussbaum, 1997; Osler, 2010; Osler & Starkey, 2005a). Both supranational approaches celebrate the multiple levels of identities that individuals inherently hold. For this chapter, however, I draw on a slightly less contested view of citizenship as a range of desirable and less desirable feelings and practices.

In a framework of maximal and minimal notions of citizenship, McLaughlin (1992) has argued that a minimal notion entails an identity limited to legal status and practices that merely abide by laws, while the maximal end comprises expressions of multiple identities and critical forms of democratic activities. As a maximal notion of citizenship, active citizenship positions individuals as agents of change (Halualani, 2010) who participate nonviolently and within principles of human rights and democracy (Hoskins, 2006). This evidence-informed description of active citizenship also posits three kinds of "good" citizens in a democratic society, which Westheimer and Kahne (2004) have presented as personally responsible, participatory, and justice-oriented. In addition to the seemingly passive activities of being "personally responsible," such as paying taxes and obeying laws, active citizens protect, examine, and employ the freedoms enshrined in human rights instruments as justice-oriented and participatory citizens. Through nonviolent activities informed by democratic and human rights principles, active citizenship celebrates diversity at individual and collective levels.

Education for Active Citizenship

Alongside an envisioned ideal notion of citizenship, educational practices and designs (e.g., learning, teaching, assessment, curriculum, and learning materials) determine to a great extent the kind of citizenship that, in reality, develops. For instance, single narrative histories (Parker, 2004) and pedagogies that uncritically transfer knowledge (Freire, 1970) would most likely foster a citizenship of a unilateral relationship serving only the state and its regime. In contrast, educational programs stemming from a pragmatist philosophy of education facilitating collaborative and reflexive learning experiences empower learners as practicing citizens (Dewey, 1916/1944) as opposed to citizens-in-waiting (Osler & Starkey, 2005a). Moreover, this democratized approach to education would support student-led and -initiated levels of participation (Hart, 1992), critical pedagogies (Giroux, 1988; ten Dam & Volman, 2004), and human rights education (Osler, 2008; Osler & Starkey, 2010).

Young people learn to be active citizens when they experience practices of active citizenship. Coordinating activities such as field trips, school governance, community service, and play would happen within a children's human rights framework (Verhellen, 2000). This means that learners take on decision-making roles in planning, implementing, and evaluating, rather than solely carrying out assigned tasks (Hart, 1992). Moreover, pedagogies for active citizenship encourage learners to collaboratively challenge and reflect on topical issues (ten Dam & Volman, 2004). Learning activities would also pay special attention to issues regarding vulnerable groups and nurture reflections of multiple identities (Osler, 2011).

Some educational approaches, however, can hinder learning for active citizenship. Civic education or civics is one program that, by design, aims to build in learners a bank of content knowledge about their constitutional rights, functions of government institutions, and responsibilities to the state (Cogan, Morris, & Print, 2002; Pratte, 1988). Although governments prioritize nationalism as a fundamental cohesive agent for inclusion and democratic participation, civics has been found to overemphasize the uncritical acquisition of content knowledge and an exclusive national identity (Akar, 2012a; Osler & Starkey, 2005b; Pratte, 1988). In an international survey, Kerr (2000) found that practices of memorization and limited understandings of citizenship were most commonly reported in civic education programs. Returning to an active-passive view of citizenship, Lawton (2000) found that students learning about the "responsibilities of a good citizen" (p. 11) and basic information about government institutions were passive and complying, while learners became active citizens by practicing democratic principles and critically examining conflicts and topical issues.

The Parameters of Civics for Active Citizenship in Lebanon

Lebanon hosts a diversity of confessional identities and cultural features from Lebanese and non-Lebanese people. The government of Lebanon identifies its 4 million Lebanese residing within the nation-state under a framework of 18 official religious sects, or sects that are eligible for political representation. The country also houses more than 100 registered political parties, 20 of which are active (Salamey, 2013). Lebanon recognizes Arabic, English, and French as main languages. With Arabic as the official state language, learning English and French languages and learning science and math in either English or French are compulsory in the national curriculum. The significant Lebanese diaspora, calculated at 4.5 million yet sometimes estimated between 6 and 8 million (Hourani, Haddad, & Sfeir, 2011), further diversifies levels of identities through the hyphenated citizenship status of families residing in and outside Lebanon. The population of people residing in Lebanon who do not hold Lebanese citizenship status includes an estimated 1.1 million registered Syrian refugees (U.N. High Commissioner for Refugees, 2015), 450,000 registered Palestinian refugees (U.N. Relief and Works Agency for Palestine Refugees in the Near East, 2014), 250,000 domestic women workers (International Labour Organization, 2015), and 200,000 Lebanese women who cannot pass on their citizenship to their children because they are married to non-Lebanese men (Alabaster, 2011).

Social scientists have long described the diversity of Lebanon as a special trait using buoyant terms such as *mosaic* (e.g., Barakat, 1973; Makhoul, Kabakian-Khasholian, El-Khoury, & El-Kak, 2013), despite social injustices and armed conflicts among religious sects and political parties. Probably the most significant and most cited civil wars took place during 1860–1864, 1958, and 1975–1990 (Khalaf, 2002; Mattar, 2007). Armed struggles continuing in the 21st century signify unresolved grievances and deep-rooted sectarian tensions (Zakharia, 2011). The diversity of religious sects and confessional groups in Lebanon is continuously linked to the roots of conflicts. Consequently, approaches to nationalism frame the citizenship education curriculum in Lebanon with the intention to create a sense of solidarity through a unifying national and pan-national identity.

The government of Lebanon shows a clear commitment to democracy, human rights instruments, social justice, and nonviolence through the national curriculum. In the national curriculum, the government has designated civics, history, and geography as the compulsory, primary subjects for citizenship education across all 12 grade levels. Moreover, only these three subjects have their textbooks and official exams prepared in Arabic, while math and sciences are instructed in English and French. Civics, officially known as "National and Civic Education" (in Arabic, "Tarbiya wataniyya wa tanshi'a madaniyya"), has a more explicit mandate toward constructing the ideal citizen than history and geography. The nine main aims of the national civics curriculum (see Table 1) encourage democratic

Table 1. Nine Main Aims of National and Civic Education in the National Curriculum

Aim
1. To prepare the student morally in harmony with the humanistic values in his or her community and country.
2. To introduce the student to the vocational world and to build in him or her a spirit for work and appreciation for workers in different fields.
3. To prepare the student, in a civil sense, to enable him or her to contribute to world development in harmony with the spirit of modernity.
4. To teach the student how to critique, debate, and accept the other and to solve conflicts with his or her peers through a spirit of peace, justice, and equality.
5. To build a social spirit so that the student feels that he or she is part of a larger community that is enriched with a diversity of ideas.
6. To raise the standards of the student's cultural, social, political, and economic contributions and encourage his or her free participation in civil life.
7. To promote the student's devotion/loyalty to his or her Lebanese identity, land, and country through a cohesive and unifying democratic framework.
8. To raise awareness of the student's Arab identity and his or her loyalty to it and a sense of Arab belonging to it that is open to the whole world.
9. To promote awareness of the student's humanity through close relationships with his or her fellow humans regardless of gender, color, religion, language, culture, and any other differences.

Note. The original text is in Arabic and gendered to males. The translation is now gender-neutral. From Akar, 2012b. Adapted from Ministry of Education and Higher Education (Lebanon), 1997a, p. 714. Translated from the Arabic by B. Akar.

practices that value diversity and active participation across a range of identities, namely, at global, regional, and national levels. This notion of citizenship appears to lean toward what McLaughlin (1992) has described as a maximal one. The aims could, however, further encourage reflections on more complex levels of identity in Lebanon, including the 18 official religious sects, scores of political parties, dual citizenship, and non-Lebanese citizenship status. As the curriculum stands, the value of diversity in Lebanon remains within the domain of a Lebanese and Arab rhetoric, which further reinforces the preamble of the Lebanese Constitution, which declares that Lebanon is for all Lebanese.

After the 1975–1990 civil war, the Education Reform Plan of 1994 revised the 1969/1971 national curriculum. Civics teachers hired by the Center for Educational Research and Development—the Ministry of Education and Higher Education's agency for curriculum development—wrote the civics textbooks for the 12 grade levels. Within a short time frame, a content-based series of civics textbooks was produced. Each grade-level textbook comprises 32 lessons, one for each hour of the 32 academic calendar weeks. The official government exams for the Lebanese program or national curriculum are administered after Grades 9 and 12 for the Lebanese Baccalaureate I and II, respectively. These exams include the national civics program of study, though the quotient is quite low compared with science and math. All public schools and an estimated 90% of students in the private sector follow the Lebanese baccalaureate track. Non-Lebanese programs are required by law to provide formal citizenship education but are not bound to the national curriculum, its textbooks, and the official exam. This chapter focuses on civics in the Lebanese baccalaureate program, which rests within a complex set of barriers of pedagogy and diversity.

The Civics Classroom: Pedagogy and Diversity

The rhetoric of education policy envisions a citizen who values the diversity of ideas and is critically engaged in resolving conflict and promoting equal opportunities. However, didactic traditions of learning and a narrow understanding of diversity seem to undermine the educational aims of the Lebanese civics program.

Civics textbooks, for example, present ideals with no opportunities for critical inquiry into topical issues (Lebanese Association for Educational Studies, 2003; Shuayb, 2015; Zoreik, 2000). Approaches to learning and teaching the civics program have also, by and large, been confined within traditional pedagogies of memorization to recite textbook content for exams (Akar, 2014; Shuayb, 2012; U.N. Development Programme et al., 2008). Many teachers even claim to avoid classroom dialogues and discussions because of fear of conflicts among students (Akar, 2012b; Zakharia, 2011). The prescriptive nature of the content in civics textbooks and long-established pedagogical traditions of memorization are among many factors that have stigmatized the learning of civics as rigid, narrow, and uncritical. Learners, therefore, have become pedagogically marginalized because they can no longer exercise freedoms in the classroom. The dominant tradition of uncritically reciting content information solely on an ideal notion of citizenship denies children basic human rights enshrined in the legally binding U.N. Convention on the Rights of the Child, namely, (1) the freedom of expression that involves seeking, receiving, and imparting information (United Nations, 1989, Article 13) and (2) "access to information and material from a diversity of national and international sources" (Article 17). Students' and teachers' self-reports on classroom pedagogies suggest that the civic education program may indeed be doing more harm than good.

The role of diversity seems to influence what and how young people learn for active citizenship inside the civics classroom in Lebanon at two interrelated levels: classroom and curriculum. A classroom with students from different backgrounds, abilities, and experiences provides an ideal environment to learn to live together. However, classrooms in sites affected by armed conflict are mostly homogeneous, whether intentionally, as in Bosnia and Herzegovina (Hromadžić, 2008), or by virtue of geographically divided communities, as in Northern Ireland (Hayes & McAllister, 2009). Lebanon, like Northern Ireland, is a site of sectarian demography where schools are culturally homogeneous by virtue of being located in communities defined by certain religious sects. Sectarian diversity in schools, however, is far more common in the urban areas of major cosmopolitan cities such as Beirut and Byblos. Moreover, many Lebanese students carry dual nationalities; speak languages other than Arabic, English, or French; and are loyal to one of scores of political parties. With the increasing number of refugees from Syria, schools are receiving a level of diversity that goes beyond Lebanon's political borders.

Curriculum and education policy can embrace, distort, or avoid diversity. Regardless of the explicit value about diversity of ideas in the social sphere (see Aim 5 in Table 1), approaches to nationalism in writing education policy have managed to concentrate primarily on Lebanese and Arab identities in the hope of fostering social cohesion. In practice, teachers discourage or avoid reflections of political and religious identities because they fear conflicts and tensions they would then need to manage (Akar, 2012b; Zakharia, 2011). It appears through policy and practice that celebrating the diversity of political, religious, and national identities is regarded as a threat to social cohesion. Consequently, the limited or few opportunities that young people have to reflect on other communities within and beyond their social ecology restrict their development of the global and cosmopolitan dimensions of active citizenship.

Maximizing this evidently narrow and passive civics curriculum would require expanding its scope to supranational and cultural levels of identity, controversial issues, and critical pedagogies, and empowering young people as citizens while learning in the classroom. Such a reform demands gradual changes at the institutional, cultural, and policy levels. This chapter explores a particular type of reform found at the bottom, grassroots level. In this chapter, I present one civics teacher's initiatives to break out of a civics program hindered by didactic traditions of learning and narrow approaches to diversity. This teacher reimagined the civics curriculum as one that encourages young people to collaboratively and critically question issues of justice and widen their positions as citizens of the world. Finding and learning from such teachers is essential to realizing new visions of learning for active citizenship in didactic, authoritarian-like curriculum cultures.

Methodology

In this methodology section, I describe the procedures of finding and selecting a teacher who appeared to demonstrate successful approaches in transforming a didactic-based civics classroom into one that allowed learners to practice an active form of citizenship inside the classroom. I also explain the qualitative methods of investigating this teacher's approaches through interviews and classroom observations.

Sample

Finding exemplary civics teachers required processes of screening interview databases and snowball sampling or networking. Since 2006, I have gathered interview transcriptions from a total of 89 civics teachers across all six governorates in Lebanon ($n = 52$ from the private sector, $n = 32$ from the public sector, $n = 5$ from U.N. Relief and Works Agency for Palestine Refugees in the Near East schools) from previous education research and development projects. I screened this database of interview transcriptions, searching for evidence of shifting from traditions of memorization to engaging learners in collaborative, dialogic, and reflexive activities that critically inquire and explore topical issues. From this sample, I found two teachers who reported creative approaches under challenging learning contexts. Unfortunately, one was from the Bekaa governorate, and due to safety issues, I chose not to travel there. So, I selected only one teacher from this database for a follow-up interview.

For the second phase, I relied on snowball sampling to identify civics teachers to interview. Snowballing helps researchers identify atypical samples by relying on connections and networks. I first drew up a list of civil society organizations, research centers, and project managers and trainers who had worked with civics teachers either through action research or professional development projects. I communicated with these individuals through e-mail, phone calls, and face-to-face conversations, inquiring about exceptional civics teachers they had observed. To include the public sector, I requested the Ministry of Education and Higher Education's permission to access public schools. Unfortunately, the ministry rejected the request.

From these two phases, eight teachers were identified and contacted; seven responded. Each of the seven received a Participant Information Sheet, which summarized the objective of the study, guaranteed anonymity, and requested consent to participate. Although permission to access public schools was denied, contacts through civil society led me to three public school civics teachers who agreed to be interviewed. The remaining four were from the private sector. All participating teachers were teaching the Lebanese civics program.

Procedure

Semistructured interviews with private school teachers took place on school grounds, while those with public school teachers took place off-campus in a coffee shop or at home. Conversations lasted 45 to 60 minutes. Teachers spoke in Arabic and English. The interviews were audio recorded. The open-ended questions were organized as follows:

1. Backgrounds and profiles

   1.a. Tell me a little bit about how long you've been teaching civics and the training you received.

   1.b. Describe your students. What do they have in common? How are they different from each other?

2. Successful activities

   2.a. Describe what you consider to have been the most successful lesson.
   2.b. What was difficult about it?
   2.c. Explain how you planned for it.

3. Learner responses

   3.a. How have learners responded to the lessons you have facilitated?
   3.b. What have you observed students struggling with the most, and have you responded?

From the seven interviews, three teachers reported pedagogies that appeared to foster active citizenship. This chapter examines in depth the approaches, rationales, and supporting factors of one teacher, Nadine, who was teaching in a private school in Saida (or Sidon), a main city of the South Lebanon governorate. Nadine granted me permission to use her real name. I was fortunate enough to be invited to observe her 10th grade civics class after our first interview. Following the 50-minute lesson, we discussed the classroom activities for another 40 minutes. The conversation further examined what Nadine thought went well and what she found challenging. She also asked me to give feedback as a peer teacher. Again, Nadine invited me to return six weeks later to observe her class during the third and final day of the performance task—creating an awareness-raising poster on child soldiers. During that second observation, I was able to walk around the groups, observe them at work, and ask them questions about their posters. Afterward, while Nadine and I talked about the class session, we were joined by the secondary school academic director, who was eager to talk about the school's curricular reforms. All interviews and classroom sessions were audio recorded. A research assistant transcribed and translated all recordings into English text. I revised all transcripts for accuracy.

In examining Nadine's approaches to teaching for active citizenship, I first present her teaching background and the student makeup of the 10th grade class. I then describe the activities Nadine facilitated, how she planned them, and how she assessed students' learning. By relating her practices to indicators of education for active citizenship, I critically review what appeared to have fostered and challenged learning for active citizenship.

Nadine, the Students, and the School Leaders

Nadine teaches civics and sociology in a private school in the South Lebanon governorate. Her qualifications include a range of formal and informal training. She completed her *licence* (bachelor's degree) in sociology and then pursued a *diplôme d'études avancées* (master's in community service and local development). After completing all the taught coursework, Nadine withdrew from the graduate program before writing her thesis to focus on her teaching career. Although she did not formally study for a written teaching qualification, she spent about a year observing Grade 5 civics and geography classrooms at the school in which she currently works.

For the 2002–2003 academic year, the school hired her as a full-time history, geography, and civics teacher for Grades 4, 5, and 6. The school at the time only reached to the sixth grade, but with every year that passed a grade was added, and Nadine was asked to teach higher grade levels. Once the school made all 12 grade levels available, the administration assigned her the civics classes for Grades 8 to 12 and the sociology classes for Grade 11, which she continued to teach in the 2014–2015 academic year.

The school is situated in a predominantly Sunni Muslim district. Nadine described her classes as very diverse at many levels. Students were from distant communities including rural areas and other religious denominations. Only one student was non-Lebanese, a Syrian girl whose family fled the conflict in Syria. She only knew Arabic, which meant that she would face difficulties adjusting in a trilingual school. Nonetheless, Nadine remembered how friendly the students were with her. The classes also had learners across a wide range of cognitive abilities. Moreover, at this school, students with special needs are only mainstreamed in civics, history, and geography classes. In this particular 10th grade class, although all 15 students were Muslim, they came from various areas of Saida and belonged to different political loyalties. Table 2 shows the distribution of gender, place of residence, religious sect, and political party. Under "Political Party," the party names follow their allegiance to either "March 8" or "March 14," the two competing alliances of the most active political parties in Lebanon. The "March 8" alliance (e.g., Free Patriotic Movement, Hezbollah, Amal Movement) was formed to show support for relations with Syria after tens of thousands protested in Martyrs' Square (Beirut, February 21, 2005) demanding that the Syrian government take responsibility for the assassination of Rafik El Hariri and remove all Syrian troops from Lebanon. One month after the assassination, "March 14" (e.g., Future Movement, Lebanese Forces, Kataeb Party) was formed and maintained resistance to Syrian involvement in government affairs in Lebanon.

While Grades 9 and 12 still follow traditional pedagogies of rote learning for the official exams, the principal and academic director have facilitated activities that supported Nadine and other teachers to reimagine their subject curriculum across the other grade levels. According to Nadine, the school principal gave "us the freedom not to adhere to the book,"

Table 2. Classroom Diversity by Gender, Place of Residence, Religious Sect, and Political Party

Gender	Place of Residence	Religious Sect	Political Party
Male	Hilalyeh (east of Saida [Sidon])	Muslim—Sunni	March 14—Future Movement
Male	Majdelyon (east of Saida)	Muslim—Sunni	March 14—Future Movement
Female	Shehim (Shouf—out of Saida)	Muslim—Sunni	March 14—Future Movement
Female	Bramieh (north of Saida)	Muslim—Sunni	March 14—Future Movement
Female	Hilalyeh (east of Saida)	Muslim—Shia	March 8—Amal Movement
Male	Wardanieh (out of Saida)	Muslim—Shia	March 8—Hezbollah
Male	Rmiehleh (out of Saida)	Muslim—Sunni	March 8—Popular Nasserite Organization
Female	Hilalyeh (east of Saida)	Muslim—Sunni	March 8—Popular Nasserite Organization
Female	Ein delb (out of Saida)	Muslim—Sunni	March 14—Future Movement
Male	Kfar Hatta (out of Saida)	Muslim—Shia	March 8—Hezbollah
Female	Sharhabel (north of Saida)	Muslim—Shia	March 8—Hezbollah
Female	Wastani (Saida)	Muslim—Shia	March 8—Amal Movement
Male	Shehim (Shouf—out of Saida)	Muslim—Sunni	March 14—Hariri
Female	Sharhabel (north of Saida)	Muslim—Sunni	March 14—Hariri

and this leadership for innovative pedagogies was taken further by Nadia, the academic director for the secondary division. Nadia was responsible for supporting teachers' professional development, student evaluation, curriculum, and classroom learning. She explained how the school engaged teachers in reshaping the Lebanese curriculum for Grades 6, 7, 8, 10, and 11 by "updating [issues and concepts] based on the global issues that are occurring around us." For the civics curriculum, the two civics teachers at the school took the government textbooks, which Nadia described as fragmented and redundant, and replaced lesson titles with broader learning objectives, deleted and added content, and extracted general concepts including "rights, environment, government, and political systems." The school's leadership, which had encouraged teachers to zoom out of their program, critically review long-running lessons, and redesign the curriculum, apparently also encouraged teachers such as Nadine to create challenging and flexible learning spaces in the civics classroom. In the subsequent sections, I present how Nadine realized this reimagined civics program through the planning and facilitation of two units on human rights.

Planning and Facilitating Activities for Active Citizenship

At the start of the academic year, Nadine receives classrooms of students with low levels of motivation and diverse academic needs, religious backgrounds, and political affiliations. The liberty to modify and rescript the civics curriculum for Grades 8, 10, and 11 gives her the upper hand to try an inspiring, inclusive, and critical inquiry–based approach to learning active citizenship. Nadine described this freedom of "going beyond the book" as really important because it allows her to update material that is "very old" and bring in topics that are more "relevant to the issues we are currently facing in our society." She also tries to ensure that assessment methods, which she referred to frequently as performance tasks, require students to participate in class rather than relying on "going home and memorizing." Students receive a rubric for assessments for projects and other similar tasks "so that they know on what basis I will grade them."

Civil and Political Rights. In a 10th grade class, Nadine remembered dedicating three months to "civil and political rights." She believed that three months was a great deal of time to spend on a single concept but also wanted to focus on the "quality of the lessons more than the quantity." She explained that, for the final assessment, students were to choose an Arab country and research how civil and political rights were violated there.

Nadine started the first session with a video on the political revolution in Egypt in 2011. Based on this documentary, the class discussed reasons why the revolution had taken place. Ideas such as poverty, political oppression, and violations of other freedoms emerged and led to discussions of human rights. At this point, she presented the "big question": "How do some Arab countries approach human rights?" A big question, according to Nadine, "does not have a [direct] answer" and requires "a great deal of research" to address. With the class, she further problematized the question by breaking it down into three concepts: "What do we mean by rights? What do we mean by responsibilities? And what do we mean by government stipulations?" For the following six sessions, she dedicated two class hours per one human right: (1) the freedom of thought and expression, (2) the right to vote, and (3) the right to resist oppression and tyranny.[2] These rights were drawn from the civics textbook, which has a lesson dedicated to each one. Nadine facilitated jigsaw activities for each of these lessons by splitting the class into groups, assigning each group a part of the lesson, and having the students regroup to explain to each other what they had read.

At the end of each session, Nadine administered a short quiz of three questions: (1) What is the importance of this right? (2) What are the names of the laws that protect this right? and (3) Under what conditions does the government have the right to regulate this right? She explained that the main aim of these short graded quizzes was to break the popular habit of not paying attention in class and waiting to go home to memorize the information. Objections to quizzes at the end of class came mainly from students who normally had the highest grades. Nadine recalled some of them protesting about not having the chance to memorize material at home: "Why, Miss, are you so unfair with us?" Although students initially complained, they quickly felt better about "not having to memorize and not having a test." A concluding session explored the type of government or society that resulted from practicing these human rights.

The final three class hours were dedicated to the assessment task: to research rights and responsibilities in one Arab country and create a video presentation. Approximately one month before, Nadine provided the students with an assessment rubric "so they have time to meet and prepare." She gave them the freedom to choose their groups. She first asked those students who were confident in using Movie Maker, a Windows film-editing program, to stand up and start choosing their team members. This way, each group had one person skilled in this application. Also, Nadine noted, "I don't interfere [in form-ing groups] so they could work freely and comfortably." She does, however, prefer that groups have no more than four members because "it becomes harder to work" when you have more than that. During the three sessions, students brought in information they had gathered and prepared presentations that showed how civil and political rights were violated in Egypt, Syria, Lebanon, and Libya. At home, they produced their video presentations.

Nadine did not recall any debates that resulted in tensions. During the presentations, however, students did comment, especially on the presentation about Syria. Debates on Syria were mainly around the extent to which human rights were being violated. Nadine's initial response to facilitating this discussion was to maintain neutrality as a facilitator because she felt that students constantly tried to find out the teacher's position. She instead believed that they should form their own positions. She then encouraged the students to try and assume a similar objective position by stating what we see in reality as "witnesses or regular citizens." She illustrated, "We see bombs falling from planes onto civilians," and, "We see that no one runs for the presidency against the president." Nadine is very clear about not encouraging political debates about positions and missions, because "you will get heavy exchanges of words, and I'm not ready for this." Despite her intentions to facilitate dialogues based on evidence and encourage learners to formulate their own arguments, Nadine shares with most civics teachers in Lebanon an anxiety about managing debates heated with emotions and personal interest (Akar, 2012b; Zakharia, 2011).

In the next example of a unit that Nadine re-created, she followed a similar structure:

- Select an issue that relates to Lebanon and the international community.

- Write one main inquiry question.

- Problematize key themes from the question.

- Create a sequence of lessons that extend the timeline normally allocated per unit.

- Dedicate several class hours for students to use information from previous lessons to produce the assessment task.

The main difference between the two unit lesson plans was that the next topic was not found in the civics curriculum. Nadine also stopped administering quizzes after each lesson.

Child Soldiers. The phenomenon of child soldiers in Lebanon has received little attention from civil society and, to date, none from formal education.[3] Working within the theme of human rights that is integrated throughout the civics textbooks (Shuayb, 2015), Nadine introduced a topic that her 10th grade students thought was a problem only in other conflict-ridden, developing countries: child soldiers. She argued that the problem was topical: "It's present. Maybe it was by chance that the video online showed children with arms in Tripoli, but it's present in all areas of Lebanon." She opened with the question: "How can societies help in protecting children against exploitation?" This big question, according to Nadine, must "not be specific, so they would not find the answer if they searched it on Google." From the question, three keywords were drawn—*society*, *children*, and *exploitation*—and the students started to brainstorm examples of child exploitation. The recruitment of child soldiers emerged and then continued to be the focus of the unit, spread across 16 class hours.

Nadine dedicated the first class hour to showing three different documentary films and set the unit question: "How do communities protect children from abuse?" Each film was purposefully selected to highlight a different location: Sierra Leone as a country of poverty, Russia as a developed country, and Lebanon as the students' home country. Documentary films, according to Nadine, are powerful media to present evidence "to [make students] believe" that a problem exists. What was demanding, however, was the time spent on gathering the resources for the lessons. Searching for and downloading materials from the Internet in Lebanon is a painstakingly time-consuming task, with Internet speed ranking among the lowest in the world (see www.speedtest.net). It took 15 full days of "hard work" to find, edit, and translate the documentary films using online sources.

After watching the documentary films, the students were given a copy of the Convention on the Rights of the Child. Over two sessions, they were asked to identify which articles were violated when recruiting children to fight in militias. In the following session, Nadine handed out a table listing countries where the recruitment of child soldiers was prevalent and a world map to color in those countries. She then facilitated discussions on apparent trends: namely, that the recruitment of child soldiers was mostly common in developing regions (e.g., the African continent, Southwest Asia, and Mexico) and that the violation of children's rights harmed national development.

Nadine had a 10th grade class on the day I visited her, and she invited me to observe the class right after the interview. The class first watched a documentary video on the civil war in Sierra Leone, read six printed extracts of individuals' personal experiences as child soldiers, and then debated whether child soldiers were victims or aggressors. I entered and sat quietly in the back of the class. The students sat facing forward in traditional desk-chair frames. Nadine introduced the context of the video and screened it to the class. The film showed graphic images of children kidnapped for military training, children and babies with amputated limbs, and children killing other people. During the conversation after class, I shared my feelings of discomfort when watching the disturbing images. While the students appeared calm and interested, I asked whether they ever complained. With the first videos, "they were frightened. They used to turn their faces and ask, 'What just happened?' and whether or not it was real." Nadine argued that students started to "take [the problem] seriously" when they saw real footage as evidence of child soldiers in and outside of Lebanon. After the video, she asked them basic comprehension questions about what they had observed. The class then read aloud testimonies from former child soldiers in Sierra Leone and Uganda. Describing a common culture of brutality, the stories displayed multiple dimensions of violence, including being forced to kill other children as part of recruitment, taking cocaine to cope with the fear, planting mines, and eating the organs of victims. When Nadine probed students about possible reasons for these acts, they suggested "exploitation" and "to get used to it."

Nadine then posed the debate question, "Are child soldiers victims or aggressors?" Students showed hands indicating their positions. She pointed to two sides of the class, one for each argument, and the students shuffled around the room dragging the heavy furniture to form groups and prepare their arguments. Nadine told them that they had only eight minutes to prepare their ideas and then she would select three students from each group to debate. Some students were concerned about whether to present in formal or colloquial Arabic. She assured them that "as long as your idea is reached," either one was fine. While the students were working together to decide on what to say, Nadine walked around and reminded them when time was nearly up. In one group, she read a comment and asked, "Why?" The student replied, and she nodded and walked off. She then gave another cue, and the students regrouped so that four tables moved to the center, with two speakers from each side facing each other and the rest of the class surrounding them. The first speaker opened the debate by stating that these children were victims because they were forced "out of their humane environment," were "denied civil rights," and "executed commands under threat." The first speaker from the opposing side then stated their position by first acknowledging the definition of "victim" as true but then showing that the acts were criminal and that, referring to the previous video on Russian child soldiers, some acts were by choice. This speaker was interrupted three times by classmates who asked, "Intervention?" The speaker objected by shaking her head and saying, "Thank you." The speaker continued. Afterward, other supporting speakers exchanged responses and were joined by the rest of the class. Hands shot up, and both sides took turns explaining their points of view. Below are excerpts of the debate:

Victims: What do you think about the children in Russia who are joining the military without being forced?

Aggressors: Children in Russia known as child soldiers are being trained to kill the enemies—not when they were young but when they become older.

Victims: There is a difference between being kidnapped from their own houses and what their parents want. We are talking about children as victims who are kidnapped from their families and are being forced to become soldiers, exposing them to beatings and torture and . . . drugs so they can kill.

. . .

Victims: The child is a victim because he's now exposed to something that makes him kill people who raised him and loved him. This of course would not be the choice of the child.

Aggressors: But killing parents is a crime. . . . It's inhumane and savage.

Victims: But he loses his sense of human nature when consuming drugs, and he wouldn't recognize he's doing something wrong to society.

. . .

Victims: I want to remind you that when the war finishes and he's in this state of being a savage, he ends up having many psychological disorders because he then realizes that he was a victim and was forced to do things.

Aggressors: He said that blood is like a morning coffee, so. . . .

Victims: After the war they would have many psychological problems; this is why they would go to hospitals for treatment.

Victims: Children, after the war, remember what happened to them and say that they were victims.

Aggressors: We just read about "Ismael," who chose to take revenge for his parents. He didn't take drugs. They killed his parents, and he had a reaction.

Victims: When he wanted to take revenge, did he become a victim right when they killed his parents?

. . .

Aggressors: But at the end he became an aggressor.

. . .

Victims: Since he was forbidden from his civil rights and education rights, since it was said that the child is drinking blood instead of water, then this all shows that he's a victim.

Nadine interjected on four occasions to (1) remind students to raise hands when interrupting, (2) raise her hand when two were talking at the same time, (3) signal to those who were quiet, and (4) bring them back to the main argument when they started to veer off topic. She brought the class to a close by asking each side to present their closing statement before asking whether anyone had changed their position after the debate. Heads shook no. Nadine then highlighted strengths in both sides and explained why, from the debate, she saw that child soldiers appeared to be more victims than aggressors.

After class, Nadine and I reflected on the activities together. Starting with what she considered went well, Nadine was very pleased with how students drew on materials from the documentary films they had watched several weeks earlier. She added that the debate also demonstrated a "deep understanding of the concept," which she saw clearly from how the students described various ways of recruiting child soldiers and argued how child soldiers could be victims, aggressors, or both. From my observations, I praised how the students structured themselves when preparing for and carrying out the debate. Nadine quickly gave credit to the Arabic teacher who ran a debate club at the school. During this interview, which took place in the teachers' lounge, the Arabic teacher happened to walk in. He explained that he had received training from a debate center in Qatar (www.qatardebate.org) and had set up a debate club in the school, of which some of Nadine's 10th grade students were active members. When I asked Nadine what she would have done differently, she said that she would like to shorten the documentary film a little more to give more time for the debate. I also expressed a little concern over the intense violence depicted in the film and how students might deal with emotional repercussions, if any. "It's reality," Nadine instantly replied.

The students had seen three other films with similar degrees of violence. During the first two, they reacted with "fear"; some "turned their faces," and others asked, "Really, is this true?" Nadine also remembered that they showed more levels of shock when they saw footage of child soldiers in Lebanon in a film documenting armed 10-year-olds in Tripoli. Although the students did not seem to have received any structured exercises to process feelings of discomfort, Nadine explained that they gradually seemed to acclimatize to the brutally graphic materials. Finally, I inquired about her role during the debate, which she described as a "judge." Though "not taking any side" during the debate, she did want to "show them who convinced me more" and explain "because of this, this, and this."

Over the following six weeks, the class was formed into four groups of three to four and researched nongovernmental organizations (NGOs) around the world that dedicated their work to rehabilitating child soldiers. Each group chose one NGO and presented to the class its objectives and activities. Nadine said, "I didn't grade them according to their presentation skills, because I didn't give them enough time to work on it, only two weeks," but she did grade on content. Afterward, they spent three sessions watching a movie on child exploitation and the diamond trade in a country in Africa. By the time I returned, the groups were on their third and last session of the final assessment, which Nadine referred to as the "performance task." In groups, they raised awareness of child soldiers by inventing an NGO (with a name and a logo) and outlining its objectives and activities for rehabilitating child soldiers. This assessment activity was done entirely in class so that "no one from home helps them."

I walked around and observed the students' work. Conscious of the limited time that they had, I tried to learn about how they had produced the objectives and poster images by spending only a minute or two talking with each group. After they briefly explained the message behind their posters, I asked how they had come up with the images and objectives. Groups referred to the information they had learned from the films they had watched, and one added the research project on the NGOs for child soldiers. They all mentioned how they collected each group member's ideas and tried to combine and edit them to create clear and coherent objectives and images (e.g., see Figure 1). A group that seemed to fall a little behind mentioned that the teacher helped them a little in writing the objectives, but they had still created their own logo and image: "Each one brought something, and we put them together." In addition to the collaboration that was evident in my observation and their reflections, the messages the students constructed also appeared to create a platform for solidarity. In Figure 1, for example, the drafted mottoes read, "Together to fight injustice; together to kill betrayal; together for a better tomorrow; together against the recruitment of child soldiers." Rhetoric on solidarity and justice, at least, seemed to have resonated from addressing a conflict experienced mostly in Sierra Leone and Russia. This sense of cohesion suggested a degree of effectiveness in consolidating cosmopolitanism within a

Figure 1. Scratch work showing how a group continuously revised text for the poster.

highly nationalistic civics curriculum and showed how the two could indeed complement rather than contradict each other (Osler, 2010).

The groups worked at their own pace. Although they did not have time to present to the class, Nadine walked around and listened to their presentations as they finished their posters. The students explained what the poster meant, and she asked questions and gave feedback on aesthetics. For each group, she carried with her a rubric to grade their work (see Table 3). Out of the four groups, three scored full marks. One group of three boys did not complete on time. Nadine told them that they could have an extra week but would have points deducted.

After class, I briefly spoke with some of the students about what they found important in the final assessment activity. One noted, "We learned that there are people not just in our country but in other countries . . . who were deprived of being children and their rights." Another added that after creating their NGO, "we felt that later we need to keep thinking about this thing, that we are still lacking organizations" to help children "who every minute and every second are killing and being killed." Another asserted that these future organizations need to make sure that "no child" is vulnerable to being recruited as a soldier. The main difficulty, according to one of the students, was in the beginning when they had to come up with a new concept for the poster: "But then we started collaborating, giving ideas . . . putting down all the ideas. It's not like we left out an idea, no, each one gave something."

Outside the classroom, Nadine expressed how pleased she was with the students' levels of creativity and how much they were able to use the information covered in class to create the posters and think about the consequences of child soldiers. She did, however, express concern over "one or two groups that need a lot of motivation." Some "don't care about the work," while others "care too much about the grade." Still, Nadine clearly did not compromise learning for time, "as long as there is deep understanding."

Nadine's Reflections on Learning and Teaching for Active Citizenship. During the interviews, Nadine reflected on her own personal views toward citizenship education. She described her childhood experiences of learning civics in school as a motivating factor to give children the freedom to explore injustices critically, collaboratively, and dialogically: "Ask me what I learned when I was young [at school], I don't remember. They vaporized. I forgot them." She remembered being scared of her teacher and having to stand up in front of the class to recite materials from the civics book. In her 9th and 12th grade classes, students memorize for the exams, but even there, she at least asks them to recite from their desk because "I don't want them to experience what I experienced." Nadine also described the

Table 3. Rubric for the Assessment of Posters

Feature	Coherent, Clear	Coherent, Unclear	Clear, Incoherent	Unclear, Incoherent
Name, motto, and vision	4	3	2	1
Specified main aims	4	3	2	1
Messages from poster (×2)	4	3	2	1
Group work and collaboration	4	3	2	1

"dull" content materials as a reason to research topics on citizenship education. "I looked at what themes they were learning [in schools] outside of Lebanon" because "I want to move away from the book, which is dull, outdated, and far from real life." Child exploitation was not in the book, but she found it fitting to the curriculum's sections on human rights and even more important and relevant when she saw examples in Lebanon.

Nadine presented her notion of an ideal citizenship as a nationalistic one, which she also struggled with considering the ongoing troubles in Lebanon. She described an inner conflict of wanting to feel patriotic to a country that has let you down. She characterized the 21st-century person as one who is "open-minded about issues in one's country and around the world" and "can solve problems" even if they are not so apparent in one's immediate surroundings. She recognizes that the presentation of an ideal citizenship lacking any engagement with topical issues challenges the integrity and purposefulness of citizenship education. However, she argued that the obvious gap between rhetoric (putting the nation first) and reality (corrupt political institutions) should drive one to learn active citizenship rather than dismiss it as a failed vision. By challenging the idealistic approach to citizenship, students can openly name surrounding conflicts so that they "do not think that this is normal" and, so, start thinking of "how to come up with a solution and implement a change."

Maximizing Civics

Nadine is a civics teacher in a country troubled with sectarian tensions, the absence of a real president, corruption, and insufficient resources for nearly 1.5 million refugees. Her students bring to the classroom a diversity of religious and political backgrounds and learning abilities. Furthermore, the established practices of citizenship education follow a minimalistic approach of memorizing the idealistic feelings and practices of a nationalistic citizenship to be recited for exams, leaving virtually no room for celebrating diverse identities and ideas. Despite such a complex and seemingly futile educational setting, Nadine has demonstrated the feasibility of creating opportunities for children to practice being active citizens in the classroom. Below, I outline a selected number of attributes that I think have contributed to her success that can be further developed in other civics classrooms in Lebanon.

Nadine reframed the function of time. The national civics curriculum and textbooks have set a timeline of 32 lessons, one for each week of the school year. Nadine has managed to break away from a task-oriented strategy of completing the book within the allotted time. Instead, she has employed time as an opportunity for students to work, think, and share about fewer topics in more depth and breadth. Using time to give students more room to work requires flexibility and respect for children's intellectual and social growth. In other words, when you give students the time to work, you are telling them that you think what they are doing is important. Hence, providing students with liberties to work (i.e., time, choice, methods, etc.) reflects the life and freedom that democratic societies strive for.

Nadine introduced discipline into the knowledge production of citizenship learning. Using higher-level thinking to build information and answer main inquiry questions reflected fundamental elements of the disciplinary approaches to history education that have developed over the past 40 years (Counsell, 2011). Indeed, Stenhouse (1968, 1971) attributed the success of the revolutionary Humanities Curriculum Project in England in the late 1960s to the writing of main questions that learners could answer after gathering and reflecting on the necessary information. Although far less structured and defined than the disciplinary curriculum of history education (see the journal *Teaching History*), Nadine's redesigned units opened with a main inquiry question to be answered using knowledge built from a sequence of lessons. Her students explored causes of human rights violations and compared and contrasted degrees of violence and rights violations among countries. The debate on child soldiers questioned the position of child soldiers as victims or killers, a question that required far more complex levels of thinking than the typical for/against dialogues. Deciding how to define these child soldiers has a life span that students can grapple with over a long period of time. Although the main inquiry questions did not reappear as explicitly as they were stated during the start of the unit, the students still used the information they gathered to address the questions. For example, their posters listed objectives that addressed multiple levels of rehabilitation and areas of human development that linked with the causes of children becoming soldiers. Also, the students consistently referred to activities and information from previous lessons when justifying their arguments during the debate and explaining their posters.

Nadine's approaches to assessment were primarily formative in nature. During the unit on civil and political rights, she gave short quizzes on comprehension after each of the jigsaw activities. In principle, assessing individual work is one key motivator to ensure reciprocal efforts during jigsaw activities (Watkins, 2005). During the unit on child soldiers, she gave only three grades over the course of three months. Nadine appeared to have taken quite a risk in significantly lessening the use of grades as an external motivation and summative measure of learning. Despite her struggles to motivate the group of three boys and respond to others' anxieties about not having graded exams, her students, by and large, still demonstrated high levels of engagement. Hence, I believe that Nadine, to a great extent, succeeded in having the students develop intrinsic motivation and a sense of learner responsibility.

Nadine modeled maximal notions of citizenship. Despite her nationalistic conceptualization of citizenship, she demonstrated to the class her values for an international and comparative approach to examining injustices and conflict. An international comparative dimension to learning history, geography, and civics is fundamental to fostering a sense of "enlightened" citizenship (Parker, 2004). This outward approach develops a construct of global citizenship (Dill, 2013; Falk, 1993). Nadine could further extend toward a more cosmopolitan form of citizenship by prompting self-reflections to strengthen multiple levels of identities as well as a shared one within the human community (Nussbaum, 1997; Osler & Starkey, 2005a). Nadine also models responsibility, curiosity, and agency by actively seeking out concepts and issues beyond Lebanon's political borders.

Nadine could further develop some of the learning activities so that the students experience a citizenship closer to being agents of change, reflective citizens, and independent learners. When creating an organization to support a child in need of conflict-related rehabilitation, students could meet activists in existing organizations to exchange views and experiences. After such meetings, learners could improve their posters and even find ways to contribute to the support of rehabilitating former child soldiers. While Nadine brought to the classroom a global outlook on critical issues, she could also encourage an inward exploration of identities. Through introspection, students could reflect on their own positions and identities in relation to child soldiers in and outside of Lebanon. Finally, I believe that the learners could also reflect on how they have learned, especially when making sense of emotive information and constructing arguments with peers.

Conclusion

In education for citizenship, civics is essentially the study of how civil, political, and governmental institutions function. Besides this rather narrow or minimalist construct of citizenship, civics classrooms around the world seem to mostly foster traditions of memorizing knowledge content (Kerr, 1999). In Lebanon, civics not only denies learners opportunities to express multiple identities and critically reflect on ideals with topical issues but also appears to do harm by reinforcing low levels of confidence in political/government institutions and a sense of helplessness (Akar, 2014). Despite didactic approaches to learning citizenship in contexts of diversity and areas affected by conflict, some teachers emerge as creative and self-initiating professionals. This chapter explored the landscape in Lebanon to seek out a civics teacher who went above and beyond her work responsibilities to design and implement for children opportunities to learn active citizenship.

Nadine emerged as a civics teacher who attempted to reimagine the civics curriculum into one that facilitated opportunities for learners to critically and dialogically engage with issues related to human rights, conflict transformation, and social justice. I learned how, with the support of the school's leadership, she designed and facilitated a unit on civil and political rights in the Arab region and another on child soldiers over the course of one year. Her students appeared to struggle with the burden of having to memorize information for exams by anxiously seeking purpose or motivation in the knowledge-building activities. She provided students with the time and resources to research cases around the world, critically analyze information drawn from videos and readings, and reorganize the information to produce new understandings of civil, political, and human rights. The children in her classroom worked in an environment that required learner autonomy, collaboration, and higher order thinking. Also, as citizens practicing their freedoms stated in the U.N. Convention on the Rights of the Child, they expressed views they had constructed (Article 13) and accessed information from a diversity of sources (Article 17).

Nadine's reflections and classroom activities clearly demonstrate an attempt to create a pedagogical shift from memorizing information in the civics textbook to critically exploring topical issues through dialogic and collaborative activities. Learning from Nadine leads to reexamining and furthering numerous approaches that aim to enhance educational programs for active citizenship. One area is the contested yet underdeveloped attempt to learn and teach active citizenship as a discipline. Although learning active citizenship is not and should not be limited to a single program, some governments around the world have designated in their curricular timetables a program specifically for active citizenship. Hence, there is great scope to draw on elements of disciplinary approaches in fields of knowledge to develop activities and questions that require more complex levels of thinking as part of learning active citizenship. Another area to further examine is the extent to which cosmopolitanism supports the aims of highly nationalistic citizenship education. When responding to injustices that affect children in places around the world, the students constructed a position showing solidarity and embraced a diversity of ideas. As a third area, we can further explore teachers' roles as curriculum writers. High-impact teachers like Nadine are critical to developing new approaches to citizenship education in Lebanon. Like many teacher professional movements around the world, a small group of high-impact citizenship education teachers in Lebanon can potentially transform how children learn to be active citizens.

Notes

1. The only exception to the post–civil war reform was the history curriculum. Efforts to officiate a single narrative failed after numerous attempts, leaving the 1971 version still in effect.

2. The "right to resist oppression and tyranny" was not established as a right in the Universal Declaration of Human Rights but, rather, incorporated in its preamble as an action of last resort. Still, the national Grade 10 civics curriculum presents it as a human right.

3. The Lebanese nongovernmental organization Permanent Peace Movement launched a campaign in 2007 titled "No More Child Soldiers." Also, some of the few reports available on child soldiers in Lebanon include Anderson, 2013, and Child Soldiers International, 2001, along with two popular video documentaries, *Beirut—War Generation* (1989) and *Sunni Extremists Raise Child Soldiers in North Lebanon to Combat Alawites* (2012), available on YouTube.

References

Akar, B. (2009). *Exploring the challenges and practices of citizenship education in national and civic education grades ten and eleven classrooms in Lebanon* (Unpublished doctoral dissertation). Institute of Education, University of London, London.

Akar, B. (2012a). The space between civic education and active citizenship in Lebanon. In M. Shuayb (Ed.), *Rethinking education for social cohesion: International case studies* (pp. 154–170). London: Palgrave Macmillan.

Akar, B. (2012b). Teaching for citizenship in Lebanon: Teachers talk about the civics classroom. *Teaching and Teacher Education, 28*, 470–480. doi:10.1016/j.tate.2011.12.002

Akar, B. (2014). Learning active citizenship: Conflicts between students' conceptualisations of citizenship and classroom learning experiences in Lebanon. *British Journal of Sociology of Education*, 1–25. doi:10.1080/01425692.2014.916603

Alabaster, O. (2011, September 30). U.N. urges Lebanon to act on stateless people. *Daily Star*. Retrieved from http://www.dailystar.com.lb/News/Local-News/2011/Sep-30/150082-un-urges-lebanon-to-act-on-stateless-people.ashx

Anderson, S. (2013, April 30). Lebanon's Sunni child soldiers. *Vice*. Retrieved from http://www.vice.com/read/lebanons-sunni-child-soldiers

Banks, J. A. (2008). Diversity, group identity, and citizenship education in a global age. *Educational Researcher, 37*(3), 129–139.

Banks, J. A., Banks, C., Cortés, C., Hahn, C., Merryfield, M., Moodley, K. A. . . . Parker, W. (2005). *Democracy and diversity: Principles and concepts for educating citizens in a global age*. Seattle, WA: Center for Multicultural Education, University of Washington.

Barakat, H. (1973). Social and political integration in Lebanon: A case of social mosaic. *Middle East Journal, 27*(3), 301–318.

Beiner, R. (Ed.). (1995). *Theorizing citizenship*. New York: State University of New York Press.

Bîrzéa, C. (2000). *Education for democratic citizenship: A lifelong learning perspective*. Strasbourg, France: Council of Europe.

Boswell, C., & Geddes, A. (2011). *Migration and mobility in the European Union*. New York: Palgrave Macmillan.

Castles, S. (2010). Understanding global migration: A social transformation perspective. *Journal of Ethnic and Migration Studies, 36*(10), 1565–1586. doi:10.1080/1369183X.2010.489381

Child Soldiers International. (2001). *Child soldiers global report 2001—Lebanon*. Retrieved from http://www.refworld.org/docid/498805e91c.html

Cogan, J., Morris, P., & Print, M. (2002). Civic education in the Asia-Pacific region: An introduction. In J. Cogan, P. Morris, & M. Print (Eds.), *Civic education in the Asia-Pacific region: Case studies across six societies* (pp. 1–22). New York: RoutledgeFalmer.

Counsell, C. (2011). Disciplinary knowledge for all, the secondary history curriculum and history teachers' achievement. *Curriculum Journal, 22*(2), 201–225.

Delors, J. (1996). Education: The necessary utopia. In J. Delors, I. Al Mufti, I. Amagi, R. Carneiro, F. Chung, B. Geremek, W. Gorham, A. Kornhauser, M. Manley, M. Quero, M. Savané, K. Singh, R. Stavenhagen, M. Suhr, & Z. Nanzhao (Eds.), *Learning: The treasure within: Report to UNESCO of the International Commission on Education for the Twenty-First Century* (pp. 13–35). Paris: UNESCO Publishing.

Dewey, J. (1916/1944). *Democracy and education: An introduction to the philosophy of education* (reprinted 1955 ed.). New York: Macmillan.

Dill, J. S. (2013). *The longings and limits of global citizenship education: The moral pedagogy of schooling in a cosmopolitan age*. New York: Routledge.

Falk, R. (1993). The making of global citizenship. In J. Brecher, B. Childs, & J. Cutler (Eds.), *Global visions: Beyond the new world order* (pp. 39–50). Boston, MA: South End Press.

Frayha, N. (2004). Developing curriculum as a means to bridging national divisions in Lebanon. In S. Tawil & A. Harley (Eds.), *Education, conflict and social cohesion* (pp. 159–205). Geneva, Switzerland: UNESCO International Bureau of Education.

Freire, P. (1970). *Pedagogy of the oppressed*. London: Continuum Publishing Company.

Giroux, H. (1988). *Teachers as intellectuals: Toward a critical pedagogy of learning*. Granby, MA: Bergin & Garvey.

Gunesch, K. (2007). International education's internationalism: Inspirations from cosmopolitanism. In M. Hayden, J. Levy, & J. Thompson (Eds.), *The SAGE handbook of research in international education* (pp. 90–101). London: SAGE.

Halualani, R. (2010). De-stabilizing culture and citizenship: Crafting a critical intercultural engagement for university students in a diversity course. In M. Smith, R. Nowacek, & J. Bernstein (Eds.), *Citizenship across the curriculum* (pp. 36–53). Bloomington, IN: Indiana University Press.

Hart, R. (1992). *Children's participation: From tokenism to citizenship*. (Innocenti Essays, No. 4). Florence, Italy: UNICEF, International Child Development Centre.

Hayes, B. C., & McAllister, I. (2009). Education as a mechanism for conflict resolution in Northern Ireland. *Oxford Review of Education, 35*(4), 437–450. doi:10.1080/03054980902957796

Hoskins, B. (2006). *Active citizenship for democracy: Report of the second research network meeting*. Strasbourg, France: Council of Europe.

Hourani, G., Haddad, L., & Sfeir, E. (2011). *Mapping Lebanese diasporas*. Paper presented at the Workshop on Lebanese Migration in the World, Lebanese Emigration Research Center, Notre Dame University–Louaize, Zouk Mikhayel, Lebanon.

Hoxsey, D. (2011). Debating the ghost of Marshall: A critique of citizenship. *Citizenship Studies,* *15*(6–7), 915–932. doi:10.1080/13621025.2011.600106

Hromadžić, A. (2008). Discourses of integration and practices of reunification at the Mostar Gymnasium, Bosnia and Herzegovina. *Comparative Education Review, 52*(4), 541–563. doi:10.1086/591297

International Labour Organization. (2015). *The ILO in Lebanon.* Retrieved from http://www.ilo.org/beirut/countries/lebanon/lang--en/index.htm

Isin, E., & Turner, B. (2002a). Citizenship studies: An introduction. In E. Isin & B. Turner (Eds.), *Handbook of citizenship studies* (pp. 1–10). London: SAGE.

Isin, E., & Turner, B. (Eds.). (2002b). *Handbook of citizenship studies.* London: SAGE.

Isin, E., & Turner, B. (2007). Investigating citizenship: An agenda for citizenship studies. *Citizenship Studies, 11*(1), 5–17. doi:10.1080/13621020601099773

Kerr, D. (1999). Citizenship education in the curriculum: An international review. *School Field, 10*(3/4), 5–32.

Kerr, D. (2000). Citizenship education: An international comparison. In D. Lawton, J. Cairns, & R. Gardner (Eds.), *Education for citizenship* (pp. 200–227). London: Continuum.

Khalaf, S. (2002). *Civil and uncivil violence in Lebanon.* New York: Columbia University Press.

Lawton, D. (2000). Overview: Citizenship education in context. In D. Lawton, J. Cairns, & R. Gardner (Eds.), *Education for citizenship* (pp. 9–13). London: Continuum.

Lebanese Association for Educational Studies. (2003). *Evaluation of the new curriculum in Lebanon* (Vol. 2). Beirut, Lebanon: Author.

Lister, R. (1997). *Citizenship: Feminist perspectives.* Houndmills, UK: MacMillan Press.

Makhoul, J., Kabakian-Khasholian, T., El-Khoury, M., & El-Kak, F. (2013). Experiments in social inclusion and connection: Cases from Lebanon. In A. Taket, B. R. Crisp, M. Graham, L. Hanna, S. Goldingay, & L. Wilson (Eds.), *Practising social inclusion* (pp. 130–140). Abingdon, UK: Routledge.

Marshall, T. H. (1950). *Citizenship and social class and other essays.* Cambridge, UK: Cambridge University Press.

Mattar, M. (2007). Is Lebanese confessionalism to blame? In Y. Choueiri (Ed.), *Breaking the cycle: Civil wars in Lebanon* (pp. 47–66). London: Stacey International.

McLaughlin, T. (1992). Citizenship, diversity and education: A philosophical perspective. *Journal of Moral Education, 21*(3), 235–250.

Ministry of Education and Higher Education (Lebanon). (1997a). Manāhij al-taʿlīm al-ʿām wa ahdāfuha [Curricula of general education and their aims]. Beirut: Center for Educational Research and Development.

Ministry of Education and Higher Education. (1997b). *The programs of general education and their aims.* Beirut, Lebanon: Author.

Nussbaum, M. (1997). *Cultivating humanity: A classical defense of reform in liberal education.* Cambridge, MA: Harvard University Press.

Osler, A. (2008). Human rights education: The foundation of education for democratic citizenship in our global age. In J. Arthur, C. L. Hahn, & I. Davies (Eds.), *SAGE handbook of education for citizenship and democracy* (pp. 455–467). London: SAGE.

Osler, A. (2010). Citizenship and the nation-state: Affinity, identity and belonging. In A. Reid, J. Gill, & A. Sears (Eds.), *Globalization, the nation-state and the citizen* (pp. 216–222). New York: Routledge.

Osler, A. (2011). Education policy, social cohesion and citizenship. In P. Ratcliffe & I. Newman (Eds.), *Promoting social cohesion: Implications for policy and evaluation* (pp. 185–205). Bristol, UK: Policy Press.

Osler, A., & Starkey, H. (2005a). *Changing citizenship: Democracy and inclusion in education.* Maidenhead, UK: Open University Press.

Osler, A., & Starkey, H. (2005b). Study on the advances in civic education in education systems: Good practices in industrialized countries. In V. Espínola (Ed.), *Education for citizenship and democracy in a globalized world: A comparative perspective* (pp. 19–61). Washington, DC: Integration and Regional Programs Department and Sustainable Development Department.

Osler, A., & Starkey, H. (2010). *Teachers and human rights education.* Stoke-on-Trent, UK: Trentham Books.

Parker, W. (2004). Diversity, globalization, and democratic education: Curriculum possibilities. In J. A. Banks (Ed.), *Diversity and citizenship education* (pp. 433–458). San Francisco: Jossey-Bass.

Pratte, R. (1988). *The civic imperative: Examining the need for civic education.* New York: Teachers College, Columbia University.

Salamey, I. (2013). *The government and politics of Lebanon.* Abingdon, UK: Routledge.

Shuayb, M. (2012). Current models and approaches to social cohesion in secondary schools in Lebanon. In M. Shuayb (Ed.), *Rethinking education for social cohesion: International case studies* (pp. 137–153). Basingstoke, UK: Palgrave MacMillan.

Shuayb, M. (2015). Human rights and peace education in the Lebanese civics textbooks. *Research in Comparative and International Education, 10*(1), 135–150. doi:10.1177/1745499914567823

Stenhouse, L. (1968). The Humanities Curriculum Project. *Journal of Curriculum Studies, 1*(1), 26–33. doi:10.1080/0022027680010103

Stenhouse, L. (1971). The Humanities Curriculum Project: The rationale. *Theory Into Practice, 10*(3), 154–162.

ten Dam, G., & Volman, M. (2004). Critical thinking as a citizenship competence: Teaching strategies. *Learning and Instruction, 14*, 359–379.

U.N. Development Programme, Ministry of Education and Higher Education, & Council for Development and Reconstruction. (2008). *Education and citizenship: Concepts, attitudes, skills and actions: Analysis of survey results of 9th grade students in Lebanon.* Beirut, Lebanon: U.N. Development Programme.

U.N. High Commissioner for Refugees. (2015). *Syria regional refugee response: Lebanon.* Retrieved from http://data.unhcr.org/syrianrefugees/country.php?id=122

United Nations. (1989). *Convention on the rights of the child.* Geneva, Switzerland: Author.

U.N. Relief and Works Agency for Palestine Refugees in the Near East. (2014). *Where we work: Lebanon.* Retrieved from http://www.unrwa.org/where-we-work/lebanon

Verhellen, E. (2000). Children's rights and education. In A. Osler (Ed.), *Citizenship and democracy in schools: Diversity, identity, equality* (pp. 33–43). Stoke-on-Trent, UK: Trentham.

Watkins, C. (2005). *Classrooms as learning communities: What's in it for schools?* London: Routledge.

Westheimer, J., & Kahne, J. (2004). What kind of citizen? The politics of educating for democracy. *American Educational Research Journal, 41*(2), 237–269.

Zakharia, Z. (2011). *The role of education in peacebuilding: Case study—Lebanon.* New York: UNICEF.

Zoreik, A. (2000). *Civics education: How do we deal with it.* Beirut, Lebanon: Arab Scientific Publishers.

Chapter 15

Diversity, Identity, and Agency: Kuwaiti Schools and the Potential for Transformative Education

RANIA AL-NAKIB

Gulf University for Science and Technology

Kuwait is a constitutional emirate with a hereditary *amir*, an appointed cabinet of ministers headed by a prime minister, and an elected 50-seat parliament. Kuwait's democratic aspirations are stated in Article 6 of the Kuwaiti Constitution (1962): "The system of government in Kuwait shall be democratic, under which sovereignty resides in the people, the source of all powers."[1] In the region, Kuwait is hailed as the most established and mature democracy, largely due to its Constitution and the distribution of powers (Abdulla, 2012).

According to the 2011 Kuwait Census, the total population is just over three million, with expatriates outnumbering nationals approximately two to one. The Kuwaiti Constitution guarantees (some) citizens their political and civil rights, as well as several social services and generous entitlements as part of the rent distribution from Kuwait's oil wealth, thus promoting nationalism and patriotism (Crystal, 1992) and feelings of superiority (Tétreault & Al-Mughni, 1995) in this group. However, the majority of the expatriate population has restricted rights and limited access to services (Parolin, 2006). This is done, Ismael argues,

> to control the immigrant population by a system of insecurity in terms of their tenure in Kuwait; on the other hand, through paternalistic policies toward the Kuwaiti population, to engender dependence on the ruling class and status distinctions between the Kuwaiti and non-Kuwaiti groups. (1993, p. 25)

The "non-Kuwaiti" designation thus puts the majority population in an inferior and subordinate position to the Kuwaitis, who are legally their sponsors. This sponsorship system, or *kafāla*, coupled with stringent naturalization laws, ensures the transience of the expatriate labor force (Longva, 1997).

Kuwait, historically a port town, has always been a multicultural society in which "the migratory flux itself constituted a constant feature of social life" (Longva, 1997, p. 34). The large-scale modernization that followed the discovery of oil in 1938 further expanded the immigrant population. However, contemporary Kuwait promotes a stratified coexistence of ethnic/cultural groups (Longva, 1997). This stratification is the result of Kuwait's theoretical and practical conceptualizations of citizenship and identity, which are based on the intricate interplay between state building, power preservation, rentierism,[2] and culture, among others.[3] The population is divided into a series of binaries: Kuwaitis/non-Kuwaitis; original/naturalized citizens; Muslims/non-Muslims; Sunnis/Shiʿa; *ḥaḍar* (townspeople)/ *badū* (bedouins); men/women; and adults/children. With these varying categories come varying degrees of legal rights and social belonging. In each binary, it is the first that is most recognized—"original" Kuwaiti, Sunni Muslim, *ḥaḍar*, male adults—a decidedly small group considering that expatriates outnumber locals approximately two to one, and women, *badū*, and youth make up the majority of the local population. This divisive approach often puts members of the various binaries into dichotomous relationships, with each falling in and out of favor with the regime at different points in history.

Kuwaiti women, who historically have been perceived as loyal and whose political participation was therefore supported by the ruling family (see Tétreault, 2000), became enfranchised in 2005, securing their political rights. However, their civil and social rights have lagged behind; for example, women who marry foreign or *bidūn* (stateless) men cannot pass their citizenship to their spouse or their children, and they lose most social benefits, such as housing. Distribution of social services through male citizens suggests that women do not have an independent status—they are daughters and then wives supported first by their fathers and then by their husbands. This inequality hinders women's capacity to compete with men in the political and economic arenas, with Islam often used to defend such barriers; in addition, though economic reasons are often cited in defense of policies that prevent women from benefiting from welfare rights for their families, this explanation conceals the real threat that full citizenship for females poses to suppressive cultural and religious practices (Tétreault & Al-Mughni, 1995).

Among the intersections of the currently less favored of the binaries are *badū* women. Al-Mughni (1993) argues that class struggles have kept women from forging solidarities to fight inequalities such as those mentioned above. She explains that in order to maintain class privileges, elite women must maintain their kinship organization; for them, privileges of class supersede gender issues (intentionally or not). Women's organizations in Kuwait have historically supported this elite group, to the detriment of women from low-income groups, who are most affected by the state's discriminatory welfare policies as well as patriarchy in both the public and private spheres (Al-Mughni, 1993).

The male *badū* population, historically used to counter the demands of the merchant *ḥaḍar* for more participatory politics, continues to face resentment. Moreover, when massive numbers of tribesmen were naturalized in the 1960s and 1970s to garner support for the rulers, it triggered a gradual shift in the demographics of Kuwait from a *ḥaḍar* majority to a *badū* one. The deep cleavage between the merchant *ḥaḍar* and the *badū* populations has been attributed to these factors, as well as perceptions of loyalty, economic privileges, and cultural differences, among others (see F. Al-Nakib, 2014; Longva, 2006). In recent years, the *badū* population has become the government's greatest opposition.

The government also encouraged sectarianism to counter opposition movements by manipulating elections and electoral constituencies in order to control parliament (Longva, 2000). Moreover, though Shiʿa citizens' legal status and rights are equal to Sunni citizens', they historically have been marginalized religiously, economically, socially, and politically (Crystal, 1990). Consequently, they are still perceived as being lower on the scale of what Tétreault dubs "Kuwaitiness" (2000, p. 33).

The use of citizenship and belonging to control the population is most apparent in Kuwait's citizenship and naturalization laws. Naturalized citizens face restricted political rights, and, unlike "original" citizens, whose citizenship can only be revoked for issues of national security, naturalized citizens can have theirs revoked for less extreme reasons, including, for example, "honor-related" and "honesty-related" crimes.[4] The Kuwaiti Constitution (1962) allows this in Article 27: "Kuwaiti nationality is defined by law. No deprivation or withdrawal of nationality may be effected except within the limits prescribed by law." The past several years have seen a marked increase in the use of this law to suppress dissent in both groups of citizens (see Human Rights Watch [HRW], 2014). The increasingly stringent citizenship laws have also made it exceedingly difficult (if not impossible) for the *bidūn* and expatriates to acquire citizenship.

This chapter explores how such increasingly singular and exclusive constructions of citizenship and identity extend into Kuwaiti schools, precluding opportunities to foster feelings of belonging and agency in the national and expatriate populations, and therefore interfering with the nation's democratic aspirations. The first section offers a brief conceptual framework to help define the key terms and highlight how they are used in and relate to the main themes in this chapter: status and identity, human rights, and agency and transformative democratic participation. Following this, the homogenized composition of Kuwaiti schools, which contrasts sharply with Kuwait's multicultural reality, is explored, and ramifications are considered. The third section presents the author's analysis of Kuwait's approach to citizenship education, including its human rights curriculum, by focusing specifically on how identity is constructed within national education policy documents. The notion of a singular national identity is problematized as ignoring the fact that citizens' and residents' identities are multi-layered and multi-leveled. The role of Islam in further excluding difference within school structures and curricula is then highlighted. The fourth section presents a case study conducted by the author; the selected school and one of its teachers will be analyzed as a critical case of possibility. The study will explore the articulation of the human rights curriculum at the school to gain insight into both its potential to expand understandings and enactments of citizenship and also some of the intractable tensions. The final section will offer concluding remarks as well as suggestions that build on the demands of Kuwaiti youth themselves.

Moving Beyond the National: Identity, Agency, and Transformative Citizenship

The tension between Kuwait's multicultural reality and its aforementioned increasingly exclusive construction of citizenship (and, indeed, identity, as will be discussed further) highlights the need for a more inclusive definition of citizenship than one rooted strictly in nationality.

Most discussions about citizenship begin with Marshall's definition: "Citizenship is a status bestowed on those who are full members of a community. All who possess the status are equal with respect to the rights and duties with which the status is endowed" (1950, pp. 28–29). Lister (2003) describes two modes of citizenship: formal (nationality) and substantive (rights and duties), pointing out that within nation-states, various groups experience varying degrees of the latter. Speaking about the United States and Europe, she argues that racist nationalism and growing fundamentalism threaten the development of a more inclusive, multicultural model of citizenship. Lister (2003) also stresses that membership and community culture are essentially contested concepts. National and citizenship identity are too often conflated, and identity and culture are not static or homogenous but rather multi-leveled (subnational, national, supranational), differentiated, and dynamic, "forged in part through struggles around membership and rights" (Lister, 2003, p. 15).

Delanty similarly argues that citizenship is enacted on different levels. He stresses the importance of the cosmopolitan public sphere in this conception, arguing that "the public sphere is a more basic form of community than the political and legal domains of civil society" (2000, p. 134). He goes on to stress that this cosmopolitan public sphere is not necessarily a global one, but is located in subnational and national public spheres whose interactions have transformed them: "The cosmopolitan moment occurs when context-bound cultures encounter each other and undergo transformation as a result" (p. 145). In diverse societies, such inclusive encounters have the capacity to reveal differential experiences of recognition and rights and then potentially to transform them. Delanty (2000) posits that this is a way to counter both false universalism and a retreat into particularism. In such a conception, human rights are universal in a way that is differentiated and interactive—they are not predetermined, but rather constructed (Delanty, 2000). Universal rights, often perceived as incompatible with a politics of difference, are, however, simultaneously necessary to accommodate difference (Dean, 1996; Lister, 2003). In this sense, universal rights are a utopian principle that can be used to counter "denials of identity and lack of recognition" (Douzinas, 2000, p. 292).

Benhabib (2008) argues that cosmopolitan norms of justice (including the various legally binding international rights agreements) have caused the local, national, and global to overlap, and that this process will continue through democratic encounters. However, rather than seeing this as a threat to democratic sovereignty, she posits that it can lead to new forms of agency, based on the interdependence between the levels.

Benhabib (2008), too, stresses the public sphere. For her, citizens of a multicultural democracy have to be able to test the limits of their overlapping consensus and that this type of cultural-political learning cannot be stifled. This process facilitates learning to "live with the otherness of others whose ways may be deeply threatening to our own"; rights must be challenged and rearticulated in the public sphere "to retain and enrich their original meaning" (Benhabib, 2008, p. 60). This process, she states, enhances the democratic dialogue. Moreover, when we shift the emphasis from consensus to ongoing moral conversation, the consequence is that universalizability evolves into "the utopian projection of a way of life in which respect and reciprocity reign"; because this is a *moral* conversation, it potentially includes the whole of humanity—every moral agent who may be affected by my actions deserves to be part of a conversation of justification (Benhabib, 1992, p. 38).

Freire defines dialogue as "the encounter between men [and women], mediated by the world, in order to change the world" (1970/1993), p. 70), pointing out that faith in people is a prerequisite for dialogue. This is rearticulated by Dean (1996), who argues that solidarity is implicit in the reciprocity of dialogue. This solidarity is not just a matter of "gestures" but is an "act of love" (Freire, 1970/1993, p. 32), requiring that "one enter into the situation of those with whom one is solidary" (p. 31). However, solidarity does not preclude mutual criticism (Turner, 2006).

Within education, such deliberation is best achieved within multicultural school settings, to which students from diverse backgrounds bring varied convictions (Gutmann, 2004). A dialogic school does not segregate (Flecha, 2009). It also does not separate students from the content of education nor from the process (Freire, 1970/1993). Human rights education provides opportunities for criticality that wider citizenship agendas often sacrifice in favor of nationalism and obedience (Osler & Starkey, 2010). Davies (2008) supports a value system for education that is created by human beings and is based on human rights, interruptive democracy, and critical idealism. She contrasts this with a value system based on religion, where obeying authority and accepting "the path" are paramount (p. 181). The latter system, she argues, cements extremist attitudes and divisions. Davies (2008) describes five kinds of criticality: critical scholarship, critical (dis)respect, critical thinking, critical doubt, and critical lightness.

Opportunities for these types of critical reflection based on a human rights framework will only be meaningful insofar as they lead to action. Both reflection and action are needed to transform the world (Freire, 1970/1993). Banks highlights an important distinction between active and transformative citizens:

> The actions taken by active citizens fall within existing laws, customs, and conventions, whereas the actions of transformative citizens are designed to promote values and moral principles—such as social justice and equality—and may violate existing conventions and laws. (2008, p. 137)

This latter type of citizenship, he argues, is the goal of education. As Tibbitts (2005) points out, the empowering quality of human rights education that facilitates individuals to make changes in themselves and their environments has the potential to support and enrich transformative learning.

Kuwaiti Schools: Differential Segregation and the Loss of the "Cosmopolitan Public Sphere"

The previously discussed layers of divisive categorization in Kuwait belie its historically cosmopolitan character as a port town, and nowhere is the abandonment of these cosmopolitan roots more apparent than in its homogenized public schools. Article 11 of the Kuwaiti Constitution (1962) states, "Education is a fundamental requisite for the progress of society, assured and promoted by the state." Article 40 (1) further states, "Education is a right for Kuwaitis, guaranteed by the state in accordance with law and within the limits of public policy and morals. Education in its preliminary stages is compulsory and free in accordance with the law." Despite what appears to be a democratic approach to educational access, in reality, Kuwait's school system is a very undemocratic one. As stated in the constitutional article above, free access to public schools is dependent on the legal status of citizenship, which means that two thirds of the country's population—the expatriates—have to pay for private education.

Castles (2004) outlines various approaches to dealing with the challenges of migration and diversity in national education systems. One approach, differential exclusion, seeks to control difference. He defines it as follows:

> The essence of this approach is partial and temporary integration of immigrant workers into society—that is, they are included in those subsystems of society necessary for their economic role: the labor market, basic accommodation, work-related health care, and welfare. Such immigrants are not meant to settle and bring in dependents and are excluded from significant areas of society, such as citizenship, political participation, and national culture. (p. 32)

He goes on to explain that the educational response for these migrants' children is either denial or stopgap measures to keep them marginalized. This describes Kuwait quite accurately. Migrant children in Kuwait (with only a handful of exceptions) are denied access to public education, as are the children of the *bidūn*. This attempt to control difference has extended to the national population through what I term, to borrow from Castles, differential segregation. Kuwaiti students are segregated based on gender most obviously, and on cultural and sectarian backgrounds more subtly.

With schools segregated by gender from primary through university levels, Kuwaiti men are more easily able to ignore the realities of women's experiences, and it becomes increasingly difficult for women to access the people and structures necessary to attain full recognition. The various additional layers of separation across schools make change even more elusive as they continue to hinder the formation of a female solidarity movement.

While districting can be defended as a practical way to organize schools, in Kuwait, district lines divide across cultural and sectarian backgrounds. Schools therefore mirror and reinforce societal divisions between Kuwaitis and expatriates, men and women, *ḥaḍar* and *badū*, and Sunnis and Shi'a. This segregation preserves the current structure by sacrificing what Freire (1970/1993) calls the "totality" in favor of the "focalized view" (p. 122), whereby people are kept largely blind to issues and injustices outside their immediate context. The danger of this segregated approach lies in its potential to perpetuate supremacist attitudes in schools that represent the dominant populations (male, Sunni, *ḥaḍar*) and reactive angry attitudes in schools that represent the marginalized populations (female, Shi'a, *badū*).

The resultant homogenized populations in Kuwaiti schools mask the country's multicultural reality. What is lost is the potential for schools to provide young people with microcosms of Delanty's (2000) aforementioned cosmopolitan public spheres and the possibility of transformative encounters with difference. The homogenization also facilitates the presentation of a singular national identity within educational curricula and ethos.

Citizenship Education: National Identity Versus Cultural Diversity and Change

Kuwait's conceptualization of citizenship education has most often been given the name "*muwāṭana*." This word, like its nearest English translation, "citizenship," is inseparable from the notion of nationality. This is perhaps even more pronounced in Arabic, since the term "*muwāṭana*" stems from the word "*waṭan*," or "nation." The word has appeared in numerous official education documents (see, for example Ministry of Education [MoE], 2008a; 2008b; 2010a), and it has often been conflated with *waṭaniyya* (translated as both "nationalism" and "patriotism"), as demonstrated by its frequent association with loyalty to, love of, and defense of the nation. Despite educational directives mentioning citizenship, however, no purposive curricular or systemic agenda for citizenship education existed at the high school level prior to 2006, when a module called *al-dustūr wa ḥuqūq al-insān* (*dustūr*)—*The Constitution and Human Rights*—was introduced as a three-year program for Grades 10, 11, and 12. This module was the result of the work of a committee set up by Kuwait's Ministry of Education in the 1990s, whose purview was to address education on human rights and the Kuwaiti Constitution. The philosophy agreed upon for this new addition to the curriculum was based on two guiding principles: the importance of the Constitution and the universality of human rights. Three sources were eventually identified for the curricular content: Islamic *shari'a*, international declarations and covenants, and the Kuwaiti Constitution.[5]

What was markedly absent from this program's name as well as its philosophical foundations, goals, and, for the most part, textbooks, was the word "*muwāṭana*" (citizenship). Rather than people being referred to as *muwāṭinīn* ("nationals" or "citizens"), they were referred to as individuals, members of society or the community, and human beings; this is significant and can be interpreted as a shift away from a strictly nationalistic conception of citizenship and identity to a more democratic one (R. Al-Nakib, 2012). Furthermore, focusing on belonging instead of national identity in the *dustūr* curricular goals perhaps marked an acknowledgement of Kuwait's contentious issues with citizenship and the resulting societal divisions. The goals also included knowledge, skills, and values promoting human rights and democracy. Significantly, the program dedicated an entire year to human rights—a radical step toward developing a more inclusive notion of citizenship and identity. This addition was a pioneering step for the region.

In 2010, the Ministry of Education released its most comprehensive plan to date on citizenship education, titled *Strategy for Reinforcing the Concepts of Citizenship, Loyalty, and Belonging Among Young People Through Educational Curricula in Kuwait* (MoE, 2010b; hereinafter, "citizenship strategy report").[6] The three main overarching goals that are listed in the report mention human rights, democracy, cultural diversity, equality, participation, dialogue, and critical thinking. Its more detailed goals also stress belonging and social pluralism. National identity is not mentioned, leaving room to expand on what has developed into an exclusive conception of Kuwaiti national identity within an increasingly young and plural society.

The report made no mention of adding anything to the curriculum to realize its goals. The *dustūr* program would therefore seem like a logical starting point to build on. The year the report came out, however, the program had been reduced from a three-year program to a one-year module for Grade 12 students only. According to the official pamphlet about the module that was presented to the UN's Office of the High Commissioner for Human Rights for Kuwait's Universal Periodic Review in 2010, "The Ministry has decided that it is much better to teach this subject in the final stage of secondary school (12th grade). The learner in this grade is ready intellectually and psychologically to [sic] such specialized [information] about democracy, [the] constitution, and human rights" (MoE, 2010c, p. 12). While this decision, as well as the reasoning behind it, seems at odds with the goals of the citizenship strategy report, a closer look at the rest of the report reveals tensions that may help to shed light on it. First, it is important to note that the goals within the report were written by one of the authors of the *dustūr* program's textbooks. The rest of the report, however, was written by other members of the committee that drafted it, and the difference in content and tone is noticeable. The report begins, for example, by outlining eight perceived challenges and threats facing the country, including multiple affiliations, demands for rights, and globalization.

The second challenge translates as follows: "the obstacles standing in the way of social integration due to multiple citizenships and ideological, tribal, or class affiliations that create cracks in the structure of the state and in the ties of national unity" (p. 24). This ignores the reality of identity as multi-layered and multi-leveled, as discussed, and instead views non-national identities—whether tribal, sectarian, etc.—as threatening to national unity. The wording implies that belonging is contingent upon leaving such identities behind. This view is particularly problematic given that these same "other" identities are strategically utilized to exclude and divide (as explained earlier). Moreover, the goal of "social integration" seems to be at odds with the homogenization of schools, which simultaneously magnifies and masks the existence of difference and limits possibilities for conversations with "the other."

The fifth challenge listed states that citizens are demanding more economic, social, cultural, health, and educational rights without fulfilling minimal responsibilities and are unwilling to accept the government's attempts to reduce this dependency on the state. By conflating rights with welfare entitlements here, the implication is that rights are already universal and equal, which is not the case. Moreover, the year after this report came out, student stipends were raised in response to student demonstrations. The Ministry again contradicted itself, responding to such protests by providing more entitlements, thereby increasing dependency while ignoring the demands for equal human rights and legal recourse and greater political participation (see HRW, 2016).

Interestingly, the only mention of the global context in the citizenship report also appears under the challenges heading: "cultural, economic, political, and intellectual effects of globalization on cultural identity, the nation state, borders, and sovereignty" (MoE, 2010b, p. 24). This focuses on preserving the national in the face of the global and conceptualizes cultural identity as desirably fixed. As discussed, this view of the global level as threatening to sovereignty is a limited one and ignores the reality of interdependence (Benhabib, 2008). Later in the report, six areas of focus for the formulation of a strategy for citizenship education are listed, and the majority of these, too, imply that culture is defined and static, including phrases such as "protecting Kuwaiti essence," "deviant behaviors that are foreign to Kuwaiti cultural identity and that threaten our intrinsic constants," and "overcoming particular affiliations" (p. 25).

Kuwait's *Education Strategy 2005–2025* also perceives change as potentially threatening. The strategy lists as its first goal "contributing to the achievement of interaction with the current age requirement of freedom of thought and response to the dynamics of change without conflict with the cultural identity of the society" (cited in MoE, 2008a, p. 28). Again, cultural identity is perceived as national, singular, and static, with the notions of thought and change conceptualized as potential threats to this status. The second goal, however, reads more inclusively: "contributing to enhancing the values of faith in the importance of dialogue and respect for human rights among the educated and providing the basis for a sound democratic life" (p. 28). This goal is echoed in the areas of focus in the citizenship strategy report: "emphasis on the value of dialogue, human rights, and respect for the opinions of others, as well as the utilization of democratic means to resolve conflicts of opinion and interest; this makes it possible for young people in the future to treat the deficiencies in political practice in society" (p. 25). Though this point stresses the role of human rights, dialogue, and democracy as *loci* for political reform, it labels students as *future* citizens rather than agents who can invoke change now, a perception that is repeated throughout the report. This is not surprising given that Kuwait delays the issuance of the *jinsiyyah*, the legal citizenship document, until the age of 18; while seemingly innocuous, this move nonetheless leaves young people without official status in Kuwait's citizenship system (R. Al-Nakib, 2011). Theoretically, this conceives of children as the property of adults and not in need of their own status. Practically, it justifies the perceptions of children as "future" citizens and therefore their exclusion from transformative decision-making processes.

This perception of children along with the focus on a "national identity" above all else perhaps make it clearer why the *dustūr* program was significantly reduced rather than built upon. As the *dustūr* module was being phased out in high school, *terbia waṭaniyya* (national education) was being added to the elementary school curriculum, marking a return to nationalistic citizenship education. Interestingly, while the "specialized content" regarding human rights was deemed too advanced for students in Grades 10 and 11 in the case of the *dustūr* program, the equally "specialized" rights content in the Grade 10 Islamic studies module continued to be taught.

Islamic Hegemony in Kuwaiti Curricula

Regional alliances between governments and religious groups against educational reforms are common and often focus on controlling what and how students learn (Faour & Muasher, 2011). By infusing national curricula with Islamic content, students are prevented from seeking out alternative perspectives and thinking critically, which further secures their passivity.

The *Education Strategy 2005–2025* includes the following objective from the Gulf Cooperation Council: "building the correct Islamic faith in the educated so that its principles become a method of thought and style, which develops the preparation of educated [people] with Arab-Islamic heritage and loyalty to the Arab-Islamic identity" (MoE, 2008a, p. 47). Not only is Islamic identity assumed to be part of the Kuwaiti and Gulf identities—the use of the word "correct" implies that there is only one such Islamic identity.

The didactic nature of the Islamic studies content and pedagogical methods in the national curriculum similarly assumes a particular patriarchal interpretation of Islam as complete, expecting obedience without discussion and debate. This leaves little or no room for anyone to interpret the religion in more egalitarian ways, including Muslim females who are attempting to change the perceived identity of women in Islam (see Karmi, 1996). The segregated school system makes it even more difficult to question and challenge gendered roles and obligations, and it justifies this separation and inequality through religion.

In the Grade 10 Islamic studies textbook (MoE, 2007a), for example, three lines state that God created everyone from mud with equal rights and responsibilities. The textbook then presents an excerpt from the *ḥadīth* against racism and another from the *Qurʾān* stating that men and women were created in the same way.[7] However, the latter does not explicitly declare equality between men and women. This is particularly problematic given that several interpretations of Islamic laws do not treat men and women equally (e.g., marriage and inheritance laws, among others). By choosing an excerpt that merely states that the genders were created in the same way leaves room to justify such unequal treatment. For example, the following chapter on punishments presents an excerpt that justifies men hitting "disobedient" women.

This chapter in the textbook, in addition to describing the various types of punishments in Islam for not obeying Islamic laws, ends with the following section, entitled "Civil Laws":

> With a quick look at the civil laws, we find they are lacking to protect the individual and society, and the proof of this is that we find an increase in crime and deviant behaviors, so either the punishments do not fit the crime or they are in excess to it. (MoE, 2007a, p. 164)[8]

To begin with, no "quick look" is taken at the existing legal system in the textbook, suggesting that the elusive "we" have deemed the laws' "lacking" as reason enough to exclude them from the book altogether.

Moreover, the chapter states that death is the Islamic punishment for apostates (MoE, 2007a). This prohibits Kuwaitis from asserting an alternative (or no) religious identity, a clear violation of Article 18 of the Universal Declaration of Human Rights (1948), which guarantees the right to change one's religion. In 2006, a decision was made to remove Article 18 from the high school curriculum. In response to this, Kuwaiti reformer Ahmad Al-Baghdadi asked,

> Why does the education ministry bother to prepare a curriculum with international contents if it plans to distort it and present it in an inappropriate manner? Moreover, why should a teacher refer to religion when teaching a curriculum on human rights? Is the Education Ministry required to introduce religion into all topics of study? If it is, then why not hand over the schools to the religious education authorities and be done with it? (translated and reported by Middle East Media Research Institute, 2007)

The 2010 citizenship strategy report lists feelings of belonging to the Arab and Muslim worlds as values to be fostered, suggesting that an Islamic identity is necessarily part of Kuwaiti citizenship. In doing so, the report ignores the tiny Kuwaiti Christian population as well as those Kuwaitis who perhaps prefer not to reveal their religious beliefs or lack thereof; it also overlooks the much larger expatriate Christian and Hindu populations.

It is not just Islam that is built into the imagined Kuwaiti identity, but particularly a Sunni perspective of Islam. In 2010, the former Minister of Education was almost forced to resign over a dispute about an Islamic studies exam. Concerns were raised by a number of Shi'a members of Parliament (MPs) over a few exam questions that they described as heretical and that they argued could contribute to sectarian tensions. The former Minister removed the questions, triggering a huge backlash from Sunni Islamist MPs. One stated, "We will not allow the Minister to amend the curricula, and nobody will dare mess with the faith of Kuwaiti people. This issue is not only a red line, it is multiple red lines together; messing with these issues could shake the whole country if the Minister does not stop" (Saeid, 2010). The quote suggests that "the faith of the Kuwaiti people" is a singular one. Another Sunni Islamist MP shared this view, stating, "Ask your father and your grandfather about the belief of Kuwaitis, and they will tell you" (Saeid, 2010), suggesting that those MPs who requested the change in the curriculum were, in his view, not "Kuwaiti."

The eight challenges listed in the citizenship strategy report do not mention extremism or what Al-Baghdadi (translated and reported by the Middle East Media Research Institute, 2007) describes as the introduction of Islam into every subject. The result is an approach to education that is rendered uncritical by the expectation of obedience that comes with religion, which is convenient for both the government and Islamists in parliament.

Kuwait's homogenized schools, its educational focus on national citizenship, and the Islamic hegemony in its curricula are all in tension with its self-proclaimed goal of demo-cratic development, as they stand in the way of recognition, agency, and civic participation. The next section examines the enactment of Kuwait's human rights curriculum at a case study school to uncover instances where these key democratic elements were present and explores the unsanctioned actions and transformations they triggered.

A Case Study

As Gandin and Apple point out, "rearticulations" of enacted policies must be studied in local contexts in order to "map out the creation of alternatives" (2002, p. 100). To this end, I carried out an in-depth case study of a local girls' public school over three academic years (2008–2011); this study coincided with the 2010 decision to roll back the three-year *dustūr* program in exchange for a one-year offering in Grade 12.

The context for the case study is significant. The school was selected for its particu-larities—for those qualities that make it atypical within the Kuwaiti school system. At first glance, this school seems like a relatively representative case: it is a Kuwaiti public school, operating within the Ministry of Education's regulations, and working from the centralized national curriculum. The case school, like all public schools, began the day with students lining up in the courtyard to sing the national anthem, while a small group marched to the flagpole in military formation to raise the flag and hail the Amir, Kuwait, and the Arab Nation. Then, a selected student read an excerpt from the *Qur'ān*. Teaching and learning were carried out in what is called a "fixed classroom," a Ministry directive; students stayed in one room for most of the day, and their teachers came to them. They usually sat in straight rows facing the teacher and were often expected to respond to questions in unison with words coming directly out of the Ministry-issued textbooks. These textbooks are distributed to teachers at the start of each academic year with a timetable indicating the exact page numbers a teacher should be covering on any given day in order to ensure that the students have memorized the information in time for what are called the two "big" Ministry exams, which make up 75% of the students' grades. The high stakes involved in this type of testing keep both teachers and students locked into the textbooks, thereby ensuring a centralized dissemination of information.

Despite these similarities to other Kuwaiti schools, the case school is located in one of the most affluent districts, and it is also a member of UNESCO's Associated Schools Project Network and has been recognized for work on human rights issues. This school's location and status make it a best-case scenario within which to explore the potential of the human rights approach to citizenship education being analyzed in this chapter. Stake succinctly supports this rationale: "My choice would be to choose that case from which we can learn the most" (2005, p. 451). Schofield similarly stresses that such cases "provide an opportunity to gain some insight into how and why [things] go well [at the case site] and into what the still-intractable problems are" (2007, p. 196).

The case study included hundreds of hours of participant observation; specifically, it spanned three academic years, with three to five weeks spent attending numerous classes, events, and meetings at the school during the spring semester each year. During the study, I also conducted workshops with 211 students to discover their perceptions of their learning on human rights, citizenship, and democracy. Thirteen interviews were carried out with the adult members involved in the study, including teachers, the principal, UNESCO representatives, and a Ministry of Education official. This chapter will focus on the embedded case of Amani, a social studies teacher who was tasked with teaching the Grade 11 human rights component of the *dustūr* program when it was first introduced.[9]

Amani: A Critical Case of Possibility

In the student research workshops I conducted, people who had positively influenced the students' learning on and experience of human rights, democracy, and citizenship at school were mentioned 40 times. One student named me, saying that I had given students a space to express their opinions freely and openly. Another mentioned the school counselor. Six mentioned an English teacher, two mentioned a second English teacher, and yet another mentioned her former English teacher. Three students mentioned Maya, and three others mentioned Wafia, the two other *dustūr* teachers. *Twenty-three* students mentioned Amani. During my observations, I often heard teachers asking Amani about various rights-related issues and her democratic teaching methods. More than once, I heard teachers encourage her to take on administrative, decision-making roles (to which she always replied that she wanted to remain in the classroom). In 2010, the principal explained to me in our interview that there were ways to work around regulations when it came to humanistic issues; she cited Amani's creation of an unofficial student government group as an example of a way to promote student rights while technically remaining within the confines of the regulations.

Wright (2007) highlights the tensions between taking seriously aspirations for a more just world on the one hand and addressing the hard constraints of reality on the other. He calls the search for emancipatory alternatives to the status quo "envisioning real utopias" (p. 27), pointing out that the viability of such alternatives is the most pressing challenge. He stresses the value of empirical studies of cases where aspects of the proposed alternatives have been attempted. Fielding and Moss build on this and argue that education research needs fewer quantitative performance assessments and more "critical case studies of possibility" (2011, p. 16). Fielding addresses Wright's notion of viability within education by linking it to prefigurative practice—that which embodies the "viability and desirability" of alternatives in its structures, processes, and relations (2007, p. 544). He identifies seven strands of such practice: overt democratic coherence; endorsement of a vibrant, inclusive public realm; interpersonal and structural integrity; radical approaches to curriculum and assessment; insistent affirmation of possibility; delight and belief in intergenerational reciprocity; and interrogative, dialogic openness. As the study began to unfold, the numerous references to Amani in my field notes, interviews, and student research workshops made it apparent that Amani was a "critical case study of possibility" (Fielding & Moss, 2011, p. 16) from whom it was important to learn.

Amani is not the stereotypical democratic teacher described by Beane:

> All too frequently, teachers who advocate for the democratic way are imagined as a certain stereotype: They are young, dress informally, have unkempt hair, wear sandals, ride bicycles to work, shop at health food stores, only watch public television, and always insist that students call them by their first names. (2005, pp. 86–87)

She is perhaps a far cry from what many would picture when speaking of radical democratic practice in the West. She also does not fit contemporary Middle Eastern stereotypes. She wears a *ḥijāb*, but her conservative clothes are bright, well-accessorized, and eclectic, mixing Eastern and Western styles. She prays five times a day, was married at a very young age, and has six sons. She also joins political groups, makes her husband do all the cooking, and is set on sending her children to the West for their college educations. Similarly, Amani's teaching also combines the stereotypical and traditional with the atypical and progressive. As a psychology major, Amani was one of the social studies teachers who had to take on the *dustūr* module with no training when it was introduced in 2006.

Enacting the Dustūr *Program: Learning Through Loopholes*

The 45-minute *dustūr* class was added to the schedule once a week for Grades 10 through 12, and teachers were given the same type of timetable for textbook coverage as they were for other classes. Interestingly, however, the *dustūr* exams, unlike those for all other social studies modules, were not written by the Ministry; schools and districts were responsible for writing their own tests, perhaps revealing something about the module's perceived status with officials. The course textbooks, which *did* come from the Ministry, were short, and all the information in them was presented as factual, even that which was based on religion. This point is particularly relevant to the Grade 11 textbook (MoE, 2007b), which presented human rights in each chapter from three perspectives: Islam, international documents, and the Kuwaiti Constitution, in that order. Each of these sections presented a "factual" perspective on the rights being discussed. However, the textbook did not provide any intentional opportunities for engagement with the tensions and contradictions among these three perspectives. In addition, since the Islamic perspective was always presented first in the textbook, the implication was that it took precedence. This was confirmed in the aforementioned official pamphlet: "There are rights that cannot be accepted as they are in conflict with *shari'a*"; the examples it provides are premarital sex, gay marriage, and equality between males and females in inheritance laws (MoE, 2010c, p. 7). This justifies allowing universal and constitutional rights to come second and third to a particular interpretation of Islamic rights. The justification does not take into account that, as signatory to the Universal Declaration of Human Rights and its related covenants, Kuwait has made a legal commitment to uphold the indivisible rights contained within them. This has been a contentious issue between Kuwait and international organizations (see HRW, 2016; United Nations High Commissioner for Refugees, 2010).

Furthermore, while the *dustūr* module aspired to include legal frameworks, this did not materialize to any significant extent in the Grade 11 textbook, which did not introduce any legal rights or discuss their potential tension with the other rights presented (Islamic, universal, and constitutional). This is particularly significant in the case of Kuwait because the Kuwaiti Constitution leaves a great deal of scope for the legal system to restrict citizens' rights (see Parolin, 2006; United Nations Development Programme, 2009). This omission led to whitewashed, decontextualized presentations of rights in the textbook. For example, in the half-page that deals with women's rights in Kuwait, it is argued that women's rights are protected because the Constitution uses the word "individual" and therefore does not distinguish between men and women. However, this fails to address the fact that women do not have equal legal rights, as discussed earlier. It also fails to contextualize women's rights struggles and successes in Kuwait. By neglecting to address legal rights, responsibilities, and consequences, the *dustūr* module did not offer a challenge to the aforementioned Islamic studies textbook's contempt for the legal system.

While it would be easy to dismiss the potential of the *dustūr* module to offer much in the way of transformative educative experiences, the short textbooks, the tensions they (perhaps unwittingly) uncovered, the absence of a Ministry exam, and even the lack of teacher training all worked together in serendipitous ways. As Amani and her class went through the Grade 11 textbook on human rights, they started to identify the aforementioned tensions and gaps within these frameworks. In an interview, Amani explained that, throughout this process, she was learning alongside her students, and they were co-constructing their curriculum. She seemed very comfortable with this approach, displaying what Fielding describes as "delight and belief in intergenerational reciprocity" (2007, p. 552).

Amani and her students decided early in the semester that, in order to address the various tensions between the Islamic framework and others, they would use a secular approach; this facilitated exploring women's rights as human rights, unburdened by patriarchal interpretations of religious expectations. They also decided to analyze lived human rights realities and violations in Kuwait. Amani explained that her students began to fill in the gaps in the textbooks using external resources (newspaper articles, videos from social media, and many others), alerting her to legal rights issues of which she admitted she was unaware. They also invited speakers to the school, including one of the first four female members of parliament and a human rights lawyer.

In 2010, Kuwaiti women were fighting for their right to become judges. During one of Amani's lessons that year, she asked her students which of them would like to be a judge one day. One student responded by saying that, in Islam, women are prohibited from being judges. Amani explained that Kuwait's Constitution does not ban women from holding such a position. The students discussed and debated this issue, and one student boldly announced that she would like to be a judge, a decision that was met with encouragement from her teacher. By creating opportunities for students to explore the tensions that were unintentionally raised by the factual presentations in the books, Amani created an environment where it was safe to question the status quo and particular religious interpretations. After further discussion about the benefits of being a judge, Amani joked with the girl who said she would like to become a judge, saying that perhaps she could do it temporarily, reap all the benefits, and then retire and repent. All the girls laughed with Amani, demonstrating Davies' concept of "critical lightness," defined as "the acceptance that ideals and their holders can be mocked" (2008, p. 182). The girls in Amani's class learned that they should be able to be judges in Kuwait despite what particular religious interpretations have taught them, and they also learned that it was fine to laugh at themselves as they worked through some of the tensions that exist among ideologies.

As the *dustūr* module textbook was short and there was no pressure from a looming Ministry exam, Amani and her students had ample time to address not only rights realities in Kuwait, but also to follow up their learning with action. They often held mock protests and demonstrations to demand restitutions. As her students designed placards, Amani encouraged the use of internationally recognized rights discourses. As they debated and argued, she highlighted the importance of dialogue and mutual respect. Amani told me about one of the first times she had her students engage in more active learning. During a lesson early in the 2008–2009 academic year, the issue of student rights came up, and the students complained that their right to voice their opinions was not taken seriously at school. "I had them draft an official complaint to the principal, starting with the line, 'Based on Article 12 of the [United Nations] Convention on the Rights of the Child . . .', and they took this down to her office during our lesson. I immediately got a call from the principal asking what this was, to which I replied, 'This is my lesson for the day.'" Amani explained that this type of teaching and learning was an eye-opening experience for her, and as the case study continued, interesting changes were revealed in both Amani and her students.

Amani's students expressed in the workshops that they felt that Amani was the only teacher who recognized their rights. For example, in 2009, one Grade 11 student wrote: "*Abla* Amani tries so hard to give us our rights, and she is the only person at the school who tries to give us our rights [. . .] I respect *Abla* Amani and I love her so much because *Abla* Amani is something different." For Amani, teaching students their rights and simultaneously violating said rights was not an option. She said in our interview in 2010, "You teach students their rights, you teach them democracy, and at the same time, you say to them, do not exercise these rights." To help correct this perceived wrong, Amani took what I term to be unsanctioned action when she decided to create a rights manifesto for the creation of a student council for female high school students at the national level, which she drafted with a human rights lawyer and then presented to the Ministry of Education. The purpose of the council was to explicitly outline the rights of students and to institutionalize their participation in education at the national level. This, she explained to me, was crucial in promoting the democratic ideals they were trying to teach and live at school, or, to use Fielding's words, to achieve "interpersonal and structural integrity" (2007, p. 548). When she presented this impressive document to the Ministry, they dismissed it, beseeching her, "Please don't open their [the students'] eyes!" However, human rights are empowering (Donnelly, 2013), and with their teacher's recognition and the sanctioned action they were taking in her classes, Amani's students' sense of confidence and agency grew. They, too, began to take unsanctioned action—action not linked to any lessons and undertaken without teacher approval.

In 2009, Amani's students decided that the absence of cafeterias in public high schools violated their right to healthy meals and also prevented them from interacting with each other. They held a peaceful demonstration outside the administration offices to protest this perceived injustice. A year later, they followed this up with a peaceful sit-in to demand a longer break, arguing that 15 minutes did not give them enough time to eat, pray, and use the restroom and was therefore a violation of their right to rest. During both these instances of unsanctioned action, the students were acting of their own volition to correct perceived wrongs. The skills they employed to execute these demonstrations and the confidence they displayed were a direct reflection of the action they were taking in their *dustūr* class with Amani. In 2011, against the backdrop of the Arab Spring, Kuwaiti students took to the streets to protest various issues, including educational reforms and corruption. Though a direct link is difficult to prove, it is safe to assume that several of these students had taken the *dustūr* modules in public schools across Kuwait.

Enacting the Dustūr *Program: Democratic Spaces and Encounters with "The Other"*

Both instances of student action above centered on the issue of space, a topic near to Amani's heart. Amani complained that school spaces were too confining for students, and she often advocated for a "school without walls." She argued that students are boxed in within school walls both physically and metaphorically, as they lack any autonomy to make decisions within them. Figure 1 (left) shows a typical classroom at the case study school, which is in one of the most affluent districts in Kuwait (a rich, oil-producing country). Because of the Ministry's aforementioned "fixed classroom" policy, students remain in their classroom for most of the day. The walls are bare. There are no computers, books, or other resources. The desks and chairs are old, mismatched, and covered in graffiti, and they face the teacher's old, rickety desk in rows. In Amani's *dustūr* classes in 2009, students were always asked to form a U-shape with the desks when she walked in. She was the only teacher to change the configuration of the room. In an interview, she explained that the rows were not conducive to the dialogue she was trying to promote surrounding human rights issues, and they did not promote democratic participation.

Figure 1. At left is a typical "fixed classroom" at the case study school. At right is Amani's "lab classroom."

By 2010, Amani had successfully lobbied for her own room, arguing that she needed a lab since she taught psychology and psychological health, which were sciences Taking full advantage of this loophole, she held all her classes, including the *dustūr* module, there. She designed the room with her students, and it was markedly different from any other in the school (Figure 1, right). There were no individual desks in the room; instead, there were three large tables, set up in a "U" shape around the room. There were posters, plants, various electronic media, games, books, snacks, and more. Each table had copies of the Kuwaiti Constitution on it, and Amani referred to it often in all of her classes. Because the *dustūr* module did not have a Ministry exam, the textbooks and workbooks remained in Amani's cabinet overnight and were not taken home by students. In almost every other class, students were given daily assignments from the textbooks and were under constant pressure to memorize everything in them for the exams.

Although Amani had an open-door policy, allowing students to leave the room whenever they wished, students rarely did; this was strikingly different from other classes I observed, where students frequently requested to leave to go to the bathroom. Their behavior was also markedly different in the "lab" than in other classrooms. For example, students were not expected to stand when responding to questions; in fact, they were specifically reminded not to. Amani confirmed that the rules that applied in every other room in the school did not apply in their "lab." This, she explained, was another reason why she wanted an independent space, one that was unburdened by preexisting notions of "good behavior." Her "lab" (not really a lab at all) arguably became the most egalitarian and democratic space on campus, developing into a "vibrant and inclusive realm" (Fielding, 2007, p. 546) where students' rights were respected, they participated in discussions and processes affecting their lives, and they developed the agency to make changes they felt were needed. This "dialogic space" (Fielding, 2007, p. 547) encouraged "interrogative, dialogic openness" (p. 553) as others became curious and excited about what was going on there and were eager to visit. I observed several teachers visiting Amani's room, both to ask about and learn from her set-up and to take a break from the monotony of the "fixed classrooms." More than once, I heard students ask their teachers if they could have their lesson (whatever it happened to be) in Amani's room. Each time I heard this, the teachers were happy to oblige, and Amani was always willing to hand over her key. By finding a way to create a space within which she could achieve an approach with greater "democratic coherence" (Fielding, 2007, p. 545), Amani again took unsanctioned action.

While the case school was as homogenized as other public schools around Kuwait, there were scattered instances of engagement with the "other," whether actual or theoretical. In 2009, for example, the English Department held its annual International Day event. Amani told me that as the day drew near, one student approached her about participating in the event. The student, one of a handful of "non-Kuwaitis" at the school, was Iraqi. Aware that her nationality might offend some people because of Iraq's 1990 invasion of Kuwait, the student still felt strongly about participating. She sought out Amani and asked her opinion. Amani, of course, encouraged her wholeheartedly, pointing out that this was an international event and that she was part of the international community in Kuwait. The student went ahead and organized her Iraq table, and when the day came, her peers shared it with the same curiosity and excitement as they did other tables. Though the Iraqi student's desire to make her ("other") national identity visible cannot be linked directly to her experiences in the *dustūr* program (though the fact that she sought out her *dustūr* teacher and no one else is interesting), the example nonetheless serves to demonstrate what allowing students the space to explore their identities and those of "the other" can do. An Iraqi table at International Day may not heal all wounds, but it offers a forum for dialogue. As the case school was making Iraq visible in its International Day, national history textbooks were leaving the invasion out altogether. This decision can be interpreted in many ways, and as official reasons were not provided, one can only speculate. A more skeptical reading would be that removing the invasion would preclude critical interrogation of the events leading up to the invasion and potential criticism of the handling of the situation from above. A more optimistic reading would be that the move was (naïvely) meant to improve relations with Iraq. The case school opted for engagement over erasure and in doing so, promoted dialogue with and understanding of the perceived "other."

Within the *dustūr* program, a significant progression took place once students experienced recognition as rights-bearers and the subsequent agency this promoted. Students began exploring the experience of "the other" in Kuwait. The students in their third year of the *dustūr* program were the only ones in any of the research workshops over three years who brought up racism and discrimination, which were mentioned by over a third of the respondents. These issues were not raised in the context of things they were learning about in school, but rather their frustration with the realities they were witnessing and experiencing:

- "We in Kuwait discriminate a lot between nationals and residents, and I think that is racism."

- "There are immigrants who are not treated well and they are not respected, and to me that is racist discrimination and I don't like it. No to racism in Kuwait!"

- "I personally am not Kuwaiti, but through my time in Kuwait, it has become clear to me that a citizen is a national . . . and maybe it is an issue of racism."

- ". . . It is clear in the majority of Arab countries that their catchwords are discrimination and racism."

After first gaining recognition and autonomy for themselves as humans, students then developed the agency to engage in the universal rights dialogue as students, young people, girls, Kuwaitis, and so forth, potentially furthering their rights in relation to these multiple conceptions of self, as well as the rights of others who had been similarly marginalized based on various other criteria. The school is a safe place to engage in this type of dialogue, which is premised on feelings of solidarity (as argued by Dean, 1996). As discussed, however, this would involve rethinking the segregated, homogenized organization of schools.

The One-Year Dustūr *Module: A Return to the Same*

When the three short *dustūr* textbooks were bound into one long volume in 2011, time and space were lost, and textbook memorization made a comeback. Below, I contrast responses of two groups of Grade 12 students during the research workshops: those enrolled in the third year of the three-year program in 2010, and those who were enrolled in the one-year program in 2011.

Students in the three-year program made links between citizenship, human rights, freedom, and democracy. They also displayed a belief in their right to be heard and an appreciation for the reciprocity built into this right, mentioning freedom of expression, dialogue, and respect for others. They identified times they felt their own rights as students and as citizens were not recognized, contrasting these experiences with those in their *dustūr* classes. What is particularly interesting is that the students voiced demands for change articulately, and they seemed quite confident in their own agency. They also expressed hope and a belief in the possibility of change. The confidence and agency reflected in the voices of these students also led them to take unsanctioned action when they felt their rights were being violated, as described previously. The students linked this learning to the *dustūr* module and their teacher.

Students in the one-year Grade 12 module in 2011 complained about the rote learning involved in the shortened *dustūr* module, and they only made vague references to learning *about* democracy, with no mention of specific knowledge or skills (which the three-year students were able to identify). These students also mentioned the Islamic studies course as a main site of their learning on human rights. The criticality and active learning that were possible within the longer *dustūr* program were again replaced with the obedience associated with religion and the passivity that comes with memorization. Like their predecessors, these students voiced concerns over their rights being violated. However, they did not link this concern to their right to be heard or to the democratic right of participation. Their tone was more compliant and less confident and forceful. They seemed less aware of their agency and their right to be part of decision-making processes, as the following two contrasting examples illustrate:

- "I demand from the state that it improves curricula . . . and the teachers." (Grade 12 student, 2011, one-year *dustūr* program)

- "I refuse to accept any regulations issued by the Ministry unless agreed upon by the students. I suggest that there be . . . an open discussion about education and how to achieve it." (Grade 12 student, 2010, final year of three-year *dustūr* program)

Despite many setbacks, Amani remained full of hope and as committed to her students as ever. As she reminded her students when they complained about how long change takes, "You may not make a difference right away, but you can at least leave your fingerprint." When asked how she stays motivated, she responded laughingly, "Because I break the rules!" This "insistent affirmation of possibility" (Fielding, 2007, p. 551) was clearly echoed during the research workshops in the responses of the students who had taken the three-year *dustūr* program.

Concluding Remarks

In March 2013, Kuwait's National Youth Project of the Diwan Al-Amiri held a conference entitled *Kuwait Listens* (*al-Kuwait tisma'*). This project is a pioneering step for Kuwaiti youth, who have had limited opportunities for institutionalized participation in the state. Among the project's strategic goals are strengthening national identity, eliminating sectarian and tribal divisions among youth, promoting social cohesion, supporting Kuwait's democratic and constitutional culture, promoting tolerance, combating extremism, and respecting freedom of speech and the diverse views of young people (translated and reported by Kuwait News Agency, 2013). In their first national conference, the group shared the findings of their research on matters of citizenship and stressed key issues in need of immediate attention. These included issues surrounding identity. The young members of the project argued that if national identity and unity are to be prioritized, then all citizens' subnational identities must be embraced as well, including religious and tribal affiliations, and the distinctions between types of citizenship (original/naturalized) should be eliminated. The members also stressed the role of education in redefining citizenship, stressing that the national curriculum should focus on teaching the constitution, critical thinking, and the values of tolerance and respect for all religions. Their findings and suggestions to the government were comprehensive and impressive, and they urged the Minister of State for Youth Affairs, present at the conference, not to "tuck [their] suggestions away in a drawer," as has historically been the case with proposed reforms.

The analysis presented in this chapter of Kuwait's policy documents and national textbooks, as well as the findings from the case study school, support the suggestions of Kuwaiti youth mentioned above. Eliminating sectarian and tribal divisions among youth and instead promoting social cohesion would be easier to do if school populations reflected the diversity of the country; this would provide opportunities for young people to confront and potentially bridge societal divisions and inequalities, as well as to gain deeper understandings of the multi-layered nature of individuals' identities. In this way, a national identity would not conflict with any other affiliations that a person may have. When schools are spaces that are free from national and religious hegemony, tolerance and solidarity can replace extremism and racism. Respecting freedom of speech and the diverse views of young people requires that students' agency be embraced, and that they are allowed time and space for active, hands-on learning. This, in turn, encourages participation not only in knowledge construction but also in unsanctioned transformative action, thereby realizing Kuwait's democratic and constitutional aspirations.

Acknowledgment

I am grateful to Chatham House, Royal Institute of International Affairs, for permission to reproduce and adapt parts of the work entitled "Education and Democratic Development in Kuwait: Citizens in Waiting" (R. Al-Nakib, 2015).

Notes

1. The excerpts from the Kuwaiti Constitution in this chapter are the official English translations.

2. Kuwait derives the majority of its national revenues from the rent of its major natural resource, oil.

3. While analyzing this interplay is beyond the scope of this chapter, some contextualization is necessary to frame the educational ramifications to be discussed.

4. Articles 13–14, 1959 Kuwaiti Nationality Law, as amended (United Nations High Commissioner for Refugees, 2017).

5. It is important to note that academic research that critically engages with Kuwait's educational reports, goals, and curricula is rare. At the time of publication, no studies in Arabic or English that analyze Kuwait's human rights initiative or the citizenship strategy have been released, apart from two articles by the author of this chapter (see R. Al-Nakib, 2011, 2012). This section therefore reflects the author's own analysis and aims to begin a much-needed conversation about citizenship education in Kuwait.

6. All excerpts from this report have been translated into English by the author of this chapter.

7. In Islam, the *ḥadīth* are those acts, sayings, etc., attributed to the prophet Muhammad rather than the *Qur'ān*.

8. All excerpts from national textbooks have been translated into English by the author of this chapter.

9. All names have been changed to protect anonymity.

References

Abdulla, A. (2012). The Arab Gulf moment. In D. Held & K. Ulrichsen (Eds.), *The transformation of the Gulf: Politics, economics and the global order* (pp. 106–124). London: Routledge.

Al-Mughni, H. (1993). *Women in Kuwait: The politics of gender*. London: Saqi Books.

Al-Nakib, F. (2014). Revisiting *ḥaḍar* and *badū* in Kuwait: Citizenship, housing, and the construction of a dichotomy. *International Journal of Middle Eastern Studies, 46*, 5–30.

Al-Nakib, R. (2011). Citizenship, nationalism, human rights and democracy: A tangling of terms in the Kuwaiti curriculum. *Educational Research, 53*(2), 165–178.

Al-Nakib, R. (2012). Human rights, education for democratic citizenship and international organisations: Findings from a Kuwaiti UNESCO ASPnet school. *Cambridge Journal of Education, 42*(1), 97–112.

Al-Nakib, R. (2015). *Education and democratic development in Kuwait: Citizens in waiting* (commissioned by Future Trends in the GCC). London: Chatham House, Royal Institute of International Affairs.

Banks, J. A. (2008). Diversity, group identity, and citizenship education in a global age. *Educational Researcher, 37*(3), 129–139.

Beane, J. A. (2005). *A reason to teach: Creating classrooms of dignity and hope*. Portsmouth, NH: Heinemann.

Benhabib, S. (1992). *Situating the self: Gender, community and postmodernism in contemporary ethics*. Cambridge, UK: Polity Press.

Benhabib, S. (2008). Another cosmopolitanism. In R. Post (Ed.), *Another cosmopolitanism* (pp. 13–80). Oxford, UK: Oxford University Press.

Castles, S. (2004). Migration, citizenship, and education. In J. A. Banks (Ed.), *Diversity and citizenship education: Global perspectives* (pp. 17–48). San Francisco: Jossey-Bass.

Crystal, J. (1990). *Oil and politics in the Gulf: Rulers and merchants in Kuwait and Qatar.* Cambridge, UK: Cambridge University Press.

Crystal, J. (1992). *Kuwait: The transformation of an oil state.* Oxford, UK: Westview Press.

Davies, L. (2008). *Educating against extremism.* Stoke on Trent, UK: Trentham Books.

Dean, J. (1996). *Solidarity of strangers: Feminism after identity politics.* Berkeley: University of California Press.

Delanty, G. (2000). *Citizenship in a global age: Society, culture, politics.* Buckingham, UK: Open University Press.

Donnelly, J. (2013). *Universal human rights in theory and practice* (3rd ed.). Ithaca, NY: Cornell University Press.

Douzinas, C. (2000). *The end of human rights: Critical legal thought at the turn of the century.* Oxford, UK: Hart Publishing.

Faour, M., & Muasher, M. (2011). *Education for citizenship in the Arab World: Key to the future.* Washington, DC: Carnegie Endowment for International Peace.

Fielding, M. (2007). On the necessity of radical state education: Democracy and the common school. *Journal of Philosophy of Education, 41*(4), 539–557.

Fielding, M., & Moss, P. (2011). *Radical education and the common school: A democratic alternative.* London: Routledge.

Flecha, R. (2009). The educative city and critical education. In M. W. Apple, W. Au, & L. A. Gandin (Eds.), *The Routledge international handbook of critical education* (pp. 327–340). Cambridge, MA: Harvard Educational Review.

Freire, P. (1993). *Pedagogy of the oppressed.* New York: Continuum. (Original work published 1970)

Gandin, L. A., & Apple, M. W. (2002). Thin versus thick democracy in education: Porto Alegre and the creation of alternatives to neo-liberalism. *International Studies in Sociology of Education, 12*(2), 99–116.

Gutmann, A. (2004). Unity and diversity in democratic multicultural education: Creative and destructive tensions. In J. A. Banks (Ed.), *Diversity and citizenship education: Global perspectives* (pp. 71-96). San Francisco: Jossey-Bass.

Human Rights Watch. (2014, October 19). *Kuwait: Government critics stripped of citizenship.* Retrieved from https://www.hrw.org/news/2014/10/19/kuwait-government-critics-stripped-citizenship

Human Rights Watch. (2016). *World report 2016: Events of 2015.* New York: Author.

Ismael, J. S. (1993). *Kuwait: Dependency and class in a rentier state.* Gainesville: University Press of Florida.

Karmi, G. (1996). Women, Islam and patriarchalism. In M. Yamani (Ed.), *Feminism and Islam: Legal and literary perspectives* (pp. 69–85). Reading, UK: Garnet Publishing Limited.

Kuwait News Agency. (2013, March 13). *HH Amir inaugurates national youth conference.* Retrieved from http://www.kuna.net.kw/ArticleDetails.aspx?id=2298178&Language=en

Lister, R. (2003). *Citizenship: Feminist perspectives* (2nd ed.). Basingstoke, UK: Palgrave Macmillan.

Longva, A. N. (1997). *Walls built on sand: Migration, exclusion, and society in Kuwait.* Oxford, UK: Westview Press.

Longva, A. N. (2000). Citizenship in the Gulf states. In N. A. Butenschon, U. Davis, & M. Hassassian (Eds.), *Citizenship and the state in the Middle East* (pp. 179–197). Syracuse, NY: Syracuse University Press.

Longva, A. N. (2006). Nationalism in pre-modern guise: The discourse on hadhar and badu in Kuwait. *International Journal of Middle East Studies, 38,* 171–187.

Marshall, T. H. (1950). *Citizenship and social class.* Cambridge, UK: Cambridge University Press.

Middle East Media Research Institute. (2007, March 2). Kuwaiti columnist: Interference of religious groups in curricula damages education. *Special Dispatch No. 1486.* Retrieved from: http://www.memri.org/report/en/print2071.htm

Ministry of Education. (2007a). *Al-terbia al-Islāmiyya lil-ṣaf al-ʿāshir* [Islamic education for Grade 10] (2nd ed.). Kuwait: Author.

Ministry of Education. (2007b). *Al-dustūr wa ḥuqūq al-insaān lil-ṣaf al-ḥādī ʿashar* [The Constitution and human rights for Grade 11]. Kuwait: Author.

Ministry of Education. (2008a). *The national report: Development of education in the State of Kuwait, 2004–2008.* Kuwait: Author and Kuwait National Commission for Education, Science and Culture.

Ministry of Education. (2008b). *Al-wathīqa al-ʾsāsiyya lil-marḥala al-thānawiyya fī dawalet al-Kuwait* [The fundamental policy for the secondary stage in the State of Kuwait]. Kuwait: Author.

Ministry of Education. (2010a). *Al-wathīqa al- waṭaniyya libinā' mehej al-ijtimaʿiyyāt fī dawlet al-Kuwait* [National policy to build the social studies curriculum in the State of Kuwait]. Kuwait: Author.

Ministry of Education. (2010b). *'Istrātijiat tekrīs mefāhīm al-muwāṭana wa al-walā' wa al-'intimā' ledā al-nesh' fī al-menāhij al-dirāsiyya bidawlet al-Kuwait* [Strategy for reinforcing the concepts of citizenship, loyalty and belonging among young people through educational curricula in Kuwait]. Kuwait: Author.

Ministry of Education. (2010c). *The State of Kuwait: Experience in the field of human rights education.* Kuwait: Author.

Osler, A., & Starkey, H. (2010). *Teachers and human rights education.* Stoke on Trent, UK: Trentham Books.

Parolin, G. P. (2006). Generations of Gulf constitutions: Paths and perspectives. In A. Khalaf & G. Luciani (Eds.), *Constitutional reform and political participation in the Gulf* (pp. 51–87). Dubai, UAE: Gulf Research Center.

Saeid, A. (2010, July 1). MPs threaten to sack education minister. *Kuwait Times*, p. 3.

Schofield, J. W. (2007). Increasing the generalizability of qualitative research. In M. Hammersley (Ed.), *Educational research and evidence-based practice* (pp. 106–120). London: SAGE.

Stake, R. E. (2005). Qualitative case studies. In N. K. Denzin & Y. S. Lincoln (Eds.), *The SAGE handbook of qualitative research* (3rd ed.) (pp. 443–466). Thousand Oaks, CA: SAGE.

State of Kuwait. (1962). *The Constitution of the State of Kuwait.* Kuwait: Author.

Tétreault, M. A. (2000). *Stories of democracy: Politics and society in contemporary Kuwait.* New York: Columbia University Press.

Tétreault, M. A., & Al-Mughni, H. (1995). Gender, citizenship and nationalism in Kuwait. *British Journal of Middle Eastern Studies, 52*(1/2), 64–80.

Tibbitts, F. (2005). Transformative learning and human rights education: Taking a closer look. *Intercultural Education, 16*(2), 107–113.

Turner, B. S. (2006). *Vulnerability and human rights.* University Park: The Pennsylvania State University Press.

United Nations. (1948). *The Universal Declaration of Human Rights.* New York: General Assembly of the United Nations.

United Nations Development Programme. (2009). *Arab human development report 2009: Challenges to human security in the Arab Countries.* New York: Author.

United Nations High Commissioner for Refugees. (2017). *Nationality Law, 1959.* Retrieved from http://www.unhcr.org/refworld/docid/3ae6b4ef1c.html

United Nations High Commissioner for Refugees. (2010). *Universal periodic review: Kuwait.* Retrieved from http://www.unhcr.org/refworld/pdfid/4c6142072.pdf

Wright, E. O. (2007). Guidelines for envisioning real utopias. *Soundings, 36*(Summer), 26–39.

Chapter 16

From Empire to Republic: Citizenship, Pluralism, and Diversity in Turkey

Hasan Aydin *and* Fadime Koc-Damgaci

Yildiz Technical University

With its rich, pluralistic Ottoman heritage, Turkey has always been an ethnically and religiously diverse country (Faltis, 2014). It consists of Kurds, Arabs, Circassians, and other Muslim ethnic groups as well as non-Muslim minorities such as Armenians, Greeks, and Jews. Located next to Syria, Turkey has found itself in the unique position of being the state that hosts the largest number of Syrian refugees from the current civil war there. According to data published by the United Nations, the number of refugees in Turkey had reached 1.7 million by March 2015; the real figure is estimated to be significantly higher if the number of unregistered refugees is added (İçduygu, 2015). Aydin (2016) argued that, in addition to the significant number of Syrian refugees, many students from other countries are registered officially with educational institutions in Turkey. Because of the highly varied cultural, linguistic, ethnic, religious, and educational backgrounds of these students, Turkey is in urgent need of an educational system that embraces cultural diversity (Aydin, 2012a). In recent years, events have pushed the issue of multicultural education to the forefront of educational policy.

The concepts of "encountering" or "familiarization" involve helping students from different backgrounds get to know each other through a process of benefiting from others' experiences—value is added to the individual's learning process (Luchtenberg, 2005). This approach occupies a key role in acquainting society at large with the situations of students in Turkey from different social backgrounds. In contrast to the education that is usually provided to immigrants, multicultural education exerts a great influence on the intellectual and spiritual development of all students, as well as on the schools that are in a diverse system. More explicit emphasis is placed on the subjects taught and the lives of students at schools than in other forms of education (Luchtenberg, 2005). Luchtenburg (2005) takes her supportive views of multicultural education further, arguing that multicultural education doubles the benefit of traditional immigrant education. She also emphasizes that today's society at large enjoys greater experience with regard to the issue of multicultural education. This is due to the fact that multicultural education enables students to become aware of the multicultural environment where they find themselves (Aydin, 2013a). Aydin (2009) argues that within the traditional framework of immigrant education, a target immigrant group is selected and an attempt is made to help its members adapt to and harmonize with the cultural differences of the new country and integrate into that society. However, multicultural education does not merely aim to integrate the immigrant into society but also to add the cultural richness and diversity brought by the immigrants to the fabric of society (Aydin, 2013b; Aydin & Ozfidan, 2014).

Studies conducted in recent years indicate that multicultural education has become a serious academic field in Turkey (Banks, 2008; Dagmaci & Aydin, 2013; Karatas & Oral, 2015). These studies have asserted the view that developments in this field have mainly taken the form of diversity and citizenship education. For example, according to Cayir and Gurkaynak (2007), citizenship education in Turkey can be regarded as a modernization project that ensures the transition of Turkish citizens between the private and public sectors. Kerr (1996), Kerr and Cleaver (2004) and Kerr, Ireland, Lopes, and Craig (2004) identified four approaches to delivering citizenship education nationally:

- *Progressing schools.* These schools are defined as developing citizenship education in the curriculum and wider community. They are purported to have the most positive school ethos related to citizenship and are regarded as the most advanced in terms of citizenship education provision.

- *Focused schools.* These schools concentrate on developing citizenship education in the curriculum, with few opportunities for active citizenship in the school and wider community.

- *Minimalist schools.* These schools are at an early stage of the development of citizenship education, with a limited range of delivery approaches and with few extracurricular activities.

- *Implicit schools.* These schools do not focus explicitly on citizenship education in the curriculum but do provide opportunities for active citizenship. With a greater focus on citizenship within the curriculum, they have the potential to become progressive schools.

Some scholars also advocate a *whole-school* approach, which includes making changes to the curriculum, community, and culture of the school (Maylor, Rose, Hutchings Rollock, & Williams, 2007, p. 49). In this context, Davies (2001) expresses concerns regarding the relationship between citizenship and citizenship education. The main question that concerns her is, "How is diversity conceptualized in the context of citizenship education?" Her other questions include the following:

- What degree of tolerance with regard to education is included in citizenship education?

- How does citizenship education manage to reach solutions on issues such as segregation, injustice, and violence?

- How does citizenship education address the key question related to the concept of diversity, such as, "What is diversity, and how can it be described and legitimized?"

- How should citizenship education be defined within the context of the various conflicting functions of the educational institution itself?

- How can conflicting or paradoxical situations be explained, such as the fact that schools encourage obedience and deference to "accepted" social norms and duties of citizenship while teaching values such as individual independence, critical thinking, and social justice?

- Do teachers expect to play the role of the loyal and tolerant citizen during the social integration process, or do they see themselves as radical defenders of the existing system?

- Can one really reconcile opposition to inequality with an individualistic and competitive school system?

- Can individualistic and competitive schooling really form the basis for collective and cooperative action?

Banks (2008) presents four key principles that may form the firm foundation of citizenship education when considered within the context of diversity. The first of these principles is that students should acquire information about local communities, nations, and the wider world, as well as about the complex relationships that exist between them, and be able to distinguish between the various interacting elements. Second, students must learn about how people in their own communities, regions, and nations are connected to and maintain communication with other groups within the context of contemporary economic, political, cultural, environmental, and technological changes. Third, students should receive information regarding the nature of democracy and democratic institutions and should learn about the opportunities offered by these institutions and democratic practices and be encouraged to think what this means for them as citizens (Dahl, 1993; Lafer, 2014). Finally, in multicultural nation-states, the teaching of human rights needs to include citizenship education courses and programs.

Citizenship

Citizenship can be defined as the legal bond or connection that delineates the relationships between the individual and the state pertaining to mutual rights, duties, obligations, and the rights established by the state in law that are granted to the individual citizen (Bozkurt, 1992; Polat, 2011). In this context, we can speak of the concept of citizenship as representing a legal definition. Citizens benefit from the opportunities presented to them by the state by exercising their rights. In the same manner, Ersoy (2014) argues that an individual who has not obtained citizenship from that state will be unable to take advantage of these legal rights and will remain subject to laws established for noncitizens. In that case, to whom does the state accord the right of citizenship? Do individuals who reside in a country where they do not possess citizenship experience an infringement of their human rights? How do those who are citizens of a given country learn about the rights that have been accorded to them?

Answers to these questions in so-called welfare or social states is offered through the provision of education and instruction. One point that must be stressed here is that citizenship education should not merely be provided in schools but should also be based and delivered in accordance with the concept of "life-long learning" (Hablemitoglu & Ozmete, 2012, p. 43). Because the majority of citizenship rights are granted on the birth of the individual citizen, the provision of citizenship education at an early age is of critical importance from the point of view of assisting individuals to learn about their rights (Crick, 1998; Yavuz, 2009). The principal aim of citizenship education is to realize a state of harmony in the society to which the individual belongs.

According to the postmodern understanding of citizenship, within the core concept of citizenship exist subconcepts of diversity and pluralism in addition to the subconcept of individualism (Bhavnani, Mirza, & Meetoo, 2005; Rattansi, 1999). For this reason, citizenship education needs to include in its framework the concepts of *diversity* and *pluralism* (Gozlugol, 2013). Diversity finds its most general expression as a biological term that is used to differentiate or encourage differences between people and groups (Damgaci, 2013; U. Gunay, 1998). Pluralism, on the other hand, strives to create an organic whole derived from the various elements that fuse together within a society (Bakker, 2003). The success of the administration of the new pluralist construct comprising various individuals with differing ethnic, religious, and cultural backgrounds and who hold differing political views is seen to be directly proportional to the citizenship rights accorded to its individual citizens. Turkey is a country that has a long tradition of uniting people with various religious, linguistic, and ethnic backgrounds and differing cultural and ideological perspectives in its territories through a common bond of "equal citizenship" (I. Kaya & Aydin, 2014). Nevertheless, because various groups have felt that their rights have been infringed—in particular with regard to culture and education—and have resorted to violence to express their opinions, education about topics such as citizenship, diversity, pluralism, and democracy in Turkey has not been as successful as might have been hoped (Aydin, 2012a; Faltis, 2014).

Citizenship in the Ottoman Empire and the Foundation Period of the Turkish Republic

During the initial years following the establishment of the Turkish Republic, subjects such as history, geography, and citizenship were all contained within a single, all-encompassing humanities course (Celik, 2008). In 1962, a subject called "Society and Country Studies" was added to the fourth and fifth grades of the primary school curriculum; the name of this subject was changed to "Social Studies" in 1968 (Ersoy, 2010). Subjects such as history, geography, and citizenship were included within the framework of this course (Ata, 2007). In primary school, while the social studies course continued to be taught after reforms to the educational program in 1990, the course was later removed from the middle school curriculum, in 1985, and replaced by separate courses in national history, national geography, history of the Turkish Revolution, and Atatürkism (Kemalism) and citizenship (Ersoy, 2013). With the transition to an eight-year compulsory and continuous education system in 1997, the decision was made to teach social studies from fourth to seventh grades, while a separate "Education in Citizenship and Democracy" course was taught in the eighth grade. The educational program of the Turkish Republic has not yet reached a stage of stability or continuity in spite of the fact that the state was established almost a century ago. With the implementation of new, far-reaching reforms every few years—reforms that were conducted with particular intensity during the last ten years—the cracks in the educational system have become evident. In research carried out regarding multicultural education in Turkey, it has been concluded that the increase in quality and standards in the system will be realized only when all parts of the system are focused on the concept of multicultural education (Aydin & Tonbuloglu, 2014). According to Cayir and Gurkaynak (2007), in Turkey, "the portrayal of any minority (for instance, Kurdish or Armenian citizens) in a citizenship textbook is still unthinkable" (p. 7). The manifestation of ethnic or religious differences in the tightly defined, state-monitored, and supposedly neutral public sphere is considered detrimental to national unity and social cohesion. In such a context, citizenship education promotes a notion of citizenship not in terms of the language of rights but of duties and responsibilities to the state and nation.

Banks (2008) notes that "multicultural societies are faced with the problem of constructing nation-states that reflect and incorporate the diversity of their citizens and yet have an overarching set of shared values, ideals, and goals to which all their citizens are committed" (p. 133). The shared values, ideals, and goals to which all individuals should be committed should include providing equal opportunity to fellow citizens, respect, and a commitment to social justice (Aydin, 2012b; Eferakorho, 2008). Put differently, the demands placed on modern states to recognize minority group identities and to accommodate these cultural differences within the larger structure of society is what Kymlicka (1995) refers to as the "challenge of 'multiculturalism'" (p. 153). Recent census figures indicate that Turkey is a multicultural society with a growing number of ethnic minority populations: Kurds (18%) and others (7% to 12%). "Others" include Laz, Circassian, Arabs, and Greeks, as well as additional ethnic minorities, which are 25% to 30% of the population of Turkey (KONDA, 2011). This phenomenon of cultural diversity is not unique to Turkey; global migration is becoming increasingly widespread. In order to meet the needs of students in an increasingly diverse, pluralistic, and global society in the 21st century, schools must equip students with the knowledge, skills, and dispositions of a multicultural citizen. Multicultural citizenship is a new concept of citizenship (Kymlicka, 1995; Taylor, 1996).

As is widely recognized, the modern Turkish Republic was founded on the reduced base of the Ottoman Empire, which had collapsed in a period of world and internal conflict. For this reason, while at a state level profound transformations were realized within the governing and administrative structures, the base of the society underwent little change (Ersoy, 2014). The communities within the borders of the new Turkish state established in 1923 managed to maintain their existence. The Turkish Republic of today consists of a total of 36 different ethnic groups within its borders.

The Ottoman Empire, whether we consider it from a north-to-south or east-to-west perspective, was not only larger in size, but also included a larger number of ethnic groups than its modern successor (I. Kaya & Aydin, 2013). However difficult it might have proved to be to govern a state with such a vast territory and such a large variety of ethnic groups, it is widely accepted that the Ottoman Empire succeeded in maintaining control over such a complex entity for many centuries (Ozturk, 2010). Although the Ottoman Empire was governed in accordance with religious provisions, both Muslim and non-Muslim subjects of the Empire were held to their laws. Few differences regarding the treatment between Muslims and non-Muslims were found in terms of the exercising or application of rights (Karatas, 2006).

According to Karatas (2006), when examining the records of courts in which sessions involving both Muslim and non-Muslim defendants and plaintiffs were held, the courts ruled in favor of non-Muslims in many trial hearings and addressed their grievances and alleviated their mistreatment. Furthermore, all common citizens enjoyed citizenship rights such as the overriding protection of the state and the accompanying guarantee of security and protection for individual life and property. Moreover, Karatas (2006) stated that the concepts of "Ottomanism" and "Turkishness" became largely synonymous, primarily because the state was founded by a community of people of Turkish origin and the characteristics of "Turkishness" came to be perceived as virtuous. The Ottoman Empire, although seeing itself as Turkish and Muslim in essence, still granted citizenship rights to individuals belonging to different religious denominations and ethnic groups (Ersoy, 2014). One of the areas in which the provision of these rights was manifested was education (Celep, 2014). For example, in the schools of the Doğubeyazıt province, which was densely populated by Kurdish ethnic communities, instruction in schools was conducted in the Kurdish language (I. Kaya & Aydin, 2013). Individuals belonging to other religious denominations, because of their status as "dhimmi" (or religious minorities) for state administrative purposes, were allowed to exercise their rights in accordance with the overruling guidelines provided to the Patriarch or Metropolitan Bishop of the confessional minority, as leaders of their religious communities (Resit, 1933).

It has been observed that the "Supreme" Ottoman Empire (Devlet-I Alliyye-i-Osmaniyye) maintained its rule over a period of more than six centuries, which can be divided into six stages or periods: (a) feudalism, (b) establishment of the state, (c) expansion of the state's power, (d) stagnation, (e) decline of the state, and finally (f) disintegration or decomposition into smaller states. As the names of these stages suggest, during the era of expansion, when the state rapidly increased the areas under its control, a saturation point was reached. The Empire proved incapable of expanding and instead endeavored merely to conserve the territories it ruled. The era of decline that followed is also widely known as the "Modernization Period" (Aktel, 1998). The most important step taken to attempt to maintain and improve the state was the proclamation of the Imperial Edict of Reorganization, or Tanzimat Fermanı, of 1839—also known as the Imperial Edict of Gülhane—that granted more comprehensive citizenship rights to non-Muslims (Erdem, 2010). As a matter of fact, the edict was in line with a long Ottoman tradition that promised its people a more just system of government (Aktel, 1998). In this edict, all Ottoman subjects, regardless of ethnic group, religion, or language, were to be accorded rights based on underlying legal principles, including protections of property, life, and personal honor; justice with regard to taxation; a fair approach to recruitment to the civil service; and specification of time spent in military service.

In the Edict of Reform, or Islahat Proclamation (1856), there is a shift to the concept of citizenship, which is different from the Ottoman understanding of the nature and rights of the subject. In this proclamation, which extends the articles established in the Edict of Reorganization (1839), other ideas about citizenship were added that emphasized (a) prohibiting religious officials from receiving money from people; (b) abolishing the *jizya,* or religious tax, for non-Muslims; (c) removing from spoken or written discourse any titles or forms of address—whether religious, ethnic, or linguistic—that implied superior or inferior social position; (d) granting the right to become state employees to all subjects without considering religious or denominational status (before this proclamation, only Muslims could become state employees); (e) granting every religious and ethnic community the right to open schools with its own minority languages as the medium of instruction; and (f) establishing nondenominational courts and recruiting non-Muslims as well as Muslims for military service. Thus, while the Proclamation of Reorganization contained legal decrees that applied to all subjects—Muslim and non-Muslim alike—the Edict of Reform further extended and expanded the citizenship rights of non-Muslims (Okandan, 1999).

Minority Education Based on Multiculturalism and Multilingualism in the Ottoman Empire

In the Ottoman Empire, Turks and Muslims enjoyed the right to open their own educational institutions, as did minority groups (Bilgiç, 2003; Gokce & Oguz, 2010). According to Uzuncarsili (1975), minorities freely spoke their own languages, practiced their faiths, developed their own cultures, and administered their own educational institutions. In addition, in a multifaith and multinational empire, educational institutions belonging to religious and ethnic minority groups were categorized as minority and foreign schools (Akyüz, 2008; Gokce & Oguz, 2010). Because of the right that was accorded to the Greek Orthodox community following the conquest of Istanbul, the Patriarch as spiritual leader of that religious minority was allowed to administer hospitals, churches, and educational institutions. In such an atmosphere, the minority schools that had been set up prior to the conquest of the city were allowed to maintain their existence and were administered in a more rational and systematic manner. The same rights were later accorded to Armenian and Jewish communities (Ergin, 1977). The minority schools can be separated into three main groups: Armenian, Greek, and Jewish schools. In these schools basic instruction in the arts, as well as in the sciences and religion, was provided. Furthermore, the Ottoman Empire provided expenses from the state budget to pay for the salaries of the Turkish language teachers employed at the Greek minority schools (Ayas, 1948). Only in the Directive of Special Schools issued in 1915 did the minority schools become subject to the state Inspectorate of Education.

Another type of non-Muslim school was the foreign schools that were opened as a result of the capitulations, or special privileges, accorded to France by the Ottoman Empire in 1536. Later these privileges were extended to other European powers. In the aftermath of the Reorganization, schools under foreign administration began to gain influence (Ayas, 1948). At the outset, these schools were only Catholic institutions. After the 18th century, because of the rights awarded to non-Muslims by the Edict of Reform (1956), non-Muslim students were able to continue their education at state-administered civil and military schools. Only on the grounds of perceived treachery of a certain number of ethnically Bulgarian subjects in the 1877 Ottoman-Russian War were non-Muslims prohibited from studying at military schools. The comprehensive rights granted to minorities and foreigners were, however, exploited in the aftermath of the weakening of the Ottoman Empire, and it was established that many members of political societies who had the intention of destroying the state had been educated at minority and foreign schools (Tasdemirci, 2001). To this day, foreign and minority schools continue their educational activities in Turkey. As an extension of the above practices, however, while non-Muslim students may attend state schools and Muslim students may study at foreign schools, admission to these schools requires passing an entrance examination.

Citizenship and Citizenship Education in Turkey

Since 1963, the concept of global citizenship education has gained recognition along with national citizenship during the process of the Turkish Republic's attempt to acquire membership in the European Union. The transition from national citizenship toward global citizenship has also brought to the forefront a new concept of European citizenship among the countries in Europe (Ersoy, 2010). According to Osler (2012), during the first decade of the 21st century there was increased interest, among both national policy makers and international organizations, in the position and status of citizenship education within school curricula. Osler (2012) stated that there was a growing debate concerning multiculturalism and multicultural citizenship, as policy makers addressed perceived tensions between the desire to promote social cohesion and the need to recognize ethnic, cultural, social, and linguistic diversity within nation-states (Banks, 2001, 2004). The National Ministry of Education has made some reforms to the national education program designed to facilitate Turkey's European Union membership integration process (National Ministry of Education, 2014). Such trends can be identified in education policy making both in societies that have readily acknowledged their cultural diversity over a long period of time and in those that have perceived themselves to be homogeneous (Osler, 2012). Interest in citizenship education and diversity at the national level has been driven by a positive recognition of diversity and dissent as essential elements in the development of a healthy democratic climate.

States in which democracy has been adopted are obliged to inform students and teach in schools human rights and basic freedoms that are essential to the well-being of all citizens (Gulmez, 2001). Ersoy (2014) states that it is necessary for individuals to learn about their own rights. Therefore, courses on the themes of citizenship rights and democracy should be provided within existing education programs. Democracy and citizenship education, in addition to enabling students to learn about personal rights, should also strive to teach responsibilities toward the state and the position of the individual with regard to laws and legislation (Buyukkaragoz & Civi, 1998).

Content pertaining to citizenship and democracy was taught as a compulsory subject in the fourth and fifth grades prior to the law that rendered eight-year continuous compulsory education, and was compulsory in the seventh and eighth grades after the transition took place (Gundem, 1996; Gozutok, 2007). Although the Citizenship and Democracy course was removed from the educational program for the 2001 academic year, it was included in the program as a cross-disciplinary subject that was an integral part of the learning process at all levels of the school as a result of reforms and alterations to the program carried out in 2004. Nevertheless, beginning in 2010 the course began to be taught again as a core subject, though only for eighth grade in primary schools.

In order to fully understand the Citizenship and Democracy course taught in Turkish schools, it is essential to be familiar with the definition of citizenship contained in the Turkish constitution. The concept of citizenship was not addressed directly in the first constitution of the Turkish Republic in 1921. In the constitution of 1924, with regard to citizenship, all people of Turkey regardless of differences in religion or ethnicity other than Turks were described as "Turks." In the 1961 constitution, a section entitled "Citizenship" was created, and all people with citizenship or who were connected to the Turkish states were thereby called "Turks." In the 1982 constitution, another section was created under the title "Turkish Citizenship," and definitions of citizenship contained in the 1961 constitution were used (Bilir, 2012). In the constitutions published in the early period of the Turkish Republic, "Turkishness" was employed as a concept pertaining to a nation rather than an ethnic group, and the citizens of Turkey were referred to as "Turks." The Turkish state equated the concept of "citizen" with that of "Turk." However, according to Kepenekci (2008), citizenship is in fact a shared connection of origin that links individuals to a state. For this reason, relating citizenship to the name of an ethnic group might be offensive to other ethnic communities living in that country. In the present age, when citizenship is defined as comprising many contrasting aspects, reducing the concept to being synonymous with a single ethnic group may be seen as simplistic.

Another factor that needs to be taken into consideration regarding citizenship is the issue of migration, which has in recent years come increasingly to the forefront of discourse. In 2011, in particular, as a consequence of the civil war that broke out in Syria, a large number of Syrian families took refuge in Turkey. In spite of this development, the first part of the Law for Foreign Nationals and International Protection only came into effect in 2013, with the second part enacted in 2014 (Mitchell, 2014). The law addresses issues concerning these refugees, such as their rights of entry into Turkey, their permission to reside in the country, conditions under which they may be expelled from the country, and the provisions to be made for the education of their children (Mitchell, 2014). It was stipulated that those who might be exposed to inhumane treatment in their countries of origin would not be expelled. The children of families who were unable to return were then granted access to education. According to the Law for Foreign Nationals and International Protection (Law No. 6458), they would be able to benefit from educational provision as described in the law, and the National Ministry of Education was called to take the necessary measures to help them access this right (Law on Foreign Nationals and International Protection, 2013).

Since 2011, Turkey has resettled and hosted the world's largest migrant community: 2.3 million Syrian refugees, approximately half of whom were school-age children at the time of entry. According to Human Rights Watch (2015), Turkey allowed Syrian refugees to attend Turkish public schools, with just over 212,000 enrolled at primary and secondary schools. However, while 90% of the children of families living in refugee camps had enrolled in schools, most refugees lived outside camps, where only 25% of school-aged children were registered; thus, 400,000 children had not yet enrolled in schools by 2015. Today, students attending Turkish schools continue to be limited in their quality of learning by the language barriers they face, as well as by the Turkish Ministry of Education's limited ability to monitor and support Syrian children in schools (Aydin, 2016).

The Democratic Context of Pluralism in Turkey

Many cultural groups currently live in Turkey. During the periods when the Ottoman Empire maintained its rule—since its territories were greater in size than those of the Turkish state today—the number of cultural groups exceeded those in Turkey today. According to Gundogan (2002), to ensure pluralism and to prevent cultural conflicts, it is necessary to place values at the foreground of the debate so that cultural groups will act positively toward each other. Tolerance is a value in itself. It is recognized that the cultural conflicts present within the Ottoman Empire were addressed in a largely tolerant manner (Bayraktar, 2013). Even Voltaire (cited in K. Gunay, 1998), one of the greatest thinkers of the Enlightenment Era, who achieved great advances in modern thinking concerning tolerance and pluralism, regarded the policy of the Ottoman Empire regarding pluralism and tolerance as an exemplary one. Dealing with the conflicts among different cultures is currently much needed on Turkey's agenda, as is the case in many regions and countries of the world. If "pluralism" in its truest sense is to be achieved, tolerance must become state policy as it was in the Ottoman Empire. In this regard, cultural conflicts will be greatly reduced, and a peaceful and stable regional and global environment will be achieved.

Assimilation and Social Dependence in the Turkish Educational System

During the final period of the Ottoman Empire, a wide range of schools of thought and political philosophies were adopted in an attempt to avert the destruction of the state. The philosophy of Ottomanism that had constituted the essential element of the Empire began to displease the Turkish subjects of the Empire, while the alternative pan-Islamism political movement was disliked by members of other religious groups. As a result, these schools lost their importance within a short time. One of the adopted trends, known as "Westernism," was also considered contrary to the spirit of Islam.

The philosophy of "Turkism" was a school of thought that gained popularity among those wishing to establish a new system of governance. The fact that the founders of the Ottoman Empire had been Turks by ethnicity and that Turks inhabited a large part of the territories remaining in the hands of the former rulers of the Ottoman Empire strengthened the positive perceptions of this trend. Consequently, the new state of the Turkish Republic was founded on the principle of Turkism. While various communities maintained their ways of life, speaking languages other than Turkish was seen as a threat to the new regime. In response, the government took prohibitive and assimilative precautions (Kubilay, 2005).

In addition, with regard to the worship practices of the majority Muslim population, those responsible for conducting religious services were pressured to lead worship in Turkish instead of Arabic. The call to prayer, or *adhân* (*ezan* in Turkish), was performed from 1932 to 1950 in Turkish (Tuncalp, 1950). This standard announcement for the service on Friday and the five daily ritual prayers (*namaz* in Turkish, or *salât* in Arabic) had always been recited in Arabic in Turkey and everywhere in the world. However, the Kemalist regime in Turkey was committed to ending that tradition. The call was recited in Turkish until June 16, 1950, when the National Assembly amended the law banning its performance in Arabic (Azak, 2008).

According to Kubilay (2005), although the multiethnic and multicultural composition of the country had been recognized during the struggle for independence, there was a change in direction, and views emerged that argued against a multiethnic basis for the state after the proclamation of the Republic. For instance, speaking languages other than Turkish in public was not only viewed as a threat but banned through legal decree following the declaration of the Republic. However, in 1991, Law No. 2932, which prohibited the speaking of languages other than Turkish, was abolished (Kubilay, 2005). After that, radio and TV channels broadcasting in languages other than Turkish were established, and the teaching of minority languages as a selective/optional subject was permitted in public schools. The concept of pluralism was adopted for the first time since the collapse of the Ottoman Empire, and great progress in democracy was made.

Democratic Adjustments/Regulations for Development of the Educational Program and Multicultural Education

Since the establishment of the Turkish Republic, the state has experienced various problems with regard to the rights of minorities. Kurdish speakers are the largest ethnic group in Turkey, comprising approximately 18% of the total population (Faltis, 2014). The founding of the proposed Kurdish Institute and the authorization for the opening of a Kurdish-language TV and radio station have been realized, and Kurdish mother-tongue education is now allowed in both public and private schools (Y. Kaya, 2015). A number of Turkish groups that had been confronted with certain groups of Kurdish provocateurs erroneously perceived education in the mother-tongue or native language as Kurdish education, and resorted to violence to oppose that right. The International Cultural Research Center report cited research finding that Turkey had entered into the process of providing elective Kurdish courses in an unfortunate and unplanned manner (Kaya & Aydin, 2013). The report recommended that Turkey immediately resolve such confusion and produce and apply permanent plans and strategies in this area. The first recommended step was to implement necessary legal arrangements and prepare a strategic action plan. The second step, one of urgent necessity, was to educate competent academicians and professionals (Kaya & Aydin, 2013).

Moreover, Damgaci and Aydin (2014) emphasized that multicultural education programs should then be developed and offered in faculties of education, and the qualifications of the teacher education programs should be designed consistent with the necessities of bilingual education. Furthermore, the shortage of relevant professionals should be immediately resolved by establishing Kurdish teaching departments (Kaya, 2015). The right to be educated in one's mother tongue is a right ensured by many international conventions (May, 2005). The Universal Declaration of Linguistic Rights, the European Charter for Regional or Minority Languages, the Framework Convention for the Protection of National Minorities, and the International Covenant on Civil and Political Rights are among the fundamental texts that support and specify language rights (Smith, 2003). These treaties and conventions guarantee a number of educational and cultural rights, primarily the right of students to learn in their mother tongues (Kaya & Aydin, 2013, p. 84).

One important language right that needs to be addressed in Turkey is the provision or introduction of Kurdish education in the mother tongue. It is the right of every cultural group to be able to receive education in its mother tongue (I. Kaya & Aydin, 2014). According to the KONDA report of 2011, Turkey now has 36 ethnic groups within its borders. All of them should be able to learn their own languages in school. In addition, citizens from various ethnic groups should be able to learn each other's languages and develop empathy for one another.

Although many steps have been taken with respect to democracy in the Turkish educational system, just as many shortcomings can be observed. For example, at certain universities, although departments for the teaching of Circassian and Georgian language and literature have been created, college programs for many of Turkey's other minority languages have still not been initiated. The fact that these departments do not teach the languages at the college level prevents the teaching of these languages for mother-tongue purposes in primary and middle schools because of a shortage of trained teachers. Furthermore, it is crucial to note that pluralism, multiculturalism, and diversity in education require autonomy in local government so that each locale can shape its language education program to meets its needs. However, the assignment of education to local governments will also create human resources problems. Therefore, the required planning of human resources should be carefully implemented.

Teacher Profile: The Profile of a Multicultural Teacher in Turkey

Ethnic minority groups in Turkey play an active role in the social, cultural, and working life of the nation and make their presence felt within the educational system. While individuals belonging to different ethnic, cultural, and linguistic groups enjoy certain choices with regard to aspects of social freedom and employment options, they remain deprived of certain opportunities within the state educational system. In the existing system, students are allocated to state schools primarily on the basis of their proximity to the school, without regard to skin color, language, or ethnic group. However, private schools, minority schools, and foreign schools are not subject to these stipulations. Students may prefer to attend private institutions with their own approaches to education by paying a set tuition fee. Foreign schools (run by the French, British, American, and Italian authorities independent of state control) admit students according to the scores and grades that candidates receive on the schools' own acceptance exams. Minority schools, such as those run by the

Greek and Armenian minorities, educate students of a specific religious denomination or minority background. The vast majority of the 53,574 primary, middle, and high schools in Turkey are operated by the state (TUIK, 2015). In Turkey, students of all types of backgrounds have the right to receive education at these schools, and 78.1% of the Turkish people are classified as being of a Turkish ethnic background (KONDA, 2011). Kurds are particularly well represented in the southeastern regions of the country. However, in classes in other regions of the country, students of a Turkish ethnic background represent the majority. The ethnic balance in today's educational context—in which both Turkish and Kurdish students feature most prominently—has also been affected by the recent increase in the number of students who are Syrian migrants.

The civil war that began in Syria on March 15, 2011, with the onset of demonstrations in the region of Dera, has greatly affected Turkey. As a result of the events originating in Dera, which were connected to the wider so-called Arab Spring movement, hundreds of thousands of people have lost their lives, cities have been destroyed, and millions of people have been forced to migrate. Because Syria shares a land border with Turkey, refugees began to migrate to Turkey in April 2011. For all countries faced with this wave of migration from Syria, including Turkey, problems with housing, food, and security have become pressing. When assessing the situation from 2011 to the present, it can be observed that the Turkish state has not formulated a clear policy with regard to the education of Syrian migrant children. A memorandum released by the Turkish Ministry of Education in 2014 concerning education for foreign students stated that the number of foreign students in Turkey had significantly increased (National Ministry of Education, 2014). A decision was made to work in coordination with civil society organizations and international institutions to establish an educational commission to enable foreign residents to benefit from the services offered by existing educational institutions. First and foremost, the commission encouraged balanced and controlled distribution of Syrian students in small numbers to state and private institutions to meet their educational requirements. Syrian students began to be admitted to various schools across the Turkish system. However, the majority of Syrian students who began to study at state and private schools—on account of existing imbalances encountered in the education and teaching systems—were unable to stay at the schools where they had started their education.

In the teacher profile for this chapter, the current situation of Syrian students is presented by examining the delivery of lessons in a class with a multicultural composition of students and describing the experiences of their teacher. It takes into account issues that directly affect the students, such as their psychological condition following their flight from a civil war, their insufficient knowledge of Turkish as a language of instruction, and their experiences of education from the perspective of foreigners. The observation for the teacher profile was conducted in 2016 at a state school situated in the Istanbul district/subprovince of Beylikduzu. The teacher was of Kurdish origin, and 22 students were ethnically Turkish, 11 Kurdish, 3 mixed, 2 Afghan, 2 Syrian, and 1 Alawite/Alevi.

For the teacher profile, we chose a highly diverse school district in Istanbul city. Then we identified a school where Syrian refugees, Kurdish, Arabs and other ethnic minorities studied together. When we visited the school, a principal recommended Mr. Ozgur because he had many different ethnic minority students in his class. He was Kurdish and spoke several languages, including English, Arabic, Turkish, and national dialects. He could use all of those languages when teaching.

Mr. Ozgur's Lessons and Citizenship Education

Some of Mr. Ozgur's students experienced problems attaining a sense of structural inclusion and empowerment in his classroom because of their home languages and cultural characteristics. Students need to experience structural inclusion, cultural recognition, and empowerment to become effective citizens. To help his students experience structural inclusion, recognition, and empowerment, Mr. Ozgur showed empathy, helped them to overcome prejudices, and reduced ethnic, cultural, and linguistic segregation among his students. He also encouraged students to use and be proud of their home languages. The culturally responsive teaching strategies used by Mr. Ozgur helped his students from diverse groups to experience a sense of structural inclusion in his classroom.

General Characteristics of the School

The school where Mr. Ozgur taught was diverse and prosperous. We list here its general characteristics:

- The standards were superior to most of those found across Turkey.

- The economic level of the students was high.

- The school received financial assistance in the form of donations from the students' families.

- All teachers in this school had at least 15 years of experience.

- In accordance with the framework of the Fatih Educational Project, conducted by the National Ministry of Education, the classroom was equipped with three boards: chalk board, whiteboard, and smartboard.

- In accordance with the system prescribed by the National Ministry of Education, lessons were delivered with the support of multimedia equipment, with activities such as matching exercises conducted to reinforce topics taught following the presentation of lesson content. The education consisted of two levels (primary).

- The school was equipped to a satisfactory level with technological support and equipment.

- It was a state school with a varied and pluralist atmosphere/environment from an ethnic and cultural perspective.

At the beginning of our observation, we asked Mr. Ozgur for information concerning the make-up of the class. He reported that students of different ethnic identities were present.

Our first question was whether there was any kind of segregation in the class, and if this was the case, how the teacher solved this problem. Mr. Ozgur answered in a clear and effective manner:

> Multicultural education starts and finishes with the teacher himself. To whatever extent the teacher is a peaceful and unifying factor, is affectionate and approaches students with empathy, then [to the same degree] the chaotic situation found in class can be resolved in a positive fashion.[1]

Mr. Ozgur's thoughts on this subject were consistent with the concepts of "reduction of prejudice and egalitarian pedagogy" introduced by Banks (2013). Banks stresses the importance of a teacher's sensitivity to cultural values and the need to pay attention to the learning styles of all students in order to ensure justice among different cultural groups and to increase academic success and reduce prejudices.

When Mr. Ozgur introduced his students to us, he asked them to introduce themselves, while he smiled, ruffled their hair, and behaved warmly toward them. Through these displays of affection, the teacher tried to demonstrate that he did not discriminate between the students. Among the students he introduced were foreign pupils, some of whom had not yet overcome certain problems related to the Turkish language. We asked him how he solved the language problem of foreign students in the classroom environment. He replied:

> The language problem disappears completely within four years. With one exception, the students have all overcome the problems they have experienced relating to the use of the language. The student who had not yet learnt the language came to my class this year. He spoke Arabic and knew hardly any Turkish. When I asked the previous class teacher why the student still had not learned Turkish, I was told that the teacher had been unable to communicate with the student because he had not learned "Syrian."

Mr. Ozgur smiled, saying that he had not heard of a language called "Syrian." He continued:

> The important thing is to get to know the child and to acknowledge his differences. Foreign students usually know English. I do not have an advanced level of English but I can write at a basic level. So as to better understand my students and teach them certain subjects, I first of all prepared texts in English; and because I was not fully confident about my English, I had the English teachers at the school check them for factual accuracy. In this way, I found a solution to the language problem, and I believe that other teachers could also solve their problems this way.

With these words, it can be seen that the National Ministry of Education had been late in establishing temporary educational centers for foreign students. Although centers began to be established in 2015, with the goal of reaching numerous learning objectives in many countries, including Turkey, it can easily be ascertained that students exposed to the education and teaching processes in operation from 2011 to 2015 experienced considerable difficulties.

One of the fundamental problems connected with the presence of students with different mother/native languages was their exclusion by students who spoke the majority language. Mr. Ozgur was asked whether he had experienced any conflicts between students because some students could not speak the majority language. He said:

> Students show a tendency to sit with successful students and wish to spend more time with them. However well Afghan and Syrian students speak Turkish, they cannot speak it as well as their native/mother languages. For this reason, they are not considered as "successful" as other students. Because they are seen as unsuccessful, they are excluded by other students.

Mr. Ozgur continued with his interpretation of the situation:

> I would like to mention a few events that I experienced in relation with the points you raise. During break time I saw that one student had dropped his notebook onto the ground and I picked it up from where it had fallen. I read what he had written in the notebook. A Turkish student had written notes about the foreign student. It was a kind of diary, including comments. In the diary, he mentioned that one of the Syrian students didn't like him. This state of affairs saddened me, and after the break period I talked to the Turkish student and said that I liked the fact that he did not discriminate among his friends. I think the message I conveyed was appropriate.

From the attitude that Mr. Ozgur showed in this situation, it can be seen that he was paying attention to the barriers to communication. Instead of warning, criticizing, or "preaching" to the student, he understood that the correct approach was to employ "I" language (personalized language).

Mr. Ozgur further stated:

> What is more, in my class, the Turkish students did not embrace certain foreign students because of their inability to fully understand Turkish. On one occasion I called two Syrian students to the board and asked them to speak to each other in their own language. Later I turned to the class and asked whether they had understood the dialogue. All the other students said that they had not understood it. I then asked the Arabic-speaking Syrian students to ask their classmates quietly what their names were. The students then turned to the class and asked their classmates in Arabic: "Ma hua ism?" As can be seen, although there are many similarities between Arabic and Turkish (in Turkish, it's "ismin ne?"), no student understood what had been said. Through their addressing the class and using an expression ("ma hua") that was very similar to Turkish and the fact that the students had not been able to understand, I tried to explain that it was very normal for them to be unable to understand a foreign

student and for a foreign student be unable to understand them. The students stated that they also agreed with this opinion.

Mr. Ozgur was able to help students overcome prejudices because he knew them well and guided their experiences. Furthermore, he always displayed a conciliatory attitude and attempted to solve the problem of segregation among students by creating a sense of empathy among them. He explained how he developed a sense of empathy:

> I have worked for 15 years as a teacher in Istanbul. I had never heard of the concept of multicultural education, whether during my university studies, my in-service training, or during my life as a teacher. I decided to undertake a master's degree qualification in order to contribute to my individual professional development and I became acquainted with the term *multicultural education* for the first time through my teacher for the master's degree course. I have always approached my immediate environment and my students with empathy; however, I could say that my feelings of empathy were limited until I heard the concept of multiculturalism. One of the most important feelings that I have gained through exposure to multicultural education is that of empathy. For this reason, multicultural education needs to be integrated into teacher-training programs to train teachers to be sensitive to different cultures.

Mr. Ozgur indicated that empathy was a characteristic essential to every teacher and that the development of feelings of empathy was connected to the acquisition of theoretical knowledge about multicultural education. In addition, he said that, by approaching students in a spirit of empathy, he had experienced a number of highly emotional moments when attempting to solve problems that immigrant students had encountered. Mr. Ozgur described one such incident, involving a twelve-year-old male student;

> A student of mine from Cizre (a city in Southeastern Turkey) and his family did not speak any Turkish. As I myself am of a Kurdish background, I tried to establish communication with him using Kurdish. I could not understand why he had said that he did not know Kurdish even though he did know the language. I invited Veysi's family to the school and spoke with them about Veysi. The family told me that they had advised Veysi not to speak Kurdish when he started school so that he would not be excluded by the teacher and his classmates and would not experience any problems. The student demonstrated extremely withdrawn behavior in class. He did not participate in class and at times alternated between aggressiveness and sadness. Whenever I tried to speak Kurdish with him, he declined to give an answer. I began to speak Turkish with him beside his mother and he began to speak with me only after the discussion with his mother.
>
> I would like to share another incident with Veysi in my class that made me sad. During break time, Veysi had an argument with a Turkish student. Both of them tore into each other. On entering the classroom, I saw that both of them were in a bad state. In particular, I asked the Turkish student why he had beaten Veysi. He explained in an

accusatory manner that Veysi had begun the argument and had sworn at him. I turned to Veysi and asked him the same question. Veysi replied in a way that I would never forget. Veysi spoke in this way: "Teacher . . . ohh . . . uh . . . ohh . . . uhh . . . ohh . . ." and then burst into tears. He cried because he was incapable of expressing himself in Turkish. I also felt helpless in this situation and felt very sad for him. There is nobody to help you when you are in an environment where education is given in another language. When I showed empathy, I saw that this situation was particularly difficult for Veysi.

As Mr. Ozgur described this incident, his voice quivered, and the degree to which he had become close to the student was palpable. I could see how this event, which was due to segregation, had affected him. In our conversation, Mr. Ozgur reiterated the fact that the language problem could only be solved through cooperation between the teacher and the student.

The delivery of education through a single language often leads to considerable difficulties for students who do not know the language. Mr. Ozgur expressed his thoughts on this subject:

As foreign and minority students are all exposed to the same type of education, they are not successful educationally until they fully learn the language of instruction. However, once they have learned Turkish, they can become successful to such an extent that they leave even Turkish students behind.

Because the same type of education was delivered to different groups, students from minority or foreign backgrounds often experienced a lack of success from an academic perspective. In addition, Mr. Ozgur, as long as he was compelled to present such a uniform educational program, was forced to teach in Turkish with students who did not know the language and therefore suffered from feelings of inferiority, and students who knew some Turkish but did not speak it as their native language. It was difficult for these students to learn the subject content (e.g., mathematics, science, history) taught within the framework of the school program. Mr. Ozgur highlighted the fact that concrete concepts are more easily taught than abstract ones and that, therefore, in classes involving students who did not know the language so well, more concrete and tangible subject matter was dealt with. Furthermore, Mr. Ozgur had to attempt to make concrete certain abstract concepts and to continue the delivery of education in this way.

We were curious about how the relative "lack of success" experienced by students of a minority or foreign background during the first years of education was reflected in the grades on their school report cards. We asked Mr. Ozgur how he went about evaluating these students. Mr. Ozgur explained how the evaluation was conducted:

The accepted grading system is not used for evaluation purposes. I try to establish a principle of equality of opportunity for students. Turkish and Kurdish students are more successful than Afghan or Syrian students. For this reason, I evaluate my students by looking at their personal achievement and efforts.

An education in which evaluation is conducted only according to results may lead to injustice even among students belonging to a particular culture. Consequently, this is a situation that needs to be taken into account, especially in classes with a multicultural student population. For this reason, an evaluation that incorporates evaluation of the learning process, the degree of readiness of the students, and the situation they have reached on completion of the process is more equitable for any class, and in particular for multicultural classes.

At the conclusion of our interviews with Mr. Ozgur, it became evident that both foreign and minority students had experienced serious problems. However, foreign students experienced the greatest difficulties. The fact that the incidents described had left indelible psychological marks on the students can be appreciated from these words by Mr. Ozgur:

Afghan and Syrian students, even more than Kurdish students, are uncomfortable with the fact that they are different. They think that this is a negative situation. Some of these students are introverted. They sometimes do not even wish to give answers to questions to which they know the answers.

From these words, it is evident that the teachers who deliver education to students from culturally diverse backgrounds need to be well trained from a pedagogical perspective; it is also evident that these students need to obtain further support from psychologists.

Another concern for foreign students in Turkish classes is acquiring identity cards/residence permits. Many students who lack identity cards and documents that indicate their exact ages have been forced to attend classes at levels improperly higher than their age. Even after staff realize that the students are younger than first assumed, many students have not been transferred to lower-age classes; the basis of such decisions is often the belief that they have become accustomed to their present class environment. For this reason, many students have been forced to try to acquire skills and abilities that are higher than those required of local Turkish students of the same age. This situation leads to an even lower level of student success and a weaker cultural and civic identity. However, the 2014 National Ministry of Education memorandum on foreign students states that students who are without a school diploma and have not yet received a Turkish identity card will be registered for schools only after taking an evaluation examination and being interviewed by school personnel to determine their academic level (National Ministry of Education, 2014). Also in 2014, the National Ministry of Education established the Data Processing System for Foreign Students. Nevertheless, because of the time needed to implement immigration law requirements and because of the inclusion of certain amendments to the definition of *migration* contained in the educational memorandum for foreign students, a large number of foreign students are experiencing serious challenges and having their cultural identity and citizenship rights denied. Furthermore, students affected by the above regulations only began to be registered (for educational purposes) in an organized and systematic way in late 2014.

Conclusion

In this chapter, we have argued that because Turkey is a linguistically, religiously, and culturally diverse society, multicultural and bilingual education are the most appropriate approaches to meeting the challenges in educating minority and immigrant children. They are slowly gaining acceptance in Turkey, especially since the Kurdish language television channel was launched and the Kurdish language has been permitted in both public and private schools in the form of elective courses. However, the large number of unregistered Syrian refugees and the large number of international students attending universities in Turkey are new challenges for the years to come. Two imminent challenges can be described as inherent in the concept of diversity: pluralism and multicultural education.

In the current curriculum, the concepts of citizenship, diversity, pluralism, and multicultural education promote a particularistic notion of citizenship, which oscillates between a will to maintain a discrete Turkish identity and to be a part of the larger world. It can be argued that citizenship education in Turkey, despite its unsatisfactory treatment of certain human rights themes, succeeds in upholding the four basic elements of the state-centric operation of Turkish modernity: a strong-state tradition, a concept of national development, an organic vision of society, and a republican notion of citizenship (Keyman & İçduygu, 2005, as cited in Cayir & Gurkaynak, 2007). In addition, Cayir and Gurkaynak (2007) argue that in Turkey the portrayal of any minority groups—such as Kurdish, Armenian, or Arab—in textbooks is still unthinkable with regard to international norms of multicultural education. They argue that such a portrayal—which would involve discussing ethnic or religious differences in the tightly defined, state-monitored, and allegedly neutral public sphere of education—would be considered detrimental to national unity and social cohesion. In such a context, citizenship education and multicultural education would need to promote the notion of citizenship not in the language of rights, but in the language of duties and responsibilities toward the state and nation.

Acknowledgment

We wish to acknowledge the helpful and thoughtful feedback we received from several colleagues while we were writing this chapter. We are grateful to James A. Banks, Stephen Lafer, Ilhan Kaya, Yiting Chu, Paul Hearn, and the anonymous external reviewers for their thoughtful comments on an earlier draft of this chapter. Also, we would like to thank Martha Yager, AERA's managing editor, for her valuable, critical, and helpful comments in the final stage of our chapter.

Note

1. The quotes from Mr. Ozgur are from conversations with the authors and were translated by the authors.

References

Aktel, M. (1998). Tanzimat Fermanının Toplumsal Yansıması [Social reflection of the imperial edict]. *SDÜ İktisadi ve İdari Bilimler Fakültesi Dergisi, 3,* 177–184.

Akyüz, Y. (2008). *History of Turkish education.* Ankara: Pegem Academy Publications.

Ata, B. (2007, March). Yeni sosyal bilgiler öğretmenliği lisans programının ilköğretim 2005 sosyal bilgiler dersi (6,7. sınıflar). Öğretim programı açısından değerlendirilmesi. [The new undergraduate program for the teaching of social sciences, social science lessons 2005 (for 6th and 7th classes). An evaluation from the perspective of the teaching program]. First International Conference on Education, Canakkale Onsekiz Mart University.

Ayas, N. (1948). *Türkiye Cumhuriyeti milli eğitimi: Kuruluşlar ve tarihçeler* [National education in the Turkish Republic: Institutions and a short history]. Ankara: Milli Eğitim Bakanlığı Yayınları.

Aydin, H., (2009). Key dynamics of assimilation among first-generation Turkish immigrants residing in Romania. *Journal of Global Initiative, 4*(2), 123–148.

Aydin, H. (2012a). Multicultural education curriculum development in Turkey. *Mediterranean Journal of Social Sciences, 3*(3), 277–286. doi:10.5901/mjss.2012.v3n3p277

Aydin, H. (2012b). First-generation Turkish immigrants' perceptions on cultural integration in multicultural societies: A qualitative case study. *US-China Educational Review B, 2*(3), 326–337.

Aydin, H. (2013a). A literature-based approach on multicultural education. *The Anthropologist, 16*(1–2), 31–44.

Aydin, H. (2013b). *Dünyada ve Türkiye'de çokkültürlü eğitim tartışmaları ve uygulamaları* [Discussions and applications regarding multicultural education in Turkey and the world]. Ankara: Nobel Academic Press.

Aydin, H., & Ozfidan, B. (2014). Perceptions on mother tongue (Kurdish)–based multicultural and bilingual education in Turkey. *Multicultural Education Review, 6*(1), 21–48.

Aydin, H., & Tonbuloglu, B. (2014). Graduate students' perceptions on multicultural education: A qualitative case study. *Eurasian Journal of Educational Research, 57,* 29–50.

Aydin, H. (2016, May). *Schooling experiences and perceptions of resettled Syrian refugee middle school students in Turkey.* Keynote paper presented at International Conference on Envisioning New Possibilities of Multicultural Education (KAME), Seoul, South Korea.

Azak, U. (2008). *Secularism in Turkey as a Nationalist Search for Vernacular Islam: The Ban on the Call to Prayer in Arabic (1932–1950).* Retrieved from https://remmm.revues.org/6025?lang=en

Bakker, C. (2003, March). Anahtar sözcük çeşitlilik dinler arası eğitim ve dini gruplar içinde belirsizlik sorunu [Keyword diversity: The problem of uncertainty within interreligious education and religious groups]. In *Din Öğretiminde Yeni Yöntem Arayışları Uluslar arası Sempozyum Bildiri ve Tartışmalar* [International Conference on New Methods in Religious and Educational Trends] (pp. 359–378). Ankara: National Ministry of Education Press.

Banks, J. A. (2001). Citizenship education and diversity: Implications for teacher education. *Journal of Teacher Education, 52*(1), 5–16.

Banks, J. A. (Ed.). (2004). *Diversity and citizenship education: Global perspectives.* San Francisco: Jossey-Bass.

Banks, J. A. (2008). Diversity, group identity, and citizenship education in a global age. *Educational Researcher, 37*(3), 129–139.

Banks, J. A. (2008). *An introduction to multicultural education* (4th ed.). Boston: Allyn & Bacon.

Bayraktar, Z. (2013). Balkanlar'da birarada yaşama kültürü bağlamında kimlik çatışmasından kültürel entegrasyona, Türk dili ve kültürünün önemi [The importance of the Turkish language and culture, from conflict of identity to cultural integration within the context of the culture of cohabitation in the Balkans]. *Karadeniz Araştırmaları Dergisi, 36,* 223–234.

Bhavnani, R., Mirza, H. S., & Meetoo, V. (Eds.). (2005). *Tackling the roots of racism: Lessons for success.* Bristol: Polity Press.

Bilgiç, V. (2003). *Minorities in the Ottoman state: Turkish-Armenian relations past and present* (Ed. İdris Bal Mustafa Çufalı). Ankara: Nobel Publications.

Bilir, F. (2012). *Yeni Anayasada vatandaşlık* [Citizenship in the new constitution]. Ankara: Adalet Yayinevi.

Bozkurt, G. (1992). Review of the Ottoman legal system. *OTAM, 3,* 115–128.

Buyukkaragoz, S. S., & Civi, C. (1998). *Genel öğretim metodları* [General teaching methods]. Konya, Turkey: Öz Eğitim Yayınları.

Cayir, K., & Gurkaynak, I. (2007). The state of citizenship education in Turkey: Past and present. *Journal of Social Science Education, 6*(2), 50–58.

Celep, O. (2014). Can the Kurdish left contribute to Turkey's democratization? *Insight Turkey, 3*(16), 165–180.

Celik, H. (2008). Cumhuriyet dönemi vatandaşlık eğitiminde önemli adımlar [Important steps taken in citizenship education in the Republican period]. *SAÜ Fen Edebiyat Dergisi, 1,* 359–369.

Crick, B. (1998). *Education for citizenship and teaching of democracy in schools: Final report of the advisory group on citizenship*. London: Qualifications and Curriculum Authority.

Dahl, R. (1993). *Demokrasi ve eleştirileri* [*Democracy and criticism*] (Trans. Levent Köker). Ankara: Yetkin Yayınevi.

Damgaci, F. K. (2013). *Türkiye'deki akademisyenlerin çokkültürlü eğitime ilişkin tutumları* [Attitudes of academicians in Turkey with regard to multicultural education]. Unpublished master's thesis, Yildiz Technical University, Istanbul.

Damgaci, F. K., & Aydin, H. (2013). Attitudes of the academicians towards multicultural education. *Electronic Journal of Social Sciences, 12*(45), 325–341.

Damgaci, F. K., & Aydin, H. (2014). An Analysis of academicians' perceptions of multicultural education: A Turkish experience. *Anthropologist. 18*(3), 817–833.

Davies, L. (2001). Citizenship, education and contradiction [Review essay]. *British Journal of Sociology of Education, 22*(2), 299–308.

Eferakorho, J. (2008). *Multicultural education and citizenship*. Paper presented at the Briefing Paper for Trainee Teachers of Citizenship Education Conference, London.

Erdem, G. (2010). Islahat fermanı'na yeniden bir bakış [A new look at the edict of reform]. *AÜ İlahiyat Fakültesi Dergisi, 51*(1), 327–348.

Ergin, O. (1977). *Türk maarif tarihi 1–2* [History of Turkish education 1–2]. Istanbul: Eser Matbaası.

Ersoy, F. A. (2010, August). *Social studies education program and textbooks in Turkey: Transition from national citizenship toward European and global citizenship*. Paper presented at the European Conference on Educational Research 2010, Helsinki, Finland.

Ersoy, F. A. (2013). Global citizenship education in social studies: Experiences of Turkish teachers and students in international conflict and war. *Journal of Qualitative Research in Education, 1*(1), 7–30. Retrieved from http://dx.doi.org/10.14689/issn.2148-2624.1.1s1m

Ersoy, A. F. (2014). Active and democratic citizenship education and its challenges in the social studies classroom. *Eurasian Journal of Educational Research, 55,* 1–20.

Faltis, C. (2014). Toward a race radical vision of bilingual education for Kurdish Usersin Turkey: A commentary. *Journal of Ethnic and Cultural Studies, 1*(1), 1–5.

Gokce, F., & Oguz, N. (2010). Minority and foreign schools on the Ottoman education system. *e-International Journal of Educational Research, 1*(1), 42–57.

Gozutok, F. D. (2007). *Öğretim ilke ve yöntemleri* [The principles and methods of teaching]. Ankara: Ekinoks Kitabevi.

Gozlugol, S. V. (2013). Avrupa çoğulcu düzeninin bir parçası olarak çoğulcu demokrasinin temel gerekleri [The basic necessities of democracy as a part of the European pluralist order]. *Hacettepe Hukuk Fakültesi Dergisi, 3*(2), 61–74.

Gulmez, M. (2001). *İnsan Hakları ve Demokrasi Eğitimi* [Human rights and democracy education]. Ankara: TODAİE Yayınları.

Gunay, K. (1998). *Anadolu'da Türk edebiyatın Osmanlı Devleti ve medeniyeti tarihi* [Anatolian Turkish literature in history of civilization and Ottoman Empire]. Istanbul: IRCICA Press.

Gunay, U. (1998). Türklerin dini tarihinde ve kültüründe çoğulculuk ve hoşgörü [Pluralism and tolerance in the religious history and culture of the Turks]. *Erciyes Üniversitesi İlahiyat Fakültesi Dergisi, 10,* 49–68.

Gundem, S. (1996). *Sosyal bilgiler öğretimine genel bir bakış: İlköğretim kurumlarında sosyal bilgiler öğretimi ve sorunları* [A general perspective of teaching of the social sciences: Teaching of social sciences in primary educational institutions and problems]. Ankara: TED Yayınları.

Gundogan, A. İ. (2002). Çoğulculuk ve değer bunalımı [Pluralism and the crisis/collapse in values]. *Muğla Üniversitesi Sosyal Bilimler Enstitüsü Dergisi, 8,* 1–9.

Hablemitoglu, S., & Ozmete, E. (2012). Etkili vatandaşlık eğitimi için bir öneri [A suggestion for effective citizenship education]. *Ankara Sağlık Bilimleri Dergisi, 1*(3), 39–54.

Human Rights Watch. (2015). *Turkey: 400,000 Syrian children not in school: Language, economic hardship keep young refugees out of class.* Retrieved from https://www.hrw.org/news/2015/11/08/turkey-400000-syrian-children-not-school

İçduygu, A. (2015). *Syrian refugees in Turkey: The long road ahead.* Washington, DC: Migration Policy Institute.

Institute of Strategic Thinking. (2012). *Türkiye'nin demokratik dönüşümü 2002–2012* [The democratic transformation of Turkey 2002–2012]. Ankara: Başak Matbaacılık.

Karatas, A. I. (2006). Osmanlı Devleti'nde Gayrimüslimlere tanınan din ve vicdan hürriyeti [Liberties of religion and conscience granted to non-Muslims in the Ottoman Empire]. *UÜ İlahiyat Fakültesi Dergisi, 15*(1), 267–284.

Karatas, K., & Oral, B. (2015). Teachers' perceptions on cultural responsiveness in education. *Journal of Ethnic and Cultural Studies, 2*(2), 47–57.

Kaya, Y. (2015). The opinions of primary school, Turkish language and social science teachers regarding education in the mother tongue (Kurdish). *Journal of Ethnic and Cultural Studies, 2*(2), 33-46.

Kaya, I., & Aydin, H. (2013). *Türkiye'de anadilde eğitim sorunu: Zorluklar, deneyimler ve iki dilli eğitim modeli önerileri* [The question/issue of mother tongue education in Turkey: Challenges, experiences, and model recommendations for bilingual education]. Istanbul: UKAM Yayınları.

Kaya, I., & Aydin, H. (2014). *Çoğulculuk, çokkültürlü eğitim ve çokdilli eğitim* [Pluralism, multicultural education, and multilingual education]. Ankara: Ani Academic Publishing.

Kaya, Y. (2015). The opinions of primary school, Turkish language and social science teachers regarding education in the mother tongue (Kurdish). *Journal of Ethnic and Cultural Studies, 2*(2), 33–46.

Kepenekci, K. Y. (2008). *Eğitimciler için insan hakları ve vatandaşlık.* [Human rights and citizenship for educators]. Ankara: Ekinoks Yayınevi.

Kerr, D. (1999). *Citizenship education: An international comparison.* London: NFER.

Kerr, D., & Cleaver, L. (2004).*Citizenship education longitudinal study: Literature review—Citizenship education one year on—What does it mean? Emerging definitions and approaches in the first year of the national curriculum for citizenship in England.* London: DfES.

Kerr, D., Ireland, E., Lopes, J., & Craig, R. (with Cleaver, E.). (2004). *Citizenship education longitudinal study: Second annual report. First longitudinal survey. Making citizenship education real.* London: DfES Press.

Keyman F., & İçduygu, A. (2005). Introduction. In F. Keyman & A. İçduygu (Eds.), *Citizenship in a global world: European questions and Turkish experiences* (pp. 50–58). London: Routledge.

KONDA. (2011). *Kürt meselesinde algı ve beklentiler* [Perceptions and expectations in the Kurdish question]. Istanbul: İletişim Yayınları.

Kubilay, Ç. (2005). Türkiye'de anadillere yönelik düzenlemeler ve kamusal alan: Anadil ve resmi dil eşitlemesinin kırılması [Regulations regarding native/minority languages in Turkey and the public sphere/space: The breakdown in the equality of native and formal language]. *İletişim Araştırmaları, 2*(2), 55–86.

Kymlicka, W. (1995). *Multicultural citizenship: A liberal theory of minority rights.* New York: Oxford University Press.

Lafer, S.(2014). Democratic design for the humanization of education. *Journal of Ethnic and Cultural Studies, 1*(1), 6-12.

Law on Foreign Nationals and International Protection (Law No. 6458). (2013). Ankara: Ministry of Interior Directorate General of Migration Management Press. Retrieved from http://www.refworld.org/pdfid/5167fbb20.pdf

Luchtenberg, S. (2005). Multicultural education: Challenges and responses. *Journal of Social Science Education, 4*(1), 31–55.

May, S. (2005). Language rights: Moving the debate forward. *Journal of Sociolinguistics, 9*(3), 319–347.

Maylor, U., Ross, A., Hutchings, M., Rollock, N., & Williams, K. (2007). *Teacher education addressing multiculturalism in Europe, England: Country Report 2.* London: DfES Press.

National Ministry of Education. (2014). *Yabancılara yönelik eğitim-öğretim hizmetlerine ilişkin 2014/21 sayılı genelge* [Memorandom concerning education and teaching activities aimed at foreigners]. Retrieved from http://kayapinar.meb.gov.tr/meb_iys_dosyalar/2014_10/31103130_genelge.pdf

Mitchell, E. (2014). *Syrian refugees: The right to education in Turkey.* Ankara: Human Right Watch Press. Retrieved from https://www.academia.edu/18207326/Syrian_Refugees_The_Right_to_Education_in_Turkey

Okandan, R. G. (1999). *Âmme hukukumuzda Tanzimat devri* [The Tanzimat (restructuring) period in our public law]. Istanbul: Tanzimat Yayınları.

Osler, A. (2012). Citizenship education and diversity, In J. A. Banks (Ed.), *Encyclopedia of diversity in education* (Vol. 1, pp. 353–361). London: Sage.

Ozturk, M. (2010). Arap ülkelerinde Osmanlı idaresi [Ottoman administration in Arab countries]. *International Journal of History, 2*(1), 325–351.

Polat, E. G. (2011). Osmanlıdan günümüze vatandaşlık anlayışı [An understanding of citizenship from the Ottoman period to the present day]. *Ankara Barosu Dergisi, 3*, 128–157.

Rattansi, A. (1999). Racism, "postmodernism" and reflexive multiculturalism. In S. May (Ed.), *Critical multiculturalism: Rethinking multicultural and antiracist education* (pp. 77–112). London: Falmer Press.

Resit, A. (1933). *Ekalliyelerin himayesi* [Protection of minorities]. Istanbul: Matbaa-i Ebuzziya.

Smith, R. (2003). Mother tongue education and the law: A legal review of bilingualism with reference to Scottish Gaelic. *International Journal of Bilingual Education and Bilingualism, 6*(2), 129–145.

Tasdemirci, E. (2001). Türk eğitim tarihinde azınlık okulları ve yabancı okullar [Minority and foreign schools in Turkish educational history]. *Sosyal Bilimler Enstitüsü Dergisi, 10*, 13–30.

Taylor, C. (1996). *Çokkültürlülük* [Multiculturalism]. Istanbul: Yapı Kredi Yayınları.

Turkish Statistical Institute. (2015). *Eğitim istatistikleri* [Educational statistics]. Retrieved from http://www.tuik.gov.tr/PreTablo.do?alt_id=1018

Tuncalp, E. (1950). *Türk-İslam çocuklarının şiirleştirilmiş Allah, din ve ahlak bilgileri* [God, religion and moral education expressed by Turkish and Muslim children through poetry]. Istanbul: HakkaDoğru Dergisi Yayınları.

Uzuncarsili, İ. H. (1975). *Ottoman history*. Ankara: Turkish Historical Institute.

Yavuz, B. (2009). Çoğulcu demokrasi anlayışı ve insan hakları [An understanding of pluralist democracy and human rights]. *Gazi Üniversitesi Hukuk Fakültesi Dergisi, 1–2,* 283–302.

Chapter 17

Diversities and Civic Education in Israel, a Society Ridden With Conflict

Zvi Bekerman *and* Aviv Cohen

Hebrew University of Jerusalem, Seymour Fox School of Education

Israel is not an easy place. The generalized categories of Jews and Palestinians that are often utilized to describe the inhabitants of this conflict-ridden area might reflect irresponsible social sciences discourse under the influence of methodological nationalism (Wimmer & Schiller, 2003) but do little to reflect the complexity in this region. Psychologized flattened ethnic national identities (Billig, 1995) might be easy to manipulate for the sake of unworthy official reports but do not truly represent intra- and inter-group diversity. Borrowing from Walt Whitman's "Song of Myself" (1855/1993, p. 113), it could be said that Jews are a "multitude" and so are Palestinians, as are non-Jews and non-Palestinians who also live in Israel (p. 113).

The entanglement of ethnicity, nationality, religiosity, and citizenship in a so-defined Jewish and democratic state has definitely determined many of the complexities of Israeli society and its political debates. Scholars have described Israeli society as ethnicized (Herzog, 1985; Levy, 2005), predominately ethnorepublican (Shafir & Peled, 2002), or nondemocratic majoritarian (Peled & Navot, 2005) and have readily explained issues of conflict and control in terms of "ethnic differences." Most Israelis consider their citizenship as being predominantly ethnic and identify themselves primarily as Palestinian Arabs or Jews before they indicate a common Israeli identity (Levy, 2005; Mizrachi & Herzog, 2012; Ram, 2008).

Western secular narratives, which dominate the Israeli scene, portray Western perspectives as heirs of the Enlightenment and as secular and rationalist (Asad, 2003) while "otherizing" and marginalizing minority discourses, both religious and cultural (e.g., Mizrachim, Ultra-Orthodox, Muslim). When adding to these marginalizing processes the liberal assimilationist conceptions of citizenship that historically have dominated citizenship education in nation-states (Banks, 2008), it becomes apparent that multicultural and citizenship matters become entangled the world over. In Israeli reality, where citizenship emphasizes both individual rights and experiences and the feelings of affiliation between the individual and the larger national Jewish entity, the term *citizen* is still highly questioned and contested (Agbaria, Mustafa, & Jabareen, 2014; Pinson, 2008).

In this chapter we first present some critical considerations regarding the entanglement between the civic and the multicultural while introducing a caveat regarding the traditional discourses of multiculturalism and its dangerous essentializing undertones, which, if not overcome, we believe will prevent any moves into possible solutions. We then present the complex historical, cultural, political, and educational backgrounds within which present Israeli civic realities are produced. Before offering some concluding remarks, we examine in depth the development of civic education in Israel and present case studies to further the understanding of the challenges and barriers that educators working in conflict-ridden contexts face when approaching citizenship and multicultural education.

Some Critical Considerations Regarding the Entanglement between the Civic and the Multicultural

The concept of *citizenship* covers a network of relationships between the state and citizens and between fellow citizens. It reflects the relationships between an individual's autonomy and his or her adaptation to life within a society. The debate about the concept of citizenship always focuses on two fundamental aspects included in the term: the legal status of being a member of a particular state, with the related rights and obligations (Choe, 2006), and a kind of identity related to the willingness to act for the benefit of a particular community.

Citizenship or civic education may be defined as the process in which the state determines the attributes of citizenship and transmits them to the younger generation (Carnegie Corporation of New York & Center for Information and Research on Civic Learning and Engagement, 2003). In general, the common denominator across studies dealing with this field is the interest in examining what types of citizens the state wants to cultivate and how to implement that concept within an educational framework (Mitchell & Parker, 2008). In the past years, following growing processes of globalization, civic education has been focused more on the issue of an individual's firm anchoring in cultural context while cultivating a sense of being a part of a whole yet diverse state population. For example, some studies have discussed the confluence and potential relevance of multicultural experiences for the civic-mindedness of students in higher education (Cole & Zhou, 2014; Verkuyten & Thijs, 2015).

The challenge of balancing diversity and unity is intensifying as democratic nation-states such as the United States, Canada, Australia, the United Kingdom, and Japan become more diversified and as racial and ethnic groups within these nations try to attain cultural, political, and economic rights (Banks, 2008). These challenges become even more accentuated in regions suffering from protracted conflict, such as Israel, where the diversity of the in-group (i.e., Jews) has been denied for the sake of nation building and the difference with the out-group (i.e., Palestinians) has been accentuated to prevent their full inclusion. This double process of alienation carries many dangers as, on the one hand, students from marginalized groups become alienated from their family and community while, on the other hand, these same students may become socially and politically alienated within the national civic culture.

Multiculturalism has been defined as a method whereby culturally diverse groups are accorded status and recognition not just at the individual level but in the institutional structures of society (Parekh, 2002). Multiculturalist perspectives have had a deep influence in the social sciences and particularly in the field of education (Phillion, He, & Connelly,

2003). While multicultural education, which evolved from ethnic studies and multiethnic education (Banks, 2004), has been framed in varied ways, leading scholars seem to agree on several key principles. Multicultural education is seen as a political move to secure social justice for underserved students through comprehensive school reform at both the classroom and the institutional levels (Gorski, 2006). Though there are strong theoretical models specifying the dimensions and value of multicultural education (Banks, 2009; Grant & Sleeter, 2011; Ladson-Billings, 2004; Ladson-Billings & Tate, 2014), there is scant empirical research examining the effects of this educational approach. Yet recent research has revealed that multicultural practices increase the academic achievement of all students (Gurin, Dey, Hurtado, & Gurin, 2002; Zirkel, 2008) at both K–12 and higher education levels. Notwithstanding, there seems to be a consensus among multicultural educational scholars that multicultural practice often fails to reflect the foundational principles of multicultural education and that ultimately it focuses more on the recognition and celebration of diversity than on equity (Whitehead & Wittig, 2004). Some scholars believe that multicultural education has surrendered to depoliticized (Gorski, 2012), static, unidirectional notions of culture and race that reinforce traditional versions of difference and (in)equality while essentializing group cultures (Gorski, 2006; Mizrachi, 2012; Paris & Alim, 2014).

Today, because of the above observations, there is a very strong connection between civic and multicultural education. The main assumption that stands at the base of this multicultural conception of civic education is the salience of social constructs in the citizen's life (Cohen, 2010). Therefore, the main goal may be seen as the need to raise awareness regarding the social reality and in particular the oppression of different social groups by stronger forces of society (Adams, Bell, & Griffin, 2007; Banks, 2004). This conception of civic education will concentrate on the ability of the individual to evaluate the social framework in which the he or she exists. Thus, the emphasis in the classroom is on the development of a thoughtful, active, and effective citizenry that relates to this diverse social reality (Ladson-Billings, 1994; Marri, 2005).

Inasmuch as traditional multiculturalism and civic education offer a solution to distinctions that engender problems in a modern world in which many cultures are situated in one social space, we maintain that such distinctions are problematic and even erroneous. Modernity did not give rise to a multiplicity of cultures but, rather, to extensive cultural/social variation. The acceptance or rejection of a particular cultural shade has never been a part of an all-or-nothing package deal demanding total rejection or total assimilation. Those who claim otherwise do not portray the historical world realistically but, rather, perpetuate an ideological school that previously served identity and culture with the purpose of consolidating priority for the ruling authority (Hall, 1996; Žižek, 1997) to identify those who resembled them and to incriminate all others. The ruling group's reasoning is obvious—accounting for otherness is preferable to accountability for it.

In Israel, for example, being Jewish or Palestinian is not destiny but an achievement, attained with the permission of all partners in efforts carried out at a given moment in history. Conceptions, beliefs, views, and especially scenarios involving multiple interactants—supporters and detractors alike—are active partners in the structuring of ethnic and civic identifications. We reiterate that this complex admixture is imparted through the vigorous social activity occurring in a particular place. "Palestinian" and "Jew" are not characteristics in people's minds but the result of work accomplished in the contexts (including educational contexts) in which these characteristics exist.

Sociohistorical-Political Background

Israel is a Western democracy where, as in other such democracies, the majority determines the identity and character of the state. Simultaneously, Israel is the declared homeland of the Jewish people and privileges Jews over other ethnic/religious minorities residing within its borders (Smooha, 2002), as exemplified in Israel's Law of Return, which, despite its multiple adaptations, is still basically understood as a Jewish repatriation law (Kravel-Tovi, 2012).

The main internationally recognized conflict of Israel, the Palestinian Israeli (in which *Israeli* is read as "Jewish") conflict can be traced to the birth of political Zionism at the end of the 19th century and to the development of Arab nationalism in response to the colonization in the Ottoman and the British empires of the 19th and 20th centuries (Abdo & Yuval-Davis, 1995). This seemingly intractable dispute resulted from at least two dominant ideological discourses, one Jewish and one Palestinian, involving control of the land and recognition of group sovereignty.

The 1948 war, called the War of Independence by the Israelis and the Nakba (the Catastrophe) by the Palestinians, was the first open military clash between the Zionist and Arab nationalist movements. Four major wars have erupted since then, in 1956, 1967, 1973, and 1982. The Intifada outbreaks in 1997 and 2000, organized in the administered territories under the flag of the Palestinian Liberation Organization, brought about even bloodier events. Even after the Oslo agreement between Israel and the Palestinian Liberation Organization in 1993 and the recent disengagement from the Gaza Strip, it is unclear whether Israel and the Palestinians will achieve peace. The 2006 second Lebanese war and the takeover of the Gaza area by Hamas, together with the 2008 attack on Gaza by Israel and more recent outbursts of violence including the 2014 summer conflict, leave little room for optimism.

Yet Jews and Palestinians do not represent dichotomous groups with respect to their historical developments and cultural resources. Nevertheless, because of the conflict's duration, they have been constructed as such: Their identities have been shaped in direct opposition to one another (Sharoni & Abu-Nimer, 2000). Both groups belong to the monotheistic religious tradition, and Muslim Palestinians (as well as Christian Palestinians) see their roots in the Jewish prophetic tradition. They share a Semitic origin for their corresponding languages, Hebrew and Arabic. Both groups include individuals representing a wide gamut of religious practices. The majority of Palestinians are Muslim; others are Christian (10%), Druze, and Bedouin (Lewin, 2012). Palestinians in Israel have chronically suffered as a putatively hostile minority with little political representation and a debilitated social and economic infrastructure (Brender, 2005; Hesketh, Bishara, Zaher, & Rosenberg, 2010). Palestinian Arab Israelis, though officially offered full rights as citizens, until 1966 had these rights negated with the institution of the military administration in 1948, which restricted their freedom of movement and economic opportunities (Hofnung, 1991; Shafir & Peled, 2002). Not surprisingly, Palestinians in Israel experience Israel as a Jewish "ethnic" state, not a democracy (Ghanem, 1998; Hammack, 2006); a dominant perspective sees Israel as a colonizing state that took their lands and curtailed their freedoms (Rabinowitz, 2001). Israel's segregationist policies toward its non-Jewish minorities have only recently been challenged in courts of justice (Gavison, 2000), and most Palestinians in Israel say that they would rather stay in Israel than move to a Palestinian state if one were to be established (Smooha, 2004).

Jews are privileged in the Israeli sphere, yet they cover a wide spectrum ranging from Ultra-Orthodox to fully secular and those with origins in Western, Middle Eastern, and African countries. Rifts and schisms exist among them as well. Ashkenazi Jews (Jews with roots in Europe, mostly Eastern Europe, but including today those with roots in English-speaking countries) hold the dominant status in Israel (Peled, 2008). Ashkenazim tend to be more secular and are proportionally overrepresented in the middle and upper classes and among supporters of left-wing and center political parties (Ben-Porat & Feniger, 2013). Mizrachim (mostly Middle Eastern and North African Jews) hold to a subordinate position in Israel. The massive influx of Mizrachi Jews to Israel occurred immediately after the war of 1948. Under the Law of Return Mizrachi Jews were granted all civil and political rights but were at the same time marginalized by being sent to populate border areas and deserted Palestinian towns; their main task was to supply unskilled labor for the country's developing industry (Peled, 2008). The state Ashkenazi elites showed little regard for the immigrants' cultural and religious traditions and tried to secularize them as part of their modernizing project (Ben-Porat & Feniger, 2013). The Mizrachim resisted these attempts and sustained a "traditional" approach based on an oral tradition in line with their cultural religious adaptation to their Muslim countries of origin (Shokeid, 1984).

Ultra-Orthodox (Haredi) Jews, who in their majority arrived in Israel with the establishment of the state as survivors of the Nazi genocide, ideologically and practically reject many aspects of Western modern life including Western-style education and values (e.g., individuality). Ultra-Orthodox Jews were at first considered a remnant of anachronistic trends that would vanish with their integration into the newly created secular Jewish state, which led to complex societal arrangements (e.g., exemption from service in the Israel Defense Forces) known as the "status quo" agreement (Stadler, 2002). Today Haredi society is composed of two major ethnic groups—Ashkenazi and Mizrachi—which in many ways replicate the tensions described before between Ashkenazi and Mizrachi Jews in Israel (Caplan, 2007; Jobani & Perez, 2014). Haredi Jews are concentrated in mostly segregated towns and neighborhoods, differentiating themselves from the larger society through their choice of distinctive dress code and lifestyle and in the case of Haredim of European origin also through their choice of language—Yiddish. Haredi groups send their children to "recognized" schools run by nonstate, nonmunicipal organizations, which though supervised by the state are subject to less regulation, and to "exempt" schools, which are subject to minimal supervision. Lower supervision levels usually entail lower public budgets (although institutions belonging to the above-mentioned Ultra-Orthodox networks are an exception to this rule; Baum, Yedidya, Schwartz, & Aran, 2014).

To summarize this reality, according to the Central Bureau of Statistics (2013a), 20.7% (1,658,000) of the total Israeli population (8,018,000) is Arab, with an additional 4.0% (318,000) counted as "others," referring to non-Arab Christians, members of other religions, and persons not classified by religion by the Ministry of the Interior. Of the Jewish population, ethnic communities that immigrated from Middle Eastern and North African regions currently constitute 50% of Israel's Jewish population, and Ashkenazi Jews primarily arriving from European and North American countries currently represent about 30% of the population (Mizrachi, 2012); of these approximately 18% make up the Ultra-Orthodox (Ashkenazi and Mizrachi) communities (Khazzoom, 2003).

Needless to say, these cultural and national differences, which stand at the basis of Israel's many social rifts, can also be interpreted and explained through structural perspectives that would easily point toward the fact that the three marginalized groups make up the low-income and poor sectors of Israeli society, and the students from these sectors obtain the lowest average grades on nationwide high-stakes tests (Connor-Atias & Abu-Hala, 2009). These three groups, Palestinians, Ultra-Orthodox, and Mizrachim, share, though at different and changing levels, other commonalities. Traditionally, they adhere to hierarchical patriarchal codes of behavior, they have large families, they are less individualistic in their outlooks, and they support group values (Baum, 2007; Shohat, 1988). In addition, they adopt traditionalist or religious perspectives and demographically live more or less segregated from the mainstream secular Jewish population (Baum, 2007; Yiftachel, 1998).

Within the Jewish state school system the total pupil population dropped by 10% in the last decade, while the shares of Ultra-Orthodox Jewish pupils and Arab pupils increased by 4% and 6%, respectively. The Ultra-Orthodox sector has grown more rapidly than the Arab sector in the recent decade and is expected to grow even more rapidly in future years. These demographic changes have significant implications. Ultra-Orthodox curricula stress religious studies over Hebrew, mathematics, English, computer literacy, and civics; thus growth in the relative size of the Ultra-Orthodox pupil population is tantamount to an increasing percentage of Israeli pupils whose educational experience fails to respond to the needs and values of Western democracies or to meet the demands of developed modern economies. Moreover, given that the Ultra-Orthodox and Palestinian population is largely poor, growth in the relative size of these populations is similar to having an increase in the percentage of pupils whose socioeconomic background is likely to have adverse effects on academic achievement.

When compared with national averages these groups score lower on national examinations, have a higher percentage of school dropouts (Central Bureau of Statistics, 2013b), and are less likely to pass matriculation examinations (Bagrut; Ministry of Education, Culture and Sport, Economics and Budgeting Administration, 2002). When they do pass, these groups are less likely to qualify for university admission. In spite of the growth in the number of students who qualify for university admission, in 2004 only half of the total 17-year-old cohort were entitled to matriculation. Out of these, 54% were Jews, and only 31% were Palestinians. In 2003, the average of entitlement to matriculation among students coming from urban areas was 63%, while for those coming from mostly Mizrachi settlements on the periphery it was 49%. For Druze students it was 41%; for Palestinians, 36%;

and for Bedouins, 26%. In 2007, most of the 17-year-old cohort who were not entitled to matriculation came from low-income neighborhoods, Palestinian villages, and periphery settlements (Swirski & Dagan-Buzaglo, 2009).

The Wider Context of Civic Education: Multicultural Education
Policy Curriculum and Language

Curriculum

Competing doctrines and practices are always at play in the formation of curricular developments because it is upon them that political forces try to construct shared cultural understandings (Apple, 2001; McEneaney & Meyer, 2000). Ben-Peretz and Zeidman (1986) have described distinctive periods of curricular development in Israel. The first is strongly related to the early days of the state and is characterized by an emphasis on ideological/cultural values; the second is typified by a more scientific approach to knowledge; and the third has been described as more attuned to humanistic values. In their own analysis, Sabar and Mathias (2003) have shown this last period as carrying less of a homogenizing force and yet limited in its response to the sectorial needs of the multiple groups that constitute the Israeli polity. More recently, Hofman, Alpert, and Schnell (2007) described Israel as a society that is undergoing radical changes and moving from being a hegemonic society, co-opted by the values of the Zionist Ashkenazi elite, to one that at least tries to confront the competing narratives and values of its conforming groups.

Modern countries have long made use of history curricula to promote a strong sense of belonging among citizens (Nash, Crabtree, & Dunn, 1998). In areas of conflict, these curricula become central tools in the prolongation of conflict (Bar-Tal, 1999). They explain the conflict from narrow, particularistic perspectives of truth and from a position of indisputable morality. These narratives also tend to exclude, dehumanize, and devalue the enemy and the accompanying narrative (Cole, 2007). In a detailed study of the Israeli curriculum, Bar-Tal (1999) found that while Palestinians were not necessarily delegitimized, they were still presented through stereotypical perspectives. At the same time, Jews were required to identify with Jewish heroism and Jewish victimization in all the various curricula produced from 1950 to 1990. Bar-Tal also found that the curriculum supported an ethos of continuity in relation to the present conflict in order to allow students to cope with the current situation.

Studies conducted by Podeh (2000), during a similar period as the one covered in Bar-Tal's studies, point toward the fact that in all aspects related to the Palestinian-Israeli conflict, the history curricula in Jewish schools have, like many other tools of socialization, acted as "memory agents" that help crystallize the Jewish nation's collective memory. In a comparative analysis conducted on the new history curriculum for junior high schools in the Jewish sector and a new experimental curriculum for senior high schools in the Palestinian sector published in 1999, Al-Haj (2002) found that there is no attempt to expose Jewish students to the rival national Palestinian narrative. However, Al-Haj further found that the curriculum fosters a feeling of identification with the Arab nation and its culture while at the same time fostering identification with the state of Israel. However, the curriculum makes neither specific reference to the Palestinian people nor any reference to the nature of the state of Israel (as a Jewish state) or to the marginalized status of the Palestinian citizens in it. These findings bring Al-Haj to conclude that Jewish curricula are still very far away from exemplifying multicultural perspectives.

In the case of Palestinians, the curricular emphasis on the Jewish character of the state has naturally marginalized them. The emphasis on this character is not universally Jewish but is tinted by the European Ashkenazi Zionist tradition and thus has also served to marginalize other Jewish groups. The ambivalence of Zionist ideology toward its non-European subjects has had grave consequences for Jews who immigrated to Israel from Arab countries—Mizrachi Jews. The prevailing education policies instituted by the reigning Ashkenazi hegemony sought to turn these immigrants into Israeli citizens through a process of cultural assimilation (Zameret, 1997). The Ashkenazi Zionist rhetoric of the "melting pot" stressed the need to assimilate the diverse Jewish populations, arriving from multiple countries and cultures, into an ideal-type Israeli citizenry with modernistic Eurocentric ideals. Basically, this meant the "melting" of the Mizrachim into the Ashkenazi pot. The justification for this process was based upon the idea of an existing cultural gap that needed to be remedied. The new immigrants were settled in peripheral areas, and schooling was the main tool used to foster Mizrachi socialization into the new state. Yet the offer was not real, because Mizrachi children were relegated to lower level schools and special education classrooms, which ultimately undermined their self-respect and marginalized them. In the late 1960s, fearing that the national unifying project was in danger, the government enacted a policy of desegregation between Mizrachi and Ashkenazi Jews with the hope of diminishing the growing inequalities. Within a decade this reform was shown to have failed, and research results showed processes of segregation taking place within the integration initiative (Dahan & Levy, 2000).

Following the dramatic political changes of 1977, the era of the 1980s and 1990s brought about a process of liberalization, with its values of individuation and market economy (Nir & Inbar, 2004). This allowed, for the first time, the organization of two alternative educational Mizrachi initiatives to evolve—Kedma and Shas. Kedma was an initiative aimed at establishing academic high schools in underprivileged neighborhoods. In addition to implementing a regular academic school program, the initiative implemented curricular projects that emphasized Mizrachi cultural heritage and attempted to reinstitute Mizrachi history in the history curriculum, whereas until then Mizrachi history was almost totally absent from Zionist historiography (similar to the case of Palestinians; Likhovski, 2010). Shas, an Ultra-Orthodox political party, established its own autonomous educational system geared toward Ultra-Orthodox Sephardi Jews and also toward low-income traditionalist Mizrachim, known in Hebrew by the name "El HaMayyan" schools. Today, both of these educational initiatives are perceived as a threat by the Zionist secular establishment, and it is yet to be seen whether and how they will develop in the future (Markovich, 2013; Mizrachi, Goodman, & Feniger, 2009).

Although there are additional examples of autonomous educational initiatives in Israel, many of which developed after the liberalizing policies adopted in the 1990s within the

Jewish educational sector (Gibton, 2011), because of space limitations, we will close this section making reference only to the Ultra-Orthodox (Ashkenazi) stream, the oldest of its kind in Israel. Today, this stream is said to have served as a model for the development of the initiatives previously mentioned. Though recognized by the state, the Ultra-Orthodox Ashkenazi stream is "nonofficial"; it gained its autonomy by refraining from openly opposing the Zionist leadership during the political struggles that preceded the establishment of the state and was rewarded by having its educational autonomy respected (Shiffer, 1999). In the curriculum, these schools reflect the traditional, pre-emancipation values of the Jewish religious community and have struggled to prevent their education from being contaminated by the Renaissance and Enlightenment values that washed over Jewish modernizing and Zionist streams (Spiegel, 2011).

Language

The imagining of a nation includes struggles with respect to language diversity; ideologies of the state are partly constructed through ideologies of language (Heller, 1999; Hornberger, 2002). The Hebrew language has traditionally been associated with Judaism and was thus considered a natural option as the national language of Jews in the period of Jewish national revival. However, Hebrew is not necessarily the language of the Jews, although it is the official language of the state. Prior to the establishment of the state, Yiddish was spoken among Ashkenazi immigrants, and Arabic and Ladino were spoken among Sephardic and Mizrachi Jews (Ben-Rafael, Shohamy, Hasan Amara, & Trumper-Hecht, 2006). Deutch (2005) has identified two main documents that shaped language rights in Israel. The first, the Israeli Declaration of Independence, suggested a strong relationship between the revival of the Hebrew language and the national revival of the Jews. Nevertheless, the document also guaranteed freedom of language to all its citizens. The second, Article 82 of the Palestinian Order in Council over the Land of Israel, which was adopted from the British mandatory law, mandated the use of English, Arabic, and Hebrew in its official publications. It was modified in Israeli law by repealing the requirement to use the English language. Thus Arabic and Hebrew remained Israel's official languages. However, these documents lack legal authority, and Hebrew has a dominant status in all aspects of communication (Spolsky & Shohamy, 1999).

The hegemonic status of Hebrew in Israel was not easily achieved, because other languages (German, English, Yiddish) were used by contesting groups in the early Jewish settlement in Palestine. By 1948, Hebrew had gained full institutional backing, which stressed the centrality of this language for the confirmation of an Israeli identity that now had to cope with the influx of major waves of Jewish immigration arriving from Arab countries. The Hebrew literacy campaign started in 1949 was successful, and by 1972, 77% of the immigrant population said that Hebrew was their principal language. In addition to this ideological claim, such success was premised on pragmatic requirements to enter the workforce.

As for Palestinians and their language, in spite of its official status, Arabic is not regularly present in all official documents or on public signs, which are normally bilingual but prefer English as the second language (Amara, 2006; Spolsky, 1994). There are Arabic radio and television broadcasts, and quite importantly, Arabic remains the language of instruction in the Arab educational system, but Hebrew literacy is a mandatory topic for all Palestinians, based on the assumption that without it they would be even more marginalized from employment opportunities. Moreover, given that higher education in Israel is only offered in the Hebrew language, a lack of Hebrew literacy would prevent Palestinians from studying at universities.

In more recent years, following the weakening of Zionist ideology and the slow but steady growth of neoliberalizing perspectives, some changes have occurred regarding language policies in Israel. The new guidelines in language education published by the Ministry of Education (1995, 1996) set multilingualism as a desirable goal while still affirming the primacy of Hebrew. In spite of these developments, Hebrew and English hegemonic power prevails, and mandatory efforts invested in, for example, teaching Arabic in Jewish schools have had little influence in helping Jews gain Arabic literacy (Shohamy & Spolsky, 1999; Spolsky, 1997). Even in special educational settings, such as the recently created bilingual integrated Palestinian Jewish schools, Jews seem not to be able to reach any satisfactory level of Arabic literacy, while Palestinians become easily and fluently bilingual (Bekerman, 2005).

The Teaching of Civics in Israel as a Case Study

In this section we present a review of the current civics curriculum standards as well as a review of research regarding the teaching of civics in Israel, highlighting the implications regarding this multicultural reality. We ask whether the current Israeli civics curriculum and its application in classrooms enable a true transformative citizenry. Furthermore, we offer an analysis of the ways in which the three cultural groups that stand at the center of this chapter (Palestinians, Mizrachim, and Ultra-Orthodox Jews) relate to these issues.

The Israeli Civics Curriculum

The current national civics curriculum standards (Ministry of Education, 2010) were approved in 1994 by the Ministry of Education and replaced the previous standards written in the 1970s. Following we offer a short overview of this curriculum's main attributes.

Population. The curriculum is taught in all of the tracks of the Israeli educational system with the aim of creating a unified conception of citizenship while respecting the cultural differences of Israeli groups.

Content. The mandatory topic to be taught is defined as "the government and politics of the state of Israel," (Ministry of Education 1995, 1996, p. 6), and it is broken down into three subtopics: (a) an exploration of the democratic and Jewish values that stand at the foundations of the state, (b) a survey of the different components and main characteristics of the Israeli government and political system, and (c) a guided discussion of different issues that are prominent in Israeli political debates, such as cultural minorities, the relation between the state and religious institutions, and socioeconomic policies.

Educational Principles. Several pedagogical principles are offered to assist the teaching of these topics, including the presentation of different opinions, the comparison of Israeli democracy with other democracies, the development of higher level thinking skills, the incorporation of current events, the incorporation of both primary and secondary documents, and the incorporation of statistical skills.

Goals. Based on these general principles, the following educational goals were defined: Students will know about the Israeli political system, will learn facts about Israeli society, will study key terms from the fields of social sciences and political thought, and will be exposed to a plethora of opinions regarding different issues and topics. The emphasis should be put on the students' ability to evaluate different social and political issues from multiple perspectives and value-based goals in order to develop their civic and national identities, respect for human rights and civil rights, and willingness to fulfill their duties as citizens while demanding their rights and participating in public issues.

Subjects. Based on these goals the curriculum writers offer a list of subjects to be taught, explaining that "the execution of these curriculum goals will lead to a political education process that will promote good intelligent citizens that are involved in the public life of the Jewish-democratic state" (Ministry of Education, 2010, p. 11). This list includes the following topics: the Israeli Declaration of Independence, Israel as a Jewish state, relationships between the state of Israel and Diaspora Jews, Israel as a democratic state, constitutional foundations, citizenship, human rights and civil rights, mass media, the parliamentary system, elections, political parties, the separation of powers, the branches of government, the role of the president, democratic supervision, local government, religious institutions, and the peace process between Israel and its neighbors.

The Academic Discourse of Civic Education in Israel

This curriculum stood at the heart of numerous academic studies throughout the years, touching on its different aspects. Most of these studies conclude that the civics classes have only minor effects on students' democratic attitudes (Perliger, Canetti-Nisim, & Pedahzur, 2006). As part of the Civic Education Study of the International Association for the Evaluation of Educational Achievement, Ichilov (1999) included an evaluation of several aspects of the teaching of civics in Israel. Her main finding was the existence of tensions between active and passive dimensions of citizenship as well as between particularistic and universal dimensions. She has explained that "these two sets of orientations may often be inconsistent and even in conflict with one another" (p. 385). Pinson (2007) has presented a critical approach to the topic of the teaching of civics in Israel, "question[ing] the democratic nature of the state of Israel and its ability to maintain its democratic character while defining itself as a Jewish state" (p. 352). She examined the ongoing tension between the inclusionary and exclusionary nature of citizenship and the difficulties of the educational system aimed at promoting democracy in such a reality. Her main argument is that, whereas the textbook displays multiple conceptions of citizenship, it makes sure to explain which approaches are legitimate and which are not. Ichilov, Salomon, and Inbar (2005) compared conceptions of democratic citizenship between Jewish and non-Jewish youth. The results of this study indicate that youth from the Arab minority suffered from a low degree of trust in political institutions, feeling of accountability of elected representatives toward citizens, and sense of political self-efficacy.

Despite the fact that, to the best of our knowledge, no studies have questioned how students from the Mizrachi cultural group perceive the civics curriculum, we may speculate on this issue based on general studies that reviewed the place of Mizrachi students in the Israeli educational system. Dahan and Levy (2000) have suggested that the founders of the already mentioned Kedma schools believed that a main cause of the marginalization and oppression of the Mizrachi population was the neglect of different facets of Mizrachi culture and history in Israeli educational and public spheres. Kedma's educational agenda has fostered, instead, a complex, hyphenated Israeli-Mizrachi identity and the creation of academic high schools in low-income neighborhoods, thus opposing the state integration policy, which had sought to bridge the ethnic gap in education by busing Mizrachi children to schools located in more affluent neighborhoods. Markovich (2013), who also studied a Kedma school, presented a pedagogical debate that occurred within the school regarding the enactment of critical pedagogy as part of the students' learning toward the Bagrut exam. She identified how some participants saw the teaching of the official civics curriculum as a barrier to creating educational opportunities for alternative educational approaches, such as critical and multicultural models, seen as essential for the unprivileged Mizrachi population.

Focusing on the Palestinian group, Agbaria (2010) has offered a critical view of the official Israeli civics curriculum as well as an analysis of four position papers authored by leading Palestinian civil society organizations. His central claim is that, whereas the civics curriculum, as taught in both Jewish and Palestinian schools, is highly influenced by identity politics, it fails to enable Palestinian students to develop and express their own cultural and political identities. The current reality, he has argued, refuses to acknowledge Arab group rights.

Spiegel (2011) conducted an ethnographic research survey of the Ultra-Orthodox educational system for boys in Jerusalem, claiming that, in fact, this system is an alternative to the general Israeli educational system and to modernity in general. In relation to civic education, Spiegel saw these institutions as an answer to the general educational system, which puts emphasis on nation building and the reinforcement of the power structures that serve the hegemonic powers of society. The alternative system empowers this cultural minority by ignoring the rules of the game offered by the general system. In this sense the author saw this alternative in a positive light, due to the fact that it offers students from the Ultra-Orthodox minority a feeling of affiliation and belonging, something that they do not feel in regard to the state.

In light of our analysis and in light of the case studies to be presented herein, we claim that the Israeli civics curriculum and its implementation at the current time are inadequate in engaging all citizens of the state in a true civic discourse. Although presented as inclusive, aimed at all students of the state, this curriculum in fact reinforces social and political injustices. The case of the Palestinian students represents the manner in which the curriculum maintains the current reality of inequality via its emphasis on a thin procedural mode of citizenship that does not provide Palestinian Arab students a true opportunity to engage in the general discourse as a minority group. The case of the Ultra-Orthodox students is an example of a minority group that does not take part in the general discourse at all, maintaining their status as an alternative to the general society, not a part of it, while the case of the Mizrachim is one of marginalization within the hegemonic Jewish sphere.

Thus, we conclude that the teaching of civics in Israel does not fulfill its potential in including all citizens of the state while enabling a transformative form of multicultural citizenship. Instead, it reinforces and maintains the current divided social and political reality, as will be demonstrated in the case studies that we will describe in the next section of this chapter.

Case Studies

In this section we present excerpts from interviews with civics teachers teaching in different branches of the Israeli educational system that reflect the complex reality they face in regard to the teaching of civic education and its entanglement with cultural, ethnic, and religious issues. The excerpts were gathered as part of studies in which teachers were interviewed about their ideologies, their personal interpretation of the official civics curriculum, and the enacted curriculum they implemented in their lessons (Cohen, 2016).

A common denominator across all interviews was the teachers' understanding that the relations between the different cultural groups that compose Israeli society make up an important issue that cannot be ignored, as expressed, for example, by one teacher who related to the current situation of Israeli democracy:

> Democracy isn't perfect, and it isn't perfect in Israel. . . . For example, the Arabs have official equal rights in legislation, but in reality there is discrimination, and I can also talk about the Haredim. I mean, there are minority groups . . . and the country has several values, but in reality I wouldn't give it an *A* grade.

One of the Arab teachers who was interviewed related to the complex reality regarding the very definition of Israel as a Jewish and democratic state. She said, "This combination is problematic, once you combine these two, that the state isn't democratic. Why say Jewish? What about the other citizens?" It was clear that this general atmosphere penetrated the classroom doors and was apparent as part of civics lessons, as one teacher described:

> And then they [the students] bring racism to class, and they do not have the understanding that the way they speak, theoretically we speak human rights . . . but in reality they really violate human rights all the time. . . . This is one of the great challenges in teaching civics.

And another example:

> We speak in the class about equality . . . and then if we speak about the Arabs in Israel, then [students say], "No, no, no, I mean they shouldn't be equal." . . . Sometimes they just say that they [the Arabs] shouldn't even exist.

When asked how they deal with this reality as part of their civics lessons, many teachers could not offer concrete examples of pedagogical practices or teaching strategies they implemented. Several exceptions where teachers followed the more critical approach could be found. For example, one teacher who taught in an elitist school whose student body was homogeneous described how he opened his first lesson in order to stimulate this critical kind of thought: "I asked my students, How many Ethiopians do we have in school? How many Arabs? How many kids of single moms? How many students are different from you?" He explained that the purpose of raising such questions was to get the students to think about the extent to which the school is or is not pluralistic in its nature. Another teacher voiced his more critical thoughts, particularly relating to his students of Mizrachi origin:

> Kedma students, the Mizrahi school, a lot of this, because they feel, you know, that they are, the country fucks them over, but they can't make this connection that the Arabs are also fucked up. . . . They can't, because they're too afraid to lose their identity as Israeli Jews, so this is the privilege that they do have; they are very much afraid of losing it.

Trying to understand this reality in which the teachers expressed the need to relate to such multicultural issues, on the one hand, but seldom did so in practice, on the other, led us to identify several barriers and obstacles that stand in teachers' way. One teacher, for example, talked about the fragile condition of Israeli democracy and particularly what he saw as the main problem his students faced—that of mistrust between them and the official institutions of the state, a problem he saw as more crucial than cultural relations. As he explained:

> To tell you the truth—and this might sound bad—I am indifferent to students saying, "Kill all of the Arabs," whereas I get mad when they say, "All of the politicians are corrupt." . . . When they say, "All of the politicians are corrupt," it is just a sign of their ignorance—and that is why I go mad. I think that this kind of statement touches a cord for me because of its implications—that it isn't worth going to vote and that all of the system is worthless.

Another obstacle was the teachers' feeling of efficacy (or lack thereof) and their self-portrayal of their role as civics teachers. One teacher offered the following confession:

> One student of mine told me about her mother who was racist, who discriminated against Arabs and Ethiopian Jews and in general made derogatory remarks toward other populations. And then, all of a sudden, I asked myself, Who am I to create conflict? I mean, what educational authority do I have?

An important third obstacle as expressed by the teachers was the civics curriculum itself. The teaching of the curriculum, in other words, preparing their students for the matriculation exam, was seen by teachers as their main educational goal. When asked, for example, what the purpose of teaching civics was, one teacher offered the narrow point of view that appeared in the curriculum: Students will know how a person is to act in the state and how the state should relate to its citizens. This narrow approach offers normative expectations for the students without touching, for example, on critical points of view or their limitations. Another teacher added:

> My goal is that the student will understand the material, and that he will connect it to reality, and, third, that we can sustain a dialogue.... But the Bagrut materials prevent us from ... it is like we teach only for the Bagrut.

As one teacher summarized: "Studying civics for the Bagrut is not studying civics."

These excerpts offer a snapshot of the reality civics teachers face in the current Israeli social, cultural, and political climate. As presented, whereas most teachers may agree on the need to deal with issues of multiculturalism, they are reluctant to do so as part of their actual civics lessons. These interviews reveal several institutional and contextual barriers that may explain this reality—the fragile condition of democracy in Israel, the teachers own feelings of self-efficacy, and the civics curriculum itself. These all lead to civics lessons that are limited in their ability to promote a transformative form of citizenship, not enabling the subject matter's full potential.

Concluding Discussion

In our conclusions we return to our opening questions regarding the possibility (or not) of seeing diversity and civic education as becoming a conduit for improving the condition of minorities in Israel. We question whether the limited citizenship and multicultural practices implemented in Israel, as presented, for example, in the excerpts from teachers mentioned above, toward the Jewish collective and those implemented toward the Palestinian minority can indeed be considered liberalizing processes. Furthermore, we wish to offer critical aspects of civic education, as presented in the case studies, as an optional answer to the current reality.

Israel's Homogenizing Education Policies

As presented, Israeli society has traditionally endorsed homogenizing policies toward its Jewish citizens with the hope of creating a strong collective shaped through ethnocultural principles. Toward its non-Jewish minorities, Israel has maintained a policy of systematic exclusion, manifesting as two main characteristics of the Israeli educational system: (a) the structural separation between Jewish and non-Jewish educational systems and (b) the mandatory curriculum standards, which prevent the development of a true cultural identity for such minority students.

While the approach toward Jewish citizens and the approach toward non-Jewish minorities seem to be radically different, their effects exhibit some similarities. Homogenizing the Jewish population meant working toward the exclusion of those elements (Mizrachi, Ultra-Orthodox) in the population that were alien to the dominant group (Ashkenazi) and trying to erase their cultural components. While acknowledging serious differences, in this sense, the process produced similar effects to the ones produced by the exclusionary practices implemented toward the Palestinian population.

Similar educational practices were implemented for the two main groups targeted—Mizrachim and Palestinians. Mizrachim were required to abandon their cultural identifications and historical heritage. Palestinians were required, though to a somewhat different degree, to abandon many of the same facets. Unlike the Mizrachim, Palestinians are allowed to be educated in their mother tongue, Arabic. However, as a language Arabic offers them little in the public sphere, particularly in terms of work opportunities and further educational opportunities. It is also true that in exchange for the abandonment of their roots, Mizrachim were supposedly offered an entrance ticket into mainstream Israeli society, and for Palestinians, this option was never available. Yet both groups have ended up constituting the lower socioeconomic strata of Israeli society (Cohen, 2014; Mizrachi & Herzog, 2012; Plaut & Plaut, 2015; Sasson-Levy, 2013).

The third group we have considered, the Ultra-Orthodox, were allowed to sustain their cultural heritage. However, they were allowed to do so while paying the high price of social marginalization and low socioeconomic status. The work invested by the sovereign powers has been so successful that these three groups are more attentive to the ethnic cultural differences among them than to the similarities they share regarding their marginalized place in society.

The rather recent emergence of multicultural schools in Israel, such as the ones described above (Kedma and the Shas schools), as well as schools dedicated to the children of Russian (Jewish) immigrants (Resnik, 2006) and bilingual integrated Palestinian Jewish schools (Bekerman, 2004, 2005, 2009), has attracted varied reactions from the authorities. While responses have ranged from criticism to indifference, in general these schools are not considered to represent a real challenge to the hegemonic national identity. As presented above, it is worth mentioning that this recent multicultural tolerance has not been directed toward schools in the Arab system.

Multicultural and Civic Education in Israel—From Theory to Practice

We questioned whether the limited citizenship and multicultural practices implemented in Israel toward the Jewish collective and those implemented toward the Palestinian minority can indeed be considered liberalizing processes. Israel has not overcome its firm position of differentiating between two separate collectives—Jews and Palestinians—while denying in-group differences. We believe that the epistemological premises that underlie present neoliberal policies in Israel make it impossible for Israel to reframe itself as a more tolerant society. Moreover, we question whether Israel can offer true recognition of its conforming groups if it stays attached to the cultural-ethnic-national differentiation it so "naturally" supports.

In his book *Culture and Society*, Raymond Williams (1958) noted that toward the end of the 18th century, five well-known terms acquired new and important meanings. In their new format, these terms—*industry, democracy, class, art,* and *culture*—reacted to and shaped the social, economic, and political changes that affect our world to this day.

At that time, the word *culture* was accorded a distinct and abstract meaning, addressing two processes taking place in developing national sovereign communities: On one hand, it reflected the Christian differentiation between moral and intellectual pursuits and the manufacture of goods and products in a world of industrial development; on the other hand, it set itself up as a human court that transcended practical human judgment. This second abstracted meaning accorded significance to the definition of *culture* posited by the British educator and philosopher Matthew Arnold: "The best which has been thought and said in the world," the best we have to learn and teach—according to Kant, however, "the best," that is, good, necessarily lacks purpose (cited in Williams, 1958, p. 89). This view allows for a ruthless differentiation between "high" culture and "popular" culture, a distinction that largely blocks the penetration of alien (i.e., nonhegemonic) cultural aspects into the pantheon of the ruling culture that putative "multiculturalism" seeks to change. Supporters of diversity may not always be aware of these meanings. It is doubtful whether their call for a change in this situation is even possible without an intensive examination of the relevant epistemological processes that sustain such a hierarchical understanding of culture and without suggesting practical measures to address them.

Culture and its reification are linked closely with the development of the nation-state. Elias (1998) and Williams (1961) shed light on the reciprocal relations between these two phenomena, a process that included a transition from the expression and representation of culture as open and constantly growing, through interpersonal and group encounters, to its conception and presentation as an organized, well-formed, closed, and fixed system of cultural items or objects, such as ideas, values, norms, texts, and ceremonies, complete and autonomous in themselves. These objects may be used to foster unity among inhabitants of a given nation-state, thereby neutralizing local-regional and linguistic variations/subcommunities said to belong to the national group. Furthermore, direct, unmediated contact may be promoted between members of this group and the state. Citizens devoid of any affiliation with ethnic, national, or religious groups will be entitled to prima facie political equality (Mendus, 1989).

Cultural identities reinforce their unity not by relying on meanings from the past but by reconstructing and reinterpreting cultural materials accessible to all in the present (Bauman, 1999). Cultural development is consolidated through translation—an act that from the outset does not address the intercultural sphere alone but also accounts for all communicative activity between human beings, even those who ostensibly belong to the same culture (Becker, 1995; Ortega & Gasset, 1957); indeed it should not be assumed that necessarily all French or Israelis today belong to the same culture. Consequently, the arguments propounded in this critique should not be perceived as an appeal against commitment to one community or another—or against differentiation among groups—but, rather, only against their conception as possessing any exclusive character.

To achieve a situation in which culture has no exclusive value requires a reevaluation of the concepts of culture and identity that have been accepted in the West over the past few centuries. It also requires a reexamination of epistemological and ontological conceptions as well as an examination of the ways in which they have shaped political and social organizations reflected in the nation-state. Modern thought has led us to understand culture as a kind of prison in which the self and its identity are incarcerated and to perceive relationships among cultural identities representing different cultures as the manifestation of a communication problem. However, the theoretical developments reviewed above point toward a different direction. Just as culture is soft, permeable, and dynamic, so too is the cultural self and its identity. This was well expressed by Bakhtin (1984) and his noncoincidence principles concerning humanity. Žižek (1997), in turn, stresses that a person's prima facie status as an unfinished entity in constant dialogue with the environment may well constitute a solution to the communication issue and not necessarily the problem.

Furthermore, the difficulties encountered have nothing to do with the linguistic constraints that preclude our understanding of one cultural language or another. The impossibility of grasping the precise meaning of a given symbol is a universal principle imprinted in all human beings (meaning is always positional, never precise). Hence, the cultural approach that undermines the civic is the one that posits that cultures exist within clearly delineated boundaries (precise meanings) that are entitled to recognition by the reigning powers. "Enlightenment" will be achieved only through a cultural conception that demands equality because all human beings are entitled to choose what they wish to be. Only such a reexamination of epistemological and ontological conceptions would accord an appropriate universal meaning in support of multicultural and civic perspectives. Following, the emphasis in the classroom should be on the development of a thoughtful, active, and effective citizenry that relates to this social reality (Ladson-Billings, 1994; Marri, 2005), faced not only outward—toward the state—but also inward—toward diverse cultural groups.

The "translation" of such ideas into the Israeli civics curriculum will result in a curriculum that enables a true discussion about students' (and teachers') cultural and civic identities, as individual citizens of the state but also as members of diverse cultural groups. Such discussions will promote an understanding of the complex and multiple roles of the students as such citizens and as members of their society, connecting these two inseparable elements.

Israel would do well to recall that most of the world's problems—hunger, disease, poverty, pollution, displacement, and the like—do not originate in the term *culture* in its axiological or symbolic sense but, rather, in culture as work or human interaction. It is this aspect of culture that ought to constitute the focus of Israel's sociocultural, political, and educational solutions. When in search of justice, redistribution is preferable to accounting for otherness.

References

Abdo, N., & Yuval-Davis, N. (1995). Palestine, Israel, and the Zionist settler project. In D. Stasiulis & N. Yuval-Davis (Eds.), *Unsettling settler societies: Articulations of gender, race, ethnicity, and class* (pp. 291–322). Thousand Oaks, CA: SAGE.

Adams, M., Bell, L. A., & Griffin, P. (2007). *Teaching for diversity and social justice*. New York: Routledge.

Agbaria, A. (2010). Civic education for the Palestinians in Israel: Dilemmas and challenges. In H. Alexander, H. Pinson, & Y. Yonah (Eds.), *Citizenship education and social conflict: Israeli political education in global perspective* (pp. 217–237). Jerusalem, Israel: Van Leer Jerusalem Institute.

Agbaria, A. K., Mustafa, M., & Jabareen, Y. T. (2014). "In your face" democracy: Education for belonging and its challenges in Israel. *British Educational Research Journal, 41*(1), 143–175.

Al-Haj, M. (2002). Multiculturalism in deeply divided societies: The Israeli case. *International Journal of Intercultural Relations, 26*(2), 169–183.

Amara, M. (2006). The vitality of the Arabic language in Israel from a sociolinguistic perspective. *Adalah's Newsletter, 29*, 1–11

Apple, M. W. (2001). Educational and curricular restructuring and the neo-liberal and neo-conservative agendas: Interview with Michael Apple. *Curriculo sem Fronteiras, 1*(1), i–xxvi.

Asad, T. (2003). *Formations of the secular: Christianity, Islam, modernity.* Stanford, CA: Stanford University Press.

Bakhtin, M. M. (1984). *Problems of Dostoevsky's poetics* (C. Emerson, Trans.). Minneapolis, MN: University of Minnesota Press.

Banks, J. A. (2004). Introduction: Democratic citizenship education in multicultural societies. In J. A. Banks (Ed.), *Diversity and citizenship education* (pp. 3–16). San Francisco: Jossey-Bass.

Banks, J. A. (2008). Diversity, group identity, and citizenship education in a global age. *Educational Researcher, 37*(3), 129–139.

Banks, J. A. (Ed.). (2009). *The Routledge international companion to multicultural education.* New York: Routledge.

Bar-Tal, D. (1999). Hashkafot dmut ha Arabi ve yachasim Yehudim-Arabim BeMikraot [The Arab-Israeli conflict as an intractable conflict and its reflection in Israeli textbooks] [Hebrew]. *Megamot, 29*(4), 445–491.

Baum, N. (2007). It's not only cultural differences: Comparison of Jewish Israeli social work students' thoughts and feelings about treating Jewish Ultra-Orthodox and Palestinian Israeli clients. *International Journal of Intercultural Relations, 31*(5), 575–589.

Baum, N., Yedidya, T., Schwartz, C., & Aran, O. (2014). Women pursuing higher education in Ultra-Orthodox society. *Journal of Social Work Education, 50*(1), 164–175.

Bauman, Z. (1999). *Culture as praxis.* London: SAGE.

Becker, A. L. (1995). *Beyond translation essays toward a modern philology.* Ann Arbor, MI: University of Michigan Press.

Bekerman, Z. (2004). Potential and limitations of multicultural education in conflict-ridden areas: Bilingual Palestinian-Jewish schools in Israel. *Teachers College Record, 106*(3), 574–610.

Bekerman, Z. (2005). Complex contexts and ideologies: Bilingual education in conflict-ridden areas. *Journal of Language Identity and Education, 4*(1), 1–20.

Bekerman, Z. (2009). Identity vs. peace: Identity wins. *Harvard Educational Review, 79*(1), 74–83.

Ben-Peretz, M., & Zeidman, A. (1986). Three generations of curriculum development in Israel. *Iyunim Bechinuch, 43*, 317–327.

Ben-Porat, G., & Feniger, Y. (2013). Unpacking secularization: Structural changes, individual choices and ethnic paths. *Ethnicities, 14*(1), 91–112.

Ben-Rafael, E., Shohamy, E., Hasan Amara, M., & Trumper-Hecht, N. (2006). Linguistic landscape as symbolic construction of the public space: The case of Israel. *International Journal of Multilingualism, 3*(1), 7–30.

Billig, M. (1995). *Banal nationalism.* London: SAGE.

Brender, A. (2005, January). *Ethnic segregation and the quality of local government in the minority's localities: Local tax collection in the Israeli-Arab municipalities as a case-study* (Bank of Israel Discussion Paper No. 2005.01). Available at https://ssrn.com/abstract=806904 or http://dx.doi.org/10.2139/ssrn.806904

Caplan, K. (2007). *Internal popular discourse in Israeli Haredi society*. Jerusalem, Israel: Zalman Shazar Center for Jewish History.

Carnegie Corporation of New York & Center for Information and Research on Civic Learning and Engagement. (2003). *The civic mission of schools*. New York: Carnegie Corporation of New York.

Central Bureau of Statistics. (2013a). *65th Independence Day—More than 8 million residents in the state of Israel* [Press release]. Retrieved from http://www.cbs.gov.il/hodaot2013n/11_13_097e.pdf

Central Bureau of Statistics. (2013b). *Statistical abstract of Israel No. 64*. Retrieved from http://cbs .gov.il/reader/shnaton/shnatone_new.htm?CYear=2013&Vol=64&CSubject=30

Choe, H. (2006). National identity and citizenship in the People's Republic of China and the Republic of Korea. *Journal of Historical Sociology, 19*(1), 84–118.

Cohen, A. (2010). A theoretical model of four conceptions of civic education. *Canadian Social Studies, 44*(1), 17–28.

Cohen, A. (2016). Between teachers' perceptions and civic conceptions: Lessons from three Israeli civics teachers. *Journal of Curriculum Studies*, 1–19. Published online December 1, 2016. doi:10 .1080/00220272.2016.1263896

Cohen, K. (2014). Mizrahi subalternity and the state of Israel: Towards a new understanding of Mizrahi literature. *Interventions, 16*(3), 380–404.

Cole, D., & Zhou, J. (2014). Do diversity experiences help college students become more civically minded? Applying Banks' multicultural education framework. *Innovative Higher Education, 39*(2), 109–121.

Cole, E. (Ed.). (2007). *Teaching the violent past: History education and reconciliation*. Lanham, MD: Rowman & Littlefield.

Connor-Atias, E., & Abu-Hala, H. (2009). *Zaka'ut lete'udat bagrut lefi yishuv* [Eligibility for matriculation by city]. Tel Aviv, Israel: Adva Center. Retrieved from http://www.adva.org/uploaded/ Bagrut2008.pdf

Dahan, Y., & Levy, G. (2000). Multicultural education in the Zionist state—The Mizrahi challenge. *Studies in Philosophy and Education, 19*, 423–444. Retrieved from http://www.ingentaconnect .com/content/klu/sped/2000/00000019/F0020005/00268738

Deutch, Y. (2005). Language law in Israel. *Language Policy, 4*(3), 261–285.

Elias, N. (1998). Civilization, culture, identity: "'Civilisation' and 'Culture': Nationalism and Nation-State Formation": An extract from *The Germans*. In J. Rundell & S. Mennell (Eds.), *Classical readings in culture and civilization* (pp. 225–240). New York: Routledge.

Gavison, R. (2000). Does equality require integration? A case study. *Democratic Culture, 3*, 37–87.

Ghanem, A. (1998). State and minority in Israel: The case of ethnic state and the predicament of its minority. *Ethnic and Racial Studies, 21*(3), 428–448.

Gibton, D. (2011). Post-2000 law-based educational governance in Israel: From equality to diversity? *Educational Management Administration and Leadership, 39*(4), 434–454.

Gorski, P. C. (2006). Complicity with conservatism: The de-politicizing of multicultural and intercultural education. *Intercultural Education, 17*(2), 163–177.

Gorski, P. C. (2012). Instructional, institutional, and sociopolitical challenges of teaching multicultural teacher education courses. *Teacher Educator, 47*(3), 216–235.

Grant, C. A., & Sleeter, C. E. (2011). *Doing multicultural education for achievement and equity*. New York: Routledge.

Gurin, P., Dey, E., Hurtado, S., & Gurin, G. (2002). Diversity and higher education: Theory and impact on educational outcomes. *Harvard Educational Review, 72*(3), 330–367.

Hall, S. (1996). Introduction: Who needs "identity"? In S. Hall & P. du Gay (Eds.), *Questions of cultural identity* (pp. 1–18). London: SAGE.

Hammack, P. L. (2006). Identity, conflict, and coexistence life stories of Israeli and Palestinian adolescents. *Journal of Adolescent Research, 21*(4), 323–369.

Heller, M. (1999). *Linguistic minorities and modernity: A sociolinguistic ethnography.* London: Longman.

Herzog, H. (1985). Social construction of reality in ethnic terms: The case of political ethnicity in Israel. *International Review of Modern Sociology, 15*(1/2), 45–61.

Hesketh, K., Bishara, S., Zaher, S., & Rosenberg, R. (2010). Inequality report: The Palestinian Arab minority in Israel. *Arab World Geographer, 13*(3), 234–284.

Hofman, A., Alpert, B., & Schnell, I. (2007). Education and social change: The case of Israel's state curriculum. *Curriculum Inquiry, 37*(4), 303–328.

Hofnung, M. (1991). Israel: Tzorchei bitachon leumat shilton ha chok [Israel: Security needs versus the rule of law] [Hebrew]. Jerusalem, Israel: Nevo.

Hornberger, N. H. (2002). Multilingual language policies and the continua of biliteracy: An ecological approach. *Language Policy, 1*(1), 27–51.

Ichilov, O., Salomon, G., & Inbar, D. (2005). Citizenship education in Israel—A Jewish-democratic state. *Israel Affairs, 11*(2), 303–323.

Ichilov, O. (1999). Citizenship in a divided society: The case of Israel. In J. Torney-Purta, J. Schwille, & J. Amadeo (Eds.), *Civic education across countries: Twenty-four national case studies from the IEA civic education project* (pp. 371–393). Amsterdam: IEA.

Jobani, Y., & Perez, N. (2014). Toleration and illiberal groups in context: Israel's Ultra-Orthodox "society of learners." *Journal of Political Ideologies, 19*(1), 78–98.

Khazzoom, A. (2003). The great chain of Orientalism: Jewish identity, stigma management, and ethnic exclusion in Israel. *American Sociological Review, 68*(4), 481–510.

Kravel-Tovi, M. (2012). "National mission": Biopolitics, non-Jewish immigration and Jewish conversion policy in contemporary Israel. *Ethnic and Racial Studies, 35*(4), 737–756.

Ladson-Billings, G. (1994). *The dreamkeepers: Successful teachers of African American children.* San Francisco: Jossey-Bass.

Ladson-Billings, G. (2004). New directions in multicultural education: Complexities, boundaries, and critical race theory. In J. A. Banks & C. A. M. Banks (Eds.), *Handbook of research on multicultural education* (2nd ed., pp. 50–65). New York: Wiley.

Ladson-Billings, G., & Tate, W. F., IV. (2014). Toward a critical race theory of education. In A. D. Dixson & C. K. Rousseau (Eds.), *Critical race theory in education: All God's children got a song* (pp. 11–31). New York: Routledge.

Levy, G. (2005). From subjects to citizens: On educational reforms and the demarcation of the "Israeli-Arabs." *Citizenship Studies, 9*(3), 271–291.

Lewin, A. C. (2012). Marriage patterns among Palestinians in Israel. *European Journal of Population/ Revue Européenne de Démographie, 28*(3), 359–380.

Likhovski, A. (2010). Post-post-Zionist historiography. *Israel Studies, 15*(2), 1–23.

Markovich, D. Y. (2013). Lessons learned from the study of a Jewish-Israeli high school: Critical pedagogy in contention. *InterActions: UCLA Journal of Education and Information Studies, 9*(2). Retrieved from http://www.escholarship.org/uc/item/5v41h8t6

Marri, A. (2005). Building a framework for classroom-based multicultural democratic education: Learning from three skilled teachers. *Teachers College Record, 107*(5), 1036–1059.

McEneaney, E. H., & Meyer, J. W. (2000). The content of curriculum. In M. T. Hallinan (Ed.), *Handbook of the sociology of education* (pp. 189–211). New York: Kluwer Academic/Plenum.

Mendus, S. (1989). *Toleration and the limits of liberalism.* New York: Macmillan.

Ministry of Education. (1995). Mediniut leshonit le chinuch BeIsrael (Policy for language education in Israel) [Hebrew]. Jerusalem, Israel: Office of Director General.

Ministry of Education. (1996). Mediniut leshonit le chinuch BeIsrael (Policy for language education in Israel) [Hebrew]. Jerusalem, Israel: Office of the Director General.

Ministry of Education. (2010). *Ezrachut: Tochnit ha-limudim ba-chativa ha-elyona le-bati sefer Yehudiim (claliim ve-datiim), Aravim ve-Druzim* [Civics: High school curriculum for Jewish (general and religious), Arab and Druze schools]. Jerusalem, Israel: Author.

Ministry of Education, Culture and Sport, Economics and Budgeting Administration. (2002). *Facts and figures about education in Israel*. Retrieved from http://meyda.education.gov.il/files/minhalcalcala/facts.pdf

Mitchell, K., & Parker, W. C. (2008). I pledge allegiance to . . . flexible citizenship and shifting scales of belonging. *Teachers College Record, 110*(4), 775–804.

Mizrachi, N. (2012). On the mismatch between multicultural education and its subjects in the field. *British Journal of Sociology of Education, 33*(2), 185–201.

Mizrachi, N., Goodman, Y. C., & Feniger, Y. (2009). "I don't want to see it": Decoupling ethnicity and class from social structure in Jewish Israeli high schools. *Ethnic and Racial Studies, 32*(7), 1203–1225.

Mizrachi, N., & Herzog, H. (2012). Participatory destigmatization strategies among Palestinian citizens, Ethiopian Jews and Mizrahi Jews in Israel. *Ethnic and Racial Studies, 35*(3), 418–435.

Nash, G. B., Crabtree, C., & Dunn, R. E. (1998). *History on trial*. New York: Knopf.

Nir, A. E., & Inbar, D. (2004). From egalitarianism to competition: The case of the Israeli educational system. In I. Rotberg (Ed.), *Balancing change and tradition in global education reform* (pp. 207–228). Lanham, MD: Scarecrow Education.

Ortega, J., & Gasset, Y. (1957). *What people say: Toward a new linguistics* (W. R. Trask, Trans.). New York: W. W. Norton.

Parekh, B. (2002). *Rethinking multiculturalism: Cultural diversity and political theory*. Cambridge, MA: Harvard University Press.

Paris, D., & Alim, H. S. (2014). What are we seeking to sustain through culturally sustaining pedagogy? A loving critique forward. *Harvard Educational Review, 84*(1), 85–100.

Peled, Y. (2008). The evolution of Israeli citizenship: An overview. *Citizenship Studies, 12*(3), 335–345.

Peled, Y., & Navot, D. (2005). Ethnic democracy revisited: On the state of democracy in the Jewish state. *Israel Studies Forum, 20*(1), 2005, pp. 3–27.

Perliger, A., Canetti-Nisim, D., & Pedahzur, A. (2006). Democratic attitudes among high-school pupils: The role played by perceptions of class climate. *School Effectiveness and School Improvement, 17*(1), 119–140.

Phillion, J., He, M. F., & Connelly, F. M. (2003). Experiential approaches to the study of multiculturalism in education: Introduction to the Special Series on Multiculturalism in *Curriculum Inquiry*. *Curriculum Inquiry, 33*(4), 341–342.

Pinson, H. (2007). Inclusive curriculum? Challenges to the role of civic education in a Jewish and democratic state. *Curriculum Inquiry, 37*(4), 351–382.

Pinson, H. (2008). The excluded citizenship identity: Palestinian/Arab Israeli young people negotiating their political identities. *British Journal of Sociology of Education, 29*(2), 201–212.

Plaut, P. O., & Plaut, S. E. (2015). Ethnic income disparities in Israel. *Israel Affairs, 21*(1), 1–26.

Podeh, E. (2000). History and memory in the Israeli education system: The portrayal of the Arab-Israeli conflict in history textbooks (1948–2000). *History and Memory, 12*(1), 65–100.

Rabinowitz, D. (2001). The Palestinian citizens of Israel, the concept of trapped minority and the discourse of transnationalism in anthropology. *Ethnic and Racial Studies, 24*(1), 64–85.

Ram, U. (2008). Why secularism fails? Secular nationalism and religious revivalism in Israel. *International Journal of Politics, Culture, and Society, 21*(1–4), 57–73.

Resnik, J. (2006). Alternative identities in multicultural schools in Israel: Emancipatory identity, mixed identity and transnational identity. *British Journal of Sociology of Education, 27*(5), 581–601.

Sabar, N., & Mathias, Y. (2003). Curriculum planning at the threshold of the third millennium: The Israeli case. In W. F. Pinar (Ed.), *International handbook of curriculum research* (pp. 381–400). Mahwah, NJ: Lawrence Erlbaum.

Sasson-Levy, O. (2013). A different kind of Whiteness: Marking and unmarking of social boundaries in the construction of hegemonic ethnicity. *Sociological Forum, 28*(1), 27–50.

Shafir, G., & Peled, Y. (2002). *Being Israeli: The dynamics of multiple citizenship*. Cambridge, UK: Cambridge University Press.

Sharoni, S., & Abu-Nimer, M. (2000). The Israeli-Palestinian conflict. In D. J. Gerner (Ed.), *Understanding the contemporary Middle East* (pp. 161–200). Boulder, CO: Lynne Rienner.

Shiffer, V. (1999). *The Haredi educational in Israel: Allocation, regulation, and control*. Jerusalem, Israel: Floersheimer Institute for Policy Studies.

Shohamy, E., & Spolsky, B. (1999). An emerging language policy for Israel: From monolingualism to multilingualism. *Plurilingua, 21*, 169–184.

Shohat, E. (1988). Sephardim in Israel: Zionism from the standpoint of its Jewish victims. *Social Text, 19/20*, 1–35.

Shokeid, M. (1984). Cultural ethnicity in Israel: The case of Middle Eastern Jews' religiosity. *AJS Review, 9*(2), 247–271.

Smooha, S. (2002). The model of ethnic democracy: Israel as a Jewish and democratic state. *Nations and Nationalism, 8*(4), 475–503.

Smooha, S. (2004). *Index of Arab-Jewish relations in Israel*. Haifa, Israel: University of Haifa, Citizens' Accord Forum, Jewish-Arab Center, Friedrich Ebert Stiftung.

Spiegel, E. (2011). *"Ve Talmud Torah KeNeged Kulam": Chinuch Charedi LeBanim BeYerushalayim* ["And the study of Torah is greater than all of them": Haredi education for boys in Jerusalem]. Jerusalem, Israel: Jerusalem Institute for Israel Studies.

Spolsky, B. (1994). The situation of Arabic in Israel. In Y. Suleiman (Ed.), *Arabic sociolinguistics: Issues and perspectives* (pp. 227–236). Richmond, UK: Curzon Press.

Spolsky, B. (1997). Multilingualism in Israel. *Annual Review of Applied Linguistics, 17*, 138–150.

Spolsky, B., & Shohamy, E. (1999). Language in Israel society and education. *International Journal of the Sociology of Language, 137*, 93–114.

Stadler, N. (2002). Is profane work an obstacle to salvation? The case of Ultra-Orthodox (Haredi) Jews in contemporary Israel. *Sociology of Religion, 63*(4), 455–474.

Swirski, S., & Dagan-Buzaglo, N. (2009, December). *Separation, inequality and faltering leadership: Education in Israel*. Tel Aviv, Israel: Adva Center. Retrieved from http://adva.org/wp-content/uploads/2015/08/education-English-20091.pdf

Verkuyten, M., & Thijs, J. (2015). Multicultural education and inter-ethnic attitudes: An intergroup perspective. *European Psychologist, 18*(3), 179–190.

Weil, S. (1996/1997). Religion, blood and the equality of rights: The case of Ethiopian Jews in Israel. *International Journal on Minority and Group Rights, 4*(3/4), 397–412.

Whitehead, K. A., & Wittig, M. A. (2004). Discursive management of resistance to a multicultural education programme. *Qualitative Research in Psychology, 1*(4), 267–284.

Whitman, W. (1855/1993). Song of myself. In *Leaves of grass* ("Death Bed" ed.; pp. 33–115). New York: Modern Library.

Williams, R. (1958). *Culture and society, 1780–1950*. New York: Columbia University Press.

Wimmer, A., & Schiller, N. G. (2003). Methodological nationalism, the social sciences, and the study of migration: An essay in historical epistemology. *International Migration Review, 37*(3), 576–610.

Yiftachel, O. (1998). The internal frontier: Territorial control and ethnic relations in Israel. In O. Yiftachel & A. Meir (Eds.), *Ethnic frontiers and peripheries: Landscapes of development and inequality in Israel* (pp. 39–69). Boulder, CO: Westview Press.

Zameret, Z. (1997). *Across a narrow bridge: Shaping the education system during the massive immigration.* Sede Boker, Israel: Ben-Gurion Research Centre.

Zirkel, S. (2008). The influence of multicultural educational practices on student outcomes and intergroup relations. *Teachers College Record, 110*(6), 1147–1181.

Žižek, S. (1997). *The abyss of freedom* (J. Norman, Trans.). Ann Arbor: University of Michigan Press.

Part 6

Mexico and Brazil

Chapter 18

Stealth Diversity and the Indigenous Question: The Challenges of Citizenship in Mexican Civic Education

BRADLEY A. LEVINSON
Indiana University

MARÍA EUGENIA LUNA ELIZARRARÁS
Secretaría de Educación Pública, Mexico

In broad brushstrokes, the story of citizenship and citizenship education in Mexico features a strongly secular, liberal, nationalist state that in the 19th century began a project to assimilate its indigenous peoples into a mainstream, mestizo national culture. This project was then inflected, but not fundamentally altered, by the revolution of the early 20th century, which came to glorify the indigenous contribution to national culture but provided few differentiated citizenship rights to indigenous peoples. Since the late 1980s this project has evolved in fits and starts toward a more inclusive, accommodating pluricultural framework. Yet there is still much more work to be done.

Three qualifications immediately must be made to such a broad narrative statement. First, until the 20th century the sense of being a citizen in Mexico was largely divorced from democratic discourse and aspiration; citizenship was largely about one's place in the social hierarchy and sense of belonging to national, regional, and local political units, or to "corporate" associations, rather than liberal democratic deliberation or participation. Only since the 1960s has citizenship focused on liberal democratic rights and obligations. Second, our characterization of citizenship as changing from a "project" to a "framework" is deliberate. It denotes the fact that until quite recently a strong federal state in Mexico, ruled by political elites, centrally dictated citizenship terms. While it is still ruled by elites, in more recent years Mexico's diverse civil society has asserted itself and forced the state "projects" of old to respond to diverse citizenship strategies and open themselves to more inclusive formulations. Third and relatedly, insofar as ethnocultural identification and membership has figured into the dynamics of modern Mexican citizenship, it has always been conceived in terms of the relationship between the mainstream (mestizo) and the indigenous. Little attention has been paid to the full racial-ethnic and religious diversity of Mexico's citizenry, including African-heritage populations; immigrants from Asia, Europe, and the Middle East; migrants and exiles from Central and South America; and return migrants from the United States. For this reason, we refer to Mexico's "stealth diversity" as those forms of ethnocultural identity and membership that remain relatively invisible in Mexico, overshadowed by the indigenous question and thus barely registering on the radar of most citizenship education programs.[1]

In this chapter, we provide an account of the shifting landscape of citizenship in Mexico, as well as the ways that Mexican educational programs and curricula have responded (or not) to such shifts. Though we try to address the full range of compulsory public education, we place most emphasis on contemporary developments at the lower secondary level (*secundaria*) since 1993, because this is where the national ministry of education has been most active in developing citizenship programs and where youth identity formation is paramount. The primary question we pose is as follows: To what extent, and in what manner, have shifting forms of racial-ethnic diversity been incorporated into Mexican school-based citizenship education? Our basic argument is that formal programs for Mexican citizenship education have slowly shifted from an emphasis on national identity and solidarity through assimilation to a multicultural (if not intercultural) emphasis on forms of democratic membership and participation. Yet such advances in education policy and curricula are limited and sometimes contradictory: They still remain firmly within a neoliberal framework of recognition without redistribution (Fraser, 1997), thus negating fuller forms of structural inclusion; and even then, they fail to adequately recognize the full range of diversity in Mexico. While some of these advances in policy and curriculum are promising, actual teacher training and practice lag sadly behind. Indeed, nongovernmental organizations have emerged to fill in the gaps and provide some of the most innovative and effective citizenship education practices, though these are often very local and therefore limited programs.

We follow Levinson's (2011) definition of citizenship as those practices "constituted by the meanings, rights, and obligations of membership in *publics*, as well as the forms of agency and modalities of participation implicated by such membership" (p. 280). Citizenship education can thus be understood as the efforts of a public to educate its members to imagine their social belonging and exercise their participation as citizens. In Mexico, as in most contemporary nation-states, the national government has attempted to monopolize the space of the "public" and organize school-based citizenship education accordingly. Yet, from a broader anthropological perspective, if we study

> how citizen identities are formed through education in the home, the community, the street, and the media (i.e., non-formal or informal domains), then we can better understand how these identities articulate with, or chafe against, the identities proposed and shaped in schools. (p. 281)

In this chapter, we argue that relatively invisible yet resurgent publics throughout Mexico have often attempted to assert their citizen identities, yet with little success against the homogenizing narrative of the state.

After the Revolution: The Vicissitudes of the State and Civic Education in Mexico

Mexico's war of independence, beginning in 1810, resulted in the declaration of formal independence from Spain in 1821. Throughout the remainder of the 19th century, politics would be defined by the battle between the Conservatives, and their penchant for centralized authority, and the Liberals, advocating federalism and the European principles of the Enlightenment. Meanwhile, the byzantine complexity of racial classification during the colonial period eventually resolved itself into a dichotomous majority of mestizos (mixed-race) and a minority of more than 70 indigenous groups (an even smaller minority, it must be said, still considered themselves *criollos* and proclaimed their European "purity"). Under the revered President Benito Juárez, the Liberals prevailed by the late 1850s, yet Juárez himself represents a leitmotif of modern Mexican citizenship: Raised as a monolingual Zapotec Indian but later adopting the Freemasons' creed, Juárez would eventually eschew his particularistic indigenous identity in favor of the universal principles of Enlightenment liberalism and the guarantees of a secular state. Ethnically speaking, he became a mestizo.

From a critical perspective, Escalante (1995) has emphasized how the liberal project of that time dismissed the indigenous population as a social sector that could participate with its customs and culture. Indeed, their participation was conditional upon the abandonment of their Indianness and their conversion into citizens conceived as individuals strongly identified with national ideals. From that time forward, any political action by indigenous communities, ranging from rebellion to peaceful social movement, was considered a subversive act that undermined the progress of civilization. Indeed, Conservatives shared in much of this discourse as well. It was during the 19th century that a range of ideologues and politicians emphasized the importance of forging an image of national unity that would foster citizen loyalty to the newly independent state. As a preeminent educational historian has demonstrated (Vázquez, 2005), early Mexican nationalism was constructed through the fusion and integration of diverse symbolic elements from pre-Columbian Mesoamerica, such as the greatness of the Aztec Empire, along with key heroic figures from the armed independence struggle.

The 1917 Mexican Constitution, forged toward the end of the revolution against the dictatorship of Porfirio Díaz, is an updated and expanded version of the original liberal Constitution of 1857.[2] It remains the law in Mexico. Although the constitution provides for a progressive federal republic—with a separation of executive, judicial, and legislative powers; a bicameral congress; and considerable state and municipal autonomy—the reality in postrevolutionary Mexico has been distinct. Deeply rooted in the habits of colonial and dictatorial rule, Mexico quickly turned into what many have called a presidentialist regime. In other words, despite the liberal spirit of the constitution, the conservative preference for centralized power prevailed. The concentration of power in the president's office led to a subordinate judiciary and a rubber-stamp legislature. By 1929, the president had formed the political party that eventually came to be known as the Institutional Revolutionary Party (Partido Revolucionario Institucional, or PRI). Drawing together different sectors of society (skilled labor, the peasantry, business groups, etc.), and built on a complex network of negotiations with regional warlords and power brokers, the PRI developed a disciplined "corporatist" machine that helped identify the party with the state and perpetuate single-party rule for more than 70 years (Joseph & Nugent, 1994; Silva-Herzog Márquez, 1999). Importantly, the national teachers' union effectively came to serve as one of the bastions of PRI support.

It was not until the late 1970s that significant electoral reforms began to open the possibility for meaningful opposition politics in Mexico. Several important mayoralties and governorships fell to opposition parties during the 1980s, and in 1988 the PRI resorted to massive electoral fraud in order to reclaim the presidency from the renegade candidate Cuauhtémoc Cárdenas. The PRI attempted to recover legitimacy throughout the 1990s by agreeing to further electoral reforms and conducting more transparent business, yet certain democratic gains were irreversible. Economic crisis deepened, and so too did the presence of new democratic actors in civil society determined to force the peaceful resolution of social problems, through civil disobedience if necessary. Chief among these nongovernmental organizations were those devoted to human rights, women's rights, indigenous peoples' rights, economic justice, and the environment.

Throughout these changes, the national ministry of public education, called the Secretaría de Educación Pública, or simply SEP, has played an important role. An ideological child of the revolution, the SEP was created in 1921 to advance the integrative and developmentalist agenda of the nascent state.[3] Modeled on the French system, and highly centralized in Mexico City, the huge bureaucracy of the SEP now controls most of the formal educational enterprise in Mexico. Through the operation of most teacher education programs, the hiring of all teachers, and the production of common textbooks for all of basic education, the SEP has historically been a key instrument of state formation and the creation of national identity (Joseph & Nugent, 1994; Ornelas, 1995). Important modernization reforms since 1993 have arguably curtailed the power of the SEP.[4] For instance, administrative decentralization has put the states in charge of budgeting and teacher hiring; and since the 1992 declaration of the *secundaria* (lower secondary, roughly ages 12–15) as part of the cycle of compulsory schooling, states can determine their own "elective" courses for two semesters of study. Still, most matters of curriculum and educational planning remain highly concentrated in the national SEP.

The formal practice of school-based civic education in Mexico has a history that is roughly coterminous with the SEP itself. Before the revolution and the creation of the SEP in 1921, Mexican liberals of the 19th century had implemented a modest civic education curriculum in public primary schools, but these only served a very small portion of the population. Because of limited resources and a highly dispersed population, only a small minority of Mexicans attended more than a year or two of primary school, if even that, and secondary schools were only available to the children of urban elites. Still, we now have accounts of important early civic instruction and political "catechism" in 19th-century schools (Roldán, 2012; Sánchez, 2008).

It was not until the period after the revolution that civics (*civismo*) became truly prominent in school life. Primary school included very basic lessons in government, but above all, civics appears to have been taught experientially through nationalist civic ceremonies, which attempted to inculcate a strong sense of national pride and identity and allegiance to the state (Vaughan, 1997). This was to be expected. Strong regional loyalties and sentiments had animated much of the revolutionary fervor, and throughout the 1920s and into the 1930s the state continued to wage a war against Christian rebels in different parts of the republic. This "hot" war was thus accompanied by a colder war of civic education for the hearts and minds of children.[5]

From early on, the SEP decided to focus much of its attention on the kind of civic education that would be imparted through the *secundaria*. In 1928 a separate Office of Secondary Education was created, and at this time the *secundaria* became explicitly conceived as an institution serving the "adolescent" life stage (Levinson, 1999; Meneses Morales, 1986). Moisés Sáenz, considered by most the founder of the *secundaria*, had studied at Columbia University with John Dewey. The Mexican *secundaria* proposed by Sáenz emphasized the importance of curtailing selfish individualism and creating a sense of social solidarity. The goal of the *secundaria* was to balance the desire for a curriculum more specialized than the *primaria*—a curriculum that would offer students the chance to explore their vocational options—with the themes of integration and national unity.

The presidency of Lázaro Cárdenas (1934–1940), the great populist reformer, oversaw significant growth in secondary enrollments. By 1937, the course in civic culture had been changed to "socialist information and practice," and students increasingly learned about class conflict and imperialism as a way of understanding Mexican history. They participated in student government and mutual aid societies to practice cooperative social work and made frequent trips to shops and factories in order to gain a fuller appreciation of working-class life (Meneses Morales, 1988). The short-lived socialist experiment ended abruptly in 1940, when presidential power changed to the more conservative Ávila Camacho. As the *secundaria* continued to expand, official educational discourse reinstated the signal importance of "national unity" and reconciliation above class struggle. This formula provided the basic continuity in policy and practice around the *secundaria* more or less until 1992. Indeed, in the period from 1950 to 1970, there was a 1,000% increase in *secundaria* enrollments, mainly due to the growing participation of female students, who came to form half the student body in most *secundarias* by the late 1970s. Then, from 1992 to 1993, a series of educational "modernization" measures included an important amendment to the constitution's Article 3, which made *secundaria* attendance compulsory, thereby raising the stakes of civic education at that level. The new law also stipulated teaching the values of critical reflection, democratic participation, and human rights.

Before continuing with our analysis of citizenship education policy and practice, we now take a short detour into a discussion of the lesser known ethnic-racial diversity and forms of citizenship that have emerged in Mexico over the last 100 years or so. This exposition will allow us to illustrate the degree of disjuncture between such diversity and ongoing reforms of citizenship education.

Forms of Ethnocultural and Racial Diversity

The revolutionary nationalism of the early 20th century, which still drives much education policy today, tempered the liberal project of assimilation with a progressive rhetoric of social justice, but the *indigenismo* that arose in the 1920s and persisted at least into the 1980s, while pretending to "empower" the indigenous population of Mexico, was still strongly assimilationist in orientation. After all, it was the first national minister of education, José Vasconcelos, who articulated the concept of the Spanish/Indian blended mestizo as the superior "cosmic race" that Mexico offered to the world. There remained a good deal of ambivalence about the value of indigenous custom and belief. In the dominant imaginary, a "good Indian" was one who shed the presumed defects of custom and superstition to join the national family and enjoy the benefits of Enlightenment modernity. One could remain an Indian in name but still needed to adopt most elements of the national mestizo culture.

Still, historians have documented the many ways that the indigenous peoples of Mexico, even going back to the 19th century, have tried to assert their full citizenship rights. While nominally citizens of a liberal democratic regime, they have always struggled socially and culturally to obtain their full "right to have rights," as Hannah Arendt (1994, p. 296) put it. Among the voluminous scholarship on the state and the education of indigenous peoples in Mexico, two recent volumes stand out for their poignant illustrations of such struggles. Tellingly, Acevedo Rodrigo and López Caballero's book is titled *Unexpected Citizens* (2012), and they have shown, for instance, how various marginalized groups, especially the indigenous, constructed and exercised a sense of social citizenship through diverse means, not least of which was the claim on the state for quality educational facilities. This theme is echoed in another recent volume (Calderón Mólgora & Buenabad, 2012), where contrary to the notion that schools are a privileged site for constructing citizenship competencies and a "civic culture," the authors have shown that throughout the early 20th-century indigenous communities were ingeniously constructing and exercising their own modalities of citizenship.

To be sure, the status of today's indigenous peoples remains relatively high on Mexico's policy agenda, and the visibility of their cause has been aided by various global human rights conventions and discourses. Estimates of Mexico's indigenous population range from 12 to 16 million (or 10% to 15% of the national population), composed of at least 62 distinct cultural-linguistic groups. Such groups range in size from Nahuatl and Yucatec Maya speakers, in the range of one to two million each, down to groups with only a handful of speakers left. In 2001, a hugely significant change was made to the country's constitutional Article 2, announcing that

> the nation has a pluricultural makeup, based originally on those indigenous peoples who descended from groups that inhabited the country's current territory at the start of colonization, and who conserve their own social, economic, cultural, and political institutions, or any part thereof.

Soon thereafter, the 2003 Law of Linguistic Rights of the Indigenous Languages recognized 62 indigenous languages as "national languages"; it presumably gives them the same validity as Spanish in the full national territory.

In this way, state-sanctioned assimilation has been effectively abolished. Yet, as Charles Hale (2006) has noted for the case of Guatemala, as well as Guillermo de la Peña (2006) and others for Mexico, these recent legal changes, while strong on recognition of indigenous rights to govern their own affairs, comport perfectly with neoliberal governments' desires to limit land claims and other material forms of redistribution, as well as more robust claims for social services as citizens of the nation and state. For this reason, Hale (2002) has called this new wave of Latin American legal reform a "multiculturalism that menaces." It is a recognition-based multiculturalism that grants limited forms of autonomy and educational-linguistic provision while still preserving indigenous peoples' subordinate status as national political subjects. The structural inequalities rooted in colonialism persist to the present day, and very few indigenous groups have achieved meaningful land reform or sustained economic development. Moreover, even societal recognition has become shallow and legally circumscribed, and as we shall see, it has a weak presence in the context of contemporary civic education programs and practices.

Beyond the fact of indigenous diversity in Mexico, we would also like to note those who constitute much smaller demographic minorities but still contribute significantly to the broader cultural fabric of the country. Many have highlighted the long-standing presence of African-origin communities in Mexico, especially along the Gulf Coast of the eastern state of Veracruz and along the Pacific coast of the state of Guerrero. While independent Mexico was never a major slaveholding economy, during the colonial period African slaves were indeed brought to Mexico; more importantly, freed or escaped African populations made their way by boat from the Caribbean region or from the United States to establish residence in Mexico.[6] While mixing with mestizo and indigenous people and contributing culturally to their practices, Afro-Mexicans have retained relatively few of their customs and have rarely sought to establish a distinct public identity. Part of this is because the dichotomous framework of Spanish/indigenous identities and the Vasconcelian notion of the "mestizo" have left little room for recognition of what some consider the "third root" of Mexican ancestry, currently estimated to be around half a million in number. Only recently have their distinctive cultural and political rights been asserted. Local and international nongovernmental organizations have taken up the cause of recognizing Afro-Mexicans' contributions to national culture and addressing the forms of discrimination to which they are often subjected. The national Council for the Prevention of Discrimination, a government-funded organization, has also taken up the Afro-Mexican cause.

While not an official "settler state" along the lines of the United States, Canada, and Australia, Mexico has nevertheless received numerous immigration flows at least since the 19th century. Small numbers of East Asian (mainly Chinese) and Eastern European (especially Polish and Jewish) immigrants arrived in Mexico during the late 1800s, mainly to work on the railroads or establish small businesses. Particularly after the revolution of the early 20th century, the progressive discourse of the Mexican state translated into a willingness to accept immigrants and refugees from many parts of the world, although an earlier logic of "racial improvement" still gave preference to Europeans (Yankelevich, 2012). In the 1920s, for instance, a group of conservative Mennonites from Canada relocated to the northern state of Chihuahua on a tract of land negotiated by President Álvaro Obregón himself. The postrevolutionary state thereby provided conditions for freedom of religious education and worship that the Mennonites could no longer obtain in Canada. Today the Mennonite community numbers around 100,000. Similarly, the Mexican government welcomed successive waves of Jewish immigration. Combining with the existing "crypto-Jews" or conversos (forced converts to Catholicism who arrived in Mexico during the earliest years of colonization), small numbers of Central European and Syrian Jews arrived between 1860 and 1910. Larger numbers were accepted during the 1920–1935 period and then again during the flight from the Holocaust during World War II (although the latter were mainly limited to relatives of those who had already immigrated to Mexico). Although their total numbers remain around 50,000, and they are mostly concentrated in Mexico City, Mexican Jews have built a strong network of religious and community organizations even as they have also actively integrated into Mexican society.

The case of Lebanese immigration to Mexico also merits discussion in this context. Most Lebanese who immigrated around the start of the 20th century were Arabic speakers displaced by the dissolution of the Ottoman Empire. Others arrived more recently as a result of conflicts around Israel in 1948 and 1967, boosting the estimated number of Lebanese Mexicans to 400,000. In contrast to Jewish immigrants, the Lebanese have assimilated much more quickly and thoroughly, with Arabic still spoken only by a small number of second-generation offspring and beyond.

Finally, Mexico has maintained a tradition of accepting political exiles and refugees, especially from other Spanish-speaking countries. This began with the welcoming of significant numbers of Spanish republicans fleeing the Franco regime in the 1930s and continued with the arrival of significant numbers of (mainly European-origin) Chilean and Argentine professionals fleeing potential persecution under military dictatorship. However, in a move that some have interpreted as classist and racist, Mexico was less welcoming of poorer Central Americans attempting to flee their militarily and economically ravaged homelands in the 1970s and 1980s. Many who tried to cross Mexico's southern border were at best placed into semipermanent refugee camps and not allowed to integrate permanently into Mexican society.

In their recent article, Acosta García and Martínez Ortíz (2015) refer to the indigenous, Afro-Mexican, and earlier immigrant populations in Mexico as constituting its "already-existing diversity,"[7] to be contrasted with more recent forms of immigrant and return-migrant diversity. They focus attention on three broad groups that merit attention: Central and South Americans, many of whom may have intended to seek refuge in the United States but eventually settled in Mexico; Asian (mostly Korean and Japanese) and European professionals eager to take advantage of opportunities in the growing tech and entertainment industries; and perhaps most interesting for our discussion of citizenship here, Mexican migrants returning from the United States after years, sometimes decades, of out-migration. Together, these groups account for a twofold increase in the number of foreign-born residents of Mexico between 2000 and 2010 (although at a million people it still represents less than 1% of the total population). Perhaps the most interesting and challenging trend from the point of view of global migration and inclusive citizenship is the rise of a generation of dual citizens made possible by the passage of new Mexican legislation in 1998. At the time motivated mainly by the political calculus of the ruling party to capture more votes from those Mexicans who had since gained U.S. citizenship (and thus had had to renounce their Mexican citizenship), the law would eventually increase different possibilities for transnational political and cultural organizing. This development combined with the 2008 economic downturn and stricter enforcement of immigration law in the United States to produce a new generation of youth born in the United States but returning to Mexico to continue their schooling and passage to adulthood. Since 2005, more than 350,000 children are thought to have returned from the United States to Mexico with their Mexican parents (Cave, 2013). In a binational collaboration, Victor Zúñiga, E. Ted Hamann, and Juan Sanchez García (Hamann, Zúñiga, & Sanchez García, 2006; Sanchez García, Hamann, & Zúñiga, 2012; Zúñiga & Hamann, 2008, 2009; Zúñiga, Hamann, & Sanchez García, 2008) have documented the presence of these transnational students and their struggles in Mexican schools. The authors collected abundant evidence about not only the academic challenges faced by returning students, some of whom had never even set foot in Mexico, but also the challenges of culture, identity, and citizenship. Although such students typically have been raised in the cultural matrix of a Mexican family, and may have mestizo racial and cultural characteristics, they have often adopted U.S. values and customs, thus creating the conditions for judgment and discrimination by their teachers and peers alike. Not only do the students occasionally require support for Spanish language study, but given some of the subtle forms of discrimination to which they may be subject (some are taunted as *gabachos*, i.e., White foreigners), the situation is ripe for reciprocal forms of citizenship education for U.S.- and Mexican-born youth alike. A 2008 publication commissioned by the SEP (Zúñiga et al., 2008) provides an accounting of how teachers and schools can and should prepare to meet these students' unique educational circumstances.

Formal Citizenship Education Since 1999

Now that we have reviewed contemporary forms of racial-ethnic diversity in Mexico, it behooves us to restate our primary question: To what extent, and in what manner, have new and shifting forms of racial-ethnic diversity been incorporated into Mexican school-based citizenship education? It is with this question in mind that we briefly resume our account of policy and curricular reform for civic education. Of course, we will also address the more general question that any analysis of contemporary civic education begs: What kind of citizen for what kind of democracy are schools enjoined to create?

After the constitutional changes and modernization accords of 1992–1993, the next serious reform of Mexican civic education began in the mid-1990s. During the previous PRI presidential administration (1994–2000), the secretary of education initiated an ambitious new civic education program for all three years of *secundaria*. The program eventually came to be known as "civic and ethical education" (*formación cívica y ética*, or FCE). An analysis of two key SEP documents—the *Annotated Program of Study* (SEP, 2000; official curriculum document) and the *Teachers' Guide* (SEP, 2001)—provides the major organizing themes and principles of the course in FCE and gives us a glimpse of the kind of democratic citizen the SEP proposes. Throughout the texts, the authors emphasized a communicative pedagogical stance and a new role for the teacher as facilitator of knowledge construction rather than provider of information. Such a new role is intimately linked to the urgent need for students to take control of their learning and to begin practicing democratic virtues:

[The program] seeks to strengthen the student's capacity for critical analysis, for group work and participation in both individual and collective decision-making processes based on the values of a democratic life.... The students will learn equally from their classmates and their teachers, manifesting in this way the importance of a dialogical and horizontal educational process. (SEP, 2000, pp. 14, 21–22)

Correspondingly, the new plan established a number of "pedagogical and didactic guidelines" for teachers. Such guidelines include clear directions to "relate themes to students' lives" and to "foment . . . attitudes of respect and acceptance that encourage freedom of expression for all, taking special care to promote gender equity" (SEP, 2001, p. 3).

Not surprisingly given Mexico's history, the values and dispositions for "democratic life" include a strong emphasis on group work, solidarity, and the collective good. This is arguably one of the key aspects of Mexican education for democratic citizenship that would seem to distinguish it from those strictly liberal models sponsored by the countries of the north, which tend to place higher emphasis on deliberation, autonomy, and the rights of possessive individualism. Mexico's strong history of collective traditions and identities may have served authoritarianism well, but a democratic education had to now balance the forces of collectivism with a focus on individual rights and conscience. Yet, in the articulation of this balance, the FCE still seems to highlight the importance of collective life and responsibilities. Individual conscience is no longer prescribed but nonetheless must be developed intersubjectively and through an "ethical" process of values clarification. The student-citizen is the subject of a political imaginary in which personal reflexivity, respectful dialogue, and collective responsibility are paramount. Nonetheless, despite the mention of "cultural pluralism" in Mexican society, there is very little attention paid to the forms of Mexican ethnocultural diversity outlined earlier.

Recent field studies in Mexico have revealed the challenges and contradictions of implementation (Araújo-Olivera, Yurén Camarena, Estrada Ruíz, & de la Cruz Reyes, 2005; Elizondo Huerta, Christiansen, & Ruíz Avila, 2009; Juárez Hernández, 2006; Landeros Aguirre, 2006; Levinson, 2004; Lozano Andrade, 2013). Most of these studies were conducted in the early 2000s, after the 1999 FCE was implemented. The single most common finding is that teachers have largely failed to adopt new pedagogical styles and methods. They may be discussing democracy, but they are not modeling it. Teachers themselves, when discussing their experiences with FCE, often call for more training and better in-service courses, which currently are only sporadically offered and of poor quality (Levinson, 2004). Later in this chapter we introduce teachers who illustrate this.

Beginning in the late 1990s, there also emerged in Mexico a strong discourse on intercultural education, which borrowed and adapted discourses circulating more broadly in Europe and South America. Laura Selene Mateos and Gunther Dietz have written most trenchantly about the ways that interculturalism has been taken up in Mexico (Dietz & Mateos Cortés, 2011). *Interculturalism* is often now used simply as a more "politically correct" term for indigenous education, but many seek to infuse it with the goal of cross-cultural communicative competencies and respect not only between the indigenous and nonindigenous but also between and among a greater number of racial-ethnic groups. In

2001, in the wake of the PRI's defeat and the first opposition government in more than 70 years, the administration of the right-wing Partido de Acción Nacional, under President Vicente Fox, helped create the first ever General Coordinating Office of Bilingual and Intercultural Education (CGEIB), headed by the revered Mexican scholar and educator Sylvia Schmelkes. With the broad intention of fostering intercultural competencies across the full educational spectrum, the CGEIB eventually focused its efforts on the creation of regional intercultural universities, designed to build on indigenous knowledge to generate new economic opportunities and create a new generation of indigenous professionals committed to empowering their communities (Gibson, 2016; Ramos, 2014). As Schmelkes has since related in her writings and interviews (Levinson, 2008), although she wished to bring intercultural competencies to the national K–12 school system, she soon learned that the bureaucratic obstacles to achieving such meaningful reform were formidable, so she focused her energies on the university initiative. Such an experience is quite telling about the inertia and resistance that characterize many efforts at meaningful education reform in Mexico, including in the area of diversity and intercultural relations.

The 2006 and 2011 Reforms and Beyond

The 1999 launching of the new civic education program in the *secundaria* was soon superseded by the 2006 reform of the *secundaria* system more generally, followed by the 2011 "Integral Reform of Basic Education," which attempted to "articulate" subject matter and pedagogical guidelines across all levels of the K–12 system (2011 was the same year that the upper secondary level was also declared compulsory in Mexico). Here we will briefly analyze some of the documents of the 2006 and 2011 reforms in order to assess their conceptions of citizenship education and the place of recognizing diversity.

In many ways, the student-centered, constructivist orientation and democratic ethos of the 1999 FCE was a precursor of the broader 2006 reform altogether. After 2006, all teachers were increasingly exhorted (and occasionally trained!) to use more dialogical, participatory, engaged methods in the classroom. In its thematic content and pedagogical orientation, the new 2006 version of FCE itself did not differ all that substantially from that of 1999. The same eight weekly hours were now distributed differently (four hours a week in each of the last two years of *secundaria*, rather than 3/2/3 across all three years of *secundaria* study, as in 1999), and changes were made mainly in thematic sequencing and pedagogical guidelines. Like the rest of the new curriculum, learning outcomes were now phrased in terms of desirable "competencies," conceived as "knowing *how to do*" rather than just knowing. One sign of the centrality of the FCE program to broader school reform was the prominence of so-called transversal themes, which had previously been "located" exclusively within FCE but which now were supposed to cut across virtually all school subjects and activities. Specifically, these transversal themes included environmental education, values education, and education about sex and gender equity.

It is quite telling that these areas of concern were identified as so-called transversal themes in the 2006 reform. The articulation of transversal themes was meant by policy makers to signal their importance across all areas of the school curriculum, indeed across school life itself (Levinson, 2008). With its new emphasis on "collegial work" (*trabajo colegiado*) and joint planning across subject areas, the 2006 reform intended for these themes to be introduced through concrete inquiry projects and school-wide activities. However, as Levinson's 2007–2008 fieldwork revealed, the growing importance of standardized subject testing at the same time, together with the fragmentation of teachers' contracts and schedules (Levinson, Blackwood, & Cross, 2013; Levinson & Casas, 2009), ensured that few schools were attending to such themes in practice.

Diversity and interculturality are referenced as one of 10 major "characteristics" of the 2006 reform, with the exhortation that "each school subject . . . incorporate themes, contents, or particular aspects related to the cultural and linguistic diversity" of Mexico (SEP, 2006, p. 30). Teachers of different subjects are told to encourage their students to "understand that human groups form parts of different cultures, with their own languages, customs, beliefs, and traditions" and to

> recognize plurality as a characteristic of their country and of the world, and that the school becomes a space where such diversity can be valued and appreciated as an aspect of everyday life. Interculturality is a proposal to improve communication and sociality between communities with different cultures, always beginning with mutual respect. (p. 30)

In addition to this mention of diversity, in the 2006 version of FCE, one of the eight key "competencies" spelled out for the *secundaria* is that of "respecting and valuing diversity." Yet, as we shall see, because they are not strongly emphasized in the curricular units themselves, and because teachers have so little experience personally and sensitively navigating Mexico's diversity (especially what we call here its "stealth diversity"), such high-minded principles are rarely translated into practice.

Likewise, one of the eight key competencies articulated as desirable outcomes for the 2006 FCE subject is "respect and appreciation for diversity" (*respeto y valoración de la diversidad*). Such a competency refers essentially to having the ability "to recognize the equality of other persons in dignity and rights, as well as to respect and appreciate differences in their way of being, acting, thinking, feeling, believing, living, and relating" (SEP, 2006, p. 195). We see, then, a progressive and inclusive statement about diversity, but again, in the specific thematic units and textbooks, one sees far fewer activities directed to developing this competency than to others. Certainly one sees virtually no mention of specific forms of ethnocultural diversity and the fraught histories of different groups' incorporation into Mexican society.

Although there appear to be very few substantive changes in content, in the 2011 version of the teachers' guidelines for FCE, we see an even more pronounced emphasis on the development of personal liberty and autonomous thinking. The first and most prominent goals of the subject mentioned are those that enjoin teachers to guide students to "make responsible and autonomous decisions in orienting the full realization of their life projects" and to "recognize the importance of exercising their liberty in making decisions responsibly and regulating their own conduct autonomously" (p. 13). In subsequent paragraphs, to be sure, there is still ample reference to the need to leaven such personal liberty with the values of solidarity and compassion, yet the overall impression is a shift away from the collective (and assimilationist?) emphasis on unity toward a rather more utilitarian expression of positive freedom. There is also seemingly no recognition of the possible contradiction between the liberal emphasis on individual autonomy and the imperative to "respect and appreciate" those cultural groups that may subordinate the value of individual autonomy to collective well-being.

With the arrival to power of a new PRI government in 2012 there was a fresh round of questioning of the Partido de Acción Nacional government's policies from 2000 forward. In particular, both in and out of the SEP, there emerged strong critiques about how complex the structure and organization of the new curricular plan would be for teachers to adapt into their practice. By 2014 the SEP was leading a National and Regional Forum (Consulta) for the Revision of the Educational Model. The forum consisted of six different regional consultations in which the opinions of teachers, researchers, experts, and parents about the need for transforming basic education were documented. Participation in each region was focused around five themes, with particular attention to the question "What basic knowledge is indispensable today?" to gather opinions and ideas about curricular content. Based on such input, the SEP undertook a revision of curriculum throughout basic education (Grades 1–9) and announced that the new curriculum would be made public in June 2014. Postponing the new curriculum various times—October 2014, August 2015—the SEP announced at the end of 2015 that it would be delayed until 2018 in order to more fully vet the proposed changes with teachers and education specialists.

Addressing Ethnocultural Diversity in Education: Current Studies and Debates

Pedagogical and political discourse and debate around ethnocultural diversity in Mexico is relatively recent. It was not really until the early 1990s and the aforementioned recognition of Mexico as a pluricultural nation in Article 2 of the Mexican Constitution that content regarding cultural diversity came to have a growing presence in primary and secondary school curricula. Yet this inclusion of themes around cultural diversity was tied to a discourse of equal rights and the struggle against discrimination, which demanded consideration of the right to cultural diversity. It was not linked to curricular content that addressed how Mexico was constituted as a nation. Such a thematic split is in concert with the long-standing tendency to exalt the folkloric contributions of indigenous peoples to Mexico's past while leaving aside any consideration of their current socioeconomic conditions or cultural beliefs (Maldonado, 2010). As Levinson has described in his study of a regional *secundaria*, indigenous students could claim substantive "equality" with mestizo students from the city, as long as they were willing to downplay their adherence to indigenous lifeways.[8] Meanwhile, a Jewish boy from Argentina and a teenager who had done much of his early schooling in California were among those students whose particular identities and experiences were never acknowledged or addressed in school (Levinson, 2001).

With the Zapatista uprising of January 1994 and later negotiations that emerged in response to the social and economic demands of southern Mexico's indigenous peoples, other needs beyond being considered part of the nation became more visible. After numerous disagreements between indigenous communities and the executive branch of the federal government, in 2001 another constitutional reform to Article 2 established indigenous rights to autonomy and self-determination. Yet such rights became further hedged in by a whole set of legal procedures that ended up limiting indigenous people's place as political subjects—as citizens—of the nation. Accordingly, scholars such as the anthropologist Guillermo de la Peña (1999) have postulated the need for a specific notion of ethnic citizenship, that is, "a cultural identity and a differentiated social organization within a state that should at one and the same time not only recognize but also protect and juridically sanction such differences" (p. 23).

In the education policies that emerged from such debates, we can see the transition from biculturalism to interculturalism.[9] This change implied a broader consideration of cultural diversity as a matter related not only to indigenous groups but to the entire country's population (Schmelkes, 2004). Likewise, interculturalism suggested "a new ethic based on respect for difference and a conviction that growth and development ought to be based in such difference" (p. 186).[10] Yet by far the majority of recent studies about sociocultural diversity in education inspired by the intercultural turn still make reference to indigenous contexts, such that interculturalism is still rarely conceived as a perspective that should be developed throughout the entire country.

Research on teachers' approaches to sociocultural diversity emerged with the founding of institutions such as the Center for Research and Higher Studies in Social Anthropology (Centro de Investigaciones y Estudios Superiores en Antropología Social)[11] and the Department of Educational Research (Departamento de Investigaciones Educativas), which in 1975 opened a program of research into school-based socialization processes among indigenous students. By the mid-1990s a group of Departamento de Investigaciones Educativas researchers had broadened this focus to include sociocultural studies of schooling.[12] As Bertely Busquets and González have reported (2004), studies about interculturalism in educational processes increased notably throughout the 1990s in comparison with the 1980s. Such studies have examined the implementation of intercultural policies from diverse angles, but the majority of them still focus on indigenous schools.[13] The fact that sociocultural diversity tends to be a matter that is studied, or for which policies and programs are created, with a focus on schools where indigenous students congregate, shows us that sociocultural dynamics are still always associated with ethnic differences and that, moreover, the idea that interculturalism is a matter that pertains to the entire population has still not come to fruition. The paucity of studies about ethnocultural diversity in urban contexts, in typical public schools, and across diverse subjects, such as civic education (FCE), history, and geography, reveals the historic weight of many years of 20th-century indigenist policy in Mexico, which is tied to an unmarked notion of *mestizaje*. The emphasis on assimilation of the indigenous to a national culture was always most evident in the fact that "indigenous education" itself was typically oriented to the eventual mastery of Spanish and mainstream knowledge (Bertely Busquets, 2009).

In recent years, according to some authors (Martínez Buenabad, 2015; Podestá Siri & Martínez Buenabad, 2003), educational discourse in Mexico has shifted from conceiving of belonging to an indigenous group as a problem, or even as a "resource," to being a right. This perspective has inspired the development of new alternative curricula. Yet one author, who occupied a key position in the CGEIB (Gallardo, 2014), has strongly criticized the way that new discourses of interculturality have been incorporated into school programs and curricula. In her analysis of the 2011 creation of a new state-level elective called "Indigenous Language and Culture," Gallardo emphasized how this ironically reinforces the superiority of the mestizo and thereby imposes a double discrimination on the indigenous world. In effect, the new subject becomes a way of locating indigenous culture in the *secundaria* as a type of diversity comparable to disability; the implicit discourse of inclusion masks the reality of inequality and submission lived by those who belong to an indigenous group. Martínez Buenabad (2015) agreed with this assessment when she claimed that "we cannot imagine an equal or equitable model of education without addressing relations of domination/submission. . . . To speak of intercultural education as a horizontal relationship is nothing more than a euphemism for masking vertical relationships" (p. 112). Likewise, the course Indigenous Language and Culture has been constructed as a marginal curricular space with few real possibilities of use, since the decision to adopt the subject is in the hands of educational authorities in each of the country's 31 states.

Gallardo (2014) continued her analysis by arguing that *mestizaje* has served as a cover for racism in Mexican education; historically, *mestizaje* was held up as a key goal of the education system as part of its glorification of national unity, and subjects such as history, geography, and civics have always contributed to this. In her assessment of the current curricula of subjects such as Spanish, natural sciences, history, and FCE, Gallardo noted that *mestizaje* is presented as a kind of static harmony in interethnic relations; it serves to hide actual power relations and therefore represents a new form of racism and discrimination toward indigenous peoples. The same author extended her critical analysis to the textbooks that the SEP produces and authorizes.

Yet, without denying that the SEP's actions instantiate a hegemonic discourse of *mestizaje*, we must also keep in mind that schools and teachers represent a social force that actively appropriates official policy and curriculum, making adjustments and even transformations not foreseen by the authorities' proposals (Rockwell, 1995), such as the case of intercultural education. As many studies in Mexico have shown (Robles & Czarny, 2003), students and teachers are co-participants in generating relationships in the classroom, and their respective sociocultural conditioning orients their manner of learning and relating to others in the school. Such studies—as well as the teaching cases we present below—reveal how it is possible to strengthen relationships between a school and its community when the community's cultural facets are integrated meaningfully into school life.

A Brief Analysis of Educational Materials

Educational materials—officially authorized textbooks, primarily, but also teachers' guides—are one of the main ways that the mandated curriculum is given concrete expression in school life, since they represent the authors' interpretations of such curriculum. Thus, we shall look briefly at some of the contents of these materials for the *secundaria*. In the three subjects of geography, history, and FCE shown in Table 1, we can see the way that themes whose contents are explicitly about, or closely related to, sociocultural diversity are articulated: As we can see, at a very general level these curricular contents do include concepts related to cultural diversity. In the case of geography, the contents highlight positive aspects of cultural diversity, while in history and civic education the conflictual aspects of such diversity are also addressed.

Table 1. Contents of Sociocultural Diversity in the *Secundaria*

Grade	Mexican and World Geography	History	Civic and Ethical Education (*Formación Cívica y Etica*)
First	Thematic Block III. —Cultural diversity of the world population: traditional, contemporary, and emergent cultures. —Multiculturalism as a current aspect of the world and of Mexico. —The importance of intercultural exchange.		
Second		Thematic Block V. —Current conflicts: ethnic and religious wars in the Middle East, India, Africa, and the Balkans. South Africa and the end of apartheid. Refugees and displaced peoples. Drug and arms trafficking. Terrorism. AIDS. Global warming and environmental movements.	Thematic Block III. —Attitudes that inhibit or worsen coexistence: ethnocentrism and discrimination based on national or ethnic origin; gender, age, or disability; socioeconomic status; health conditions or pregnancy; language, religion, or opinions; or sexual preference, marriage status, or anything else.
Third		Thematic Block V. —Culture, national identity, and globalization: cultural homogenization. Globalization and the defense of pluricultural identity. Mexican culture in the United States.	Thematic Block II. —Plurality as the peaceful coexistence of ideas. Cooperation, solidarity, and co-responsibility as part of our social and political commitment to address situations that affect communities, nations, and all of humanity. Thematic Block III. —Cultural differences that enrich the nation: plurality and diversity. Recognition and valuing of the pluricultural nature of the country. Empathy, dialogue, and negotiation, in the search for intercultural relationships.

With regard to educational materials for the *secundaria*, we find quite a bit of variation for each subject in regards to how the thematic blocks of the curriculum are actually expressed and treated. In what follows we present a few randomly chosen excerpts to give a brief overview of the treatment given by such texts to cultural diversity.

- *The Importance of Intercultural Exchange*

The term *cultural exchange* [*convivencia*] is used to refer to acts of communicating, dialoguing, and exchanging knowledge, beliefs values, customs, opinions, and points of view between people from distinct cultures.

In a condition of cultural exchange, nobody loses their identity; rather, it's a matter of establishing frank and open communication between individuals of different ethnic, social, and professional groups, and of distinct genders.

In order to achieve intercultural exchange, it is important to participate actively in the social development of our places of residence and surroundings, respecting both our own culture and that of others. (Heras & Heras, 2013, p. 140)[14]

Just as occurs in the official curriculum itself, here the advantages of cultural diversity are highlighted without being problematized and without referring to specific situations affecting different populations.

- *Indigenism*

Discrimination against indigenous peoples originated in the Spanish conquest of America and was reinforced during the colonial period. In Mexico, as in other countries, it was not until the early part of the 20th century that a concern for improving the living conditions and protecting the cultural values of indigenous peoples became state policy.

Indigenism was such a policy that aimed to conserve customs and beliefs [*usos y costumbres*]; in addition, the policy aimed to integrate indigenous people into modern life. A lot of people criticized this policy, arguing that such aims were contradictory when the very same customs and beliefs were seen by authorities as the reason for such peoples' backwardness [*atraso*].

Today, in Mexico as in almost all Latin American countries, the richness of cultural diversity is recognized and constitutional amendments have been made to include such diversity as a fundamental right. Nevertheless, in reality indigenous peoples continue to be subject to all kinds of discrimination, ranging from [policies that produce] abject poverty to lack of respect for their rights, which makes difficult their inclusion in the development of each country. (García, Portillo, & Pérez, 2013, p. 242)

In this history textbook, the more critical aspects of cultural diversity in Mexico are addressed, with emphasis placed on the discrimination and economic inequality that have prevailed among the indigenous up to the present moment. In this case, the text updates the importance of cultural diversity and eclipses the perspective that for so long held sway: that the culture of indigenous peoples was only valuable as part of the past. Yet we must note, as well, that the "richness of cultural diversity" here is used only in reference to the indigenous and not the fuller range of groups making up Mexico's true ethnocultural diversity.

- *Cultural Differences That Enrich the Nation: Plurality and Diversity*

Thanks to intercultural exchange, diversity is possible, since exchange favors all cultures; in Mexico, both indigenous peoples and those people who've arrived from other countries have made significant contributions to our culture. *Cultural diversity* refers to the great variety of forms through which the cultures of different groups and societies are expressed, exchanged, and shared.

. . . Over time the indigenous groups in our country have re-created their way of viewing life with Christian ideas and traditions; for example, the Mayos, whose name means "people of the riverbank," and who live on the border of the states of Sonora and Sinaloa, celebrate Easter with a festival that lasts 40 days. In the festival they use goatskin and pigskin masks that enable them to dance; and all members of the community participate and have a role to play.

One thing that's made life difficult for Mexico's indigenous cultures is that a large portion of their population has had to migrate to the cities, or to the United States. In the process the visible symbols of their identity, such as traditional garments or the everyday use of their mother tongue, have vanished or been hidden. In general, this is a result of the discrimination to which they have been subject throughout history. To learn about, recognize, and value these cultures is a task incumbent upon all of us, insofar as we are a diverse country that must construct conditions for dialogue and for integrating harmoniously and respectfully the diversity that characterizes it. (Latapí, 2014, pp. 136–137)

In this example from an FCE textbook, we can see mixed together an abstract discussion of the advantages of cultural diversity with some attention to its folkloric manifestations. It also seems a bit paradoxical that the description of the current situation of the country's original peoples, called here "indigenous cultures," emphasizes the discrimination that they appear to suffer while migrating to the United States, thereby overlooking the discrimination exercised against them in Mexico.

Through this brief analysis, we can see that there still persists in both the curriculum and educational materials a hesitant, confused notion of cultural diversity. Clearly, such materials still have a long way to go for sociocultural diversity to become a theme that invites discussion about the local conditions that students are living and experiencing in each school context.

The Struggles of Teaching With/Through/About Diversity

As we have already noted, numerous empirical studies in Mexico have shown that *secundaria* teachers rarely have the training, support, or inclination to implement new intercultural topics and activities envisioned by the official curriculum. To further illustrate some of these challenges, we interviewed several *secundaria* teachers. Due to space considerations, we concentrate here on a teacher who works in a *telesecundaria* in a rural area of Mexico's northern region, within hours of the U.S. border.[15] This young teacher, whom we call Esteban, has been in the profession for three years and has expressed particular interest in exploring relationships between students of different ethnic origins. We supplement the case of Esteban with reflections and insights from two female and rather more experienced teachers of geography and civic education, Marta and Lupita, both of whom work in the west-central Mexican state of Michoacán.

Although he has already been working at the *telesecundaria* for three years now, it took a year for Esteban to realize that many of his students come from families that still speak an indigenous language (interview with author, September, 2015). He did not even learn of this situation when, upon arriving at the school, he conducted a survey in which it was necessary to document how many students spoke an indigenous language or belonged to an indigenous community. Indeed, it was only through invitations made to him and his fellow teachers to attend events in different communities that he realized how many of his students were indigenous. At these events, Esteban noted that most adults would speak an indigenous language among themselves in the household but still speak Spanish to children and youth. Accordingly, the children could understand the language but not speak it.

Despite his own urban mestizo background, Esteban set out to investigate the origins of the indigenous groups that reside in his state. In this way, he identified one group of Nahuatl speakers who are native to the region, along with another group that came from the northern part of the state based on a 1970s state migration policy that relocated some settlers to the catchment zone of the *telesecundaria*. Esteban admitted his own dismay about the alienation of the youth from their families' native languages, so he conducted a kind of census among them and thereby determined that in addition to Nahuatl and Totonac, and because of internal national migration, there are also families that speak languages from the south and central parts of Mexico, namely, Hñähñu and Zoque.

Nahuatl and Totonac parents informed Esteban that the mestizo teachers who staffed the first elementary schools in the region asked students not to speak their native languages, with the argument that it would delay their ability to read and write. Such teachers also urged students to change their traditional dress so that when they sought out work potential employers would take them seriously and not think less of them. Thus, discrimination comes largely from outside the community, though clearly many have adapted to it by encouraging their young people to follow these suggestions.

Esteban has recognized the need to adapt nationally standardized curricular contents to be in concert with his observations of cultural life in the community. His knowledge about his students' lives has come largely from these observations outside the school (though he has also obtained some from his everyday classroom interactions); since he resides permanently in the community in the "teachers' house," he has been able to gradually incorporate himself into everyday life. After three years, there appears to be a mutual acceptance, signified by the fact that community adults are not ashamed to speak their native language in his presence.

In terms of curriculum, Esteban uses subjects such as civic and ethical education, geography, and history to work on topics relating to cultural diversity and interculturality. As part of civic and ethical education, Esteban devised an activity in which the male students were encouraged to wear a turban during recess, in order to sensitize them to differences. Yet only two students dared to wear the turbans for fear of being made fun of by their peers. Esteban also inspired reflection about the veil that women wear throughout the Middle East and asked students whether they thought that being made to wear the veil violated the women's human rights. In another activity he invited representatives from different religious groups in the community (Catholic, Protestant/Pentecostal, Jehovah's Witness) to present to the students key characteristics of their religion. He then reflected with the students about the respect that varied religious beliefs deserve, especially in light of the fact that Pentecostal and Jehovah's Witness students abstained from participating in the community's Day of the Dead celebration.

Through the subjects of Spanish and geography, Esteban exhorts his students to take an interest in the indigenous languages spoken in the community. In Spanish, students tape interviews with community members about their origins. These interviews are then later used as resources to learn about types of phrases and conversations used in the community. In the subject of geography, Esteban reinforces the topic by teaching about the national distribution and number of speakers of different native languages.

In the current school year, Esteban has decided to teach the state elective course Indigenous Language and Culture as a means of promoting among his students an appreciation and awareness of the diverse languages spoken in the community. In this subject he utilizes the same interviews his students completed in previous years of their Spanish class, supplemented with materials developed by the National Commission for the Development of Indigenous Communities, which mainly consist of videos and electronic links through which students can locate the regions of the state where indigenous-speaking communities reside. As part of this class Esteban's students also invite various adults to narrate the founding of their community and to speak their indigenous language, so that students can have an opportunity to listen to key words and understand their significance. Given the multi-ethnic nature of the community, Esteban guides the students to appreciate the efforts of the community's founders, especially those that have permitted a fruitful coexistence between the two main original groups: Nahuatl and Totonac.

At a technical *secundaria* in the Mexican state of Michoacán, one of our other interviewees, Marta, has been teaching subjects such as geography and civic education for nearly 30 years (interview with author, December, 2015). About 25% of the students in most of her classes are from the local Purépecha indigenous group, and she often takes class time for these students to share aspects of their culture with other students. Since most of the Purépecha students no longer actively speak their language, their classroom contributions focus on themes such as traditional foods, dress, and music.

When asked whether he teaches about migrant or immigrant students, Esteban answered that he considers it important to raise the consciousness of his students about the situation faced by Central American migrants who have been passing through or near the community in an effort to evade primary migration checkpoints. He believes that the topic of interculturality can be a starting point for discussing why these migrants are seeking a better life. He noted that some of the migrants may take the same bus routes as the students and their families or stay in the community for short periods of time when heavy rains close the roads. Most community members are hospitable but confess that they do not really know how to treat these passing strangers.

One thing Esteban shares with our other interviewee, the geography teacher Lupita, also from Michoacán, is an attempt to generate discussion about Central American migrants by using a documentary film about "The Beast," the primary north-south freight train on which migrants often make the dangerous journey across Mexico toward the U.S. border (interview with author, December, 2015). Without invoking interculturality, Lupita discusses The Beast in her geography unit on globalization and borders, when her students also watch videos and discuss readings about migrants. The school where Lupita works also has many returning students from the United States. They are migrants of a different sort. In order to help these students integrate into the group and experience a kind of solidarity and compassion from the group, Lupita uses a narrative technique: She asks them to relate their "successes and failures," their most positive and negative experiences, while living in the United States. And lest these mere words fail, Lupita enjoins the former U.S. residents to share with the class something of their tastes and habits acquired in the United States: their style of dress, their musical tastes, their food. We should not fail to note the same strategy is used by Marta with her Purépecha students in the same region of Mexico.

Like many other teachers Levinson encountered in 2008, these three teachers mainly resort to their own devices in addressing issues of citizenship and interculturality in the classroom. Esteban echoed a common lament when he said that topics around diversity and interculturality remain prominent in the official curriculum—there are even standards developed to guide student evaluation—but that they tend to remain in the discursive realm. Teachers are given little training for *how* to creatively translate the topic of diversity into the classroom. Moreover, what few guidelines are given seem scripted by the dominant culture, said Esteban: "Those who make the curriculum and try to address interculturality don't know the field, or they only know a single reality, but there are many realities in this country." Teachers who work in contexts other than those imagined by the curriculum writers must make adjustments on their own. And Esteban feels that indigenous peoples and other ethnic minorities should be the authors of curriculum. At the very least, their opinions and experiences should be actively consulted and reflected.

Teachers do not need a recipe book for interculturality, Esteban made clear. They need support and guidance, training and camaraderie, and more coherence among local, state, and federal expectations. He is aware that, in some regional supervision districts, the authorities are asking for evidence of results or activities that differ substantially from those laid out in federal guidelines. And echoing another common teacher lament, Esteban recounted how his request for assistance from the district's "Technical Pedagogical" department to teach the Indigenous Language and Culture class met with complete silence. There is very little support or follow-up from authorities who might be in a position to supply resources or ideas.

Some Final Thoughts

As we have seen, Mexican teachers struggle to meaningfully incorporate exercises and activities that engage students with deep and relevant questions about Mexico's ethnocultural diversity. They may creatively embellish and modify textbooks that are inadequate and policies that are, at best, ambiguous and, at worst, still racist. Ever mindful of the need for more and better professional training, in the best of cases they may try to enact a kind of bottom-up, community-based citizenship education, drawing upon local publics to contest official discourses and foster alternative citizen identities (Levinson, 2011). Many others may simply glide over these topics altogether, effectively denying indigenous worldviews and maintaining a status quo of stealth diversity. As Martínez Buenabad has said, drawing on another author (Muñoz, 2009), "The transformation or appropriation of the intercultural approach in indigenous regions of Mexico principally will emerge from school realities and practices, to the degree that policy implementation is democratized through forms of community control" (Martínez Buenabad, 2015, p. 123). Accordingly, Martínez Buenabad (2015) has proposed a new paradigm of citizenship formation for bilingual intercultural education that goes well beyond the classroom and school to implicate the whole society in education for and about diversity.

As Walter Parker (2003) has compellingly argued and demonstrated, there can be no effective teaching for democracy without including the full diversity of perspectives and voices that presumably constitute a democratic society. Such inclusion in the official realm of a society's knowledge production and transmission must be accompanied by meaningful and enduring forms of structural inclusion, which includes full enfranchisement and legal rights, land reform, and economic development, along with equality of opportunity for socioeconomic mobility. We hope to have made one modest contribution toward Mexico's ongoing efforts to provide an education that truly honors its diversity.

Notes

1. We focus on ethnocultural diversity because of this book's focus on global migration, which most often occurs along ethnic lines. Spaniards were the original "immigrants" to the New World, where they quickly subdued the "original peoples" of the Americas, as the indigenous are often called in Mexico, and converted them to Christianity. More recent immigrants to Mexico also have had strong religious as well as ethnic identities (Bonfil Batalla, 1993), and like ethnicity and social class, religion is often made invisible in Mexican public discourse.

2. Among the key differences between the 1857 and 1917 constitutions are that (1) in the 1857 constitution rights inhere in man and the state recognizes such rights, while in 1917 the state becomes the granter of rights, and (2) the 1917 constitution includes important new articles on national and collective control of land (Art. 27), labor rights (Art. 123), and restrictions on the role of clerics in political participation (Art. 130), all of which represent important grievances inspiring the revolution (Arroyo, 2001).

3. The institutional antecedents to the SEP include the prerevolutionary Ministry of Justice and Public Instruction and the Secretariat of Public Instruction and Fine Arts.

4. But see Ornelas, 2008, for a demonstration of how so-called decentralization measures (called "federalization" in Mexico) have actually reconcentrated certain forms of power in the federal executive branch.

5. Regional cultural diversity is very important to address in the Mexican context. According to a noted historian (Florescano, 1996), Mesoamerican biodiversity led to a great deal of cultural and linguistic diversity among indigenous peoples before the time of the Spanish conquest. Mexican history is also characterized by strong regional loyalties and distinctive cultures of the north, center, and south (González y González, 1982; León-Portilla, 1976). Such regional and indigenous cultural diversity, however, is much

more adequately represented in Mexican textbooks and classrooms than the forms of ethnocultural "stealth diversity" we discuss in this chapter.

6. Others who may have adopted an Afro-Mexican identity include more recent immigrants from independent African countries or from Latin American countries such as Cuba, the Dominican Republic, and Colombia, which are known to have strong Afro-descendant populations.

7. Although space is limited here, one would also have to include a discussion of the presence of U.S. citizens migrating to Mexico as well. While there has been a significant number of expatriates (many of them retirees) living in Mexico for decades, and perhaps even more who study in Mexico for a summer or more, only recently has the number of non-Mexican U.S. citizens living and working legally long-term in Mexico seen a significant upward shift—to an estimated 70,000 in 2012 (Cave, 2013).

8. See other studies for similar accounts of dilemmas faced by indigenous students in the urban contexts of Guadalajara and Monterrey (Durin, 2007; Martínez Casas, 2000).

9. As Schmelkes (2004) has noted, "In 1997 elementary education offered to indigenous groups changed its name from 'bilingual bicultural education' to 'intercultural bilingual education.'"

10. As Schmelkes (2004) went on to note, though, it is necessary to recognize that most primary and secondary schools neither "attend to indigenous peoples as such, nor are they conscious of or sensitive to their cultural and linguistic diversity. Such schools are often sites for the reproduction of discriminatory and racist attitudes" (p. 187).

11. In 1973 the Center for Higher Research of the National Institute of Anthropology and History was founded, later to be restructured in 1980 as the Centro de Investigaciones y Estudios Superiores en Antropología Social.

12. Other institutions that have developed programs of research on diversity and intercultural education include the National Pedagogical University, the Graduate Division of Pedagogy of the National Autonomous University of Mexico, the Center for Adult Education in Latin America, the University of Guadalajara, and the Western Technological Institute of Advanced Research (Bertely Busquets & González, 2004).

13. For an important exception, see the work of Gabriela Czarny (1995), who studies interactions between teachers and students from varied ethnocultural backgrounds in an urban elementary school.

14. We have translated the Spanish term *convivencia* here into "exchange." This is a notoriously difficult term to translate. The term *conviviality* exists in English, but it is little known and used. In Spanish, *convivencia* refers to a kind of "living together," which goes beyond mere "coexistence" to active exchange and togetherness.

15. The *telesecundaria* in Mexico serves more than 15% of all *secundaria* students. It is a model developed in the 1970s that relies on distance technologies (originally satellite television, today the Internet) to impart the curriculum, thus obviating the need for larger school buildings and staff. In this way, fewer teachers with small buildings can still serve remote rural areas.

References

Acevedo Rodrigo, A., & López Caballero, P. (2012). *Ciudadanos inesperados: Espacios de formación de la ciudadanía ayer y hoy* [Unexpected citizens: Spaces of citizenship formation yesterday and today]. Mexico City, Mexico: Colegio de México/CINVESTAV.

Acosta García, R., & Martínez-Ortíz, E. (2015). Mexico through a superdiversity lens: Already-existing diversity meets new immigration. *Ethnic and Racial Studies, 38*(4), 636–649.

Araújo-Olivera, S. S., Yurén Camarena, M. T., Estrada Ruíz, M. J., & de la Cruz Reyes, M. (2005). Respeto, democracia y política, negociación del consenso: El caso de la formación cívica y ética en las escuelas de Morelos [Respect, politics and democracy, and the negotiation of consensus: The case of civic and ethical education in the schools of Morelos]. *Revista Mexicana de Investigación Educativa, 10*(24), 15–42.

Arendt, H. (1994). *The origins of totalitarianism*. New York: Harcourt.

Arroyo, J. A. (2001). La Constitución Mexicana: ¿Reforma o cambio? [The Mexican Constitution: Reform or change?]. In D. Valadés & R. Gutiérrez (Eds.), *Justicia: Memoria del IV Congreso Nacional de Derecho Constitucional* [Justice: Proceedings of the Fourth National Conference on Constitutional Law] (pp. 251–262). Mexico City, Mexico: Universidad Nacional Autónoma de México.

Bertely Busquets, M. (2009). Education for intercultural citizenship: The Maya teachers of Chiapas in the construction of alternative citizenships from below. *Inter-American Journal of Education for Democracy, 2*(2), 179–210.

Bertely Busquets, M., & González, E. (2004). Experiencias hacia la interculturalidad de los procesos educativos [Experiences toward the interculturality of educational processes]. In I. Hernaiz (Ed.), *Educación en la diversidad: Experiencias y desafíos en la educación intercultural* [Education about diversity: Experiences and challenges in intercultural education] (pp. 19–106). Buenos Aires, Argentina: IIPE-UNESCO.

Bonfil Batalla, G. (Ed.). (1993). *Simbiósis de culturas: Los inmigrantes y su cultura en México* [Symbiosis of cultures: Immigrants and their culture in Mexico]. Mexico City, Mexico: Fondo de Cultura Económica.

Calderón Mólgora, M. A., & Buenabad, E. (Eds.). (2012). *Educación indígena, ciudadanía y estado en México: Siglo XX* [Indigenous education, citizenship, and the state in Mexico: The 20th century]. Mexico City, Mexico: El Colegio de Michoacán and Benemérita Universidad Autónoma de Puebla.

Cave, D. (2013, September 21). For migrants, new land of opportunity is Mexico. *New York Times.* Retrieved from http://www.nytimes.com/2013/09/22/world/americas/for-migrants-new-land-of-opportunity-is-mexico.html?_r=0

Czarny, G. (1995). *Acerca de los procesos de interculturalidad: Niños de origen mazahua en una escuela pública en la Ciudad de México* [On processes of interculturality: Mazahua children in a Mexico City public school] (Unpublished master's thesis). Center for Research and Advanced Studies of the National Polytechnic Institute, Mexico City, Mexico.

de la Peña, G. (1999). Territorio y ciudadanía étnica en la nación globalizada [Territory and ethnic citizenship in the globalized nation]. *Desacatos: Revista de Antropología Social, 1*(1), 13–27.

de la Peña, G. (2006). A new Mexican nationalism? Indigenous rights, constitutional reform and the conflicting meanings of multiculturalism. *Nations and Nationalism, 12*(2), 279–302.

Dietz, G., & Mateos Cortés, L. S. (2011). *Interculturalidad y educación intercultural en México: Un análisis de los discursos nacionales e internacionales en su impacto en los modelos educativos mexicanos* [Interculturality and intercultural education in Mexico: An analysis of national and international discourses and their impact on Mexican educational models]. Mexico City, Mexico: Secretaría de Educación Pública.

Durin, S. (2007). Promotores interculturales y agentes étnicos: Las dos caras del maestro bilingüe en el medio urbano [Intercultural promoters and ethnic agents: The two faces of the bilingual teacher in an urban context]. In G. Dietz, R. G. Mendoza Zuany, & S. Téllez Galván (Eds.), *Multiculturalismo, educación intercultural, y derechos indígenas en las Américas* [Multiculturalism, intercultural education, and indigenous rights in the Americas] (pp. 151–173). Quito, Ecuador: Abya-Yala.

Elizondo Huerta, A., Christiansen, A. S., & Ruíz Avila, D. (2009). Democracia y ética en la escuela *secundaria*: Estudio de caso [Democracy and ethics in the *secundaria*: A case study]. *Revista Mexicana de Investigación Educativa, 14*(40), 243–260.

Escalante, F. (1995). *Ciudadanos imaginarios* [Imaginary citizens]. Mexico City, Mexico: El Colegio de México.

Florescano, E. (1996). *Etnia, estado y nación: Ensayo sobre las identidades colectivas en México* [Ethnic group, state, and nation: An essay on collective identities in Mexico]. Mexico City, Mexico: Aguilar.

Fraser, N. (1997). *Justice interruptus: Critial reflections on the "postsocialist" condition*. New York: Routledge.

Gallardo, A. L. (2014). *Racismo y discriminación en el sistema educativo mexicano: Claves desde las reformas a la educación básica nacional en el siglo XXI (2006 y 2011)* [Racism and discrimination in the Mexican educational system: Key clues in 21st century reforms of basic education] (Unpublished doctoral dissertation). National Autonomous University of Mexico, Mexico City, Mexico.

García, S., Portillo, A., & Pérez, O. (2013). *Historia universal. Segundo grado*. Mexico City, Mexico: Trillas.

Gibson, T. (2016). *Partial democracy and compromised multiculturalism: The fate of the intercultural universities in Mexico*. (Unpublished doctoral dissertation). Indiana University, Bloomington, IN.

González y González, L. (1982, November). El linaje de la cultura mexicana [The lineages of Mexican culture]. *Vuelta, 72*, 14–23.

Hale, C. R. (2002). Does multiculturalism menace? Governance, cultural rights and the politics of identity in Guatemala. *Journal of Latin American Studies, 34*(3), 485–524.

Hale, C. R. (2006). *Mas que un indio: Racial ambivalence and the paradox of neoliberal multiculturalism in Guatemala*. Santa Fe, NM: School of American Research Press.

Hamann, E. T., Zúñiga, V., & Sanchez García, J. (2006). *Pensando en Cynthia y su hermana*: Educational implications of United States–Mexico transnationalism for children. *Journal of Latinos and Education, 5*(4), 253–274.

Heras, Á., & Heras, J. G. (2013). *Geografía de México y del mundo. Tierra*. Mexico City, Mexico: Editorial SM.

Joseph, G. M., & Nugent, D. (Eds.). (1994). *Everyday forms of state formation: Revolution and the negotiation of rule in modern Mexico*. Durham, NC: Duke University Press.

Juárez Hernández, A. F. (2006). *Estrategias de enseñanza en formación cívica y ética en secundaria* [Teaching strategies for civic and ethical education in the *secundaria*] (Unpublished master's thesis). Center for Research and Advanced Studies of the National Polytechnic Institute, Mexico City, Mexico.

Landeros Aguirre, L. G. (2006). *Trayectorias y concepciones educativas en profesores de la asignatura formación cívica y ética para la educación secundaria* [Career trajectories and educational beliefs of teachers of the civic and ethical education subject in the *secundaria*] (Unpublished master's thesis). Center for Research and Advanced Studies of the National Polytechnic Institute, Mexico City, Mexico.

Latapí, P. (2014). *Comprometidos con la convivencia solidaria. Formación cívica y ética. Tercer grado*. Mexico City, Mexico: McGraw-Hill/Interamericana Editores.

León-Portilla, M. (1976). *Culturas en peligro* [Cultures in danger]. Mexico City, Mexico: Alianza Editorial Mexicana.

Levinson, B. A. (1999). "Una etapa siempre difícil": Concepts of adolescence and secondary education in Mexico. *Comparative Education Review, 43*(2), 129–161.

Levinson, B. A. (2001). *We are all equal: Student culture and identity at a Mexican secondary school, 1988–1998*. Durham, NC: Duke University Press.

Levinson, B. A. (2004). Hopes and challenges for the new civic education in Mexico: Toward a democratic citizen without adjectives. *International Journal of Educational Development, 24*(3), 269–282.

Levinson, B. A. (2008). Interculturality as a pivotal aspect of education for democracy: A dialogue with Sylvia Schmelkes. *Inter-American Journal of Education for Democracy, 1*(2), 205–218.

Levinson, B. A. (2011). Toward an anthropology of (democratic) citizenship education. In B. A. Levinson & M. Pollock (Eds.), *A companion to the anthropology of education* (pp. 279–298). Malden, MA: Wiley-Blackwell.

Levinson, B. A., Blackwood, J., & Cross, V. (2013). Recipients, agents, or partners? The contradictions of teacher participation in Mexican secondary education reform. *Journal of Educational Change, 14*(1), 1–27.

Levinson, B. A., & Casas, C. (2009, February). *From curriculum to practice: Removing structural and cultural obstacles to effective secondary education reform in the Americas.* Paper presented at the Organization of American States Working Papers for the Sixth Meeting of Ministers of Education, Guayaquil, Ecuador.

Lozano Andrade, I. (Ed.). (2013). *Currículum oculto y vida cotidiana en la escuela secundaria: Significados de los actores en el contexto de las reformas* [Hidden curriculum and everyday life in the *secundaria*: The meanings of actors in the context of reform]. Mexico City, Mexico: Díaz de Santos.

Maldonado, I. (2010). De la multiculturalidad a la interculturalidad: La reforma del estado y los pueblos indígenas en México [From multiculturalism to interculturality: The reform of the state and indigenous groups in Mexico]. *Andamios, 7*(14), 287–319.

Martínez Buenabad, E. (2015). La educación intercultural y bilingüe (EIB) en México: ¿El camino hacia la construcción de una ciudadanía democrática? [Intercultural and bilingual education in Mexico: The path toward the construction of a democratic citizenry?]. *Relaciones, 36*(141), 103–131.

Martínez Casas, R. (2000). Nuevos espacios para las lenguas y culturas indígenas: Los otomíes en Guadalajara [New spaces for indigenous language and culture: The Otomí in Guadalajara]. *Nueva Antropología, 17*(57), 43–55.

Meneses Morales, E. (1986). *Tendencias educativas oficiales en Mexico, 1911–1934* [Official educational trends in Mexico, 1911–1934]. Mexico City, Mexico: Centro de Estudios Educativos.

Meneses Morales, E. (1988). *Tendencias educativas oficiales en Mexico,1934–1964* [Official educational trends in Mexico, 1934–1964]. Mexico City, Mexico: Centro de Estudios Educativos.

Muñoz, H. (2009). Política pública y educación indígena escolarizada en México [Public policy and school-based indigenous education in Mexico]. *Cadernos CEDES (Campinas, Brazil), 19*(49), 39–61.

Ornelas, C. (1995). *El sistema educativo Mexicano* [The Mexican educational system]. Mexico City, Mexico: Secretaría de Educación Pública/Centro de Investigación y Docencia Económica.

Ornelas, C. (2008). *Política, poder, y pupitres: Crítica al nuevo federalismo mexicano* [Politics, power, and school desks: A critique of the new Mexican federalism]. Mexico City, Mexico: Siglo XXI.

Parker, W. C. (2003). *Teaching democracy: Unity and diversity in public life.* New York: Teachers College Press.

Podestá Siri, R., & Martínez Buenabad, E. (2003). Sociolinguística educativa [Educational sociolinguistics]. In M. Bertely (Ed.), *Educación, derechos sociales y equidad (Tomo I)* [Education, social rights, and equity (Vol. 1)] (pp. 105–123). (Vol. Colección: La Investigación Educativa en México 1992–2002, Vol. 3). Mexico City, Mexico: Consejo Mexicano de Investigación Educativa.

Ramos, F. J. (2014). *Appropriating policy, practicing identity: College student experiences of intercultural education in Veracruz, Mexico* (Unpublished doctoral dissertation). Indiana University, Bloomington, IN.

Robles, A., & Czarny, G. (2003). Procesos socioculturales en interacciones educativas [Sociocultural processes in educational interactions]. In M. Bertely (Ed.), *Educación, derechos sociales y equidad (Tomo I)* [Education, social rights, and equity (Vol. 1)] (pp. 125–138). (Vol. Colección: La Investigación Educativa en México 1992–2002, Vol. 3). Mexico City, Mexico: Consejo Mexicano de Investigación Educativa.

Rockwell, E. (1995). *La escuela cotidiana* [The everyday school]. Mexico City, Mexico: Fondo de Cultura Económica.

Roldán, E. (2012). La escuela Mexicana decimonónica como iniciación ceremonial a la ciudadanía: Normas, catecismos y exámenes públicos [The 19th century Mexican school as a ceremonial induction into citizenship: Norms, catechisms, and public exams]. In A. Acevedo & P. López (Eds.), *Ciudadanos inesperados* [Unexpected citizens] (pp. 36–69). Mexico City, Mexico: El Colegio de México/CINVESTAV.

Sánchez, C. (2008). *Educando al ciudadano: Los catecismos políticos oaxaqueños del siglo XIX* [Educating the citizen: Oaxacan political catechisms of the 19th century]. Oaxaca, Mexico: Universidad Benemérita de Oaxaca.

Sanchez García, J., Hamann, E. T., & Zúñiga, V. (2012). What the youngest transnational students have to say about their transition from U.S. schools to Mexican ones. *Diaspora, Indigenous, and Minority Education, 6*(3), 157–171.

Schmelkes, S. (2004). La política de la educación bilingüe intercultural en México [Policy for intercultural bilingual education in Mexico]. In I. Hernaiz (Ed.), *Educación en la diversidad. Experiencias y desafíos en la educación intercultural* [Education for diversity: Experiences and challenges of intercultural education] (pp. 185–196). Buenos Aires, Argentina: IIPE-UNESCO.

Secretaría de Educación Pública. (2000). *Formación cívica y ética: Programas de estudio comentados* [Civic and ethical education: Annotated curriculum]. Mexico City, Mexico: Author.

Secretaría de Educación Pública. (2001). *Formación cívica y ética, educación secundaria: Libro para el maestro* [Civic and ethical education for the *secundaria*: Teachers' guide]. Mexico City, Mexico: Author.

Secretaría de Educación Pública. (2006). Acuerdo número 384 por el que se establece el nuevo Plan y Programas de Estudio para Educación *Secundaria* [Accord 384, which establishes the new structure and curriculum for secondary education]. *Diario Oficial* (Mexico City), May 26.

Silva-Herzog Márquez, J. (1999). *El antiguo régimen y la transición en México* [The old regime and the transition to democracy in Mexico]. Mexico City, Mexico: Planeta/Joaquín Mortíz.

Vaughan, M. K. (1997). *Cultural politics in revolution: Teachers, peasants, and schools in Mexico.* Tucson, AZ: University of Arizona Press.

Vázquez, J. (2005). *Nacionalismo y educación en México* [Nationalism and education in Mexico] (2nd ed.). Mexico City, Mexico: El Colegio de México.

Yankelevich, P. (2012). Mexico for the Mexicans: Immigration, national sovereignty, and the promotion of mestizaje. *The Americas, 68*(3), 405–436.

Zúñiga, V., & Hamann, E. T. (2008). Escuelas nacionales, alumnos transnacionales: La migración México/Estados Unidos como fenómeno escolar [National schools, transnational students: U.S.-Mexico migration as a school phenomenon]. *Estudios Sociológicos, 26*(76), 65–85.

Zúñiga, V., & Hamann, E. T. (2009). Sojourners in Mexico with US school experience: A new taxonomy for transnational students. *Comparative Education Review, 53*(3), 329–353.

Zúñiga, V., Hamann, E. T., & Sanchez García, J. (2008). *Alumnos trasnacionales: Las escuelas mexicanas frente a la globalización* [Transnational students: Mexican schools facing globalization]. Mexico City, Mexico: Secretaría de Educación Pública.

Chapter 19

Citizenship and Education in Brazil: The Contributions of Black and Indigenous Peoples

Douglas Verrangia *and* Petronilha Beatriz Gonçalves e Silva
Federal University of São Carlos

This chapter discusses the Brazilian Black and Indigenous movements' contributions to education and citizenship, highlighting a possible change in the educational public-policy community. The chapter's central idea is that since the publication of *Diversity and Citizenship Education: Global Perspectives* (Banks, 2004), there have been important events in Brazil concerning citizenship, education, and racial relationships. The primary objective of this chapter is to describe these institutional changes and to discuss obstacles to and advances in building educational systems in Brazil that are engaged in furthering social justice.

In the first part of this chapter, we present information about educational policies (primarily during the 20th century) concerning Black and Indigenous populations to illustrate how diversity has been considered in Brazil at the governmental level. We emphasize the 1990s, when the idea of citizenship education began to appear in official documents.

The second part of the chapter describes education legislation related to diversity and citizenship in Brazil since the beginning of the 21st century. We discuss events such as approval of laws and implementation of curricular documents that marked significant changes in educational policies. After more than 10 years since the publication of *Diversity and Citizenship Education: Global Perspectives* (Banks, 2004), some important legislative and administrative changes have occurred at the level of Brazil's federal government, which have the potential to both change social structures and reduce inequalities.

In the third part of the chapter, we identify and analyze the positive societal effects of these educational policies. On the basis of our analyses, we describe some remaining challenges that must be addressed if Brazil is to make advances in citizenship education connected with social demands and oriented toward social justice.

In the fourth part of the chapter we describe some of what we are still learning from Black and Indigenous peoples' struggles for education in Brazil. We identify new questions and horizons related to the interactions of education, citizenship, and diversity.

The final part of this chapter describes a lesson taught by Solange Bonifácio, an elementary school teacher. Bonifácio explains how she incorporates African and African-Brazilian culture when teaching literacy skills, which involves encouraging students to write and read autobiographical texts written by their classmates.

Introduction

Brazil is one of the largest multiracial societies in the world, and more than half of its population is of African descent. According to the Instituto Brasileiro de Geografia e Estatística (Brazilian Institute for Geography and Statistics [IBGE, 2011]), the 2010 national census indicates that Brazil has a population of 190,755,799—84.4% of whom live in urban areas. Among these urban residents, 47.7% consider themselves White, 50.7% Black (*pretos* and *pardos*),[1] 1.1% Asiatic, and 0.4% Indigenous. In addition, the sociocultural diversity of Indigenous people has been recognized. More than 220 distinct groups of Indigenous people live in 628 official Indigenous lands and in urban centers in most of the states in Brazil, including communities that are not yet recognized by the government. More than 60% of Brazil's Indigenous population is concentrated in the Amazon area. Brazilian's current diversity is rooted in the colonialist invasion in the 15th century and the transatlantic slavery trade. Even before colonial times, however, diversity was a reality in South America. Researchers estimate that the Indigenous population living in "Brazilian" territory before colonialism might have been between two and four million, comprising approximately 1,500 ethnic groups (Ribeiro, 1957). This population was systematically exterminated, initially by the Portuguese and then by national economic forces, at such a high rate that researchers believe that more than 80 ethnic groups disappeared during the first half of the 20th century. The total population of these groups decreased from one million to 200,000 during that period (Ribeiro, 1957).

As Hébrard (2013) stated, Brazil was the last country in the Western world to abolish slavery, and Portugal was "one of the first European empires to make slavery the primary tool of its colonization of the Atlantic world" (p. 48). Moreover, Brazil was the European colony that received the most Africans during the colonial period:

> By 1570, the first slave ships had arrived in Brazil, and they did not stop arriving until 1850, when the trans-Atlantic transfer of captives to Brazil was finally effectively outlawed. Between these two dates, four to five million Africans were shipped overseas to work and live as slaves in the plantations, mines, and cities of Brazil. (Hébrard, 2013, p. 49)

After the end of formal slavery, the interest of many Brazilian intellectuals turned to the "Black man" rather than the former slaves. They adopted a perspective strongly influenced by eugenics and wondered what to do with the African portion of society and how to protect the population from that group's alleged "defects" (Hébrard, 2013, p. 50). It is interesting that Brazil—a society that passed laws to prevent Africans and people of African descent from being educated, to own land and properties, and even to live in urban areas that were reconstructed and expanded during the 20th century—was internationally recognized as a "racial paradise" until the 1950s (Martins et al., 2004).

It was only in 1955 that findings of a UNESCO study (developed by Roger Bastide and his Brazilian colleagues, especially Florestan Fernandes) began to demolish the premise that a "racial democracy" existed in Brazil. The authors made the following argument:

In the state of São Paulo, where an archaic world on its way out converged with a new world that had not known slavery, prejudice based on color was not erased, it simply changed its role. The racist ideology that had been used to justify the enslavement of Africans had become a means of essentializing class hierarchies. (UNESCO & Anhembi, 1955, as cited in Hébrard, 2013, p. 50)

During the 1960s, sociologists such as Cardoso and Ianni (cited in Hébrard, 2013) further contributed to the understanding of the slavery system as both a mode of production and a form of social organization, arguing that characteristics of Brazilian society would no longer be expressed in moral or psychological terms, but in economic ones. Moreover, they added that abolition was less the result of human effort than the consequence of an economic collapse (Hébrard, 2013).

From 1964 to 1989, Brazil was ruled by a military dictatorship with six governments (one of them civilian): It was a period marked by political repression, violence, censorship, and suppression of social demands (Cohen, 1987). As Lebon (2007) explains, by the late 1970s, as the dictatorship was easing its grip on academic life, a few pioneers such as sociologists Carlos Hasenbalg (1979/2005) and Nelson Silva (1978), following in the footsteps of Florestan Fernandes, set out to demonstrate the fallacy of the "racial democracy"myth[2] through statistical data that showed stark inequalities in income and living standards. It is important to stress that the work of two Black female scholars and activists, Sueli Carneiro and Thereza Santos (1985), who focused on the living conditions of women of African descent (Lebon, 2007, p. 6), attracted less attention. The Black movement, for instance, has denounced the racial democracy myth, which was used by the authoritarian state to justify banning the gathering of racially disaggregated data from the 1970 census, leading to a gap in such information for almost 20 years (Berquó, 2001). In the same context, the Brazilian state discouraged politicized Indigenous identification during the 1980s and 1990s and—as in almost all Latin American countries—the state's Indigenous policies encouraged assimilation (Jackson &Warren, 2005).

Until the 1990s, Brazilian scholars were still faced with an indifferent census administration that was unable "to disseminate timely statistical data on race and to disaggregate socioeconomic indicators by race (or gender)" (Reichmann, 1999, p. 26, as cited in Berquó, 2001). Telles (2003) stated that, in the 1990s,

> government support for human rights and the fight against racism was in the large part pure rhetoric, since the government did little to try to honor its international commitments in the country. Therefore, the educational policy of the 1990s hadn't visualized concrete affirmative action that has produced any significant impact in the fight against "racial" inequalities in Brazil. (p. 90)

Obviously, the slavery system, the systematic extermination of native people, and the politics that followed the formal colonial period left a profound mark on the Brazilian social structure. To this day, Brazilians who are minorities in terms of their power to govern and influence—Blacks and Indians, among others—continue to suffer from social injustice.

Blacks and Indigenous peoples have arisen against injustices since the very beginning of the colonial period. For example, it was the large-scale *marronage* (*maroons*—communities of runaway slaves), not revolts, that initially drew the most attention to Africans' resistance to slavery. The Portuguese empire had experienced the first serious phenomenon of this type at Palmares (or Quilombo dos Palmares), a community that resisted colonial power from 1605 to 1694. The estimated population of that region was approximately 20,000, including Africans, Indigenous people, and other excluded people. The full breadth of slave resistance became ever clearer, as "the *quilombo* no longer seemed to be the exception, but the rule" (Hébrard, 2013, p. 61). Hébrard (2013) cited other examples of similar developments from around the country and, considering the movement's continuity as most important, argued that "this resistance movement never seemed to abate" (p. 62).

Indigenous movements also arose in other Latin American nations struggling with constitutional reforms. It was only in the 1990s that countries such as Argentina, Brazil, Colombia, Ecuador, Guatemala, Mexico, Nicaragua, Paraguay, Peru, and Venezuela were recognized as multicultural nations (Jackson & Warren, 2005). Van Cott (1995, as quoted in Jackson & Warren, 2005) characterized the goals of Latin American Indigenous movements as follows:

> self-determination and autonomy, with an emphasis on cultural distinctiveness; political reforms that involve a restructuring of the state; territorial rights and access to natural resources, including control over economic development; and reforms of military and police powers over indigenous peoples. (p. 12)

Cultural identity became central to the Indigenous movement, and explicitly development-oriented goals—for example, access to training, development of resources to modify traditional subsistence modes, improvement of educational quality and health conditions—were articulated "in terms that insist[ed] on these goals being accomplished in culturally appropriate ways" (Jackson & Warren, 2005, p. 554). Recognizing the potential value of the symbolic and political capital attained through the resignification of "Indigenous culture," Indigenous leaders increased their effort to revive and strengthen their institutions.

The contributions of social movements for education were discussed by P. B. G. Silva (2004), who described what could be learned by educators from these movements. She described centuries of discriminatory and racist policies in Brazilian society. The struggle of Indigenous peoples for citizenship and Blacks' search for citizenship and identity were also emphasized. P. B. G. Silva (2004) argued that groups that have been deliberately excluded should "seek to establish their own participation in the broader society in much the same way that they participate in their communities of origin" (p. 204).

Social movements and intellectuals linked to them have been producing demands, struggles, and knowledge to fight against Brazil's societal model, which remains connected (for example, through institutional racism) to practices that originated during the slavery colonial period. Afolabi (2012), discussing the concept of *quilombismo* (*marronage*), and Martins et al. (2004) related the struggle for educational equality for Blacks today in Brazil with the struggles of the *maroon* communities during slavery, which were established to provide a racism-free environment for the people who established them and for others who wished to live there.

It is important to stress that there are differences between Black and Indigenous people's social conditions and struggles for education in Brazil and that differences exist even within each group.[3] Whereas most African Brazilians attend regular public schools, vocational or technical courses, and adult education courses, more than 200,000 Indigenous people (approximately 238,113 in 2013) attend Indigenous schools in most Brazilian states (Instituto Nacional de Estudos e Pesquisas Anísio Teixeira, INEP, 2013).

However, some aspects of the struggles are shared by both groups. For example, all current social indicators—produced both by official governmental institutions such as IBGE and by academic researchers—describe educational disparities between White and non-White populations. The data reveal that recent changes in Brazil have had little positive effect on the Black and Indigenous people, who remain at the bottom of society. Unfortunately, studies have shown that Blacks are experiencing increased disadvantages in terms of quality of life, infant mortality, life expectancy at birth, social mobility, participation in the labor market, distribution of income, and education (Santos & Coelho, 2014). This contradictory situation shows the importance of initiatives to address how much Brazilian society has advanced and how far it is away from social and racial justice.

Racial Relationships and Contemporary Educational Policies in Brazil

In light of the racial relationships in Brazil, the period between 1988, the year the Constitution was ratified, and 2003, when Law No. 10.639 was approved, is extremely important in any effort to understand the social changes in progress in national and international contexts (Silvério & Trinidad, 2012). After the end of the 1990s, a new configuration in educational policies began. This change is not disconnected from the massification of education oriented toward the neoliberal economic model, in which the major concern about diversity is described in terms of reducing social and economic inequalities (Santos & Coelho, 2014). Advances were also made after 1995, when the Black movement—following the "March Against Racism and for Racial Equality, Citizenship and Life" in Brasília—delivered a document to the president of the Republic, Fernando Henrique Cardoso, who made an unprecedented statement acknowledging that there was racial discrimination against Blacks in Brazil.

After the Third Conference against Racism, Racial Discrimination, Xenophobia, and Related Intolerance in 2001 in Durban, South Africa, significant changes in curriculum policy were made to take "race" relations into account. At that conference, Brazil officially recognized the existence of racism as an important cause of social inequalities and proclaimed that the nation "promised to make changes to enhance social justice" (P. B. G. Silva, 2011, p. 132). For example, proposals made during the conference influenced the creation of two governmental positions related to ethnic-racial issues, education, and diversity during the tenure of President Luis Inácio "Lula" da Silva (2003–2011). The first was for a special federal, ministerial-level Secretary of Racial Equality, the second for a Secretary of Continuous Education, Alphabetization and Diversity, to be administered by the Ministry of Education.

Another objective that was achieved under Lula's government was the approval of Law No. 10.639 of 2003, which established the education system's obligation to teach about African and African-Brazilian culture and history from preschool through high school. To obtain the fundamental materials needed to comply with the law, the National Council of Education (CNE) consulted with Black movement participants, university professors, schoolteachers, educational system managers, students, parents, and other citizens who advocated for equal rights. The CNE noted that Law No. 10.639 would require reeducation about ethnic and racial relations, guided by the following principles: historical and political awareness of diversity, strengthening of identities and rights, and educational activities to fight against racism and discrimination. In 2004, the Council issued the "National Curricular Guidelines for Ethnic-Racial Education and the Teaching of African and African-Brazilian Culture and History" (Conselho Nacional de Educação, 2004; *Diretrizes Curriculares Nacionais para a Educação das Relações Étnico-Raciais e para o Ensino de História e Cultura Afro-Brasileira e Africana*; Conselho Nacional de Educação, 2004).

In 2012, the Council, in response to demands by the *quilombola* communities, established the "National Curricular Guidelines for Quilombo/Maroons Schools in Basic Education"[4] (*Diretrizes Curriculares Nacionais para a Educação Escolar Quilombola na Educação Básica*; Conselho Nacional de Educação, 2012).This legal document includes Black communities both in the countryside and in the cities, many of them remnants of organized communities established by former slaves who had fled from subjugation in distant places that were difficult to access. The guidelines state that the education provided in such institutions should be based on (a) collective memory; (b) diversity of languages; (c) civilization landmarks; (d) cultural practices; (e) technologies and forms of producing work; (f) collections and oral repertoires; (g) the festivities, customs, traditions, and other elements that make up the cultural heritage of the *quilombo* communities across the country; and (h) territoriality. All of these should be accounted for without neglecting students' preparation to continue their studies beyond the elementary level.[5]

A set of laws and opinions of the boards of education at the federal, state, and municipal levels offers legal support for guaranteeing the Black population's rights. Moreover, these laws and opinions mandated opportunities for all Brazilians to be educated as citizens of an egalitarian, anti-racist society. Some important public policies that concern Brazil's Black population and that focus on the full exercise of citizenship rights are expressed in the form affirmative actions, including the following:

- Law No. 12.288 (2010), or the Statute of Racial Equality, which in its first article not only guarantees the Black population equal opportunities and individual and collective ethnic rights, but also prohibits discrimination and other forms of ethnic intolerance.

- Law No.12.711 (2012), which governs admission[6] to federal universities and federal institutions of mid-level technical education and other measures. The first article states that the federal institutions of higher education linked to the Ministry of Education will reserve, in each selective admission for undergraduate students, a minimum of 50% of their seats for students who have completed their education in public schools.

- Law No. 12.990 (2014), which reserves for Blacks 20% of the positions offered in *concursos publicos* (civil service examinations) for the occupation of public positions within the federal government, local authorities, public foundations, public companies, and joint stock companies controlled by the Brazilian state.

In the history of education policies for Indigenous peoples, the last two decades of the 20th century were marked by legal achievements intended to ensure, as part of what are now called r*ecognition* or *identity* policies, the right to be different. In this sense, Jackson and Warren (2005), referring to Indigenous peoples in Latin America, affirm that many of the "most marginalized pueblos gained the most basic right: the 'right to have rights' as citizens." In Brazil, this new political horizon with a plurality of ideas—including diversity, interculturality, specificity, and differentiation as structuring principles of Indigenous education projects—gains strength and is associated with the political processes of identity affirmation (Oliveira & Nascimento, 2012).

At the national level, one important example of policy related to Indigenous identity and culture is the *Referenciais para a Formação de Professores Indígenas* (References for Indigenous Teachers' Education), which identifies principles and pedagogical and curricular proposals for Indigenous schools (Ministério da Educação, 2002). This reference work also provides orientation to help education systems to construct and develop policies guided by the ideas of specificity, differentiation, interculturality, bilingualism, and school community.

In general, the growth of Indigenous education over the last 10 years can be expressed quantitatively. During this period, based on data from the Educational Census, the number of Indigenous schools almost doubled, from 1,392 in 1999 to 2,698 in 2008—an increase of 93.8%—with 238,113 enrolled students in 2013 (INEP, 2013). Since 2004, Indigenous enrollment has shown stable growth, increasing in a period when the total Basic Education enrollment was decreasing (INEP, 2008). As noted above, in 2012, the Council of Education, in consultation with Indigenous Movement leaders and other social activists, established the *National Curricular Guidelines for Indigenous School Education* (*Diretrizes Curriculares Nacionais para a Educação Escolar Indígena*; Conselho Nacional de Educação, 2015).

The guidelines' primary goals were to help Indigenous schools and their pedagogical projects to construct normative instruments, such as Indigenous-specific education in multilingual programs and intercultural community organizations. The document highlights the importance of considering each community's sociocultural and economic practices and of promoting Indigenous teacher-training programs. It also regulates the functioning of Indigenous education, requiring collaboration with experts in Indigenous knowledge. The right to differentiated education is characterized by the emphasis on social equality and pedagogical relevance; cultural, linguistic, environmental, and territorial cohesion; and the logic, knowledge, and perspectives of Indigenous peoples (Brazil, 2012).

This normative context described above has attracted the attention of sociologists interested in racial relationships. For example, Silvério (2015) makes the following argument:

> We live in Brazil in a process of transition from a racial integration model based
> on the foundational idea of "mestizo nation" to a model which seeks to recognize

different ethnic and racial identities present in Brazilian social formation, which began to question their "erasure" in the political field through organized social movements. (p. 40)

It is impossible to deny the changes that are occurring in Brazil. However, as Silvério and Trinidad (2012) ask, "Is there anything new to say about racial relationships in contemporary Brazil?" (p. 891). This question enables the reader to be aware of the tension surrounding diversity in Brazilian society and the level at which its legal recognition has contributed to recreating the social, cultural, and political order.

Citizenship, Educational Policies, and Diversity Today

Educational legislation and legal texts that guide elementary and secondary education emphasize the relationship between education and citizenship.[7] For example, Law No. 9.394 (Guidelines and Bases of National Education; Presidência da República, 1996)—the most important educational document that establishes the social function of school education in Brazil—contains the following statements in two articles:

Education, Family and State duty, based on the principles of freedom and ideals of human solidarity, is intended to fully develop students, their preparation for the exercise of citizenship and qualification for work. (Presidência da República, 1996, p. 1)

Basic education has the objective of developing the student, ensuring the indispensable common preparation for citizenship and providing the means to progress at work and in later studies. (Presidência da República, 1996, p. 7)

In general, the wider educational guidelines in Brazil highlight the importance of social relationships in education, which are considered as a preparation for full citizenship. These legal provisions, targeted at specific areas of knowledge, are reaffirmed by several scholars who discuss education and citizenship. For example, Silva and Araújo-Oliveira (2004) write:

Citizens are men and women who take the story of the groups to which they belong in their hands and undertake a struggle in order that everyone can be recognized in their particularities, accepted and respected, and guaranteed to participate in decisions that will forward the destiny of their community, in the nation where they exercise their citizenship, the continent where they live. (p. 6)

The laws and regulations mentioned above and the researchers cited noted the importance of social relationships in citizenship education. Education is integral to the process of becoming citizens and should contribute to creating citizens who seek to experience and produce ethical social relationships. A variety of groups in Black and Indigenous social movements originated in the early 20th century, highlighting that it is not enough to think only in terms of social relationships in cultivating critical citizens. These groups called for the consideration of specificities of racial relationships in citizenship education.

Based on his experience as a professor and his reflections on educational processes, Paulo Freire (2005) emphasizes that no one offers or provides education for anyone else. Instead, each person, through her or his life experiences and mutual coexistence, constructs her or his own education. This idea is also emphasized by the research of James Banks (2008), whose scholarship significantly contributes to the study of the relationships between different social groups.

Banks (2004) and his colleagues have sought, in the United States and worldwide, to identify not only the people and groups whose particularities constitute society but also the ways that schools and universities educate citizens in their respective political spaces (see Nascimento, 2008). One of Banks's most important contributions is his concept of *equity pedagogy* (Banks, 2016). Equity pedagogy consists of procedures and pedagogical interactions that not only valorize and encourage the expression of the peculiarities of distinct social and cultural groups but also promote consistent exchanges among those groups.

Consistent with Banks's (2016) concept of equity pedagogy, some of Brazil's current educational policies highlight the recognition of differences and the need to correct historical distortions. One element we consider very important is the introduction, in the Brazilian legal field since 2004, of the concept of *reeducation in ethnic-racial relations*. This concept brings an important element to educational actions because it addresses the complex issue (often ignored in schools) of the ethnic-racial relationship lived by all educational actors (students, relatives, teachers, principals, and coordinators). The concept addresses daily relations between different social groups and individuals in those groups, guided by concepts and ideas about differences and similarities regarding individual and collective belongings and all of the consequences of those belongings. Such consequences remain informed by false racial hierarchies, against which the Black movement has been fighting through its history, affirming Black identity and promoting Black empowerment.

The actions of the Brazilian Indigenous and Black movements, along with the public policies of recognition and affirmative action, must be seen in their historical context not only in Brazil but also in the region as a whole. During the 20th century, the Black movement in Brazil, with the diverse entities that comprised it, proposed and fought for public policies that recognized and resolved both inequalities and the deprivation of rights, which persisted even after the promulgation of Imperial Law No. 3353 (1888), which abolished slavery. Unfortunately, no policies were established for the benefit of the former slaves' citizenship, housing, employment, or schooling. At the same time, a tacit policy was established—which continues on a daily basis—to "whiten" Brazilian society, even though the idea of Brazil as a "racial democracy" became widespread and institutionalized.

One important consideration imposed by the current educational/curriculum legislation is the need to include school-specific content related to African and African-Brazilian history and culture. Educational systems have been charged with the task of managing the specific relationships within social practices that bring together Blacks, Whites, Indigenous people, and Jews, among many others—people who are classified into categories that have been created throughout human history to differentiate people, especially according to their ethnic-racial origins.

The current legislation advocates a society that can go beyond tolerance, beyond a naive (and/or exclusionary) multicultural conception—a society formed by citizens engaged in promoting a radical intercultural process, oriented toward recognizing and appreciating differences. This is a political stance that, until recently, was rarely adopted by the Brazilian state: affirmative action for developing identity, memory, and culture claimed by Black, Indigenous, and other social movement activists who participate in the anti-racist struggle (Gomes, 2011). However, the implementation of this type of public policy has been a tense, complex process. Even with important programs and actions that have the potential to support policies from a broader, more inclusive perspective,

> its effectiveness will depend on the necessary mobilization of civil society in order to guarantee the right to ethnic and racial diversity in schools, curricula, political-pedagogical projects, teacher training, educational policies, etc. (Gomes, 2011, p. 116)

This is because, as noted previously,

> these laws and practices clash with the racial imaginary present in the structure and functioning of Brazilian education, such as the myth of racial democracy, ambiguous racism, the whitening ideology and the naturalization of racial inequalities. (Gomes, 2011, p. 118)

In support of this vision, one of the few national studies on pedagogical practices related to ethnic-racial relationships in the schools has shown that the legally mandatory teaching of African and African-Brazilian culture and history has helped reinforce existing anti-racist practices (Gomes & Jesus, 2013). Simultaneously, it promotes the building of novel practices, bringing new challenges for school management, teachers, and teacher preparation programs. The same research also reveals that

> there is no uniformity in the process of 10.639/2003 Law implementation in the education systems and in the public schools participating in the research. It is a context still marked by tensions, advances, and limits. (Gomes & Jesus, 2013, p. 32)

Thus, one can see the importance of strategic educational policies and actions for the democratic implementation of this set of laws and policies as the result of historic struggles.

Another important issue is that the context created by these policies opens space for both a broader debate (for example, in the news) and new studies in this area. In this sense, Santos, Silva, and Coelho (2014) show that research on education and race relations has expanded in the last decade. They observe a noticeable expansion of post-graduate programs in Brazil in the field of education, along with an increasing interest in research involving various aspects and themes of education pertaining to race relationships both in schools and in nonschool educational environments (Santos et al., 2014).

Despite a significant advance in public policies concerning cultural diversity as an important element of differentiation, there are problems that need to be considered. For example, an official statistical analysis of enrollment in "Indigenous schools," based on the 2005 general School Census, indicates an increase in Indigenous schools and students enrollment. At the same time, enrollment in the secondary level at Indigenous schools remains low, which reveals the low educational levels in Indigenous territories (INEP, 2007). There are also serious problems with these schools. For example, more than half of Indigenous students are older than expected for the grade in which they are enrolled. In addition, the schools' structures are in critical condition: 50% do not have access to electricity, only 11% are connected to a public water supply, and almost 48% have no adequate sewer system.

Without more recent, officially systematized data,[8] researchers, the press, and institutions such as the Ministério Público Federal (MPF; Federal Public Ministry) are highlighting the difficult situations in several Indigenous schools. An MPF research project shows that only 54.4% of such schools are regulated by the government: The rest did not pass the admission process, which considers the pedagogical project, council, or local educational institution that is responsible for each school (MPF, 2015). The same project finds that one third of the schools lack a building; students must work under trees or in their homes. Another problem is the lack of high-quality drinking water, as 58.4% of the schools do not even have treated water (MPF, 2015).

In the case of the African-Brazilian population, qualitative studies such as the one conducted by Louzano (2013) continue to describe the negative school environment experienced by Black children. Louzano analyzed the 2001 and 2011 results of the National Exam of Basic Education for the fifth year of elementary school. The study revealed that there were substantial differences in school performance between Black and non-Black children. According to Louzano,

> although a slight improvement over the last decade has been seen, to be Black further reduces the possibility of academic success. In 2011, 43% of Black students in the 5th year have already failed or dropped out of school at least once. Moreover, even controlling for factors such as gender, parental education and geographic region, Black students are far behind their peers, especially Whites. (2013, p. 125)

Thus, we see the importance of strategic educational policies and actions in order to implement the aforementioned multicultural education legislation, which is the result of historic struggles. At the same time, it is important to note that different types of affirmative action have been taken to reinforce major sociostructural corrections, including in non-educational areas, such as the recognition of *quilombolas* and indigenous lands, economic redistribution, and social mobility.

Challenges in Educating Black and Indigenous Students for Citizenship

Educators can learn important lessons from Black and Indigenous social movements, which are fundamental to consider if we want our society, so deeply multicultural, to be less unequal. Centuries of struggle produced knowledge of both cultural diversity and Brazilian inequalities, along with ways to overcome them. Such struggles show that even in the current society, which is more favorable to social justice, much remains to be done. It would be very difficult to note all of the knowledge that we have received from these movements.

Therefore, we will highlight some relevant aspects revealed by our studies and social context analysis.

The Persistence of Institutional Racism

The more we deepen our studies, the more we realize the complexity of the web of facts, relationships, projects, and worldviews that interpose, shock, and even complement each other in the field of multicultural experience. At the same time, we realize the complexity of the processes of transmutation and adaptation that racism creates to guarantee its persistence. One of the most important lessons that social movements teach us as a society is to keep our "eyes wide open." That is, we cannot fall into the traps created by the false idea of racial democracy. Sometimes, even by hoping for a better place to live, we could be attracted to some interpretations that minimize the role of race in social relationships. One example is the frequent discussion about whether to include racial identification in official documents. It is interesting that a significant proportion of Brazilian society argues in favor of excluding racial characterizations. However, data analysis provides an understanding (as taught by social movements) of the danger in this mindset, which must be avoided.

Research on the 2013 national census shows that the people who benefit the most from income-transfer policies have dark skin. According to data released by Tereza Campello, secretary of the Ministry of Social Development and Fight against Hunger, 73% of those registered in the BolsaFamília[9] program (one of the most important—and criticized— federal government programs) are Black (Presidência da República, 2013). For other benefits, the proportion is even higher.

Regarding inequalities, according to the Laboratory of Economic, Social and Statistical Analysis about Racial Relationships (Laboratório de Análises Econômicas, Sociais e Estatísticas das Relações Raciais), which cited various sources, including the Ministry of Health, the number of homicides in Brazil increased from 1980 (13,910) to 2007 (47,707; Paixão, Rossetto, Montovanele, & Carvano, 2010, "Annual Report on Racial Inequality in Brazil, 2009–2010"). If we take, as a tragic example, the murder rates for young people in Brazil, we will see that the rate is higher for Black males aged 5–9 years old: Black children in that age group represented 4% of the total homicides in 2007, as compared with 2.7% for White children. In the age range of 10–14 the differences increase (17.3% for Black children, 8.2% for White children), and other age groups confirm the nonrandom direction of violent deaths: 15–17 years, 51.4% Black and 31.4% White; 18–24 years, 52% Black and 32.5% White. For females, the situation is similar, but less pronounced (Paixão et al., 2010). In contrast to the explicit violence of the various types of death that occur daily, other forms of oppression, often unspoken and symbolic, are created in educational contexts, generating both exclusion and violence.

Even though affirmative action grants Black and Indigenous students entry and sometimes maintenance in high-quality public universities, strategies of resistance to democratization are produced at both institutional and individual levels, whether consciously or not. There are reports of situations and processes that maintain a type of privatization of public resources benefiting privileged groups in these universities. Such situations involve, for example,

- Strained relations between teachers and affirmative action students, who are considered to be (and often openly accused of being) less capable than other students (Plá, 2009, among others);

- Strained relations between affirmative action students and other students, who are, in some contexts, excluded from study groups, projects, or programs that rely on interview-based selection (Nery & Costa, 2009, among others);

- Strained relations with regard to learning materials that exclude African, African-Brazilian, and Indigenous contributions to constructing the human heritage and society in Brazil (Gomes, 2012, among others).

Social movements have continued to demonstrate that education researchers and society overall cannot abandon making systematic observations of social/racial relationships. Such observation is important in the effort to keep identifying and fighting against existing inequalities.

Contradictory Policies

The struggles of Brazil's Black and Indigenous peoples show educators that contradictory or disconnected policies, as much as universal policies, act to favor the society's strong resistance to fairer educational practices. It is important to highlight the need for a coherent set of laws and public policies, and also to consistently evaluate the actions implemented to effectively promote the improvement of ethnic-racial relationships. We highlight the relationships between evaluation policies, teaching materials, working conditions, and teacher training conditions and their impact on the education of Black and Indigenous people.

Since 2003, the federal government has noted important social paths through a difficult process of transforming agreements into official documents and laws. Ultimately, we can see the emphasis on recognizing and valorizing of differences and the need to correct historical distortions. However, the context that produced Brazil's race relationships and its laws and curricular documents—such as Law No. 10.639 (2003) and its guidelines—is extremely complex. From the point of view of social actors (policy makers, social activists, executors, teachers, and others), this complexity is a challenge in efforts to understand racial relationships. Moehlecke (2009) identified three sometimes contradictory meanings of "diversity" in policy-related documents, programs, actions, and reports produced during the first period of President Lula's government (2003–2006). According to Moehlecke, these three meanings were

> a) social inclusion; b) affirmative action; c) policies of difference. We note that, although the so-called diversity policies have reached a higher degree of institutionalization in the Lula government, the concepts that guide related actions are still very mismatched and adopted in a fragmented way by government departments. There is evidence of internal disputes in the government regarding the definitions of educational projects, with different proposals that respond to the demands of social movements for the recognition of diversity. (Moehlecke, 2009, p. 461)

Other researchers have also noted the contradictions at the core of the meanings in the legislation texts (Santos & Coelho, 2014). These contradictions result from the difficult political process that underlies educational curriculum production.

The meanings attributed to Basic Education by the Brazilian Constitution—preparation for citizenship, work, and further studies[10]—and its relation to standardized processes of evaluation and formal mechanisms to access education at the university level are constantly discussed. For example, the National High School Exam (ENEM) has changed from a test used to test high school achievement to one intended to evaluate the educational system (and its results) and to promote access to professional (technical) education and to public and private universities through scholarships or financial aid.

According to Viggiano and Mattos (2013), in 2011, ENEM had approximately 4.5 million subscribers.[11] This elevated number of participants qualified the test to influence high school classrooms, school organizations, and curricula. After a 2009 restructuring, ENEM also began to take on additional functions, such as awarding equivalency diplomas to students over 18 years old who had not completed a high school education. The contents evaluated in the exam were presented in a Reference Matrix (*Matriz de Referência*) based on the concepts of competence and ability. According to official sources, this conception was innovative compared to the "vestibular" tests for access to higher education that traditionally had been applied and developed by colleges and universities. However, it is important to analyze this content in comparison with the previously mentioned laws that guide education related to ethnic-racial relationships. In general, ENEM's contents refer to a few conceptual (factual) aspects of African, African-Brazilian, and Indigenous history and culture but do not explicitly engage students in reeducation with regard to ethnic-racial relationships. Consequently, the exam has contributed little to implementing these guidelines at the school level. Within the current, massive evaluation programs, it is important to remember Silva's (2004) argument that "assistance measures, formulated and executed without any ethical criteria of recognition of plurality and diversity, must be rejected" (p. 203). Educators must learn, as Freire (2005) argues, that one cannot use the instruments of domination to achieve liberation. In this sense, Black and Indigenous movements have noted the need to review official history as presented in student textbooks and other didactic materials.

Important changes are occurring, for example, promoted by the adoption of specific criteria—related to eliminating ethnic-racial discrimination and valorizing African, African-Brazilian, and Indigenous cultures and history—by a national textbook evaluation program, Programa Nacional do Livro Didático (PNLD). The program is helping change the scenario noted by studies such as Rosemberg, Bazili, and Silva (2003), which show the absence of critical perspectives on these histories and cultures. However, the program has not yet produced a review of the Eurocentric perspective that is still present in these teaching materials. Inconsistencies were found by comparing federal legislation with curricular materials produced by specific public education systems at the state and city levels. For example, studies conducted by Constancio (2012) and Bonifácio (2015) show either the absence, or the merely incipient presence, of content involving reeducation about ethnic-racial relationships in curricular materials produced in the state of São Paulo.

In the case of Indigenous schools, the most recent official data show that fewer than 41.5% have educational materials specifically addressing ethnic-racial relationships and that important differences exist among regions (INEP, 2007). The same research shows that in the northern region, where more than 50% of Brazil's Indigenous schools are located, 33% use specific related materials, whereas in the southeast, where there are far fewer schools, 79.6% have this resource. More recent information (MPF, 2015) confirms the absence or lack of specific and adequate teaching materials in several schools.

Teacher Preparation

School is not the only institution responsible for education about ethnic-racial relationships. Education is provided by families, cultural groups, and communities and occurs in social life in general, influenced by the media. At the same time, the school is a privileged environment for a reorientation on ethnic-racial relationships because it is in the schools that one can see the remarkable presence of Brazilian diversity. Research has shown that initial teacher preparation and continuous preparation courses generally do not prepare teachers to adequately address the ethnic-racial relationships that exist in schools (Gomes & Jesus, 2013; Verrangia & Silva, 2010; and many others). There have been some advances in institutions for teacher preparation in efforts to critically address ethnic-racial relationships and African, African-Brazilian, and Indigenous history and culture. For example, some of the criteria that the government has adopted in university accreditation and evaluation processes are connected to these issues. Consequently, institutions have been forced to consider and reflect upon how to address these questions, which in several cases have been completely ignored in formal curriculum and classroom practices.

Educators cannot ignore the remaining challenges to changing teacher preparation curricula and practices, especially considering the structural gaps. For example, fewer than 13% of educators teaching in Indigenous schools have university degrees (INEP, 2007). This situation is worrying, but might improve because of the current affirmative action programs that guarantee the entry of Indigenous students into universities, along with the recently published "National Curricular Guidelines for the Preparation of Indigenous Teachers."[12]

Another challenge is consideration of ethnic relationships in preparing teachers from different backgrounds (especially in mathematics and the natural sciences). Our studies found a difficult situation related to science education. Verrangia (2009), through contact with hundreds of teachers participating in continuing education courses in the state of São Paulo, found that most teachers did not see a relationship between their classes and the school's planned activities to discuss and promote positive ethnic-racial relationships. When asked about activities and content for promoting positive ethnic-racial relationships among students, most of these teachers stated that they were unprepared and/or insecure, and were afraid that they would "make the situation even worse" (Verrangia, 2009, p. 237). From the perspective of preparing for citizenship, it is critical to uncover and analyze the absence of discussions about ethnic-racial relationships in the Brazilian (and even international) literature on science education. In addition, we found that the few science teachers who decided to discuss these relationships in their classrooms were using inappropriate teaching materials and working without specific orientation materials or guidelines.

Conclusion

As we attempt to show, the effects of colonialism can still be observed in contemporary Brazilian society. Since the formal end of the colonial period (in the 19th century), Indigenous people, Africans, and African-Brazilians have been forced to fight for social justice, including for the right to high-quality, fair schooling. During the 20th century, these struggles passed through different periods, achieving more or fewer goals, according to society's evolution. Social movements experienced a military dictatorship, a period of violence, and small advances in the institutionalization of human rights. We view the 1990s as a moment of redemocratization and slow, but progressive, advances in the consideration of ethnic-racial diversity in educational policies. During this period, Brazilian governments began to officially recognize the important role of diversity in the development of citizenship and the obvious inequalities among various ethnic-racial groups. Even when recognizing these realities, Brazil's governments did not institutionalize critical policies to combat educational inequalities; instead, they created "universally" oriented programs that did not concretely address diversity and racial inequalities.

Our main argument in this chapter is that, in the year 2000, there was an important change in official government discourse involving the adoption of diversity policies such as affirmative action in public universities and specific curricular guidelines. We have observed a more institutionalized process to fight against racism and to consider ethnic-racial diversity in education. Many laws and normative documents, and several federal government institutions and departments, are specifically responding to education-related demands from Black and Indigenous movements.

In this chapter, we highlight the importance of institutionalized policies on diversity as a way to fight inequalities and to recognize—more fairly—the diversity of Brazil's people. At the same time, it is necessary to stress the important role played by the government and independent social movements in denouncing inequalities and identifying ways to overcome these threats. In particular, we have mentioned the prevalence of structural racism, the presence of contradictions among educational policies, and the need for teacher preparation and teaching materials to address curricular guidelines that incorporate critical citizenship education.

In the coming years, social movements must be aware of the danger of losing what they have achieved. The constant debate about affirmative action and the increased number of affirmative action opponents (both intellectuals and other citizens) indicate the tentativeness of the arrangements to maintain political gains involving reparations. It is necessary to move forward and accomplish the current goals of the multicultural legislation. This means supervising the implementation of laws and normative documents while producing critical revisions to avoid contradictions. It is very important to provide a better understanding among the general public about laws and programs related to citizenship education and diversity because the mainstream press is openly against "race"-based affirmative action. In the field of curriculum, there is an intense debate about the power to review official national history, which in some way has been crystallized by previous curricular policies. As Silva (2004) argues, becoming a citizen, along with becoming a fully developed human being, is a dynamic, incomplete process that advances over time. In the field of educational policies, this reality is the same for social movements—societal evolution is an incomplete process, achievements are not stable, and constant struggle is necessary.

A Teacher Describes Reading Lessons That Include Content About African and African-Brazilian Culture

BY SOLANGE BONIFÁCIO

The lesson described below was taught to second-grade children, aged 7 to 8, in a public state school located in the outskirts of a medium-sized city in the countryside of São Paulo State. This primary school had classes from first to fifth grades and students from four neighborhoods, which required public transportation to transport students to the school. In two periods there were 350 students, mostly Whites (about 50%), Blacks, and *Pardos*, who identify as mixed or *mestizo*. The family socioeconomic status varied from medium lower-class to poverty, with most students coming from working-class families. In some cases, information about families was incomplete. Many students were living with siblings and their mother, with no information reported about their father. Some students belonged to families that had recently migrated from the northern part of Brazil.

The Lesson

Nine years have passed since I received my degree in pedagogy; returning to the university inspired many feelings. Experiencing both joy and fear, I joined the professional master's program in education, the context in which the work described here was conducted.

The working assumption is that in the writing activities, the child must have the opportunity to express his or her experiences, feelings, and thoughts, and that it is this type of experience "that, necessarily, allows the 'I' to get out of a fixed position in the imaginary to switch to a subject-author position in order to sculpt [in the writing] his real traits" (Aguiar, 2010, p. 17).

The intervention involved reading, interpreting texts and images, and producing drawings and texts to educate students about human relationships that are just and humane. Many readings were taken, conversation circles (*roda de conversa*) were conducted, and opinions were registered about books that adequately addressed African-Brazilian history and culture, informative texts, musical lyrics that addressed racial discrimination, facts about the African continent, learned impressions, and a game of African origin (*labirint,* from Mozambique). The children made many observations of images of Black people, non-Black people, and themselves. From the material, they produced drawings, texts (some rewritten) about Africa, African names, autobiographies, new versions of stories, and self-portraits. In addition, they danced to African and Brazilian music, looked at elements of history and culture, and explored movements and interactions. They also played games and watched a short film.

From the teaching perspective, the intervention attempted to promote shared analyses of images with positive references to people—children and adults—with different skin shades and hair styles. At the same time, to mediate reading and promote reflections on African and the African-Brazilian culture, the children were encouraged to write and to read auto-biographical texts produced by other children that addressed their ethnic-racial belonging. The intervention's perspective was that reading and writing were moments called "exercise of children's speech by writing" (Smolka, 2012, p. 154), which emerged both from their lived ethnic-racial relationships and from intervention moments.

During the project planning, ten activities were initially organized. However, from literature studies and, more importantly, interactions with the children, 15 classes were developed (and the children asked for more at the end). The data used in the research were collected through filming, children's productions, and a field diary.

I think it is important to stress that during the project I did not fail to deliver the content and exercises presented in the "Reading and Writing Program"(*Programa Ler e Escrever*),[13] providing an explanation about it to parents and guardians and asking for their free, informed consent. However, to achieve the objective of educating students about racial relationships through reading and writing, it was necessary to organize various activities, because contents proposed in the program omitted this type of discussion. The material was inconsistent with educational legislation—such as the Law No. 10.639 (2003)—that does not promote reflection on ethnic-racial relationships and ignores African and African-Brazilian culture and history. For example, almost all of the stories presented are of European origin, and the model of "competent writing" that was adopted disregarded the diversity present in the classroom, which was markedly intercultural.

Results and Thoughts

Addressing issues of ethnic-racial relationships in a school context created opportunities to rethink and rebuild children's and adults' identities. However, during the work I realized that these issues involved pain and that, therefore, it was essential to establish a welcoming space. With children, it was noticeable that, unlike adults, they appropriated the goals, understanding that the activities had specific purposes and engaging so that the initial forecast of activities was expanded to 15.

The school setting is challenging, especially because it involves a day full of attitudes such as "here, there is no prejudice," "it is all in your head," "we are all equal," or "a person who is paid by the government must apply its programs without question." In addition, the school setting is full of suspicious looks and small gestures, showing that the presence of people who "dare" to ask questions is bothersome.

From the didactic procedures, speeches, observations, and reflections, it was possible to conclude that teaching involved organization; guidance; questioning; providing historical context; sharing personal stories, values, and experiences; and constant pedagogical reflection. The practice is enriched when it is influenced by children's actions, interactions, and particular ways of producing texts, which are not characterized by homogeneity. In that sense, this work highlights the contradiction present within federal educational policies—for example, the National Curricular Guidelines for Education on Ethnic-Racial Relationships and Law No. 10.639 (2003)—and São Paulo State's prescribed curriculum, which can prevent the development of work like that which took place in my classroom.

The work's purpose of articulating education on ethnic-racial relationships and the production of texts (in the context of literacy training) enabled reflections on identity, extended students' historical knowledge, and allowed learning not only from curricular content but also about and with *the other*, enabling perceptions of other voices, in the words of these children. The intervention development allowed children to feel safe to talk about themselves and each other, to loosen their curls, to write, and to play with words. Even in the presence of an initial strangeness, boys and girls gradually discovered ways to respect, to listen, to relate to each other, and to write. The children showed a remarkable desire to continue the project, as expressed through both words and gestures (such as "Aunt, today can we mess up our hair?") and in attitudes such as meeting the teacher at the school entrance to talk, share family pictures, request songs, and deliver letters and notes.

Finally, I emphasize that the significations produced in lived relationships provided meaning to the concepts of "I" and "other." Given the results of this work (Bonifácio, 2015), it is possible to argue that just as it is not enough to know the letters to read and write, it is not melanin concentration that defines a Black person. Due to the peculiarities of ethnic-racial relationships in Brazil, being Black is a complex "becoming" process involving identity so that we can become "writers of our own words."

Notes

1. In the complex Brazilian racial system, skin coloration terms are used by IBGE to collect information about racial identity (self-definition). The institute uses the words *Preto* (Black) and *Pardo* (Brown), both of which relate to skin color, to collect data, and then add the numbers to define racial categories (see Hanchard, 1999).

2. "Brazil was long upheld as a racial democracy, a thesis which argued that racial inequality was due basically to poverty and class differences, and would disappear with development. However, the "continuing racial gaps in socioeconomic status following the period of rapid economic growth from 1960 to 1980, and the growth of a black middle class, which still suffers from racial discrimination, have weakened a belief in racial democracy" (Safa, 2007, p. 94).

3. See Mc Sweeney and Jokisch (2015) on studying urbanization processes among Native Amazonians.

4. In Brazil, the mandatory Basic Education runs from elementary school (*ensino fundamental*) through high school (*ensino médio*).

5. Resolution CNE/CB 8/2012—Basic Education Chamber of the National Council of Education.

6. For additional information about affirmative action at universities and its impacts in Brazilian society, see, e.g., Daflon, Feres Júnior, and Campos (2013) and Telles and Paixão (2013), which provide an analytical landscape of the debate, some results of the implemented policies, and an assessment of their relevance.

7. Even in Brazilian Basic Education there is no mandatory curricular component intended to inculcate a "civic education"; that was abolished after redemocratization.

8. In response to the need for actualized data, the Ministério Público Federal (Federal Public Ministry; MPF) suggested to the INEP, related to the Ministério da Educação (Ministry of Education), that a specific census of Indigenous education must be developed.

9. This is a federal governmental assistance program that provides financial aid to low-income families, primarily those with children attending public school.

10. Constitution of the Federative Republic of Brazil, ratified on October 5, 1988.

11. In the 2015 edition, the number of subscribers was more than 7.7 million, according to the Ministry of Education on its official website (http://www.brasil.gov.br/educacao/2015/10/enem-tem-25-5-de-abstencao-menor-taxa-desde-2009).

12. These guidelines objectify, for purposes of regulation, initial and continuous Indigenous teachers' education programs and courses, both in state and city educational systems and in universities and normative councils (Brazil, 2015).

13. According to the São Paulo State Educational Secretary, the Programa Ler e Escrever (Secretaria de Estado da Educação de São Paulo, 2015) is a set of coordinated lines of action that includes training, monitoring, preparation, and distribution of teaching materials and other subsidies which seeks to promote improvement of education across the state educational system (Secretaria de Estado da Educação de São Paulo, 2010). A critical analysis, pointing out the standardization—ignoring cultural diversity of students—promoted by the program is seen in Constâncio, 2012.

References

Afolabi, N. (2012). Quilombismo and the Afro-Brazilian quest of citizenship. *Journal of Black Studies, 43*(9), 847–871.

Aguiar, E. A. de. (2010). *Escrita, autoria e ensino: Um diálogo necessário para pensar a constituição do sujeito-autor no contexto escolar* [Writing, authorship and teaching: A necessary dialogue to think about the constitution of an author-subject in school context]. Unpublished doctoral thesis in education, Faculdade de Educação, Universidade de São Paulo, São Paulo.

Banks, J. A. (Ed.). (2004). *Diversity and citizenship education: Global perspectives.* San Francisco: Jossey-Bass.

Banks, J. A. (2008). Diversity, group identity, and citizenship education in a global age. *Educational Researcher, 37*(3), 129–139.

Banks, J. A. (2016). Multicultural education: Characteristics and goals. In J. A. Banks & C. A. M. Banks (Eds.), *Multicultural education: Issues and perspectives* (9th ed., pp. 2–23). Hoboken, NJ: John Wiley & Sons.

Berquó, E. (2001). *Perfil demográfico das chefias femininas no Brasil* [Demographic profile of female bosses in Brazil]. Paper presented during the meeting "Estudos de gênero na sociedade brasileira," da Fundação Carlos Chagas, Itu/SP.

Bonifácio, S. (2015). *Educação das relações étnico-raciais e produção de textos na escola: Traços, letras, cores e vozes das crianças* [The education of ethnic-racial relationships and the production of texts at school: Traces, letters, colors and children's voices]. Unpublished master's dissertation in education, Programa de Pós-Graduação Profissional em Educação, Universidade Federal de São Carlos.

Carneiro, S., & Santos, T. (1985). *Mulher Negra* [Black woman]. São Paulo: Nobel and Conselho Estadual da Condição Feminina.

Cohen, Y. (1987). Democracy from above: The political origins of military dictatorship in Brazil. *World Politics, 40*(1), 30–54.

Conselho Nacional de Educação. (2004). *Parecer CNE/CP n.º 3, de 10 de março de 2004: Diretrizes curriculares nacionais para a educação das relações étnico-raciais e para o ensino de história e cultura Afro-Brasileira e Africana* [Parecer CNE/CP No. 3 of March 10, 2004: National curriculum guidelines for the education of racial-ethnic relationships and the teaching of Afro-Brazilian and African culture and history]. Brasília: Ministério da Educação. Retrieved from http://portal.mec.gov.br/

Conselho Nacional de Educação. (2012). *Resolução CNE/CB 13/2012* [CNE/CB 13/2012 Resolution]. Brasília: Conselho Nacional de Educação/Câmara de Educação Básica [National Council of Education/Basic Education Chamber]. Retrieved from http://portal.mec.gov.br/

Conselho Nacional de Educação. (2015). *Diretrizes curriculares nacionais para a formação de professores Indígenas* [National curricular guidelines to the preparation of Indigenous teachers]. Brasília: Conselho Nacional de Educação/Conselho Pleno [National Council of Education/Full Council]. Retrieved from http://portal.mec.gov.br/

Constâncio, A. R. (2012). *A padronização do trabalho docente: Crítica do Programa Ler e Escrever* [The standardization of teaching: Reading and Writing Program critics]. Unpublished master's dissertation in education, Pontifícia Universidade Católica de São Paulo, PUC-SP. Retrieved from http://www.sapientia.pucsp.br/

Daflon, V. T., Feres Júnior, J., & Campos, L. A. (2013). Ações afirmativas raciais no ensino superior público brasileiro: Um panorama analítico [Racial affirmative action in Brazilian higher education: An analytical landscape]. *Cadernos de Pesquisa, 43*(148), 302–327.

Dos Santos, R. A., & Coelho, W. de N. B. (2014). Política curricular e relações raciais no Brasil: Entre textos e discursos [Curriculum policy and racial relationships in Brazil: Between texts and speeches]. *Revista Teias, 15*(38), 122–146.

Dos Santos, R. A., Silva, R. M. de N. B. e, & Coelho, W. de N. B. (2014). Educação e relações raciais: Estado da arte em programas de pós-graduação em educação (2000–2010) [Education and race relations: State of the art in education post-graduation programs (2000–2010)]. *Revista EXITUS, 4*(01), 111–141.

Freire, P. (2005). *Pedagogy of the oppressed* (30th anniversary of the 1st ed.). New York: Continuum Education.

Gomes, N. L. (2011). Diversidade étnico-racial, inclusão e equidade na educação Brasileira: Desafios, políticas e práticas [Ethnic and racial diversity, inclusion and equity in Brazilian education: Challenges, policies and practices]. *RBPAE, 27*(1), 109–121.

Gomes, N. L. (2012). Relações étnico-raciais, educação e descolonização dos currículos [Ethnic-racial relationships, education and decolonization of curricula]. *Currículo sem Fronteiras, 12*(1), 98–109.

Gomes, N. L., & Jesus, R. E. de (2013). As práticas pedagógicas de trabalho com relações étnico-raciais na escola na perspectiva de Lei 10.639/2003: Desafios para a política educacional e indagações para a pesquisa [The pedagogical practices with ethnic-racial relationships in schools from the perspective of 10.639/2003 Law: Challenges for educational policy and questions for research]. *Educar em Revista, 47*, 19–33.

Hanchard, M. (1999). *Racial politics in contemporary Brazil*. Durham, NC: Duke University Press.

Hasenbalg, C. (2005). *Discriminação e desigualdades raciais no Brasil* (2nd ed.). [Discrimination and inequalities in Brazil]. Belo Horizonte/Rio de Janeiro: Editora UFMG/Iuperj/Ucam. (Original work published 1979)

Hébrard, J. M.(2013). Slavery in Brazil: Brazilian scholars in the key interpretive debates. *Translating the Americas, 1*, 47–95.

Instituto Brasileiro de Geografia e Estatística. (2010). *Censo demográfico 2010: Aglomerados subnormais: Informações territoriais* [Demografic Census 2010: Subnormal agglomerates]. Retrieved from http://www.ibge.gov.br/home/estatistica/populacao/censo2010/aglomerados_subnormais_informacoes_territoriais/default_informacoes_territoriais.shtm

Instituto Nacional de Estudos e Pesquisas Anísio Teixeira. (2007). *Estatísticas sobre educação escolar indígena no Brasil* [Statistics on indigenous school education in Brazil]. Brasília: Diretoria de Estatísticas Educacionais. Retrieved from http://www.oei.es/

Instituto Nacional de Estudos e Pesquisas Anísio Teixeira. (2008). *Um olhar sobre a educação Indígena com base no Censo Escolar de 2008* [A look at Indigenous education based on the 2008 School Census]. Brasília: Diretoria de Estatísticas Educacionais. Retrieved from http://www.inep.gov.br/

Instituto Nacional de Estudos e Pesquisas Anísio Teixeira. (2013). *Censo Escolar da Educação Básica 2013: Resumo técnico* [*Basic Education Scholar Census 2013: Technical resume*]. Brasília: Diretoria de Estatísticas Educacionais. Retrieved from http://www.inep.gov.br/

Jackson, J. E., & Warren, K. B. (2005). Indigenous movements in Latin America, 1992–2004: Controversies, ironies, new directions. *Annual Review of Anthropology, 34,* 549–573.

Lebon, N. (2007). Beyond confronting the myth of racial democracy: The role of Afro-Brazilian women scholars and activists. *Latin American Perspectives, 34*(6), 52–76.

Louzano, P. (2013). Fracasso escolar: Evolução das oportunidades educacionais de estudantes de diferentes grupos raciais [School failure: Evolution of educational opportunities for students from different racial groups]. *Cadernos Cenpec, 3*(1), 111–133.

Martins, S. de S., Medeiros, C. A., & Nascimento, E. L. (2004). Paving paradise: The road from "racial democracy" to affirmative action in Brazil. *Journal of Black Studies, 34*(6), 787–816.

McSweeney, K., & Jokisch, B. (2015). Native Amazonians' strategic urbanization: Shaping territorial possibilities through cities. *Journal of Latin American and Caribbean Anthropology, 20*(1), 13–33.

Ministério Público Federal. (2015). *Levantamento do MPF revela situação precária das escolas indígenas no país* [MPF survey reveals precarious situation of indigenous schools in the country]. Brasília: Procuradoria Geral da República. Retrieved from http://http://www.pgr.mpf. mp.br/

Moehlecke, S. (2009). As políticas de diversidade na educação no governo Lula [Education diversity policies in Lula's government]. *Cadernos de Pesquisa, 39*(137), 461–487.

Ministério da Educação. (2002). *Referenciais para a Formação de Professores Indígenas* (References for Indigenous teachers' education). Retrieved from http://portal.mec.gov.br/seb/arquivos/

Nascimento, E. L. (2008). *A matriz Africana no mundo* [The African matrix in the world]. São Paulo: Selo Negro.

Nery, M. da P., & Costa, L. F. (2009). Política afirmativa racial: Polêmicas e processos de identidade do cotista universitário [Racial affirmative policy: Polemics and identity processes of university scholarship students]. *Psico-USF, 14*(2), 211–220.

Oliveira, L. A., De, & Nascimento, R. G. do. (2012). Roteiro para uma história da educação escolar indígena: Notas sobre a relação entre política indigenista e educacional [Road map to a history of indigenous education: Notes on the relationship between indigenous and educational policies]. *Educação & Sociedade, 33*(120), 765–781. Retrieved from www.scielo.br/pdf/es/v33n120/07.pdf

Paixão, M., Rossetto, I., Montovanele, F. & Carvano, L. M. (Eds.). (2010). *Relatório anual das desigualdades raciais no Brasil, 2009–2010: Constituição Cidadã, seguridade social e seus efeitos sobre as assimetrias de cor ou raça* [Annual report on racial inequality in Brazil, 2009–2010: Citizen Constitution, social security and its effects on color or race asymmetries]. Rio de Janeiro: Laboratório de Análises Econômicas, Históricas, Sociais e Estatísticas das Relações Raciais (LAESER). Retrieved from http://www.laeser.ie.ufrj.br/

Plá, S. (2009). *Os cotistas negros nas universidades: Perfis e representações* [Black scholarship students in universities: Profiles and representations]. Unpublished master's dissertation in education, Universidade Estadual de Ponta Grossa, Paraná, Brazil.

Presidência da República. (1996). *Lei Nº 9.394, de 20 de dezembro de 1996: Estabelece as diretrizes e bases da educação nacional* [Law No. 9.394, of December 20, 1996: Establishes the guidelines and bases of national education]. Brasília: Casa Civil, Subchefia para Assuntos Jurídicos. Retrieved from http://www.planalto.gov.br/

Presidência da Republica. (2013). *Maioria dos beneficiários do Bolsa Família é composta por mulheres e negros, afirma Tereza Campello* [Majority of Bolsa Familia beneficiaries is composed of women and blacks, affirms Tereza Campello]. Retrieved from http://blog.planalto.gov.br/

Ribeiro, D. (1957). Culturas e línguas indígenas do Brasil [Indigenous cultures and languages in Brazil]. *Educação e Ciências Sociais, 2*(6), 1–102.

Rosemberg, F., Bazili, C., & Silva, P. V. B. (2003). Racismo em livros didáticos brasileiros e seu combate: Uma revisão da literatura [Brazilian textbooks and the fight against racism: A literature review]. *Educação e Pesquisa, 29*(1), 125–146.

Safa, H. (2007). Challenging *mestizaje:* A gender perspective of indigenous and Afrodescendant movements in Latin America. *Critique of Anthropology, 25*(3), 307–330.

Secretaria de Estado da Educação de São Paulo. (2010). *Ler e escrever: Livro de textos do aluno* [Read and write: Students' textbook]. São Paulo: Fundação para o Desenvolvimento da Educação. Retrieved from http://lereescrever.fde.sp.gov.br/

Secretaria de Estado da Educação de São Paulo. (2015). *Programa Ler e Escrever* [Read and Write Program]. São Paulo: Fundação para o Desenvolvimento da Educação. Retrieved from http://lereescrever.fde.sp.gov.br/

Silva, N. do V. (1978). *White-nonwhite income differentials: Brazil, 1960.* Unpublished doctoral thesis, University of Michigan, Ann Arbor.

Silva, P. B. G. e. (2004). Citizenship and education in Brazil: The contribution of Indian peoples and Blacks in the struggle for citizenship and recognition. In J. Banks (Ed.), *Diversity and citizenship education: Global perspectives* (pp. 185–214). San Francisco: Jossey-Bass.

Silva, P. B. G. e. (2011). Education on ethnic-racial relations from the perspective of Afro-descendants: Agenda for knowledge production. *Revista Interamericana de Educación para la Democracia/ Interamerican Journal of Education for Democracy, 4*(1), 73–86.

Silva, P. B. G. e, & Araújo-Oliveira, S. E. (2004). Cidadania, ética e diversidade: Desafios para a formação em pesquisa [Citizenship, ethics and diversity: Challenges for preparation in research]. In Bosio, B. G. de. (Ed.), *Actas del VI Encuentro corredor de las ideas del cono sur "Sociedade civil, democracia e integración."* Montevideo: Editora Universidad de la República, Uruguai.

Silvério, V. R. (2015). Relações étnico-raciais e educação: Entre a política de satisfação de necessidades e a política de transfiguração [Ethnic-racial relations and education: Between the politics of fulfillment and the transfiguration policy]. *Revista Eletrônica de Educação, 9*(2), 35–65.

Silvério, V. R., & Trinidad, C. T. (2012). Há algo novo a se dizer sobre as relações raciais no Brasil contemporâneo? [Is there something new to say about racial relationships in contemporary Brazil?] *Educação & Sociedade, 33*(120), 891–914.

Smolka, A. L. B. (2012). *A criança na fase inicial da escrita: A alfabetização como processo discursivo* [The children in the initial process of writing: Literacy as a discursive process]. São Paulo: Cortez.

Telles, E. (2003). *Racismo à Brasileira: Uma nova perspectiva sociológica* [Brazilian racism: A new sociological perspective]. Rio de Janeiro, Brazil: Relume-Dumará–Fundação Ford.

Telles, E, & Paixão, M. (2013). Affirmative action in Brazil. *Lasa Forum, 44*(2), 10–12.

UNESCO & Anhembi. (1955). *Relações raciais entre negros e brancos em São Paulo, ensaio sociológico sobre as origens, as manifestações e os efeitos do preconceito de cor no município de São Paulo, sob a direção dos professores Roger Bastide e Florestan Fernandes* [Racial relationships among Blacks and Whites in São Paulo, sociological essay over the origins, manifestations and effects of color prejudices in the city of São Paulo, under the direction of professors Roger Bastide and Florestan Fernandes]. São Paulo: Editora Anhembi.

Verrangia, D. (2009). *A educação das relações étnico-raciuis no ensino de ciências: Diálogos possíveis entre Brasil e Estados Unidos* [The education of ethnic-racial relationships in science education: Dialogues between Brazil and the United States]. Unpublished doctoral thesis in education, Universidade Federal de São Carlos, São Carlos, Brazil.

Verrangia, D., & Silva, P. B. G. (2010). Cidadania, relações étnico-raciais e educação: Desafios e potencialidades do ensino de ciências [Citizenship, racial-ethnic relationships and education: Challenges and potential of science teaching]. *Educação e Pesquisa, 36*(3), 705–718.

Viggiano, E., & Mattos, C. (2013). O desempenho de estudantes no ENEM 2010 em diferentes regiões brasileiras [Students' performance on 2010 ENEM among different Brazilian regions]. *Revista Brasileira de Estudos Pedagógicos, 94*(237), 417–438.

Part 7

Diversity and Citizenship Education: Implications of Theory and Research for Teaching

Chapter 20

Toward a Powerful Human Rights Curriculum in Schools: Problems and Possibilities

Walter C. Parker

University of Washington, Seattle

This concluding chapter revisits the goal of the conference and book and addresses it in two ways—first by considering obstacles to the goal's realization and then by evaluating a curriculum recommendation that emerged: human rights education (HRE). The chapter does not introduce readers to HRE or the reasons why it is important, nor does the chapter explore the ways that HRE is a site of struggle over the meanings and practices of human rights, justice, recognition, and living together peacefully. These contributions have been well made by several authors in this book (e.g., Moodley, Starkey, Bashir, and Osler) and elsewhere (e.g., Bajaj, 2011; Bowring, 2012; Gaudelli, 2016; Osler, 2015; Said, 1993; Spivak, 1998; Starkey, 2012; Suárez, 2007a). This chapter takes up a different concern and aims to make a different kind of contribution to HRE theory and practice: First, it considers HRE in the context of curriculum reform, and then it deploys recent scholarship from the critical sociology of knowledge to address the question, *What HRE knowledge should be taught in schools?* Finally, the chapter suggests the kind of work that is needed to make HRE a more robust curriculum initiative.

The premise of this chapter is that the central mission of schooling and the driving purpose of the school curriculum is to provide students with equitable access to knowledge—and not just any knowledge but what in this chapter is called powerful knowledge. This requires educators to distinguish among forms of knowledge and then to consider how the more powerful forms are allocated to students of varying social status.

Goal

As James Banks stated in his preface to this book, a conference was held in Seattle in June 2015. The goal of the conference and this book was for "educators in different parts of the world . . . [to] share perspectives, issues, theories, research, and strategies for *implementing citizenship education courses and programs in schools*" (Banks, 2015a, p. 2). I emphasize the final words to stress that the meeting and book have a practical goal. They are geared not only to analyzing a phenomenon but to doing something about it. This something, the goal statement continues, consists of "courses and programs in schools" that have a particular aim. That aim is to "facilitate the structural inclusion of students from diverse ethnic, cultural, linguistic, and religious groups into their societies and nation-states" (p. 2). As we can see, then, the goal is not theoretical but practical. It is aimed at improving practice in schools.

Further, the goal assumes that schools are instrumental for social cohesion. This is a warranted, long-standing assumption. As social scientists have demonstrated, schools serve national purposes (Beadie, 2016; Green, 1990). In a nation's early years, its school system devotes its powers to nation-building and cultural integration—to developing a national community unified by common beliefs, ideals, and customs. Later, the system turns to reproducing these in subsequent generations. An exemplar in the United States is when politician Horace Mann (1846) persuaded fellow Bostonians (White, Protestant, and male) to fund free primary education for children, especially immigrant children whose Roman Catholic parents were thought to be ignorant of or indifferent to a liberal-democratic ethos.

Citizenship education in any nation-state, not only democracies, is "relative to regime type" (Galston, 2001, p. 218). It is not suspended above the fray but integral to it. Nazi Germany had extensive citizenship education programs, both in school and out, tailored to the cultivation of Nazis. Plato had quite a different idea about citizenship education. He had a fair and just regime in mind for Athens but doubted citizens' ability to rule. In a liberal-democratic political culture, such as in Canada or South Korea, the animating idea is that ordinary citizens themselves are the governors. That is, "we the people" create governments to secure our rights, and we *consent* to be governed. Citizens need not only to comply with authorities but to become authorities, not only to obey laws but to make them, not only to abide by judges' rulings but to become judges, serve as jurors, and deliberate public policy with other citizens. It follows that there can be no democracies without democratic citizens. Democratic modes of association are constructed by citizens who have some idea of what they are doing. These citizens, too, are constructs; they are not born already inclined toward tolerating let alone respecting fellow citizens whose beliefs and practices may be sharply different. These inclinations are not found in our genes but are social, moral, and intellectual attainments. It is on this basis that educators are expected to mobilize curriculum and instruction in schools toward the formation of democratic citizens (Parker, 2003, 2014).

The conference goal—"citizenship education courses and programs in schools that will facilitate the structural inclusion of students from diverse ethnic, cultural, linguistic, and religious groups into their societies and nation-states" (Banks, 2015a, p. 2)—is not, then, radical or utopian, at least not in most of the societies represented in this volume. Instead, it is conventional and unremarkable. It is a conservative goal in that it aims to preserve and strengthen democratic institutions, not replace them. As such, it can serve as a resonant and practical goal for teachers, curriculum developers, and policy makers in societies that are aiming to be robust liberal democracies.[1]

This chapter will address this goal in two ways. In both, the theoretical perspective is sociological. First, the chapter will identify obstacles that impede achievement of the goal. Stated positively, the chapter will appraise the conditions and constraints within which progress toward the goal will be made. "This is the world as it is. This is where you start," argued activist Alinsky (1989, p. 14) in his famous book *Rules for Radicals: A Primer for*

Realistic Radicals. Extant conditions and forces may be ignored by dreamers and romantics but not by realists and activists who want to get things done. Gecan (2002) has clarified:

> As an organizer I start from where the world is, as it is, not as I would like it to be. That we accept the world as it is does not in any sense weaken our desire to change it into what we believe it should be—it is necessary to begin where the world is if we are going to change it to what we think it should be. (p. 38)

Second, the chapter will evaluate what I believe is the primary curricular recommendation to emerge, both explicitly and implicitly, from this conference and book: human rights education. I am interested in whether it is likely to succeed as a curriculum reform initiative—Does it have a chance? But I am interested also in whether it is *powerful*. By this I mean, with Young (2008, 2013), courses and programs that are generative and liberatory, that help students think the unthinkable and learn what they are unlikely to learn elsewhere. These are courses and programs that help students transcend the everyday, experiential knowledge with which they come to school, supplementing it with disciplinary knowledge—Durkheim's (1912/1965) esoteric knowledge or Vygotsky's (1986) scientific knowledge. This is, after all, why parents send their children to school: not to rehearse what they learn at home, temple, and neighborhood but to learn what they do not know, to broaden their horizons, to develop their capacity to think the "yet to be thought" (Bernstein, 2000, p. 30).

"This Is Where You Start"

The first obstacle is the tendency to inflate the potential of school reform and see it as a solution to social problems that originate in other institutions. The second is the abandonment of curriculum-making by curriculum scholars.

Swimming Upstream

We should not deceive ourselves about schools' place in society. Grubb and Lazerson (2004) have pointed to an "education gospel" that generates a continuous stream of exaggerated hope and hyperbole about the effectiveness of *school* reform as an instrument of broader *social* reform. Baker (2014) demonstrated that the gospel has spread worldwide, but Tyack and Cuban (1995) believed it to be a particularly American ideology of societal improvement *through the schools*. Cremin (1990) called it a "device." To contend that social problems can be solved by educational reform "especially educational reform *defined solely as school reform*, is not merely utopian and millennialist, it is at best a foolish and at worst a crass effort to direct attention away from those truly responsible for doing something" (p. 103; emphasis added). It is nonetheless widespread. Labaree (2012) called it the "school syndrome" and believed it to be hegemonic:

> We can understand the whole grand educational enterprise as an exercise in formalism. We assign formal responsibility to education for solving our most pressing social problems in light of our highest social ideals, with the tacit understanding that by

educationalizing these problem-solving efforts we are seeking a solution that is more formal than substantive. We are saying that we are willing to accept what education can produce—new programmes, new curricula, new institutions, new degrees, new educational opportunities—in place of solutions that might make real changes in the ways in which we distribute social power, wealth, and honour. (p. 154)

As Dewey wrote, "The reality of education is found in the personal and face-to-face contact of the teacher and the child"; however, "the conditions that underlie this contact dominate the education situation" (quoted in Westbury, 2008, p. 1). Dewey was accounting for the failure of progressive education proposals to take root in schools, and his explanation is that institutional structures and relations (really do) constrain and shape the practices of schooling. Agreeing, longtime editor of the *Journal of Curriculum Studies* Ian Westbury (2008) concluded that "the architecture of school systems is carefully designed to impede reform initiatives from above or outside" (p. 3). Whether centrally planned in national school systems or locally planned in states, school reforms such as those advocated in the book before us must swim upstream, against structural currents that are dedicated to sculpting the school into its present form: "Top-down curriculum construction can design new objects and systems, but can never give its developments an authentic institutional agency. Bottom-up development can yield agencies in local places, but cannot provide the conditions necessary for institutionalization of the new agencies" (p. 3).

Consequently, it is unlikely that schools can do much to "facilitate the structural inclusion of students from diverse ethnic, cultural, linguistic, and religious groups." The locus of the problem is outside the school system, residing mainly in the legal system, the political economy, and the cultural norms and folk beliefs of families, religions, and ethnic enclaves. On the other hand, schools can do *something* toward that end. After all, schools have potent resources that are institutionally unique to them: classrooms, teachers, curriculum, instruction, assessment, materials, and students whose parents have sent them to school for the purpose of learning its curriculum. It is within this agentic space that "citizenship education courses and programs" are created and will have whatever effects they can.

Global education in U.S. schools serves as a case study. There is a global education movement recently under way in local school districts across this country. "International" public schools are appearing in many U.S. cities. Typically, a school inserts the word *international* into its preexisting name. Alexander Hamilton Middle School becomes Alexander Hamilton International Middle School. Fueling the movement are calls to action from government and corporate leaders, prizes for excellence in global education, and an array of nongovernmental organizations providing materials and programs. There is a vision that students will come to know and care not only for Americans but for peoples everywhere; there is anxiety over the United States losing its competitive edge on a new, "flat" playing field; and there is much hyperbole about creating "global citizens." In a study of this movement, I found that *nationalism*, counterintuitively, is structuring the movement (Parker, 2011). A discourse of national security dominates, and it has both economic and military dimensions. The economic way to secure the nation is to improve its economic competitiveness; the military way is to strengthen its armed forces and intelligence community. In both, a problem is framed (flat world and terrorism), a corresponding solution is identified (school reform), and anxieties are mobilized to create a sense of urgency.

Alongside the dominant national security discourse are weaker discourses at the margins, jockeying for position. One, Global Perspective, gives global education a transnational, cultural meaning. Another, Cosmopolitanism, gives it a transnational political meaning. A third, International Student Body, gives it a cultural meaning again but in a decidedly student-centered way. These discourses may be described as follows:

- *Global Perspective*: Multiculturalism is rescaled from the nation to the globe, and some attention is paid to global connections and systems. Historically, this derives from an earlier wave of global education in U.S. schools in the 1960s and 1970s (Hanvey, 1978).

- *Cosmopolitanism*: Schools shift students' primary allegiance from the nation to the human family and Earth—from national citizen to global citizen. This is an ancient Greco-Roman idea recently revived by Nussbaum (2002).

- *International Student Body*: Immigration is putting the world into the classrooms, hallways, cafeterias, and playgrounds of public schools today. Seizing the opportunity, an "international" school is formed on the basis of its "international" students.

Of these, Cosmopolitanism is the weakest in relation to the discourse of national security and sometimes, therefore, is rejected outright. Case in point: Voting against proposed legislation for increased global education in Utah schools, a state senator explained that she was

> opposed to the anti-American philosophy that's somehow woven into all the classes as they promote the U.N. agenda. . . . I would like to have *American citizens* who know how to function in a global economy, not *global citizens*. (quoted in Fulton, 2008; emphasis added)

Global Perspective and International Student Body stand a better chance of challenging or at least surviving the dominant, nationalistic discourse because they are able to mobilize the instrumentalism of national security discourse. They can present themselves as solutions to the existential threats to the nation posed by globalization and terror. Moreover, both are comfortably nested in the mainstream multiculturalism that has settled into the nation's schools (Zimmerman, 2002). They can use multiculturalism's moderate rhetoric of inclusion as a resource to move a little from the national container: Global Perspective toward the world at large and International Student Body to the world at home—to the "glocal" scene of the underfunded and overstressed urban public school where structurally excluded immigrant students are most likely to be found.

I share this case to illustrate how curriculum reform efforts are structured by downstream, institutional forces. Here the force is nationalism, which carries even a potential corrective, global education, in its current. This conclusion is hardly original with me. Examples from earlier movements to institutionalize global education will illustrate. Writing between the two world wars in a volume entitled *International Understanding Through the Public School*

Curriculum, Kandel (1937) cautioned that a global education that wants to be more than national security education operating under an assumed name will have to emerge from *within* the national school system, recognizing and complying with its logics. It cannot be transplanted wholesale from another orbit. In the same vein, Boulding (1968) wrote a generation later that the question is not whether an alternative to nationalistic education can be imagined but

> whether we can develop an image of the world system which is at the same time realistic and also not threatening to the folk cultures within which the school systems are embedded; for if educators do not find a palatable formula, the "folk" will revolt and seek to divert formal education once again into traditional channels. (p. 650)

The Seattle conference goal faces a similar downstream current that will make it difficult for the desired school reform to gain traction. For if "citizenship education courses and programs in schools" are to be implemented in such a way that they facilitate the structural inclusion of students currently excluded or marginalized, they will somehow have to engage with the institutional forces that are creating the problem in the first place. Cremin, as we saw, considered this to be wishful thinking. Labaree believed that such a reform, were it to occur, would likely be formal rather than substantive. This is where you start.

Knowledge Blindness in Curriculum Scholarship

I turn now to a second obstacle to achieving the goal of the conference and book. The main concern of this chapter, recall, is the subject matter of HRE; consequently, the second obstacle is the widespread abandonment by curriculum scholars of precisely this concern—subject matter. The reason this is a salient obstacle is plain enough: Persons with the pertinent expertise (historical, comparative, theoretical, and practical) to assist with the development and implementation of the desired "citizenship education courses and programs in schools" are, generally speaking, attending to other things. Despite the hyperbole surrounding the contemporary "knowledge society" and today's "knowledge economies" and the "information age," the actual selection of knowledge and skills for teaching and learning in schools (i.e., the curriculum) is largely ignored by experts. Maton (2014) has called this "knowledge blindness" (p. 3). Knowledge is believed to be (re)shaping every aspect of contemporary social life today, he observed, "yet, *understanding knowledge* is not viewed as crucial to *understanding society*" (p. 1). He gave as an exemplar Castells's three-volume work *The Information Age,* where the definition of knowledge is relegated to a footnote as "a set of organized statements of facts or ideas" (quoted at p. 2). Castells, despite the title of his work, treats information as homogeneous and having no inner structure with properties or powers of its own, as if the forms knowledge takes are of no consequence. So, the very thing that is apparently now central to every aspect of our lives is itself not theorized or well understood.

How is it that knowledge blindness extends to the one field where it should be addressed explicitly and deliberately—education, particularly the curriculum field? There are a number of likely causes. It is due in part to the neoliberal juggernaut launched during the

Thatcher-Reagan years. Its testing-and-accountability imperative, coupled with its drive to privatize public schools, had the effect of commodifying knowledge and credentializing learning (Labaree, 2012). Curiously, knowledge itself is treated as a homogenous mass. Bernstein saw this, writing that knowledge in the so-called information age is believed to flow like money. "Indeed knowledge is not like money," he wrote, "it *is* money" (quoted in Maton, 2014, p. 2).

Knowledge blindness is due also, and more directly, to the rise of discourses in the education field that have redirected scholars' attention to other matters. Foremost are a *critical* discourse, a *learner* discourse, and a *learning* discourse. The first of these is a discourse of educational criticism that reveals how school curricula are formed in ways that reproduce the distribution of power in the surrounding society. Featured in this discourse is the unequal class- and race-based distribution of educational assets. This discourse produces findings of educational inequality, analyses thereof, and demands for equal access to schools and, within them, to knowledge. This is good as far as it goes, but it does not attend to the forms and other structural characteristics of the knowledge thus distributed. The question left unasked is *Access to what?*—to which knowledge? This discourse has become mainstream in educational scholarship, despite its radical origins, and is today's orthodoxy. The seminal works in England were by Bernstein (1971) and Young (1971) and then a bit later in the United States by Bowles and Gintis (1976), Apple (1979), and Giroux (1979). Mostly neo-Marxist, but not exclusively (e.g., Pinar, 1975), this critical discourse focuses mainly on political-economic factors that are external to the education sector of society but structure what goes on there. Moore and Muller (1999) have summarized: "Knowledge relations were transcribed [first] as class relations" (p. 190) and soon thereafter as gender relations and then race relations.

The second discourse concerns the *learner*. This discourse is child-centered and progressive. It places the learner in familial, ethnic, and other primary cultural contexts and identifications and uses these referents to help students see themselves in the curriculum and to help them learn. Learners have cultures, not deficits; they have funds of relevant and usable knowledge, not disadvantages. Contemporary exemplars of this literature are Gay (2000) and Howard (2010). This discourse appears now to be even more mainstream than critical discourse, particularly in the wide-ranging discussions of culturally relevant pedagogy and differentiated instruction, both now standard fare in teacher education programs.

The third, a *learning* discourse, draws attention to the psychology of learning. It is dominated currently by a new education discipline, learning sciences, that is quickly replacing educational psychology, at least in name. This discourse achieved prominence with the publication of a National Academies of Science report, *How People Learn* (Bransford, Brown, & Cockling, 2000). In this discourse, teaching is for and about learning; and learning includes learning processes, learning environments, and learners' sociocultural and familial referents. *Knowledge* in this discourse is, as above, like money: homogeneous and interchangeable. Deng (2015) has summarized:

> The relative absence of attention to knowledge or content . . . has something to
> do with a remarkable rise of a learning discourse which has impacted our way of

thinking and talking about education—a language that construes teaching as facilitation of learning. (p. 723)

Learning in this discourse is intellectual labor done by the learner him- or herself—this is constructivism—but it is facilitated and scaffolded, assessed and evaluated, by the teacher. Additionally, learning is enhanced by new media and information technologies, which are valorized in this discourse. In all of this, Deng concluded, "knowledge is merely a tool, with no educational value or significance in itself" (p. 723).

I have simplified these three education discourses. There is actually a good deal of overlap among them and variation within them, but each highlights a crucial facet of the educational enterprise: schools' allocational role in distributing power, wealth, and status; the child, understood as a social being; and processes of learning.

For present purposes I note that the three discourses, while important in their own ways, do not attend to knowledge—its forms and attributes—nor do they propose curriculum: a selection of subject matter that students should learn at school. This is a problem because, since not everything can be taught, choices have to be made and inevitably are made. This choosing involves expertise, ideology, power, tradition, inertia, serendipity, and more. It is anything but neutral, as Young (1971) and Apple (1979) established long ago. The curriculum is a social construct; this is now a truism. As such, it relays power relations from the surrounding society into the school. Still, a curriculum is needed if the school is to be a school, for the curriculum is the school's defining characteristic, its raison d'être. It is the asset that anchors and justifies the others: teachers, instruction, students, classrooms, assessment, parent-teacher conferences, administrators, cafeterias, and custodians. Save for its curriculum, there is no need for the school. And the Seattle conference goal, recall, concerns the school curriculum.

McEneaney and Meyer (2000) have explained that "research inattention to curricular content arises, not because scholars think the matter unimportant, but because they tend to see it as obvious." Scholars take curriculum for granted because "the necessary content of modern education . . . is mostly established" (p. 191). It may have been necessary for the likes of Dewey and Durkheim, writing at the peak of the industrial age, to spell out a theory of content selection for schools, but today we accept more or less without question that schools teach math, science, social studies, literature, and language. *This* is the curriculum—these are the school subjects. The matter is settled, more or less around the world (Baker, 2014), and the urgent questions are about other things: achieving equal access to the curriculum (whatever it is), achieving equal learning of it (whatever), better understanding how people learn it (whatever), and increasing its (whatever) rigor and depth.

There are forms of knowledge, some more powerful than others. Yet scholarly inattention to the matter has thrown schools and curriculum standards into a fog. Schools' efforts to close racial and class achievement gaps and, quoting the conference goal, to "facilitate the structural inclusion of students from diverse ethnic, cultural, linguistic, and religious groups into their societies and nation-states" must proceed without curricular expertise. The curriculum field, having been drawn to noncurricular objects (neoliberalism, reproduction, learners, learning), is of little help to the aims of this conference and book.

Illustrating the extremity of the situation, the Curriculum Studies division of the world's largest educational research society, the American Educational Research Association, has few papers on curriculum. Papers in the "curriculum" division focus instead on the political economy, on students and their identities and funds of knowledge, or on learning processes—on society, learners, and learning—rather than on knowledge: everything but the curriculum.[2] The field is mired in a rearticulation mode—restating the seminal, critical work of the 1970s and reapplying it to contemporary policy contexts and identity groups: "The main move is to attach knowledge to categories of knowers and to their experience and subjectivities" (Moore & Muller, 1999, p. 190). This is, indeed, important work, but the project does not end there. Curriculum-making is needed, but the curriculum field has surrendered curriculum-making to other communities—to policy makers whose testing-and-accountability initiatives have narrowed the curriculum in many schools and to the various subject-area professional organizations that perennially (re)develop lists of "curriculum standards."

A body of recent scholarship by sociologist Michael Young and colleagues has addressed this lacuna directly. This is the same Young who, in a 1971 book called *Knowledge and Control*, launched the critical discourse discussed earlier—the very discourse that jettisoned knowledge from the curriculum field by transcribing the field as power relations. Young (2013) has now called the situation a "crisis" (p. 101) because curriculum practice is left without expertise and curriculum theory is left without epistemology—a theory of knowledge for content selection—even though this is the distinguishing object of the school and the field. While Young laments his role in creating the problem, he is keen to solve it. The next section will introduce his current analytic framework, and then I will apply it to what emerged from the conference as a central curriculum recommendation: human rights education.

Powerful Knowledge and Human Rights Education

In this section, I evaluate HRE as a curriculum proposal. I do so in light of the conference goal and the two obstacles examined above. To begin, I consider sociological scholarship on the question *Which knowledge is of most worth?* From this, we can ask whether the knowledge in HRE has achieved the epistemological strength needed to do the work required of it.

Powerful Knowledge

Young's theory of school curriculum—the knowledge selected for teaching and learning in schools—builds on the foundation laid by Durkheim (1912/1965), Bernstein (1971), and Vygotsky (1986). Young's theory centers on the koanic dyad "knowledge of the powerful" versus "powerful knowledge." The intent of the theory is to vindicate and strengthen the radical social justice aim of critical curriculum studies (e.g., his earlier work, 1971). This requires rescuing critical curriculum studies from the clutches of an overly simplistic social constructivism that has consumed critical curriculum studies. The means by which this recue is effected is (to put it positively) to reintroduce knowledge as a social justice imperative or (to put it negatively) to not undermine education's social justice aim with knowledge blindness. Moore (2013) has interpreted the earlier error this way:

> Radical forms of social constructionism . . . fitted the theoretical space in which "official" school knowledge was being problematized [in the 1970s] but did so in ways that . . . tended towards a form of relativism that ultimately undermined the radical political aspirations of many associated with the new sociology of education. (p. 32)

In terms of Young's dyad, we can say that curriculum theory after the early 1970s began to focus one-dimensionally on knowledge of the powerful, that is, on Marx's axiom, "The ideas of the ruling class are in every epoch the ruling ideas" (Marx & Engles, 1846/1970, p. 64; also Bourdieu & Passeron, 1977). This was a limited effort because it ignored a second question that needs to be asked in tandem: Which forms of knowledge make a better school curriculum? Put differently, if equal *access* to the school curriculum were to be achieved for historically excluded groups, would not the *substance* of that curriculum—its particular knowledge and skills—matter? Or is the goal equal access to *whatever*? Because the goal is decidedly not "equal access to whatever," the struggle for access must be paired, if it is to be coherent and liberatory, with the struggle to define the substance to which access is sought. By analogy, were a juggler to keep only one ball in the air, the audience would rightly complain that this was not juggling at all. Two balls, at the very least, must be kept in the air at once: the social construction of knowledge and the forms of knowledge thus produced.[3]

Eisner (2002) clarified that schools cannot teach all the knowledge that is valuable; the array of curricular possibilities is too vast. There is inevitably a giant "null curriculum" (p. 97): the curriculum that is not taught. Accordingly, a small sample of subject matter needs to be selected for teaching and learning in school. This is inexorably a political and social process. The resulting selection is a construct coming neither from the gods nor from nature but from social beings who live, move, and are moved by particular relations of meaning (the symbolic order) and power (the political order). But this fact does not eliminate the need for knowledge selection—for a curriculum. The error was to take up the one concern without also taking up the second. Accordingly, curricularists sidelined a crucial question: What knowledge should be featured in the school curriculum?

Endeavoring to correct this error of omission, Young (2008, 2013; Young & Lambert, 2014) now brings knowledge back into the equation explicitly and makes a social justice argument for teaching powerful forms of knowledge at school. He identifies three attributes. First, powerful knowledge is different from the knowledge children learn at home and in the neighborhood. Let us call this "everyday" knowledge, and it is dense, textured, and context-dependent. Children come to school generally to learn a different kind of knowledge—knowledge that is more abstract, more generalizable, more context-independent. In Bernstein's (1999) well-known typology, these two kinds of knowledge, together with their social bases, are called horizontal and vertical discourses, respectively. Schools evolved to teach vertical discourse or what Vygotsky (1986) called "scientific" concepts— in today's education jargon, "disciplinary knowledge." This is knowledge that children generally do not learn at home (some do, of course, which gives them an advantage at school). Second, origins: Powerful knowledge is produced through argumentation in somewhat autonomous communities of specialists who value evidence and disputation and whose processes and products depend on transparency (publication). Why? So that findings and arguments are available for interrogation and replication. Typically, these specialist communities are research labs, studios, seminars, think tanks, guilds, and universities. Third, powerful knowledge is complex, requiring a coherent network of relationships among core and peripheral concepts.

Powerful knowledge, then, in this particular usage, is differentiated, specialized, and organized. It is a more powerful form of knowledge for school teaching and learning than the context-dependent, familiar, everyday knowledge of home because of the reliability of its explanations and the generative ways of thinking about the world that it promotes. It is "indispensable to enabling students to transcend the limitations of everyday experience *and* develop critical awareness of the forces structuring their own lives" (Beck, 2013, p. 187; see also Freire, 1981). Powerful knowledge is specialized, not general, but it has what Young (2013) has called "generalizing capacities" (p. 108). It predicts, it explains, and it enables us to imagine alternatives. As examples, consider how evolutionary theory explains the diversity of life on Earth or, in this volume, Castles's explanation of migration and Levinson and Luna Elizarrarás's explanation of civic education in Mexico.

Let us take the three attributes in turn. The claim that knowledge is differentiated is based on Durkheim's "magnificent insight into the relationships between symbolic orders, social relationships and the structuring of experience" (Bernstein, 1971, p. 133). Studying the place of religion in premodern societies, Durkheim saw differences between everyday knowledge and esoteric knowledge. The former was context-dependent; the latter, abstract. The former was knowledge of known people, things, and forces (e.g., kin, neighbors, tools, farm, wind), and the latter, "sacred"—religious beliefs and principles, often unseen, a province regulated by priests. Durkheim's "magnificent insight" was that this epistemological distinction persisted through the Scientific Revolution until this day, albeit transformed in substance. Muller (2001) has commented:

> Durkheim makes the argument, more strongly as the book progresses, that science, far from making a break with superstition and religion, is formally isomorphic with religious thought. Both are sacred modes of cognition. . . . On the formal level they are equivalent. (p. 132)

The sciences and their agents (natural and social scientists, professors and teachers) trade in esoteric knowledge (*foreign policy, cell division, 17th-century empires, algebra, plate tectonics, literary theory, citizenship*), while everyone (teacher and student alike, scientist, priest, and parishioner) trades in everyday knowledge. Schools evolved to teach children and youth decontextualized symbolic orders that are abstracted from the familiar and the everyday. Teachers must, of course, build bridges between students' personal, cultural, everyday knowledge and the specialized, disciplinary knowledge schools are trying to teach. This is instruction, not to be confused with curriculum, and it is the learning of the curriculum that is the aim of building the bridge in the first place. The central purpose of schooling, then, is "to provide students with equitable access to powerful knowledge that is ultimately capable of taking them beyond their experience" (Rata & Barrett, 2014, p. 3). For Dewey (1902), as for Vygotsky (1986), similarly, students are helped *at school* to take the step from personal experience to abstract forms of thought, from "spontaneous" (everyday) to "scientific" concepts, as Vygotsky called them (p. lx). "The strength of scientific concepts," Vygotsky wrote, "lies in their conscious and deliberate character." By contrast, spontaneous concepts "are strong in what concerns the situational, empirical, and practical" (p. 194). In this way, powerful knowledge can help students reflect on the near and the familiar, but also it can liberate them from its enclaves. The two, as Moll (1990) has written, "are interconnected and interdependent; their development is mutually influential" (p. 10). He explained:

> One cannot exist without the other. . . . That is, everyday concepts *mediate* the acquisition of scientific concepts. However, Vygotsky . . . proposed that everyday concepts also become dependent on, are mediated and transformed by the scientific concepts; they become the "gate" though which conscious awareness and control enter the domain of the everyday concepts. . . . [They] "blaze the trail for the development of everyday concepts" upward toward the scientific. (p. 10)

This is the emancipatory potential of powerful knowledge. This is how it frees students to think the "yet to be thought" (Bernstein, 2000, p. 30). It is precisely the reason why parents send their children to school but also why they clash with educators over the contents of the school curriculum. Looking at their child's science or history class, parents are conflicted: They want their children to have access to powerful, worldly knowledge, but not when it draws them away from the beliefs and bonds of the home. Parents want their children to be exposed to a range of beliefs, but not those that undermine their own convictions. They want their children to be taught to think critically, but not when the tools of critical thought are used to interrogate the parents' values. They want the school to open windows on the world, but they want it to mirror and affirm the home, too. In liberal-democratic societies where parental consent is valued alongside scientific inquiry and personal freedom, this is material for routine parent-school conflict, and it is *curricular* conflict.[4]

Moving to the second attribute, let us consider what it means to say that powerful knowledge is specialized. Specialized knowledge is not general knowledge. It is narrower and deeper, as in a division of labor. Its boundaries are well marked, and its substantive structure is helpfully insulated from other divisions. These boundaries mark a field's focus and objects of study—its categories and concerns. Biology and chemistry overlap, but they are distinct, each with its own concentrations, journals, university departments, students, academic societies, and debates. (To be privy to these debates, one needs to attend the society's meetings and read and contribute to its journals.) The same is true of poetry and rhetoric, history and economics, filmmaking and craft beer making, journalism, and so forth. Young (2013) has clarified: "This does not mean that boundaries are fixed and not changeable." After all, they *are* social constructs. "However, it does mean that cross-disciplinary research and learning depend on discipline-based knowledge" (p. 108).

Further, powerful knowledge is specialized in how it is produced and communicated. Its production occurs in knowledge-generating communities: members of academic associations and university departments, filmmakers, craft beer makers. Before the Scientific Revolution, that community was the upper reaches of the Christian church. The pope decided whether the moon had mountains. He decided it did not, that it, like other heavenly orbs, was perfectly smooth and spherical. When Galileo observed something different through his telescope, the Inquisition brought him to Rome and had him recant. The Scientific Revolution gradually replaced the church with the academy and doctrine with observation as the legitimate authorities for interpreting nature and society. Today, Pluto is no longer a planet, a decision rendered not by priests (or parents, generals, or government officials) but, independent of these, by the voting members of the International Astronomical Union at their 2006 convention in Prague.

What is haiku poetry, and what forms can it take? Is Earth warming, and is human activity causing it? What are the structural conditions needed for a struggling democracy to thrive? The answers to these questions are, in the current epoch, to be found (and interrogated and revised) in knowledge-generating communities where transparency (publication, exhibition), criticism, and fallibility are established conventions. The acceptance of those findings is by no means guaranteed, clearly,[5] but the school subjects stand more or less ready to recontextualize them for general education in schools when the dust settles. Banks (1993) illustrated this—the ongoing production/revision of powerful knowledge— when he argued more than two decades ago in a specialist community's flagship journal, *Educational Researcher*, that "the curriculum should be reformed so that it will more accurately reflect the histories and cultures of ethnic groups and women" (p. 4). By criticizing "Western traditionalist" scholars who believed "that Western history, literature, and culture are endangered in the school and university curriculum because of the push by feminists, ethnic minority scholars, and other multiculturalists for curriculum reform and transformation" (p. 4), Banks pushed the scholarly consensus toward curriculum reform and transformation. Of what? Of powerful knowledge itself.

I turn now to the third attribute of powerful knowledge, its organization. Vertical discourse features core ideas and tensions that are related systematically. This is the "conceptual framework" and "literature" that graduate students are required to master as they move toward proposing a dissertation. Study of the discipline of history, for example, requires entry to its unique substantive and syntactical structures, the latter involving thinking like historians—interrogating sources, corroborating accounts, and using evidence and warrants to support a thesis. To understand a concept, whether sourcing, corroboration, or thesis, is to understand the attributes shared by multiple examples of the concept. To understand the concepts in their conceptual network signals expertise.

Advanced secondary school courses, such as Advanced Placement courses in the United States, present teachers and students with a vast number of concepts for teaching and learning but little in the way of guidelines as to how they should be organized (grouped, sequenced, and paced) for instruction. In a program of research on these courses, I collaborated with teachers to distinguish core and peripheral concepts (Parker & Lo, 2016). This study permitted core concepts to be singled out for recursive, cyclical teaching, strengthening them over time and across examples. In this way, advanced courses can be something more than test-prep gauntlets, achieving in-depth learning of core ideas. To begin to bring this around to HRE, let me just indicate that for an HRE curriculum to approach this level of organization there needs to be guidance from the specialist HRE communities on core and peripheral subject matter.

Let me reiterate that powerful knowledge is a construct and that its construction is embedded in power relations (a novel idea in the 1970s, an axiom today). But that is not the whole story. Knowledge not only is constructed but has forms and features. Knowledge is real. There is declarative and procedural knowledge (knowledge and skills); there is esoteric and everyday knowledge (science and common sense). Questions then arise about whose knowledge and which forms of knowledge schools should teach. Young's response, building on Bernstein, Vygotsky, and Durkheim, is that schools should teach forms that are (a) more transferable and transformative than everyday knowledge or common sense; (b) produced, critiqued, and revised in specialized communities with transparent norms of inquiry and argumentation; and (c) organized into coherent symbolic orders, such as the disciplines of geography and biology. Young summarized these under the name "powerful knowledge." In a justly famous essay, especially important to the U.S. context, Delpit (1988) called powerful knowledge "codes of power." She has argued "that we must take the responsibility to teach them . . . to students who do not already possess them" (p. 293). Young (2013) called them a learner's "entitlement" (p. 107). This is the social justice imperative for identifying and teaching not just any knowledge but powerful knowledge.

Multiple objections can be raised to this conception of powerful knowledge. They range from familiar arguments for curriculum tracking (the curriculum should respond to students' capabilities or vocational prospects) to relativist-constructivist arguments that all knowledge is arbitrary and, therefore, all content selection is merely ideological. The former had a broad and diverse constituency across the 20th century, from parents and progressive educators to political and business leaders. It thrives today. The latter has been fashionable since the 1970s but, preoccupied with debunking, offers few alternatives. Straddling these two objections is a currently popular "21st-century skills" narrative that sees knowledge as fluid and changing so quickly that schools should not attempt to single out any particular slice of it for instruction beyond literacy and mathematics and, instead, teach students how to use search engines, how to collaborate, and how to think.

A different sort of objection concerns the tension Dewey tried to resolve in his famous 1902 essay *The Child and the Curriculum*. Advocates of child-centered education (e.g., the learner discourse above) may not warm to Young's curriculum-centered argument. Yet Young is child-centered, too, in arguing that instruction needs to bridge the gap between the child's known world and the not-yet-known, the world of family and the public space, the everyday and the theoretical. This bridging is instruction's famous task, and it requires the teacher both to know and to respond to the child. Dewey was famously opposed to intemperate child-centered experiments carried out in his name, where the curriculum catered to children's interests. But he was opposed as well to the opposite extreme where schooling was rote, grinding, and ignorant or dismissive of children's actual lives. The point to be emphasized here is that while the school's moral and intellectual obligation is to provide students with access to the more powerful forms of knowledge to which they are entitled and for which they have been sent to school, this does not entitle teachers to dismiss or devalue students' lived experience and home life (see Gay, 2000; Noddings, 2003). The two are to be valued in tandem and treated not as two things but as two dimensions of one thing—education.

Let me address one more objection, which will transition us to the next section. It is that the disciplines should not dictate the school curriculum. I agree with this assertion, but I do not regard it as a salient objection to the curriculum theory outlined in this chapter. The objection may arise because the academic disciplines serve as exemplars of powerful knowledge. They epitomize specialist communities that, via evidence-based argumentation protocols, aim to produce reliable, organized, and transferable knowledge. But we should recognize that there are specialist communities outside the university as well. Craft beer makers were given earlier, as were artists and journalists. The important point is that specialist communities, whether or not the academic disciplines, valorize knowledge growth, transparency, cross-examination of evidence and interpretations, argument, fallibility, and revision. If they do not have peer-reviewed journals, as the disciplines must, they do have other regulatory discourses for vetting claims—competitions and exhibitions in art and the Pulitzer Prize in journalism, for example. While the academic disciplines exemplify knowledge-generating communities, and this is why they have come to be institutionalized in the school curriculum, they are nevertheless *resources* for the school curriculum, not its master (Tyler, 1949). The reason is that the ultimate purpose of schooling is not to produce disciplinary experts but to produce democratic citizens—people who can pursue the common good alongside private goods, fulfilling their obligations as wise members of a democratic public (see Thornton & Barton, 2010). In democracies at least, this is precisely why HRE is needed and why the strength of its knowledge base needs to be ensured, not assumed.

Human Rights Education

With this sociological conception of powerful knowledge in hand, we can ask whether HRE's knowledge base is powerful. In this section, I venture my tentative answer. I do so as a friend of HRE, and an advocate, but a nonspecialist. I hope that HRE specialists can generate a more nuanced answer.

First, *is it differentiated?* I would say yes. Human rights knowledge is not everyday knowledge or common sense. Its standards and principles are esoteric, not taken for granted or everyday. They are abstract and, therefore, transferable from case to case. It is on the basis of these abstractions that violations are recognized as such, as something more than negative and demeaning, and then corrective, collective action is taken. What I gather are the core concepts of human rights knowledge—human rights, universal respect, struggle, freedom, peaceful coexistence—are not confined to learners' daily contexts. They transcend experience. The discourse is imaginative and theoretical; the grammar, subjunctive. The development of these human rights concepts, each involving a diverse set of concrete examples, requires education. But we should note that the interdependence of everyday and schooled concepts, the way one mediates and elaborates the other, is especially useful in

HRE, where rights, protections, and violations are as personal and local as they are universal and cosmopolitan.

Second, *is it specialized?* Somewhat. Human rights knowledge is grounded and codified in international law and justice and several academic disciplines. There are by now hundreds of international declarations, covenants, and conventions that constitute this body of knowledge, at the center of which is the Universal Declaration of Human Rights (UDHR), adopted by the General Assembly of the United Nations in 1948. Human rights knowledge is regulated by scholarly societies (international law is a professional field with meetings, codes, journals, university departments, professors, and students). Also, human rights is a scholarly arena within and among several disciplines, such as moral philosophy, international relations, law, sociology, and political science. Secondary schools generally do not have human rights departments or specialist teachers of human rights, certainly not in the same way they have math departments and algebra teachers; instead, human rights is likely to be a topic or unit, usually in a social studies course (e.g., world history, current affairs).[6] In higher education, on the other hand, courses and programs can be found at universities around the world. Interdisciplinary centers exist, such as the Institute for the Study of Human Rights at Columbia University and the Center for Human Rights at the University of Washington. The former offers an undergraduate major in human rights, and the latter, an undergraduate minor.

Third, *is it organized?* Again, only somewhat. While lacking the systematic organization of fields such as biology and geography, human rights knowledge does have a rough conceptual framework—a network of concepts and principles—and a corresponding literature at the center of which is a core text of global reach, the UDHR, and several secondary texts (the International Covenant on Economic, Social and Cultural Rights; International Covenant on Civil and Political Rights; and Convention on the Rights of the Child). As an example of the conceptual network, we can say that *human rights* are rights, they are plural, and they are universal. Moreover, they have priority (violations are matters of grave injustice); they are inalienable (they cannot be removed); and they are conceptualized and practiced on both moral and legal platforms (Nickel, 2014). Or in the words of the United Nations (U.N. High Commissioner for Human Rights, 2016), these

> are rights inherent to all human beings, whatever our nationality, place of residence, sex, national or ethnic origin, colour, religion, language, or any other status. We are all equally entitled to our human rights without discrimination. These rights are all interrelated, interdependent and indivisible.

We can imagine that the *knowledge* taught in HRE would comprise these core texts and concepts, the histories of their development, biographies of key actors and their struggles, and an array of examples and nonexamples, including those from the students' own communities but also those from far away in both space and time.

Each of the three criteria is debatable, as is the extent to which HRE satisfies them. But let us return finally to the two obstacles introduced earlier and ask how HRE fares in light of them: the structural constraints that make curriculum reform unlikely and curriculum scholars' inattention to content selection—knowledge blindness.

Swimming upstream. HRE is grounded in a normative vision of freedom, justice, and the peaceful coexistence of people around the world. As Starkey (this volume) stated, it is fundamentally a vision of "learning to live together." The vision is utopian, but there are significant structural developments already under way that support it. First, the world's largest intergovernmental organization, the United Nations, has formally agreed to it. Its declaration, the UDHR, spells out the vision's concepts, standards, and principles. Second, the ratification of the UDHR spawned what Bashir (this volume) called "the human rights revolution." It is integral to a modern cultural model that is nearly worldwide and includes the normalization of a human rights discourse, mass schooling, and participatory citizenship. McEneaney and Meyer (2000) have observed a rising tide of mass schooling in modern sensibilities such that modern "educational systems are fundamentally engaged in a project of constructing individuals who understand themselves and others as having interests and the capacity to act rationally on them" (p. 193). This model involves an institutionalized framing of the appropriate ways for a state to proceed in such areas as mass education, and it has circulated globally. Similarly, Baker (2015) has demonstrated that "a schooled society" (p. 765) has arrived, worldwide. "Most people in most nations" now go to school for considerable amounts of time: "A robust culture of education influences fundamental processes that construct society—from the labor market to political action and personal identity." There has been an education revolution with widespread cultural effects involving the family (e.g., parenting), the organization of religious communities, the professions, political culture, and definitions of personal success, including the new cult of lifelong learning: "The education revolution has created a new, global, educated population, a condition thought improbable as recently as 50 years ago" (p. 765). As a rising tide lifts all boats, so HRE should be lifted accordingly. As modern mass schooling spreads human rights discourse such that greater numbers of secondary school students are actually reading and applying the UDHR, there should be greater curricular accommodation for HRE.[7]

Yet realism cautions that in nationalistic political cultures such as the United States, France, and China, the downstream current of nationalism will swamp a cosmopolitan project such as HRE. Even though globalization has supported an education revolution along with what Bashir (this volume) called "new regimes of citizenship" existing above and below the Westphalian nation-state, and even though the new regimes are reterritorializing citizenship particularly in the Levant and the Indian subcontinent today, civic education is normally tied to the territorial nation-state. A prime example was given in the account of "global education" presented earlier in this chapter. Another is the civil rights narrative in the United States, where the familiar historical referents are *national* referents. They are from the founding era of the nation-state and the civil rights movement of the 20th century: Martin Luther King, Jr., Malcolm X, George Wallace, and Rosa Parks. Students read not the UDHR but the Declaration of Independence, the Bill of Rights, and King's "Letter from a Birmingham Jail."

Bashir's argument is that civic education among regional populations with diverse and interconnected histories can, perhaps, loosen civic education from its national container and promote multiple identifications and affinities. However, nation-states do exist; they do take their sovereignty seriously; they do expect their schools to serve national, not cosmopolitan, purposes; and they will not be loosening their grip on education anytime soon. Indeed, they are eager to beat other nations on the international tables. This is not to say that there are no transnational initiatives under way in local places, but as emphasized earlier in this chapter, the local agencies (such as the teacher cases presented in this volume) cannot provide the structural conditions necessary for their institutionalization (Westbury, 2008).

Knowledge blindness. The general solution to "knowledge blindness" is presented in the title of Young's 2008 book *Bringing Knowledge Back In*. This means that curricularists need again to recognize knowledge as the central feature of education, as did Dewey (1902) before it was marginalized as merely an artifact of power by the critical curriculum studies movement that was initiated, ironically, by Young (1971) himself. What "bringing knowledge back in" means for HRE is reclaiming the radical social justice dimension of knowledge itself—in this case, of the concepts, standards, and principles associated with human rights. Further, it means engaging in curriculum-making rather than only curriculum critique—that is, developing HRE courses and programs. This entails selecting, organizing, and sequencing subject matter and then, as Delpit (1988) admonished, teaching it.

Fortunately, a good deal of work has already been accomplished by various organizations. Prominent are the various initiatives under way by Amnesty International (2014); the U.N. Educational, Scientific and Cultural Organization; an international organization called Human Rights Education Associates (Suárez, 2007a); and the U.N. High Commissioner for Human Rights. From the latter, a World Programme for Human Rights Education (U.N. High Commissioner for Human Rights, 2014) is currently under way. It was proclaimed in 2004 by the General Assembly with the goal of "advancing the implementation of human rights education programmes" (p. 4) around the world. There are seven objectives:

1. To promote the development of a culture of human rights;

2. To promote a common understanding, based on international instruments, of basic principles and methodologies for human rights education;

3. To ensure a focus on human rights education at the national, regional, and international levels;

4. To provide a common collective framework for action by all relevant actors;

5. To enhance partnership and cooperation at all levels;

6. To survey, evaluate, and support existing human rights education programmes, to highlight successful practices, and to provide an incentive to continue and/or expand them and to develop new ones;

7. To promote implementation of the United Nations Declaration on Human Rights Education and Training. (p. 4)

The World Programme is now in its third phase. The first (2005–2009) "was dedicated to the integration of human rights education in the primary and secondary school systems"

(U.N. High Commissioner for Human Rights, 2014, p. 5). The second (2010–2014) "focused on human rights education in higher education and human rights training for teachers and educators, civil servants, law enforcement officials and military personnel at all levels" (p. 6). The third (2015–2019) is a plan of action "to strengthen implementation of human rights education in the primary and secondary school systems and in higher education, and human rights training for teachers and educators" (p. 6). According to the plan, human rights education encompasses

(a) Knowledge and skills—learning about human rights and human rights mechanisms and acquiring skills to apply them in a practical way in daily life;

(b) Values, attitudes, and behavior—developing values and reinforcing attitudes and behavior which uphold human rights;

(c) Action—taking action to defend and promote human rights. (p. 4)

The question remains whether the knowledge, skills, values, and action are powerful. They are stated in such general terms that it is difficult to make a determination. I leave it to those with greater knowledge of the World Programme to judge the epistemological power of what it aims to teach. My primary interest here is to proffer a set of criteria by which its power can be assessed: its differentiation from everyday knowledge, its production and criticism in knowledge-generating communities with the necessary expertise and protocols for criticism and revision, and the internal organization of its concepts and principles. The fact that there are "instruments," as the program calls them—texts that can be studied and which are grounded in international communities, debates, and agreements—bodes well for the educative power of the World Programme.

Conclusion

What is HRE, why is it needed, and in what ways is it a site of contention and struggle? These questions are addressed in several chapters in this book and in many works beyond it. I have addressed a different sort of question: What is the knowledge students are expected to learn in HRE, and is it robust? If it is robust, or can be made so, can it then be institutionalized in the school curriculum, negotiating the conditions that constrain curriculum reform?

The approach taken here to answer these questions is critical (emancipatory) in that it attends to power and the power–knowledge relationship, and it seeks to free students from oppressive conditions. Yet it diverges from mainstream critical pedagogy by attending also to the structural forms and features of knowledge. That is, it does not veer off into knowledge blindness. Two balls are juggled; the baby is not thrown out with the bathwater. I am aware that this attention to knowledge and its forms risks being branded as conservative, elitist, masculinist, or traditionalist, but that is precisely the reductionist error made earlier, in the 1970s, which this approach seeks to correct. Knowledge cannot be reduced to knowers, nor can it be reduced to power; the relationship is more complicated and potentially more fruitful, as I have tried to show. Knowledge matters, and it is not homogeneous "like money."

HRE is only one of many proposals made for the school curriculum (see "education gospel"; Grubb & Lazerson, 2004). I believe that its knowledge base requires additional development and specification before it can secure a stable place in the school curriculum. Progress is being made, but it is impeded on several fronts. Not only is there competition from reform proposals that promise to affect more directly the economic security of the nation-state, but too often the knowledge base of HRE is assumed, as though no specification were needed, as though we share a common understanding of which knowledge and skills students should learn in the domain of human rights. Moreover, HRE is embroiled in debates that question its legitimacy. Its ties to Western colonialism, its faux neutrality, its individualism, its hollow appropriation by governments, its dependence on a constitutive Other with resulting rescue narratives—these are open issues (see American Anthropological Association, 1947; Bajaj, 2011; Bowring, 2012; Said, 1993). These debates are needed, for they are precisely what specialist communities do to refine, specify, and remodel their domains, in both substance and syntax. Yet, at the same time, they cast doubt on the validity of HRE.

In my judgment, it is difficult to find a more attractive curricular alternative for schools than human rights education when the goal is to implement "citizenship education courses and programs in schools that will facilitate the structural inclusion of students from diverse ethnic, cultural, linguistic, and religious groups into their societies and nation-states." On-the-ground curriculum alternatives, let us be clear, are the coin of curriculum-making. A *what* needs to be selected—subject matter, a curriculum—to which culturally relevant instruction (bridging) can be applied. Multicultural education as conceived by Banks (2013) is certainly a viable curriculum alternative in many nations. It is closely related to HRE, but its origin is not only Western but more specifically national. In the United States, for example, it derives from the civil rights movement of the 1950s and 1960s (see Banks's [2015b] account). For this reason its global reach may be limited. HRE, on the other hand, is structurally advantaged in several ways: its sponsorship by no less than the United Nations, its grounding in international texts and organizations (e.g., the UDHR, the World Programme, Amnesty International), the advent of a worldwide "schooled society," and the codification of human rights knowledge in international law.

Summarizing, schools cannot do much to "facilitate the structural inclusion of students from diverse ethnic, cultural, linguistic, and religious groups into their societies and nation-states." Structural conditions that precede and envelop schooling constrain reform initiatives in schools. This is where you start. Still, schools can do something. They can, above all else, teach a curriculum. The premise of the chapter is that there is such a thing as powerful knowledge (it exists objectively and can be defined and distinguished from less powerful knowledge) and that the purpose of schooling is to provide students with equitable access to it. Students are *entitled* to it (Young, 2013). Like all knowledge, powerful knowledge is a contingent, social construct. Less obvious is that its being a construct in no way mitigates the need to select, organize, and sequence it and then to distribute it broadly rather than to only a privileged few. As Delpit (1988) wrote, there are codes of power, and justice demands that we teach them to students who do not already possess them. Put differently, and now pulling the argument together, the social justice goals of radical educators require us to address the distribution of not just any knowledge in schools but the most powerful, emancipatory knowledge we have.

Something schools can do, then, to facilitate the structural inclusion of students into their nation-states is to teach them robust forms of human rights knowledge. Schools generally have the resources to do this: teachers, curriculum, and instruction. Additional work in specialist communities (e.g., the U.N. Educational, Scientific and Cultural Organization, universities, advocacy groups, the conference that led to this book) is needed to debate and organize its knowledge base, but selecting, organizing, and sequencing powerful human rights subject matter in schools appears to me to be the uniquely *curricular* priority to emerge from this book. This knowledge base will likely include the core texts (UDHR, Convention on the Rights of the Child), the histories of their production (individuals, movements, setbacks), the core concepts they embrace (suggested earlier), and vivid examples and nonexamples of each of them (case studies) to ground the abstractions in concrete realities. No doubt, there are other things that can be done in schools, and outside of them, too; but a powerful human rights curriculum is well within the purview of schools.

Acknowledgment

I am grateful to James Banks, Yiting Chu, Keith Barton, David Lambert, and three anonymous reviewers for helpful suggestions on an earlier draft of this chapter.

Notes

1. There are no ideal democracies. That liberal democracies fall short of their aspirations is obvious and is the motive behind social movements (and conferences such as the one that led to this book) that aim to close the gap between the real and the ideal.

2. Consider the division's call for papers for a recent annual meeting. The proposal categories were

> Culture and Commentary (The Reading/Making of Curriculum)
> Histories and Futurities (The Moment[s] of Curriculum)
> Methodologies and Ethics (The Shapes of Curriculum)
> People and Politics (The Who of Curriculum)
> Place and Praxis (The Places of Curriculum)
> Decolonization and the Next Hundred Years (The Desires of Curriculum)

3. Bernstein's critique of Bourdieu, whom he otherwise admired, is that he kept one ball in the air (knowledge as social practice) but not the other (knowledge as form, as real). See Muller, 2001. In addition to juggling, a useful metaphor is throwing the baby out with the bathwater.

4. See Zimmerman's (2002) historical analysis, Binder's (2002) sociological analysis, and watershed U.S. court cases such as *Tennessee v. John Scopes* (1927) and *Mozert v. Hawkins County Board of Education* (1987).

5. See the previous note.

6. There are exceptions. Bajaj (2011) has reported that in India thousands of teachers have been trained by a nongovernmental organization called the Institute for Human Rights Education to provide HRE with specialized HRE textbooks in nearly 4,000 schools.

7. I do not mean to overgeneralize. See, for example, Suárez, 2007b.

References

Alinsky, S. (1989). *Rules for radicals: A pragmatic primer for realistic radicals.* New York: Vintage.

American Anthropological Association. (1947). Statement on human rights. *American Anthropologist, 49*(4), 539–543.

Amnesty International. (2014). *Human rights education: Engaging new target groups.* London: Author.

Apple, M. W. (1979). *Ideology and curriculum.* New York: Routledge-Falmer.

Bajaj, M. (2011). Human rights education: Ideology, location, and approaches. *Human Rights Quarterly, 33*(2), 481–508.

Baker, D. P. (2014). *The schooled society: The educational transformation of global culture.* Stanford, CA: Stanford University Press.

Baker, D. P. (2015). A note on knowledge in the schooled society: Towards an end to the crisis in curriculum theory. *Journal of Curriculum Studies, 47*(6), 763–772.

Banks, J. A. (1993). The canon debate, knowledge construction, and multicultural education. *Educational Researcher, 22*(5), 4–14.

Banks, J. A. (2013). Approaches to multicultural curriculum reform. In J. A. Banks & C. A. M. Banks (Eds.), *Multicultural education: Issues and perspectives* (8th ed., pp. 181–199). Hoboken, NJ: Wiley.

Banks, J. A. (2015a). *Global Migration, Structural Inclusion, and Citizenship Education Across Nations: A conference sponsored by the Center for Multicultural Education* [Conference program]. Seattle, WA: University of Washington.

Banks, J. A. (2015b). Multicultural education. In J. D. Wright (Ed.), *International encyclopedia of the social and behavioral sciences* (2nd ed., pp. 18–21). Amsterdam, The Netherlands: Elsevier.

Beadie, N. (2016). The federal role in education and the rise of social science research: Historical and comparative perspectives. *Review of Research in Education*, 40, 1–37.

Beck, J. (2013). Powerful knowledge, esoteric knowledge, curriculum knowledge. *Cambridge Journal of Education, 43*(2), 177–193.

Bernstein, B. (1971). *Class, codes and control* (Vol. 1). London: Routledge & Kegan Paul.

Bernstein, B. (1999). Vertical and horizontal discourse: An essay. *British Journal of Sociology of Education, 20*(2), 157–173.

Bernstein, B. (2000). *Pedagogy, symbolic control and identity: Theory, research, critique.* Lanham, MD: Roman & Littlefield.

Binder, A. (2002). *Contentious curricula: Afrocentrism and creationism in American public schools.* Princeton, NJ: Princeton University Press.

Boulding, K. E. (1968). Inside Spaceship Earth. *Social Education, 45*(7), 648–656, 669.

Bourdieu, P., & Passeron, J. (1977). *Reproduction in education, society, and culture.* Cambridge, UK: Cambridge University Press.

Bowles, S., & Gintis, H. (1976). *Schooling in capitalist America: Educational reform and the contradictions of economic life.* New York: Basic Books.

Bowring, B. (2012). Human rights and public education. *Cambridge Journal of Education, 42*(1), 53–65.

Bransford, J., Brown, A. L., & Cockling, R. R. (2000). *How people learn: Brain, mind, experience, and school.* Washington, DC: National Academies Press.

Cremin, L. A. (1990). *Popular education and its discontents.* New York: HarperCollins.

Delpit, L. D. (1988). The silenced dialogue: Power and pedagogy in educating other people's children. *Harvard Educational Review, 58*(3), 280–298.

Deng, Z. (2015). Michael Young, knowledge and curriculum: An international dialogue. *Journal of Curriculum Studies, 47*(6), 723–732.

Dewey, J. (1902). *The child and the curriculum*. Chicago: University of Chicago Press.

Durkheim, E. (1965). *The elementary forms of religious life*. New York: Free Press. (original work published 1912)

Eisner, E. W. (2002). *The educational imagination* (3rd ed.). Columbus, OH: Merrill/Prentice Hall.

Freire, P. (1981). *Education for critical consciousness*. New York: Continuum.

Fulton, B. (2008, February 23). Students say good things about IB. *Salt Lake Tribune*. Retrieved from http://archive.sltrib.com/story.php?ref=/ci_8343648

Galston, W. A. (2001). Political knowledge, political engagement, and civic education. *Annual Review of Political Science, 4*, 217–234.

Gaudelli, W. (2016). *Global citizenship education*. New York: Routledge.

Gay, G. (2000). *Culturally responsive teaching*. New York: Teachers College Press.

Gecan, M. (2002). *Going public: An organizer's guide to citizen action*. Boston, MA: Beacon.

Giroux, H. A. (1979). Toward a new sociology of curriculum. *Educational Leadership, 37*(3), 248–252.

Green, A. (1990). *Education and state formation*. London: Macmillan.

Grubb, W. N., & Lazerson, M. (2004). *The education gospel: The economic power of schooling*. Cambridge, MA: Harvard University Press.

Hanvey, R. G. (1978). *An attainable global perspective*. New York: Center for Global Perspectives.

Howard, T. (2010). *Why race and culture matter in schools*. New York: Teachers College Press.

Kandel, I. L. (1937). Intelligent nationalism in the school curriculum. In I. L. Kandel & G. M. Whipple (Eds.), *Thirty-sixth yearbook of the National Society for the Study of Education, Committee on International Understanding, Part II: International understanding through the public school curriculum* (pp. 35–42). Bloomington, IL: Public School Publishing Co.

Labaree, D. F. (2012). School syndrome: Understanding the USA's magical belief that schooling can somehow improve society, promote access, and preserve advantage. *Journal of Curriculum Studies, 44*(2), 143–163.

Mann, H. (1846). *Ninth annual report of the Secretary of the Board of Education, Boston, December 10, 1845*. Boston, MA: Dutton and Wentworth.

Maton, K. (2014). *Knowledge and knowers: Towards a realist sociology of education*. New York: Routledge.

Marx, K., & Engles, F. (1970). *The German ideology*. New York: International Publishers. (original work published 1846)

McEneaney, E. H., & Meyer, J. W. (2000). The content of the curriculum: An institutionalist perspective. In M. T. Hallinan (Ed.), *Handbook of the sociology of education* (pp. 189–211). New York: Kluwer.

Moll, L. C. (Ed.). (1990). *Vygotsky and education*. New York: Cambridge University Press.

Moore, R. (2013). *Basil Bernstein: The thinker and the field*. New York: Routledge.

Moore, R., & Muller, J. (1999). The discourse of "voice" and the problem of knowledge and identity in the sociology of education. *British Journal of Sociology of Education, 20*(2), 189–206.

Mozert v. Hawkins County Board of Education, 827 F.2nd 1058 (6th Cir. 1987)

Muller, J. (2001). Intimations of boundlessness. In A. Morais, I. Neves, B. Davies, & H. Daniels (Eds.), *Towards a sociology of pedagogy: The contribution of Basil Bernstein to research* (pp. 129–151). New York: Peter Lang.

Nickel, J. (2014). Human rights. In E. N. Zalta (Ed.), *The Stanford encyclopedia of philosophy*. Retrieved from http://plato.stanford.edu/archives/win2014/entries/rights-human/

Noddings, N. (2003). *Happiness and education*. Cambridge, UK: Cambridge University Press.

Nussbaum, M. C. (2002). Patriotism and cosmopolitanism. In J. Cohen (Ed.), *For love of country?* (pp. 4–17). Boston, MA: Beacon.

Osler, A. (2015). Human rights education, postcolonial scholarship, and action for social justice. *Theory and Research in Social Education, 43*(2), 244–274.

Parker, W. C. (2003). *Teaching democracy: Unity and diversity in public life.* New York: Teachers College Press.

Parker, W. C. (2011). "International education" in U.S. public schools. *Globalisation, Societies and Education, 9*(3–4), 487–501.

Parker, W. C. (2014). Citizenship education in the United States: Regime type, foundational questions, and classroom practice. In L. P. Nucci, D. Narvaez, & T. Krettenauer (Eds.), *The handbook of moral and character education* (2nd ed., pp. 347–367). New York: Routledge.

Parker, W. C., & Lo, J. (2016). Content selection in advanced courses: Deep learning amid the "hundred million things." *Curriculum Inquiry, 46*(2), 196–219.

Pinar, W. (Ed.). (1975). *Curriculum theorizing: The reconceptualists.* San Francisco: McCutchan.

Rata, E., & Barrett, B. (2014). Introduction. In B. Barrett & E. Rata (Eds.), *Knowledge and the future of the curriculum: International studies in social realism* (pp. 1–20). New York: Palgrave Macmillan.

Said, E. W. (1993). *Culture and imperialism.* New York: Knopf.

Spivak, G. C. (1988). Can the subaltern speak? In P. Williams & L. Chrisman (Eds.), *Colonial discourse and post-colonial theory: A reader* (pp. 66–111). New York: Columbia University Press.

Starkey, H. (2012). Human rights, cosmopolitanism and utopias: Implications for citizenship education. *Cambridge Journal of Education, 42*(1), 21–35.

Suárez, D. F. (2007a). Education professionals and the construction of human rights education. *Comparative Education Review, 51*(1), 48–70.

Suárez, D. F. (2007b). Human rights and curricular policy in Latin America and the Caribbean. *Comparative Education Review, 51*(3), 329–352.

Tennessee v. John Scopes, 154 Tenn. 105 (1927)

Thornton, S. J., & Barton, K. C. (2010). Can history stand alone? Drawbacks and blind spots of a "disciplinary" curriculum. *Teachers College Record, 112*(9), 2471–2495.

Tyack, D., & Cuban, L. (1995). *Tinkering toward utopia: A century of public school reform.* Cambridge, MA: Harvard University Press.

Tyler, R. W. (1949). *Basic principles of curriculum and instruction.* Chicago: University of Chicago Press.

U.N. High Commissioner for Human Rights. (2014). *Plan of action for the third phase (2015–2019) of the World Programme for Human Rights Education.* New York: U.N. General Assembly, Office of the High Commissioner for Human Rights. Retrieved from http://documents-dds-ny.un.org/doc/UNDOC/GEN/G14/099/55/PDF/G1409955.pdf?OpenElement

U.N. High Commissioner for Human Rights. (2016). *What are human rights?* New York: U.N. General Assembly, Office of the High Commissioner for Human Rights. Retrieved from http://www.ohchr.org/EN/Issues/Pages/WhatareHumanRights.aspx?

Vygotsky, L. S. (1986). *Thought and language.* Cambridge, MA: MIT Press.

Westbury, I. (2008). Curriculum in practice. In F. M. Connelly, M. F. He, & J. Phillion (Eds.), *SAGE handbook of curriculum and instruction* (pp. 1–4). Thousand Oaks, CA: SAGE.

Young, M., & Lambert, D. (2014). *Knowledge and the future school: Curriculum and social justice.* London: Bloomsbury.

Young, M. F. D. (1971). *Knowledge and control: New directions for the sociology of education.* London: Collier-Macmillan.

Young, M. F. D. (2008). *Bringing knowledge back in: From social constructivism to social realism in the sociology of education*. London: Routledge.

Young, M. F. D. (2013). Overcoming the crisis in curriculum theory: A knowledge-based approach. *Journal of Curriculum Studies, 45*(2), 101–118.

Zimmerman, J. (2002). *Whose America? Culture wars in the public schools*. Cambridge, MA: Harvard University Press.

Citizenship Education and Global Migration: A Bibliography

Abrajano, J., & Hajnal, Z. L. (2015). *White backlash: Immigration, race, and American politics.* Princeton, NJ: Princeton University Press.

Adam, H., & Moodley, K. (2015). *Imagined liberation: Xenophobia, citizenship, and identity in South Africa, Germany, and Canada.* Philadelphia: Temple University Press.

Appadurai, A. (1996). *Modernity at large: Cultural dimensions of globalization.* Minneapolis: University of Minnesota Press.

Appadurai, A. (2006). *Fear of small numbers: An essay on the geography of anger.* Durham, NC: Duke University Press.

Appiah, K. A. (2006). *Cosmopolitanism: Ethics in a world of strangers.* New York: Norton.

Arthur, J., & Cremin, H. (Eds.). (2012). *Debates in citizenship education.* New York: Routledge.

Arthur, J., Davies, I., & Hahn, C. (Eds.). (2008). *The Sage handbook of education for citizenship and democracy.* Thousand Oaks, CA: Sage.

Banks, J. A. (Ed.). (2004). *Diversity and citizenship education: Global perspectives.* San Francisco: Jossey-Bass.

Banks, J. A. (2007). *Educating citizens in a multicultural society* (2nd ed.). New York: Teachers College Press.

Banks, J. A. (Ed.). (2009). *The Routledge international companion to multicultural education.* New York: Routledge.

Banks, J. A., Banks, C. A. M., Cortés, C. Hahn, C., Merryfield, M., Moodley, K., ...Parker, W. C. (2005). *Democracy and diversity: Principles and concepts for educating citizens in a global age.* Seattle: University of Washington, Center for Multicultural Education. Retrieved from https://education.uw.edu/sites/default/files/cme/docs/pdf/_notes/DEMOCRACY%20AND%20 DIVERSITY%20pdf.pdf

Banks, J. A., Suárez-Orozco, M. M., & Ben-Peretz, M. (Eds.). (2016). *Global migration, diversity, and civic education: Improving policy and practice.* New York: Teachers College Press.

Bauder, H. (2011). *Immigration dialectic: Imagining community, economy, and nation.* Toronto, Canada: University of Toronto Press.

Benhabib, S. (2004). *The rights of others: Aliens, residents, and citizens.* New York: Cambridge University Press.

Benhabib, S. (2006). *Another cosmopolitanism.* New York: Oxford University Press.

Benhabib, S., Shapiro, I., & Petranovic, D. (Eds.). (2007). *Identities, affiliations, and allegiances.* New York: Cambridge University Press.

Ben-Porath, S. R. (2006). *Citizenship under fire: Democratic education in times of conflict.* Princeton, NJ: Princeton University Press.

Berger, P. L., & Huntington, S. P. (Eds.). (2002). *Many globalizations: Cultural diversity in the contemporary world.* New York: Oxford University Press.

Bhabha, J. (2014). *Child migration and human rights in a global age.* Princeton, NJ: Princeton University Press.

Bloemraad, I. (2006). *Becoming a citizen: Incorporating immigrants and refugees in the United States and Canada*. Berkeley: University of California Press.

Bosniak, L. (2006). *The citizen and the alien: Dilemmas of contemporary membership*. Princeton, NJ: Princeton University Press.

Bowen, J. R. (2007). *Why the French don't like headscarves: Islam, the state, and the public space*. Princeton, NJ: Princeton University Press.

Calhoun, C. (2007). *Nations matter: Culture, history, and the cosmopolitan dream*. New York: Routledge.

Carens, J. H. (2000). *Culture, citizenship, and community: A contextual exploration of justice as even-handedness*. New York: Oxford University Press.

Carens, J. H. (2013). *The ethics of immigration*. New York: Oxford University Press.

Castles, S., & Davidson, A. (2005). *Citizenship and migration: Globalization and the politics of belonging*. New York: Routledge.

Castles, S., de Haas, H., & Miller, M. J. (2015). *The age of migration* (5th ed.). New York: Palgrave Macmillan.

Cesari, J. (2013). *Why the West fears Islam: An exploration of Muslims in liberal democracies*. New York: Palgrave Macmillan.

Chebel d'Appollonia, A., & Reich, S. (Eds.). (2008). *Immigration, integration, and security: America and Europe in comparative perspective*. Pittsburgh, PA: University of Pittsburgh Press.

De Blig, H. (2009). *The power of place: Geography, destiny, and globalization's rough landscape*. New York: Oxford University Press.

Favell, A. (2001). *Philosophies of integration and the idea of citizenship in France and Britain* (2nd ed.). New York: Palgrave Macmillan.

FitzGerald, D. S., & Martin, D. C. (2014). *Culling the masses: The democratic origins of racist immigration policy in the Americas*. Cambridge, MA: Harvard University Press.

Foner, N., & Fredrickson, G. M. (Eds.). (2004). *Not just Black and White: Historical and contemporary perspectives on immigration, race, and ethnicity in the United States*. New York: Russell Sage Foundation.

Foner, N., Rumbaut, R. G., & Gold, S. J. (Eds.). (2000). *Immigration research for a new century: Multidisciplinary perspectives*. New York: Russell Sage Foundation.

Fredette, J. (2014). *Constructing Muslims in France: Discourse, public identity, and the politics of citizenship*. Philadelphia: Temple University Press.

Freedman, A. L. (2000). *Political participation and ethnic minorities: Chinese overseas in Mayalsia, Indonesia, and the United States*. New York: Routledge.

Gerges, F. A. (2016). *ISIS: A history*. Princeton, NJ: Princeton University Press.

Gonzales, R. G. (2016). *Lives in limbo: Undocumented and coming of age in America*. Oakland: University of California Press.

Gutmann, A. (2003). *Identity in democracy*. Princeton, NJ: Princeton University Press.

Hargreaves, A. G. (1995). *Immigration, 'race,' and ethnicity in contemporary France*. New York: Routledge.

Huntington, S. P. (2004). *Who are we? The challenges of America's national identity*. New York: Simon and Schuster.

Isin, E. F., & Nyers, P. (Eds.). (2014). *Routledge handbook of global citizenship studies*. New York: Routledge.

Joppke, C. (2010). *Citizenship and immigration*. Malden, MA: Polity Press.

Kasinitz, P., Mollenkopf, J. H., Walters, M. C., & Holdaway, J. (2008). *Inheriting the city: The children of immigrants come of age*. New York: Russell Sage Foundation.

Kennedy, J., Lee, W.O., & Grossman, D. L. (Eds.). (2010). *Citizenship pedagogies in Asia and the Pacific.* New York: Springer.

Koopmans, R., Statham, P., Giugni, M., & Passy, F. (2005). *Contested citizenship: Immigration and cultural diversity in Europe.* Minneapolis: University of Minnesota Press.

Kymlicka, W. (1995). *Multicultural citizenship: A liberal theory of minority rights.* New York: Oxford University Press.

Kymlicka, W. (2001). *Politics in the vernacular: Nationalism, multiculturalism, and citizenship.* New York: Oxford University Press.

Kymlicka, W., & Norman, W. (Eds.). (2000). *Citizenship in diverse societies.* New York: Oxford University Press.

Law, W. W. (2011). *Citizenship and citizenship education in a global age: Politics, policies, and practices in China.* New York: Peter Lang.

Levinson, M. (2012). *No citizen left behind.* Cambridge, MA: Harvard University Press.

Lucassen, L. (2005). *The immigrant threat: The integration of old and new migrants in Western Europe since 1850.* Urbana: University of Illinois Press.

Malin, H., Ballard, P. J., Attai, M. L., Colby, A., & Damon, W. (2014). *Youth civic development and education: A conference consensus report.* Stanford, CA: Stanford University, Center on Adolescence, and Seattle: University of Washington, Center for Multicultural Education. Retrieved from https://education.uw.edu/sites/default/files/cme/images/Civic%20Education%20report.pdf

Martin, S. F. (2011). *A nation of immigrants.* New York: Cambridge University Press.

Massey, D. S. (2008). *New faces in new places: The changing geography of American immigration.* New York: Russell Sage Foundation.

Massey, D. S., & Sánchez, R. M. (2010). *Brokered boundaries: Creating immigrant identity in anti-immigrant times.* New York: Russell Sage Foundation.

May, S., & Modood, T. (2011). Education for national citizenship in the context of devolution and ethno-religious conflict. *Ethnicities, 11*(3), 267–407 [Special issue].

Minow, M., Shweder, R. A., & Markus, H. R. (Eds.). (2008). *Just schools: Pursuing equality in societies of difference.* New York: Russell Sage Foundation.

Modood, T. (2007). *Multiculturalism: A civic idea.* Cambridge, UK: Polity Press.

Modood, T., Triandafyllidou, A., & Zapata-Barrero, Z. (Eds.). (2006). *Multiculturalism, Muslims and citizenship: A European approach.* New York: Routledge.

Motomura, H. (2006). *Americans in waiting: The lost story of immigration and citizenship in the United States.* New York: Oxford University Press.

O'Brien, P. (2016). *The Muslim question in Europe: Political controversies and public philosophies.* Philadelphia: Temple University Press.

Olsen, L. (2008). *Made in America: Immigrant students in our public schools.* New York: New Press.

O'Neill, M., & Austin, D. (Eds.). (2000). *Democracy and cultural diversity.* New York: Oxford University Press.

Ong, A. (1999). *Flexible citizenship: The cultural logics of transnationality.* Durham, NC: Duke University Press.

Ong, A. (2003). *Buddha is hiding: Refugees, citizenship, the new America.* Berkeley: University of California Press.

Osler, A. (2016). *Human rights and schooling: An ethical framework for teaching for social justice.* New York: Teachers College Press.

Osler, A., & Starkey, H. (2005). *Changing citizenship: Democracy and inclusion in education.* New York: Open University Press.

Parekh, B. (2006). *Rethinking multiculturalism: Cultural diversity and political theory*. New York: Palgrave Macmillan.

Parker, W. C. (2003). *Teaching democracy: Unity and diversity in public life*. New York: Teachers College Press.

Portes, A., & Rumbaut, R. (2014). *Immigrant America: A portrait* (4th ed.). Oakland: University of California Press.

Ramadan, T. (2010). *What I believe*. New York: Oxford University Press.

Rhoads, R. A., & Szelényi, K. (2011). *Global citizenship and the university: Advancing social life and relations in an interdependent world*. Stanford, CA: Stanford University Press.

Rosaldo, R. (Ed.). (2003). *Cultural citizenship in Island Southeast Asia*. Berkeley: University of California Press.

Sassen, S. (1998). *Globalization and its discontents*. New York: New Press.

Sassen, S. (1999). *Guests and aliens*. New York: New Press.

Schierup, C. U., Hansen, P., & Castles, S. (2006). *Migration, citizenship, and the European welfare state*. New York: Oxford University Press.

Sen, A. (2006). *Identity and violence*. New York: Norton.

Smith, L. T. (2012). *Decolonizing methodologies: Research and Indigenous peoples* (2nd ed.). New York: Zed Books.

Soyal, Y. N. (1994). *Limits of citizenship: Migrants and postnational membership in Europe*. Chicago, IL: University of Chicago Press.

Spellman, W. M. (2008). *Uncertain identity: International migration since 1945*. London: Reaktion Books.

Suárez-Orozco, C., Suárez-Orozco, M. M., & Todorova, I. (2008). *Learning a new land: Immigrant students in American society*. Cambridge, MA: Harvard University Press.

Suárez-Orozco, M. M. (Ed.). (2007). *Learning in the global era: International perspectives on globalization and education*. Oakland: University of California Press.

Torres, C. A. (2009). *Globalizations and education: Collected essays on class, race, gender, and the state*. New York: Teachers College Press.

Waters, M. C., & Pineau, M. G. (Eds.). (2015). *The integration of immigrants into American society*. Washington, DC: National Academies Press.

Waters, M. C., & Ueda, R. (Eds.). (2007). *The new Americans: A guide to immigration since 1965*. Cambridge, MA: Harvard University Press.

Yoshikawa, I. (2011). *Immigrants raising citizens: Undocumented parents and their young children*. New York: Russell Sage Foundation.

Young, I. M. (2000). *Inclusion and democracy*. New York: Oxford University Press.

Zolberg, A. R. (2006). *A nation by design: Immigration policy in the fashioning of America*. Cambridge, MA: Harvard University Press.

Name Index

Subject Index

The letter f following a page number denotes a figure, the letter n denotes an endnote, and the letter t denotes a table.

About the Contributors

Editor

James A. Banks holds the Kerry and Linda Killinger Endowed Chair in Diversity Studies and is the founding director of the Center for Multicultural Education at the University of Washington, Seattle. His research focuses on multicultural education and diversity and on citizenship education in a global context. His books include *Cultural Diversity and Education: Foundations, Curriculum, and Teaching* (6th ed., Routledge, 2016), and *Race, Culture, and Education: The Selected Works of James A. Banks* (Routledge, 2006). He is the editor of *Diversity and Citizenship Education: Global Perspectives* (Jossey-Bass, 2004) and of the *Encyclopedia of Diversity in Education* (Sage, 2012). Banks is a past president of the National Council for the Social Studies and the American Educational Research Association. He is an AERA fellow and a member of the National Academy of Education.

Authors

Bassel Akar is an associate professor at the Faculty of Humanities and Director of the Center for Applied Research in Education at Notre Dame University, Louaize, Lebanon; *bassel.akar@gmail.com, bakar@ndu.edu.lb.* His research focuses on learning and teaching for active citizenship in Lebanon and other areas affected by armed conflict. He designs pedagogical methods of inquiry that engage young people in open-ended learning activities. Akar also carries out consultative work for local and international NGOs in Lebanon and the Arab region. His projects include supporting history teachers in transforming a culture of memorization to one of learning history as a discipline, and conducting research studies investigating the quality of education for Syrian refugee children from early childhood through secondary school. Akar has recently coauthored "Influences of Nationalisms on Citizenship Education: Revealing a 'Dark Side' in Lebanon" (in press) and authored "Dialogic Pedagogies in Educational Settings for Active Citizenship, Social Cohesion and Peacebuilding in Lebanon" (2016, *Education, Citizenship and Social Justice*, vol. 11, no. 1).

Rania Al-Nakib is an assistant professor at the Gulf University for Science and Technology, Department of Humanities and Social Sciences in Kuwait, where she teaches courses in education, human rights, and citizenship; *alnakib.r@gust.edu.kw.* She has a Ph.D. from the Institute of Education, University of London, an M.Ed. in NK–8 education from Marymount University in Virginia, and an M.S. in theoretical linguistics from Georgetown University in Washington, D.C. Her research focuses on human rights and education for democratic citizenship in Kuwait. Current research interests include the influence of religion on regional curricula and the gendered educational experiences of Kuwaiti female students. She has published articles in *Education Research* and the *Cambridge Journal of Education*.

Hasan Aydin is an associate professor of multicultural education at Yildiz Technical University, Istanbul, Turkey; *aydinhytu@gmail.com*. His research focuses on multicultural education, curriculum development, citizenship education, diversity, and democracy. He is an author of several books and has published many articles. He is currently a chief editor of *Journal of Ethnic and Cultural Studies (eJECS)* and has translated books by James A. Banks and Geneva Gay into Turkish.

Angela M. Banks is a professor of law at William & Mary Law School. She is an immigration and citizenship expert whose research focuses on membership and belonging in democratic societies. Her scholarship has appeared in leading American law review journals such as the *Emory Law Journal* and the *William & Mary Law Review*. Prior to joining the William & Mary faculty, Banks was the Reginald F. Lewis Fellow for Law Teaching at Harvard Law School. She has also served as a legal advisor to Judge Gabrielle Kirk McDonald at the Iran–United States Claims Tribunal; as an associate at Wilmer, Cutler & Pickering in Washington, D.C.; and as a law clerk for Judge Carlos F. Lucero of the U.S. Court of Appeals for the Tenth Circuit.

Bashir Bashir is a senior lecturer in the Department of Sociology, Political Science, and Communication at the Open University of Israel and a research fellow at the Van Leer Jerusalem Institute. His primary research interests are nationalism and citizenship studies, multiculturalism, democratic theory, and the politics of reconciliation. His publications include "Reconciling Historical Injustices: Deliberative Democracy and the Politics of Reconciliation" (2012, *Res Publica*, vol. 18, no. 2); "On Citizenship and Citizenship Education: A Levantine Approach and Reimagining Israel/Palestine" (2015, *Citizenship Studies*, vol. 19, nos. 6–7); with Amos Goldberg, "Deliberating the Holocaust and the Nakba: Disruptive Empathy and Binationalism in Israel/Palestine" (2014, *Journal of Genocide Research*, vol. 16, no. 1); and, coedited with Will Kymlicka, *The Politics of Reconciliation in Multicultural Societies* (2008, Oxford University Press).

Zvi Bekerman teaches anthropology of education at the Hebrew University of Jerusalem, Seymour Fox School of Education, and is a faculty member at the Mandel Leadership Institute in Jerusalem; *zvi.bekerman@mail.huji.ac.il*. His main interests are in the study of cultural, ethnic, and national identity, including identity processes and negotiation during intercultural encounters and in formal/informal learning contexts. Bekerman is particularly interested in how concepts such as culture and identity intersect with issues of social justice, intercultural and peace education, and citizenship education. In addition to publishing articles in a variety of academic journals, Bekerman is the founding editor of the refereed journal *Diaspora, Indigenous, and Minority Education: An International Journal*. Among his most recent books are *The Promise of Integrated and Multicultural Bilingual Education: Inclusive Palestinian-Arab and Jewish Schools in Israel* (2016, Oxford University Press); and *Teaching Contested Narratives: Identity, Memory and Reconciliation in Peace Education and Beyond* (coauthored with Michalinos Zembylas), (2012, Cambridge University Press).

Géraldine Bozec is an associate professor of sociology at the University of Nice Sophia Antipolis (France) and member of the Unité de Recherches Migrations et Sociétés (Migration and Research Unit), specializing in the study of migrations and interethnic relationships; *geraldine.bozec@unice.fr*. She teaches in the Department of Sociology as well as the Teacher College of Nice. Her research focuses on citizenship education in primary and secondary schools, the construction of national belonging at school, and issues related to cultural, ethnic, and religious diversity in education in France from a comparative perspective. Her current research explores the construction and the role of race and religion in children's identity construction and relationships.

Stephen Castles is Honorary Professor in Sociology at the University of Sydney. He is a sociologist and political economist and works on international migration dynamics, global governance, multiculturalism, transnationalism, migration and development, and regional migration trends in Africa, Asia, and Europe. His research and publications have made an influential contribution to the development of interdisciplinary migration research for many years. His books include *The Age of Migration: International Population Movements in the Modern World* (5th ed., coauthored with H. de Haas and M. Miller, 2013, Guilford Press) and *Social Transformation and Migration: National and Local Experiences in South Korea, Turkey, Mexico, and Australia* (coedited with D. Ozkul and M. Cubas, 2015, Springer).

Yun-Kyung Cha is a professor of the sociology of education at Hanyang University, Seoul, South Korea; *yunkyung@hanyang.ac.kr*. He is a founding member and former president of the Korean Association for Multicultural Education, and is currently serving as chief editor of its international journal, *Multicultural Education Review,* a Routledge journal indexed in Scopus. Cha has also been a member of the Korean government's advisory and monitoring committees, including the Multicultural Family Policy Committee and the Immigration Policy Committee. He has recently published an edited book that provides a "glocal" perspective on cultural diversity and educational inclusion: *Multicultural Education in Glocal Perspectives: Policy and Institutionalization* (with Jagdish Gundara, Seung-Hwan Ham, & Moosung Lee, 2017, Springer Singapore).

Saba Nur Cheema is director of educational programs at the Anne Frank Educational Centre in Frankfurt; *scheema@bs-anne-frank.de*. She was trained as a political scientist and currently is a Ph.D. candidate in educational science at Goethe University, Frankfurt. She is a qualified trainer in human rights education and anti-racism. Her work and research relates to discrimination and marginalization of Muslims living in White, Christian, secularized Germany. She works with youths to empower and raise awareness of everyday forms of discrimination. She also counsels, trains, and empowers teachers and other educators in addressing and reflecting on discrimination, racism, and processes of political radicalization among youths.

Aviv Cohen (Ph.D.) is a lecturer at the Hebrew University of Jerusalem, Seymour Fox School of Education. His major areas of teaching and research are democratic civic education, teacher education, social studies teaching, educational theory, and the use of qualitative methods in education research. Cohen's recent publications are based on his dissertation, which dealt with the manifestations of conceptions of citizenship and civic education in three Israeli civics classrooms. His current research project, funded by the MOFET Institute, focuses on the challenges facing teacher educators preparing Israel's future civics teachers.

H. Julia Eksner is a professor of education at the Frankfurt University of Applied Sciences, School of Social Work; *eksner.julia@fb4.fra-uas.de.* She was trained as an anthropologist and as a learning scientist, thus connecting sociocultural, developmental, and educational perspectives in the study of youth development. Eksner investigates how urban youths from marginalized groups experience, interpret, and navigate the opportunities and barriers posed to them by the environments in which they come of age, and ways to empower marginalized youths to respond to these environments and ultimately change their lives for the better. Eksner has for many years been engaged in designing learning environments concerned with issues of social justice, diversity, citizenship, and intergroup conflict.

Muhammad Faour is a professor and dean of the College of Arts and Sciences at Phoenicia University in Sarafand, Lebanon. He was formerly a senior associate at the Carnegie Middle East Center, where his research focused on education reform in Arab countries, with an emphasis on citizenship education. Prior to that, Faour was vice chancellor/president of Dhofar University in Oman and deputy vice president for Regional External Programs at the American University of Beirut. Faour is the author of several monographs, including *A Review of Citizenship Education in Arab Nations* and (with Marwan Muasher) *Education for Citizenship in the Arab World: Key to the Future.* His books include *The Silent Revolution in Lebanon: Changing Values of the Youth* (1998, American University of Beirut) and *The Arab World After Desert Storm* (1993, US Institute of Peace Press). Faour is the co-author (with Adnan El-Amine) of *University Students in Lebanon: Background and Attitudes* (1998, Lebanese Association for Educational Studies).

Seung-Hwan Ham is an assistant professor of educational administration and policy at Hanyang University, Seoul, South Korea; *hamseunghwan@gmail.com.* Before joining Hanyang University's College of Education, he taught at Michigan State University and worked as a research professor at Pohang University of Science and Technology. His scholarly interests focus on school organization and multilayered structural and institutional arrangements, especially in relation to their effects on educational equity and well-being for diverse students. His recent research projects have been examining the effects of different types of government policies for multicultural inclusion/integration on various aspects of schooling, with particular analytical attention given to educational leadership practices and student learning experiences.

Rahil Ismail is an associate professor at the National Institute of Education, Nanyang Technological University, Humanities and Social Studies Education Academic Group; *rahil.ismail@nie.edu.sg.* She earned her history honors degree at the National University of Singapore, a postgraduate certificate in education from the Institute of Education, University of London, and both her master's degree and Ph.D. in international studies from the Institute for International Studies, University of Leeds. Her current research interests are in international relations and multicultural and heritage studies. Her teaching responsibilities include contemporary American history and modern international history.

Reva Joshee is an associate professor in the Department of Leadership, Higher and Adult Education, of the Ontario Institute for Studies in Education (OISE) at the University of Toronto, where she teaches courses in multicultural education and policy analysis in both the graduate and initial teacher education programs. She is director of the Center for Leadership and Diversity at OISE. Her research examines issues of diversity and policy in India, Canada, and the United States. She is also the chair of the Advisory Council for the Mahatma Gandhi Canadian Foundation for World Peace.

Fadime Koc-Damgaci is a doctoral student in the curriculum and instruction department at Yildiz Technical University, Istanbul, Turkey; *fdamgaci@gmail.com*. Her research interests are multicultural education, curriculum studies, and teacher training for culturally responsive teaching and human rights.

Will Kymlicka is the Canada Research Chair in political philosophy at Queen's University and a visiting professor in the Nationalism Studies program at the Central European University in Budapest. His publications include seven books published by Oxford University Press: *Liberalism, Community, and Culture; Contemporary Political Philosophy; Multicultural Citizenship: A Liberal Theory of Minority Rights; Finding Our Way: Rethinking Ethnocultural Relations in Canada; Politics in the Vernacular: Nationalism, Multiculturalism, and Citizenship; Multicultural Odysseys: Navigating the New International Politics of Diversity;* and *Zoopolis: A Political Theory of Animal Rights*.

Wing-Wah Law is a professor at the University of Hong Kong, Faculty of Education; *wwlaw@hku.hk*. His research contributes to the understanding of the interplay between globalization and localization on education and development in various areas (including educational policy, citizenship and citizenship education, educational and curriculum reforms, culture and leadership, and music education and social change); his work serves as a bridge for the exchange and development of educational research between China and the world. Law's publications have appeared in international journals such as the *Cambridge Journal of Education, Comparative Education,* the *Comparative Education Review, Compare,* the *International Journal of Educational Development,* the *International Journal of Music Education,* the *Journal of Curriculum Studies,* and *Teachers College Record*. He served as an associate editor of the *International Journal of Educational Development* between 2013 and 2016, and has been a member of the *Comparative Education Review*'s Advisory Board since 2012.

Bradley A. Levinson is a professor of education policy studies at Indiana University, where he holds adjunct appointments in Anthropology, Latino Studies, and Latin American

Studies; *brlevins@indiana.edu.* He studies youth identity, secondary education reform, education policy, and democratic citizenship education comparatively, especially in Mexico and Latin America. Among his published works are the books *We Are All Equal: Student Culture and Identity at a Mexican Secondary School* (2001, Duke University Press), *Schooling the Symbolic Animal* (2000, Rowman and Littlefield), *Reimagining Civic Education* (2007, Rowman and Littlefield), and *Beyond Critique: Exploring Critical Social Theories and Education* (2015, Routledge).

Mi-Eun Lim is a Russian-language teacher at Suwon Foreign Language High School and a doctoral student at Hanyang University, Seoul, South Korea; *mila26@korea.kr.* She received a bachelor's degree in Russian language from Hankuk University of Foreign Studies and a master's degree in teaching Korean as a foreign language from Seoul National University. She is currently pursuing a Ph.D. in multicultural education at Hanyang University, with a focus on global citizenship education for both students and teachers. In addition, she is serving as a member of the National Teachers Network for Civic Education and the Suwon City Civic Education Study Group to improve the practice of civic education in Korea.

María Eugenia Luna Elizarrarás is a curriculum specialist and ethnographer of citizenship education; *maruluna45@prodigy.net.mx.* She has coordinated the development of programs in civic education for both primary and secondary schools in the Secretaría de Educación Pública (SEP) of Mexico and has authored civic education textbooks for secondary students. She is now an advisor to the Office of Educational Materials of the SEP.

Kogila Moodley is professor emerita of sociology at the University of British Columbia, Vancouver, Canada, where she was the first holder of the David Lam Chair in Multicultural Education. She has served as president of the International Sociological Association's Research Committee on Racism, Nationalism and Ethnic Relations (RC05) and currently serves on the editorial board of several journals, including *Ethnic and Racial Studies.*

Audrey Osler holds a chair in education at the University College of Southeast Norway and the University of Leeds, United Kingdom, where she was founding director of the Centre for Citizenship and Human Rights Education; *a.h.osler@leeds.ac.uk.* Her research addresses sociopolitical aspects of education, focusing on children's human rights, participation, and citizenship, in both established democracies and postconflict societies. Osler has written 19 books. The latest, *Human Rights and Schooling: An Ethical Framework for Teaching About Social Justice*, was published by Teachers College Press (2016). Osler has held visiting professorships at various universities, including Beijing Normal University and Hong Kong University of Education; the UN University of Peace, Costa Rica; and the University of Washington and Utah State University. Her work is translated into Japanese, Mandarin, and various European languages. Osler was awarded a Japan Society for the Promotion of Science Invitation Fellowship in 2015. She holds a Ph.D. in education from the University of Birmingham, United Kingdom.

Walter C. Parker is a professor of education and, by courtesy, political science at the University of Washington, Seattle; *denver@uw.edu*. His books include *Teaching Democracy* (2003, Routledge), *Social Studies Today: Research and Practice* (2015, Routledge), and *Social Studies in Elementary Education* (2017, Pearson). He is an AERA fellow as well as a fellow of the Center for Ethics and Education at the University of Wisconsin, Madison. Currently he conducts design-based research aimed at bringing deep conceptual learning to purportedly advanced high school courses, particularly in U.S. government and politics. This work has been published in the *American Educational Research Journal, Curriculum Inquiry, Democracy & Education,* and the *Journal of Curriculum Studies.*

Petronilha Beatriz Gonçalves e Silva is a professor emerita in education and racial-ethnic relations at the Federal University of São Carlos, Brazil; *pbgs@terra.com.br*. She also holds the title Dame of the National Order of Merit in recognition of her contributions to education in Brazil. Representing the Black movement, she also served on the National Council of Education and in this position was Rapporteur of the Commission on the National Curriculum Guidelines for Education of Racial-Ethnic Relationships and the Teaching of African and Afro-Brazilian History and Culture. She is a founding member of the International Research Group on Epistemology of African Roots and Education and of the World Education Research Association, representing the Association of Brazilian Black Researchers and the National Association of Research and Graduate Studies. In 2014–2015 she was Tinker Visiting Professor and Visiting Scholar in the College of Education at Georgia State University.

Hugh Starkey is professor of citizenship and human rights education at the University College London (UCL) Institute of Education, where he is founding co-director of the International Center for Education and Democratic Citizenship. His research focuses on education for democratic citizenship, human rights, and social justice in a globalizing world. He is coauthor (with Audrey Osler) of *Teachers and Human Rights Education* (2010, Trentham, UCL IOE Press) and editor of the *London Review of Education*. He has led European-funded projects on citizenship and human rights education and has acted as a consultant for several governments and the Council of Europe, UNESCO, the European Commission, and the British Council.

Monica Thomas is a teacher in the Edmonton Public Schools in Edmonton, Alberta, Canada. She has a master's degree in education from the University of Alberta and a certificate from the Mahatma Gandhi Summer Institute for Building Peaceful Communities. She continually applies her understandings of Gandhian thought to her parenting and teaching.

Douglas Verrangia is a professor at the Federal University of São Carlos, Department of Teaching Methodology; *douglasverrangia@gmail.com*. As an undergraduate he studied biology and science teacher education. He did a semester of doctoral studies in education at Medgar Evers College of The City University of New York, working in the research group led by Mwalimu Shujaa. Recently he did postdoctoral work in Spain with a grant from the São Paulo Research Foundation. As a professor he has worked in teacher education and teacher preparation, focusing on teaching techniques and methodology; curriculum development in science education; social relationships, especially interethnic and interracial relationships; and the connections between science education and culture.